Troubling Arthurian Histories

Medieval and Early Modern French Studies

Series Editor
NOËL PEACOCK

VOLUME 5

PETER LANG

Oxford • Bern • Berlin • Bruxelles • Frankfurt am Main • New York • Wien

Troubling Arthurian Histories

Court Culture, Performance and Scandal in
Chrétien de Troyes's *Erec et Enide*

JAMES R. SIMPSON

PETER LANG
Oxford • Bern • Berlin • Bruxelles • Frankfurt am Main • New York • Wien

Bibliographic information published by Die Deutsche Bibliothek
Die Deutsche Bibliothek lists this publication in the Deutsche National-
bibliografie; detailed bibliographic data is available on the Internet at
‹http://dnb.ddb.de›.

British Library and Library of Congress Cataloguing-in-Publication Data:
A catalogue record for this book is available from *The British Library*,
Great Britain, and from *The Library of Congress*, USA.

ISSN 1661-8653
ISBN 978-3-03911-385-9

© Peter Lang AG, International Academic Publishers, Bern 2007
Hochfeldstrasse 32, Postfach 746, CH-3000 Bern 9, Switzerland
info@peterlang.com, www.peterlang.com, www.peterlang.net

All rights reserved.
All parts of this publication are protected by copyright.
Any utilisation outside the strict limits of the copyright law, without
the permission of the publisher, is forbidden and liable to prosecution.
This applies in particular to reproductions, translations, microfilming,
and storage and processing in electronic retrieval systems.

Printed in Germany

Contents

Acknowledgements		vii
Editions and Translations of *Erec et Enide*		ix
Introduction	Troubling Arthur: A Courtier Behaving Strangely	1
Chapter One	Before or After the King? The Hunt as Court (Re-)Composition	77
Chapter Two	Court Beauty Turns Ugly: A Young King and His Maiden(s)	125
Chapter Three	The Neighbour's Ugly Joy: Laluth	167
Chapter Four	'Just Right for a Maiden': Approaches to Marriage at Court	217
Chapter Five	'Misfortune Brought You There': History (and Geography) in the *Boudoir*	251
Chapter Six	'If You Don't Do What [We] Do, Why Are You Here?': Queering the Quest	303
Chapter Seven	'As If You Were My Secretary': Scripting Enide's Histories	353
Chapter Eight	Illusions and Consolations: Joys of the Court	399
Conclusion	Arts of Spinning and Dazzling: The Coronation	447
Bibliography		471
Index		515

Acknowledgements

This book would not have been possible without the insight and encouragment of various friends and colleagues. I would therefore like to record my warm thanks to Bill Burgwinkle, Emma Campbell, Ellie Ferguson, Charles Forsdick, Oranye Fradenburg, Simon Gaunt, Jane Gilbert, Miranda Griffin, Mary Heimann, Sylvia Huot, Sarah Kay, Gary McCaw, Caroline MacAvoy, Caroline Palmer, Simon Pender, Helen Philips, Wendy Scase, Helen Swift, and, if last then certainly not least, Neil Wright. I would particularly like to thank my medievalist colleagues in Glasgow, for their help and support over the years: Alison Adams, Stuart Airlie, Peter Davies, Andrew Roach, Graeme Small, Debra Strickland and Matt Strickland all made invaluable suggestions at various points. A number of medievalist graduate students, past and present, also made contributions above and beyond the call of duty, and I would therefore like to thank Michael Amey, Eilidh MacDonald, Kate Maxwell, Kathleen O'Neill and Lucy Whiteley. From among my colleagues in French, thanks go to Keith Reader, and especially to Wullie Dickson and Noël Peacock, for their unstinting encouragement, support and advice over the years. I would also like to acknowledge the generous support of the University of Glasgow John Robertson Bequest and the Faculty of Arts Strategic Research Fund.

Editions and Translations of *Erec et Enide*

This study chiefly centres on the version of *Erec et Enide* preserved in the manuscript Bibliothèque Nationale fonds français 1376. Accordingly, unless indicated otherwise, references to *Erec et Enide* are to the edition of Jean-Marie Fritz (ed. and trans.), *Chrétien de Troyes, 'Erec et Enide': édition critique d'après le manuscrit B. N. fr. 1376*, Lettres Gothiques (Paris: Livre de Poche, 1992) reprinted in *Chrétien de Troyes: Romans*, La Pochothèque (Paris: Livre de Poche, 1994). For editions based on other manuscript versions, see Wendelin Foerster (ed.), *Kristian von Troyes, 'Erec und Enide'*, rev. edn (Halle: Niemeyer, 1934); Mario Roques (ed.), *Les Romans de Chrétien de Troyes édités d'après la copie de Guiot (Bibl. Nat. fr. 794): 'Erec et Enide'*, Classiques Français du Moyen Age (Paris: Champion, 1981) and Peter Dembowksi (ed.), *Erec et Enide*, La Pléiade (Paris: Gallimard, 1994). Unless indicated otherwise, references to other works attributed to Chrétien are also to the editions reproduced in the Pochothèque volume. For commentary on the manuscript tradition see notably Alexandre Micha, *La Tradition manuscrite des romans de Chrétien de Troyes* (Geneva: Droz, 1966) the introductions to the editions cited above and also the essays and other materials in Keith Busby et al. (eds), *Les Manuscrits de / The Manuscipts of Chrétien de Troyes*, 2 vols (Amsterdam: Rodopi, 1993)

Given the prominence accorded the 'Guiot copy', it is logical enough that English translations of Chrétien have mainly been based on Roques's or Foerster's editions, as is the case for William W. Kibler and Carleton W. Carroll (trans.), *Chrétien de Troyes, Arthurian Romances* (London: Penguin, 1991), Ruth Harwood Cline (trans.), *'Erec et Enide' by Chrétien de Troyes* (Athens GA and London: University of Georgia Press, 2000) and Dorothy Gilbert, *Chrétien de Troyes: 'Erec et Enide'* (Berkeley and Oxford: University of California Press, 1992). Burton Raffel's translation, based on both Dembowski's and Fritz's editions (see *Erec et Enide, Chrétien de*

ix

Troyes (Newhaven Conn.: Yale University Press, 1997), pp. ix–x), is something of a textual composite and, although elegant, is therefore not suitable for my purposes here. Unless indicated otherwise therefore, translations of *Erec et Enide* are mine after Fritz's, Carroll's and Raffel's versions, adapted to fit Fritz's base text or where my understanding differs from theirs.

As Evelyn Mullally commented back in 1988, 'Chrétien scholarship is so extensive that it is impossible to do it justice in the confines of a study such as this' (*The Artist at Work: Narrative Technique in Chrétien de Troyes*, Transactions of the American Philosophical Society, 78:4 (Philadelphia: American Philosophical Society, 1988), p. 1). The situation has got no easier with the passing of time. For bibliography, see Douglas Kelly (ed.), *Chrétien de Troyes: An Analytic Bibliography*, Research Bibliographies and Checklists, 17 (London: Grant and Cutler, 1976), with Kelly and others (eds), *Chrétien de Troyes: An Analytic Bibliography (Supplement 1)*, Research Bibliographies and Checklists, New Series 3 (London: Grant and Cutler, 2002). For a useful *état présent* in 1980, see René Ménage, '*Erec et Enide*: Quelques pièces du dossier', *Marche Romane*, 30:3–4 (1980), 203–21. For a more recent survey of directions in scholarship, see Norris J. Lacy, 'Arthurian Research in a New Century: Prospects and Projects', in *New Directions in Arthurian Studies*. ed. by Alan Lupack, Arthurian Studies, 51 (Cambridge: Brewer, 2002), 1–20.

Henry: 'Dear Kate, you and I cannot be confin'd within the weak list of a country's fashion: we are the makers of the manners, Kate; and the liberty that follows our places stops the mouth of all find-faults.' (Shakespeare, *Henry V*, act 5, scene 2)

Let the prince [...] act to conquer and to maintain the state; his methods will always be judged honourable and will be praised by all; for ordinary people are always deceived by appearances and by the outcome of a thing; and in the world there is nothing but ordinary people. (Niccolò Machiavelli, *The Prince*, trans. by Peter Bondella and Mark Musa, World's Classics (Oxford: Oxford University Press, 1984), p. 60)

'Nothing that is acquired by force and violence can ever be held legally by anyone.' (Geoffrey of Monmouth, *The History of the Kings of Britain*, trans. by Lewis Thorpe (London: Penguin, 1966), p. 232)

Mout s'entredonent grant colees
Qui *de rien nule ne se feignent*. (*Erec et Enide*, ll. 882–3, my emphasis)

They fought ferociously, cutting hard at one another's necks, for this was no make-believe combat.

'Onques encore *ne me soi faindre*
De lui amer, ne je ne doi.' (*Erec et Enide*, ll. 6300–01, my emphasis)

'I never yet did know to feign or be fainthearted in my love for him. And nor should I.'

What lies under the surface of Mock [Medieval speech and language in films etc.], the thing that makes it sound all right even though only a moment's reflection exposes its ludicrous conceit, is the unspoken sense that medieval people were odd and they knew it. Mock has the effect of casting medieval men and women as the dimly self-aware spokespersons of a sense of difference and detachment that in reality, of course, only exists in our modern perception of them, not in their own contemporary awareness. They probably could not quite put their finger on it, so Mock implies, but they somehow sensed they were primitive, crude, or whatever stereotype one wants to apply, and that better times, progress, lay somewhere in the future. Mock, in other words, makes medieval people sound like actors in their own costume drama. (Marcus Bull, *Thinking Medieval: An Introduction to the Study of the Middle Ages* (Basingstoke and New York: Palgrave MacMillan, 2005), p. 138)

Introduction
Troubling Arthur:
A Courtier Behaving Strangely

My target is a medieval courtier who is behaving strangely.[1]

The prevailing law threatened one with trouble, even put one in trouble, all to keep one out of trouble. Hence, I concluded that trouble is inevitable and the task how best to make it, what best way to be in it.[2]

'Doing (a Bit of) an Arthur':
Making a Performance at Court

Arthurian literature was clearly a major source of aristocratic behavioural scripting in central and late medieval court circles.[3] However, to take one's cue from such an archive was not a guarantee of success. The fifteenth-century Burgundian chronicler Georges Chastellain gives an account of the knight Philippe Pot greeting an out-of-humour Philip the Good, just returned from the forest having fled there in a rage following an argument with his son: 'Good morning, your majesty, good morning! And what is this? Are you playing at King Arthur now or is it Sir Lancelot?'[4] Philippe Pot's phrase for 'playing at King Arthur' – 'faites-vous *du roy Artus*?' – seems to indicate that 'doing a bit of an Arthur', to render the partitive construction more literally, could readily cover some of the more extreme and dramatic shows of royal displeasure, the knight's teasing comment inviting his lord to reflect on whether he was taking things too seriously or too far in a mangling imitation of Arthur unlikely to strengthen his political authority. In so doing, Philippe Pot – noted as a 'power behind the throne' at the Burgundian court – affirms his

1

status as judge and orchestrator in a political theatre he does not want to see devolve into a mere imperial fashion show. Such a consideration was especially important given Philip's role in asserting Burgundy's independence from French royal interests.[5]

Medieval aristocratic fascination with figures such as the once and future king or other members of the pantheon grouped together under the heading of the *neuf preux* – the 'nine worthies' drawn from Antiquity and accounts of the early Middle Ages – is that courtly performance is above all citational, looking to the words and deeds of departed greats to steal a little of their glory or even rival and outdo them.[6] However, the fact that – both chronologically and mimetically – the performance is always 'after' a model brings its own anxieties of influence.[7] Philip's 'doing a bit of an Arthur' might thus sin against a view that royal behaviour should be a one-off, suffused with a singular presence that is the unique stamp of a successful performance by a cultural leader and figurehead, not a tired and out-of-place echo. But then, the model might be of debatable value: while in some sources Arthur embodies everything that was best and brightest about medieval kingship, he could, as Donald Maddox neatly resumes, also appear 'depressed, lethargic, hesitant, powerless, concupiscent, incestuous, short-sighted or even apparently senile'.[8] Thus, whether the clearly mischievous Pot thought 'playing at Arthur' was a description of royal performance as citational practice or just part of everyday royal dysfunctionality and delusion is not entirely clear.

The puzzlement aroused by Philippe's Arthurian stylings, the sense that there was something strange, even exotic about his fits of pique or gestures – such as what historian Johan Huizinga sees as his 'caliph-like' insistence that his other courtiers have their heads shaven like him – emphasise the extent to which 'courtly' ways were perceived as outlandish in more than one sense. Their 'second nature', a remaking of the raw stuff of unschooled new arrivals, focused on the sublimated and indirect expression of 'spontaneous' impulses, clearly took some time to insinuate itself, to get under the skin of medieval aristocrats seemingly at ease with spitting gristle back into their plates, defaecating in palace stairwells or stabbing someone in a quarrel.[9] However, once they did inculcate themselves, the transforming effect had the potential to be rapid and alienating.

Huizinga's comments on episodes such as this in his examination of Burgundian court culture, *Autumn of the Middle Ages*, bear witness to an enduring perception, filtered through observers such as Jean de la Bruyère (1645–1692), for whom court manners epitomise all that is most baroquely byzantine, cynically calculating, disingenuously indirect, superfluously over-refined or just plain cruel in human behaviour:

> Un homme qui sait la Cour, est maître de son geste, de ses yeux et de son visage; il est profond, impénétrable; il dissimule les mauvais Offices, sourit à ses ennemis, contraint son humeur, déguise ses passions, dément son coeur, parle, agit contre ses sentiments: tout ce grand raffinement n'est qu'un vice, que l'on appelle fausseté, quelquefois aussi inutile au Courtisan pour sa fortune que la franchise, la sincérité et la vertu.[10]

Pungent with the courtly savours of cynicism and paradox, La Bruyère's comments reduce its world into a decadent *jus* of sharply, bitterly distinct notes: the courtier is a creature of artifice cultivated to the nth degree; for all its art, that artifice is still no better than a lie; lies sometimes turn out to be no more useful to the courtier than naturalness and virtue. In that nest of vipers, it seems, you are damned if you do and damned if you don't, so good job it's only a century until the French Revolution. Such perceptions of the court as blasphemous moral topsy-turvey were of course already being articulated in words contemporary with Chrétien, such as Walter Map:

> Men who have to gird themselves against [backbiting at court] must of necessity suppress their virtues and arm themselves with faults. They must keep each carefully in its place so as to appear righteous to the good and very evil to the wicked. (*The Courtier's Trifles*, dist. 4, chapter 13, p. 373 in edition)

If La Bruyère sees the court as offering a catalogue of the vices to be exposed in the manner of Theophrastus's *Characters*, the model for his text, Walter points forward to Dante, the court structured after the pattern of hell, its various circles reserved for the motley train of flatterers and backstabbers who make up its *dramatis personae*.

Huizinga's sense of estrangement from the emotional styles of the Burgundian court, refracted through the biliously tinted glasses of an anti-court tradition, forms a key thread in the long history of social performance. In this, the court is presented as a key social 'Other', our history presented as a lurch from primitive barbarism to decadent over-refinement that now rights itself in our enlightened modernity in some neat sequence of thesis–antithesis–synthesis, where the history of 'our' acquisition of *la distinction* is either conveniently forgotten or strategically occluded.[11] And yet that sense of 'natural' behaviour has been long in the making, marinaded in 'microphysics' of various kinds and slow-cooked into a 'second nature' of subjection and internalisation, traced in histories unpicking how we are not 'naturally and inevitably' born – as Simone de Beauvoir puts it – but culturally and contingently *become* what we are.[12] In this it draws on courtly ideals such as the avoidance of excessive show or obvious artifice encompassed in Shakespeare's myriad variations on the opposition of appearance and substance or in French idealisations of *le naturel*.[13] Of course, such an over-valorisation of the historical foreignness to us of such manners leaves us overlooking the strangeness of those ways to the Middle Ages, the extent to which – from medieval perspectives – they were a source of hostility, incomprehension, not to mention moral and sexual panic.[14] In that sense, courtly ways, not unlike manners more generally are troubling, caught between regulation and licence, discipline and corruption – as Edmund Burke put it in 1780, 'manners are more importance than laws [...] they aid morals, they supply them or they totally destroy them'.[15] Burke's comment provides a key microcosmic history, even suggestion that rather than being confined to a secondary existence as the ephemeral and contingent surface structure of behaviours in particular places and times, it is manners that form the frame within which morals flourish or wither. Variations on Burke's brief history can be seen in various contexts, one being the vision of the court and the palace as forming a social hothouse in which young men would be shaped and formed for good or ill. This tradition springs from the political and cultural ambitions of the Carolingian court, the urgency of its language stoked further by late-ninth century uncertainties about Charlemagne's legacy sparked by conflicts between his immediate descendants. That discourse, still discernable in eleventh- and twelfth-century assertions about court life and values in the Latin historiography and panegyric produced in the ecclesiastical and secular *curiae* of France and

Germany, is clearly reflected in early vernacular romance, the change of language effectively 'burying' this cultural coding behind the apparently 'what you see is what you get' presentation that is the surface narrative of its *contes d'aventure*.

A central text in this debate, Hincmar of Rheims's *The Order of the Palace* (*De Ordine Palatii*), a vision of the properly ordered court written for Carloman, son of Louis III in 882, offers a paradigmatic and influential vision of ideals echoed extensively in comment on aristocratic societies.[16] His treatise summed up a tradition of comment on the place of the court in shaping aristocratic society by 'disciplining' the young aristocrats schooled there, principles already articulated in an earlier letter from Hincmar to Louis in 858:

> The king's court is properly called a school [scola], that is a course of discipline, not because it consists solely of schoolmen [scolastici], men bred on learning and well trained in the conventional way [disciplinati et bene correcti], but rather a school in its own right [potius ipsa scola], which we can take to mean a place of discipline, that is correction, since it corrects men in their dress, deportment, speech and actions [habitu, incessu, verbo et actu], and in general holds them to the norms of restraint appropriate to a good life [atque totius bonitatis continentia corrigat].[17]

As Janet Nelson makes clear, Hincmar's letter comes at a period when Charles was in conflict with Robert of Anjou and also under pressure to deal with Viking raids in the North of his territories, pressures which seem to have led to the raising of demands for tribute.[18] Hincmar's distinction between the disciplines of the palace and the school draws sanction from his use within the same letter of Christ's words 'render unto Caesar that which is Caesar's' (Matt. 22:21) as part of a concern to see that the temporal powers be not merely active in defence of the realm but also properly administered in a time of crisis.[19] Thus, while Hincmar's admonition to Louis here is part of a call for fiscal prudence rather than intended to characterise the cultural distinctiveness of a lay but clerically-informed curial milieu. Nonetheless, already here we have an image of court culture as akin to but different from that of the schools: its discipline is both like and unlike that associated with the Church, and, although in effect 'aping' the model of the cathedral schools – the court's ways being something other than the 'good' conventions that make ecclesiastical schoolmen the *bene correcti* – still has a legitimacy of its own.

Although a considerable chronological gap separates the Carolingian courts reflected in these early sources and the later circles in which figures such as Chrétien and his contemporaries moved, as Stephen Jaeger nonetheless makes clear, there is a significant continuity between the terms Hincmar uses and the values of later court cultures:

> [Hincmar] departs from [ecclesiastical] language by omitting any reference to sacred learning, scripture or divine law. *Habitus, incessus, verbum* and *actus* are not common among the topics of praise of Carolingian clergy, but they will loom large in the eleventh century.[20]

Comments such as Hincmar's, seemingly out-of-time in their own day, thus almost presciently pave the way for later distinctions between the cultures of 'clergie' and 'chevalerie' fundamental to the court cultures that later shaped and produced vernacular romance.[21] In that sense, although Hincmar's use of the term 'school' might suggest a top-down educational organisation, Jaeger points out that, in Merovingian sources, *scola* commonly designates the court entourage, the term denoting 'a group with common characteristics, habits and interests', thus less a school per se than a 'school of thought', or, if not of fish, then some animal amenable to discipline and dressage, such as a horse.[22] In that sense, the discipline of the school encompassed both mind and body, or, in modern educational terms, both cognitive and motor skills. Key concerns here were values such as the pursuit of virtue (*cultus virtutum*), moderation (*bonus modus*), dignified seriousness (*gravitas*) and utility in service of the greater good (*utilitas rei publicae*), all of which would be reflected in the eloquence of elegant, charismatic performance either through words (*verbo*) or through bearing (*actu*).[23] Through such influence, the inculcation of knowledge as well as more embodied disciplines, the court became a centralising instrument shaping collective identity through the functional specialisation of a warrior, administrative or cultural elite operating more or less sporadically as a more or less coordinated political and legislative body, 'increasingly governing continuously rather than in brief spurts', as Tim Reuter puts it.[24]

Although the shaping discipline of the court aimed at educating (*prodesse*) new arrivals and producing community and similarity in virtue, it also inevitably created difference that would allow individuals to distinguish themselves (*praesse*). In pursuing excellence through a grasp of the rules either of language or 'the game', a schoolman might make himself less a countryman of his compatriots than a citizen of that other country of Rome and its *res publica*. In its more domesticated form, that cult of singularity was already present in Hincmar's vision in the pursuit of excellence that might lead some men to be lauded as exemplars, as 'our Plato', 'our Socrates' or 'a second Cicero'.[25] However, this translation of the self could take on a potentially runaway dimension in the secular sphere. Just as for Hincmar the ways of the court were distinct from the norms of the well-schooled, an association emerges between courtliness and the valorisation of strategic rule-breaking and improvisation later to be described by Shakespeare's Henry V as 'making manners' (see epigraph above), or by as Pierre Bourdieu as 'conducts of honour' – not 'the product of obedience to rules or submission to values (which they also are, since they are experienced as such), but [...] the product of a more or less conscious pursuit of the accumulation of symbolic capital'.[26] As Jaeger puts it:

> The curriculum of institutional identity and the pedagogy of individual charisma were as strongly in force at worldly courts as in monasteries or cathedrals. The possibilities for diversity were far greater at court, however. There is no ideal of uniform dress and behaviour (*aequalitas morum*). On the contrary, there is a tendency towards personalised and individualised forms of behaviour that grew stronger in the course of the high and late Middle Ages, and became a striking feature of Renaissance courts. Fashion and a tendency towards the aestheticising of behaviour, hence towards artificiality, are features of European court life that distinguish it from customs of religious communities.[27]

While discipline provided a regulatory body of rhetorical, ethical and moral ideals its cult of virtue often appears as a cult of virtuosity. Thus, just as the hagiography of martial artist Bruce Lee charts his progress through the study of various combat disciplines to a transcendent synthesis he described as 'no style', so rhetoricians would look beyond the limits of mimetic performance: as the chronicler and biographer Sigebert of Gembloux (b. 1028/1029) put it, 'There is no need for examples. You yourselves are the example'.[28] Although the pursuit of fame is a topos in early medieval ecclesiastical writings, in the secular sphere the guaranteeing *gravitas* of the churchman's sense of Christian mission seems not always to find a ready translation. Indeed, cultural innovation in the secular court pushes at the frames of reference that provide for the cultural intelligibility of behaviours, such that celebrated courtly or aristocratic performances often have a tendency not so much demonstrate as make, or rather *re*make, manners, seeming to rule in what had been ruled out as part of an assertion of dominance.[29] In this widening gap between ecclesiastical nervousness about a tension between what one might characterise as the forces of 'authority' and 'reason' on the one hand and a secular orientation towards the competitive pursuit of innovation and distinction on the other, we have the appearance of two cultures sometimes divided by a common language of panegyric.

To re-emphasise Susan Crane's opening gambit (and thereby, alas, mangle its delightful prosody), 'my target is *a* medieval courtier who is behaving strangely', which we might take not merely as 'strangely' relative to non-court cultures but also – not uncommonly – to the other courtiers around him. That is to say that the pursuit of courtly distinction carried with it the potential for getting 'lost in *translatio*': to do a bit too much of an Arthur (or a Socrates or an Alexander) was to risk looking not so much honestly 'Roman' as suspectly 'Greek' – or, in English or German contexts, a bit too *French*. In that regard, court culture's nature as a quasi-grammatical and rhetorical discipline shaping the courtier's performance both at an intellectual and an embodied level could lead to 'sport' – that is to say play of a sort that could seem not just disturbingly ludic or baroque in its strangeness or hybridity but even queer – in various domains, pushing at the boundaries of either meaning or avowability. One manifestation of court accomplishment (*urbanitas*) was the exercise of wit (*lepor* or *hilaritas*) through jokes (*facetiae*): thus, when Ruotger praises Brun of Cologne for improving the quality of Latin at the court of Otto the Great, then this is attributed to his 'courtly grace' ('domesticus lepor'), that is to say a command of the language sufficiently exemplary in its grasp and precision to form the basis for a play with nice distinctions in which wit still remained the seasoning salt of conversation rather than the substantive food.[30] Likewise, were Walter Map to praise the notedly larky Henry II for his capacity for 'facetiae', then this would not necessarily be the rhetorical 'nerd' – to evoke the opposition conventionally used to described the agonistic, 'two cultures' division of American campus life – collusively finding a way to put an ennobling spin on the tyranny of a bullying, 'jock'-ish pseudo-prankster, but rather a praise of Henry in terms to which John's fellow *clerici* could subscribe. That said, *The Courtier's Trifles* is sufficiently multi-layered and larded with damning anecdotes disarmingly and ostensibly told in praise, that it would be impossible to be sure. Likewise, the almost impenetrable ironies of some troubadour poetry – its cultivation of a poetics ostensibly 'open' to the lay body of the court linguistically, but 'closed' by dint of its baroque layerings of irony, its hyper-sophisticated game-playing – paints a picture of other milieux in which courtiers seemed prepared to risk their audiences saying it was 'all Greek' to them.[31]

The acquisition of the social language of charisma could also be perceived as overbalancing into the pursuit of suavity of other kinds, a suspicion expressed in the accusations of sodomy frequent in accounts of court life. In that sense, Walter Map's citing of sexual slanders against Bernard of Clairvaux (see dist. 1, chapter 24) has a double edge: the imputation of deviance is compounded by the clumsy, indecorous gestures that mark his failure to internalise and embody court ideals of *elegantia*. Just as Cistercians, required to forego undergarments to cool their ardour, seem fated to the indignity of tripping over and exposing their nether regions in the presence of kings (an anecdote Walter recounts in dist. 1, chapter 25), so Bernard awkwardly prostrates himself full-length on unresponsive boys. As Walter comments on the monk who embarrassed himself by falling backside over heels in front of Henry II, 'the monk who tumbled down would have got up again with more dignity [honestius surrexisset] had he had his breeches on' (dist. 1, chapter 25, p. 103 in edition). Although noisily famed abroad as a charismatic leader,

Walter's anecdotes about the Cistercians constantly return to details that reflect badly on their mastery of court discipline, in a world where converts to the order are delivered to the order's houses in farm-carts (dist. 1, chapter 24, p. 77–9 in edition).

In its charting of the collapse of ideals associated with earlier court circles, the degradation of their *virtutes* (whether rhetorically or morally), Jaeger's account of the changing perceptions of court culture between the ninth to the twelfth centuries reads in part as a narrative of decadence and decline. In that sense, the ambiguity of this moment appears as a sort of forerunner of that summed up in Johan Huizinga's title, *The Autumn of the Middle Ages*, ambiguously caught between fruiting and plenty on the one hand and putrescent decline on the other.[32] Thus, although the 'twelfth-century Renaissance' appears as a cultural flowering, that sense of vigour and renewal is doubled by discourses of pessimism, decadence and lament: old values seem to have fossilised into the dead hand of received wisdom and *auctoritas* while what passes for innovation is denounced as style triumphing over substance in a world rife with accusations of Pharisaical fraud and intellectual imposture.[33] Beyond that lies a more uncertain terrain in which the relation of words to values seemed less certain. By the time we reach Alan of Lille, we find ourselves faced with a virtuosic Latinist apparently panicked to the point of arguing that any syntax other than Subject–Verb–Object is tantamount to sodomy, and that – in a seeming reversal of the logic of discipline associated with the earlier schools – the effete corruption of literary language carries within itself, and indeed 'embodies' the possibility of sexual deviance: a passive construction *is* sodomitical, deponent verbs, passive in form but active in meaning (*locutus sum* –'I spoke') , *are* hermaphroditic.

The problem with the school of the court as a world of what René Girard would term 'mimetic desire' is that in proposing the undiscovered country of a second nature, it seems to open too many doors, to offer too many different possibilities for self-fashioning, to expose the self too radically to the risks of remaking.[34] In that regard, the fruitfully cornucopian relation of court performances to the allure of their 'scripts' rather resembles Judith Butler's vision of gender performance as caught between the identification with and citational reproduction of perceived norms on the one hand, and, on the other, transgressive and parodic play with those same models. Its various manifestations – be they advanced Latinity, exotic materials or new possibilities of desire – trouble and make strange the seemingly known terrain of the self in an encounter with 'foreignnesses' that raises the spectre of forces disavowed and repressed in its construction. What the reactions of courtiers against the institutions and discourses that shaped them reveal is the measure in which court culture offers a sort of grey area in which the influx of new information and influences threaten and trouble identity at various levels, intellectually, culturally, physically or sexually. In that sense, medieval presentations of court culture find themselves caught between history and libel in a logic neatly summarised by Mary Douglas:

> The regular strategy of rejection starts with the libel. The simple food libel (foreigners eat disgusting foods), the sex libel (the demeaned category is promiscuous, effeminate, incestuous), escalate to violence and perversion, and, if the determination to exclude is fixed, it resorts to the blood libel (the enemy is murderous and even murders children). The culminating infamy that incites ethnic persecution combines blood, sex, food and religion.[35]

All of these aspects are repeated in medieval denunciations of court culture. Court food is either decadent or awful. For example, in the *Roman de Renart*, the fox tempts the bear – sent to summon him to appear before the lion-king, Noble – by contrasting how badly courtiers are served with the fact that he himself has just eaten a 'marvellous *French* dish' peas and bacon, followed by honey (ed. by Dufournet, Br. 1, l. 504–37), tantalising his listener by the thirty-line gap between the initial mention of the culinary marvel and his eventual revelation of what was on the menu. Message: whatever they serve at the court might be *haute*, but it isn't *cuisine* as you and I know it. Needless to say, after this, the bear is only a few octosyllables from being putty in Renart's diabolical paws. As for the sex libel, since a vast bibliography of sources relating to the court could be cited in evidence, I will limit my comments to noting that all of human life is in Walter Map's catalogue of life in the place he compares to hell. The 'blood libel' effectively combines all of the above, especially in the person of the tyrant as centre of the court's infamy, a figure capable of murder, sexual impropriety and cannibalism, sometimes simultaneously, whether in alleged fact or because the various domains become assimilable to one another such that once one kind of mud sticks, every kind does. Thus, portraits of Richard the Lionheart as court sodomite go hand-in-hand with stories of him eating Saracen flesh.[36]

What these various voices tell us is that to be a courtier was to be troubling, to be subject to the envy and admiration, defamation and disapproval that were the marks either of outsiders looking in or the jaundiced reflections of the alienated insider. However, does this mean that the courtier is simply travestied by being made the scapegoat for everything that appears strange in culture? After all, it is also clear that court culture's apparent courting of rejection through the discourses of nature and sincerity it spawned and nurtured is the reflection of a mode of behaviour that thrived on sowing uncertainty from a position of exception. In this, the question is one of balance of power, of leverage, and also of owning that power as the subject of a certain discourse, rather than being reduced to the constructed object of censure, or, as Judith Butler puts it, the object threatened with trouble is, at the same time, a source of trouble.[37] In the court milieu, as Machiavelli notes (see chapter epigraph), troubling the audience of 'find-faults', making them uncertain of the value of the consensus to which they hold, is sometimes supremely useful, especially given that collectives are usually persuaded by outcomes or appearances rather than genuine understandings of cause, reason or right. Although often tarred as the damnable inventor of modern political cynicism, it is nonetheless clear Machiavelli was not the first to think along such lines, his sin perhaps being to spell out the underlying (lack of) principles. For example, in Geoffrey of Monmouth, the tensions between the high ground of Arthur's reaction to Rome's demand for renewal of tribute (see epigraph) and his own recent career as a conqueror, are – as Lewis Thorpe notes – glaringly apparent.[38] Does this make him a despotic fraud or just less egregious a sinner than his Roman competitors? Although, as I will argue, the answer is probably the latter, the impression – if only transitory – of disingenuousness on Arthur's part is cause for thought, his history haunting and troubling the ostensible concern with right and justice conventionally associated with his reign.

Text and Context: Vernacular Prosopopoeia

> With regard to Caesar's memoirs Cicero, also in the *Brutus* speaks in the following terms: 'He wrote memoirs which deserve the highest praise; they are naked in their simplicity, straightforward yet graceful, stripped of all rhetorical adornment, as of a garment [nudi sunt, recti et venusti, omni ornatu orationis tamquam veste detracta]; but while his purpose was [dum voluit] to supply material to others, on which those who wished [qui vellent] to write history might draw, he haply gratified silly folk, who will try to use the curling-irons on his narrative [qui illa volent calamistris inurere], but he has kept men of any sense from touching the subject.' (Suetonius, *The Deified Julius*, § 56)[39]

> What is the role of prosopopoeia in ethical thinking and doing? Why do both thinking about ethics and the act of ethical choice always involve some act of personification?[40]

From the work of scholars such as John Benton, Ad Putter and others, we have a reasonably detailed picture of the literary and artistic culture of the court of Champagne under Count Henry the Liberal (1127–1181) and his wife, Marie de Champagne (1145–1198), daughter of Eleanor of Aquitaine. I say 'reasonably' because although Chrétien may be 'très présent dans son oeuvre' (as Carleton Carroll puts it), whenever a piece of evidence emerges that seems to point to a person who might have been Chrétien – such as the canon 'Christianus' who appears in the records of Saint-Loup-de-Troyes in 1173 or another (or perhaps the same) canon bearing the same name mentioned in the records of Henry's church of Saint-Maclou at Bar-sur-Aube – further examination seems to open a hall of mirrors in which any hope of finding the man himself vanishes.[41] Indeed, Sarah Kay's re-examination of the various occurrences of the name in French works from the period suggests that Chrétiens can seem almost as numerous as Spartici at the end of *Spartacus*, depending on how you interpret the evidence.[42] This question of authorship and authorial identity may not be entirely incidental or decoratively prefatory to my consideration of *Erec et Enide*: the poem alludes frequently to matters of history, evidence and identity, asking questions about the relation between what we know about the past and the uses we make of that supposed knowledge. What that suggests is a highly informed 'historical literacy' underpinned the court of Champagne's culture industry, very much interested in what the Romans (or the Greeks, or Arthur or whoever) did, or – more importantly, perhaps – could still do for us. Thus, whoever he was, I suspect that, although the 'Chrétien' of *Erec et Enide* would have been gratified by his critical afterlife, he would have been, above all, amused to find that what was being written about 'him' some 900 years later begged many of the same biographical and historiographical questions and assumptions evoked in 'his' work.

Thus, if character study can be seen as one of the duller and more outmoded strands of romance criticism, this is arguably because the context of its concern with portraiture in larger traditions of cultural and historical debate and in medieval jockeyings for pre-eminence through their equalling and surpassing of the examples of Antiquity has been overlooked. Although it is far from certain who Chrétien was, whether that name actually designates a single individual responsible for all the works commonly attributed to him or, indeed, exactly when those works were written, it nonetheless seems reasonably clear that the poems attributed to him reflect an interest, also attested elsewhere, in the court as a social milieu and particularly in the 'rules' by which its 'games' were played and in how the actions of key players might either impact on or be interpreted in that milieu.[43] Of course, this is not to say that Chrétien's world announces itself as all spin and artifice: the narrator of *Erec et Enide* stresses that combats are not faked, love is not feigned (see chapter epigraph above). Yet, as will become apparent, neither of these statements can be taken at face value. In that sense, Chrétien can be seen as interrogating how people perform in their social roles and what different varieties of distance might exist between the person and a given mask in a particular place and a particular time. Thus, although Marcus Bull rightly highlights that modern representations of the Middle Ages as speaking a parodic 'Mock Medieval' pidgin (see epigraph above) amount to a refusal to see what was 'native' to them, it is also evident that medieval people knowingly engaged in citational practices, appropriating and adapting discourses and behaviours from other cultures and times. In that sense, their native 'Medieval' can often be seen as interrogating its cultural endebtedness, the extent to which it was 'Mock Antique' or 'Mock Oriental'. For example, at what point if ever might it have occurred to twelfth-century French courtiers that a room decked out in rugs, silks and other finery might look less like an affirmation of the prestige of that milieu than evidence of medieval vernacular cultures as acquisitive, shoulder-chipped *wannabes* in relation to the wealth and sophistication of their Byzantine and Islamic neighbours?[44] The question that then arises is how self-conscious that appropriation was, how alive or occluded the strangenesses internal to the senses of self they constructed were as well as how evolved was the reflection on how troubling or useful different sources of strangeness could be.

The extent to which othernesses admirable and even imitable were a source of anxiety in the construction of the mandate that might found a 'vernacular' medieval aristocratic self is clearly apparent from texts such as the parody chanson de geste, *Le Pèlerinage de Charlemagne à Constantinople* to see the venerable king of the Franks cast as leader of a band not of heroic crusaders but crass, vandalistic yokels.[45] The poem's vision of the twelve peers of France slack-jawed in amazement at emperor Hugh blithely leaving his golden plough unattended before the city gates in order to escort them back to his palace crystallises in eloquent miniature a 'cultural cringe' that takes in not merely embarrassment at the Franks' crass assumptions about their own status but indeed at an entire literary tradition. In a moment that anticipates Voltaire's vision of a world where everyone seems more charitable than European Christians or *The Return to the Planet of the Apes*'s depiction of chimpanzees more sympathetically humane than people, Hugh utterly wrong-foots the French *chevaliers* by appearing in the guise of a peasant-king (*rex laborans*) whose generosity and ease targets the authority of a warrior aristocracy founded in the assumed pre-eminence of 'second order' *bellatores*, making Roland and his companions look like unformed *parvenus*. Indeed, the scene's central joke seemingly sweeps the rug out from under the feet of the *Pseudo-Turpin Chronicle's* legend that it was those members of Charlemagne's expeditionary force in Spain who asked leave to return to France thereby becoming the first serfs, the social Other whose baseness defined the Franks as free-born.[46] Further questions then attach to the very form and language of the poem: the discourse and conventions of the French chansons, works that played an important role as crusade propaganda, are here unmasked as the crude, overweening soundtrack of supremacist backwardness. In this poem, if anything, Western Europe expresses a wish to become more 'foreign' in relation to its present identity.

Arthurian romance appears as one of the key elements in this literature of court 'strangeness'. Although he clearly served as a pattern for the kings – fictional or flesh-and-blood – who followed after him, Arthur himself was no less prone to 'doing a bit of a'..., well, himself. Thus it is that Chrétien's opening scenario in *Erec et Enide*, one of the earliest surviving vernacular representations of his court, presents a king endangering the cohesion of his court through what seems like a whim. In Arthur's desire to reinvoke the custom of the hunt of the White Stag, we have a moment of wilfulness that throws the court sufficiently off balance for it to take almost 7,000 lines for it finally to right itself. Yet, although seemingly irrational, that assertion of will can be seen as central to the matter of Arthur, both in terms of the picture Chrétien paints of court life and how he positions his own poetic production in relation to the literary and historiographical traditions that inform his work. Chrétien's narrative presents itself as a puzzle in many respects, not least regarding how the sense of what we are told depends on after-the-fact judgements about motivation. Key issues are the reticence of Erec and his treatment of Enide, with many essays dealing with what our understanding of his motivation and judgement should be, or what her motivation in speaking out or her actual 'forfait' might have been.[47] When Erec returns to court, the narrator abridges the hero's account of his adventures, especially insofar as these might provide an explanation of what Erec set out to do:

> Cuidiez vos or que je vos die
> Quex acoisons le fist movoir?
> Naie; que bien savez le voir

> Et de ce et de l'autre chose,
> Si con je la vos ai esclose. (ll. 6470–4)

> I hope you're not now expecting me to tell you the occasion for his setting out? No indeed, for full well do you know the truth both about this and the other matter, just as I have disclosed it to you.

Unhelpfully, puzzlingly, the narrator positions the audience in the midst of a range of directions and objects. Even as Chrétien dashes any expectation that the truth of Erec's quest might be revealed, we are immediately distracted by the statement that this is because we 'already' know this as well as that concerning 'the other matter'. When precisely did we learn this truth, and what is the 'other matter' the narrator refers to in his conspiratorial nod? Did we actually miss *two* things instead of one somewhere along the line, or is the narrator mischievously trying to distract us from one object by introducing an extraneous red herring? Which avenue should we follow? Of course, the word 'quest' would be somewhat abusively applied here, reflecting a narratology of romance shaped by texts such as *Le Conte du graal*. Instead, the term Chrétien uses is simply 'movoir', a term that in itself covers a range of senses: what moved him to set out, or 'what caused him to move', or even, 'to make a move'. This then posits a relation of two terms: the movement and its 'occasion', its cause. Chrétien's formulation seems to posit the two as separate in nature: 'occasion' gives rise to a motion, but it is in some way distinct from it in the sense that although cause and effect can be part of a single perceived event, they are nonetheless distinct elements. However, as the comment makes clear, Erec's move is also a motion in time, its truth recoverable in retrospect, a vision that then problematises our sense of the primacy of the cause. We seem invited to look back from our perspective at the point he occupies sighting back down a line of motion to a point of origin presented as containing that direction. Can any of these assertions of relation or perspectival alignment be taken at face value? One person who claims an insight into what moved Erec is Enide. It is for this reason that my reading highlights the importance of the version contained in B. N. fonds fr. 1376.[48] Where the Guiot copy and related versions present her concluding comment on Erec's fate as 'Amis, con mar fus'

('Friend, how great a misfortune for you'), in fonds fr. 1376 it appears as '[Tant] mar *i* fus' ('It was such great misfortune that you happened to be there.', l. 2503).[49] Her reading of the sense of his journey at this point is tragic. However, that reading is both reiterated and contested throughout the poem. Erec's questioning of her – 'why did you say misfortune brought me there?' – provides precisely the permanent open-endedness of this particular dialogue, the lack of assurance to its claims regarding the sense of Erec's adventure.

In part, Erec's motion reflects both an observation of and intervention in the *mouvance* of vernacular literary traditions. As Simon Gaunt observes, 'Chrétien does not invent Arthurian romance, rather he *reshapes* it'.[50] While, as far as we can know, Chrétien's first romance may inaugurate a career, if not a genre, at the same time it can be read as a response to other traditions and other debates, a response located in specific literary and cultural contexts and taking the genre in a particular direction. In that sense, the impetus of the 'acoisons [qui] le fist movoir', located either in the past as cause or as irruption in the present, is the focus of a biographical or prosopopoeic project – *prosopopoeia*, being the 'ascription of a voice or face to the absent' – that not only looks to uncover character, cause and motive but also to examine how the 'naked' truth that emerges is that biographical subjects like Julius Caesar might also have wished to retain some fig-leaf of enigma.[51] In the citation from the historian Suetonius above, a group of great minds and first-hand observers – Cicero, Brutus and Suetonius himself – scratch their heads at a man who, though dead, seems able to cover himself sufficiently not to be laid bare to history. As successive generations and cultures look back over those shoulders to the accounts of Caesar, overlaying their will and purpose on his, the play of perspectives does not get any simpler. What I will argue here is that to look at movement in *Erec et Enide* taps into a vast range of relations – literary, cultural and historical – looked at from the perspective of a late twelfth-century court milieu. In that regard, if courtly performance is imitative or referential in character, then its reference to past cultures can be seen to either dissimulate agency in the present and to mystify it by present it as springing from a source that cannot be recovered.

Yet, if Chrétien's first romance carries with it a great deal of historical baggage, it also carries it lightly. One image gives some sense of how that relation is envisaged: when we first meet Erec (ll. 81–104), he is described as much loved at court (ll. 85–6), beautiful (ll. 87–8), riding a warhorse (l. 94), clad in elegant, exotic robes (ll. 97–100) and carrying no equipment other than his sword (ll. 103–4). If we read Chrétien's description against the language of courtly values emanating from of medieval cathedral schools and courts from the ninth century on, we see a number of key background signals about Erec's status and cultural competences. Erec's charm and good manner in company (*urbanitas, affabilitas*) – his elegance in dress (*elegantia habitu*) being merely a first impression – have engendered bonds of friendship (*amicitiae*) that open doors at a political level. Thus, although he appears here alone in a forest, he is nonetheless intimately connected to a wider court world in which he has earned the favour of key players. If anything needs doing, Erec is dress-coded and has the medieval aristocratic equivalent of exactly the right mobile phone, credit card and car to see that it gets done. What we have here is the idealised vision of a young aristocrat whose appearance of ease and assurance is the product of a great deal of disciplinary work that, we are given to understand, happened off-stage. Among these we might list the economic exploitation that paid for everything, the training that made him able to use horse and sword together, not to mention the investment of labour and skills as well as the trade activity that brought him his clothing. What we learn later in Laluth is that Erec has spent three years at Arthur's court (l. 654). It is this not insignificant period of careful networking at court that has brought him the influence and access he clearly enjoys as the Queen's chosen companion for the day, a position – given that he is not Lancelot – that also implies the King's permission.[52] Though neither past labour nor future threat seem to weigh too heavily here, it was that work which brought us to this place.

The same applies to Chrétien's appearance on the literary stage: critical opinion worries about what baggage the tale carries and how. Should we see the tale of Erec as an *oeuvre de jeunesse* whose influences are borrowed rather piecemeal? To what extent is it a reflection of scholastic traditions? Although it would be wrong to underplay the problems with identifying Chrétien or seeing him as the author of the range of works attributed to him, my argument here does take as an assumption the conventional association of *Erec et Enide* with the court of Champagne in the late twelfth century.[53] Critics, most prominent among them Beate Schmolke-Hasselmann, have scented hints of Plantagenet sympathies in possible allusions to figures associated with the court of Henry II (1133–1189), notably 'Brian of the Isles' ('Brïanz des illes', l. 6722), thought to be Brian Fitz Count, lord of Wallingford (d. ca 1150) and 'Yvain de Cavaliot' (l. 1705), possibly based on Owein Cyfeilog (1130–1197).[54] However, more recent studies have taken issue with these claims, Karen Broadhurst concurring with Ian Short's view that attempts to associate 'Chrétien de Troyes with Henry's court are doomed to remain conjectural'.[55] Likewise, as Broadhurst tellingly reminds us, 'if Henry or Eleanor had solicited this text from Chrétien, there is no mention of it in the romance'.[56] However, allusion to events and evidence of patronage are not the same thing, as both D. D. R. Owen's cautious assessment of Chrétien's contact with the Plantagenet court and Broadhurst's concession make clear: 'it is certainly possible that Chrétien was inspired by the Christmas court at Nantes and maybe that he even left out the French at the festival described in his romance'.[57] My reading here echoes work that sees Chrétien's poem as a reflection of relations between those courts, although – for reasons that will become clear – I remain agnostic with regard to the exact dating of the text.

A significant proportion of opinion sees *Erec et Enide* as having been composed in 1170, in part based on the view that Erec's coronation reflects the investiture of Henry II's son Geoffrey (1158–1186) as Duke of Britanny in Nantes, although 1165 has also been suggested as a possibility. However, although widely accepted, the 1170 dating is difficult to reconcile with what Claude Luttrell and others have seen as the influence of works associated with the so-called 'School of Chartres' and thought to have been produced in the 1180s, such as Alan of Lille's *Anticlaudianus*.[58] Given that the similarities adduced by Luttrell are striking to say the least, this is potentially problematic.[59] However, not only is the dating of the Chartrean texts Luttrell cites not secure, as Tony Hunt demonstrates, but also one might equally see sources for them, perhaps drawn on in common with Chrétien, in the work of earlier authors such as Bernardus Silvestris or even Macrobius, as well as in troubadour lyric.[60] It is also possible that a good deal of Chrétien's reflection on cosmogony and fate may well simply reflect scriptural sources or such staples as Boethius's *Consolation of Philosophy*, 'after the Bible, the most-read book of the entire Middle Ages', as Ruth Firestone comments, following Frederick Pickering.[61]

Another avenue opened by a later dating is to see in Chrétien's poem reflections – positive or negative – of the actions of Henry II's first son, Henry (1155–1183), Duke of Normandy, known as the 'Young King'.[62] Henry's activities in the late 1170s were a source of some comment, as we can see from Walter Map's *The Courtier's Trifles* (*De Nugis Curialium*) as well as from the extensive chronicle sources associated with the King's reign.[63] Richard Barber summarises as follows:

> [Henry] had spent four years, between 1176–1180, in a series of great tournaments in Northern France, with no thought of politics, while his brothers Richard and Geoffrey were serving a hard apprenticeship in real warfare. His nature was better suited to such diversions than to more serious work. Universally popular, he was on the other hand too easily swayed by flatterers and bad counsellors.[64]

With this view of the young Henry in mind, Chrétien's portrait of Erec takes on rather a different tint: Erec's *recreantise* might read as a distant reflection of the Young King's lack of military activity. However, this could be seen as inconsistent with the fact Erec is begged both by his father and by Arthur to remain at court rather than to go out and risk his life in tourneys and combats. One possible avenue here would then be to see *Erec et Enide* as a propagandist attempt to secure Henry's reputation by repositioning him as the hero of a work set in the context of a genre and period where there just happened to be no wars. Although such a suggestion is – as Ian Short comments – likely to remain only a conjecture, the possibility of Chrétien offering a reflection on the 'Young King' problem is nonetheless intriguing. Other critics have argued for later datings locating the poem in the context of relations between the Plantagenet and Champenois courts in spite of the tensions created by Eleanor's siding with the revolt of Henry's younger sons in the early-mid 1170s and thereafter that of the Young King himself in the early 1180s. Joseph Duggan makes the interesting point that an identification of Plantagenet interests need not be incompatible with a later dating sometime after the marriage of Geoffrey and Constance in 1181.[65]

Of course, excessive focus on the importance of a specific moment might distact us from looking at another aspect of the poem's context: while Chrétien has been read as taking specific events as a focus, it may also reflect larger histories. Thus, the near, although not immediate horizon for Chrétien's work could comprise histories of family and diplomatic relations as well as literary traditions centring on Eleanor of Aquitaine, all potential sources of scandal in the family closet. As is emphasised in recent studies by Richard Barber and Dan Power, Eleanor's personal history, 'a focal point of the gossip and intrigues at court', was the object of rumour and speculation whose racy propagandist use extended well beyond her own lifetime.[66] Such influence as scandalous inspiration may overshadow the role attributed to her as patron: as Ruth Harvey argues, despite considerable claims having been made for her patronage in Occitania, the actual literary evidence is mixed at best, with only Bernart de Ventadorn seeming to accord her real significance.[67] However, as Harvey notes, if her beauty and largesse did not have the inspirational effect she is sometimes credited with, rumours about her private life – a heady brew of political intrigue, adultery and incest – seemingly did.[68] The relation between literary production and personal scandal is then further complicated by the flagrantly scandalous character of some of the literary production directly associated with her ancestors (a case in point being William IX's poem 'Companho, farai un vers covinen', whose possible influence I discuss in chapter four).[69] This is not to say that I am proposing to follow Richard Barber's suggestive parallel between Eleanor's reputation and contemporary celebrity scandal by offering a 'tabloid' decoding of Chrétien's romance as a *roman à clef*. However, some of the spice of Chrétien's tale may lie in what Peggy McCracken sees as his teasingly 'oblique' treatment of such matters, a subject-matter still probably less directly dangerous than the Lancelot-Guinevere affair.[70] Indeed, the latter in comparison might seem too solidly unspectral: such skeletons – perhaps open secrets in various court circles – that might haunt the family closet offer the best hope of producing what we might think of as a (sufficiently visible but decently diaphanous) intertextual or hyper-textual shadow.[71]

While Eleanor's family history offered its own salacious tang, other houses may have tried to lay claim to a more settled, less scandal-ridden view, commissioning works that located particular family histories of conflict, disgrace and succession in a larger context. In that regard, literary and family histories sometimes evolved in parallel, as Simon Gaunt comments:

> The group [of poems] formed by the *Eneas*, the *Roman de Troie* and the *Roman de Thèbes* was probably composed between 1150 and 1165. They may have been composed for Henry II of England; they certainly circulated in his continental territories under the patronage of someone wishing to promote Plantagenet interests, for with Wace's *Roman de Rou* and *Brut* they form a sequence of narratives which shows how the new royal house of England could trace a direct line of descent back to the royal house of Troy, through Arthur and Julius Caesar. Amongst the earliest surviving romances, the *romans antiques* are precursors both in terms of form and content of Chrétien de Troyes and Arthurian romance. Indeed, in one manuscript (B.N. fonds français, 1450) all of Chrétien's romances are interpolated into the *Brut*, which follows the *Eneas* and the *Roman de Troie*, suggesting a high degree of continuity and cohesion between the *romans antiques* and Chrétien.[72]

What we might understand from Gaunt's comments is that the work of weaving Plantagenet history into a larger tapestry continued alongside the events of Henry II's reign. Thus, Chrétien's poem does not simply narrate events subsequent to the settlement of Britain or Arthur's early conquests: it also reflects back on the family history that continued to unfold in the 15 to 20 (or more) years between the composition of the *Roman d'Eneas* and *Erec et Enide* as well as on the evolving 'historiographical project' that sought to legitimise Plantagenet claims. Of course, during this interval the two great households – apparently perfectly capable of manufacturing more history than they could consume at home – scarcely needed more publicity to secure them their place in the annals. In this period, the history of Eleanor's marriage to Henry moved from the shared interest of the early years following her divorce from Louis in 1152 to the rather less happy events of 1173–1174 when Henry led her into captivity following her siding with his sons in rebellion against him. In this conjuncture, the events narrated in the *romans antiques* associated with the Plantagenets and those of Henry's reign and his union with Eleanor continue to look back at one another, the course of events in the foreground providing shifting resonances and significances to the literary backdrop.

From such a long-view vantage, Chrétien's synthesis of these various strands was almost bound to become playful rather than dutiful. But how playful? The problem here lies in reconciling ludic elements with views of the tone of *Erec et Enide*. However, preconceptions here might have led to possibilities being overlooked. For example, although earlier criticism sees the influence of the *Roman d'Eneas* mainly in the later sections, such as the description of the saddle Guivret gives Enide (*Erec et Enide*, ll. 5322–45), I will suggest the earlier work operates as an intertextual backdrop throughout.[73] The reason this might have been neglected lies in its scandalous nature: what I see as a principle point of reference is the horse imagery used by Lavine's mother in her slandering of Eneas as a sodomite (*Roman d'Eneas*, ll. 8588–95), a use that leaves Chrétien's text subversively 'haunted' by scandal and impropriety. While such readings may seem provocatively or modishly lurid, what I intend to show is that Chrétien's poem functions in terms of a sort of recursive logic of confirmation: over the sequence of Erec's adventures we see patterns of allusion and suggestion retrospectively confirmed in later scenes. One key example of this practice is to be found in the sequence from Erec's encounter with the giants and rescue of the abducted Cadoc of Tabriol to his subsequent collapse and Enide's lament for him ('Con mar i fus'). Taken in this context, the line recycled from earlier now appears as a climactic echo of Helena's nurse's warning to Arthur ('Misfortune brought you here') in Geoffrey of Monmouth's account of the King's slaying of the giant of Mont-Saint-Michel, an allusion that then highlights the sexual dimension of the tortures inflicted on Cadoc earlier (see chapter seven). Another instance is the suggestion that the key to the riddle of Arthur's controversial decision to relaunch the custom of the hunt may lie in a (botched) plan to exploit the general amazement and confusion as a backdrop to the court theatre that would be the announcement of Erec's betrothal to the handmaiden accompanying Guinevere.

Chrétien's romances explicitly present themselves as part of a definitve cultural and historical shift, the transference (*translatio*) of political power (*translatio imperii*) and intellectual pre-eminence (*translatio studii*) from Roman antiquity to the kingdoms of the medieval West. By incorporating or encoding family histories of Eleanor's kin and the Plantagenets into vernacular revisionings of the ancient past, romance texts arguably strengthen a historical and genealogical 'middle ground', reinforcing the compositional weave of what might otherwise seem like a more distant relation in which there would be nothing between the immediate present's foreground mime of a remote background past. The gesture is both one of projection (they are intimately contextualised in, or *translated into* that history) and appropriation (because they are in it, it belongs to, or is 'carried across' /*translated to* them). As with Erec's relation to the court, they do not just 'love' History, abjectly waiting on its regard: History 'loves' them, too. This context emphasises both lineage and seriousness of their cultural claims. Here, the 'long view' from the fall of Troy to the founding, flourishing and decline of Rome – whether in the context of the civil war and the end of the Republic or the later barbarian invasions – is shaped by the reflections of authorities such as Cicero, Virgil, Lucan, Ovid, Boethius and Augustine on questions of merit and virtue, reward and disregard, loss and exile, reflection and consolation.[74] It also engages with questions in biographical and prosopopoeic traditions, such as the fate of Julius Caesar, who leaves to history *two* bodies – one of writings, the other bloodied and twitching on the marble floor of the Senate – either or neither of which may give the full sense of what made and moved the man himself. Chrétien's poem engages with these larger historiographical and philosophical reflections through a focus pulling us back towards the here-and-now (or there-and-then) of Enide's 'mar i fus', echoing traditions of lament and consolation literature that includes Ovid's exile poetry, Cicero's lost tract on the death of his daughter, Augustine's *City of God* and Boethius's *Consolation of Philosophy*. One of the key aspects of consolation literature is its dual perspective: the macrocosmic sweep of universal forces counterpoints the microcosmic detail of individual cases; emphasis on the inevitability, and even banality of human misfortune counterpoints the singular poignancy of individual experiences. Without the pathetic effect, the larger vision appears as empty philosophising; without the shaping frame of principle, all we have is a mire of despair and pity.

This emphasis on the intersection of cosmic patterns and the particularity of location or individual trajectory is fundamental more generally to Chrétien's vision of the relation between culture, history and desire and to his engagement with antecedent sources such as Geoffrey of Monmouth's *History of the Kings of Britain* or the Old French *Roman d'Eneas*. Both of these works deal with place in the sense of migration and cultural shift at different levels. First, both take the tale of Aeneas's wanderings as their point of origin and use them as a way of looking back at Roman history from a medieval perspective, contextualising assumptions of primacy and certainty in a larger vision of transition and change. Second, both position the medieval present as informed by a distinctive and legitimate cultural identity and value-system in contradistinction to a Rome viewed as alienly republican or simply tyrannical. The *Roman d'Eneas* thus bears witness to the trouble of carrying over ancient narratives of migration and foundation manifest in Virgil's *Aeneid* and in its response to the propagandist assertions associated with the reign of Caesar Augustus, assertions that in their turn can be seen as an attempt to settle out the turbulent vision of historical dialectic that are the myths of Rome's strife-torn pantheon of gods, particularly, as Sarah Spence comments, Juno.[75] Eneas is the founder of a feudal history which, according to the prophecy of his father whom he encounters in the underworld, will encompass the Senate's regicide of Eneas's great scion, Julius Caesar. As for Geoffrey, Rome is presented as a leviathan hybrid, the will of the Senate represented in the imperialist discourse of a legate who harks back to relations of subservience and tribute established by Caesar. That Arthur is (albeit ambiguously) praised for his 'Ciceronian eloquence' – thus, the key attribute of Caesar's great enemy – makes it clear the emperor is viewed here as tyrant.

My argument here is that one way of understanding Chrétien's poem is as a knowing, jocular and singularly unfazed response to and reflection on potential hostages to fortune in both a specific family history as *cause célèbre* and also more generally in the genealogical models and narratives associated with medieval aristocratic appropriations of classical tradition. His rhetorical and referential fireworks, his disarmingly daring in-jokes, appear both subversive and yet at the same time perhaps counterintuitively useful as a response to the propaganda problems facing his putative masters. Thus, while informed by long traditions of writing about change and identity, agency and origin, Chrétien's sense of place – whether that of his work or of his audience in history – clearly also focalises at a particular point and a particular time.

Locating Agency:
Perversity, Anxiety, Subalternity, Anamorphosis

> Cinema is the ultimate pervert art. It doesn't give you what you desire – it tells you how to desire.[76]
>
> L'émoi est trouble, chute de puissance [...] c'est le trouble, le se troubler en tant que tel, le se troubler le plus profond dans la dimension du mouvement.[77]
>
> The project of provincialising Europe [...] cannot be a project of cultural relativism. [...] For the point is not that Enlightenment rationalism is always unreasonable in itself, but rather a matter of documenting how – through what historical process – its 'reason', which was not always self-evident to everyone, has been made to look obvious far beyond the ground where it originated. If a language, as has been said, is but a dialect backed up by an army, the same could be said of narratives of 'modernity' that, almost universally today, point to a certain 'Europe' as the primary habitus of the modern.[78]
>
> Poems are necessarily sequential, whereas we see pictures all at once. Narrative is predisposed to suit the historical imagination, whereas pictoral art more readily serves ecological, systemic, a-historical habits of mind.[79]

If Chrétien's poem can be located in the context of particular political, historical and cultural relations, it is simultaneously implicated in a history of the subjectivity and desire foundational to a number of 'theoretical' discourses. With this in mind, my treatment of *Erec et Enide* here draws on a range of approaches which, although ostensibly separate, are arguably connected in their illumination of how performance and troubling shape and interrogate our sense of place and history. The first of these is the vision of courtly romance as a literature of what Jacques Lacan terms perversity. The second relates to Freudian and Lacanian discussions of the notion of anxiety (*Angst, angoisse*). The third plank is the notion of 'subalternity', which has been a highly productive field of inquiry and debate in postcolonial criticism, as well as more specifically in the field of medieval studies.[80] What links all three of these aspects is a focus on the relation between the subject, its agency and the object of desire, and especially with regard to an access to a 'true' subjective status marked by what Lacan terms 'full speech' ('la parole pleine') in which the subject articulates and assumes the 'truth' of its own desire or actions.[81] In this matter, the question of anamorphosis, the use of perspectival distortion as a visual riddle, highlights the way in which words and acts may be pulled at and haunted by other scenes and other forces that make vain and provisional any claim to plenitude. Relating these terms provides us with a way of understanding the particular places of Chrétien's vision of medieval kingship as well as of the relation between cultures, both synchronically and diachronically, specifically in his interrogation and contestation of particular historicising gestures fundamental to the Arthurian legend and to the larger narrative of *translatio imperii*. In these relations, condensatory structures such as 'locations of culture' or the figure of the king constitute troubling 'exceptions' open a dialogue between medieval and modern theoretical debates regarding issues such as universality and relations of cultural dominance. This provides a range of ways of thinking about the fantasy construction of both history and geography, the indebtedness to elsewheres and elsewhens in romance's elaboration of a cultural 'Subject position' for the medieval literary vernacular.

This dialogical relation between the medieval and the modern is apparent in Lacanian examinations of subjective interpellation, the question of how the Subject accepts the 'logic of castration' and subordinates itself to the Law (a.k.a. Superego, a.k.a. 'Name of the

Father') even as the Law itself – in its 'uncastrated' tyrannical irrationality – is then paradoxically an 'exception' to its own absolute legalistic rationality.[82] A medieval version of this discussion can be found in the doctrine of 'the king's two bodies' elaborated by medieval political theorists, notably John of Salisbury: here the king is both free of the law and yet at the same time voluntarily subject to it, subordinating his 'private' person and will ('privata persona' / 'privata voluntas') to the demands placed on him as a 'public' person.[83] While aimed at providing a regulatory framework, such nuanced presentations of the king's sovereign status, nonetheless only dance politely around the fundamental truth articulated as a witticism in Patrice Leconte's (dir.) vision of pre-Revolutionary Versailles: *Ridicule*: 'le roi n'est pas un sujet'. The exceptionality and sovereignty associated with royal status cut across all three aspects of my treatment of Arthur here. If a king is not a subject, this is because kings do not defer, a reflection that points to the central role of such exceptions to the Law as objects of both perverse investment and anxiety. The concentrations associate with such libidinal investments then map our geographies and histories, locating cultures, centres and frontiers. In Leconte's film, the palace of Versailles and the Pays des Dombes, the hero's home, stand in opposition. As one character comments, both were swamps originally. However, in the pre-revolutionary moment of the film, it seems in effect as if the Pays des Dombes is now a muddy, disease-ridden provincial backwater *because* Versailles is a palace. The centre, thrilling and vibrating with presence, drains the nation of life and possibility, leaving only the mud that is the base, lumpen materiality of the provinces.

Spatial and psychic organisation go hand-in-hand. In different ways, both perversion and anxiety highlight the tensions inherent in the relation of the subject to both the pleasure principle (*le plaisir*) and its desired-but-threatening beyond, *jouissance* (conventionally but not unproblematically translated as 'enjoyment'). Perversion characterises the fundamental ambivalence to the object underpinning the subject's actions: while proximity to the object satisfies desire, distance from it sustains it.[84] For example, the conventions of romantic desire Lacan sees as underpinning the ritualised love poetry of the Middle Ages school the (masculine) Subject in the investment of mechanisms of deferral – what Freud refers to as *Vorlust* ('fore-pleasure' or foreplay) – with 'surplus enjoyment' (*plus-de-jouir*).[85] Indeed, such an operation is typical of what Žižek presents as art's 'pervert' nature: instead of giving the Subject the object of his/her desire, artistic representations teach how to desire in a fetishisation of deferring language and activity.[86] In that sense, fetishism represents one of the more successful versions of what Lacan terms as 'le plaisir d'éprouver un déplaisir': the libidinal dividend derives less from some 'final' attainment than from the performative 'experiencing of a non-pleasure' that is the patterning of one's desire in line with the rules implicit in representations of the desired object or objects.[87] For the perverse Subject, actual *jouissance* happens elsewhere. Thus, rather than enjoying in his own name, the pervert makes himself the 'instrument of the Other's *jouissance*', thus effacing his/her own agency whether in the infliction of cruelty or the excitement of pleasure. Alternatively, the Subject invests another person (e.g. 'savages', 'heretics', 'terrorists') or another time (the 'Wild West', the Middle Ages) with the disavowed *jouissance*, leaving them to enjoy 'in our name'. Such operations of deferral/distancing and appropriation are most commonly not explicitly acknowledged by the perverse Subject and commonly exhibit a logic of sacrifice or scapegoating. For example, the other can become the person who *believes* in our place (e.g. religious fundamentalists as the support of tolerant, rational Western liberals) or who suffers (e.g. disaster victims), or indeed can become a 'thief of enjoyment'.[88] This perverse projection onto the fundamentalist or terroristic other forms the basis of our contemporary 'beautiful soul complex', with the liberal West denying its complicity in the turbulence of the wider world.[89] Similarly, in a flip-side of this relation, we have the obsessional neurotic, who perceives the loss of *jouissance* as a theft and looks for a culprit, a structure which Žižek sees exemplified in nationalist politics: the nation presents itself as robbed of its *jouissance*, its 'glory' or 'secret treasure' (Lacan here referring to Socrates's use of the Greek term *agalma*), its rightful greatness by 'the foreigner'. The Jew appears as a scapegoated agent who, having 'robbed' the nation-Subject of its 'rightful' enjoyment or in designing to corrupt its 'purity', can then be persecuted in what is then referred to as *plus-de-jouir* or 'surplus enjoyment'.[90]

In anxiety, the Subject is inhibited by the proximity (actual or imagined) of the other's *jouissance*, forcing it into an uncomfortable awareness of its own position 'between desire and enjoyment'. Such a construction helpfully illuminates the complex affective transactions of collectivities where 'exceptions to the rule' reign, whether in figures such as the king or more generally as 'the neighbour', whose disturbing 'foreigness' and 'thieving' appropriations appear as troubling exceptions to the Law. Both Freud and Lacan elaborate very different models at different points, returning to themes and models sidelined in their earlier writings. Thus, in Freud's initial accounts, anxiety is associated with undischarged libidinal energies, a view he then turns away from but which Lacan reprises in his arguments about the line between pleasure and *jouissance* as late as the seminar of 1974–1975.[91] Another enduring theme is the question of objects: where for Freud fear is a response to a specific stimulus, anxiety appears as a sense of threat to the Ego.[92] However, Lacan suggests that anxiety is not 'objectless', but rather that the object is in fact the object-cause of desire, *objet petit a* – a view that fits with his emphasis elsewhere on the latter's substanceless, non-positive character.

The experience of anxiety is characteristically inhibitory, with the condition of *émoi* leaving the anxious moved... not to move, manifesting as a 'trouble in the dimension of movement' (see above).[93] In masochism, for example, as Lacan comments, although the ostensible goal of the masochist is to provide for the Other's enjoyment, what he secretly wishes is to provoke anxiety in the Other through the disclosure of desire – a structure which underpins Arthur's manipulation of his court (see chapter two below).[94] Trouble reveals the problem inherent in investing another with enjoyment, in that what emerges is a disturbing insight into *jouissance's* alien, uncanny dimension: an example here is the stereotype of male anxiety at the 'faraway' look of the 'enraptured' woman, her implication in some relation of desire that reveals her as 'not all' ('pas toute') in relation to the man.[95] That said, anxiety can be a spur, as in the case of phobia, where the Subject substitutes a real object for *objet petit a* (analogous to the manner in which the fetishist 'supplies' an object in place of the missing maternal phallus), a condition more tolerable than the anxiety of wondering 'what might be out there'.[96] Equally, we can see in this an entire logic of cultural opposition and constructions of the Other, as in Žižek's discussion of the relation between paganism and Christianity:

> When [G. K. Chesterton] writes that 'Christianity is the only frame for pagan freedom', this means that, precisely, this frame – the frame of prohibitions – is the only frame within which we can enjoy pagan pleasures: the feeling of guilt is a fake enabling us to give ourselves over to pleasures – when this frame falls away, anxiety arises.[97]

Thus, the perverse regulatory mechanisms created by the pagan-Christian binary allow us to enjoy while remaining conveniently blind to our desires. Of course one problem here is the inevitably divided location of a given moment: Arthurian romance is in effect the vision of an early Christian Europe, while simultaneously appearing as a form whose debt to the arts of antiquity marks it as 'pagan' in its literary modernity.[98] In that sense, it demonstrates a temporal fracture indicative of a culture 'capable of living in several centuries at once', as Chakrabarty puts it à propos of modern India.[99] This chiastic relation offers a two-way infolding of one culture into the other: the values of medieval vernacular cultures are projected back into the past, while at the same time, through appropriating the cultural clothing of that past, those cultures also experience themselves as dislocated in their own present. These two operations are interdependent, creating a sort of temporal and cultural bilocation that I will explore in greater detail below.

Part of a larger tradition of organisatory fantasy expressed through models of both history and geography, romance's relation to the monstrous and exotic objects of its quests reflects back on aristocratic constructions of the self and opening a terrain in which to explore the limits and truths of its desire. The operation of displacement here is apparent from the difference between the German original and French translation of a remark of Erich Köhler's: 'der Dichter des Artusromans spiegelt in seinem Werk eine *entfremdete Wirklichkeit* als Entfremdung seiner Gestalten wider', rendered in Eliane Kaufholz's French translation as 'l'auteur du roman arthurien donne dans ses oeuvres le reflet d'une réalité *déroutante*'.[100] As a translation of *entfremdet* ('alienated', 'estranged'), *dérouté* can have the sense of 'distanced' in the manner of a house situated away from a main road, while *dérouter* also has the sense of 'to throw off track', 'to disconcert'. However, Kaufholz's translation, 'déroutante', shifts both voice and aspect, from an *estranged* reality to an *estranging* one that looks troublingly, defamiliarisingly back at the Subject.[101] Such is precisely the sense of the encounter between the hero and the serpent creature in the 'ordeal' of the 'fier baiser', the 'big, scary kiss', in Renaut de Beaujeu's *Le Bel inconnu* (ll. 3127–252), a monstrous vision that appears as the very embodiment of all that is alien in human desire.[102] Having spared the wyvern and received the kiss, Guingalain is seized by great uncertainty and prays (ll. 3204–11), claiming that the kiss was against or not of his will ('j'ai baissié otre mon gré', l. 3210), even though his decision not to kill the serpent is presented as a series of carefully-considered evaluations and actions (ll. 3155–62; ll. 3165–71; ll. 3174–8). What we have here in the hero's momentary impotence to act is a vision of what happens when enjoyment fails to happen elsewhere: its proximity in either thought or appearance unsettles.

That that borderline between the elsewhere of desire and our place is a thin one is apparent from the fate of another Freudian term, the neighbour, from the biblical injunction to 'love thy neighbour as thyself' ('diliges *proximum tuum* tamquam te ipsum', Romans 13:9, my emphasis). The German translation of the Latin *proximus*, as used by Freud, is 'der Nächste' (the near/next person). As Žižek puts it:

> Here one should [distinguish] between the neighbour (*der Nächste*) and the 'near/proximate thing' (*das Nächste*): the neighbour is the intriguing *object* of desire, in front of us, while 'the near thing' is the *(object-)cause* of desire, that which from within us, from behind our back, out of our sight, pushes us toward the object, making it desirable, account for the urgency in our approach to the object.[103]

The problem revealed in anxiety is that although *objet a* as object-cause of desire is invisible to us, its substanceless entity reveals the world as only apparently solid, as pulled at and made plastic by more and different desires we can ostensibly account for. That desire can be alien in that it belongs to another person, *der Nächste*, but it can also be alien in the sense that *das Nächste*, the object-cause, appears as a 'foreign' element that is 'in us more than ourselves', the source of an agency that is ours but which we either do not or are not minded to own. In that sense, if anxiety is the place of the Subject caught between desire and *jouissance*, then the point is that these two are both fundamentally alien (or 'extimate'), even if the desire is ostensibly that of Subject.[104] This ambiguity in the location of the object-cause arguably problematises the strong association between anxiety and inhibition Lacan sees in the term *émoi*, tracing it back to roots such as Germanic *es-magan* that, like English *dismay* (and Old French *esmaier*) indicate a loss of capacity or power.[105] This is certainly apparent in Guingalain's perplexity in the lead-up to the *fier baiser*:

> 'Bien sai que ne puis longes durer,
> Car je ne sai quel part aler,
> Ne mon destrier mie ne sai,
> Et neporeuc por ce m'esmai.
> De rien ne me doi m'esmaier,
> Ce n'afiert pas a chevalier
> Qu'il s'esmait por nul aventure.' (ll. 3107–13)

> 'I know I cannot last long, for I do not know where to go. Nor do I know anything of my horse. And yet on account of that I am dismayed. I should not be dismayed on any count: it is not fitting that a knight should be dismayed, whatever the adventure might be.'

Crucially, Guingalain's uncertainty – the *émoi* focalised in the loss of his horse – is resolved by divine intervention in the form of the disembodied voice that answers his prayer (ll. 3217–42). Speaking in good Lacanese, its response addresses the central issues of Guingalain's *angoisse* with regard to the object-cause of his desire:

1. Here is your name (l. 3233).
2. Here is the name of (the /your) father (l. 3235).
3. Don't panic – your mission has an agreed object which implies that prohibitions do obtain and that you have rightly

conquered your lady (ll. 3239–42). Rejoice therefore, for you are heterosexual.

Although Guingalain's indecision fits with Lacan's vision of anxiety as a loss of power, as an inhibition with regard to motion, it is clear that motion can be part of anxiety, albeit robbed of a secure sense of purpose and direction. In that sense, troubled and indecisive motion, worrying in circles, the directionless milling of a collective are all indicative of anxiety, as are arguably then their verbal and emotional correlates: whether mutter or sudden instabilities of mood and feeling. Thus, although the distinction targeted by Lacan is a key one, it is perhaps less simple to divide cleanly between emotion as an interior movement and anxiety as the troubling of that motion. Indeed, had Lacan looked beyond Bloch and von Wartburg's *Dictionnaire étymologique* and examined the uses of *émoi* in Old French texts, he would have found a more complex picture, differing senses of fear, emotion and inhibition jumbled together in Töbler and Lommatzsch's entry for *esmoi-esmai* like pottery shards from different vessels buried in a ditch.[106] That jumbling proximity points in and of itself to the permanent haunting of the perceptual world by our desires, occasionally glimpsed in perplexing, uncanny encounter.

As part of this tendency toward disavowal, we can see kingship and court societies as sustained by perverse fantasy structures. This is bound up with what René Girard sees as the fundamentally sacrificial character of kingship: 'the king only reigns by virtue of his future death', meaning that he is invested by the collective with an enjoyment that must be seen to be redeemed.[107] Arthur's destruction is the *jouissance* of that sacrificial relation. As Victoria Guerin has argued, what is clear from the appearance of Arthurian romance is that, once Arthur's future doom was fixed by Geoffrey of Monmouth, an entire work went into forestalling that end.[108] Where Geoffrey's version of Arthur's reign has his court enjoying the high point of its flourishing in the seven years of peace, Chrétien sets out to extend that period or blur its outlines. In *Cligés*, for example, those seven years seem suddenly to be extended over two generations. In *Le Chevalier de la charrette*, although Lancelot has appeared his relationship with Guinevere is consummated in the course of the tale, he is nonetheless not the threat posed by Meleagant.[109] We can also see this mechanism at work in Arthur's contemplation of the paintings and lettering in the chamber of images (§ 51–2) in *La Mort le roi Artu*, the scene's climax – his recognition of the proof of Guinevere's adultery – painfully slow because of Arthur's limited literacy: 'Li rois Artus savoit bien tant de letres qu'il pooit *auques* un escrit entendre' (§ 51, my emphasis). Cable's translation ('King Arthur knew his letters well enough to be able to make out the meaning of a text.') misses the qualifying force of the 'auques' ('to an extent'), a haltingness implicitly contrasted with Morgane's quasi-sorcerous capacity for speed-reading. This mechanism of deferral is then given its cosmic context in the vision granted Arthur of himself on top of Fortuna's wheel, the moment of his fall delayed by her hand.

Such representations of Arthur speak of a cultural version of the '*fort-da* game' in which – like the spool of thread with which Freud's grandson plays – the king is cast away and then retrieved.[110] However, in line with a re-evaluation of the significance of the scene, this act positions Arthur not as the traumatically lost object whose absence must be overcome but as a cipher for the opening of a 'space of desire' in the political life of the court. And yet representations of Arthur reveal his function as more subtle that the *fort-da* game. When the child throws away the bobbin, with the cry of 'Fort!' ('Away!'), and then pulls it back with a cry of 'Da!' ('There!'), we have a simple alternation, with the child's agency supplying absence in a 'neurotic' defence from the mother's overwhelming presence. However, Arthur – famously 'once and future king' (*rex quondam et futurus*) – thereby appears as 'Away!' (*quondam*) and then not yet here (*futurus*), the problem of an onerous royal presence vanishing in neat ellipsis, even as the mechanism of the king's 'retrieval' is more akin to a yo-yo or a rubber band, any sense of agency displaced onto universal forces seeming to act by themselves. This 'elasticity' in Arthur's place in the fantasy economy of medieval kingship positions him as a convenient means of sustaining some of its more glaring economic irrationalities and subterfuges in charismatic kingship, a subject with a long history in the observation of court cultures, particulary in the work of sociologists Max Weber and Norbert Elias.[111] The latter's work in particular returns frequently to the opposition between charismatic and patrimonial kingship, Louis XIV, the architect of Versailles emerging in Elias's account as a plodding conservator of royal authority, a leader who thrived in prudently regimented Versailles but would have failed at Camelot: 'had he been a man of genius and vigour, the slow, complex machine would have made him impatient, he would have broken it'.[112] Charismatic communities appear as idealised visions of high-risk elite groups, their giddy, grasshopper nonchalance set in contrast to the ant-like prudence of 'patrimonial' kings.

Although Elias's account does not name a charismatic leader, various aspects of his characterisation sound suspiciously Arthurian: his remark that 'if the ice breaks, drowning him and his followers, he is likely to pass into history as an unsuccessful adventurer' seems more than a little reminiscent of one of Arthur's engagements with the invading Saxons.[113] The charismatic leader thus finds himself the head of an enterprise so perilous as to preclude rational assessment, his followers 'conceal[ing] from themselves the uncertainty and the size of the risk, which might be unbearable if clearly contemplated, by faith in the special grace enjoyed by their leader, his "charisma"'.[114] Although folly in many respects, such a capacity for snowballing makes at least short-term sense, transforming charisma's most obvious disadvantage: the very fact charismatic leaders go out to 'break the bank' is a guarantee of uncompromising authenticity in a world where merely to survive is nothing, the core drama of this theatre of state deriving precisely from the fact the entire structure gives every appearance of teetering on the verge of collapse.

One arguable weakness with Elias's presentation is that it perhaps makes or suggests too much of a binary of the opposition between patrimony and charisma. All kings, even the comparatively staid Louis XIV, are exceptions to the system: as Girard puts it, they all 'escape through the roof'.[115] Arthur just happens to be more exceptional (and slightly more fictional) than most. As a fantasy construct widely appropriated by medieval kings, he represents an extreme position in the latitude for manoeuvre available to a royal figure. As Clifford Geertz comments, in Balinese court society, a king's success in securing high status leads paradoxically to his 'ritual deactivation', his place at the heart of ceremonial life curtailing his capacity to act unilaterally.[116] Elias's description of Louis XIV's 'constantly threatened elbow-room' points to a similar effect in the context of Versailles.[117] This 'damping effect' reflects anxieties about royal agency as an exception to the law and the court as the location of a culture that focalises a certain exceptional energy in the person of the king.

If the Middle Ages has been claimed as the point of origin for the discourses of *fin'amor* that structure Western experiences of desire, similar claims can be advanced for the field of 'subaltern studies', a branch of postcolonial theory whose central term derives from Antonio Gramsci's *Prison Notebooks* and 'refers to subordination in terms of class, caste, gender, race, language and culture and was used to signify the centrality of dominant/dominated relationships in history'.[118] The central strategy of subaltern studies is then the interrogation of the relation between dominant and subaltern cultures, in particular questioning the claims to either centrality or universality underpinning dominant-culture narratives, a project encompassed by Dipesh Chakrabarty's use of the term 'provincialisation'. The problem of the subaltern as a 'subject of history' is neatly summed up in the title of Gayatri Spivak's article 'Can the Subaltern Speak?'.[119] In the context of colonial and post-colonial India, this then encompasses the view of 'peasant' uprisings as failed attempts to enact the sort of resistance advocated by Mahatma Ghandi.[120] A corresponding blindness is also found in historiography which overlooks subaltern agency, ascribing it instead to historical forces or to notions of 'cause' not intuitively available to the group.

Interestingly, the concern of subaltern studies with both intercultural relations and with marginalised castes and categories, such as 'the peasant', as exemplified in Dipesh Chakrabarty's work, draws in part on historians dealing with medieval and early modern Europe.[121] In that regard, Chakrabarty's work complements work both in medieval social history – such as that of Paul Freedman – and in cultural relations and cultural identity under the banner of 'postcolonial medieval studies'.[122] Some sense of the vitality of the connection here is apparent from the very fact that Chrétien's first articulation of the ideas of *translatio studii* and *imperii* is 'li vilain dit' (l. 1): 'the peasant says'. Both he and Chakrabarty have as their prime focus *vilain* agency and speech.

Where the connection between subaltern and romance studies becomes apparent is in the relation of the subaltern groups to the cultures that dominate them. Chakrabarty presents nineteenth- and twentieth-century Bengali writers struggling with the place of England and Englishness as an imaginary referent and object of their literary and poetic discourse.[123] The tensions brought to the surface in the citation and re-use of poetic forms or discourse and the principles that underpin them give rise to an emergent modernism that negotiates between the centre as model and the 'contingent' conditions of urban India. One phrase in particular stands out from an 'anonymous' poem written by an Indian poet in 1951:

> To the memory of the
> British Empire in India
> Which conferred subjecthood on us
> But withheld citizenship;
> To which yet
> Everyone of us threw out the challenge
> 'Civis Britanicus Sum'
> Because
> All that was good and living
> Within us
> Was made, shaped and quickened
> By the same British colonial rule.[124]

Chakrabarty's emphasis on the issue of 'translation' in both its broadest and most specific senses – whether interrelating and passing between not merely different languages, but also different disciplines, cultures and times – productively illuminates Chrétien's vision of romance and its engagements. In referring to British citizenship in the language of Rome, the poem targets not merely the historical foundation of 'British' ideals in a sense of timeless universality, but, in paying homage, also foregrounds how the 'subaltern' status of ancient Britain undercuts its self-positioning as singular beneficiary of – what one might cast in terms most familiar to medievalists – a one-strand narrative of *translatio studii* and *imperii*.[125] The various gestures of appropriating the ancient past in all of the various contexts implied here, whether postwar colonial India, nineteenth-century

British models of classical studies or indeed late twelfth-century France, all raise their particular problems as historicisations.

Although postcolonial approaches have most commonly been applied to representations of the Orient in medieval sources, some attention has also been paid to narratives of *internal* colonisation, a key example being the *roman d'aventure*, whose 'exoticisation' of milieux such as the forest can be seen as an extension of the narratives of settlement of Geoffrey of Monmouth and Wace. To thereby contextualise in a longer tradition of the poetic (re)locating of cultures the relation between emergent national identity and literary modernism in post-imperial India suggests that a 'subaltern' reading of medieval vernacular sources is far from some arbitrary projection of a fashionable critical paradigm back into the remote past. Of course, the sense of distance from the dominant culture and indeed the conditions of knowledge are different: for example, manuscript illuminations typically do not represent Romans as different in armour or marks of ethnicity from European knights, and thus see them as belonging to the same world. However, I would argue there is a parallel between India's vision of Britain and Europe's vision of ancient Rome, between the 'echoes of Milton and seventeenth-century radicalism' that make up 'colonial pastiche' on the one hand and the obsessive citation and imitation of classical authors such as Cicero and Lucan by medieval writers working either in Latin or in the vernacular.[126]

Traditionally, a tension is often perceived between postcolonial and psychoanalytical approaches in the field of cultural studies – especially those associated with Lacan whose assimilation to Enlightenment universalist positions adds fuel to arguments regarding its cultural specificities. However, a common ground emerges perhaps in work such as Žižek's *Welcome to the Desert of the Real* and *Iraq: The Borrowed Kettle*, both of which appeared after Chakrabarty's initial essay and subsequent book. Here Žižek takes particular issue with Western failures to think through the radical consequences of events such as the attacks on the World Trade Centre:

> Either America will persist in – even strengthen – the deeply immoral attitude of 'Why should this happen to us? Things like this don't happen *here!*', leading to more aggressivity towards the threatening outside – in short, a paranoiac

acting out. Or America will finally risk stepping through the fantasmatic screen that separates it from the Outside World, accepting its arrival in the Real world, making the long-overdue move from 'A thing like this shouldn't happen *here*!' to 'A thing like this shouldn't happen *anywhere*!'. That is the true lesson of the attacks: the only way to ensure that it will not happen here again is to prevent it happening anywhere else. In short, America should learn humbly to accept its own vulnerability as part of this world, enacting the punishment of those responsible as a sad duty, not an exhilarating retaliation.[127]

Žižek's comments outline the common ground between 'Republican' visions of a radicalised universalism and Chakrabarty's project of 'provincialisation'. That sense of an evacuation of presence associated with the critique of locations of culture in effect operates in both paradigms as can be seen from Žižek's comments on the social and material conditions in Cuba as manifesting both absence and presence:

> The counterpart of the Event is the growing inertia of social being/life: a country frozen in time, with old buildings in a state of decay. It is not that the revolutionary Event was 'betrayed' by the Thermidorian establishment of a new order; the very insistence on the Event led to the immobilisation at the level of positive social being. The decaying houses *are* the proof of fidelity to the Event. [...] When eternity intervenes in time, time comes to a standstill. No wonder that the basic impression of Havana in 2001 was that the original inhabitants had escaped, and *squatters had taken it over* – out of place in these magnificent buildings, occupying them temporarily, subdividing large spaces with wooden panels and so on. [...] This obscene inertia is the 'truth' of the revolutionary Sublime.[128]

Žižek's emphasis on the bathos of 'actually occurring Revolution' returns as a frequent theme in his writings on French Republicanism.[129] However, it also introduces a problem also emphasised in Chakrabarty's work. For all that, as Walter Benjamin argues in his 'Theses on the Philosophy of History', the failure of past revolutionary attempts are redeemed in any present success, the very appearance of absence in the bathos of 'actual' revolutionary gestures at the same time relegates them to a 'not yet'.[130] The Cubans are at the same time *either* faithful revolutionaries *or* peasant squatters. Indeed, they may even warp anamorphically between the two identities, between banal ugliness and beautiful sublimity. This can be compared with Lacan's question of the 'subversion of the subject in the dialectic of desire': to what extent does the issue of desire problematise subjectivity as a locus of what he refers to in his earlier writings as 'full speech'?

This question of the intelligibility of a history shaped by both visible and invisible forces and presences is something that unites in a range of courtly productions, epitomised for critics from various disciplines in Hans Holbein's painting, *The Ambassadors* (1533).[131] Here the opposition in the face-on view between the distorted form of the skull and the main body of the composition – consisting of the two emissaries, Jean de Dinteville and Georges de Selve, positioned in front of a table covered with various objects – only resolves into view as the viewer moves round to the right of the canvas. This motion of the view *vis-à-vis* implied by the queering intersection of perspectives in the painting forms a basis for a conversation about the nature of history while simultaneously pointing to its inevitable failure. The objects themselves speak of division and disharmony – a treatise on mathematics open at a page about division, the lute with a broken string emblematic of discord. However, this self-answering 'surface' message, with its concession to the vanity of human striving, finds a further answer in the distorted shape of the skull, highlighting the ultimate failure of such topoi to bring the central question into focus. The elaborate allegorical and emblematic language of the painting thus remains fundamentally, humanly blind to the unseen forces cutting across the perspective of the picture, its world-encompassing eloquence and erudition either a vain attempt to articulate the warping effect of that other element or a snapshot capture surprising a normally unseen presence. In terms of the 'perverse' relations I highlight here, the skull appears as a motif of the permanent queering of the world that is the gravitational field of desire. In terms of the place of anxiety, the skull appears as a figure of *das Nächste*, the unseen object-cause. In terms of subaltern studies it speaks of the striving and failure to pin the shape of the world in time, even through apparent concessions to and knowledge of the possibility of that failure.

We can see Chrétien offering a reflection on this in his own context through the use and re-use of key terms, notably *la parsome* (a compound of intensifying prefix (*par-*) plus noun (*some*, from Latin *summa*), 'the final sum/account', a term that appears three times in the romance. The first occurrence is at a key point in the celebration of Erec's wedding, where Arthur takes a momentary delight in the contemplation of his courtiers as a unified body:

> Li rois Artus *a la parsome*,
> Quant assemblé vit son bernage,
> Mout en fu liez en son corage. (ll. 2008–10, my emphasis)

> When King Arthur *finally* saw his lords and barons assembled, his heart rejoiced.

For all this moment it finally draws together the interlaced threads and conflicts of the *premiers vers* into the smoothly-spun affirmation of Arthurian unity, the very fact this central term is repeated reminds us that the efforts required to bring this unity yield only a transitory reward, the vantage point from which Arthur beholds his courtiers taking its place in a process of attempting to hold together in a harmonious body an entirely heteroclitic assemblage nobles drawn from the four corners of the great King's territory. Nonetheless, for all this appearance of unity is delusive, the note of finality speaks eloquently of the fascination exerted by that contemplation. However, the other two occurrences reveal the term's darker overtones, the second underscoring the finality of Erec's refusal to heed his father's plea that he should not leave Carnant without escort:

> Erec respont *a la parsome*,
> Et se li dit tot a devise
> Coment il a sa voie emprise:
> 'Sire', fait il, 'n'en puet el estre.' (ll. 2712–15, my emphasis)

> At length, Erec replied, telling him why he was making this journey: 'My lord', he said, 'I have no other choice.'[132]

The third occurrence is in Evrain's dire warning to Erec against seeking the Joy of the Court: 'Even you yourself, when it's over, will be dead and mangled' ('Vos meïsmes *a la parsome* /En serez morz et afolez.' ll. 5604–05, my emphasis). Of course, for all the spookiness,

43

the seeming *fatalité* of the recurrence, rumours of Erec's imminent demise turn out to be exaggerated. What the three occurrences yield *a la parsome* is a 'final vision' of the movement of the king through a space shot through with uncanny snapshot moments presaging both glory and doom, a present tense thrillingly subtended by a future perfect – this is what the sense of your actions *will have been* – both sombre and joyous.

Thus, although frequently invoked in more general discussion, *The Ambassadors* is a product of the court, an observation of how it is structured and organised whether in terms of its spaces, its ceremonial time or the forms of knowledge that focus there. Its techniques translate themes given analoguous expression in other media associated with the courtly milieu. While its composition 'ritualises' the space before it, at the same time it subjects that space to the continual shocks inherent in the dissonance between the picture's main body and the skull-anamorphosis. In that sense, we may see its message as an assertion of the inevitable and even necessary permanence of danger in ritualised gatherings of the great and the good.[133] My argument here will be that *Erec et Enide* can be seen as an early literary exploration of a similar effect, its warp and woof (the textile terms reflective of Chrétien's frequent evocations of tapestry and embroidery both as glorifying amplification of the material culture of the court and compositional metaphor) intersecting with and haunted by other productions and other histories, interrogated and mocked in terms sinister or obscene. Moreover, perhaps more than his other works, this is a text about the organisation and orchestration of courts, the relation between how courtiers move, what forces move them and what might be the place in the cosmos of those mechanisms. Accordingly, the perspectival distention of the anamorphosis is answered in Chrétien by plays with time and perception, the stoppings, stretchings and intensities Augustine referred to as 'distentio temporis' (of time) and 'distentio animi' (of the mind), the pull and ripple of these intersecting desires and insistent wills partly operating blindly and partly moulded by dimly intuitable logics glimpsed as it were 'through a mirror darkly'.[134]

What this confluence of ideas suggests with regard to relations between the medieval and the ancient world is a challenging of the recourse to narratives that imply a centre-periphery construction of historical change. In particular, I will argue, Chrétien's contestation of the primacy of the Trojan narrative as model history of the aristocratic desiring subject frames a strategic questioning of the location – both temporal and spatial – of 'culture', not merely resisting any positioning of medieval European 'vernacular' cultures as *vilain* subalterns in relation to Rome, but also disputing synchronically the attempts of any single milieu or lineage to claim something like literal descent from Aeneas. What was at stake for the court of Champagne is readily apparent here: distanced in time and space from Plantagenet appropriations of the Aeneas-theme, its courtiers had leisure to reflect on the hostages to fortune that might result from scrambling to appropriate a narrative of legitimisation that – like some comedy rug – was all too ready to be pulled out from under their feet. Although Chrétien's first romance does not have the geographical sweep of *Cligés*, the cultural history in which it needs to be located, I argue, highlights a tension between fundamentally contrasting models of historical identity that can be polarised in terms of various oppositions: ancient versus modern, Trojan versus Greek. My contention is that *Erec et Enide's* sense of the place of Arthurian fiction on the cultural stage of the French Middle Ages is broader than has previously been allowed.

For all that *Erec et Enide* seems self-contained in its vision of geography and history, it is linked to Chrétien's other works by its questioning of when and where courtly literature speaks from. In particular, I compare Chrétien's location of love and marriage negotiations in *Erec et Enide* with the histories contained in his lyric works and in his treatment of the *Philomena* story, surviving in the verse *Ovide moralisé*. Chrétien's emphasis in these works on the nature of desire and on the practicalities and problems in the sphere of aristocratic marriage foregrounds tensions between different histories and temporalities. Comparisons here show Chrétien's critical attitude to historical models associated with the matters of Troy and Britain, contesting simplistic or over-hasty appropriations of the narrative as a legitimising foundation myth. In that sense, what emerges is a 'provincialising' of cultural relations in which the interweaving and coexistence of histories of conflict and desire undermine any claims to centrality. Such a move can clearly be seen as a response to the propagandist strategies associated with the Capetians, even if, as Theodore Evergates points out, relations between Champagne and the Capetians in the reign of Louis VII were good, emphasising that it cannot be assumed that such productions are evidence for a 'culture war' of unvarying and unremitting temperature between the two houses.[135] However, it also reads as a more general and more profound comment on the place of medieval 'modernities' with regard to their antecedent cultural models, a relation in which Chrétien can be seen both to explore and contest any sense of 'subaltern' status. In that regard, although the model of history associated with northern European appropriations of Virgilian tradition can be seen as the result of a series of 'translations', both linguistically and spatially, Chrétien's final move in this process seems then to be to (back-)translate a 'Trojanised' or 'Trojanising' history into a past that seems more 'Greek' in terms of the fractured, plural temporalities which he presents in his *Philomena* and lyric poetry. Chrétien's contestation of the model of *translatio imperii* elaborated in the *Roman d'Eneas* is based on an entirely pragmatic insight into the difficulty posed by dynastic marriage practices for the construction of propagandist narratives. The presence of such skeletons in the closet, whether in fact or merely suspected, undercuts attempts to elaborate unassailable assertions of pre-eminence. In this regard, we can see Chrétien both as an observer of court life in his own time and also the historiographical traditions of classical antiquity.

Through these references Chrétien presents a vision of scandalous history as both problematic and useful, in that while such rumours can undermine claims to legitimacy, they can also be deployed to 'face down' opponents. This practice is part of Chrétien's 'audacity' as a repositioning of the political culture of a courtly 'modernity' freed from being a literature of the civilising process to explore potential strategic and terroristic uses of rhetorical effect, a strand that is then counterpointed and given legitimacy by the strongly Boethian themes running through his work. The seeming irrationality, the profligacy of energy and wealth associated with the fantasy/model of charismatic kingship emblematised by Arthur is offset by a compensatory future doom.

'*Erec et Enide*, Interrupted': The Shape and Structure of the Book

Having outlined the historical and theoretical background, this section outlines the plan of the rest of the book. Starting at the beginning and working its way slowly to the end, its organisation follows the linear model of other *in extenso* commentaries on *Erec et Enide*, such as those of Jean Frappier, Reto Bezzola, Leslie Topsfield, Zara Zaddy, Glyn Burgess, Peter Noble or Claudia Seebass-Linggi.[136] In that regard, to write (yet another) commentary seems potentially redundant, or at least unfashionable compared to the exuberant 'exploded' logic of partly linear, partly thematic treatments by scholars such as Joseph Duggan or Donald Maddox.[137] However, what I hope to do here is revisit that question of structure in a perhaps less straightforward manner than elsewhere. For instance, chapter divisions do not always follow what might seem like 'natural' divisions in Chrétien's text – even if the work's structure has been a matter of some debate: bipartite (the *premerains vers*, ending at l. 1840 with the bestowal of the kiss, and then the rest) or tripartite (taking the Joy as a distinct part)?[138] For example, chapter four splits the Sparrow-Hawk tournament off from the negotiations with the Count of Laluth that evening, running together the latter parts of the events at Laluth with the preparations for Erec and Enide's wedding, while chapter five takes in the bedchamber 'crisis scene' and the events of the first day of the quest following Erec's departure from Carnant, splitting these from my reading of the second through fourth days. Such plays with structure reflect a probing of closure and identity at least quite loudly implicit in the contrast between the *premerains vers*' use of interlace and the more straightforwardly linear organisation of the remainder of the narrative. While such a leaden following of narrative logic seems a conservative trait, I would argue that Chrétien's sense of structure and proportion – his highlighting of the importance of elegance in structure and composition ('une mout bele conjunture', l. 14) and his refusal to 'mangle' or 'dismember' (depecier', l. 21) its unities in the manner of *jongleurs* or indeed to repeat accounts of particular episodes given for the benefit of internal audiences (notably on Erec's return to court at the end of his quest) – points to a playful interrogation of the line of courtly beauty in which linear direction is very much a live issue.

Chrétien's linear construction is self-consciously set against various 'queering' forces, to use a term that encompasses both issues of desire and identity on the one hand and the interrogation, interruption and disturbance of line on the other (*queer* thus possibly cognate with Germanic *quer*, 'crossways', 'diagonally', giving Modern German *queren*, 'to cross'). Indeed, the centrality of Enide's lament in the form '[Con / tant] mar i fus' – 'Misfortune brought you here.' – points precisely to the prominence Chrétien gives to the crossing of paths and to the ordering of events whether in life's journey or in nature. These paths relate to the riddling of desire, queer theory, as Warren Hedges puts it, 'attend[ing] carefully to what characters *want* and do', that 'care' in particular targeting tensions between 'straight minds' and 'queer wishes' where queering appears as a disturbance of and challenge to culturally-ordained hierarchies and constellations of active-passive, masculine-feminine and so on.[139] In a manner reminiscent of the vituperations of Alan of Lille, such contradictions are neatly described by Fanny Hill, heroine of John Cleland's *Memoirs of a Woman of Pleasure*, as a 'project of preposterous pleasure', Cleland's phrase providing the germ for Glenn Burger and Steven Kruger's introduction to their volume, *Queering the Middle Ages*.[140] Moreover, as will become apparent, the unfolding thrust of Chrétien's narrative is perhaps most troublingly answered by recurring looks back over the shoulder in which the glimmers and hauntings of particular allusions in a given scene are 'outed' in a subsequent one. One key example is Chrétien's arguable confirmation of the sexual dimension of the giants' attack on Cadoc in Enide's lament for the fallen Erec, a moment which points strongly to Geoffrey of Monmouth's version of the abduction of Helena by the giant of Mont-Saint-Michel. Such a logic can be seen to go hand-in-hand with a more general strategy of allusion to scandals in the family or literary closet associated with the houses of both Henry and Eleanor, hinting perhaps that all aristocratic histories are shadowed by 'queer' presences of one kind or another, as well as to a more general investigation on Chrétien's part of the location – whether in space or history – of Arthurian culture and its narratives, and indeed, more generally, of the nature of desire. In this regard, I hope to offer something of a counterpoint to Jeffrey Cohen's oppositional characterisation of *Erec et Enide* as a (boring) 'consensual' narrative that 'silences' social scripts of agreement and desire to *Le Chevalier de la charrette*, construed as (interestingly) sado-masochistically 'contractual', fetishising and making explicit of such ritual behaviours.[141] What I will argue is that *Erec et Enide* is perhaps more explicit about the silent subtexts of its presentation of aristocratic power and marital relations than Cohen allows.

The first chapter deals with the prologue and opening. Both can be seen as assertions of a will cast against various possible classical exemplars that nonetheless subtly positions Arthur in relation to a long tradition of representations. Arthur's gesture conjures the spectres of various scenes in later versions, notably both his death and Erec's. At the same time it forms an interrogation of the split in political and cultural values of republican and imperial Rome by echo of representations of the death of Julius Caesar as a problematic 'final sum' ('parsome' in Chrétien's terms) to the Emperor's career. This coded representation also has parallels elsewhere in representations of Henry II, a key figure in the history of political irrationality through his defence of royal anger as a mode of display. In this, we can see Chrétien offering a vision of a political and literary modernity refusing to be dismissed as simply subaltern.

In the second chapter we move to the encounter between Guinevere and her handmaiden and the young Erec, their meeting only apparently accidental and arguably staged for the purposes of royal matchmaking. However, for all the decorum, the scene's emphasis on horsemanship reveals a rather less decorous textual backdrop, its hints of possible union haunted by the horse imagery in the slandering of the hero by Lavine's mother's in the *Roman d'Eneas* – a text associated with the court of Henry II. Although Yder's interruption offers an opportunity for the young woman to prove herself, she overplays her hand, entailing disgrace for the Queen and for the unarmed Erec. Erec's intervention thereafter is conditioned by a need to forestall disgrace for Arthur, the implication emerging that the announcement of his betrothal was perhaps scheduled as the centrepiece of the resolution of the hunt of the White Stag, with the court already having been forced to engage in stalling tactics through the setting up of Gauvain's privy counsel. Erec plays his part by elaborating a narrative that will then buy the King a stay of execution during which the botching of the initial plan might yet be rectified.

The third chapter then takes us to Laluth, the initial encounter between Erec and Enide's father readable as a counter-narrative to Chrétien's version of the Philomena story recounted in Ovid's *Metamorphoses* (book 6, ll. 412–674). One key difference here is that where Philomena has licence, Enide knows to submit herself to paternal control. Yet, at the same time, Enide's father's description of her flirts self-consciously with forces hidden in *Philomena*, his paternal vigilance daringly but codedly foregrounding the concerns he might entertain regarding the newly-arrived young stranger. In similar wise, Erec then directly but tactfully raises the question of his host's impoverished circumstances, carefully flagging that such an apparently tactless intervention is intended for the latter's ultimate good. This deployment of subtexts on both sides marks the beginning of a relation of trust and accord between the two men that will be concretised in the betrothal, Enide's silence arguably marking a shrewd assessment of the skills deployed on both sides. Erec's combat with Yder then repeats this pattern of text and subtext, with Erec's participation in the show combat effectively a Trojan Horse tactic in his quest for revenge. Yet at the same time his behaviour also shows a concern with the theatre of the tournament that has not been satisfied in the previous years, Yder having taken the title unchallenged. The combat then pushes that theatre to its limits in the savagery of the attacks on both sides, and yet both participants show a subordination to the rules of the game: Yder recognises Erec's performance as the sign of some wrong on his own part, while the latter accepts his plea for mercy.

In chapter four we trace the arc from Erec's negotiations with the Count of Laluth to the marriage itself. Here again my reading underscores the importance of literary subtexts in the family closet. Erec's rejection of the dress is received as a disgrace to the Count, forcing the intervention of his redoubtable niece. Erec for his part seems in no mood simply to allow the richer branch of the family to make last minute amends for their attempt to force Enide's father to marry her off on less advantageous terms. However, this is not made explicit. In the absence of any explanation as to what moves him into such a confrontational stance, the niece, for her part, makes the conciliatory but forceful offer of the palfrey, a speech again haunted by lurid subtexts from the family literary closet. The niece's discussion of the merits of various possible mounts arguably echoes not only the *Roman d'Eneas* but also other works associated with the houses of Henry and Eleanor, notably her grandfather William IX's poem 'Companho, farai un vers covinen'. These meditations on what is 'just right for a maiden' imply a derisive evaluation of her kinswoman as a sexual partner and a tacit suggestion Erec might want to look elsewhere for a creature of more fiery and interesting temperament. Here Erec chooses discretion as the better part of valour and tactfully confines himself to praise of the horse, allowing the negotiations to conclude peacefully and to the joy of all. The return to Arthur's court then continues Chrétien's flirtation with disturbing subtexts, Arthur staging his possibly lecherous regard for Enide much in the manner that a knight might perform 'hatred' on the tournament field even as this nod to the fateful role of *lecherie* in the Arthurian legend provides a useful thrill of anxiety. Indeed, Arthur's courting of disaster in the hunt means that his speech on the rights and duties of kings, a summing up he probably would have given even if Erec's original union had come about, is now invested with new energy. Thus, Arthur's gesture reveals how twists of all kinds, such as the perverse investments of collective desire, may be harnessed. With Enide accepted into the Queen's household, the preparations for the wedding ceremony lay bare the wider cultural play surrounding such events. Crucially, Chrétien emphasises the permanent capacity of interaction to aggrieve or cause pain (*grever*): Erec asks for the wedding to be brought forward, as long as this does not aggrieve Arthur too much, while, on the wedding night itself, Enide bears the pain of her defloration, a silencing that stands in contrast to earlier imagery pointing to the 'bestial' noise of intercourse censured in various clerical sources. This contrast between 'noise' and 'silence' is also apparent in Chrétien's evocation of the hubbub of the preparation of the wedding bed, the festivities working towards and centring on a sexual act discreetly concealed or elided as a 'soreplus' even as it remains to haunt as the object of sexual fantasy. This haunting shows a persistence of 'nature' in the midst of acculturating artifice, a persistence that still 'speaks' even as it is seemingly passed over in silence.

Chapter five deals with the events of the crisis following Enide's revelations to Erec of the discontent among his followers, emphasising the importance of the version of the text contained in fonds fr. 1376. Enide's lament that 'misfortune brought you there' ('[Tant /Con] mar i fus') – rather than more generally bewailing his fate ('Con mar fus') – foregrounds once again the importance of place and motion in Chrétien's vision. Indeed, her contemplation of her husband, interweaving desire and regret, manifests an anamorphic blurring of temporal perspectives akin to that seen in Erec's arrival in Laluth. Erec's response then capitalises on this presentation. Deploying both the deadly insistence of his legalistic language and the image of his own possible future death, the young king dismays and drives to distraction the very courtiers who criticised him. The pathos of such a departure is then intensified by Erec's indifference to his father's earnest concerns and entreaties, a show of displeasure deriving its charge from the fact – more than just a dramatic irony – that he will indeed never see this man again during his lifetime. This display of force continues with his early travels in the forest, the encounters with the robber knights serving as an object lesson in political terror and interrogating the bound between conscious and unconscious actions, the cocksure bands of brigands not merely destroyed but also thrown into disarray by Erec's deadly and implacable control of the space around him.

In chapter six, following on from the demonstration of Erec's terroristic will, Chrétien elaborates a number of troubled or troubling visions of the libidinal economy of court life answered or fulfilled by the monstrous vision of the giants. Faced with the vision of his squire seduced by Erec's 'beauty', Galoain's behaviour appears as a puzzle. Initially drawn to and jealous of Erec's charisma, he then transfers his attentions to Enide, a displacement that glosses over some potentially inconvenient libidinal subtexts, since what is notable about Galoain's court is the absence of women and the emphasis on men looking at men as objects of desire and envy. In that sense, the image of Galoain's court fits with other homophobic characterisations of the milieu in medieval sources as a place in which sodomy is the paradigmatic example of a range of outlandish practices associated with such an unfamiliar place. Guivret then appears as a hyper-condensation of chivalry's turbulent vigour: in spite of his need to assert his might over a conflict-torn frontier and his redoubtable neighbours – the Irish – he still has energy to burn, his thunderous charge an extreme example of the noisiness of man on horse. From this terrifying vision, we move to its burlesque replay in the encounter with Kay, joy-riding Gauvain's renowned horse, 'Le Gringalet', the variation here being that we are faced with the hybrid of one man delighting in trying out another's mount. Here as at Laluth, Chrétien's playfully suggestive handling of the moment contrasts with Erec's tactful refusal to probe too deeply the libidinal conundrums before him. However, Erec's arrival in Arthur's camp then reverses the look, presenting the wounded but insistent Erec, from the court's perspective driven by an unfathomable energy, as a contradictory object of joy and pathos, the use of Morgane's magical salve to treat him an acknowledgement of the troublingly exorbitant and unnatural appearance of his *chevauchée*. From here, Erec passes beyond and exceeds the limits set by Arthur, encountering not just a giant (as per the accounts of Arthur's encounters in Geoffrey), but giants. The abduction of Cadoc of Tabriol seems to offer the final, most apocalyptic replay of the *Eneas* scenario. This attack constitutes an irruptive resurgence of the monstrous depravity of precolonisation Britain in the Arthurianised present, an attempt to undo chivalric modernity. Through the sexualised torture and murder of a knight before witnesses humiliated by their physical and legal impotence, this scene haunts the Arthurian world, pointing to the sum of its fears and disavowed enjoyments. Through their repeated and echoing gestures of castration, exhaustion and annihilation, Erec's adventures form an interrogation of what it is that moves knights, giants and dwarves to act, its 'bestial', inhuman dimension embodied in the relation to the horse. That interrogation is not merely ongoing, but is also revisited, the queering libidinal foundations of key scenes disavowed in their present and emerging only retrospectively.

Chapter seven examines how both Erec and Enide affirm their claim to sovereignty through encounters with future (or past) death. With Erec's collapse, a key piece of the puzzle seems to fall into place: Enide's phrase 'mar i fus', now seemingly uttered in earnest, and which – in its context of a knight dying in a heroic encounter with a giant – appears as an allusion to Geoffrey's encounter with the giant of Mont-Saint-Michel, a scene in which he is greeted with the lament of Helena's nurse: 'Unhappy man, what misfortune brought you here?' ('O infelix homo, quod infortunium te in hunc locum subvectat?'). The tragedy we are then presented with is a heroic figure who has lost his life in an attempt to pattern himself after Arthur the giant slayer, and who has therefore failed in that he has lost his life and succeeded in that he has outdone his model and mentor. This allusion to Geoffrey also retroactively confirms the obscene sexual subtext of the encounter with Cadoc: Helena's nurse clearly implies that the giant's killing of Arthur is an act born of sexual frustration at not having been able to work his will on the body of the young girl, the 'flower of [Arthur's] youth' destined to serve as substitute. However, for all such a conjuncture speaks of sense and understanding, it is also marked by the gravest of misrecognitions: Enide's lament offers an object lesson in the danger of misusing one major part of Boethius's legacy to the Middle Ages, namely personification allegory. From her self-effacement before the prior claims of the figures she invokes – beauty, largesse and wisdom – her train of thought leads her to a more problematic interlocutor: Death. Her drawing of Erec's sword can then be seen partly as this object, first glimpsed in Erec's encounter with Guinevere as the agent of her destruction, echoing Dido's lament over Eneas's armour and weapon in the *Roman d'Eneas*: 'Alas that I ever saw these trappings: they were the beginning of my death and destruction' (ll. 2128–30). However, just as the picture seems to be falling into place, assuming a shape and a sense previously hidden by its anamorphic distortions, so now another strand points forward with the arrival of Oringle of Limors. Enide's forced marriage raises the spectre of sexual violence foreshadowed in her suicide attempt, paying implicit homage to the debate surrounding the example of Lucretia: Chrétien's narrative points to Augustine's discussion of her suicide and the history of Stoic exemplarity in *City of God* book 1, arguing that, since the rape was a unilateral act, Lucretia had no reason to kill herself – unless she took from it some 'secret pleasure', a shameful enjoyment she felt unable to live with. From here, Augustine questions the moral value of Cato's suicide, offering a counter-example: the Roman general Marcus Regulus, captured by the Carthaginians and sent back to negotiate for his release. In an assertion of Roman courage and principle, having exhorted the Senate not to agree to Carthage's terms, Marcus returned to his captors and was put to death, a fate that assimilates him to Job. However, in Enide's behaviour we can arguably see a challenge to Augustine's line of thought: the convincing nature of her contemptuous provocation of Oringle depends for its force on her earlier suicide attempt, Chrétien problematically bringing together in one person models which Augustine kept carefully separate to reveal the fundamentally dangerous nature of royal will. This exploration continues with the revival of Erec, the suspension of whose volition during his faint continues in the barely reflective, 'automatic' nature of his killing of Oringle, the terroristic, 'undead' dimension of this act causing the Count's courtiers to flee. Having set all this in train, it is unsurprising that his 'pardoning' of Enide should play fast and loose with the question of what her 'forfeit' was: in the bewildering discursive and historical hypercondensation of the scene at Limors, questions of action and intention intersect with a density that defies any rational assessment. As a coda we then have a further testing for Enide in the second encounter with Guivret, the young woman beating back a knight she had previously thought of as utterly terrifying in his approach. From here we then move back to the castle where Erec's carefully managed treatment and convalescence is carried out under the direction and watchful eye of his wife, an affirmation of her capacity to assume a controlling role in court life. However, the description of her saddle presented to her by Guivret with its carvings telling the tale of Dido and Aeneas positions her ambiguously as either a domesticated scion of the Trojan narrative or an embodiment of its permanent 'Junoian' dimension.

Chapter eight deals with the Joy of the Court as offering a further lesson in royal manipulations of the irrational economy of spectacle. If Enide's saddle provided a vision of the problematic foundation of aristocratic society in the Troy narrative, the description of Brandigan, surrounded by turbulent torrents and waters, has been seen as similarly marked by its troubling, but useful instability. The approach to the castle reprises themes carefully rehearsed in the narrative so far, Erec's companions concerned for his well-being and at his absolute determination to pursue the Joy of the Court even to the point of (almost) certain doom. Here again, we see Erec's beauty as an object of lament and feared loss expressed through the flagrantly self-contradictory discourse of the townspeople, cursing the name of the Joy. However, for all the combat is terrifyingly violent, rather than injuring or killing one another, the two exhaust one another, their swords conveniently disappearing as they fall to grappling with one another, their vigour spent. Here again, the scene is mocked by its libidinal dimension: Maboagrain's love of the maiden may have omitted nothing, yet satisfaction with a woman eludes him. Indeed, the erotic subtext of the scene may well suggest that this is then the last version we see of the *Eneas* scenario of a knight using a woman to attract another man, now either appearing in its giant-slaying form as the defeat and censure of the energies embodied in the giants faced earlier by both Arthur and Erec or in retrospect as a form of festivity whose carnival elements had initially appeared as cruel mockery. Yet, if Erec's victory is said to bring him unparalleled fame, it is perhaps Enide's role that is more significant. Her speech to Maboagrain's *amie*, the tale of how she arrived at such heights ('tele hautece') – an inversion of the 'mar i fus' lament as *con buer i fui* – is a carefully weighted mixture of consolation, rebuke and carefully deployed hubris as she seeks to reassure her kinswoman not all is lost. Indeed this part of the narrative emphasises the shifting fortunes within the house of Laluth, with kinswomen once seemingly more fortunate and favoured than Enide and her immediate kin now eclipsed by her but at the same time gaining by their association with her. Where previously in the forest her use of Boethian tropes such as personification allegory had led her in the direction of self-destruction, her apparent pride now appears as a forceful rhetorical subterfuge. Such a gesture then also reflexively highlights the provisional and incomplete perspective of the work as a whole in the context of a wider Arthurian history, but without at the same time implying any sort of despairing capitulation.

The conclusion examines various themes drawn together in the latter part of the poem. If the victory of the Joy implied a dramatic or personal resolution promising any kind of 'end of history' in terms of Erec or Enide's personal histories, the events leading up to the coronation re-establish the motion of the wheel. Accordingly, Chrétien offers a counterpointing range of scenarios: the restoration of the fortunes of Enide's parents; the death of Erec's father and the coronation of the royal couple. The fate of the two sets of parents, although contrasting as sources of grief versus joy, are nonetheless connected in that Chrétien stresses that neither Erec nor Enide was in a position to translate inward truth into outward show. Courtly decorum militates against Erec giving expression to his grief, while Enide is simply unable to manifest the full sense of the joy she feels. Thus, the intersecting and contrasting rhythms of fortune and misfortune are then doubly counterpointed by the opposition of interior and exterior. Contesting earlier arguments about the baselessness of astrology, Chrétien's presentation of the coronation robe, with the emphasis on the (personified) art of Astronomy reflects a renewed interest in cosmology. However, the narrator's comments beg a further reading: if Astronomy takes her counsel from the stars and 'from no other quarter in any matter', she provides a pattern for the dazzling, high-risk tactics of Arthurian charismatic authority, a blinding and disorienting effect also reflected in the excessive splendour of the crowns which Arthur presents to the couple. Kings are better to trust to their own counsel or even the stars before they give too much heed to the counsellors around them. Chrétien's description of the two thrones as identical stands in sharp contrast to his emphasis hitherto on the uniqueness of the precious artefacts and their singular histories, on the seeming impossibility of duplication in carving and casting (as in his earlier evocation of Nature's creation of the inimitable Enide). This leads us to re-evaluate Enide's role at this point – if less prominent than in the latter stages of the quest, then perhaps not as reduced as some critics have commented, and certainly no more constrained than Arthur's position as master of ceremonies. Her delay in setting out for the coronation ceremony, her staying of the time, can be seen as a means of claiming her due 'elbow-room' through the 'stretching' of ceremonial time.

Notes

1   Susan D. Crane, *The Performance of Self: Ritual, Clothing and Identity During the Hundred Years War*, The Middle Ages (Philadelphia: University of Pennsylvania Press, 2002), p. 1.
2   Judith Butler, *Gender Trouble: Feminism and the Subversion of Identity*, Thinking Gender (New York and London: Routledge, 1990), p. vii.
3   See Roger Sherman Loomis, 'Arthurian Influence on Sport and Spectacle', in *Arthurian Literature in the Middle Ages: A Collaborative History*, ed. by Loomis (Oxford: Clarendon, 1959), pp. 553–9; L. O. Aranye Fradenburg, *City, Marriage, Tournament: Arts of Rule in Late Medieval Scotland* (Madison, W: University of Wisconsin Press, 1991), pp. 153–71; Michael Evans, *The Death of Kings: Royal Deaths in Medieval England* (London and New York: Hambledon and London, 2003), pp. 147–73 (chapter: 'Once and Future Kings'); Michel Pastoureau, *Une histoire symbolique du Moyen Age occidentale*, La Librairie du XXIe Siècle (Paris: Seuil, 2004), pp. 293–305 (chapter: 'Jouer au roi Arthur').
4   'Bonjour monseigeur, bonjour. Qu'est cecy? Faites-vous du roy Artus maintenant ou de mesire Lancelot?' (Georges Chastellain, *Oeuvres*, ed. by Kervyn de Lettenhove, 8 vols (Brussels: Heussner, 1863–6), III, p. 279). Translation cited from Johan Huizinga, *The Autumn of the Middle Ages*, trans. by Rodney J. Payton and Ulrich Mammitzsch (Chicago: Chicago University Press, 1996), p. 11. For discussion, see Huizinga, pp. 11–12.
5   As Henri Pirenne comments on Philip's reign: 'désormais ce n'est plus en France ni par la France, c'est hors de la France et contre la France que la maison de Bourgogne poursuivra l'accomplissement de ses desseins' (Pirenne, *Histoire de Belgique*, 8 vols, rev. edn (Brussels: Lamertin, 1922–32), II, p. 238). For commentary on Philip and Chastellain, see Graeme Small, *Georges Chastellain and the Shaping of Valois Burgundy: Political and Historical Culture at Court in the Fifteenth Century* (Woodbridge: Boydell, 1997).
6   Donald Maddox, *The Arthurian Romances of Chrétien de Troyes: Once and Future Fictions* (Cambridge: Cambridge University Press, 1991), p. 3 and note 5.

7   On the many possible senses of 'being after', see in particular Nicholas Royle, *After Derrida* (Manchester: Manchester University Press, 1995), pp. 2–7. On anxiety in this context see Harold Bloom's influential *The Anxiety of Influence: A Theory of Poetry*, rev. edn (Oxford: Oxford University Press, 1997). On the relation between gender and performance, see introduction, above.

8   Maddox, *Arthurian Romances*, p. 3.

9   On all of which see notably, Norbert Elias, *The Civilising Process: Sociogenetic and Psychogenetic Investigations*, trans. by Edmund Jephcott, ed. by Eric Dunning, Johan Goudsblom and Stephen Mennell, rev. edn (Oxford and Malden, MA: Blackwell, 2000). Although influential, Elias's work has been considerably criticised (see, for example, the reviews by Keith Thomas, *The New York Review of Books*, 25:3 (1978), 28–31 and George Mosse, *New German Critique*, 15 (1978), 178–83). On court behaviour and culture since Elias, in addition to Crane, see especially C. Stephen Jaeger, *The Origins of Courtliness: Civilising Trends and the Formation of Courtly Ideals, 939–1210* (Philadelphia: University of Pennsylvania Press, 1985), Jaeger, *The Envy of Angels: Cathedral Schools and Social Ideals in Medieval Europe, 950–1200*, The Middle Ages (Philadelphia: University of Pennsylvania Press, 1994) and Jaeger, *Ennobling Love: In Search of a Lost Sensibility* (Philadelphia: University of Pennsylvania Press, 1999) as well as Aldo Scaglione, *Knights at Court: Courtliness, Chivalry and Courtesy from Ottonian Germany to the Italian Renaissance* (Berkeley and Oxford: University of California Press, 1991). For a fascinating study of the problem of 'civilising' the Normans see Emily Albu, *The Normans in their Histories: Propaganda, Myth and Subversion* (Woodbridge: Boydell, 2001). On the court and sexual mores in the period in question, see especially Bill Burgwinkle, *Sodomy, Masculinity and Law in Medieval Literature: France and England, 1050-1230*, Cambridge Studies in Medieval Literature (Cambridge: Cambridge University Press, 2003). See also Jeffrey Jerome Cohen, notably *Of Giants: Sex, Monsters and the Middle Ages*, Medieval Cultures, 17 (Minneapolis and London: University of Minnesota Press, 1999) and *Medieval Identity Machines*, Medieval Cultures, 35 (Minneapolis and London: University of Minnesota Press, 2003).

10 Jean de la Bruyère, 'De la cour', in *Les Caractères de Théophraste traduits du grec avec les caractères ou les moeurs de ce siècle*, ed. by Marc Escola (Paris: Honoré Champion, 1999), pp. 319–48 at p. 319; for discussion, see Elias, *The Civilising Process*, p. 398–9.

11 On the sociology of manners and taste, see of course Pierre Bourdieu, *Distinction: A Social Critique of the Judgement of Taste*, trans. by Richard Nice (London and New York: Routledge, 1986). On the history of manners, see also essays in Alain Montaudon (ed.), *Dictionnaire raisonné de la politesse et du savoir-vivre du Moyen Age à nos jours* (Paris: Seuil, 1994), notably Claude Roussel, 'Courtoisie', pp. 175–96. For more period-specific studies, see Anna Bryson, *From Courtesy to Civility: Changing Codes of Conduct in Early*

Modern England (Oxford: Clarendon, 1998), especially her comments on the 'importation' of manners into England from continental handbooks (pp. 75–106; chapter: 'The Rules of Civility: Decency and Deference'), Jorge Arditi, *A Genealogy of Manners: Transformations of Social Relations in France and England from the Fourteenth to the Eighteenth Century* (Chicago and London: University of Chicago Press, 1998).

12 'One is not born, but rather becomes, a woman' (Simone de Beauvoir, *The Second Sex*, trans. by H. M. Parshley (London: Vintage, 1997), p. 295. For de Beauvoir's original formulation, see *Le Deuxième Sexe*, 2 vols (Paris: Gallimard, 1949), II, p. 13 (opening of the first chapter of her section 'Formation'). Although Parshley's translation considerably abridges de Beauvoir's original text and has many flaws (on which see Margaret Simons, 'The Silencing of Simone de Beauvoir: Guess What's Missing from the *Second Sex?*', *Women's Studies International Forum*, 6:5 (1983), 559–64), her oft-quoted, less commonly fully-referenced formulation has had a rich afterlife, notably in Monique Wittig's essay, 'One is Not Born a Woman', from her *The Straight Mind* (see *'The Straight Mind' and Other Essays*, ed. by Louise Turcotte (Hemel Hempstead: Harvester Wheatsheaf, 1992), or the excerpt 'One Is Not Born a Woman', in *The Lesbian and Gay Studies Reader*, ed. by Henry Abelove and others (London and York: Routledge, 1993), pp. 103–09 (references are to this edition)) and Judith Butler's highly influential examination of gender and performance, *Gender Trouble*. For the purposes of my present study, see also Butler's later *The Psychic Life of Power: Theories in Subjection* (Stanford, CA: Stanford University Press, 1997). Interestingly, given the context here in discussion of 'cultural' translation, the lack of referencing may have helped nurture the wildfire uncertainty among Anglophone, especially US readers as to whether the phrase cited above offered yet another instance of Parshley's 'mangling' of de Beauvoir (for examples, follow relevant threads at www.amptoons.com/blog/archives accessed on 28/08/07). The anxieties expressed by readers here are indicative of de Beauvoir's text itself becoming a 'lost object' or lost original script of feminist ontology, with claims that the 'actual' formulation was more abstrusely philosophical: 'I had a bilingual professor who would regularly point out the mistranslations when we studied de Beauvoir. They really do make a huge difference in interpreting the text. Y'know that famous quote "One is not born, but becomes a woman," apparently should be translated as "Woman is a becoming."' (ibid.).

13 On performance in Early Modern English cultures, see notably Stephen Greenblatt, *Renaissance Self-Fashioning: From More to Shakespeare* (Chicago: University of Chicago Press, 1980).

14 On court behaviour as the object of homophobic anxieties see especially Burgwinkle and also Simon Gaunt, *Love and Death in Medieval French and Occitan Courtly Literature: Martyrs to Love* (Oxford: Oxford University Press, 2006).

15 Edmund Burke, *Letters on a Regicide Peace*, cited from Bryson, p. 43.
16 Hincmar of Rheims, *De Ordine Palatii*, ed. by T. Gross and R. Scheiffer, Monumenta Germaniae Historica: Fontes Iuris Germanici Antiqui, 3 (Hanover: Hahn, 1980). The bibliography is understandably extensive. See among other, J. Fleckenstein, 'Die Struktur des Hofes Karls des Grossen im Spiegel von Hincmars *De Ordine Palatii*', *Zeitschrift des Aachener Geschichtsvereins*, 83 (1976), 5–22. For a translation, see *On The Governance of the Palace*, in *The History of Feudalism*, ed. and trans. by David Herlihy, The Documentary History of Western Civilisation (London: MacMillan, 1970), pp. 208–27.
17 'Et ideo domus regis scola dicitur id est disciplina; quia non tantum scolastici, id est disciplinati et bene correcti, sunt, sicut alii, sed potius ipsa scola, quae interpretatur disciplina, id est correctio, dicitur, quae alios habitu, incessu, verbo et actu atque totius bonitatis continentia corrigat.' ('Quierzy, Nov. 858', in *Concilia Aevi Carolini DCCCXLIII–DCCCLIX*, ed. by Wilfried Hartmann, Monumenta Germaniae Historica: Concilia, 3 (Hanover: Hahn, 1984), pp. 403–27, here at p. 420; translation after Jaeger, *The Envy of Angels*, pp. 27–8). See also Jaeger's comments on the letter and other comments on 'courtly' deportment in Carolingian sources (pp. 27–35).
18 J. L. Nelson, *Charles the Bald*, The Medieval World (London and New York: Longman, 1992), pp. 188–9. On the letter, in addition to Jaeger, *Envy of Angels* (refs above), see Matthew Innes, ' "A Place of Discipline": Carolingian Courts and Aristocratic Youth', in *Court Culture in the Middle Ages: The Proceedings of the First Alcuin Conference*, ed. by Catherine Cubitt, Studies in the Early Middle Ages (Turnhout: Brepols, 2003), pp. 59–76.
19 See 'Quierzy, Nov. 858', p. 420.
20 Jaeger, *The Envy of Angels*, p. 29.
21 On this, in addition to Jaeger's works, see, also John F. Benton, 'The Court of Champagne as a Literary Centre', *Speculum*, 39 (1961), 551-91 (reprinted in *Culture, Power and Personality in Medieval France*, ed. by T. N. Bisson (London: Hambledon, 1991), pp. 3–43); Ad Putter, 'Knights and Clerics in the Court of Champagne: Chrétien de Troyes's Romances in Context', in *Medieval Knighthood V: Papers from the Sixth Strawberry Hill Conference 1994*, ed. by Steven Church and Ruth Harvey (Woodbridge: Boydell and Brewer, 1995), pp. 243–66 as well as Sarah Kay, 'Courts, Clerks and Courtly Love', in *The Cambridge Companion to Medieval Romance*, ed. by Roberta L. Krueger (Cambridge: Cambridge University Press, 2000), pp. 81–96.
22 Jaeger, *The Envy of Angels*, p. 28.
23 Jaeger, *The Envy of Angels*, p. 32 and pp. 76–117.
24 Texts such as this document the values of good order underpinning the laments of later chroniclers and commentators such as Walter Map and Gerald of Wales. On Hincmar and the political function of the court, see notably Tim Reuter, 'Assembly Politics in Western Europe from the Eighth Century to the Twelfth', in *The Medieval World*, ed. by Peter Linehan and Janet L. Nelson

(London and New York: Routledge, 2001), pp. 432–50 rev. edn in *Medieval Polities and Modern Mentalities*, ed. by Nelson (Cambridge: Cambridge University Press, 2006), pp. 193–216, here at p. 194.
25 Jaeger, *The Envy of Angels*, p. 47.
26 Bourdieu, *The Logic of Practice*, trans. by Richard Nice (Stanford: Stanford University Press, 1990), p. 16.
27 Jaeger, *The Envy of Angels*, pp. 28–9.
28 'Non opus exemplis. Exemplum vos magis estis.' (*Sigeberts von Gembloux Passio Sanctae Luciae Virginis und Passio Sanctorum Thebeorum*, ed. by Ernst Dümmler, Akademie der Wissenschaften, Berlin, Philologische-Historiche kleine Abhandlungen, 1 (Berlin, 1893), cited and discussed in Jaeger, *The Envy of Angels*, pp. 189–90.
29 On Bourdieu and manners in medieval culture in this regard, see in particular Mark Addison Amos, ' "For Manners Make Man": Bourdieu, de Certeau and the Common Appropriation of Noble Manners in the *Book of Courtesy*', in *Medieval Conduct*, ed. by Kathleen Ashley and Robert L. A. Clark, Medieval Cultures, 29 (Minneapolis and London: University of Minnesota Press, 2001), pp. 23–48.
30 Jaeger, *The Envy of Angels*, pp. 102–03.
31 On the cultivation of irony and ambiguity in troubadour poetry see notably Simon Gaunt, *Troubadours and Irony*, Cambridge Studies in Medieval Literature, 3 (Cambridge: Cambridge University Press, 1989).
32 Huizinga's *Herfsttij der Middeleeuwen: Studie over Levens- en Gedachtenvormen der Veertiende en Vijftiende eeuw in Frankrijk en de Nederlanden* (Haarlem: Tjeenk Willink, 1919) was originally translated in abridged form into English under the more '*Decline and Fall of the Roman Empire*'-inflected title of *The Waning of the Middle Ages: A Study of the Forms of Life, Thought and Art in France and the Netherlands in the Fourteenth and Fifteenth Centuries*, trans. by F. Hopman (London: Penguin, 1955), a more one-sided rendering that that reflected in Payton and Mammitzsch's retitled and expanded version. I am grateful here to my colleague, Graeme Small, for discussions of Huizinga's work.
33 See Jaeger, *The Envy of Angels*, pp. 199–236.
34 See René Girard, *Violence and the Sacred*, trans. by Patrick Gregory (Baltimore and London: Johns Hopkins, 1979), pp. 143–92.
35 Mary Douglas, *Risk and Blame: Essays in Cultural Theory* (London and New York: Routledge, 1994), p. 86.
36 On Richard's alleged cannibalism, see Geraldine Heng, 'The Romance of England: *Richard Coer de Lyon*, Saracens, Jews and the Politics of Race and Nation', in *The Postcolonial Middle Ages*, ed. by Cohen, The New Middle Ages (Basingstoke and New York: MacMillan, 2000), pp. 135–71 and Michael Uebel, *Ecstatic Transformation: On the Uses of Alterity in the Middle Ages*,

The New Middle Ages (London: Palgrave MacMillan, 2005), pp. 44–51. On Richard's reputation as a sodomite, see Burgwinkle, pp. 73–85.

37   On Sartre, see Butler, *Gender Trouble*, p. vii. De Beauvoir returns frequently to the parallels and differences between gender and ethnic difference, and the problematic experience of that difference in a single contingent locality: 'Thus it is that no group ever sets itself up as the One without at once setting up the Other over against itself. If three travellers chance to occupy the same compartment, that is enough to make vaguely hostile "others" out of all the rest of the passengers on the train. In small-town eyes all persons not belonging to the village are "strangers" and suspect; to the native of a country all who inhabit other countries are "foreigners".' (*The Second Sex*, p. 17).

38   *The History of the Kings of Britain*, trans. by Thorpe, p. 232, note. 'Nichil enim quod ui et uiolentia adquiritur iuste ab ullo possidetur.' (Geoffrey of Monmouth, *Historia Regum Britannie: Bern, Burgerbibliothek, MS. 568*, ed. by Neil Wright, The Historia Regum Britannie of Geoffrey of Monmouth, 1 (Woodbridge: Brewer, 1985), p. 114 (§ 159)).

39   For edition and translation, see Suetonius, *Lives of the Caesars*, ed. by T. E. Page et al., trans. by J. C. Rolfe, Loeb Classical Library, 2 vols (Cambridge MA and London: Heinemann, 1954).

40   J. Hillis Miller, *Topographies*, Meridian: Crossing Aesthetics (Stanford: Stanford University Press, 1995), pp. 57–79, here at p. 57.

41   See Carleton W. Carroll, 'Quelques observations sur les Reflets de la cour Henri II chez Chrétien de Troyes', *Cahiers de Civilisation Médiévale*, 37 (1994), 33–9 at p. 33. See also Benton, *Culture, Power and Personality*, p. 13 and Putter, 'Knights and Clerics', pp. 253–5.

42   Sarah Kay, 'Who Was Chrétien de Troyes?', *Arthurian Literature*, 15 (1997), 1–35. For a less sceptical examination, see Joseph J. Duggan, *The Romances of Chrétien de Troyes* (New Haven CT: Yale University Press, 2001), pp. 4–8 and (regarding dating) pp. 8–23. However, there are or have been alternative views, on which see especially Claude Luttrell, *The Creation of the First Arthurian Romance: A Quest* (London: Edward Arnold, 1974) and Tony Hunt's probing but broadly supportive examination of Luttrell's arguments ('Redating Chrestien de Troyes', *Bulletin bibliographique de la Société Internationale Arthurienne*, 30 (1987), 209–37), and discussion below. For more recent arguments for an earlier dating, see Claudia Seebass-Linggi, *Lecture d''Erec': traces épiques et troubadouresques dans le conte de Chrétien de Troyes*, French Language and Literature, 211 (Bern: Peter Lang, 1996), pp. 162–8 for her discussion of F. Pirot, *Recherches sur les connaissances littéraires des troubadours occitans et catalans des XIIe et XIIIe siècles*, Memorias de la Real Academia de Buenas Lettras de Barcelona, 14 (Barcelona: Real Academia de Buenas Lettras, 1972).

43   See, for example, Laurel Amtower, 'Courtly Code and Conjointure: The Rhetoric of Identity in *Erec et Enide*', *Neophilologus*, 77:2 (1993), 179–89.

44 See notably James G. Harper, 'Turks as Trojans; Trojans as Turks: Visual Imagery of the Trojan War and the Politics of Cultural Identity in Fifteenth-Century Europe', in *Postcolonial Approaches to the European Middle Ages: Translating Cultures*, ed. by Ananya Jahanara Kabir and Deanne Williams, Cambridge Studies in Medieval Literature (Cambridge: Cambridge University Press, 2005), pp. 151–79.

45 For edition and translation, see *'The Pilgrimage of Charlemagne' and 'Aucassin and Nicolette'*, ed. and trans. by Glyn S. Burgess and Anne Elizabeth Cobby, Garland Library of Medieval Literature, 47 (New York: Garland, 1987).

46 Paul Freedman, *Images of the Medieval Peasant*, Figurae: Reading Medieval Cultures (Stanford: Stanford University Press, 1999), pp. 110–14.

47 See for example, A. Castellani, 'La "Parole" d'Enide', *Cultura Neolatina*, 18 (1958), 139–49; Gabriel J. Brogyanyi, 'Motivation in *Erec et Enide*: An Interpretation of the Romance', *Kentucky Romance Quarterly*, 19 (1972), 407–31; Lacy, 'Narrative Point of View and the Problem of Erec's Motivation', *Kentucky Romance Quarterly*, 19 (1972), 355–62; Zaddy, pp. 1–23; Glyn S. Burgess, *Chrétien de Troyes: 'Erec et Enide'*, Critical Guides to French Texts (London: Grant and Cutler, 1984), pp. 54–7; René Ménage, 'Erec et les intermittences du coeur', in *Marche Romane*, 32:2–4 (1982), 5–14; Peggy McCracken, 'Silence and the Courtly Wife: Chrétien de Troyes's *Erec et Enide*', *Arthurian Yearbook*, 3 (1993), 107–26; Liliane Dulac, 'Peut-on comprendre les relations entre Erec et Enide?', *Le Moyen Age*, 100:1 (1994), 37–50; E. Jane Burns, *Bodytalk: When Women Speak in Old French Literature*, The Middle Ages (Philadelphia: University of Philadelphia Press, 1993), pp. 151–202; René Pérennec, 'La "Faute" d'Enide: transgression ou inadéquation entre un projet poétique et des stéréotypes de comportement?', in *Amour, mariage et transgressions au Moyen Age: Actes du colloque des 24–27 mars 1983, Université de Picardie, Centre d'Etudes Médiévales*, ed. by Danielle Buschinger and André Crépin, Göppinger Arbeiten zur Germanistik 420 (Göppingen: Kümmerle, 1984), pp. 153–9.

48 In Foerster's original stemma, fonds fr. 1376 is designated as Ms. B. In terms of content, it pairs *Erec et Enide* with Aimon de Varennes' romance, *Florimont*. Although Foerster and Roques follow Micha in taking the manuscript to be one of the older ones in the tradition, dating it to the early 1200's, Fritz has suggested a considerably later dating of the end of the that century (see Fritz's introduction at p. 59). For commentary on the manuscripts and transmission of *Erec et Enide* in addition to Micha and the introductions to the editions see also Tony Hunt, 'Chrestien de Troyes: The Textual Problem', *French Studies*, 33:3 (1979), 257–71; Françoise Gasparri, Genevieve Hasenohr and Christine Ruby, 'De l'écriture à la lecture: réflexion sur les manuscrits d'*Erec et Enide*', in *Les Manuscrits de Chrétien de Troyes*, I, pp. 97–148 and Roger Middleton, 'Coloured Capitals in the Manuscripts of *Erec et Enide*', in *Les Manuscrits de Chrétien de Troyes*, I, pp. 149–93. See also Carleton W. Carroll, 'A Reappraisal

of the Relationship between Two Manuscripts of *Erec et Enide*', *Nottingham French Studies*, 30:2 (1991), 34–42; Sandra Hindman, *Sealed in Parchment: Rereadings of Knighthood in the Illuminated Manuscripts of Chrétien de Troyes* (Chicago and London: University of Chicago Press, 1994). For an edition of *Florimont*, see Alfons Hilka (ed.), *Aimon de Varennes, 'Florimont': ein altfranzösicher abenteurroman*, Gesellschaft für romanische Literatur, 48 (Göttingen: Gesellschaft für romanische Literatur; Halle: Niemeyer, 1933). For studies, see notably Douglas Kelly, 'The Composition of Aimon de Varennes's *Florimont*', *Romance Philology*, 23 (1969), 277–92 and Alison Adams, 'Destiny, Love and the Cultivation of Suspense: The *Roman d'Eneas* and Aimon de Varennes's *Florimont*', *Reading Medieval Studies*, 5 (1979), 57–69.

49 My emendation here reflects the original reading of l. 2503 in fonds fr. 1376 which Fritz rejects in favour of that in B. N. fonds fr. 375 (Ms. P in Foerster's stemma). For further comment, see chapter five below.

50 Gaunt, *Gender and Genre in Medieval French Literature*, Cambridge Studies in French, 53 (Cambridge: Cambridge University Press, 1995), p. 92, my emphasis. Contrast this with Anthime Fourrier: 'A-t-il existé en français avant Chrétien de Troyes des poèmes narratifs qui mettaient en oeuvre la "matière de Bretagne" sous sa forme arthurienne? On l'ignore, mais ce que l'on sait bien, en revanche, c'est qu'avec lui cette matière a connu son suprême épanouissement: il a été, sinon l'inventeur, du moins l'initiateur incontesté du genre.' (*Le Courant réaliste dans le roman courtois en France au Moyen Age*, 2 vols (Paris: Nizet, 1960), I, p. 111–12). The difference between the two comments, flowering versus reshaping, is slight but telling.

51 On prosopopoeia, see Miller, pp. 57–79, here at p. 57. On medieval biography, see, among others, Michael Goodich, 'Biography 1000–1350', in *Historiography in the Middle Ages*, ed. by Deborah Mauskopf Deliyannis (Leiden and Boston: Brill, 2003), pp. 353–85, as well as David Bates, Julia Crick and Sarah Hamilton, 'Introduction', in *Writing Medieval Biography, 750–1250: Essays in Honour of Professor Frank Barlow* (Woodbridge: Boydell, 2006), pp. 1–13 and, in the same volume, Janet L. Nelson, 'Did Charlemagne have a Private Life?', pp. 15–28.

52 My comments here are influenced by M. Victoria Guerin's *The Fall of Kings and Princes: Structure and Destruction in Arthurian Tragedy*, Figurae: Reading Medieval Culture (Stanford: Stanford University Press, 1995). Guerin's study centres on what she sees as a suspension of the forces of fate that foreshadow the twilight and ruin of the Arthurian idyll. These, she argues, are most apparent in works such as *Cligès* and *Le Chevalier de la charrette*. My contention here is that such a reading can be extended to *Erec et Enide* as well.

53 See note above.

54 On Brian and Owein, see Jessie Weston, 'Who Was Brian des Illes?', *Modern Philology*, 22 (1924), 4–11; Beate Schmolke-Hasselmann, 'Henry II Plantagenet, roi d'Angleterre, et la genèse d'*Erec et Enide*', *Cahiers de Civilisation*

Médiévale, 24:3–4 (1981), 241–6 and *The Evolution of Arthurian Romance: The Verse Tradition from Chrétien to Froissart* (Cambridge: Cambridge University Press, 1998), pp. 238–40; Carroll, 'Quelques observations', p. 35, as well as Duggan, *The Romances of Chrétien de Troyes*, pp. 10–11 and pp. 136–82.

55   Broadhurst, p. 65, citing Ian Short, 'Patrons and Polyglots: French Literature in Twelfth-Century England', *Anglo-Norman Studies*, 14 (1991), 229–49 at p. 239.
56   Broadhurst, p. 64.
57   Broadhurst, p. 64. See also Owen, *Eleanor of Aquitaine*, pp. 184–5.
58   On the question of whether there actually was a School of Chartres, see Hunt, 'Redating', p. 208 and note 2.
59   As part of this, I am also struck by the similarities between the attitudes of sadness and repose shown both by Enide's father (ll. 373–80) and Hymenaeus, Nature's estranged husband, in prose 8 of Alan of Lille's *The Plaint of Nature* (trans. by James J. Sheridan, Medieval Sources in Translation, 26 (Toronto: Pontifical Institute of Mediaeval Studies, 1980), pp. 196–7) and that of Enide's father. On Hymenaeus, see Michael D. Cherniss, *Boethian Apocalypse: Studies in Middle English Vision Poetry* (Norman, Oklahoma: Pilgrim, 1987), pp. 68–9 and discussion in chapter 4 below.
60   Hunt, 'Redating', pp. 214–31.
61   One intriguingly specific example of possible scriptural influences is W.A. Nitze's 'Erec and the Joy of the Court', *Speculum*, 29:4 (1954), 691–701, in which he highlights the possible importance of Psalm 44 ('Eructavit'), a commentary on which was written for Marie de Champagne (for edition see T. A. Jenkins (ed.), *Eructavit: An Old French Metrical Paraphrase of Psalm XLIV* (Dresden: Niemeyer, 1909)), excerpts from Psalm 45 incorporated into the coronation ceremony for the kings of France and England (see Jenkins, *Eructavit*, p. xix). On the reception of Nitze's arguments, see Emmanuel J. Mickel, 'A Reconsideration of Chrétien's *Erec*', *Romanische Forschungen*, 84 (1972), 18–44. For edition and translation of the *Consolation of Philosophy*, see *Boethius: The Theological Tractates and the Consolation of Philosophy*, ed. by E. H. Warmington, trans. by S. J. Tester, Loeb Classical Library, 74 (Cambridge MA: Heinemann, 1973), pp. 130–435). For another translation, see *The Consolation of Philosophy*, trans. by V. E. Watts (London: Penguin, 1969). On the reception of Boethius generally, see Pierre Courcelle, *La 'Consolation de Philosophie' dans la tradition littéraire: antécédents et postériorité de Boèce* (Paris: Etudes Augustiniennes, 1967), Cherniss, passim and Winthrop Wetherbee, *Platonism and Poetry in the Twelfth Century: The Literary Influence of the School of Chartres* (Princeton: Princeton University Press, 1972). On Boethius and Chrétien, see Ruth H. Firestone, 'Chrétien's Enide, Hartmann's Enide et Boethii *Philosophiae Consolatio*', *Amsterdamer Beiträge zur alteren Germanistik*, 26 (1987), 69–106, cited here at p. 70. Firestone's

reference is to Frederick P. Pickering, *Augustinus oder Boethius? Geschichtsschreibung und epische Dichtung im Mittelalter und in der Neuzeit*, Philologische Studien und Quellen, 39 and 80, 2 vols (Berlin: Schmidt, 1967–1976), I, p. 88. As Firestone points out, more systematic study has been devoted to Hartmann von Aue's Middle High German adaptation, which seems to offer a more sustained use of Boethius (Firestone, p. 74).

62   On Henry and his sons in this period, see W. L. Warren, *Henry II*, Yale English Monarchs (New Haven and London: 2000), pp. 559–93.

63   Walter Map, *The Courtier's Trifles*, ed. and trans. by M. R. James; revised by C. N. L. Brooke and R. A. B. Mynors, Oxford Medieval Texts (Oxford: Clarendon, 1983). On the intellectual and political culture of Henry's court, see, among others, Egbert Türk, *Nugae curialium: le règne d'Henri II Plantegenêt (1145–1189) et l'éthique politique*, Hautes Etudes Médiévales et Modernes, 28 (Geneva: Droz, 1977).

64   Richard Barber, *Henry Plantagenet* (Ipswich: Boydell, 1964 [2001 reprint]), p. 205. Barber cites Walter as his source here, although I can find no mention of the Young King as prone to being easily swayed there. However, William of Newburgh makes reference to the circle of conspirators surrounding the Young King (see *The History of William of Newburgh*, ed. and trans. by Joseph Stevenson (London, 1856 [repr. Felinfach: Llanerch, 1996]), book 3, chapter 7, pp. 521–2 in translation). I am also very grateful to Matthew Strickland for kindly providing me with a copy of his as yet unpublished work on the Young King ('On the Instruction of a Prince: The Upbringing of Henry, the Young King').

65   See Duggan, *The Romances of Chrétien de Troyes*, pp. 12–13

66   On contemporary chronicle sources, see Richard Barber, 'Eleanor of Aquitaine and the Media', in *The World of Eleanor of Aquitaine: Literature and Society in Southern France between the Eleventh and Thirteenth Centuries*, ed. by Marcus Bull and Catherine Léglu (Woodbridge: Boydell, 2005), pp. 13–27, here at p. 26. On later slanders and their sources in earlier stories, see Dan Power, 'The Stripping of a Queen: Eleanor of Aquitaine in Thirteenth-Century Norman Tradition', ibid., pp. 115–35. See also D. D. R. Owen, *Eleanor of Aquitaine: Queen and Legend* (Oxford: Blackwell, 1993). See also Peggy McCracken, 'Scandalising Desire: Eleanor of Aquitaine and the Chroniclers', in *Eleanor of Aquitaine: Lord and Lady*, ed. by Bonnie Wheeler and John Carmi Parsons, The New Middle Ages (New York and Basingstoke: Palgrave MacMillan, 2003), pp. 247–63 as well as Parsons, 'Damned If She Didn't and Damned When She Did: Bodies, Babies and Bastards in the Lives of Two Queens of France', in *Eleanor of Aquitaine*, ed. by Wheeler and Parsons, pp. 267–99 and Tamara F. O'Callaghan, 'Tempering Scandal: Eleanor of Aquitaine and Benoît de Sainte-Maure's *Roman de Troie*', in *Eleanor of Aquitaine*, ed. by Wheeler and Parsons, pp. 301–17.

67   See Ruth Harvey, 'Eleanor of Aquitaine and the Troubadours', in *The World of Eleanor of Aquitaine*, pp. 101–14. See also Karen M. Broadhurst, 'Henry II of England and Eleanor of Aquitaine: Patrons of Literature in French?', *Viator*, 27 (1996), 53–84.

68   Harvey, p. 104.

69   For edition, see *Guglielmo IX d'Aquitainia: Poesie*, ed. and trans. by Nicolò Pasero (Modena: Mucchi, 1973). For translation, see Alan R. Press (ed. and trans.), *Anthology of Troubadour Lyric Poetry*, Edinburgh Bilingual Library, 3 (Edinburgh: Edinburgh University Press, 1971). However, the text and translation cited reflect Simon Gaunt's comments on the transmission of the poem (*Troubadours and Irony*, p. 19). As Gaunt points out, 'there is a lacuna of one syllable in the first line. As the text is preserved in the manuscripts, Guilhem claims that he will compose a 'seemly' poem. [...] Various interpolations have been suggested for the first line, but the simplest solution is to leave the manuscript reading as it stands even thought it is hypometric. In the manuscripts, the line is clearly ironic: it so patently contraditcts the facts that the real or intended eamning must be the opposite of the literal or pretended meaning. In other words *covinen* is intended to convey *descovinen*.' (pp. 19–20). For discussion of the poem or William's work more generally, see Gaunt, *Troubadours and Irony*, pp. 19–31 and also Jean-Charles Huchet, *L'Amour discourtois: la 'fin'amors' chez les premiers troubadours*, Bibliothèque Historique Privat (Toulouse: Privat, 1987), pp. 59–123 (on 'Companho farai un vers covinen', see in particular, pp. 65–73).

70   Peggy McCracken, *The Romance of Adultery: Queenship and Sexual Transgression in Old French Literature*, The Middle Ages (Philadelphia: University of Pennsylvania Press, 1998), p. 2. For an account of the shifts in status and influence of the queens of France in this period, see pp. 3–15. On Chrétien's possible reservations about the Lancelot-Guinevere narrative, see notably David F. Hult, 'Author/Narrator/Speaker: The Voice of Authority in Chrétien's *Charrete*'; in *Discourses of Authority in Medieval and Renaissance Literature*, ed. by Walter Stephens and Kevin Brownlee (Hanover and London: University Press of New England, 1989), p. 76–96, especially at pp. 86–8.

71   By inter- or hypertextuality I mean allusions to antecedent sources that supply elements left unstated in the later work. See notably Gérard Genette, *Palimpsestes: la littérature au second degré*, Poétique (Paris: Seuil, 1982), pp. 7–19, and, for discussion, Mary Orr, *Claude Simon: The Intertextual Dimension* (Glasgow: University of Glasgow French and German Publications, 1993).

72   Gaunt, *Gender and Genre*, p. 76.

73   For edition, see *Le Roman d'Eneas*, ed. and trans. by A. Petit, Lettres Gothiques (Paris: Livre de Poche, 1997). For studies on both the work itself and its relation to either Chrétien or *Erec et Enide*, see Joseph S. Wittig, 'The Aeneas-Dido Allusion in Chrétien's *Erec et Enide*', *Comparative Literature*, 22 (1970),

237–53, Giovanna Angeli, *L' 'Eneas' e i primi romanzi volgari* (Milan: Riccardo Riccardi, 1971), Raymond J. Cormier, 'Remarques sur le *Roman d'Eneas* et l'*Erec et Enide*', *Revue des Langues Romanes*, 82 (1976), 85–97, Jean-Charles Huchet, *Le Roman médiéval*, Littératures Modernes (Paris: Presses Universitaires de France, 1984). See also Lee Patterson, *Negotiating the Past: The Historical Understanding of Medieval Literature* (Madison: University of Wisconsin Press, 1987), pp. 157–95 (chapter: 'Virgil and the Historical Consciousness of the Twelfth Century: The *Roman d'Eneas* and *Erec et Enide*'). Interestingly, Patterson reads the *Eneas* as 'unproblematic', a 'propagandistic resolution' (p. 180). On the *Aeneid* and the *Roman d'Eneas* as narratives of genealogy and foundation, see also notably Gayle Margherita, *The Romance of Origins: Language and Sexual Difference in Middle English Literature* (Philadelphia: University of Pennsylvania Press, 1994) and Zrinka Stahuljak, *Bloodless Genealogies of the French Middle Ages: Translatio, Kinship, and Metaphor* (Gainsville: University Press of Florida 2005).

74 On which see in particular Sarah Spence, *Rhetorics of Reason and Desire: Virgil, Augustine, and the Troubadours* (Ithaca and London: Cornell University Press, 1988).

75 'Augustus presumably knew of the powers of Juno and all she stood for; otherwise he would not have suppressed rebellion with such vigour and would not have insisted on the superiority of reason. While I agree that the *Aeneid* is not a celebration of the status quo and that it does indeed introduce the problems of the darker forces, I would not argue that these forces need to be viewed as negative. I would propose rather that Virgil is working within the current rhetorical system, and the is trying to suggest the limits of that system and, perhaps subconsciously, to escape from such a system, an effort in which he all but succeeds.' (Spence, p. 23).

76 Slavoj Žižek, *The Pervert's Guide to the Cinema*, dir. Sophie Fiennes (2006).

77 Lacan, *Le Séminaire X*, pp. 21–3, citation from p. 22.

78 Dipesh Chakrabarty, *Provincializing Europe: Postcolonial Thought and Historical Difference* (Princeton and Oxford: Princeton University Press, 2000), p. 43.

79 James Simpson, *Sciences of the Self in Medieval Poetry: Alan of Lille's 'Anticlaudianus' and John Gower's 'Confessio Amantis'*, Cambridge Studies in Medieval Literature, 25 (Cambridge: Cambridge University Press, 1995), p. 248.

80 For an overview of 'Subaltern Studies', see Gyan Prakash, 'Subaltern Studies as Postcolonial Criticism', *American Historical Review*, 99:5 (1994), 1475–90. Central to the field here is Homi K. Bhabha's *The Location of Culture* (London and New York: Routledge, 1994). On subalternity in medieval studies, see especially Kathleen Biddick, 'Bede's Blush: Postcards from Bali, Bombay, Palo Alto', in *The Past and the Future of Medieval Studies*, ed. by John van Engen, Notre Dame Conferences in Medieval Studies, 4 (Notre Dame and London:

University of Notre Dame Press, 1994), pp. 16–44, rev. edn repr. in *The Shock of Medievalism* (Durham NC and London: Duke University Press, 1998), pp. 81–101 (all references to this edition) especially her comments on language and translation in Bede (*The Shock of Medievalism*, pp. 96–101).

81   The question of speech is notably treated in Lacan's first seminar, where, as he puts it 'full speech is speech *that performs*' (*The Seminar of Jacques Lacan (Book I): Freud's Papers on Technique (1953–54)*, ed. by Jacques-Alain Miller, trans. by John Forrester (London and New York: Norton, 1991), p. 107, my emphasis), a rendering of the original expression 'qui fait acte'. For discussion, see Dylan Evans, *An Introductory Dictionary of Lacanian Psychoanalysis* (London and New York: Routledge, 1996), pp. 190–2.

82   On which see notably Ernst Hartwig Kantorowicz, *The King's Two Bodies: A Study in Medieval Political Theology* (Princeton: Princeton University Press, 1957).

83   Kantorowicz, pp. 94–7.

84   For an overview of Lacan's discussion of the structure of perversion, see Evans, *Introductory Dictionary*, pp. 138–40. Lacan returns frequently to the subject – for principle treatments, see *Le Séminaire de Jacques Lacan (livre IV): la relation d'objet (1956–1957)*, ed. by Jacques-Alain Miller, Le Champ Freudien (Paris: Seuil, 1994), 'The Subversion of the Subject and the Dialectic of Desire in the Freudian Unconscious', in *Ecrits: A Selection*, trans. by Bruce Fink (New York and London: Norton, 2004), pp. 280–312, 'Kant avec Sade', in *Ecrits*, Le Champ Freudien (Paris: Seuil, 1966), pp. 765–90 and *Le Séminaire de Jacques Lacan (livre XI): les quatre concepts fondamentaux de la psychanalyse (1963–1964)*, ed. by Jacques-Alain Miller, Le Champ Freudien (Paris: Seuil, 1973), pp. 159–69. In Žižek's work, see for examples of discussion *The Plague of Fantasies*, Wo Es War (London and New York: Verso, 1997), pp. 13–16 (on Foucault's 'perverse implantation' and sex in the Garden of Eden) and pp. 86–126 (chapter: 'Fetishism and its Vicissitudes'); *The Ticklish Subject* (London and New York: Verso, 2000), pp. 247–57; *The Puppet and the Dwarf: The Perverse Core of Christianity*, Short Circuits (Cambridge MA and London: MIT Press, 2003), passim, and *How to Read Lacan* (London: Granta, 2006), pp. 105–24 (chapter: 'The Perverse Subject of Politics: Lacan as a Reader of Mohammad Bouyeri'). See also Alenka Zupančič, *Ethics of the Real: Kant, Lacan*, Wo Es War (London and New York: Verso, 2000), pp. 58–62 and pp. 107–21 (on Valmont in *Les Liaisons dangereuses*).

85   On courtly love as a key perverse structure, see notably Lacan, *Le Séminaire de Jacques Lacan (livre VII): l'ethique de la psychanalyse (1959-1960)*, ed. by Jacques-Alain Miller, Le Champ Freudien (Paris: Seuil, 1986) and Žižek, *The Metastases of Enjoyment*, pp. 89–164 (Chapter: 'Courtly Love or Woman as Thing'). See also Jean-Charles Huchet, notably here *L'Amour discourtois: la "fin'amors" chez les premiers troubadours* (Paris: Privat, 1987); *Essais de clinique littéraire du texte médiéval*, Medievalia (Orléans: Paradigme, 1998),

notably pp. 71–84 ('La Jouissance romanesque'), *Littérature médiévale et psychanalyse: pour une clinique littéraire*, Ecriture (Paris: Presses Universitaires de France, 1990) and *Le Roman médiéval*, Littératures Modernes (Paris: Presses Universitaires de France, 1984). See also Kay, *Courtly Contradictions: The Emergence of the Literary Object in the Twelfth Century*, Figurae: Reading Medieval Culture (Stanford: Stanford University Press, 2001), pp. 257–99.

86   In fetishism, an object is supplied as the substitute for the maternal phallus – the missing object *par excellence*. For an account of the evolution of Lacan's thought in this area, see Evans, *Introductory Dictionary*, pp. 63–4.

87   Lacan, *Le Séminaire VII*, p. 182.

88   On fundamentalism, see also Žižek, *On Belief*, Thinking in Action (London and New York: Routledge, 2001).

89   On the notion of the 'beautiful soul', in Lacan's thought, see Evans, *Introductory Dictionary*, p. 16.

90   On anti-Semitism in Žižek, see for example, *The Sublime Object of Ideology*, Phronesis (London and New York: Verso, 1989), pp. 64–6, *Enjoy Your Symptom!: Jacques Lacan In and Out of Hollywood* (London and New York: Routledge, 1992), pp. 89–90, pp. 132–4 and *The Plague of Fantasies*, Wo Es War (London and New York: Verso, 1997), pp. 76–7.

91   See Evans, *Introductory Dictionary*, p. 12.

92   See Freud, 'Inhibitions, Symptoms and Anxiety', in *The Standard Edition of the Complete Psychological Works of Sigmund Freud (Volume XX)*, ed. and trans. by James Strachey and others (London: Hogarth), pp. 75–175 at p. 140. Lacan follows this sense of the term in his earlier writings on the subject.

93   See Lacan, *Le Séminaire X*, pp. 21–3, citation from p. 22. Also Žižek, *The Puppet and the Dwarf*, pp. 59–91 and Salecl, *On Anxiety*, pp. 2–5.

94   See Žižek, *Welcome to the Desert of the Real*, pp. 21–2 and discussion below.

95   On which see especially Lacan, *Le Séminaire de Jacques Lacan (livre XX): encore (1972–1973)*, ed. by Jacques-Alain Miller, Le Champ Freudien (Paris: Seuil, 1975).

96   This later presentation again has points in common with Lacan's earlier accounts in *Le Séminaire IV*, especially the commentary on the case of Little Hans, where Hans's phobia of horses saves him from the anxiety produced by the absence of paternal intervention, thus substituting for a (missing) symbolic 'castration' in the form of the Law that would have separated him from mother. Lacan's reflections here then effectively pave the way for his later accounts of anxiety as 'the lack of a lack', in which sense we can see anxiety as opening a space much as in the same way that, for Lacan, the 'fort-da' game (the child's pushing away of the toy and pulling it back) recounted and analysed by Freud, is less to do with overcoming loss than with making desire possible through the introduction of *manque*.

97   Žižek, *The Puppet and the Dwarf*, p. 57.

98 On the debate of the 'Ancients' and the 'Moderns' in the twelfth century, see, among others Ernst Robert Curtius, *European Literature and the Latin Middle Ages*, trans. by Willard R. Trask (London: Routledge and Kegan Paul, 1979), pp. 251–5; Elisabeth Gössman, *Antiqui und Moderni im Mittelalter: eine geschichtliche Standordbestimmung*, Veröffentlichungen des Grabmann-Institutes, New Series, 23 (Munich: Schöningh, 1974), pp. 81–101 and Bernard Ribémont, *La 'Renaissance' du XIIe siècle et l'encyclopédisme*, Essais sur le Moyen Age (Paris: Honoré Champion, 2002).

99 Chakrabarty, *Provincialising Europe*, p. 49. See also Jeffrey Cohen, 'Introduction: Midcolonial', in *The Postcolonial Middle Ages*, ed. by Cohen, The New Middle Ages (Basingstoke and New York: Palgrave MacMillan, 2000), pp. 1–17.

100 Erich Köhler, *Ideal und Wirklichkeit in der höfischen Epik: Studien zur Form der frühen Artus- und Graldichtung*, Beihefte zur Zeitschrift für Romanische Philologie, 97 (Tübingen: Niemeyer, 1956), p. 242 and *L'Aventure chevaleresque: idéal et réalité dans le roman courtois*, trans. by Eliane Kaufholz, Bibliothèque des Idées (Paris: Gallimard, 1974), p. 276, my emphases.

101 On estrangement or defamiliarisation, see Viktor Shlovsky, 'Art as Technique' in *Modern Criticism and Theory: A Reader*, ed. by David Lodge (London and New York: Longman, 1988), pp. 15–30.

102 For edition, see Renaut de Beaujeu, *'Le Bel Inconnu': roman d'aventures*, ed. by G. Perrie Williams, CFMA (Paris: Champion, 1983).

103 Žižek, *The Puppet and the Dwarf*, p. 57, note 31 (at p. 178), original emphasis.

104 On 'extimité' ('extimacy'), see Evans, *Introductory Dictionary*, pp. 58–9.

105 See O. Bloch and W. von Wartburg, *Dictionnaire étymologique de la langue française*, rev. edn (Paris: Presses Universitaires de France, 1991), p. 219.

106 Adolf Töbler and Erhard Lommatzsch, *Altfranzösisches Wörterbuch* (Wiesbaden: Steiner, 1954), III, cols 1105–09.

107 Girard, *Violence and the Sacred*, p. 107

108 Guerin, pp. 89–90.

109 On which, see notably Guerin, pp. 102–07.

110 On this rereading of Freud's account, see Žižek, *The Puppet and the Dwarf*, pp. 59–60.

111 On charisma, see Max Weber, *Economy and Society: An Outline of Interpretative Sociology*, ed. by Gunther Roth and Claus Wittich, trans. by Roth, Wittich and others, 3 vols (New York: Bedminster, 1968). See also Norbert Elias, *The Court Society*, pp. 117–26.

112 Lavisse, cited from Elias, *Court Society*, p. 127.

113 Elias, *Court Society*, p. 125.

114 Elias, *Court Society*, p. 123.

115 'But what about the king? Is he not at the very heart of the community? Undoubtedly – but it is precisely his position at the centre that serves to isolate

him from his fellow men, to render him casteless. He escapes from society, so to speak, via the roof, just as the pharmakos escapes through the cellar.' (Girard, p. 12).
116   Clifford Geertz, *Negara: The Theatre State in Nineteenth Century Bali* (Princeton and Guilford: Princeton University Press, 1980), pp. 132–3.
117   Elias, *Court Society*, p. 3.
118   Prakash, p. 1476.
119   See Gayatri Chakravorty Spivak, 'Can the Subaltern Speak?', in *Marxism and the Interpretation of Culture*, ed. by Cary Nelson and Lawrence Grossberg (Urbana: University of Illinois Press, 1988), pp. 271–313.
120   See Shahid Amin, 'Ghandi as Mahatma: Gorakhpur District, Eastern UP, 1921–1922', *Subaltern Studies*, 3 (1984), 1–61.
121   For examples, see Chakrabarty, *Provincialising Europe*, pp. 27–8 and pp. 109–11.
122   See Freedman, especially his comments on alterity as a catch-all category (pp. 300–02). For examples of explicitly postcolonial approaches to medieval studies, see the essays in *The Postcolonial Middle Ages*, ed. by Cohen and also those in *Postcolonial Approaches to the European Middle Ages*, ed. by Kabir and Williams.
123   See Chakrabarty, *Provincialising Europe*, pp. 30–4.
124   Cited from Chakrabarty, *Provincialising Europe*, pp. 32–3.
125   On 'translation' in subaltern studies, see Chakrabarty, *Provincialising Europe*, pp. 72–96. Tantalisingly, Chakrabarty does not refer to the medieval notion of *translatio*, although the extensive referencing of medieval scholarship in the context of his overall argument about translation is suggestive. In this connection, see also Biddick's remarks on the reception in India of the publication of the Early English Texts Society ('Bede's Blush', pp. 25–9).
126   Chakrabarty, *Provincialising Europe*, p. 33.
127   Žižek, *Welcome to the Desert of the Real*, p. 49, original emphasis.
128   Žižek, *Welcome to the Desert of the Real*, p. 8, original emphasis.
129   See notably Slavoj Žižek, 'Robespierre or the "Divine Violence" of Terror', in *Virtue and Terror*, ed. by Jean Ducange, trans. by John Howe, Revolutions (London and New York: Verso: 2007), pp. vii–xxxix.
130   On Benjamin in this regard, see Žižek, *Welcome to the Desert of the Real*, pp. 22–5.
131   Holbein's painting is central to Lacanian discussions of anamorphosis as a visual rendering of the warping effects of desire and the Law on the space of the Symbolic and of fantasy, see Lacan, *Le Séminaire VII*, pp. 139–42 and *Le Séminaire XI*, pp. 75–84. Žižek makes frequent reference to Holbein. For examples of notable discussions, see *Sublime Object*, pp. 98–100, *Enjoy Your Symptom!*, pp. 134–40, and, *How to Read Lacan*, pp. 61–78. On Holbein see also Greenblatt, *Renaissance Self-Fashioning*, pp. 17–26.

132   Carroll's translation is perhaps slightly misleading here, in that the force of the phrase, in this line that follows directly on from Erec's father's speech (ll. 2693–711) is to indicate Erec's rejection of all attempts at persuasion.
133   On ritual in this regard, see, among others, Philippe Buc, 'Political Rituals and Political Imagination in the Medieval West from the Fourth Century to the Eleventh', in *The Medieval World*, ed. by Linehan and Nelson, pp. 189–213. On danger in ritual, see especially Buc, *The Dangers of Ritual: Between Early Medieval Texts and Social Scientific Theory* (Princeton: Princeton University Press, 2001). See also Gordon Kipling, *Enter the King: Theatre, Liturgy and Ritual in the Medieval Civic Triumph* (Oxford: Clarendon, 1998), and Reuter, 'Political Assemblies in Western Europe'.
134   On 'distentio' in Augustine's *Confessions*, see Paul Ricoeur, *Temps et récit*, L'Ordre Philosophique, 3 vols (Paris: Seuil, 1983–1985), I, pp. 19–53.
135   Theodore Evergates, 'Louis VII and the Counts of Champagne', in *The Second Crusade and the Cistercians*, ed. by Michael Gervers (New York: St Martins, 1992), pp. 109–17. See also Putter, 'Knights and Clerics', pp. 244–5.
136   See Reto Bezzola, *Le Sens de l'aventure et de l'amour: Chrétien de Troyes* (Paris: La Jeune Parque, 1947); Jean Frappier, *Chrétien de Troyes*, Connaissance des Lettres, rev. edn (Paris: Hatier, 1968); Zara P. Zaddy, *Chrétien Studies: Problems of Form and Meaning in 'Erec', 'Yvain', 'Cligès' and the 'Charrete'* (Glasgow: Glasgow University Press, 1973); Leslie T. Topsfield, *Chrétien de Troyes: A Study of the Arthurian Romances* (Cambridge: Cambridge University Press, 1981); Peter S. Noble, *Love and Marriage in Chrétien de Troyes* (Cardiff: University of Wales Press, 1982) and Glyn S. Burgess, *Chrétien de Troyes: 'Erec et Enide'*, Critical Guides to French Texts (London: Grant and Cutler, 1984).
137   See Duggan, *The Romances of Chrétien de Troyes* as well as Maddox, *The Arthurian Romances of Chrétien de Troyes* and *Structure and Sacring*.
138   On the structure of *Erec et Enide*, see among others, Gaston Paris (review of *Erec und Enide* (ed. Foerster), *Romania*, 20 (1891), 148–66, pp. 158–9), who, somewhat perversely regards the work as tripartite (1) 'Premerains vers' 2) Crisis and quest 3) Joy of the Court) with the coronation as a fourth part or coda. For further variations on the triptych theme, see W. A. Nitze ('Erec and the Joy of the Court', *Speculum*, 29:4 (1954), 691–701 at p. 692) and Jean Frappier (*Chrétien de Troyes*, p. 90), albeit with differences as to exactly how the poem divides. As Zara Zaddy points out in her summary of previous critical accounts (pp. 60–71), E. Hoepffner (' "Matière et sens" dans le roman d'*Erec et Enide*', *Archivum Romanicum*, 18 (1934), 433–50) divides the romance into *three* structurally (1) Winning of Enide 2) Crisis and quest 3) Joy), but *two* thematically (1) Winning 2) Crisis, reconciliation and coronation), a division echoed by Bezzola (Bezzola, p. 81). On structure, see also Douglas Kelly 'La Forme et le sens de la quête dans l'*Erec et Enide* de Chrétien de Troyes', *Romania*, 92 (1971), 326–58; Wolfgang Brand, *Chrétien de Troyes: zur*

Dichtungstechnik seiner Romane, Freiburger Schriften zur romanischen Philologie, 19 (Munich: Fink, 1972); R. G. Cook, 'The Structure of Romance in Chrétien's *Erec and Yvain*', *Modern Philology*, 71 (1973), 128–43; Volker Roloff, ' "Parole" und "teisir" in Chrétien de Troyes *Erec et Enide*', in *Reden und Schweigen: zur Tradition und Gestaltung eines mittelalterlichen Themas in der franzözischen Literatur*, ed. by Volker Roloff, Münchener Romanistische Arbeiten, 34 (Munich: Fink, 1973), pp. 117–38; Pierre Gallais, 'L'Hexagone logique et le roman médiéval', *Cahiers de Civilisation Médiévale*, 18 (1975), 1–14 and 113–48 and 'Hexagonal and Spiral Structure in Medieval Narrative', *Yale French Studies*, 51 (1974) 115–32, which formed the basis for his later *Dialectique du récit médiéval: Chrétien de Troyes et l'hexagone logique*, Faux Titre, 9 (Amsterdam: Rodopi 1982) (on *Erec et Enide* see notably pp. 83–175); Donald Maddox, 'The Structure of Content in Chrétien's *Erec et Enide*', in *Mélanges de philologie et de littératures romanes offerts à Jeanne Wathelet-Willem*, ed. by Jacques de Caluwé, (Liège: Cahiers de l'A. R. U., 1978), pp. 381–94; and his *Structure and Sacring: The Systematic Kingdom in Chretien's 'Erec et Enide'* (Lexington KY: French Forum 1978); François Suard, 'La Réconciliation d'Erec et d'Enide: de la parole destructrice à la parole libératrice (*Erec*, 4879–4893)', in *'Bien dire et bien aprandre': Bulletin du Centre d'Etudes Médiévales et Dialectales de l'Université de Lille III*, Bien Dire et Bien Aprandre, 1 (Lille: Centre de Gestion de L'Edition Scientifique, 1978), pp. 86–105; Marla W. M. Iyasere, 'The Tripartite Structure of Chrétien's *Erec et Enide*', *Mediaevalia*, 6 (1980), 105–21; Allard, pp. 13–37; Roger Middleton, 'Structure and Chronology in *Erec et Enide*', *Nottingham French Studies*, 30:2 (1991), 43–80 as well as Brigitte Burrichter, 'Ici fenist li premiers vers' (*Erec et Enide*), Noch einmal zur Zweiteilung des Chrétienschen Artusromans', in *Erzählstrukturen der Artusliteratur: Forschungsgeschichte und neue Ansätze*, ed. by Friedrich Wolfzettel and Peter Ihring (Tübingen: Niemeyer, 1999), pp. 87–98.

139 Warren Hedges, 'Queer Theory Explained', (at www.sou.edu/English – for full reference see bibliography below), my emphasis. See also Simon Gaunt, 'Straight Minds / Queer Wishes in Old French Hagiography: *La Vie de Sainte Euphrosine*', in *Premodern Sexualities*, ed. by Louise Fradenburg and Carla Freccero (New York and London: Routledge, 1996), pp. 155–73.

140 On John Cleland, see Glenn Burger and Steven F. Kruger, 'Introduction', in *Queering the Middle Ages*, ed. by Burger and Kruger, Medieval Cultures, 27 (Minneapolis and London: University of Minnesota Press, 2001), pp. xi–xxiii, at pp. xi–xiv. For the purposes of my discussion here see also Susan Schibanoff, 'Sodomy's Mark: Alan of Lille, Jean de Meun and the Mediveal Theory of Authorship', in *Queering the Middle Ages*, pp. 28–56.

141 Cohen, *Medieval Identity Machines*, pp. 88–91.

Now I have finished my work, which nothing ever can destroy –
Not Jupiter's wrath, nor sword, nor devouring time.
The day which has no power except over this body of mine
May come when it will and end the uncertain span of my life,
[*cum volet*, illa dies, quae nil nisi corporis huius
ius habet, incerti spatium mihi finiat aevi:]
But the finer part of myself shall sweep me into eternity,
Higher than all the stars. My name shall never be forgotten.
Wherever the might of Rome extends in the lands she has conquered,
The people shall read and recite my words. Throughout all ages,
If poets have vision to prophesy truth, I shall live in my fame.
    (Ovid, *Metamorphoses*, book 15, ll. 971–9, my emphasis)

'O how sacred and immense the task of bards! You snatch everything
From death and to mortals you give immortality.
Caesar, do not be touched by envy of their sacred fame;
Since, if for Latian Muses it is right to promise anything,
As long as honours of the Smyrnaean bard endure,
The future ages will read me and you; our Pharsalia
[Venturi me teque legent; Pharsalia nostra]
Shall live and we shall be condemned to darkness by no era.'
    (Lucan, *Civil War*, book 9, ll. 980–6)

To point to elements of staging and of ritualised or symbolised collective behaviour is not necessarily to deny the existence of more *ad hoc* and less structured elements, and hence ways of 'reading' these gatherings which legitmately treat the layer of staging and symbolic action as transparent and go through it and beyond it. Anyone familiar with meetings of an analoguous kind in our own culture (for example, meetings of political parties at all levels, parliaments and councils, boards of firms or universities or hospital trusts) will know that these too are staged occasions with their own rituals and expectations, but will also know that that does not preclude either the unpredictable, or the open and often quite unstructured debate, or even conflict. Yet our culture expects and allows for these: we accept the existence of staging and ritual in our gatherings when it is pointed out to us, but we perceive them primarily as places of functional interaction. Participants in assembles in the period we are dealing with here probably saw the staging and ritual as primary, and were more troubled than we might be when consensus and unanimity failed to materialise. (Reuter, 'Assembly Politics in Western Europe', p. 202)

Chapter One
Before or After the King?
The Hunt as Court (Re-)Composition

It is no coincidence that a recent – and purportedly 'authentic' – film version of the Arthurian legend, *King Arthur*, relocates the story from the typical Hollywood backdrop of central or later medieval castles, armour, pageantry and cod forsoothing to a world more recognisably late (or post-) Roman in character.[1] In this vision, Arthur's appropriation of the 'engineered' quality of Roman strategic innovation on the battlefield appears in a context of not merely political and military 'bricolage' but also ethnic and social *métissage*, themes that go hand-in-hand with visual echoes of *Spartacus's* narrative of slave-revolt seasoned with the post-feminist, post-punk chic of Guinevere's leather armour. What we have here is an Arthurianised vision of post-*pax Americana*, multicultural, post-class Britain whose anxious revisiting of the question 'What have the Romans done for us?' blends into contemporary anxieties about the future shape of society in the fading of old certainties. Crucially, its narrative ends with the death of a Lancelot who never entered into any liaison with Guinevere, and thus with an implicit question: in the absence of the seeming certainties of the legend as generally known, what does (did) the future hold, what should (or did) Arthur do next? How did he organise the band of followers around him or attempt to govern the country?

This question of Arthur's agency, its debts and belatedness at a cultural level, is central not merely to modern but also medieval visions of the King's place in history. Accordingly, in this chapter, I argue Chrétien's presentation of Arthur offers a reflection on the fundamentally transgressive nature of any assertion of cultural or historical subject status. Can a community's will to legitimate its cultural 'acts' overcome the anxieties of influence attending on them or be reconciled with with inhibitory logic of castration subsumed in phrases such as Norbert Elias's problematic 'civilising process' – a theme that will underpin the rest of the book.[2] If that process is something that happens to 'barbarians' (not to mention peasants or pagans), one of the common corollaries is that those subjected to it are incapable of offering a critical or reflective account of that experience: any such awareness would appear either as an anachronism or be dismissed as some sort of fumbled misunderstanding. The problem here is that in order to shake off the 'barbarian' tag, the Northern kingdoms found themselves caught in something of a cleft stick. To be 'civilised' was to be Romanised, caught in an impasse similar to the historiographical and ethnographical traditions that had looked to them as a model of energy to set against Rome's corruption and decadence – chief examples here being texts such as Tacitus's *Germania* or Caesar's accounts of his campaigns in Gaul and Britain. But then, of course, to refuse Romanisation was to remain barbaric.

Medieval attempts to elaborate a history 'after Rome' risked placing Northern Europe in a subaltern bind that would leave any claims to be a/the 'Subject of history' undermined by permanent self-doubt. I would therefore suggest that one way of reading the evolving Arthurian tradition is as part of a deconstructive project to transcend Rome's opposition between exemplars of rationality and self-mastery (such as Cicero) and figures of irrationality (such as Caesar) by drawing on those aspects of Roman historiography that highlighted Rome's disavowed instability and irrationality and refusing to take at face value either assertions of Republican *virtus* or the foundational narratives associated with the reign of Augustus.[3] In that regard, Chrétien's response is one of ironic reflection: his retrospective construction of the Arthurian court as a self-aware vernacular past legitimises the transcendent cultural positioning of a central medieval subjectivity. In so doing, he thereby completes a process of renegotiation associated with medieval receptions of the *Aeneid* – such as Geoffrey of Monmouth's *History of the Kings of Britain* or Wace's *Roman de Brut* – in which the conquest and colonisation of Britain moved from being an exoticist narrative of the wild frontier to one in which it offered the foundation of the post-Roman Self.

Triumph of the [Subaltern] Will: Chrétien's Prologue

> Think! Caesar lives in the mighty praises of Lucan, Aeneas in those of Maro, largely by their own merits, and yet not least by the alertness of the poets [vigilancia poetarum]. For us the troupe of buffoons [scola mimorum] keeps alive the divine fame of the Charlemagnes and Pepins in popular ballads [vulgaribus ritmis], but of our modern Caesars, no one tells: yet their characters, with their fortitude and temperance and admiration of all, lie ready to the pen. (Map, *The Courtier's Trifles*, dist. 5, chapter 1, p. 406 in edition)

As various commentators have noted, Chrétien's opening gambit, 'Li vilain dit en son respit' (l. 1), disturbs proprieties and exclusions foundational to a rhetoric of *courtoisie*.[4] The 'bloody peasant' famously berated by an exasperated Arthur in *Monty Python and the Holy Grail* is there from the outset, the first of many unwelcome intrusions that determine the character of the narrative. As Claudia Seebass-Linggi points out, such a prominent mention of the 'vilain' can be read as a taunting allusion to the prologue to the *Roman de Thèbes* ('Ne parlerai de peletiers, /Ne de vilains ne de bouchiers [...]', ll. 17–18).[5] Chrétien's stripping back of the list to its principal player highlights what the earlier work's heavy-handed rhetoric betrays. Enumerating at such length the very characters excluded might seem not merely a waste of time, but also either crassly self-asserting or insecure: what does it imply about the literary ambitions of a medieval literary culture if all it can list of its own in a prologue is a range of ignoble professions? Moreover, it leaves medieval courtly and aristocratic cultures in unreflective thrall to the values of a pagan age. Although Seebass-Linggi sees these excluded figures as being given first place, another way of reading Chrétien's opening lines is to see in them the assertion that error lies not in the earlier work's actual mentioning of 'the v***** word', but rather in its clumsily unimaginative and self-sabotaging harping on it.[6] But then peasants are not necessarily to be located solely outside the court: concern with *vilains*, both as subject matter and potential audience members, is clearly signalled in productions such as William IX's 'Companho, farai un vers covinen', the poet deeming anyone incapable of understanding his work a base peasant ('tenhatz lo per vilain, qui no l'enten', l. 4). Moving on from William's poem, Chrétien's opening appears as a deliberate indiscretion, in keeping with what R. Howard Bloch identifies as a general thematicisation of speech in vernacular romance as inherently transgressive.[7]

This sense of social clash is strengthened and dramatised in other aspects of the presentation of Chrétien's text in fonds fr. 1376. As Sandra Hindman points out, the three illuminations in the version of *Erec et Enide* contained in B. N. fonds fr. 24403 – a collection in which it appears between two chansons de geste, *Garin de Monglane* and *Ogier le Danois* – highlight the work's epic dimension, focusing on the combat scenes in the forest.[8] By contrast, fonds fr. 1376's (admittedly minimal) programme of one image arguably emphasises the centrality of court ritual and ceremony to the life of medieval romance: a blue historiated initial on folio 95 at l. 1 – thus, the L of 'Li vilains...' – shows a crowned figure, presumably Arthur, hunting a white stag.[9] This image raises many questions about the ordering and organisation of ceremony as a reflection and performative enactment of both history and social hierarchy. Who *came* first, who *goes* first and what do precedence and priority signify? How open is ritual to play and disturbance? Is the success of it to be gauged by how well the spectacle seems to proceed or what is concluded off-stage in the vast textual penumbra away from that central focus? Indeed, literary discourse's mimicking of ceremonial order can seem to create considerable problems of etiquette: in *Erec et Enide* not only does Chrétien precedes the King, the first word out of his mouth is 'the peasant'. Moreover, at this microsequential point in the text in fonds fr. 1376, Arthur and the peasant are collapsed *together*, the King reduced to acting as a visual prologue to his ostensible inferior.

However, as Hindman comments, we are perhaps given little time to reflect on such *faux pas*: 'even the formal composition of the miniature launches the action of the story in the forest, in part through the momentum of the riders, the stag and the dog'.[10] Although dealing with the same subject, the two illuminations show some slight but possibly telling differences, the scene in fonds fr. 24403 having a less cramped, more open composition: Arthur has a horn to his lips and the hounds are stretched in full chase. In comparison, fonds fr. 1376's figures are more constrained and upright, Arthur's gesture, his finger raised, clearly echoes the scenes of debate and counsel depicted in the illuminations accompanying *Florimont* (fol. 1; fol. 64v).[11] In that sense, if we are to glean anything much from the limited programme in fonds fr. 1376, then what emerges is that unlike the dynamic 'epic' cast of fonds fr. 24403, what we have in Arthur's formal, reflective gesture is a collapsing together of scenes of hunt and counsel: this is a vision of the business of the forest as the continuation of the space of the palace, thus quite unlike fonds fr. 24403's vision of it as 'a locus of spontaneous, haphazard adventure'.[12] In fonds fr. 1376, Arthur seems to be not so much hunting the stag, embodiment of the wild and witchy forces of destiny and the Celtic-inspired *merveilleux*, as trying to organise a meeting with it.

What the opening to the prologue demonstrates is that history is a difficult thing, that the fact that any given sequence can be construed in multiple ways means nothing begins without some problem or impropriety. Thus, Chrétien's show of assurance in slimming down the *Roman de Thèbes's* list of people who should not be allowed to mix with the in-crowd of the great, the good and the beautiful who actually belong in romance – an encounter dramatised in fonds fr. 1376's single illumination for the text of *Erec et Enide* – exemplifies an eagerness in early French literature to assert vernacular cultural identity as more than merely barbarous or belated, as not doomed to embarrassingly trip over its own ceremonial toes before anyone has even got into the palace. Not content with being a subaltern reflection of the ancient past, this age also dreams of its own immortality:

> Des or comencerai l'estoire
> Que toz jors mais iert en memoire
> Tant con durra crestïentez.
> De ce s'est Crestïens ventez. (ll. 23–6)

> And here I begin the story that will be in memory for evermore, as long as Christendom lasts – of this did Chrétien boast.

In lines eerily reminiscent of the boasts found in Ovid or in the speech Lucan attributes to the local guide conducting Caesar around the ruins of Troy (cited above), 'Chrétien' further justifies what Walt Whitman would have termed his "barbaric yawp" with the assertion that the tale he is about to tell has been corrupted and mangled by 'those who try to live by storytelling' (Carroll's translation of 'Cil qui de conter vivre vuelent', l. 22).[13] And yet the danger here is that Chrétien's intervention risks marking him as little more than an upstart successor to the author of the *Roman de Thèbes*, only innovating in that he replaces the cavalcade of tradesmen with a sideswipe at the ignorant butchering of tales perpetrated by (shudder!) mere *jongleurs*. However, as Michel Zink points out, where previous authors had insisted on the authority, authenticity and quality of their sources, Chrétien turns the mangling of his model to his advantage.[14] It is their aesthetic massacre that is redeemed in what Patricia Harris Stabelein neatly casts as Chrétien's virtuoso cannibalisation of sources vernacular and ancient.[15] However, there is arguably more to it than simple arrogance. To fully understand the force of Chrétien's assertion here, we need to look both back to the opening of his prologue and forward to some of the comments on royal authority made by Arthur at the conclusion of the hunt of the White Stag. Rather than the nouns, the choice of modal verb here is all: 'Cil qui de conter vivre *vuelent*' (l. 22, my emphasis) could perhaps be rendered more grandiloquently as 'those *whose will/ desire* it is to live by storytelling'.[16] How, indeed, does one 'live' by storytelling, especially when it seems that to enter into the world of vernacular composition is precisely *not* to 'live', indeed, to risk one's soul, as Denis Piramus, a figure associated with the court of Henry and Eleanor, laments in his *Vie de saint Edmund le rei*:

> Trop ai usee ma vie
> Et en peché e en folie.
> Kant court hanteie of les curteis,
> Si feseie les serventeis,
> Chanceunettes, rimes, saluz
> Entre les druz et les druz. [...]
> Ceo me fist fere l'enemi.[17]

> I have greatly used up my life in sin and folly. When I frequented the court with all those courtly folk, I composed *serventeis, chançonetes, saluts d'amour* and various other poems in the company of lovers. [...] The devil made me do it. (trans. Hult)

Denis's rueful self-positioning as 'recovering poet' is, as David Hult comments, more generally expressive of the situation of the vernacular author as an 'in-between character caught between the library and the court, the Church and lay society, between a Latin culture and the particularities of vernacular expression', uncertain about his authority, any will or intention subordinated to his patron and only distinguishable from it in coded assertion.[18] In that world where he is not quite sure whether what he did was a matter of his own rational volition, the devil is probably a good person to blame.

Chrétien's denigration of such base acts of will begs the question of whether there is any on his part. From what we will see later, so much of what Arthur has to say on the subject of royal authority revolves around the problematic relation between right and duty, will and desire.[19] It is in this regard the text affirms a long-standing connection between rhetorical method and political ideals and propaganda attested in the educational activities of the court of Charlemagne: '[Alcuin's] *Rhetoric* is made up of rhetorical doctrine, not because Alcuin wanted to write a rhetorical treatise, but because he wished to describe the *mores* of Charlemagne as those that ought to serve as examples to his subjects'.[20] For good or ill, all assertions of claim or status, royal or authorial, are ultimately founded in some kind of *voluntas propria*, some singular or exceptional will. Consequently, the application of the verb *voloir* to those Chrétien here supplants paints them as literary tyrants and usurpers, coveting literary pre-eminence for the base goal of mere survival in the here-and-now. And yet, another understanding may be that there is no power, great or small, that does not depend on volition or desire. Rather than some blanket censure of anything resembling hubris, the criteria for judgement he seems to imply are the ambition demonstrated and the effective deployment of means. One echo of Ovid's boast from the epilogue to the *Metamorphoses* (a passage following directly on from the apotheosis of Julius Caesar discussed in the below), is precisely this contestation with oblivion and decay: 'the day [...] may come *when it will* [cum volet]'. Why should time have an uncontested monopoly on volition or agency?

Of course, if we set Chrétien's prologue alongside Lucan's boast about the power of bards, the chord darkens: with no less a backdrop than the ruins of ancient Troy, Caesar's guide's speech stands in bitterly ironic counterpoint to the picture painted of the emperor's deeds – central among which his role in the civil war – as the great abomination of Roman history. To speak of the great afterlife of 'our Pharsalia' is to speak of Caesar's desecratory trampling of the ground of Rome's Trojan ancestors. The will to appropriate history is always at least in part an ugly, *vilain* thing. Yet Chrétien's gesture stands further along a chain of modulations in historical necessity – the force Lucan's prologue sees as generative of the cruellest of paradoxes and begging the great question ('if the Fates could find no other way /[...] then we have no complaint.', *Civil War*, book 1, ll. 33–7) – now seen from a perspective where its sense, although certainly not apparent to unreflective observation, is nonetheless clearer. In that sense we are presented with a move akin to the presumed procession through the space adorned by Holbein's *The Ambassadors*: Lucan in effect occupies the space directly before the picture, caught in baffled and horrified contemplation of the skull's monstrous stain. His is the poetry of a world robbed of sense by the events he observes. Chrétien's position is more akin to the viewer who has moved to the left of the picture. He sees the skull. But then the resonances of his work imply an awareness of the shift of perspective that brought him to that place. Where Lucan casts Rome's history as a very sick joke, Chrétien sees the post-Troy narrative of *translatio imperii* and *studii* as offering a less live, but still present, sense of trauma that can fuel both historical understanding and – in its more domesticatable form – the odd clever pun. Although Eric Auerbach presents Chrétien as inaugurating an independent courtly aesthetic, we might see in Chrétien's distance from the grand view of history here a reflection of what Auerbach regards as an 'attenuation' of classical literature's sublime narrative of historical forces in the 'middle' or 'pleasing' style of medieval adaptations such as the *Roman d'Eneas*.[21] However, although we might regard Chrétien as independent from models such as Lucan, the latter's weighty vision of history here seems implicitly contrasted with Chrétien's breezier octosyllables.

Chrétien's interesting mix of humility and defiance is combined with an ostentatiously brassy assertion of the enduring nature of his contribution to the *matière de Bretagne*. But then, his very 'Christian name' both asserts an identity and yet at the same time melts into the texture of the historical continuum of Christendom, abnegating itself almost without trace. In that sense, here is an identity that does and does not seek to 'live' through storytelling; rather, the 'estoire' – an ambiguous term that could designate either Chrétien's version or the pre-existing structure that is his source – is what is will be remembered. Doubly then, in the assertions of name and life, Chrétien appears to boast only so that the force of that boast can be undercut by ludic self-abnegation. However, there is more to this position than ironic undercutting of a standard authorial fanfaronade. Instead, Chrétien's *auctoritas* positions itself as a spectral presence, his authorial voice the unearthly interpellation of an audience it always already addresses as its future. However, what is then concealed is the very idea that, by conflating the text's immediate reception with its survival through time, Chrétien presents his work as always already having survived, his past tense boast ('De ce *s'est* Crestïens *ventez*', l. 26, my emphasis) always already fulfilled. In making due concession to time Chrétien performs an exorcism analogous to his nuanced rehabilitation of authorial will.

In mentioning the things one should not mention, Chrétien's prologue offers a microcosmic reflection of the politics of trust and promise we will see enacted in the rest of the work. However, arguably, the effect of his self-presentation is simultaneously reassuring and not. In bolstering his position by acting out the most disingenuous manipulations in public, he assimilates himself to figures such as that most audacious of medieval rhetoricians, Renart the fox, a creature perfectly able to construct a trap even as its future victim, sceptical throughout, looks on. Such a play of mirrors seems unlikely to engender trust, unless the confidence earned is the audience's faith in the speaker's ability to play with appearances. Indeed, the self-conscious speciousness of the fireworks Chrétien deploys is central to the lesson: the fact that Arthur is either dead or a fiction seems to have little power to harm the appeal of his legend. If neither textual nor political authority is much more than a play of mirrors, there is presumably nothing the audience might feel it urgent to dispute. Indeed, the reassuring rehearsal of an apparent temporal divide that has already been bridged posits the satisfaction of that trust. If Chrétien boasts, then the other ghost that haunts his discourse is the belief that he can deliver, even if at this point there is no absolute basis for certainty given that the position he takes up only differs by dint of the paradoxical combination of its hubris and, his tactful dissimulation of his own personality and *voluntas*. In that sense, the boast is disarmingly self-undercutting: like his chief model, Arthur, all Chrétien can do is hold back the inevitable, his literary excellence potentially as fragile as the King's political power. Chrétien's boast is both 'before' and 'after' Arthur, the narrator preceding him in the organisation of the narrative and yet following him both as narrative of events past and as imitation of his example.

The prologue thus celebrates the capacity of narrative's *ordo artificialis* to confound and stay – if only for a moment – the inexorable linearity of time. No coincidence therefore that Chrétien accompanies mentions of speech with key temporal markers: we might compare his 'From this point [= 'Des or...'] I will begin the tale that will live in memory ever more', Chrétien's utterance seeming to leap from some sort of inchoate or virtual state directly into the future, dwelling not at all in the present. Of course, this is all very well, but it does create a problem in terms of the actual practicalities of court business: for example, how do you *contredire* – that is 'speak against', 'contradict' or 'raise objections against' – a pronouncement if you may not do so *once the king has spoken it*? In that sense, this is what marks out the kinship and the difference between *Erec et Enide* on the one hand and the text that precedes it in fonds fr. 1376, *Florimont*. Its hero is the grandfather of Philip of Macedonia, the latter father of Alexander the Great, a figure to whom both Erec and Arthur are prominently compared in Chrétien's text (for Erec, see ll. 2265–6; for Arthur, ll. 6669–77). In documenting a past at several generations remove from a key phase in an already remote Antiquity, Aimon de Varennes opens a similar terrain to Chrétien's, albeit one whose possibilities for cultural shock are diminished by the historical and genealogical 'distances' involved: in keeping to a territory remote from *li vilains* of medieval modernity, these figures simply do not monopolise history in the way both Chrétien and his model claim to do. And yet, as Alison Adams argues, Aimon de Varennes's use of motifs from the *Roman d'Eneas*, such as the tension between Fortune and Destiny, sow a fair degree of romance-style trouble in the antique history of Alexander's ancestor.[22] Thus, after Sandra Hindman's reading of the presentation of *Erec et Enide* in fonds fr. 24403 as 'epic', a possible common thread linking the two texts in fonds fr. 1376 would then be to see them as forming a diptychal reflection on the *Roman d'Eneas's* vision of history, encompassing both the ancient and Arthurian worlds and interrogating the earlier text's account of historical forces.

The Hunt:
Interruption and Intrusion as Ritual Revitalisation

> And with what does not belong to you or to your subjects you can be a more liberal giver, as were Cyrus, Caesar and Alexander; for spending the wealth of others does not lessen your reputation but adds to it; only the spending of your own is what harms you. And there is nothing that uses itself up faster than generosity, for as you employ it, you lose the means of employing it, and you become either poor and despised or else, in order to escape poverty, you become rapacious and hated. (Machiavelli, *The Prince*, pp. 54–5)

> All events are not equal. Some seem almost charismatic in their ability to absorb the opposing charges of competing ambitions and then spin them off again, organised and hence powerful.[23]

The scandalous collapse of social and historical distance and difference in the 'opening credits' continues with the entry into the narrative matter itself. If Chrétien's prologue imitates Arthur's general model, Arthur's opening gesture echoes Chrétien, taking the latter's defiance of the rationalities of linear temporality as a pretext for play with other economies:

Un jor de Pasque, au tens novel,
A Caradigant son chastel
Ot li rois Artus cort tenue.
Onc si riche ne fu veüe,
Car mout i ot boens chevaliers,
Hardiz et corageus et fiers,
Et riches dames et puceles,
Filles de rois, gentes et beles.
Mais ançois que la corz fausist,
Li rois a ses chevaliers dist
Qu'il voloit le blanc cerf chacier
Por la costume ressaucier.
Mon seignor Gauvain ne plot mie
Quant il ot la parole oïe:
'Sire', fait il, 'de ceste chace
N'avroiz vos ja ne gré ne grace.
Nos savommes bien tuit pieç'a
Quel costume li blans cers a.
Qui le blanc cerf ocirre puet,
Par raison baisier li estuet
Des puceles de vostre cort
La plus bele, a que que il tort.
Maus en porroit avenir granz:
Encor a il ceanz .vc.
Damoiseles de hauz parages,
Filles de rois, gentes et sages,
Et n'i a nule n'ait ami
Chevalier vaillant et hardi,
Que chascuns desranier voudroit,
Ou fust a tort ou fust a droit,
Que cele qui lui atalante
Est la plus bele et la plus gente.' (ll. 27–58)

One Easter day, in springtime, King Arthur was holding court at Cardigan his castle. So splendid a one was never seen, for there were many good knights, brave and bold and fierce, and rich ladies and maidens, noble and beautiful daughters of kings. But before the court disbanded, the King told his knights that he wanted to hunt the White Stag in order to revive the tradition. These words did not bode well. When my lord Gauvain heard about it, he was strongly displeased. 'My lord', he said, 'Your knights are in great uproar. They are all talking about this kiss. They all say it will never be granted without there being arguments and fighting.' My lord Gauvain was not a bit pleased when he heard this. 'Sire,' said he, 'from this hunt you will gain neither gratitude nor thanks.

> We have all known for a long time what tradition is attached to the White Stag: he who can kill the White Stag by rights must kiss the most beautiful of the maidens of your court, whatever may happen. Great evil can come from this, for there are easily five hundred damsels of high lineage here, noble and wise daughters of kings; and there is not the one who is not the favourite of some valiant and bold knight, each of whom would want to contend, rightly or wrongly, that the one who pleases him is the most beautiful and the most noble.'

Is there any good way to end a wonderful party? It all depends on the relation of the host to the guests. Moreover, in the case of a court, the question is how to make the gift-giving fundamental to the social interaction in that milieu both meaningful and sustainable.[24] How do you pick up the bill discreetly enough to avoid crass ostentation but without allowing those present to ignore the generosity with which they have been favoured? How can you leave them wanting more, but in the right way: eagerly agog rather than deadeningly parasitic? Perhaps there is no 'real-world' solution: Machiavelli's comments on generosity offer a bleak outlook in which no gifting to the world can be sustained in the face of its ingratitude, although from a slightly earlier Christian perspective, this smacks of the apathy of despair faced with the futility of earthly striving. His words reflect the inevitable self-depletion of the culture of charisma, the entropic burn-out of the royal sun. It is this sense of exhaustion that to some extent accounts for Machiavelli's vision of political life, predicated on the exercise of spectacle and brutality in what becomes a sort of anti-economy or anti-theatre of state.

There is apparently a world of difference between Machiavelli's vision of court life and the first glittering image of the royal court at the opening of *Erec et Enide*. The splendour of the Arthurian court is reflected both here and in the many descriptions of lavish spectacle and generosity that follow later: the wedding feast, the tournament at Danebroc and Erec's eventual coronation. However, although seemingly a celebration of peace and order, it is also a memory of violence: the economy depends on conquest, such that fruitful peace only exists because of Arthur's success in war. It is this spectre of violence and instability that then returns in Arthur's decision to revive the hunt of the White Stag, reminding the court that the shows of largesse so central to *Erec et Enide* are bankrolled through conquests that have already taken place off-stage. All questions regarding the past or future acquisitions underpinning such spectacle are for now silenced or held in abeyance – except insofar as the King chooses to flirt with them, or as Burgess puts it, to 'channel' those pent-up energies.[25]

Of course, wealth and exchange are also marks of the buoyancy of the psychic economy of chivalry: not just material riches, but arguably more importantly the *Glanz*, the glamour and presence that sustain court society, here underscored in the emphasis on the beauty and high status of the female courtiers. That passions run high at this point is evidence of the energising closeness of contact between King and court, an affective bond standing in sharp contrast to the remoteness of Machiavelli's Prince. If Arthur's courtiers hang on his every word, constantly looking to him to set the tone of the proceedings, it is obviously significant that this first intervention appears such a clangingly monumental blunder, compounded by his brusque squashing of Gauvain's suggestion that he reconsider. Such an error flies in the face of key strands of classical wisdom on the subject of crowd-management. In a notable simile from book 1 of the *Aeneid*, Virgil describes Neptune's return to calm from rage as the effect of the orator on the rabble: 'he rules their minds with speech and soothes their souls' ('ille regit dictis animos et pectora mulcet', book 1, l. 153). For Virgil, Plato and Cicero, the ideal leader, such as Aeneas, pours oil on the waters, and, through the use of good speaking (*bene dicere*) reasserts the primacy of reason over the emotions so as to bring order to the polis.[26] Arthur, by contrast, thoughtlessly seems to sow disorder in a work whose prologue praised precisely those ideals of good speaking ('bien dire', l. 12), stirring up cupidity among his knights in the manner of Juno's seduction of Aeolus (*Aeneid*, book 1, ll. 65–75), a scene Virgil presents as emblematic of the abuse of rhetorical skill.[27] If this is the leader who in the *History of the Kings of Britain* famously opposed himself to the rule of Rome, then here he seems the very antithesis of those values of civic order, the negative image of Geoffrey's fount of Ciceronian virtue.

Gauvain's choice of terms is of capital importance here: to insist that the King will earn no thanks raises precisely the problem described by Machiavelli. Courtly largesse only really has one possible outcome, a collapse stemming from the fundamental *ingratitude* of people always wanting more. In short, no one will thank Arthur for this, but then what good are thanks anyway when it comes to filling the royal coffers? Moreover, the circulation of gifts is not an entirely closed circuit in that wealth does not return either in its entirety or at the same rate. If to thank someone is to honour them with the token of a will to reciprocate, then there are problems: such a gift exchange may not be reciprocable there and then (as in those cases where the return is military support) or should not be immediately reciprocated. After all, were a gift met immediately with an identical counter-gift, any resultant relation between the two parties would be annulled.[28] Thanks and good-will thus oil the wheels, addressing the deferral necessary to such exchanges while promising a future return. However, this necessary suspension in the gifting process implies a bankrolling that begs the question of how the tendency towards draining unilateralism can be sustained in a world where the King lavishes material goods in exchange for the service that is the means to acquire more wealth. Indeed, the fact that we seem to be presented with two sorts of sublimity complicates rather than solves the problem. The descriptions of the intricate working and expensive or exotic materials associated with the artefacts exchanged hints moreover at an intense cultural 'cooking process', that is to say, the massive addition of value through specialised labour. However, the violence appears doubly sublimated not only in the sense that its knightly practitioners are highly skilled and use equally high-status artefacts to fulfil their purpose but also in that their labour in the form of 'value-added' violence – more effective, brutal and, hopefully, discriminating than the 'raw' variety – is effectively banked for the future.

Although Arthur contemplates the court and they him, that relation is not symmetrical or 'feudal' in its libidinal exchange. In that regard, Chrétien presents gap and doubt – the space of desire – as just as necessary to the political relations he represents as to private, erotic ones. Such an imbalance is perhaps more explicitly framed in *Cligés* and in Chrétien's lyric poetry, which – as I will show in the next chapter – suggest that, while figurations of love's amorous fusion with the beloved can be found in imagery such as the symbiotic relation of hazel and honeysuckle in various Tristan narratives, desire is never straightforwardly 'mutual' or 'reciprocal'. Although two individuals may yearn for one another with what seems like a similar degree of passionate intensity, neither party actually has direct experience of the other's feelings: as Lacan puts it 'you never look at me from where I see you' ('Jamais tu ne me regardes là d'où je te vois').[29] The object of desire is necessarily not in the position to return the Subject's regard at that point.

It is of course not impossible to narrate mutual regard and appreciation, but the moment can quite easily fall into or lend itself to comedy, as can be seen in the opening of *Aucassin et Nicolette* with the (possibly intentionally twee) mirroring of the two young, blond, beringleted darlings. The experience of beauty and largesse is therefore inscribed into a model that begs the question of how and whether that experience of Arthurian largesse and regard can and will be returned. At this point, if all redress is predicated on the ultimate of courtly spectacles – namely, war – then some alternative to simply breaking the spell of the moment needs to be found. However, Arthur has to balance the potential economic benefits of both peace and war while avoiding the potential disadvantages of both states. It can be argued that his solution is neatly Machiavellian, Arthur's gesture effectively breaking with the draining aspect of the economic cycle. Gifting in its banal, craven guise as placatory bestowal of honour and wealth is replaced with an energised, edgy dance with danger and difference.

Arthur's intervention thus disrupts two fixing, specular relations – subject to king and lover to lady – his intervention troubling both the collective and singular attachments of his courtiers. Thus, even as the King ostensibly desires to escape from his position at the focus of various looks, he paradoxically forces his way back into the picture of the court, caught and stretched between its capacity to sustain and to disrupt itself. What appears as the central problem is the concurrence of several economies operating both *at the same time* and *out of time*: speaking, giving and desiring all play with temporality, depending on future echo or return, Chrétien already suggesting particular directions for subsequent exploration and amplification. And yet, at the same time, Arthur's reply to Gauvain highlights precisely this question of how courtiers should be 'after the king' in a negative:

> Li rois respont: 'Ce sai je bien,
> Mais por ce n'en lairai je rien
> Car ne doit estre contredite
> Parole puis que rois l'a dite.' (ll. 59–62)
>
> The King replied: 'I'm well aware of that, but I'm not backing down one jot. Once a king has spoken, no one's allowed to argue.'

In their transgressive dimension, all true *paroles*, all speech *acts*, admit of response, and yet, at the same time appear as troubling singularities cutting across the fixing ceremonial organisation of the court. As Philippe Walter puts it, *H*istory in the making cannot simply appear as the routine of the social calendar. Accordingly, Arthur's words emphasise the absolute and totalitarian nature of his demand: although perfectly aware of rational objections and possible dangers, he will not give up *on any aspect* of his intention ('n'*en* lairai je *rien*' l. 60, my emphasis). The fact his words *make no sense* (i.e. that any future intelligibility or 'sens' appears unimaginable) is precisely the point. As Miha Pintarič puts it of Gauvain's response: 'ce sage chevaleresque pense en moderne: il n'a aucune chance de réussir'.[30] Part of the temporal positioning of Arthur's utterance is the intrusion into modernity of an absolutist, unaccommodating insistence, a violent denial of other models of history and historicity.[31] Moreover, the libidinal basis of his words is apparent, its assertion of desire a reaffirmation of 'la virilité monarchique', as Gérard Chandès puts it.[32] The ordering of elements and temporal structure – not rendered in Carroll's translation – also seems central to the emphatic effect: 'there should be no arguing with a pronouncement once it has been made by a king'. Thus the first part of the statement – 'ne doit estre contredite /parole' – is clearly debatable, with the clause 'puis que rois l'a dite' providing crucial qualification, as well as a syntactic reflection of the proper order of business. There are two possible readings, more or less illiberal. According to the first, which would make Arthur sound rather like a despot, a courtier should never argue with anything a king says. This seems to be supported by the apparent dismissiveness of his response. According to the second, which offers a quick glimpse into Arthurian protocol, you can have *parole* and *contredit* (thus proposals and then the objections or debates they give rise to) but, *once the king has spoken*, the proverbial fat lady has sung. After that, the customary thing is to be corporate and toe the line. Arthur's implication is obvious enough: the time to speak up against a given *parole*, he implies, is *before* the king has pronounced on it. Gauvain's objection is not therefore wrong in itself, but rather out of place in terms of the order of business. In that sense, he finds himself caught in the problematic relation of the court to time as explored in the opening of Walter Map's *The Courtier's Trifles*, a ludic reworking of Augustine's well-known comments on the nature of time from the *Confessions*: 'In time I exist and of time I speak. [...] What is time, I know not'.[33] Of course, Walter also goes on to liken the court to Hell, only 'aggravated'... Long before Hamlet observed that 'the time is out of joint' (*Hamlet*, act 1, scene 5), the court appears as a place of temporal warps, folds and lurches.[34]

Of course, the tension inherent in the scenario Chrétien presents us with centres on the question of how anyone can speak *before* a king pronounces when his utterances seem to be the spontaneous and unpredictable products of private whim rather than of careful thought and consultation. Like a sudden flash of beauty, this political 'process' was over before anyone had a chance to participate. The other question is to do with what Arthur implies about what happens *after* the royal pronouncement. If you cannot *contredire* a royal pronouncement after the event, are there other ways of 'countering' it? Indeed the text seems to place great pressure on the room for manoeuvre in contestatory or questioning speech. Various other compounds of *–dire* come into play: the scene in which Enide is forced to reveal what she knows of the complaints regarding Erec's *recreantise* foregrounds the question of legal denial based on objection or alibi (*escondit*), while other encounters dramatise the notion of *redit* (an answer given under compulsion or stipulation). The idea that there is no unsaying what has been said, that all statements in effect 'burn their bridges', is apparent both here and in Erec's reponse to Enide's fateful words: 'Bien ai *la parole* entendue' (l. 2519, my emphasis). There seems to be little latitude.

However, paradoxically, room for manoeuvre is precisely the point: Arthur has been the absolute focus of the events of the plenary court, and now there needs to be a way of breaking the spell, of moving out from the court's static body to the dynamism of the chase, its headlong rush the very vision of the charismatic *career* (in various senses). Arthur's actions thus spring from the tension between charisma and the established order of custom (what Hegel would refer to as 'Sittlichkeit'), seeking to avoid a disabling collapse into the inertia Johan Huizinga was later to present as characteristic of its 'waning' or 'Autumn'.[35] Charismatic power thus derives from the almost excessive quickness of the body politic, the potential powder-keg explosiveness of a standing army constrained only insofar as its members are entertained and honoured. However, royal power is also paradoxically dependent on the patrimonial 'deadness' of the social order, its customs and structures, for stability and continuity. The contradiction is quite simply that the court has to be, to modify Chakrabarty, 'capable of living in [at least two ages] at once': one of order and one of disorder. In that respect, what Arthur seemingly seeks to do is to resurrect precisely the problem Gauvain hoped and thought they had successfully done away with, blaming his king for stirring it up once more through the cultivation of a violence founded in libido. By presenting the custom of the hunt as something Arthur effectively re-innovates, Chrétien offers a vision of how spectacle can have its cake and eat it. Arthur's desire to revive the hunt of the White Stag 'por la costume ressaucier' (l. 38) emerges just at the point when it seemed that the whole issue of violence was being successfully conjured by the niceties of court ceremonial. Arthur's gesture thus spicily problematises the very notion of *coustume*, here appearing less as the customary basis of law than as something more unreasoningly atavistic. Court culture then appears as authentically self-shattering rather than some mere mime, as an unconditional openness to adventure in all its undomesticatable danger, as Bezzola comments, thus an irrational, terroristic threat of disorder necessarily internal to the rule of law.[36]

It falls to Gauvain to speak up. No small moment as Chrétien's evocation of his reaction ('Quant mes sire Gauvains le sot /Ce sachiez, mie ne li plot.' ll. 299–300) gives a snapshot of the collective dismay that greets his anger in later works such as *La Mort le roi Artu*, where his Achilles-like approach to the palace following the death of Gaheriet clearly leaves the bystanders pale and quaking at the explosion of black fury to come (*La Mort le roi Artu*, § 100).[37] Looking back, we might well see in his blunt intervention here an echo of counsel scenes such as that found in the Oxford *Roland*. However, here Gauvain finds himself uncertainly positioned between potential assimilations either to Roland, defender of absolutism, or to Ganelon the pragmatist.[38] As Charles Foulon emphasises, the strength of his relation with Arthur is illustrated by his fearless intervention as spokesman here.[39] The very fact that Gauvain, the most senior male courtier in terms of rank and closest to Arthur in terms of family connection, is silenced after having expressed the strongest reservations about the proposed course of action indicates a useful demonstration of a royal prerogative that transcends the bonds of kin. What Arthur's response to Gauvain highlights are the theatrical and dialectical dimensions of a court culture attempting to reconcile conflicting opinions and interests in such a way as to satisfy internal debate while, at the same time, producing a show of authority supporting the will of the monarch. The message is dual in its address, fostering cohesion internally and radiating outwards in order to convince, compel and impress outsiders. In that respect, Gauvain can be seen as a convenient focus for the internal opposition which Arthur then overcomes as part of his assertion of sovereignty. In that sense, the King's behaviour appears as a radical and disturbing vision of what Pierre Bourdieu terms 'officialising strategy', the goal of which, as Paul Strohm puts it, is to 'transmute particular and private interests into disinterested, collective, publicly avowable interests'.[40] However, such a moment of transmutation can leave both roles and individuals at the door, as Strohm argues the regarding the public humiliation of the royal champion, John Dymmock, coronation of Richard II. When John appeared at the due moment in order to offer the Champion's time-honoured assertion of the King's rightful succession, he was apparently told to come back later. For Strohm, this snub marks the symbolic reduction of a significant player to a 'mere individual'.[41] As things stand at this point in the proceedings, Gauvain, treated rather dustily in his assertion of support for the King's position, seems to have fared much like his later counterpart. However, for Strohm the sense of the the slight to John is undecidable: Richard's gesture could be an accidental oversight, reflect a desire to rebuke the champion or constitute a potentially dangerous play with the order of ritual designed to dramatically emphasise the king's central place by publicly clearing a prominent second fiddle from the stage. Likewise, Gauvain's anxiety with regard to the potential consequences of Arthur's decision might be either genuine or a show. After all, Gauvain's intervention provides an ideal cue for Arthur to evoke the 'esfroi' – in effect through an unsettling play with the 'ritual time' allotted to his reign – that could endanger his authority. The court is thereby caught amazed as what first appeared self-sabotage on the part of the King now spreads out in a shockwave that shakes the courtiers into activity. First of all, it is clear that Gauvain's response does effectively emphasise the king's exceptional status. The hunt is clearly the sort of high-risk enterprise Elias describes as characteristic of charismatic leadership. Although reckless, the decision clearly does not test the love that is the social and legal bond between nephew and lord to destruction... For now.

Mangling Histories: Arthur, Caesar, Erec

'Vos meïsmes a la parsome
En serez morz et afolez.' (ll. 5604–05)

'Even you yourself, when it's over, will be dead and mangled.'

I *must* have a body, [...] And in the first place I must have a body because an obscure object lives inside me. [...] The mind is obscure, the depths of the mind are dark, and this dark nature is what explains and requires a body. We call 'primary matter' our passive power or the limitation of our activity. [...] And, in effect, if the monad Caesar clearly expresses the crossing of the Rubicon, is it not because the river maintains a relation of proximity with his body? [...] Each monad condenses a certain number of unique, incorporeal, ideal events that do not yet put bodies in play, although they can only be stated in the form, 'Caesar crosses the Rubicon, he is assassinated by Brutus...'. [...] These unique events included in the monad as primary predicates constitute its zone of clear expression. [...] It is because we have a clear zone that we must have a body charged with travelling through it or exploring it, from birth to death.[42]

Il faut être économe ou César.[43]

Arthur's 'wobbly moment' in Chrétien's first romance is part of a longer tradition of thought that the great king is never exactly 'balanced' – whether physically, politically or economically. Geoffrey of Monmouth's Arthur appears as a conqueror whose military career is at least potentially inconsistent with his pronouncements about right, his grand statement that 'nothing that is acquired by force and violence can ever be held legally by anyone', sitting, as Lewis Thorpe puts it, very uncomfortably with the narrative of conquest that precedes it. The cosmic foundation of this lack of balance is notably envisioned in the slightly later prose text, *La Mort le roi Artu*. In Arthur's famous dream, Fortuna shows the King the image of himself paused momentarily on top of her wheel, his place only a fleeting concession, a staying of the forces that will cast him down:[44]

> 'N'il i a granment chose dont tu n'aies esté sires jusques ci, et de toute la circuitude que tu voiz as tu esté li plus puissanz rois qui fust. Mais tel sont li orgueil terrien qu'il n'i a nul si haut assiz qu'il ne le conviegne cheoir de la poesté del monde.' Et lors le prenoit et le tresbuschoit a terre si felenessement que au cheoir estoit avis au roi Artu qu'il estoit touz debrisiez et qu'il perdoit tout le pooir del cors et des menbres. (*La Mort le roi Artu*, § 176)

> 'Of all the circle you can see you have been the most powerful king there ever was. But such is earthly pride that no one is seated so high that he can avoid having to fall from power in the world.' Then she took him and pushed him to the ground so roughly that King Arthur felt that he had broken all his bones in the fall and had lost the use of his body and limbs. (trans. by Cable)

The nature of Arthur's powerlessness here is of key symbolic importance: he is given to feel what it is to be a broken thing unable to act. Just as Boethius presents Philosophy clad in a tattered garment from which men have torn shreds and patches (*Consolation of Philosophy*, book 1, prose 1), so the King now appears as a bag of broken pieces into which future kings – such as Philippe – will dip, hoping to season their leadership styles with a workable charge of singular, energetic defiance. Insofar as his body is shattered, but his consciousness endures, Arthur here offers a more human image of the effect of time and other cosmic forces on bones than something like the skull anamorphosis in Holbein's *The Ambassadors*. In that image, the problem of historical perspective twists and distorts the *momento mori* into a nightmarish stain that forces the viewer through a reflection on human striving perhaps not so far removed from those lessons that might be learned from the mangling experienced by the *dépecié* Arthur in a moment more lucid but not unlike Roland Barthes's description of a floored wrestler offering '[le] spectacle intolérable de son impuissance'.[45] Powerless he may be, but the experience of the place in which the (un)dead know and speak is granted to only a very select few in history.[46] Indeed, following Carolyn Walker Bynum's work, we see here a saint experiencing his own fragmentation into a corpus of relics in what is posited as the transcendent vision of his own body in effect 'resurrected' in the beyond of its destruction and dispersal.[47]

One way of thinking through the sense of this gesture is to see in it a medieval reflection on classical accounts of the death of Julius Caesar and its place in debates about history and the human passions, about government and self-government. To raise this question and to negotiate with these models is then to engage with key stress points that affirm the 'subaltern' status of the Middle Ages. Just as illustrations of Fortune's wheel not uncommonly show historical processes in terms of a succession of individual figures experiencing rise or fall, so Arthur's fate takes its place in and appears as a response to other visions of the uncertain foothold granted to the great and good through the ages.[48] Arthur's cosmic smackdown, his living of the simultaneous destruction of body and reign contrasts with the accounts given of his great Roman archetype and enemy, Julius Caesar, who, betrayed and dying, legendarily drew his toga over his head. Explanations of this gesture vary, fitting perhaps with Caesar's place in a political culture dystopically torn between ideals of *amicitia* and the prevalence of *inimicitia*, enmity or factional feuding, fundamental to Roman public life.[49] According to Suetonius – widely read in the Middle Ages –

Caesar then adjusted his garments so that his lower body would not be exposed when he fell (*The Deified Julius*, § 82).[50] In his account, the gesture is indicative of a concern with the dictates of *honestas*, a view reflected in Emmanuel Levinas's reading of the scene as an assertion of human identity in the face of the unmanning indecency of death, the moment when 'nous *ne pouvons plus pouvoir*'.[51] Plutarch – an important source for John of Salisbury – gives a rather different explanation (*Life of Caesar*, § 66).[52] In his account, the events of the assassination seem more dictated by chance than noble design, and so his covering of his head is presented as a despairing reaction at the sight of Brutus among the conspirators, a loss of control that foreshadows the image of Caesar's dying body lying at the foot of Pompey's statue 'quivering from a multitude of wounds' ('*perispairontoζ upo plηθouζ traumatωn*', *Life of Caesar*, § 66).

Caesar's downfall echoes in other notable death scenes, forming part of a more general debate about the relation between ideals of virtue and the political economy of late and post-Republican Rome. Lucan's *Civil War* – a work revered by medieval poets – is incomplete, and it is uncertain whether his design for the poem would have taken the narrative as far forward as the Ides of March.[53] It is therefore speculated that Cato's suicide at Utica is the more likely dramatic climax, the final assertion being one of Stoic heroism. However, even though either the surviving poem – or, indeed, any putative completed version – might give no actual account of the death of Caesar, it is hard not see in some of its key scenes an adumbration of Lucan's vision and understanding of the assassination. Key among these possible foreshadowings are the brutal butchery of Pompey (book 8) and Cato's subsequent elegy for him (book 9), a speech which praises the man both for his skills of command and for the mastery of his passions and appetites:

> 'Civis obit' inquit, 'multum maioribus inpar
> *Nosse modum iuris*, sed in hoc tamen utilis aevo,
> Cui non ulla fuit iusti reverentia.' (book 9, ll. 190–92, my emphasis)

> 'A citizen has died', he says, 'far inferior to our ancestors *in knowledge of the limit of power*, but valuable to this age yet which has no respect for justice.'

There is much in Cato's eulogy that might resonate with later, perhaps especially medieval audiences, especially given Lucan's high reputation.[54] Notable here is his extended reflection on the tensions between the ideals of civic life and the possibilities, both for good and ill, afforded by personal wealth and power in an apparently barbaric modernity. The Rome he evokes appears as a belated reflection of its former self, and yet not deprived of value. Caught between still-cherished values and tempting means, his heroes appear as archetypes for those who followed in a world where Rome and what it represented appeared a far more distant memory. Geoffrey's vision of Arthur especially, caught between his imitation of Cato and Cicero on the one hand and Caesar on the other, is a case in point. I will return to Geoffrey's treatment of Arthur in more detail presently.

Differences over Caesar's capacity to orchestrate his final moments appear emblematic of a more general debate regarding the extent to which the emperor was either master of his fate or a tyrant puppet of universal forces and his own passions.[55] Treatments of his life thus either brazen it out with regard to questions such as his sexual preferences, as is the case with Suetonius's account of rumours regarding his sexuality, which begin with mention of the 'lasting reproach [and] insults from every quarter' ('perenni opprobrio et ad omnium convicia exposito', *The Deified Julius*, § 59) to which he was exposed and which ends rather more defiantly and jokingly with the song purportedly sung by his soldiers following his triumph in the Gallic wars:

> 'Gallias Caesar subegit, Nicomedes Caesarem:
> Ecce Caesar nunc triumphat qui subegit Gallias,
> Nicomedes non triumphat qui subegit Caesarem.' (*The Deified Julius*, § 59)
>
> 'All the Gauls did Caesar vanquish, Nicomedes vanquished him; Lo, now Caesar rides in triumph, victor over all the Gauls, Nicomedes does not triumph, who subdued the conqueror.'

Suetonius's bare-faced approach contrasts markedly with Ovid's apotheosis of Caesar (*Metamorphoses*, book 15, ll. 745–870). In an account much more concerned with immortal rather than mortal agencies, just as Suetonius had the deified Julius cover himself, so he draws a pudic veil over the actual events of the murder subtended by a conspiracy whose power is as nothing compared to the grim purpose of the Fates. For Ovid, Brutus and his companions appear as mere shadows in history, only intruding through the reference to Caesar's 'slain body' (l. 840), the presence and actions of the conspirators, reduced from any noble sense of purpose to mere henchmen (l. 800). The ugliness of the moment is rapidly left behind as – consoled by Jupiter's account of the glories which the Fates have decreed will follow under Augustus (ll. 816–40) – the goddess catches Julius's soul and bears it up into the heavens, where, its virile energy undimmed by death, it escapes the maternal care of her bosom and assumes its own place in the firmament.

Patristic sources typically take a negative line. In Augustine's *City of God*, Julius's divine descent is treated as a matter of collective delusion (book 3, chapters 3–4) and his ambition censured as no more than a bloodthirsty lust for glory (book 5, chapter 12). Meanwhile, Augustine effectively downplays the mystery of Caesar's passions and purposes, subordinating the doings of this apparently exceptional man to his grander theme of the consideration of the unknowability of the workings of Providence. The relation between the virtues and fortunes of all ancient kings is known only to God (book 5, chapter 21): 'He who gave power to Marius gave it also to Caius Caesar; He who gave it to Augustus also gave it to Nero'. Medieval visions of Caesar appear as divided as their classical forebears.[56] Use of Caesar as a cipher in reflections on the ephemerality or obscenity of worldly power, and on the untrustworthiness of those who seek it, continue in later tradition in that moral commentary in the central Middle Ages: 'references to Caesar [...] operated like references to the Trojans', both of them appearing as the embodiments of passionate deregulation and double-dealing.[57] John of Salisbury's *Policraticus*, which presents the death of Caesar as the paradigm of tyrannicide, also reprises the song mentioned by Suetonius (see above) as part of his reflection on sexual *mores* at court.[58] However, later vernacular representations of Caesar's career in the *matière de Rome* shows a range of perspectives, not all of them critical, and indeed a number seemingly endorsing and celebrating Caesar's strength of purpose. In Le *Roman d'Eneas*,

Anchise's prophecy of the future glories of Rome refers to him in brief but at least apparently glowing terms:

> 'De la lignie Romuli
> Et de la ton filz Julii
> Yert Julïus Cesar li prous:
> De prouesce sormontera touz,
> Sor la monde ert sa poëstés
> Et puis l'occira li Senez.' (ll. 3038–43)

> 'Of the line of Romulus and your son Iule will come the worthy Julius Caesar. He will outshine all in his valour and have the world at his command, and then the Senate will kill him.' (trans. mine)

In this short narrative, what was tyrannicide for other sources reads rather more like Fortune felling the great conqueror. Indeed, the intimation may be that medieval audiences did not always think of the Roman Senate as benign guardians of civic values, their major function from that perspective having been to kill Caesar. This lends a rather more sinister tinge to the description of Dido's Carthage, a civilisation so advanced it had 'already' invented the Capitol and the Senate as legislative and judiciary bodies (ll. 506–09). In light of Anchise's later words, the implication is that another sinister fate might well have awaited the conquering Dido if Eneas had not appeared. This seeming valorisation of Caesar in the vernacular traditions continues to contrast with the comments found in clerical sources, whether dealing with Caesar himself or his symbolic descendants, such as Richard the Lionheart, referred to by Gerald of Wales as a 'New Caesar'.[59]

In the highly influential *Le Fait des Romains*, dating to 1212–1214 and based on a combination of Sallust, Suetonius and Lucan, the description of Caesar's death is sourced to Suetonius. The passage repeats the detail of Julius covering and pulling down his toga and making little sound as he was attacked:[60]

> Il envelopa son chief de sa togue et covri ses cuisses aval a sa main senestre dou chief de la togue par desoz por chaïr plus honestement; ne voloit pas chaïr espars ne descoverz, sanz nule voiz de parole. Lors reçut .xxiii. plaies sans mot soner, ne mes que il gemit a la premiere plaie. Li un dient que Brute apela il

> traître, quant il le vit acorre vers lui por ferir. (ed. by Flutre and Sneyders, I, pp. 740–1)

> He wrapped his head in his toga and, with his left hand, covered his thighs below with the top of his toga in order to fall more decently: he did not want to fall indecently or with his clothing in disorder. Then he received 23 wounds without uttering a word, except that he groaned a little at the first wound. Some said that he called Brutus a traitor when he saw him run at him to strike. (trans. mine)

Again, unlike the 'twitching heap' of Plutarch, it is simply said that Caesar's body lay on the ground ('il remest ilec gisanz et peestanz une piece', I, p. 740). Interestingly, in this second-hand digest of sources, his involuntary comment about Brutus becomes a rumour put about by an anonymous 'some', the further layering of possible additions and adornments of first-hand accounts now clearly standing between the audience and Caesar's thoughts and deeds.

The *Roman de Jules César*, dated to the latter part of the thirteenth century, again paints a portrait of a brooding, driven individual.[61] Based on Lucan's *Civil War* and Caesar's own *Commentaries*, it therefore does not take Caesar's story as far forward as the conspiracy and murder, closing instead on the fulfilment of his ambitions:

> Et adonc fu Cesar esluz et elevez,
> A empereour fu de Rome couronnez,
> S'oult donc li ber emplies ses pluseurs volontez
> Puis que de Rome fu emperere apelez. (ll. 9390–3)

> And then was Caesar elected and raised up, crowned emperor of Rome. And so had the worthy man accomplished the various things he wished to do in that he was named emperor of Rome. (trans. mine)

In a sense, there is reason – apart from the epilogue's appeal for the audience's indulgence on the grounds that it was composed in a hasty four months (ll. 9410–19) – to regard the *Roman de Jules César* as a rather inferior consideration of the issues raised by its hero's deeds and career. Its reconciliation of Lucan's dark vision of the blasphemies of civil strife with Caesar's own accounts of his various campaigns removes the sense of horror that gives the *Civil War* its colour and energy. But then, in an age that venerated Charlemagne for his military and political achievements, the desire to be proclaimed emperor of Rome – as indeed Charles was on Christmas Day 800 CE – would not invariably appear a monstrous design. In a literary world inflected by the preoccupations and stylistic traits of the chanson de geste, and where the news of Pompey's betrayal is received with a leonine sigh and shake of the head straight out of the *matière de France* ('Quant Cesar oï ce, le chief en a crollé /et d'ire et de torment de parfont souspiré', ll. 314–15), Caesar's imperial will begs fewer questions. This impression is bolstered by Charlemagne's direct assimilation of Ganelon's treachery to Caesar's assassination in the Châteauroux version of the *Chanson de Roland* (ed. by Duggan, ll. 3112–26).

A man of both contradictions and suspect expenditures, the accounts – in all senses – of Julius Caesar give us another way of looking at Arthur. At every level, neither man 'adds up', baffling their enemies and alarming their supporters with shows of unpredictability and profligacy. However, although both cast long, enigmatic shadows over the Middle Ages, only one of the pair bequeaths to history his own account of events along with a range of other detailed, apparently eyewitness biographies.[62] While the sense of Caesar's actions might have been received as a riddle summed up in the comment attributed to Brutus that 'we will never know the truth of him', and Augustine may have poured scorn on the legend of his divine descent, there was no real debate in the Middle Ages as to whether Julius Caesar had actually existed. The same cannot be said for Arthur, who hovers differently between legend and history in various national literatures and historiographical traditions.[63] As the narrator of *La Naissance du chevalier au cygne* puts it: 'The tales of Arthur were mere fables or faery' ('Co fu fable d'Artu u co fu faerie', l. 3292).[64] Even the famous 'discovery' of his Glastonbury tomb in 1190 or 1191 cannot be taken as an unambiguous assertion of his existence. Indeed, the precise point of the gesture was arguably to show that Arthur was 'not real' in the sense that he would not return from Avalon to usher in a revival in Celtic fortunes.[65] The finding of Arthur's old and broken bones targets the power of the fiction. As Madeleine Blaess puts it, 'the fact is that from 1191, and in spite of localised belief in his return, Arthur was dead and buried'.[66] That said, as a problem case in medieval debates about the relation between 'historiography' and 'fiction', the figure of Arthur stirs interest considerable interest, protestations about his fictional status indicative of perceptions of literary genre.[67] The narrator of the *Roman de Brut* therefore laments the impossiblity of telling truth from fiction in his adventures:[68]

> [...] a fables sunt aturnees:
> Ne tut mençunge ne tut veir,
> Ne tut folie ne tut saveir.
> Tant unt li cunteür cunté
> Et li fableür tant flablé
> Pur lur cuntes enbeleter,
> Que tut unt fait fable sembler. (*Roman de Brut*, ll. 9792–8)
>
> [...] they have become the stuff of fiction: not all lies, not all truth, neither total folly nor total wisdom. The raconteurs have told so many yarns, the story-tellers so many stories, to embellish their tales that they have made it all appear fiction. (trans. by Weiss)

Questions of fictionality are central to medieval receptions of the Arthur legend in various ways. However many question-marks may have hung over Caesar's financial arrangements, military exploits, sexual practices or motivations, the fundamental issue that concerns both his contemporaries and the authors of his various lives is how he achieved the extraordinary things they knew him to have achieved. This is not to say that accounts of Caesar never take liberties in the matter of cast or character: for example, whereas in Plutarch's account of events following the murder of Pompey the prinicipal figures are his former slave, Philip, and an anonymous old man, Lucan's (*Civil War*, book 8, ll. 712–93) introduces the figure of Cordus. Nonetheless, with Caesar as the great riddle at their centre, the differences between the various versions of him seem to be taken as stemming from a generalised sense of uncertainty about the nature of events and individuals than purely cavalier invention. By contrast, the more Arthur achieves, the more doubts are sown about his existence. Too good to be true, his historical stock appears as a matter of speculation in a way Caesar's did not.

As we move forward and backward in this literary and political genealogy that follows on from the collapse of the Roman Republic, and especially as we encounter the beginnings of the matter of Britain, what we see emerging is a reflection on the basis and the embedding of medieval northern Europe's 'cultural cringe' with regard to the values of its great historical model. This sense is most apparent in Geoffrey of Monmouth's vision of Arthur defying Rome and questioning its claims to superiority. Arthur's response to Rome's demands, and especially his statement 'nothing that is acquired by force and violence can ever be held legally by anyone', clearly glosses over some aspects of his own career, while at the same time paying tribute to Rome through his echo of Cicero criticisms in *On Duties* of government sustained and enforced through fear rather than love.[69] The appreciative reaction of Arthur's fellow kings and nobles, voiced by Duke Hoel of Britanny, is an important plank in the presentation of his hero:

> 'Even if every one of us [...] were to take the trouble to turn all these things over in his mind and to reconsider each point deep within himself, it is my opinion that no one could find better advice to give than what has emerged from your own experienced and highly-skilled wisdom. Your speech, adorned as it was with Ciceronian eloquence [Tulliano liquore], has anticipated exactly what we all think.'[70]

Hoel's tribute makes a crucial divide between substance and style, thereby highlighting the fact that Arthur's speech shows judgement and principle that can entirely stand scrutiny through reflection, while being at the same time pleasingly 'adorned [...] with Ciceronian eloquence'.[71] The Duke does not thereby imply the King's intervention is mere sophistry, but rather emphasises his appreciation that this deployment of oratorical skill springs from a sincere wish to persuade rather than to manipulate his fellows, bringing out and giving voice to shared views rather than supplying and inculcating them. There is clearly no danger of the 'inarticulate public feeling' Cicero denounces as one of the possible effects of tyrannical repression here.[72]

Obviously, such a vision of love could well disguise murkier undersides and inconvenient facts glossed over. After all, what Thorpe renders as 'eloquence' is not the Latin word from which it is derived, *eloquentia*, but rather *liquor*, a highly ambiguous term that encompasses eloquence, fluidity and indeed liquid of various kinds, from wine to (quite commonly) clear spring-water to seawater to the fluid products of putrefaction. Thus Hoel's comment leaves us uncertain whether Arthur's companions are refreshed, intoxicated or corrupted by the heady 'liquor of Tully': does Arthur's deliberation constitute a dissecting analysis of the rights and wrongs of cases or a blurring and dissolution of key distinctions? Is it a beneficent potion or a sinister poison?[73] Compared to stealing shreds from the coat of Philosophy or bits of Arthur, this sounds rather more slippery, reading indeed as a version of Plato's presentation of the idea of 'the *pharmakon* or noble lie, which is designed to inoculate us against the vitiating consequences of the recognition that justice is impossible'.[74] However, seen in a broader context, Arthur's position can be defended in that it effectively positions the king as a sort of Diomedes to Rome's Alexander as much as it does as a David to their Goliath. One solution lies with the argument Lucan attributes to Cato: whatever concerns there might be about the legitimacy of Arthur's conquests, whatever grounds we might have for agreeing with Cato's conjecture that he might be 'far inferior to our ancestors in the knowledge of the limit of power', he is still a citizen. Any reservations are dwarfed by those that attach to the actions of the tyrannical Romans, a leviathan-like collective whose appetites dwarf the cannibal giants of which Arthur is the legendary slayer.

Thus, in a way that makes Arthur's stance look distinctly like the lesser of two possible evils, Rome's claims clearly reflect the darker strands of their own history. Although the procurator, Lucius Hiberius, presents himself ostensibly as the delegated mouthpiece of the Senate and the Republic, he is also referred to as emperor and is presented as being able to command the support of kings in the manner of a feudal lord. Moreover, to compound this confusion, republican Rome is further assimilated to its imperial past through the demand that Arthur renew the custom of paying tribute to Rome established and enforced by the conquering Julius. The complex play of mirrors here is of great political importance to Geoffrey's vision of a *translatio imperii* in process, a central reversal of the dominant-subaltern relation being

Arthur's denial of Rome's claims to pre-eminence and to tribute from the Britons by recalling his ancestor Belinus's conquest of the city. What thus emerges in the king's speech is a Ciceronian vision now mapped onto a Europe where no one nation dominates by tyranny. It is crucial in that regard that the Roman emperors Arthur cites are also the villains of the piece in Cicero's own account, with Caesar as the legendary conqueror of Britain and dictator of Rome at the head of the list. In that sense, what Geoffrey presents us with here is a watershed moment in the shaping of what will be the legacy of Rome to the West: *studium* or *imperium*? It is also crucial that the apparently younger nations are presented as playing a key role in that process of reception, rejecting violent imposition in favour of a dialogue of equals. What is fundamental to this new Troy patterned after Rome, however, is its public reflection on the place of desire and will in the political order. Geoffrey may present us with a world in which Arthur is in direct conflict with the 'dark side' of the Roman political imaginary, but of course his account and his positioning of Arthur is still 'after Rome' at a temporal and historical level.

Arthur is in that sense a creature both of his time and out of time: he embodies and is the agent of a medieval cultural identity both in debt to and in conflict with Roman models of will and desire. Caesar was represented by Suetonius as moved first to tears and then to action by the deeds of Alexander, the conquest that ensued was that of northern Europe. Geoffrey's Arthur, by contrast, asserts the values of a medieval Europe romanised, but not Rome's subaltern puppet. Moreover, any claims Rome might advance on the basis of historical precedent or assumed cultural superiority are correspondingly undermined from Arthur's side through Geoffrey's presentation of Rome as a fudged hybrid of democracy and tyranny. This creature can claim no high ground on the basis of purity of principle. Indeed, in that sense what we might see here is Geoffrey's Arthur's, through his own potentially highly ironic assertions about right and claim and through his use of the 'liquor of Tully' as targeting a cultural anxiety at the heart of the Roman tradition, a tradition torn in the figure of Cicero, on the one hand, between rhetoric's association with philosophy and principle and, on the other, its darker incarnation as the seductive force whose honeyed subterfuges can unleash the irrational passions of the vulgar mob. The other manifestation of that anxiety about the place of passion and conflict in history lies precisely in debates about the role of Juno, malign, jealous persecutor and stirrer of storms. Just as Jacques Derrida was to question Francis Fukuyama's announcement of the 'end of History' following the fall of the Berlin wall and the fragmentation of the former Soviet Bloc, so authors such as Virgil and later Augustine can be seen as raising the question of whether Juno was as ready to be written out of history as those eager to assert the triumph of the stabilising values of Augustan Rome, notably Vitruvius, would have seemed to wish. In short, if Arthur had not done something to shake the palace to its foundations, it just wouldn't have been a proper Arthurian romance.

Regarding Henry II:
Royal Anger and Vernacular Politics

Arthur's imperious decision to relaunch the custom of the hunt not merely reasserts the place of the irrational in political life but also contests any attempt to dismiss that move as an unreflective barbarism. Although the picture it paints is one of past civilisation threatened by arbitrariness and violence, this is not to say that Chrétien's contemporaries would have inevitably viewed themselves as the 'civilised descendants' of 'barbaric forebears'. Rather, there is evidence to suggest that court culture in the late twelfth century was re-evaluating the role of those forces that had been seen as inimical to good government either of the collective or of the self. One of the interesting connections between a range of sources, not merely *Erec et Enide*, but also works such as Walter Map's *The Courtier's Trifles* or the writings of Peter of Blois and John of Salisbury, is the picture these paint of the court of Henry II as a place of turbulence central to reflections on the history and sociology of the emotions and emotional display in medieval aristocratic cultures. Accordingly, in this section I will explore Henry's place in the history of royal anger, perhaps the most striking instance of passionate irrationality in political life. Moreover, locating Chrétien in this context has the advantage of avoiding potential over-generalisation of the value of a particular milieu: what I am not suggesting here is that we need to regard this confluence as part of some grand cultural shift but rather that it is shaped by more specific engagements. That said, it is tempting to discern a shift from what seems a more 'closed' culture of emotional display in the early Middle Ages to one that was more open to reflecting on the relation between performance and experience, regulation and excess.

Reflections on royal anger have their place in a more general preoccupation with the origin, nature and regulation of violence and violent impulses evident from historiographical and ethnographical accounts as well as in fictional works. One example can be seen in Orderic Vitalis's account of the volatile temperament of the Normans, figures both admired and feared, simultaneously politically central and barbarically marginal.[75] The consequences of the persistence of such energies are mapped extensively in vernacular romance, where, as Richard Kaeuper argues, violence and prowess are the objects of profound ambivalence, spawning contradictory views, prowess endowed with a 'power akin to fire: if noble, necessary and useful, such violence [nonetheless] requires much care and control'.[76] The darkness of this reflection is particularly apparent in the later prose romances, a world in which chivalric violence, partly controlled and harnessed and yet at the same time out of control, permeates the world in the manner of a 'brooding fear', a poisoning 'radiation' as Kaeuper puts it.[77] Other metaphors spring to mind: it is tempting to think of Arthurian romance as a reflection on chivalry's 'addiction' to violence: while reasonably clear about how much is too much, and more than capable of painting the effects of that excess in the bleakest and most haunting of tones, it seems less certain as to how much is enough, or, for that matter, good fun. Indeed, chivalry's culture of outdoing means that prowess in even the most apparently antisocial of its manifestations is 'codependently' recuperated and celebrated, as can be seen from the case of Balin in the *Suite du Merlin*, praised by the crowd, but, according to Arthur, 'not a man knight like other mortal knights, but a man born on earth for human destruction'.[78]

Thus, although romances seem to valorise the virtues of *mesure* and stability, or at least are eloquent on the consequences of their absence, they consistently lionise characters who fail to behave in accordance with the restraint they advocate.[79]

Concern with the regulation of the royal passions is central to the vision of the palace as a civilising milieu. In the eighth century, Alcuin of York, adviser to Charlemagne, argued that anger, 'the eighth vice', must be controlled by reason lest it turn into raging fury.[80] Accounts of Charlemagne thus seem to inaugurate a tradition valorising mercy and piety and associating anger with royal injustice and tyrannical iniquity. Yet, although the ideal king appears as an exemplar, Alcuin's position does not take any account of a performative dimension, of a distance between interior experience and external effect, in the king's behaviour: the gap foregrounded is that of imitator from model rather than of self-reflectiveness. Indeed, Alcuin's vision is based instead on a strict analogy between individual and collective. The passions of the king directly shape the mood of the court: deregulation at a microcosmic level translates into public disorder and conflict, which means that the good of the collective begins with self-mastery. Indeed, there is an extent here to which Charlemagne – the barbarian warrior king embracing the transformative values of education and educational reform for himself, his people and for a larger empire – becomes an embodiment of the change associated with a civilising process presented as far from complete. Under Alcuin's tutelary gaze, it seems there are subtleties and strategies Charlemagne is subalternly 'not yet' ready to incorporate into his royal persona.[81]

Alcuin's emphasis on rational control had a long and stately afterlife in medieval debate, echoed in later writings such as the *Policraticus* of John of Salisbury. For John, the king is both unbound or unfettered by the laws insofar as his status as the embodied spirit of the law places his authority above them and then subject to them insofar as he willingly submits to be governed.[82] Yet, as Stephen White notes, some sense of a challenge to this regulatory view can be seen in writings from the later period:

> When public displays of anger are located in eleventh- and twelfth-century political narratives, they do not provide evidence of emotional instability; instead, they reveal the position occupied by displays of anger in a relatively stable, enduring discourse of disputing, feuding, and political competition. Anger, in other words, has a well-defined place in political scripts in which other emotions figure as well.[83]

From having been the fire that would destroy the palace, anger becomes part of the heat and life of the system, its performance a key social strategy. Accordingly, Parzival's shows of anger in Wolfram's reworking of *Le Conte du graal* are less marks of his uncourtliness than his instinct for justice.[84] However, although White's comment paints an extremely useful and far from misleading picture of the sociology of royal power, there is a potential problem with his assertion that that system was 'relatively stable'. We could risk overly domesticating the phenomenon of royal anger and thereby overlook the necessary dimensions of excess much as we might fail to see the persistence and function of danger in the apparently fixed grammar of ritual.[85] Although it is more than arguable that social systems tend not to view catastrophic instability as entirely desirable, it is clear that that instability, or at least the convincing appearance of it, has its uses. As Gerd Althoff puts it:

> Communication in medieval public life was decisively determined by demonstrative acts and behaviours. [...] Many of the mannerisms of medieval communication, which may appear to us over-emotionalised, were bound up with this demonstrative function – especially the demonstration of anger.[86]

'Over-emotionalisation', as part of the question of what is 'enough' and what is 'too much', is thus not just a figment of modern misperception, rather it is a key part of the game as played, part of the necessary denial that this 'game' is indeed a game at all. Althoff's presentation underlines the ambiguity and difficulty inherent in the situation and its observation. Thus, although Mirrors for Princes typically advocated the mastery of self, of emotions and impulses, this did not mean that they exclusively set out to restrain kings.[87] For Althoff, the history of these expressions is one that is hidden in medieval sources. What emerges from this consideration is the thought that writers on Christian kingship in the Middle Ages advocated rules that were not, and to a large extent *could* not, be followed in practice.[88]

This general history has some highly specific focuses. As both Richard Barton and Michel Senellart note, Henry II – thought to be the addressee and model of Chrétien's poem – plays a key role in the revisioning of the dramatic function of royal anger.[89] In the dialogue treatise attributed to Peter of Blois, Henry appears in discussion with a clerical figure, the abbot of Bonneval. As Barton puts it:

> Peter, speaking through [the abbot], attempts to persuade King Henry II and the reader to abandon vengeance, pride and anger, and to embrace more 'Christian' virtues. Not surprisingly, Peter has the abbot win the disputation, and he has Henry reluctantly agree that meekness, temperance and humility are preferable. But, in the course of the dialogue, Peter puts into Henry's mouth arguments that seem very close to what actual laymen might have thought about anger and vengeance.[90]

As Barton goes on to show, the arguments Henry presents make use of a full range of justifications, anger appearing as a 'safety valve' preferable to actual vengeance, as a legitimate response to treachery and as sanctioned by its echo of Old Testament kings. In Peter's dialogue, the Church wins the day, even if Peter's choice not to put himself in the room with Henry marks his wary distance from too close a confrontation on this point.

Such ambivalence and ambiguity with regard to the dance with the devil that would be any accommodation of the less readily domesticated aspects of royal power is also reflected in Walter Map's likening Henry's court to Hell. Here the distance from the utopian ambitions of Alcuin's vision of the Carolingian palace could not be more extreme. From a cultural point of view, what this distance represents is the sense that the shape of the political future could not be encompassed as part of clerical culture at court. However, what it may also mark is the increasing room for manoeuvre afforded temporal powers in the reign of Henry (a latitude that infamously overbalances into savage hubris with his call for the removal of Thomas Becket in 1170).

Chrétien's location of Arthur in the past marks a distanciation not merely from that past but may also reflect a distance between the courts of Champagne and Anjou, a tribute that locates Henry in the mythical west of the Arthurian past, and, in producing that portrait, locates the court of Champagne as a key beneficiary of the precedent created by the King's innovatory act of will. Here the relation is a two-way street. Chrétien's allusive positioning of Arthur challenges any move to present Henry's political stance as manifesting subaltern 'irrationality' or a lack of pedigree. The long intertwining of the histories of Arthur and Caesar and the substantive questioning in Geoffrey of Rome's assertions of principle and prior claim had already marked an emergent refusal to accept second-class status on which Chrétien now capitalises in an assertion of the claims of vernacular modernity. Through that act of reflection, Champagne also positions itself in an after-time that secures it both political and cultural licence. And yet again, there is a distance: just as Peter puts a fictional alter-ego in dialogue with Henry, so Chrétien's slippery use of temporal markers suggests something other than wholehearted identification. Champagne's regard for Plantagenet Anjou looks both across and back at Arthur. Such a perspective may be both one of legitimising veneration or sly irony.

Notes

1 *King Arthur*, dir. Antoine Fuqua (2004). On Fuqua's film and various other popular adaptations of the Arthurian legend, see Bull, *Thinking Medieval*, pp. 7–41. On cinematic representations of the Middle Ages, see also Stuart Airlie, 'The Middle Ages in the Cinema', in *The Medieval World*, ed. by Linehan and Nelson, pp. 163–83.
2 On chivalry and kingship in the Matière de Bretagne as a narrative of assumed castration, see notably Cohen, *Of Giants*.
3 See notably Spence, pp. 22–51.
4 On the prologue, see especially Seebass-Linggi, pp. 23–9 and Tony Hunt, 'The Rhetorical Background to the Arthurian Prologue: Tradition and the Old French Vernacular Prologues', *Forum for Modern Language Studies*, 6 (1970), 1–20 and his 'Tradition and Originality in the Prologues of Chrétien de Troyes', *Forum for Modern Language Studies*, 8 (1972), 320–44, as well as M.-L.

Ollier, 'The Author in the Text: The Prologues of Chrétien de Troyes', *Yale French Studies*, 51 (1974), 26–41. See also John F. Plummer, '*Bien dire* and *bien aprandre* in Chretien de Troyes's *Erec et Enide*', *Romania*, 95 (1974), 380–94 and Köhler, *L'Aventure chevaleresque*, pp. 59–64. On *conjointure*, see, among others, Douglas Kelly, 'The Source and Meaning of *Conjointure* in Chrétien's *Erec*, l. 14', *Viator*, 1 (1970), 179–200. For a recent, in-depth treatment of Chrétien's rhetorical practices, see Danièle James-Raoul, *Chrétien de Troyes: la griffe d'un style* (Paris: Honoré Champion, 2007), pp. 132–60 on the prologue to *Erec et Enide* and the antecedent tradition.

5   Seebass-Linggi, p. 23.
6   Seebass-Linggi, p. 26.
7   On indiscretion in romance poetics, see Bloch, *Medieval Misogyny*, pp. 123–9.
8   See Hindman, pp. 131–3.
9   For reproduction, see Busby et al., *The Manuscripts of Chrétien de Troyes*, II, plate 296. Given that a similar image is one of the three associated with the version contrained in fonds fr. 24403 (at fol. 119) – the other two being Erec jousting with a knight (fol. 140v) and Erec attacking the giants (fol. 155) – Hindman's view of the sequence as 'epic' in character might seem a little skewed. Of course, that the definite article should be a likely client for decoration does not seem too surprising: as Roger Middleton's study of coloured capitals makes clear, *Li* is the word most commonly decorated with coloured capitals in fonds fr. 1376 (12 out of 86 instances – see Middleton, 'Coloured Capitals', p. 191), although the fact that l. 1 has the only historiation in that version of *Erec et Enide* points to the possibility of singular pungency.
10 Hindman, pp. 132–3.
11 For reproductions, see Busby et al., *The Manuscripts of Chrétien de Troyes*, II, plates 292 and 295.
12 Hindman, p. 132.
13 'I too am not a bit tamed, I too am untranslatable, /I sound my barbaric yawp over the roofs of the world.' Walt Whitman, 'Song of Myself' ll. 1332–3, in *Leaves of Grass, Authoritative Texts, Prefaces, Whitman on his Art Criticism*, ed. by Sculley Bradley and Harold W. Blodgett (New York and London: Norton, 1973), pp. 28–89.
14 Michel Zink, *The Invention of Literary Subjectivity*, trans. by David Sices, Parallax: Re-Visions of Culture and Society (Baltimore and London: Johns Hopkins University Press, 1999), p. 29.
15 See Patricia Harris Stabelein, '*Erec et Enide*: l'ouverture du sacrifice arthurien', in *Erec ou l'ouverture du monde Arthurien: Actes du colloque du Centre d'Etudes Médiévales de l'Université de Picardie-Jules Verne, Amiens 16–17 janvier 1993*, ed. by Danielle Buschinger and Wolfgang Spiewok, WODAN, 18 (Greifswald: Reineke, 1993), 51-61.
16 On the use of *voloir* and *devoir* in *Erec et Enide*, see notably Maddox, *Arthurian Romances*, pp. 25–32.

17 Text and translation cited from Hult, 'Author /Narrator /Speaker', pp. 81–2.
18 Hult, 'Author /Narrator /Speaker', at p. 82 and pp. 90–2.
19 On will in this section of the text, see notably, Mullally, *The Artist at Work*, pp. 42–3.
20 Wallach, cited in Hunt, 'Rhetorical Background', p. 15.
21 Eric Auerbach, *Literary Language and its Public in Late Latin Antiquity and the Middle Ages*, trans. by Ralph Mannheim (London: Routledge and Kegan Paul, 1965), pp. 183–233 (on the *Eneas*, see especially pp. 186–91; on Chrétien, pp. 215–20).
22 Adams, pp. 63–9.
23 Geoffrey Koziol, *Begging Power and Favour: Ritual and Political Order in Early Medieval France* (Ithaca and London: Cornell University Press, 1992), p. 4.
24 On gifts and gifting, see Marcel Mauss, *The Gift: The Form and Reason for Exchange in Archaic Societies*, trans. by W. D. Halls (London: Routledge, 1990). See also Marilyn Strathern, *The Gender of the Gift: Problems with Women and Problems with Society in Melanesia* (Berkeley and London: University of California Press, 1988), Maurice Godelier, *The Enigma of the Gift*, trans. by Nora Scott (Cambridge: Polity, 1999) and Jacques Derrida, *Given Time 1) Counterfeit Money*, trans. by Peggy Kamuf (Chicago: Chicago University Press, 1992) and *The Gift of Death*, trans. by (Chicago: Chicago University Press, 1992). On gifting in Derrida, see John D. Caputo, *The Prayers and Tears of Jacques Derrida: Religion without Religion* (Bloomington and Indianapolis: Indiana University Press, 1997). See also Gaunt, *Love and Death*, pp. 20–43. Interestingly, Gaunt's emphasis, following Derrida, that the 'gift of death' is fundamental to ethical responsibility makes a curious case of the king, who, as Girard comments, 'reigns only by virtue of his future death', a formulation that raises the question of whether kings who may or may not be fictional may or may not be ethical.
25 Burgess, *Erec et Enide*, p. 19.
26 Spence, pp. 11–14.
27 Spence, pp. 19–21.
28 Derrida, *Given Time*, pp. 37–43.
29 Lacan, *Le Séminaire XI*, p. 94–5.
30 Miha Pintarič, 'Le Rôle de la violence dans le roman médiéval: l'exemple d'*Erec et Enide*', in *La Violence dans le monde médiéval*, Senefiance, 36 (Aix-en-Provence: CUERMA, 1994), pp. 413–23, here at p. 416.
31 In that regard, I would see Maddox's carefully elaborated reading of the scene (*Arthurian Fictions*, pp. 14–32) as almost underplaying the traumatic, ahistorical imperative that is the kernel of the hunt. On the scene see also Köhler, *L'Aventure chevaleresque*, pp. 105–08.

32 Gérard Chandès, *Le Serpent, la femme et l'épée: recherches sur l'imagination symbolique d'un romancier médiéval: Chrétien de Troyes*, Faux Titre, 27 (Amsterdam: Rodopi, 1986), p. 23.
33 Walter Map, *The Courtier's Trifles*, dist. 1, § 1–9 (pp. 2–9 in edition, citation from p. 3).
34 On Hamlet and 'time out of joint', see Jacques Derrida, *Specters of Marx: The State of the Debt, The Work of Mourning and the New International*, trans. by Peggy Kamuf (New York and London: Routledge, 1994), pp. 17–32.
35 Huizinga, see for example pp. 60–124 (chapter: 'The Heroic Dream').
36 Bezzola, p. 96.
37 On Gauvain in *Erec et Enide*, see particularly Charles Foulon, 'Le Rôle de Gauvain dans *Erec et Enide*', *Annales de Bretagne*, 65 (1958), 149–58 and Keith Busby, *Gauvain in Old French Literature*, Degré Second, 2 (Amsterdam: Rodopi, 1980), pp. 50–4.
38 Gauvain thus speaks ostensibly as a figure assimilable to that of traitors such as Ganelon and, ultimately, Judas, both of whom speak as defenders of the material interests of their lord or their cause, Ganelon in the sense that it was he resists who the idea of pursuing the war further at the fruitless cost of their lives, Judas in that was he who questioned the use of the ointment used to anoint Christ's feet ('not because he cared for the poor, but because he was a thief' John 12. 6). Whether this is done innocently or disingenuously matters comparatively little compared to the overall effect.
39 Foulon, p. 150.
40 See Paul Strohm, *Theory and the Premodern Text*, Medieval Cultures, 26 (Minneapolis and London: University of Minnesota Press, 2000), p. 42. Strohm's references to Pierre Bourdieu are to *Outline of a Theory of Practice*, trans. by Richard Nice (Cambridge: Cambridge University Press, 1977).
41 See Strohm, pp. 39–41 and also p. 42, citing Bourdieu on demotion at p. 40.
42 Gilles Deleuze, *The Fold: Leibniz and the Baroque*, ed. and trans. by Tom Conley (London and New York, Continuum, 2006), pp. 97–8, original emphasis. In tandem with Deleuze's comments here on Caesar and biography, see Carolyn Dinshaw's comments on Barthes, biography and desire (*Getting Medieval: Sexualities and Communities, Pre- and Postmodern* (Durham NC and London: Duke University Press, 1999) pp. 40–54): here, in her reading of the relation between Barthes and the nineteenth-century French historian, Jules Michelet, of whom Barthes was an avid reader, Dinshaw focuses on the queering dimension of the biographical project, Barthes the would-be biographer 'lending' Michelet, 'the author I love', the 'biographemes', the select details whose 'distinction' and 'mobility' are his vision of his subject appear as a more dialogical version of Deleuze's 'ideal events'. Obviously, on the question of the biographeme as an object of exchange between the biographer as 'the one who writes' and the one who does not, see also Jacques Derrida's *La Carte postale: de Socrate à Freud et au-delà*, La Philosophie en

Effet (Paris: Flammarion, 1980). Derrida's focus here is the inversion in Matthew Paris's illumination of *Prognostica Socratis Basilei* (Bodleian Library, Ms. Ashmole, 304, fol. 31v) of Plato seemingly overseeing and correcting Socrates in a scriptorium.

43   Albert Camus, 'Entretien avec Pierre Berger', in *Essais*, La Pléiade (Paris: Gallimard, 1965), p. 743.

44   For edition and translation, see *La Mort le roi Artu*, ed. by Jean Frappier, Textes Littéraires Français, rev. edn (Geneva: Droz, 1964) and *The Death of King Arthur*, trans. by James Cable (Harmondsworth: Penguin, 1971). On the wheel of fortune motif, see in particular Jean Frappier, *Etude sur 'La Mort le roi Artu'*, Publications Romanes et Françaises, 70, rev. edn (Geneva: Droz, 1972), pp. 248–64. On Fortuna see also Christoph Cormeau, 'Fortuna und andere Mächte im Artusroman', in *Fortuna*, ed. by Walter Haug and Burghart Wachinger (Tübingen: Niemeyer, 1995), pp. 23–33, and, in the same volume, Haug, 'Eros und Fortuna: der höfische Roman als Spiel von Liebe und Zufall' (pp. 52–75).

45   Roland Barthes, 'Le Monde où l'on catche', in *Mythologies*, Points (Paris: Seuil, 1971), pp. 13–24, here at p. 14.

46   On 'dead knowing', see Žižek, *How to Read Lacan*, pp. 91–104.

47   Caroline Walker Bynum, *Fragmentation and Redemption: Essays on Gender and the Human Body in Medieval Religion* (New York and London: Zone, 1992).

48   On images of Fortune's wheel, see especially Walter Haug, 'O Fortuna: eine historisch-semantische Skizze zür Einführung' in *Fortuna*, ed. by Walter Haug and Burghart Wachinger (Tübingen: Niemeyer, 1995), pp. 1–22, at pp. 1–2 and the references in notes 4 and 5.

49   On *inimicitia*, see David F. Epstein, *Personal Enmity in Roman Politics 218–43 BC* (London and New York: Croon Helm, 1987).

50   '[L]'étroite dépendance de l'histoire, de la morale et de la rhétorique eut du moins pour résultat que l'histoire ancienne fut bien connue au Moyen Age. Tite-Live, Lucain, Salluste, Suétone, Valère-Maxime, d'autres encore, furent abondamment lus, copiés et traduits.' Bernard Guenée, *Histoire et culture historique dans l'Occident médiéval* (Paris: Aubier Montaigne, 1980), p. 28.

51   Emmanuel Levinas, *Le Temps et l'autre* (Paris: Quadrige and Presses Universitaires de France, 1996), p. 62. 'When he saw that he was beset on every side by drawn daggers, he muffled his head in his robe, and at the same time drew down its lap to his feet with his left hand [simul sinistra manu sinum ad ima crura deduxit, quo honestius caderet etiam inferiore corporis parte velata], in order to fall more decently, with the lower part of his body also covered. And in this wise he was stabbed with three and twenty wounds, uttering not a word, but merely a groan at the first stroke, though some have written that when Marcus Brutus rushed at him, he said in Greek, "You too, my child?"' (Suetonius, *Life of Caesar*, § 82).

52 Edition and translation taken from Plutarch, *Lives: Demosthenes and Cicero, Alexander and Caesar*, ed. by E. H. Warmington and others, trans. by Bernadotte Perrin, Loeb Classical Library (Cambridge MA and London: Heinemann, 1917 [1967 printing]).

53 For an edition, see Lucan, *The Civil War*, ed. and trans. by G. P. Goold and J. D. Duff, Loeb Classical Library, 220 (Cambridge MA and London: 1988). For a translation, see *Civil War*, trans. by Susan H. Braund, World's Classics (Oxford: Oxford University Press, 1992). On the possible intended shape of the work, see Braund's introduction. Neil Wright in particular sees the influence, both stylistic and as a world-view, of Lucan on medieval historiographical epic as extensive (Neil Wright (ed. and trans.), *Gesta Regum Britannie*, The Historia Regum Britannie of Geoffrey of Monmouth, 5 (Woodbridge: Brewer, 1991), p. xv and the overview of sources on pp. 289–323).

54 Summed up neatly by Bernard Guenée: 'surtout les oeuvres de Salluste et de Lucain s'imposèrent partout comme livres de lecture fondamentaux. Leur succès fut prodigieux. Les copies en furent aussi nombreuses que celles des historiens chrétiens les plus répandus. A simplifier les choses, on peut dire que le XIIe et XIIIe siècles furent le temps de Flavius Josèphe et d'Orose d'une part, de Lucain et de Salluste de l'autre part' (p. 304).

55 This can be seen as reflected in the various debates regarding Caesar's character and private life, and notably the questions raised regarding various 'secret shames', such as personal vanity and financial profligacy. Prominent among these questions, are the imputations of homosexuality and adultery expounded on notably in Suetonius (*The Deified Julius*, § 49–51), who presents Caesar's sexuality as a determining factor in his foreign policy and military adventures, as well as a 'dirty secret' in Rome. Similar uncertainties can be seen in Plutarch's frequent reference to Caesar's dissembling, his 'appearance of humanity'. The same goes for Caesar's later career, where sources return repeatedly to the question of whether particular actions were the result of design or whims of the moment.

56 On the death of Caesar in medieval sources, see Joachim Leeker, *Die Darstellung Cäsars in den romanischen Literaturen des Mittelalters*, Analecta Romanica, 50 (Frankfurt-am-Main: Vittorio Klostermann, 1986), pp. 249–57.

57 Burgwinkle, *Sodomy*, p. 80.

58 Burgwinkle, *Sodomy*, p. 80.

59 Burgwinkle, *Sodomy*, p. 80. On Richard more generally, see pp. 73–85.

60 For edition, see *Li Fet des Romains*, ed. by L.-F. Flutre and K. Sneyders de Vogel, 2 vols (Paris: Droz and Groningen: Wolters, 1938).

61 *Le Roman de Jules César*, ed. by Olivier Collet, Textes Littéraires Français, 426 (Geneva: Droz, 1993). On Rome in thirteenth-century French vernacular historiography, see particularly Catherine Croizy-Naquet, *Ecrire l'histoire romaine au début du XIIIe siècle*, Nouvelle Bibliothèque du Moyen Age, 53 (Paris: Honoré Champion, 1999).

62   Guenée stresses the importance of Caesar's historical writings for his medieval reputation (pp. 77–8).
63   On this most vast of subjects, see, among many others and from various perspectives, Brigitte Burrichter, *Wahrheit und Fiktion: der Status der Fiktionalität in der Artusliteratur des 12. Jahrhunderts*, Beihefte zu Poetica, 21 (Munich: Fink, 1996); Rodney Castleden, *King Arthur: The Truth Behind the Legend* (London and New York: Routledge, 2003) and Fran Doel, Geoff Doel and Terry Lloyd, *Worlds of Arthur: King Arthur in History, Legend and Culture* (Stroud: Tempus, 1998). For a brief, but thoughtful keek at the problem from a Scottish perspective, see Rhiannon Purdie and Nicola Royen (eds), 'Introduction: Tartan Arthur?', in *The Scots and Medieval Arthurian Legend*, Arthurian Studies (Woodbridge: Brewer, 2005), pp. 1–7. For a consideration of the medieval literary sources, see Rosemary Morris, *The Character of King Arthur in Medieval Literature*, Arthurian Studies, 4 (Woodbridge: Brewer, 1985).
64   Jan A. Nelson and Emmanuel Mickel Jr. (eds), *The Old French Crusade Cycle 1: 'La Naissance du Chevalier au cygne'* (Alabama: University of Alabama Press, 1977).
65   On the finding of Arthur's tomb, see W. A. Nitze, 'The Exhumation of King Arthur at Glastonbury', *Speculum*, 9:4 (1934), 355–61 and also Geoffrey Ashe, *From Caesar to Arthur* (London: Collins, 1960), pp. 206–33.
66   Madeleine Blaess, 'The Public and Private Face of King Arthur's Court in the Works of Chrétien de Troyes', in *Chrétien de Troyes and the Troubadours: Essays in Memory of Leslie Topsfield*, ed. by Peter S. Noble and Linda M. Patterson (Cambridge: St Catherine's College, 1984), pp. 238–48, at p. 245.
67   On which see Hans Robert Jauss, 'Chanson de geste et roman courtois: analyse comparative du *Fierabras* et *Le Bel Inconnu*', in *Chanson de geste und höfischer Roman*, ed. by Pierre le Gentil and others, Studia Romanica, 4 (Heidelberg: Winter, 1963), pp. 61–77, Robert W. Hanning, *The Vision of History in Early Britain: From Gildas to Geoffrey of Monmouth* (New York and London: Columbia University Press, 1966); Paul Zumthor, 'Roman et histoire: aux sources d'un univers narratif', in *Langue, texte, enigme* (Paris: Seuil, 1975), pp. 237–48; Donald Maddox, 'Pseudo-Historical Discourse in Fiction: *Cligés*', in *Essays in Early French Literature Presented to Barbara M. Craig*, ed. by Norris J. Lacy and Jerry Nash (Columbia SC: French Literature, 1982), pp. 9–24; Douglas Kelly, '*Matiere* and *genera dicendi* in Medieval Romance', *Yale French Studies*, 51 (1974), 147–59; Sara Sturm-Maddox, ' "Tenir sa terre en pais": Social Order in the *Brut* and in the *Conte du Graal*', *Studies in Philology*, 81:1 (1984), 28–41; Suzanne Fleischmann, 'On the Representation of History and Fiction in the Middle Ages', *History and Theory*, 22:3 (1983), 278–310 and Peter Ainsworth, 'Legendary History: *Historia* and *Fabula*', in *Historiography in the Middle Ages*, pp. 387–416.

68   Text and translation from Judith Weiss (ed. and trans.), *Wace's 'Roman de Brut': A History of the British (Text and Translation)*, Exeter Medieval Texts and Studies, rev. edn (Exeter: University of Exeter 2002).

69   Thorpe sees Arthur's assertions are potentially undercut by his own record as a conqueror: 'In view of Arthur's recent activities in Europe, this is a very bland statement.' (p. 232, note).

70   'Licet unusquisque nostrum totus in se reversus omnia et de omnibus omni animo retractare valeret, non existimo eum prestantius consilium pose invenire quam istud quod modo discretion sollertis providentie tue redoluit. Provide etenim providit nobis tua deliberatio Tulliano liquore lita unde constantis viri affectum, sapientis animi effectum, optimi consilii profectum laudare indesinenter debemus.' Wright, *Historia*, p. 114 (§ 160); Thorpe, p. 233.

71   The rendering of Hoel's speech in Wace is much reduced: 'mult paroles raisnablement' (l. 10911).

72   Cicero, *On Duties*, book 2, § 7, para 24.

73   On which ambiguity, see Jacques Derrida, *La Dissémination* (Paris: Seuil, 1972), pp. 108–33 (on Plato and the *pharmakon*).

74   Stanley Rosen, *The Quarrel Between Poetry and Philosophy: Studies in Ancient Thought* (London and New York: Routledge, 1988), p. 26.

75   See Albu, pp. 193–5.

76   Richard Kaeuper, *Chivalry and Violence in Medieval Europe* (Oxford: Oxford University Press, 1999), p. 143.

77   See Kaeuper, *Chivalry and Violence*, p. 168 and pp. 26–7.

78   Cited from Kaeuper, *Chivalry and Violence*, pp. 159. One might also cite Sagremore the Unruly, styled a veritable devil in his uncontrolled fury, and yet, because of that, the darling of the crowd, praised as a model of knighthood and virility in a number of later prose romances (see Kaeuper, *Chivalry and Violence*, pp. 143–4).

79   Lancelot is the obvious case in point. Like Gawain in *Le Chevalier au lion*, he is more than capable of not adhering to the advice he himself gives. Although he asserts the primacy of court-administered royal justice over private chivalric retribution, he is entirely happy to mete out punishment himself without reference to any other authority and with it entirely unclear as to whether he is to be construed as acting as an exemplary king or exemplary knight (see Kaeuper, *Chivalry and Violence*, p. 97).

80   Alcuin, *Liber de virtutibus et vitiis*, Patrologia Latina, 101, cols 613–38, at col. 634. For discussion, see Richard E. Barton, ' "Zealous Anger" and the Renegotiation of Aristocratic Relationships in Eleventh- and Twelfth Century France', in *Anger's Pasts*, ed. by Rosenwein, pp. 153–70.

81   On the question of 'not yet', of the refusal of political agency and 'maturity' in historicism, see Chakrabarty, *Provincialising Europe*, pp. 7–9.

82   Kantorowicz, pp. 94–7.

83 Stephen D. White, 'The Politics of Anger', in *Anger's Pasts: The Social Uses of an Emotion in the Middle Ages* ed. by Barbara H. Rosenwein (Ithaca and London: Cornell University Press, 1998), pp. 127–52, at p. 142.
84 Notable examples here are his outrage at Kay's mistreatment of Cunneware and Antanor (see Wolfram von Eschenbach, *Parzival*, trans. by A. T. Hatto (Harmondsworth, Penguin, 1980), p. 87), as well as his fury at not finding his sword to hand in the grail castle (p. 122)
85 On which, see notably Buc, *The Dangers of Ritual*.
86 Gerd Althoff, '*Ira Regis*: Prolegomena to a History of Royal Anger', in *Anger's Pasts: The Social Uses of an Emotion in the Middle Ages* ed. by Barbara H. Rosenwein (Ithaca and London: Cornell University Press, 1998), pp. 59–74, p. 74.
87 Althoff, pp. 61–7.
88 Althoff, p. 61.
89 Barton, pp. 160–1 and Michel Senellart, *Les Arts de gouverner: du 'regimen' médiéval au concept du gouvernement*, Des Travaux (Paris: Seuil, 1995), pp. 111–26. For the text of Peter's dialogue, see *Dialogus inter regem Henricum secundum et abbatem Bonevallis*, ed. by R. B. C. Huygens, *Revue Bénédictine*, 68 (1958), 87–112.
90 Barton, p. 160.

Chapter Two
Court Beauty Turns Ugly:
A Young King and his Maiden(s)

First Impressions: The (Social) Death of a Princess

> Erec stands aside from the hunt. Self-indulgent in soft raiment, he is committed to no damsel who would involve him in the chase of the stag.[1]

> Young and pretty, the slaves of the harem are always the same in the Sultan's embrace.[2]

Although Arthur may have managed to mar the end of a party, another future king is about to show us that part of court spectacle is knowing when and how to make an entrance.

> Aprés aus monte la roÿne,
> Ensamble o li une meschine,
> Pucele estoit, fille de roi,
> Et sist sor un blanc palefroi.
> Aprés les siut a esperon
> Uns chevaliers, Erec ot non.
> De la Tauble Reonde estoit,
> Mout grant los en la cort avoit.
> De tant con il i ot esté,
> N'i ot chevalier plus amé;
> Et fu tant beax qu'en nule terre
> N'esteüst plus bel de lui querre.
> Mout estoit beax et prouz et genz,
> Se n'avoit pas .xxv. anz.
> Onques nuns hom de son aage
> Ne fu de greignor vasselage.
> Que diroie de ses bontez?
> Sor un destrier estoit montez:

Afublez d'un mantel hermin,
Vient galopant par le chemin. (ll. 77–96)

Afterwards the Queen mounted, accompanied by an attendant maiden – a king's daughter – who sat upon a white palfrey. A knight came spurring after them: his name was Erec. He was of the Round Table and had received great honour at court: as long as he had been there no one had been so highly praised, and he was so handsome that there was no need to seek a man of finer looks anywhere. He was very handsome and valiant and noble, and he was not yet twenty-five years old; never was any man of his youth so accomplished in knighthood. What should I say of his virtues? Mounted on a charger, he came galloping along the road; he was dressed in a fur-lined mantle.

Erec's lateness is often cited as one of the reasons as to why he does not participate in the hunt, and thus a propensity not to live up to the masculine values of court society.[3] In spite of all his good qualities, he appears last in the list of the courtiers mentioned and lags behind the hunting party, an apparent tardiness that allegedly foreshadows his later *recreantise*. However, the question here is as to whether his lateness might not mark the striking use of a minor transgression, marking him as a maker rather than follower of fashion and throwing qualities such as his beauty into sharp relief, even though critics have not uncommonly looked past Erec's entry to Chrétien's introduction of the peerless Enide.[4] Aristocratic societies seem in that regard torn as to whether the best way to stand out is to follow the rules or bend, perhaps even break, them: after all, clothes, to take one key status-marker in courtly societies, only 'make' the people who need making in the first place.[5] Erec's arrival thus raises a similar question: to arrive on time is to be functionally 'invisible' or 'silent', whereas in arriving late, he draws attention to himself. Maybe such was precisely the point given that the passage emphasises the capacity of his beauty – clearly a key plank in his suitability as a future monarch – to disrupt the collective's attention, to produce 'distentions' (*distentiones*) of both time and thought (*temporis et animorum*).[6] This experience of beauty as temporal suspension is apparent as Erec catches up on the royal party, the narrator filling out the 'camera-movement' by telling us both about our hero's appearance and the impression he has made at court, colluding with Erec's seeming disturbance of the structures of court behaviour, a transgression merely providing a further pretext to advertise himself and affirm that the court's time belongs to him.

Part of Erec's 'beauty' is thus his capacity to deploy the resources he has – both physical and material – to spectacular effect. The sense of suspension is therefore also marked in Chrétien's sighing admission of defeat, the self-interrupting, quasi-parenthetical rhetorical question ('que diroie de ses bontez?' l. 93) introducing his comments on Erec's garb and equipment, the waves of seduction breaking over us again and again. Although the term 'bontez' is generally taken to designate personal qualities (Carroll: 'What shall I say about his qualities?'; Fritz: 'Que dirais-je de ses qualités?'), Chrétien then proceeds to describe his clothes, which may suggest a less abstract and more material sense. Accordingly, as with Hincmar's use of the term *bonitas*, 'bontez' could also encompass the outward manifestation of his *biens*, which is to say his actual goods and wealth, then implying an assessment of his discrimination and fashion sense as a barometer of his use of his wealth. We can also find support for this split in and multiplication of the senses of beauty in the love that Erec elicits. As I noted earlier, this is both indicative of the strength of personal bond he is capable of creating with his peers and superiors and also the 'love' in the sense of *amicitia* that will be the basis of his future authority and diplomatic power.[7]

Questions of the future are of paramount importance here: to be able to suspend the present is to lay claim to time – especially the future. However, the sheer purity of impression here – foregrounded in Chrétien's introduction both of his eponymous hero and, later, of Enide – begins with the beauty of face that is the root manifestation of charisma, or, as the sociologist Georg Simmel puts it, the most 'theoretical':

> The face brings about a situation in which a person is already being understood from his or her appearance, and not first from their actions. The face, viewed as an organ of expression is, as it were, of a completely theoretical nature. It does not *act*, like the hand, the foot or the entire body, it never supports the inner practical behaviour of people, but rather it only *tells* others about it.[8]

Insofar as it merely tells or promises, the worth which the face betokens appears as a form of unsecured credit, it implies a sort of historical suspension, a sigh, which it implicitly claims it will resolve.

Chrétien's is not the only work in which we see male beauty cause time to stand still, a suspension creating problems further along the line, as we can see from the mid thirteenth-century chanson de geste, *Anseïs de Carthage*:

> Tout le resgardent, Alemant et Frison,
> Dist l'uns a l'autre (de coi parleroit on?)
> 'Chis ne fu fais se pour esgarder non.' (*Anseïs de Carthage*, ll. 86–8)
>
> Everyone was looking at him, the Germans and the Frisians. They said to one another – and what else would they talk about? – 'Surely he was just made to be looked at.' (my trans.)

Again, the court catches its collective breath. What were we talking about? You know, I don't remember. In a text that – through explicit reference to performances and readings of works such as *Graelent* as courtly entertainment, through the treatment of desire and of the casuistry of love, as well as through a plethora of descriptive motifs – shows clear romance influence, it is tempting to wonder to what extent the introduction of Anseïs marks a debt to works like *Erec et Enide*. Here, Anseïs's youthful beauty is the quality that seals his acclamation as the king of Spain following Charlemagne's return to France, the poem then exploring the extent to which the promise it contains is fulfilled.[9] However, what is also examined, even though the events that follow are in large part the result of his own errors, is the extent to which that 'first impression' burdens him with an albatross-like expectation that he can only disappoint in the harsh realities of war: held back for a moment, the flood smashes down on him with greater violence as he is driven across Spain city by city in an interminable series of sieges. In the case of Anseïs, the theory seems to weigh down the practice in a disabling manner: the ugly realities of political life in *Reconquista* Spain will bring Charlemagne back to help but then crucially chastise his young, beautiful protégé. The events that follow on from his rapturous acclamation reveal royal duty to be a much less simple matter than royal beauty.

That beauty is both a source of promise and disappointment is made clearly apparent in other medieval sources. Walter Map's *The Courtier's Trifles* presents the Young King – like Erec, a man of charm and manifold accomplishments – as offering the promise of Absalom:

> [...] vir nove adinvenciones in armis, qui miliciam fere *sopitam excitavit* et *ad summum* usque perduxit. Eius possumus *virtutes*, qui eum vidimus ipsius amici et familiares, et *gracias* describere. *Speciosus erat pre ceteris statura et facie, beatissimus eloquencia et affibilitate, hominum amore gracia et favore felicissimus, persuasione in tantum efficax* ut fere omnes patris sui fideles in ipsum insurgere fefellerit. Absalon eum, si non maior hic vero fuit, comparare possis. (*The Courtier's Trifles*, dist. 4, § 1, pp. 280–1 in edition, my emphasis)

> [...] A man fruitful of new devices in war, who roused chivalry from *something like slumber*, and raised it *to the height*. We who saw him as friends and intimates are in a position to tell of his *grace and manly gifts*. *He was fairer than the children of men in stature and in face, richly endowed with eloquence and charm of address, blest with the love and favour of his fellow men*, so powerful to persuade that he beguiled almost all his father's liegemen to turn against him. You might liken him to Absalom if indeed he was not superior to Absalom.

The general point here is how neatly Walter turns the evocation of charm into a tale of bitter disappointment. However, more narrowly, were a later date for *Erec et Enide* to gain greater acceptance, the prominence that Chrétien gives to Erec's graces could read as a potentially disquieting echo of descriptions of the Young King.[10] That said, this passage raises a particular problem: as Christopher Brooke points out, although the bulk of Walter's ragbag text is probably datable to 1181–1182, some passages – including this one, with its obituary-like tone – may have been added as late as 1191, well after the death of the Young King in 1183. This would make for some very moveable goalposts with regard to *Erec et Enide*. Of course, there are other possibilities here that do not require us to consider such a case exclusively. Chrétien's description is larded with the generalities of praise poetry, topoi also present in soured form in Walter's retrospective evocation. It is not impossible that his description of Henry echoes romance celebrations of chivalry and its virtues.

129

However, Walter's perspective on the present can be hard to gauge. Although elsewhere a defender of *modernitas* in the face of an oppressive cult of the ancients, his comments on the 'barbarousness' of contemporary *mores* and poetry following his description of Henry (see dist. 4, § 2, pp. 282–9) read as a dystopic, Lucanian take on things new – whether generations, courtly ways or literary production: 'the times deserve such poets' ('Talium tempora sunt poetarum.' dist. 4, § 2, pp. 286–7).[11] One side thought of which we can be reasonably sure is that in any event, there might well have been courtiers in Plantagenet or Champenois circles for whom *Erec et Enide* would have seemed a much darker text after 1180.

The 'promise' of Chrétien's evocation also extends in other directions, a possible untold story here being of a missed encounter between Erec and an unnamed (and critically neglected) handmaiden.[12] Young women were sent to court in the hope of making advantageous matches, with the Queen – head of the part of the household that received these newcomers – acting in the role of match-maker. The status of the maiden is clearly significant: 'pucele estoit, fille de roi' (l. 79). At a court where, as Gauvain commented earlier, for every fair lady there was a handsome knight ready to fight for her beauty (ll. 55–9), such a personal advertisement rings out clearly enough: 'King's daughter, maiden, great sense of decorum, seeks...'. Indeed, *Cligés* presents precisely that scenario, the Queen's maiden companion, Soredamors, conveniently introduced as the obvious partner for the new court favourite, Alexander. In terms of both birth and social connection, she is a court insider ostensibly far more Erec's equal than Enide; like Enide (but unlike Soredamors), she is unnamed at this point in time. Moreover, if – in her guise as royal *entremetteuse* – Guinevere engineered the encounter, it may have been envisaged as a solution to the hunt of the White Stag: since Erec has just been introduced as the most excellent of all the knights at court, one might well suppose that his chosen love would be the beauty about whom all others would agree.

But – crucially – at this point the text is silent and makes no explicit comment. This gives rise to a certain amount of critical debate as to whether Erec's presence here is the result of accident or design.[13] Maddox argues we are to see him as originally having intended to catch up with the King's hunting party, but having been left behind on his slower mount.[14] Possibly, but Erec choosing the wrong horse is about as likely as some young, hawkish corporate counterpart choosing the wrong tie. Then again, as Reto Bezzola points out, he may be ineligible to participate: 'il n'avait pas d'amie, comment aurait-il pu honorer la coutume?'.[15] In either event, accompanying Guinevere presents its own opportunities.[16] As that later observer of French court life, the Duc de Saint-Simon, was to comment, in this milieu knowing how to sieze the moment is all.[17] Indeed, Erec's greeting to the Queen – 'Je ne ving ci por autre afaire /Fors por vos compaignie faire' (ll. 109–10) – either keeps any other designs concealed or affects a deliberate casualness in his arrival on the scene at this point. Although the hunt could potentially be a place to distinguish himself or bond socially with the King, business can still be done with the Queen who controls access to the women at court. Unlike Actaeon's encounter with Diana and her maidens, the picture is perhaps then that of a young noble finding himself in – at the very least – *not* the wrong place at the wrong time, and demonstrating a certain suave opportunism spiced with the most perfect smirk of *naturel* ('What a delightful coincidence! There you are, and here I am.'). This is meant to look like an accident. Whether it really is one is another question.

The divorce between word and intention is indicative of, and may well respond to, other gaps and concealments in the text. If, as Jane Burns comments, the great silence of this work, and indeed of much of vernacular romance, is the crudely direct evocation of sexual desire and activity – apparent in accumulated echoes of the syllable designating the obscure object of romance desire, *le con* (so, *le con-te*, *con-ter* and so forth) – then Erec is clearly here for something he is courtly enough not to put in so many words, an end to which he does not intend to proceed directly. Moreover, he marks himself as courtly precisely insofar as he carefully conceals – to recall the sexual subtext of Shakespeare's title – the 'much ado about nothing', the great (but normally socially invisible) activity brought to bear in the pursuit of the object Burns names.[18] Indeed, the next time the poem presents Erec, the Queen and a 'pucele' together (i.e. at Erec's wedding), then the focal point will be precisely that. Thus, although it does not feature as explicitly on the agenda at this point as it will later, sex may indeed be the 'autre afaire' which Erec denies is on the agenda.

Erec's presence and his self-presentation are thus, I would suggest, not marks of laxness or self-indulgence, but rather his part in a formalised game of seduction, a ritual carried out on the social stage, but still – and, indeed, perhaps because of that – charged with a rippling undercurrent of desire:

> La roÿne Guenievre estoit
> Ou bois, qui les chiens escoutoit,
> Lez li Erec et *sa pucele*
> Qui mout estoit cortoise et bele. (ll. 125–8, my emphasis)

> Queen Guinevere was in the woods listening to the dogs; beside her was Erec and her maiden, who was extremely courtly and beautiful.

Erec et '*sa pucele*': whose maiden exactly? It is more than possible to read the ambiguity of the possessive pronoun in l. 127 as a narratorial joke at Erec's expense, a sort of sly, playful insinuation. However, in terms of the syntactic organisation, this 'pucele' is presumably the Queen's rather than Erec's, just as in l. 151 and l. 158, 'sa pucele' is the maiden belonging to the knight Yder. The shifting sense of this phrase fits suspiciously with other details. While the reduction of the hunt to a background noise raises the question of which scene should be regarded as the main event, its persistence in the collective music at this point in space and time has its own dramatic importance. The possible allusion to Ovidian hunt-scenes, in which the paths that might allow one to lose or trap the prey become a key metaphor for narrative directness and indirectness, is arguably a sign that 'the hounds' – in the form of both courtiers and, possibly, readers – have been put off the scent. By means of a displacement of attention through the virile business of the chase, the Queen has the opportunity to head the main party off at the pass.[19] However, this does not mean that the hunt is excluded from her purposes, her carefully contrived show of preoccupation with the distant noise indicating that, like the rest of the court, her attention is elsewhere for the moment, tactfully leaving space for another party to take the initiative.

However, what breaks the suspense is not what the Queen perhaps expected: another party – another knight, accompanied by a maiden and a dwarf – ambles into view.[20] Yet, although this intrusion initially queers the mood of the moment, it is rapidly assimilated as offering its own possibilities:

> La roÿne Guenievre voit
> Le chevalier bel et adroit,
> Et de sa pucele et de lui
> Vuet savoir que il sont andui.
> Sa pucele commande aler
> Isnelement a lui parler:
> 'Damoisele', fait la roÿne,
> 'Cel chevalier qui la chemine
> Alez dire qu'il viegne a moi,
> Et s'amaint sa pucele o soi.'
> La pucele va a l'ambleüre,
> Vers le chevalier a droiture. (ll. 149–60)

> Queen Guinevere saw the handsome and elegant knight, and she wanted to know who they were, he and his maiden. She told the maiden to go quickly to speak to him. 'Damsel', said the Queen, 'go and tell that knight riding there to come to me and bring his maiden with him.' The maiden set off at an amble straight towards the knight.

Once again, Chrétien's description emphasises the knight's beauty – again not just of physical appearance, but also of deportment: 'bel *et adroit*' (l. 150, my emphasis). However, Guinevere's admiration of the knight is not simply desire or a giddy, beguiled admiration. Indeed, her 'inspection' of the new arrival may raise questions about the point(s) of view from which Erec's entry and initial description was observed. Guinevere's view is that of the experienced court dame, the *pucele's* that of a potential partner, the text possibly braiding separate strands of savvy appreciation and raw desire.

This mix of perspective continues in a vision of calculation and effect not unlike that found in a chess game.[21] The Queen does not answer Yder with a knight's move, except in the indirectness of her thinking: in response to his spectacular entrance, she sends her maid. Guinevere's actual instruction is to proceed 'isnelement', which, obediently enough, the maid does, moving 'a droiture'. However,

133

the character of her motion is the leisurely catwalk saunter of 'a l'ambleüre' denotes an unhurried pace whose gentle sashay is the stereotypical allure of such characters as Chaucer's Wife of Bath ('Upon an amblere esily she sat', *General Prologue*, l. 469), a lilting, *Girl from Ipanema*, come-hither seductiveness one of whose aims is to lure the knight to join the royal party.[22] Thus, the disjuncture between the Queen's instruction and the maid's motion does not mark unwillingness (as in the maid sent to entertain the knight in *Le Chevalier qui fist parler les cons*), but rather an understanding of courtly ways. Instructed to set about something post haste, she rightly intuits that the appropriate thing is to proceed according to her status and in accordance with the dictum, *festina lente* – 'Hurry slowly'. Her motion thus answers the knight's beauty, advertising the status and *savoir-faire* of the Arthurian court. However, her message also has its internal addressees, her performance marking her out to both Erec and the Queen as Erec's potential equal in her note-perfect performance of courtly *oisiveté*.

What we see here is a feminised version of what Jeffrey Cohen brilliantly describes as the 'becoming animal' of chivalry, the incorporation of the horse into knightly identity to the point of creating a single weapon.[23] As Cohen points out, the knight appears as a satyr-like hybrid, the horse an extension of himself, assimilated prosthetically into his body image to a degree where he commands the creature as he would his own limbs. However, what Cohen's reading also underscores is the erotology of the relation of knight to horse. As Isidore of Seville comments:

> The spiritedness of horses is great. They exult in battlefields; they sniff the combat; they are excited to the fight by the sound of a trumpet. [...] They are miserable when conquered and delighted when they have won. They recognise their enemies in battle to such an extent that they go for their adversaries with a bite.[24]

Obviously there is an element of transposition and anthropomorphism here, a sort of feedback circuit of the passions: the horse manifests the character of the knight, the knight that of the horse. While Isidore emphasised spirit and aggressivity, representations of equine energy also foreground the sexual: in a small corner of the Bayeux tapestry that is perhaps forever Robert Mapplethorpe's, William the Conqueror's charger sports a not very discreet erection.[25] Augustine, for whom male sexual arousal was a 'bestial movement', might have seen this as an allegory of the fundamental depravity of human sexual desire.[26]

Romance discourses about gender and sexuality locate themselves precisely at this fork in the road. Indeed, a potentially unhallowed mix queers the scene here, intimations of physical arousal, noisy animal delirium and perverse voyeurism forming the background chatter and noise of other texts, key here a skeleton in the Plantagenet family closet: the *Roman d'Eneas*. As Simon Gaunt comments, the Old French reworking can be read as an account of the nature of object choice, offering a policing critique of the sexual mores depicted in Virgil.[27] Central here is the diatribe by Lavine's mother against Eneas:

> 'S'il lo pooit par toi atraire,
> Nel troveroit ja si estrange
> Qu'il ne feïst asez tel change
> Que il feïst son bon de toi
> Por ce qu'il sofrist de soi;
> Bien lairoit sor toi monter,
> S'il repuet sor lui troter;
> Il n'aime pas poil de conin.' (*Roman d'Eneas*, ll. 8588–95)

> 'If he could procure him through you, he would not find it so strange to do a deal, whereby he [the lover] would have his way with you because he [Eneas] was allowed to have him; he would let him mount you if he could ride behind: he does not like rabbit hair [i.e. pussy].' (trans. by Gaunt)

Assimilating sodomy to bestial copulation is part of a stock-in-trade of masculine insult attested in the sorts of slander discussed by Joyce Salisbury, notably from the Old Norse text, 'Ale-Hood':

> You didn't notice the fat stallion Steingrim had till it was up your backside. That skinny mare you were on faltered under you [...] and I've never been able to make up my mind whether it was you or the mare that got it. Everybody could see how long you were stuck there, the stallion's legs had got such a grip on your cloak.[28]

Reflective of wider traditions of homophobic abuse, the terms chosen by Lavine's mother are clearly significant: Eneas is painted as a grotesque, satyr-like travesty of a knight and a man, incapable of understanding the proper grammar of relations between men or between men and beasts. Eneas's *chevalerie*, his 'horse-manship', is debased by a fundamental and obscene confusion of categories: instead of 'manning' the horse, he 'horses' the man. Worse still, her account of the Sadean tableau she paints for her daughter, with its emphasis on permutation and the swapping of mounts, indicates that this is not simply an inversion, but rather that for Eneas there is no difference between his performance on a horse and on another man. Given the importance of the *Roman d'Eneas* as a pre-history of chivalric values associated with the court of Henry II, the suggestion that Eneas's knightly strivings spring from an animal articulation of same-sex affection undercuts the entire sense of the historical mission of chivalry. Lavine's mother effectively sketches a counter-history of the line of men that will be engendered by this ur-stallion of European lordship.[29] This crossroads moment is then vital to the emphasis the poem places on fixing Eneas's lawful heterosexuality, lest the Imaginary archetype unleashed create nothing more than a great line of lords linked in a parody of what Zrinka Stahuljak refers to as the 'bloodless genealogy' by something less lofty than descent and shared ideals. If Erec is like Eneas, then, as in the original slander, the tableau here is that Erec would be indifferent as to whether his horse 'mounts' (*monter sor*, l. 8593), in the sexual sense, the palfrey *or the maid*, just as he himself would be as to whether he mounts the maid *or his own horse*. However, what is not clear at this point is whether we have before us a coded but slanderous imputation or merely the carnivalesque horseplay observed in the collective *Vorlust* of wedding preparations.

Our understanding of the scene is not helped either by its other theme of 'becoming palfrey', the maiden's command of dressage allowing her to replicate mounted an allure that would otherwise have been restricted to the corridors of the palace. Of course, she makes it look perfectly natural.[30] However, this air of nonchalance only serves to counterpoint the fundamental ambiguity of Chrétien's presentation of the scene: we could be witness to understated courtly flirting or an encounter whose subtexts are rather more lurid and transgressive. The change in *dramatis personae* from two men and a woman – as in the *Roman d'Eneas* – to two women and a man potentially does little to help matters. As with the confusions of the *Eneas*, so here we have an element of contaminatory contact between discrete areas of experience in the possibly perversely voyeuristic dimension of Guinevere's behaviour. That contact may also operate diachronically, the encounter here either hinting at some budding desire or instead foreshadowing an immoderate, bestial abandon. Indeed, any animal presence can appear problematic in this regard, the signs of unregulated impulse: as Albertus Magnus comments, human sexual behaviour is 'discreet, rational, prudent and bashful', in contrast with animals, who 'bray and holler greatly as if in a fury' ('multum canunt et clamant quasi furiosa'), Albert singling out cockerels and horses in this regard.[31] What we are therefore invited to consider is that either this particular hypothetical wedding night would owe its sexual decorum to a perverse projection of bestial *jouissance* onto stallion and palfrey, or whether the horse is then the symbol of an unregulated abandon. Indeed, one might wonder therefore what exactly was meant by Chrétien's description of Enide as being 'made more bold by love' on her wedding night. After all, the position that is sketched out seems to offer problems on either hand: either she endures the ordeal with patience or we are to understand that her desire and curiosity overcome fear and pain leaving her open to suspicion of a potentially culpable sensuality, a participation in the *luxuria* of sexual pleasure that consisted in submitting to the usurpation of rationality by what Peter the Lombard described as the 'despot ['tyrannus'] in our members', the 'law of the flesh' ('lex carnis') that is desire.[32]

For both Lavine's mother and Chrétien to target this moment through such a slander is to fragment, interrupt and subvert a widely appropriated grammar of genealogy in a way that was then to sow anxieties for Arthurian romance, evident in the recurring emphasis on interruption in both lineage and communication highlighted by Donald Maddox.[33] But then, maybe the 'bloodlessness' of the genealogy is less of a disadvantage. Literal ideas of connection expressed through blood may foreground authentic continuity and vitality. However, such connections are also supremely vulnerable to the sowing of doubt. Moreover, although later romances of the 'fair unknown' model – such as *Le Bel inconnu* and *Le Conte du graal* – teach the lesson that blood will out in spite of the suppression of explicit knowledge of origins in the social sphere, this can then be seen as a falling back on biology rather than culture as a vector or repository of knowledge and continuity. This vision of the wasteland, in which not only the location and purpose of the Grail but also Perceval's identity are mysteries, reflects a world in which metaphorical discourses of kinship are bereft of currency once their foundation, the certainty of genuine genealogical continuity, has been supplanted and devalued through excessive reliance on the 'next best thing'. But then the problem is revealed through the crisis of collective knowledge as 'bloodless'. It is here that the question of knowledge and recognition become paramount: the ideal of literal genealogy restates itself through the reiteration of the self-same. For all Alan of Lille compares coïtus and lineal descent to grammar and knowledge, the two spheres are not the same: dissonance, contradiction and reordering may beget knowledge that is not just a perverse act or its issue in the form of a 'sport' or *jocus*. Thus, to engage in what Alan refers to as the 'true script of Venus' is to write in the sense that all 'proper' writing, as Jacques Derrida puts it, 'repeat[s] without knowing'.[34] Against this, in *Erec et Enide*, the potential for subversive overdetermination in the encounter in the forest places the accent on knowledge, making discontinuity fundamental to the scene, its remembering of the *Eneas* less an invention or begetting than a reshaping founded in choice even if the senses that haunt that scene are a source of *angoisse*.[35]

Of course, another interesting consideration here is that insofar as this scene effectively opens the parenthesis of an intimate encounter – a moment that will only be closed with Erec and Enide's wedding night – the evocation of the *Roman d'Eneas* has a certain relevance. Just as Eneas would have been prepared to use Lavine as a female version of a 'teaser' (in animal husbandry, 'an inferior stallion or ram used to excite mares or ewes', OED) to attract and excite other men, so here Erec is perhaps initially beguiled by a horsewoman who is not Enide and finds himself constrained by circumstances to change mounts, a theme that will reappear in his dealings with the Count's niece in Laluth. In that sense, the slanderous portrait of Eneas fits him more closely than might have appeared. This means that the entirety of what is to follow in the *premiers vers* falls under the banner of Freud's early modelling of anxiety as undischarged affect, especially that which is the 'dissatisfaction' arising from 'unsatisfactory discharges' such as through masturbation or *coïtus interruptus*.[36] Freud's narrative here of course appears as a modern descendant of medieval accounts of sexual regulation. Yet, at the same time, what it reveals is the measure of anxiety that subtends this scene as a break in the closed but vulnerable cycle of a perversely extended *Vorlust* that continues in pregnant anticipation.

But then the maid encounters the dwarf:

La damoisele avant s'est traite,
Passer vuet outre, a force faite,
Car le nain ot a grant despit
Por ce qu'ele le vit petit. (ll. 175–8)

The maiden moved forward, intending to push her way past. She felt great contempt for the dwarf because she saw how little he was.

Although she has mastered the courtly game in terms of adopting an appropriate demeanour in going about her duties, the next move is more taxing: the force of the Queen's instruction re-emerges when her progress is blocked by the dwarf, causing her to push on without thinking through the next few moves, reckoning that a certain *hauteur* would be all that would be required to deal with her importunate opponent. Nonetheless, sometimes an obstacle is just an obstacle: the dwarf will not be moved.

When her maiden returns injured and in tears, Guinevere settles any potentially open issue of appropriation, presenting the treatment of '*ma* pucele' (l. 196, my emphasis) as an affront to herself in what appears as a rehearsal of Arthur's desperate plea for counsel to Gauvain. However, just as Gauvain will find himself stumped for a different answer, Erec is ordered to replay the same scene again, and indeed can do little different. Key elements of the Queen's instructions, although artfully framed, remain basically constant (ll. 201–04 cp. with ll. 155–8). Her lament for the wrong done to her maiden (ll. 195–200) serves as a form of *captatio benevolentiae*, with the repeated interpellation 'Beax amis Erec' (l. 201 cp. l. 195) an appeal to his sense of decorum and his capacity for action, both of which may provide the basis for a fairer outcome. Although Burgess wonders whether Erec should have intervened on his own initiative rather than wait to be asked, the Queen's complaint regarding the wrong done to her in the body of her maiden alludes to shared values and the diplomatic bonds of *amicitia*.[37] For all this incident takes place in the wild space of the forest, it emphasises the formalities of cooperation and duty, civilising ideals undercut by the attack on the maiden and whose reaffirmation begins with the Queen's insistence on due protocol. Erec's subordinate status is carefully underscored by her request: Yder will answer to the Queen rather than to Erec himself. Any licence Erec has in this situation is, as with the maiden, in the area of supplementary effect: this is the same message to some extent, but it is now to be delivered in more emphatic form. Just as the maiden's ambling approach represented one possible embellishment, Erec's more forceful delivery is underscored by his spurring of his horse:

> Erec cele part *esperone*,
> Des *esperons* au cheval done,
> Vers le chevalier *point* tot droit.' (ll. 205–08, my emphasis)
>
> Erec spurred off, urging his horse on, and rode straight towards the knight.

The insistent accumulation of 'esperonne'/ 'esperons'/ 'point' represents everything Erec has to add by way of ornamentation to Guinevere's message. The maiden's approach having initially been that of beauty and *amitié*, Erec's is a carefully advertised show of force. Yet, although Erec's behaviour is like that of the maiden in that both young courtiers look to act in accordance with the dictates of beauty, the *savoir-faire* that governs court life, things are about to turn rather ugly. Instead of leading to some sort of exchange of challenges, Erec's picture-perfect approach bogs down in a laughably undignified pantomime 'Oh yes I will!', 'Oh no you won't!' argument before the final sting of the lash. Indeed, as Erec himself comments slightly further on, 'or est plus lait' (l. 234).

Critical censure of Erec at this point not uncommonly hinges on the fact that he is not armed and thus not in a position to defend the

Queen's honour there and then.[38] Although he is riding a warhorse rather than a hunter, he is not unprepared for the wider ritual and spectacle of the hunt in terms of his dress: a hunt may be a training for war, but it is not war. Illustrations of deer hunting, such as those found in Gaston Fébus's lavishly illuminated *Livre de la chasse*, do not show the nobles taking part clad in full battle armour.[39] Criticism of Erec founded on the assumption that the courtiers participating in the hunt, riding 'chaceors' (l. 74) and armed with bows and arrows (l. 76) are either better or even as well prepared for the sort of encounter the young knight faces may therefore be misplaced.[40] Indeed, the dress-code combination of his mount – the very embodiment and symbol of chivalric masculinity – and his sword arguably reflect his intentions for the day: he is here to put on an appropriate degree of elegant show, playing his part by providing fitting company for the ladies.

Moreover, to emphasise, implicitly or otherwise, the contrast with Yder's apparel is to miss the fortuitous nature of the encounter between the two parties. After all, what grounds are there for assuming that armour is the default dress code for knights venturing forth from court? Yder is on his way to a tournament, after all, and is thus not entirely or even very much like the robber knights whom Erec encounters later. Consequently, any arguments for an error of judgement on Erec's part (or even a more general presumption by the court as a whole that the space in which they move is entirely controlled and domesticated) would have to take into account the fact that Yder's dress is in its own way ceremonial rather than a mark of a sensible adequation to the demands created by the lawlessness of the outside world. Equally, although Bezzola describes Yder and his party as 'symbolic', which is to say the manifestation of some archetypal figure, we might also understand their role more in terms of the Lacanian Imaginary. Thus, Yder enters as an actor already 'in character' (so, identifying with his role) as part of Laluth's own ritual theatre, a participant in a ritual he is 'more or less conscious' rather than magically or irrevocably trapped in what Marcus Bull might term some kind of 'Mock *Matière de Bretagne*'.[41] The problem is that they have accidentally wandered into the ritually public bedroom of the Arthurian court. And indeed, this is precisely the point: in the context of the hunt the forest has been transformed into a quasi-palatial space, with the main body of knights engaged in the public business of the chase, and this small group, by contrast, closeted away in a privvy chamber but still the object of a certain collective attention.

Moreover, although Erec might have been asked to produce a fairer show, to redress the injustice of this spectacle, his performance is in large part entailed by earlier circumstances. The key error is arguably the maiden's, acting without thinking out the next move or two. Chrétien gives us two hints as to the sort of violence she deploys. First there is the literal mention of 'force' (l. 176), and then the comment on her contempt for the dwarf. Of course, we were warned in the very first lines of the prologue about the dangers of thoughtless shows of *despit*, although clearly not everyone was paying attention. In her thoughtless contempt, the maiden fails to give sufficient consideration, to tailor her actions to the circumstances. For a start, if Erec was not armed, then what we might be being invited to weigh up from a strategic point of view is whether the young woman had any business deploying violence without considering whether she could look to him to back her up. The maiden is thus guilty of a 'folie' that Erec subsequently avoids (l. 231), and thereby in large part the author of damage done both to his reputation and the Queen's.

Part of the ugliness of the scene lies in its mechanistic compounding of the offence done to the Queen. Erec's attempt is the act of a man caught in a machine: he repeats the mission with the same end in view, himself knowing full well that, although he has a sword, he is not really equipped to fare any better than the maiden had done. Thus, from a certain point of view, the problem lies in the fact that the tales of the maiden and Erec are *insufficiently dissimilar*, that he and she at this point are too (although not entirely) equal in disgrace and that there has been no satisfactory progression. The compensatory *Steigerung* then occurs in his farewell speech to the Queen (ll. 234–71) in which he outlines his plan, undertaking to produce a fairer tale or die trying. The point is that the consequences of the maiden's error cannot be concealed, an impossibility that can be contrasted with the comparatively minor issue of Erec being possibly late for the hunt, at which point he was more than able not merely to save face but indeed enhance his 'beauty' by putting a positive spin on circumstances. Erec has been harmed not only because he realises he is unable to act decisively in this situation to resolve the issue, and so is made to look ill-prepared faced with a conflict that could have been avoided. A greater harm lies in the fact that he has been constrained to admit as much himself in a discursive space that is now effectively public, addressing a potential disgrace in which he will have to answer the reproaches of his peers ('Mais nuns nou me doit reprochier, /Que trestoz desarmez estoie.' ll. 238–9). Burgess argues that, in the light of Erec's later demonstrations of exemplary valour against seemingly impossible odds, we might see him here as having acted too cautiously.[42] However, the counter-argument here is that his later exploits might equally suggest his judgement here was based on an informed risk-assessment.

The neglected role played by the Queen's maid problematises many of the assumptions that have been made about opposition in this part of the narrative. After all, the maid, as the daughter of a king, is as much a 'pucele de grant estre' (l. 144) as the one accompanying Yder. If this is the case, then there is every reason to understand Chrétien's presentation of the party accompanying Yder as something more than, as Bezzola argues, a simple 'symbolic' mirror image of the party accompanying the Queen in which Yder's maiden is reduced to a figure of 'orgueil'.[43] After all, it was the Queen's maiden who showed 'despit'. Bearing this in mind, Chrétien's conception of opposition and reflection thereby takes on a more dialogical character. Indeed, it is tempting here to term his presentation of the situation as more 'human' – no more woodenly 'symbolic' than it will be at Laluth. In spite of the otherworldly air of the encounter, the 'pucele de grant estre' is no more a monster than Enide is a fairy, and indeed, in her anguished concern for the safety of her lover, will become Enide's exact double at the Sparrow-Hawk contest.[44] As a consequence, what emerges is that, although she is also to be lamented, the Queen's maiden is perhaps no less a candidate for the title of 'monster' – if there actually is one in a narrative where the convivial reception of Yder at court (ll. 1141–1239) is contrasted with the defeat of the far less tractable Morholt (ll. 1245–53). The difference between all these maidens is then not so much how they appear, but how they act, a consideration that has considerable implications for our understanding of the role played by the Count's niece (see below).

Of course, the problem is that now Yder has unknowingly put a spanner in the works: the maiden's lack of sense and failure here to negotiate the scene as she should have done possibly disqualifies her as a potential partner for the excellent Erec, removing her from further appearances in a manner possibly more to do with jockeying for position than simply a general silencing of the feminine in the text, as Jane Burns argues.[45] There is a certain cruelty of fate here: sent into a situation requiring experience and understanding she clearly did not have, the maid ended up brutally punished for no more than being in over her head. Arguably, the fate of this young woman provides some clue as to the sorts of blurring Chrétien will play with in his text from here. In Kathryn Gravdal's analysis of the staging of rape in Chrétien's works, there is a striking emphasis on the ugliness of such scenes, most notably in the abduction and rape of Helen by the giant of Mont-Saint-Michel described by Wace. And indeed, a kind of 'laidure' has been done here: partly to Erec, as the Queen's subsequent account of the dwarf's actions makes clear ('dou nain felon et petit /Qui de la corgie [...] ot ferue tot ausiment /Erec ou vis mout laidement' ll. 326–30), and partly in the sense that the courtiers have been forced into a position of impotent witnesses, a scenario we will see traumatically repeated in the abduction of Cadoc of Tabriol. Although comparatively minor, the wounding of the maiden has a clearly sexualised quality, not merely in the sense that 'force' was done, but also that it happened under the eyes of third parties, who, like Chrétien's readers find themselves in the uncomfortable position of witnesses who are not sure if they are not also *voyeurs*. First, there is Erec, who observes the scene in its horror and is moved to act to avenge it, and to whom the most humiliating violence is done under the eyes of Yder, who observes both attacks callously and impassively. Third, there is the Queen, who sees in the scene the disfigured image of her own plans and desires, having handed over this maiden for a knight's enjoyment, although with events having had an outcome entirely different from that which she intended. Fourth, there is the maiden, who sees in her failure and Erec's injury the extinction of certain possibilities. In that sense, there is also a dialectical contrasting of this scene, not directly witnessed by the rest of the court with the king's more public discomfiture. The scene inevitably unfolds in momentary disarray. As the Queen clearly understands, all the King's horses and all the King's men – though within earshot – could not put this party together again, meaning any solution will come less than directly or speedily ('isnelement'). Erec's wound cannot be healed at once any more than Arthur can immediately call in the gratitude he is owed for his gifts and mastery of spectacle. The *laidure* done to Erec becomes the very form of suspension in the narrative. But then the 'ugliness' of cause is part of the point, without which there would have been no elegant resolution to the hunt for the White Stag. Chrétien's vision of the hunt thus provides an echo of Lucan's 'if it was by this alone [...] then we have no complaint'. Interestingly, the exclusion of an internally-generated solution to the hunt, a critique of the potentially quasi-endogamous aspect of courtly match-making re-emerges in the marriage politics of Laluth. As for the maiden, critics seem to have taken their cue from Erec, who as per Roland with Aude, does not think of her again. However, her apparent failure to make more of an impression may suggest she would not have been the one to resolve the crisis. That said, Erec could quite probably have affirmed her beauty through might, as we see from the outcome of the tournament at Danebroc. However, this would perhaps have been too explicit an assertion of dominance. The foundation of spectacle in some sort of genuine consensus binds Arthur's court to the quest for a suitable *bel objet*.

'Cicatricosa Facies': Erec Scarface

> Turbari memoria vel continuandi verba facultate destitui nusquam turpius, cum vitiosum prohoemium posit videri *cicatricosa facies*: et pessimus certe gubernator qui navem dum portu egreditur impegit. (*Institutio Oratoria*, book 4, chapter 1, 61, my emphasis)
>
> There is no place in speech where confusion of memory or loss of fluency is more shaming: a faulty prooemium is like a badly scarred face, and it is a bad pilot indeed who runs his ship aground while leaving harbour.

Obviously, the use of body imagery as a means of describing textual organisation, proportion and literary aesthetics is extremely common, Quintilian notably comparing a poor opening or prologue to a scarred face.[46] That Erec is marked early on clearly has resonance at a textual level. Just as in *Le Chevalier au lion*, Chrétien's prologue (ll. 1–42) is doubled or supplemented by the workmanlike but perhaps more pedestrianly formulaic *captatio benevolentiae* offered by Calogrenant (ll. 149–74), so the injuries inflicted on Erec mirror the 'scarring' of the poem's opening, with its *vilain* aspect (l. 1). Although the injuries done to Erec and the maiden are unjustly inflicted, they are not devoid of meaning, but rather part of a cultural inscription especially apparent in medieval systems of judicial punishment. The maiden's unwisely deployed show of force receives its reproof in that domain in the form of the lash, a vision seen in other works where the hand functions as the very embodiment of the capacity for action and violence. In the *Chanson de Roland*, the Saracens proudly boast that Roland's death will deprive Charlemagne of his right arm (ll. 596–7), only for Marsilie to then lose his own right hand and son in combat with Roland (ll. 1902–05), dying partly of that wound and partly of his rage and grief at the failure of his plan (ll. 3644–7). The maiden suffers a less extreme reproof, this time arguably in the form of a lesson: think again. Erec's failure is then entailed, so it is similar to the maiden's, but there is also progression in that he is struck in the face, a public, potentially permanent marking that compounds the 'laidure', the immediate physical damage and wrong done to the respective parties. What is perhaps evoked here are instances of shaming through facial mutilation and scarring in epic, such as the injury to William's nose in his duel with the pagan champion Corsolt in the *Couronnement de Louis*. Crucially, quick to salvage the moment with a quip as to how the scar will redound to his glory, William does not lose face, however: 'my nose has been shortened a little, but my name will be lengthened because of it' (ed. by Langlois, ll. 1157–60).[47] However, to say that the whipping they receive is 'written on the body' is to miss its force. Erec's face is not so much marked as *destroyed* or *dismembered* ('tot m'a le vis *depecié*' l. 236, my emphasis), his beauty now shattered like Arthur's body in *La Mort le roi Artu*. Unlightened by any such show of verve or zest, Erec's crude, stigmatic injury goes unanswered where his face had previously been the promise of justice, decorum and *savoir-faire*.

There is a key element of chiastic inversion in the distribution of injuries: the maid is wounded in the hand and Erec in the face. If men act and women appear, opposing masculine prowess to feminine beauty, then the *jeu parti* would ask us to consider whether the alternative scenario of the maiden disfigured and Erec impaired would have been better or worse. Although the outcome is not ideal, such a scenario would arguably have permanently destroyed the maiden's value as a marriage prospect and disabled Erec in the coming adventures. Instead, the *pucele* is given a salutary warning about reflection and action. Her physical beauty remains without question, but her intervention in the encounter with Yder's party was less than 'bel et adroit' in that it caused Erec and the Queen to lose face. One lesson we might take from this scene is then the sense that both the maid and the young knight have been acting somewhat outside the general repertoire of their gendered behaviours at court, testing out new skills in a milieu where men appear by acting and women act by appearing.

However, for all the incident is renarrated, neither Erec's wound or any mark of it are mentioned again. Why? Obviously, Erec's disfigurement reflects Arthur's marring announcement of the hunt, an event that will itself be smoothed and rationalised to eliminate the sting of potential shame Arthur brings on himself. Yet, if Arthur's debasement of himself in the announcement of the hunt is in some way essential to his political survival, then the public nature of such 'laidures', whether the wound Arthur inflicts on his own standing and the one inflicted by Yder on Erec's face, become reminders of the excessive and disfiguring aspects of collective life. Of course, the Arthurian tradition provides the most notable example of this in the form of the wound of the Fisher King. As Žižek comments, the centrality of that wound is neatly captured in Hans-Jürgen Syberberg's film version of Wagner's *Parsifal*, where Amfortas's wound is actually externalised and carried around on a pillow, much in the manner of the grail itself. The spectacle of the wounded king offers a key insight into the 'obscene' or 'feminine' nature of totalitarian power.[48] In that regard, although critics have gone so far as to describe

Erec's appearance as unmanly or even effeminate, one way of reading the wound he receives here is as a foreshadowing of the Fisher King's. Although Žižek's reading of Wagner relates to a very different cultural and political context from the vision Chrétien presents (see *Le Conte du graal*, ll. 3023–359), it is arguably possible to map the genesis of that tradition in Erec's disavowed wound, the mark by which Yder should have been able to recognise him. As we will see in Erec's no-holds-barred handling of his opponent in the Sparrow-Hawk contest, that wound is then arguably the mark of a capacity for violence and brutality ostensibly at odds with the fair face of justice and decorum he presented on his first appearance, his leisurely manner there the fair face of equanimity. Beauty here gives way to the *laidures* of disfigurement, disgrace and cruelty.

However, although Erec is positioned initially as passive bystander, his status will become that of agent, the savage *jouissance* apparent in the momentum and cruelty we will see systematically elaborated in later sections. The wound of enjoyment thus marks the charismatic king as the one who seeks to provoke anxiety in the Other. Erec's marred beauty presents the scar in the vision of royal charisma much in the manner of the anamorphic skull in Holbein's *The Ambassadors*. Lacan's reading of this painting is that the skull both disfigures and explains the picture. In the same way, Erec disfigured reminds us that royal beauty in the form of the exercise of charisma inevitably has its stain of ugliness and desire. This is the traumatic lesson whose truth will be necessarily passed over in silence in the remainder of the narrative. Interestingly, Jane Burns reads the reductions and omissions in subsequent accounts of the incident as a silencing of the disruptive feminine voice, a reassertion of a controlling masculine subjectivity.[49] Against this, it can be argued that the scene's mangling *laidure*, blazoned across Erec's face for all to see (except that no one mentions it), bears witness to a dark, uncomfortable open secret at the centre of court life, bearing the ugliness of his avenging will into the scenes to come.

Arthur's Masochistic Diversions

> Toute la cour est en émoi.[50]

Chrétien's warping play with what is 'before' and what is 'after' continues with the switch back to court, now in uproar. Just as Erec's humiliation by Yder's dwarf follows on from a scene subtended by a history of compromising secrets and associations, the vision of a group of courtiers surprised while engaged in the perversely voyeuristic contemplation of possible future couplings, so the scene that follows back in Arthur's court is potentially no less disturbing. Indeed, from a certain perspective, his initial, potentially calamitous decision furnishes the 'primal scene' of Arthurian self-destructiveness. The relatively brief interlude in which Arthur and his knights appear as no more than a distant commotion in the background of Erec's encounter with Guinevere only forestalls briefly the consequences foreseen by Gauvain. With dissent brewing, it seems as if Arthur has outdone even himself:

> 'Beax niés Gauvains, consoilliez m'en,
> Sauve m'onor et ma droiture,
> Que je n'ai de la noise cure.' (ll. 308–10)
>
> 'Dear nephew Gawain, advise me in this. Save my honour and rightful rule, for I do not care for discord.'

Instead of offering a neat solution to the problem of charismatic leadership, the King's enterprise teeters on the brink of failure. At least apparently dismayed, he calls on his chief magnates and counsellors to help pour oil on the troubled waters. The term 'noise' in particular has potentially disturbing resonances in that it is also the term used in the *Chanson de Roland* (l. 3842) by the traitor champion Pinabel, scornfully seeking to silence the hubbub following Thierri's limpidly brilliant and humane intervention in support of the beleaguered Emperor. There as here both desperate appeal and noise seem to mark the bankrupting of the economy of feudal kingship. Of course, the difference is that Pinabel's assertion is supported directly by threat of force, a dark energy threatening to supplant the emperor, whereas Arthur appears lost and uncertain even though his plea to Gauvain is made 'wisely' ('par sen', l. 307).[51] Yet, Arthur's turn to his nephew is in keeping with the economy of honour and status operating at the court: his advice rejected earlier, Gauvain is now called on to convene a privy council of the great and the good (ll. 311–20). However, whatever 'plan B' was here does not appear to bear fruit: the Queen returns with her news *before* the council reports (ll. 321–2). Her narrative of the injury done to her maid and to Erec, the conclusion of which repeats his boast to avenge his shame or to increase it (ll. 323–34), displaces attention away to the exterior and provides a useful breathing space.

There are thus several possible perspectives here, either from the point of view of our understanding of the narrative or the political structures Chrétien represents. One question here is whether we should see such a seemingly fortuitous encounter of the two parts of the Arthurian household as mere coincidence:

> Tant ont la parole tenue
> Que la roÿne i est venue. (ll. 321–2)
>
> Discussion went on and on until finally the Queen arrived.

The 'tant' is all: does this mean Gauvain and his cronies rack their brains and debate for so long that the Queen returns in the meantime or that the debate is sustained with a view to buying the Queen's party more time? If the latter, then further suspicions emerge in retrospect: for a start, Erec's parting address to the Queen (ll. 234–71), carefully insistent on certain details, takes on a different possible significance. Both the specification of three days – perhaps more than the simple forward planning of follow-fight-return – and the careful dramatic and rhetorical shape of his narrative become part of a 'live-fire' elaboration of whatever collusive game had been played between the two of them earlier. If the goal of the Hunt was to distract the court while a royal marriage was arranged, that plan has now gone awry, with the possibility that the danger latent in court ritual might be catastrophically released. If we are invited to suspect Erec knew all along such was the nature of the game, then he also understands the danger facing Arthur if no surprise resolution can be produced from the royal hat. With that in mind, the young prince substitutes another tale, underwriting it with the spectacularly compelling possibility of his own destruction. Making the Queen his messenger, he improvises for her a 'pilot prologue' she can bring back to the court. While this may seem like mixture of fanciful over-reading and conspiracy theory, subsequent developments may add weight to the argument.

Another perspective – which abstracts for now any behind-the-scenes dealing – may reveal the method in Arthur's apparent madness: the economic underpinnings of his charismatic leadership and the place of the darker side of collective fantasy in it. Here Chrétien pairs the aristocratic economy of gift (bankrolled by previous conquests that have happened 'off-stage') with one of collective regard. Both of these are in effect predicated on reward for past merit and on future obligation, leaving the present subject to a steady economic haemorrhaging at either the psychic or material level. However, too facile a solution might not have the binding, compelling force necessary: for the hunt to succeed as economic subterfuge and redress the imbalance inherent in charismatic authority, the King must assert his place as the chief manipulator of the collective fantasy life of the court even at the price of appearing as an object of pity or bafflement. It is this fantasy dimension that is fundamental to the dual appearance of events at court: Chrétien's sophisticated observation of the court's dependence on the managing of 'personal magic' suggests that only the whiff of real danger can appease an audience discerning and experienced enough to sniff out the fakery of artifice and pantomime. The uncertainty as to whether things are or are not as bad as they look generates a certain dynamic energy. The extremity of the scenario presented is of vital importance. Arthur's apparent impotence faced with a problem of his own creation operates as a piece of masochistic theatre staged for courtiers all the more thoroughly implicated in the psychic life of the court for witnessing it.

That the economy of interaction in the courtly sphere is conceived of as an 'erotology' by audiences of the time is readily apparent from a range of medieval sources. Visions of aristocratic

largesse also seem suggest a masochistic structure, the giver placed in a 'feminised' position possibly reflective of the gender inversion apparent in representations of image of male authority figures as mothers, a recurrent motif in biblical and monastic discourse.[52]. The quasi-maternal nature of duty of care was clearly sufficiently generally understood to be worth exploiting as a comic theme. Compassion and largesse place the king in an apparently passive, even feminised position, as literally is the case in *Aucassin et Nicolette*, where the young hero finds the king of Torelore lying in childbed having, he claims, recently given birth (*Aucassin et Nicolette*, § 30).[53] Aristocratic self-abasement and self-depletion is perhaps most dramatically exemplified in the trickster tale/fabliau motif compendium *Trubert*, where the Duke, as part of his sense of *noblesse oblige*, finds himself paying for the same commodity twice, in this case a pseudo-*merveille* in the form of a painted goat. Economic and sexual exploitation are combined in quasi-Sadean tableaux that see him offering the hairs from his backside to Trubert in payment only for the anti-hero to take the opportunity to stab him repeatedly in that area with a bradawl. This pattern of vicious humiliation continues as he is beaten again and again, on one occasion having first been smeared with dog excrement.[54] In Lacanian terms, we can consider the relation of monarch and subjects as having the potential to become hystericised in either direction. Either side can be characterised by images of devouring and depletion, whether in the form of tyrannical royal cannibalism, as described by Jeffrey Cohen, or in the form of impoverishment,
as described by Machiavelli and also, as we will see, Enide's father. If masochism is alive and well in medieval texts, it thus has a clear political content: scenes of the kind found in *Trubert* and other works may attest to a 'gender trouble' expressive of anxieties about the 'openness' characteristic of the claims of lordly care, a potentially limitless sense of duty set against a more neatly defined chivalric masculinity. Left prone to rage and fainting fits at the mere mention of his persecutor's name, Trubert's Duke clearly appears hystericised, the dehumanised, desubjectivised 'support' of the Other's monstrous *jouissance*.

This is, of course, not the first suggestion that Chrétien's romances elaborate libidinal economies characteristic of masochistic fantasy, although such arguments have typically been applied to later works. As Jeffrey Cohen illustrates, elaborating on comments by Michel Foucault, Lancelot's devotion to Guinevere is clearly a worthy antecedent of *Venus in Furs*, demonstrating the 'contractual' character of the masochist's negotiations with the dominant party identified by Gilles Deleuze.[55] Lancelot's submission to Guinevere's shows of coldness and cruelty towards him – exemplified by her insistence he lose rather than win in tournaments or by her arbitrary withdrawal of favour – appear as part of the game-logic of masochism. Cohen then contrasts *Erec et Enide* as 'consensual' in structure, following critics such as R. Howard Bloch who also sees it as a narrative of 'successful consensual union'.[56] However, such an opposition invites us to overlook the subversive nature of the earlier text's treatment of what is at stake in the notion of 'consent'.[57] For a start, consent is not exclusively rational, but rather can spring from what Peter the Lombard refers to as the 'law of the flesh' ('lex carnis') rather than that of the mind and will (see below for further discussion).[58] Moreover, consent is not necessarily the exclusive prerogative of an individual, but rather a matter for parents and guardians concerned with the business of familial alliance: as various critics and historians have pointed out, *Erec et Enide* was composed at a time when the balance accorded to the wishes of an individual as opposed to those of elder kin in marriage arrangements was in practice far from settled. In that regard, it is arguably at least as important that Enide's father – as opposed to Enide herself – agree to sexual relations with Erec. Lastly, 'consent' implies free will rather than domination and constraint, a consideration profoundly at odds with a culture in which a marriage could effectively be compacted through a process initiated by forced sexual relations.[59] To relegate the text's interest by presenting Erec and Enide as a pair of 'consenting adults' thus overlooks significant assymmetries of power in terms of gender. However, as I will show, Cohen is right in the sense that Chrétien's treatment of the wedding highlights the political dimension of consent in the relations between Erec, Enide and Arthur, that language suggesting a continuity between the apparently separate domains of public and private.

Moreover, to present 'consent' and 'contract' in binary opposition is to miss the relation between the two terms, both of which have their roles in a potentially fragile social theatre: contractual arrangements provide frameworks within which consent can operate. However, problems remain: although the contractual element provides the appearance of robust limits, part of masochism's charge lies in its constant flirtation with the traumatic dimension of *jouissance*, with the idea that the game can go too far. In that sense, both parties in the relation can be seen to 'lie' in the sense that they conform to a suspect logic of appearances. Thus, the masochist is not simply a passive victim, but rather seeks to manipulate the Other while disavowing his or her own agency. At the same time, the 'sadist' in the masochistic fantasy relation is not an *actual* sadist, but in effect is required to act *as if* he or she were such a creature. The relation then collapses when it is revealed that things are not in fact as they appear: for example, the masochistic Subject becomes hystericised by the idea that the dominator/dominatrix is simply using them for their own sadistic pleasure. However, this refusal in itself is a 'false' disavowal of a 'hidden truth': the 'withdrawal from fantasy' occurs when the masochistic subject shrinks from the realisation of their desire in the form of a violence too degrading and disturbing for mere pleasure.[60] As Žižek emphasises, it is not the violence per se that is traumatic, but rather the extorted acknowledgement of their consent to debasement: thus the temporality of the 'yes' is ambiguous, appearing as either disavowed in the past or retroactively projected back into it.[61] This is especially apparent in *Trubert* where the Duke's horrified reactions at the successive revelations of his persecutor's identity speaks of a gnawing, shaming sense of having somehow fatefully allowed himself to be fooled once more.

This question of what the masochist chooses not to acknowledge leads us to other possible questions of 'bad faith' in the contract. As Žižek points out, the disavowed goal of the masochistic subject is to provoke *anxiety* in the Other, that is to say a troubling uncertainty produced by proximity to the disturbing 'truth' of their own *jouissance*:

In his [...] seminar on anxiety (1962–1963), Lacan specifies that the true aim of the masochist is not to generate *jouissance* in the Other, but to provide its anxiety. That is to say: although the masochist submits himself to the Other's torture, although he wants to serve at the Other, he himself defines the rules of his servitude; consequently, while he seems to offer himself as the instrument of the Other's *jouissance*, he effectively discloses his own desire to the Other and thus gives rise to anxiety in the Other – for Lacan, the true object of anxiety is precisely the (over)proximity of the Other's desire.[62]

One vision of the motive here is that masochistic desire is effectively predicated on the permanent neurotic suspicion that the desire of the sadist-as-Other is not amenable to regulation and that their participation in the contract is therefore a sham. The masochist's position is thus a 'passive-aggressive' lie, their actions structured by the suspicion that the contract is a fraud. Likewise, Arthur's behaviour in *Erec et Enide* reveals or depends on what the Arthurian tradition already knows: that its climax, its *jouissance* is the King's destruction. The libidinal 'pay-off' of the external audience is displaced onto the internal audience, namely the turbulent mass of Arthur's courtiers. Through a blurring of these internal and external perspectives, the question of the King's death as an object of collective desire hovers between being as yet unknown and unglimpsed on the one hand and a 'known unknown' when viewed from the perspective of the external audience.

What we see here is that the fantasy basis of either collective or individual life is genuinely and fully traumatic to the point that those participating will rarely wish to test or contemplate too closely the limits of that theatre. The threat of Arthur's debasement and loss of face interrupts the potentially impossible, draining cycle of charismatic largesse by presenting the ugly face of the relation between monarch and subjects and by allowing the possible shadow of a sexualised humiliation to obtrude. Arthur's sowing the tumult and fear of 'esfroi' (l. 302) among his courtiers indicates that his 'masochism' provides for a transfer of anxiety, an operation in which Gauvain, faced with his uncle's apparently self-destructive actions, has the function of witnessing guarantor. Gauvain's presence as both kin and courtier creates a dual perspective in which we are invited to read the scene as the public playing out of a family secret, a betraying avowal we have no business witnessing. If, as Lacan comments, love is offering someone the gift of something you do not possess, then Gauvain is placed here in the position of not being able to return the gift that has been given to him in terms of his own status, faced with the spectacle of being upstaged by a comparative newcomer in the form of Erec. The guarantee of the authenticity of his failure can be found in the fact that this moment serves as a link forward to the role of Arthur's nephew in the end of the Arthurian realm. Gauvain's response is 'lacking' in a way that will be repeated in later representations of his role in the conflict with Lancelot, a conflict that will be his to resolve. However, once again, there is a dual perspective: the image of Gauvain's portentous failure to find a solution is also part of the spectacle. The fact there seems to be no way out makes possible the suspension of disbelief.

The force of Arthur's gesture is to face the courtiers with the unreasoning limitlessness of the desire that is their engagement in the charismatic economy. Here, Arthur clearly stands in relation to not merely individual eyes, but the court collective whom he places at the origin of the 'look of love' that could reduce him to nothing but the instrument of the court's enjoyment. To avoid that collapse, the court must be given something else to focus on, even at the price of a potentially uncontrollable eruption of violence. Arthur's apparent self-debasement thus binds his courtiers to him in a manner that exempts him from dependence. As Žižek points out with regard to the function of concentration camps in Nazi Germany, eliciting collusion in the economy of the 'dirty secret' appears as a singularly effective means of securing the compliance and obedience of followers in a way that seems to provide neat exemption from either the Law or the pleasure principle.[63] Such submission provides sufficient freedom from normal 'moral gravity' that they are often happy commit the most horrific of crimes in the name of the cause.[64] Although Arthur's actions in the medieval tradition do not mark him out as a monster of this unprecedented kind, the court is nonetheless seems to be united by a commitment to the exorbitant material and energetic cost of his mission that is not simply founded in rational consent or seductive, compelling beauty, but rather also in some of the ugliness of human experience.

What seems like Arthur's madness is then precisely a sort of 'court rationality' that seeks to free the structure of social life as rooted in the relations between members of the elite from the parochial vagaries of individual attachment and whim, thereby making the forces harnessed in this vision of the body social both manageable and calculable. Of course, what the limited longevity of the Arthurian ideal reminds us is that no settled structure can be produced. In that sense, Chrétien's presentation here can be seen as something quite removed from the 'Classicism' of Louis XIV's court. However, part of what is being suggested in this early section is that the release cannot be too controlled. Chrétien is presenting us with something a little more refined than the image of characters tailoring their actions to play to the gallery while not appearing to do so. For this reason the text insists throughout on the question of feigning, or rather, *not* feigning. The relation of social reality to the 'order of fictions' is explored in a manner far more subtle and far-reaching than envisaged in Huizinga's laments on decadence and ritualised game-playing. If Arthur forms the court into a 'masochistic' tableau, positioning his followers as Other and the agent of the gaze, he thereby averts the risk of a 'hysterical' reaction, the depletion, disintegration and revolt that would be the result of exposing the fundamentally excessive and tyrannical demands on either side. The satisfying theatrical illusion must be maintained, however: the anamorphic skull must appear as more than a conceit. In the same way, the difference between traumatic enjoyment and desire is distance, but desire has no savour or promise without the spectre of enjoyment to haunt the picture. In these twistings of perspective, the King stands central as the manipulator of the order of fictions. What we will see unfold later is a reflection on how Erec in turn uses appearance and performance to keep his audiences in suspense and anxiety, the practitioner of strategic manipulations of collective emotion through means both expected and unexpected, whether beauty or violence.

Notes

1. Topsfield, p. 29.
2. De Beauvoir, p. 740.
3. For summary, see Burgess, *Erec et Enide*, pp. 20–1.
4. See for example Allard, pp. 37–48.
5. On clothing in romance, see notably E. Jane Burns, *Courtly Love Undressed: Reading Through Clothes in Medieval French Culture*, The Middle Ages (Philadelphia: University of Pennsylvania Press, 2002). On clothing and status in medieval and early modern Europe, see Alan Hunt, *Governance of the Consuming Passions: A History of Sumptuary Laws* (London: MacMillan, 1996).
6. On this section and on Erec's beauty, see notably Alice M. Colby, *The Portrait in Twelfth Century French Literature: An Example of the Stylistic Originality of Chrétien de Troyes* (Geneva: Droz, 1965), pp. 104–12 and H. Genaust, *Die Struktur der altfranzösischen antikisierenden Lais* (Hamburg, 1965), pp. 115–22. Karl-Heinz Bender ('L'Essor des motifs du plus beau chevalier et de la plus belle dame dans le premier roman courtois', in *Lebendige Romania: Festschrift für Hans-Wilhelm Klein*, ed. by A. Barrera-Vidal and others, Göppinger Akademische Beiträge, 88 (Göppingen: Kümmerle, 1976), pp. 35–46) sees masculine beauty as well-developed motif, but not to the point of enjoying 'thematic' status in romance texts (p. 44). See also Marie-Madeleine Castellani, 'La Description du héros masculin dans *Erec et Enide* de Chrétien de Troyes', in *La Description au Moyen Age: Actes du colloque du Centre d'Etudes Médiévales et Dialectales de l'Université de Lille III*, ed. by Aimé Petit, Bien Dire et Bien Aprandre, 11 (Lille: Centre de Gestion de L'Edition Scientifique, 1993), pp. 105–17.
7. Of course, this notion of love can be seen early on in Old French literature as being represented in an ambiguous way. Ganelon's 'Jo ne vus aim nïent' (*La Chanson de Roland*, l. 306) can be read as an exasperated but ineffectual show of pique. However, in context, it is also indicative of the breaking of bond with his stepson, who is now no longer protected by the bonds of love that bind the clan-based aristocratic elite together, thus the remark constitutes a formal *défi* tantamount to a Mafioso 'kiss of death'.
8. Georg Simmel, 'Culture of Interaction', in *Simmel on Culture: Selected Writings*, ed. by David Frisby and Mike Featherstone, Theory, Culture and Society (London: Sage, 1997), pp. 109–35, here at p. 113.
9. For edition, see *Anseïs von Kathargo*, ed. by Johann Alton, Bibliothek des literarischen Vereins in Stuttgart, 194 (Stuttgart: Bibliothek des literarischen

Vereins in Stuttgart, 1892). For study, see Simpson, *Fantasy, Identity and Misrecognition*, pp. 89–132.

10   On the Absalom comparison, see further below.
11   On Walter as a 'modernus', see Türk, p. 161.
12   She attracts no comment whatsoever in Noble or Burgess. Bezzola devotes more space to the scene, even to the point of commenting that Erec is present because he is unattached, but then draws no conclusions about the presence of the maiden in relation to Erec.
13   See, for example, Burgess, *Erec et Enide*, pp. 20–1.
14   Maddox, *Structure and Sacring*, p. 84.
15   Bezzola, p. 109. Against Topsfield, see Burgess, *Erec et Enide*, p. 20.
16   Bezzola, pp. 96–7 and also, here, at p. 109.
17   Saint-Simon, *Mémoires*, cited from Elias, *Court Society*, pp. 202–03.
18   See E. Jane Burns, *Bodytalk: When Women Speak in Old French Literature*, The Middle Ages (Philadelphia: University of Pennsylvania Press, 1993), pp. 159–62.
19   As Frappier points out (*Chrétien de Troyes*, pp. 90–1), another possibility here is that Chrétien is highlighting the conventionality of the theme of the hunt for the marvellous White Stag as a 'motif un peu suranné déjà' (p. 91), thus kindly and tactfully sparing his audience the narrative cliché by placing the action off-stage.
20   On Yder's party, in addition to Bezzola, Burgess and others, see also Joan Brumlik, 'The Knight, the Lady, and the Dwarf in Chrétien's *Erec*', *Quondam et Futurus*, 2:2 (1992), 54–72
21   For an extensive exploration of chess as an explanatory metaphor, see Ursula Katzenmeier, *Das Schachspiel des Mittelalters als Strukturierungsprinzip der 'Erec'-Romane*, Beiträge zur Älteren Literaturgeschichte (Heidelberg: Winter, 1989).
22   References to Chaucer's works are to *The Riverside Chaucer*, ed. by Larry D. Benson et al., rev. edn (Boston: Houghton Mifflin, 1987).
23   Cohen, *Medieval Identity Machines*, pp. 35–77. On horses in Chrétien, see also A. Eskenazi, '*Cheval* et *destrier* dans les romans de Chrétien de Troyes', *Revue de linguistique romane*, 53 (1989), 397–433.
24   Isidore of Seville, *Etymologies*, book 12, chapter 1, § 43. For edition, see *Isidori Hispalensis Episcopi Etymologiarum sive Originum Libri XX*, ed. by W. M. Lindsay, Scriptorum Classicorum Bibliotheca Oxoniensis, 2 vols (Oxford: Clarendon, 1911). Translation cited from Joyce E. Salisbury, *The Beast Within: Animals in the Middle Ages* (London and New York: Routledge, 1994), p. 30. For discussion of horses, see Salisbury, pp. 28–35 and R. H. C. Davis, *The Medieval Warhorse* (London: Thames and Hudson, 1989). On animal sexuality, see Salisbury, pp. 78–83.

25 See Salisbury, pp. 40–1 and Davis, p. 18. As Davis points out, this is probably a symbolic detail rather than a representation of fact: it was more common to use mares and geldings as chargers.
26 'Members are good which we move with the decision of the will, with the exception of the reproductive members, although they also are the work of God and are good. They are called *pudenda* because lust has greater power to move them than reason, although we do not permit them to commit the acts to which they urge us, since we can easily control the other members'. Augustine, *Against Julian*, trans. by M. Schumacher, The Fathers of the Church, 35 (New York: Catholic University of America Press, 1979), p. 199. For discussion, see Salisbury, p. 79.
27 Gaunt, *Gender and Genre*, pp. 75–85.
28 'Ale-Hood', in *Hrafnkel's Saga and Other Stories*, trans. by Herman Pálsson (Harmondsworth: Penguin, 1970), pp. 82–93, here at p. 90. For discussion, see Salisbury, pp. 94–5.
29 See Huchet, *Le Roman médiéval*, pp. 175–222 and Stahuljak, passim.
30 The analogue that would reveal the potential pantomime drag-act strangeness of the maiden's horsewomanliness is perhaps to be found in the animated film, *Shrek* (dir. Andrew Adamson and Vicky Jenson, 2001), where a character voiced by a tall, slim, African-American actor (Eddie Murphy) is estrangingly embodied in carnavalesque form as a short-legged, wide-bottomed donkey with long, fluttering eyelashes, a winning smile and, when viewed from behind, a suggestive wiggle only further spiced by the slightly perilous, high-heeled teeter of his hooves. What the resonances of *Eneas* and *Erec et Enide* emphasise is the queer history of the look at Donkey's ass. Interestingly, in *Shrek 2* (dir. Adamson and Kelly Ashbury, 2004), the hybrid offspring of Donkey and the dragon appear as paradigmatic examples of what both Horace and Alan of Lille, not to mention Bernard of Clairvaux, would have described as grotesque 'sports' (see Michael Camille, *Image on the Edge: the Margins of Medieval Art* (London: Reaktion, 1992), pp. 17–55 and Simpson, *Fantasy, Identity and Misrecognition*, p. 135).
31 Albertus Magnus, 'Quaestiones de Animalibus', in *Alberti Magni Opera Omnia: 'De Nature et Origine Animae', 'De Principiis Motu Processivi', 'Quaestiones de Animalibus'*, ed. by E. Filthaut, (Aschendorff: Westphalian Monastery, 1955), XII, book 1, question 13 ('Quare omnia animalia sunt multi strepitus in coitu praetor hominem?'). For translation and discussion see Salisbury, p. 79.
32 See James A. Brundage, *Law, Sex and Christian Society in Medieval Europe* (Chicago and London: University of Chicago Press, 1987), pp. 268–88. On sex in the thought of Augustine, Peter the Lombard and Thomas of Chobham, see John Baldwin, *The Language of Sex: Five Voices from Northern France around 1200* (Chicago and London: University of Chicago Press, 1994), p. 116–21.

33 See Donald Maddox, 'Lévi-Strauss in Camelot: Interrupted Communication in Arthurian Fictions', in *Culture and the King: The Social Implications of the Arthurian Legend (Essays in Honour of Valerie M. Lagorio)*, ed. by Shichtman and Carley (Albany NY: State University of New York Press, 1994), pp. 35–53.

34 'On commence par répéter sans savoir – par un mythe – la définition de l'écriture: répéter sans savoir.' (Derrida, *La Dissémination*, p. 84).

35 Gaunt, *Gender and Genre*, p. 92.

36 Freud, 'Inhibitions, Symptoms and Anxiety', p. 141. See also Roberto Harari, *Lacan's Seminar on 'Anxiety': An Introduction* (New York: Other, 2001), pp. xxiv–xxvi.

37 Burgess, *Erec et Enide*, p. 23.

38 See, for example, Burgess: 'Certainly, although he cut a dashing figure, he was not properly equipped as a knight' (p. 21). Also Alfred Adler, 'Sovereignty as the Principle of Unity in Chrétien's *Erec*' *Publications of the Modern Language Association*, 60 (1945), 917–36, p. 918; Colby, *The Portrait*, p. 109 and Maddox, *Structure and Sacring*, p. 83.

39 In addition to the miniatures of Arthur hunting in fonds fr. 1376 and 24403, see, for example, *The Hunting Book of Gaston Phébus (Manuscrit français 616, Paris, Bibliothèque Nationale)*, ed. by Marcel Thomas, François Avril and Wilhelm Schlag, Manuscripts in Miniature, 3 (London: Harvey Miller, 1998), illuminations on f. 68r, f. 73r, f. 73v and f. 77r.

40 Which, if we follow Bezzola, who presents the hunt as the very invocation of *aventure* (pp. 93–7) is arguably a more serious lack of preparation: in terms of the scene's possible Ovidian sources, it is they who are in the 'front line'.

41 Bezzola, pp. 105–06. Zink makes a similar point with regard to 'mythic' interpretations of Old French epic, such as Joël Grisward's work on Indo-European structures – 'no one would think of applying the same investigations and demonstration [...] to Proust's *Remembrance of Things Past*.' (Zink, p. 4) – the presumption being that medieval texts are inevitably tradition-bound to a degree that makes them less amenable to being read as 'subjective' expression.

42 Burgess, *Erec et Enide*, p. 22.

43 Bezzola, p. 98.

44 See Bezzola, p. 114.

45 Burns, *Bodytalk*, p. 164.

46 Hunt, 'Rhetorical Background', p. 15.

47 *Le Couronnement de Louis*, ed. by E. Langlois, in *Le Cycle du Guillaume d'Orange*, ed. by Dominique Boutet and others, Lettres Gothiques (Paris: Livre de Poche, 1996).

48 'In the film version of *Parsifal*, Hans-Jürgen Syberberg demonstrated – by a series of changes to Wagner's original – that he was well aware of this fact. First there is his manipulation of the sexual difference: at the crucial moment of inversion in the second act – after Kundry's kiss – Parsifal changes his sex: the male actor is replaced by a young, cold female; what is at stake here is no

ideology of hermaphroditism but a shrewd insight into the feminine nature of totalitarian power: totalitarian Law is an obscene Law, penetrated by enjoyment, a Law which has lost its formal neutrality. But what is crucial for us here is another feature of Syberberg's version: the fact that he has *externalised* Amfortas's wound – it is carried on a pillow beside him, as a nauseous partial object out of which, through an aperture resembling vaginal lips, trickles blood.' Žižek, *The Sublime Object of Ideology*, pp. 76–7. Žižek returns to this episode in his *Tarrying with the Negative: Kant, Hegel and the Critique of Ideology* (Durham NC: Duke University Press, 1993), pp. 164–99. His discussion here expands on the question of hermpahroditism.

49 Burns, *Bodytalk*, pp. 164–5.
50 Bezzola, p. 100.
51 See Busby, *Gauvain*, p. 50.
52 On biblical and monastic images of male maternity, see Caroline Walker Bynum, *Jesus as Mother: Studies in the Spirituality of the High Middle Ages* (Berkeley and London: University of California Press, 1982), pp. 110–69.
53 On *Aucassin et Nicolette*, see Jane Gilbert, 'The Practice of Gender in *Aucassin et Nicolette*', *Forum for Modern Language Studies*, 33:3 (1997), 215–28. As Gilbert puts it: 'The pregnancy of Adam, far from undermining his gender position by rendering him effeminate, is the basis of his supremacy as a male. [...] Another possibility would be to see the king of Torelore as engaged in an *imitatio Adami*, his lying in as a representation of the orthodox structure of medieval western society, and as embodying its various hierarchies (generational, theocentric, class and gender) in their proper form.' (pp. 220–1).
54 See *Trubert*, in *Fabliaux érotiques: textes de jongleurs des XIIe et XIIIe siècles*, ed. and trans. by Luciano Rossi and Richard Straub, Lettres Gothiques (Paris: Livre de Poche, 1992), pp. 348–529. For commentary, see Simpson, *Fantasy, Identity and Misrecognition*, pp. 191–236.
55 Cohen, *Medieval Identity Machines*, p. 88.
56 See R. Howard Bloch, *Etymologies and Genealogies: A Literary Anthropology of the French Middle Ages* (Berkeley and London: University of California Press, 1983), pp. 189–90 here at p. 190.
57 On consent in marriage in the period in question, see Georges Duby, *Love and Marriage in the Middle Ages*, trans. by Jane Dunnett and others (Chicago: University of Chicago Press, 1994), pp. 19–20; Christopher Brooke, *The Medieval Idea of Marriage* (Oxford: Oxford University Press, 1991), pp. 137–52 and Brundage, pp. 235–42. On marriage in *Erec et Enide*, see Dorothea Kullmann, 'Hommes amoureux et femmes raisonnables: *Erec et Enide* et la doctrine ecclésiastique du mariage', in *Arthurian Romance and Gender / Masculin / Féminin dans le roman arthurien médiéval/Geschlechterrollen im mittelalterlichen Artusroman*, ed. by Friedrich Wolfzettel (Amsterdam: Rodopi, 1995), pp. 119–29.
58 On Peter, see Brundage, pp. 268–88.

59 On which, see, among others, Kathryn Gravdal, *Ravishing Maidens: Writing Rape in Medieval French Literature and Law* (Philadelphia: University of Pennsylvania Press, 1991), p. 11.

60 In that respect, Arthur's position here is potentially not unlike that of the Isabelle Huppert character in Michael Haneke's film *The Piano Teacher*. Here, the revelation of her masochistic tendencies to her lover leads fatefully towards her death: 'Things take a fateful turn and start to slide towards the inexorable tragic ending, (the teacher's suicide) at the precise moment when, in answer to the boy's passionate sexual advances, the 'repressed' teacher violently opens herself up to him, writing him a letter with a detailed list of her demands (basically, a scenario for masochistic performances: how he should tie her up, force her to lick his anus, slap and even beat her, and so on). It is crucial that these demands are written – what is put on paper is too traumatic to be pronounced in direct speech: her innermost fantasy itself. When they are thus confronted – he with his passionate outbursts of affection and she with her cold, impassioned distance – this setting should not deceive us: it is she who in fact opens herself up, laying her fantasy bare to him, while he is simply playing a more superficial game of seduction. No wonder he withdraws in panic from her openness: the direct display of her fantasy radically changes her status in his eyes, transforming a fascinating love object into a repulsive entity he is unable to endure. Soon afterwards, however, he becomes perversely attracted by her fantasmatic scenario, caught up in its excessive *jouissance*, and, at first, tries to return her own message to her by enacting elements of her fantasy (he slaps her so that her nose starts to bleed, kicks her violently); when she breaks down, withdrawing from the realisation of her fantasy, he passes to the act and makes love to her in order to seal his victory over her.' (Žižek, *Welcome to the Desert of the Real*, pp. 20–1).

61 On which, see *Metastases of Enjoyment*, pp. 119–22.

62 Žižek, *Welcome to the Desert of the Real*, pp. 21–2. See also Lacan, *Le Séminaire X*, pp. 122–9 and Harari, pp. 138–45.

63 Žižek illustrates how unthinkable elements, such as the use of 'dirty secrets' are fundamental to collectives, instilling them with their sense of purpose. One illustrative example is a detail of *Fight Club* that Žižek does not discuss in the context of his analysis in *Welcome to the Desert of the Real*. The revelation at end of the film that the Brad Pitt character – apparently the charismatic centre of the 'Fight Club' network – is nothing more than a figment of Edward Norton's imagination is followed by a sequence of flashback revisions of earlier scenes. Most notable among these is the founding moment of the 'Fight Club': Norton and Pitt's experimental brawl outside a bar. This moment, which draws their first group of 'acolytes', is now replayed and reviewed as the grotesque and incomprehensible scenario of Norton beating himself up. Thus, what we are only given to understand at the last moment is that what attracted the men who became his followers was not the predictable latent homoeroticism of the

sweaty, bare-knuckle bout, but in fact a masochistic scenario that was always already the object of their perverse curiosity and fascination. The psychoanalytical rationalisation the film then suggests for this scene, too traumatic to be represented either by the Norton character to himself or in the diegetic bulk of the film, then had to be disguised through a delusional split and dissimulated as an image of ludic, exploratory jockishness. The paradox of the film's 'ugly secret' remains: for all Norton's followers did not see and could not bear to see what really happened that night, they were bound to him nonetheless. Indeed, so successful is Norton's trick of charisma that his own agalma appears in externalised, embodied form as the Brad Pitt character, exempted from real-world constraints on charismatic energy to the point that he is able to travel the country setting up 'Fight Clubs' in every city.

64 Nazi Germany seems to offer the most extreme illustrations of this sort of psychology. Himmler, for example, in a speech to SS officers in 1943, defended the murder of Jewish women and children on the grounds that the killing of Jewish men alone would have been indefensible if the Nazis had not been prepared to take the next step. (On Himmler's justifications of the Final Solution, see Ian Kershaw, *Hitler 1936–1945: Nemesis* (London: Penguin, 2001), pp. 604–05. For commentary, see Žižek, *Welcome to the Desert of the Real*, pp. 30–2). And indeed, Himmler seemed to go further still in offering explicit acknowledgement of the obscenity of this action in describing it as a page in German history that 'has never been written and never can be written' (Himmler, speech to SS leaders in Possen, October 4th, 1943. See Kershaw, p. 604–05). In that regard, the nightmarish nature of the action is not merely a surgical rooting out that has no moral weight, but, as an actual crime unspeakable beyond the dreams of Herod, unifies the German people. As Hitler himself is quoted as saying the day after Himmler's speech, 'the bridges have been destroyed behind them; only the way forward remains' (Kershaw, p. 606). Actions that break the bounds of moral, political and other economies, if sufficiently bewildering in nature or scale, seem to point towards future solutions in the manner of a debt deferred. If Žižek is right here, then what is utterly obscene is the 'moral suicide' the Nazi persecutions entailed.

The world of Laluth lacks [the] quality of *savoir*. It esteems outward show, the appearance of beauty and prowess. It acclaims Erec as immoderately as it did Yder. (Topsfield, p. 37)

It is Angevin chronicles that first begin to celebrate counts as chivalric heroes, Angevin princes (most notably the sons of Henry II) who were the most renowned for their devotion to chivalric pursuits; and from Anjou comes the earliest complete description of a great prince being dubbed a knight: Geoffrey le Bel, future count of Anjou, in 1128. [...] When Geoffrey le Bel discovered four knights in his prisons, he personally ordered their release. He ate with them at his table. He returned their horses and arms. Finally, he freed them, showing them such magnanimity [...] simply because they were knights, like him, and as such shared his 'profession'. 'For if we are really knights', said the count, 'we should show compassion to knights, especially those who have been defeated'. (Koziol, p. 287)

But the other consciousness, the other ego, sets up a reciprocal claim. The native travelling abroad is shocked to find himself in turn regarded as a 'stranger' by the natives of neighbouring countries. As a matter of fact, wars, festivals, trading, treaties and contests among tribes, nations and classes tend to deprive the concept *Other* of its absolute sense and to make manifest its relativity; willy-nilly, individuals are forced to realise the reciprocity of their relations. (De Beauvoir, *The Second Sex*, p. 17)

The ultimate horror occurs [...] not when the mask of innocence disintegrates [...] but when the sublime text is (mis)-appropriated by the wrong, corrupted speaker. [...] At the level of ethnic identity, something similar happens when a subject who is not 'one of us' learns our language and endeavours to speak it, to behave as part of 'our' community; the automatic reaction of every proper racist is that the stranger, by doing this, steals from us the substance of our identity. (Žižek, The Plague of Fantasies, pp. 69–70)

Chapter Three
The Neighbour's Ugly Joy: Laluth

If the ways of Arthur's court seem strange, Erec's departure takes us out into a wider world stranger still. This encounter with foreign ways is quite often presented as something of a one-way street, one of the recurring tropes in critical studies being that this world mirrors Erec and his values in the negative, Chrétien's narrative a differentiating and rehabilitatory account of socially-useful chivalry, the creatures and individuals Erec meets are 'othered', reflecting repudiated aspects of himself, and most particularly, his old self. Thus, for Leslie Topsfield, Laluth is 'out there' as an undiscriminating provincial backwater (see chapter epigraph). Likewise, Erich Köhler sees the rationale and function of the Sparrow-Hawk custom as different in kind to that underpinning the hunt of the White Stag.[1] However, it can also be argued that Chrétien presents a more nuanced picture of Erec's encounter with this new world, showing a young aristocrat both seeking to understand the fault-lines in the geography he enters and to exploit its rituals and rules to make the most effective entrance.

Although interpretations emphasising the 'symbolic' aspects of Laluth risk overlooking the fine detail of the shifting landscape Chrétien describes, such a focus is not inevitably blind to underlying issues, the 'symbolic' languages of ritual also having their place and role in the 'real world'. For all larger courts sought to focus collective attention on their ritual and ceremonial life – thereby dispossessing smaller communities of cultural capital, 'local' court cultures, centring on houses of lesser rank (if not ancestry), clearly aspired to symbolic expression as part of their political life. As Geoffrey Koziol argues, although ritual displays may advertise themselves as universal and timeless, they are also the language through which local cultures negotiated conflict and change. For Koziol, appeals for pardon and shows of humility are a key example, the conventions of performances of supplication or penitence varying from one area to another, high-status figures seeking to placate the offended while avoiding damaging humiliation for themselves.[2] Yet, social change led to modifications of the rules of the game, Koziol contrasting the jealous safeguarding of ancestral dignity on the part of Angevin counts with the more dynamically fraternal conventions associated with knighthood. In that regard, it is perhaps no coincidence that Erec's participation in the Sparrow-Hawk contest pits him against a knight and a *count*. Allegiances between the counts and royalty were shaped both by the to-and-fro of conflicts between the Capetians and Plantagenets – counts and countesses looking to secure the favour of whoever might best further their local interests – as well as by shifts of power internal to particular houses.[3] A comital family with various branches, eager to assert its place in the cultural and political life of its region might well provide a more complex backdrop than was expected. In that sense, the slap in the face Erec receives from the dwarf – cat's paw to the Count's own cat's paw, Yder – can be read as a reminder of the energies, tensions and claims that might be dissimulated in the world of tournaments but which reflect the concern of such apparently 'provincial' players to maintain their own elbow-room or the extent to which apparently parochial conflicts could erupt onto a wider stage.

Moreover, to posit a strongly oppositional relation between the courts of Arthur and of Laluth is to disregard the 'uncanny' dimension of Erec's encounters, the interpenetration of self and other troubling distinctions of self and other, familiar and unfamiliar, before and after. Indeed, Chrétien's exploration of opposition and hostility attaching to individuals and communities 'external' to the world of Arthur's court reflects back on the internal tensions and ambivalences revealed in the hunt. Just as the encounter between Guinevere, the maiden and Erec was subtended by queering allusions to the *Roman d'Eneas*, so Chrétien's vision of Laluth offers a study of diplomacy and history-making as improvisation within a continuum rippling with the shocks, reflections and echoes of earlier and later scenes, earlier and later intensities. His presentation of conflict between individuals and communities reflects tensions and shifts of perspective inherent in an evolving psychodynamic of interaction that passes from hostility to resolution to alliance requiring Erec to manifest his capacity for not merely functional but effectively also temporal multi-tasking. Functionally, the young knight is a mix of implacable avenger and rule-bound judge, while also caught between different vantage points in the process of conflict and reconciliation. The subjective and intersubjective turbulence of such interactions, troubled by collective investments as well as by individual passions and quests for revenge, reveals a process whose driving energies are often out-of-joint with the goal of engineering concord between aristocratic houses or the production of publicly consumable histories of the dangerous transition from conflict and cultural difference to negotiated union.

Erec's arrival in Laluth brings into play the range and intensity of emotions and attitudes that form the basis for Chrétien's examination of performance and theatricality in the remainder of the work. In tracing a path from 'hatred' and mortal conflict to union in a context in which the present is haunted by both past and future, Chrétien vision of a two-way temporal and emotional continuum, highlighting the permanent dis-ease in the relation with our proximate others. This tension is explored by Freudian and Lacanian traditions in discussions of the neighbour, a term Freud takes from Paul's injunction to 'love thy neighbour as thyself' ('diliges *proximum tuum* tamquam te ipsum', Romans 13:9, my emphasis). Freud's sees this as encapsulating the fundamental paradox of 'civilised morality': the pathogenic effect of regulatory mechanisms. Here, the demand to love the neighbour appears as a counterpoint to the question of giving ground with regard to one's desire, except that the matter on which the Subject gives ground is the 'fundamental hostility'. What Chrétien's presentation of the relation between Erec and Yder makes clear is that while antagonism energises the work, we also see the shocks characteristic of the uncanny encounter. What we reject or what we choose not to recognise in our 'neighbour' is fundamental to our relation with ourselves, the close-to-home uneasily caught between the foreign and the familiar. When Chrétien evokes Erec's first encounter with Laluth's noise and bustle, we are not so far from seeing that perception modulate into something rather more rebarbative. The joyous throng becomes the ugly mob, local ceremony appears as garish and uninvolving pantomime in which outsiders and newcomers have neither place nor leverage.

Yet, at this stage, the animation of Laluth's cast of thousands smacks of an energy ready to be harnessed in frenetic, in many respects perfectly laudable industry manifest in the cornucopia of courtly activities and occupations evoked by the narrator (ll. 348–60), its body social clearly working to the production of the 'mout grant joie' (l. 348) Erec witnesses. However, what really catches his eye is a note of abstraction in the midst of all this joyous bustle:

> Un petit est avant alez
> Et vit gesir sor uns degrez
> Un vavasor auques de jorz,
> Mais mout estoit povre sa corz.
> Biauz homs estoit, chenuz et blans,
> Debonaire, gentis et frans.
> Iluec estoit toz sous assis,
> Bien resembloit qu'il fust pensis. (ll. 373–80)

> He went on a little further and saw an elderly vavassor sitting on the steps of a shabby house. He was a handsome man, grey-bearded, white-haired, well-born and noble. Seated alone, he seemed obviously deep in thought.

In spite of the 'but' regarding the vavassor's poverty (l. 376), the narrator passes on quickly to the enumeration of his physical qualities as an embodied guarantee of his standing. As Köhler notes, the attitude of being *pensif* – in Chrétien's work and more generally in vernacular lyric – speaks not merely of a history of events but also a process of rationalisation and accommodation: '"pansif" désigne un choc douloureux venu du destin irrévocable, auquel il ne reste plus à se soumettre si on ne veut pas tomber dans "la folie" où on risque de s'anéantir'.[4] In short, we already know that the vavassor has had some reason to internalise the teachings of Boethius on worldly fortune. Of course, there is more to such thoughtful reticence than just thought: the stance itself is designed to attract attention, which is indeed what happens: 'Erec pensa que cil estoit /Proudon' (ll. 381–2). Appearing as Erec's observation and thoughts, Chrétien's doubles his interruption of the narrative flow by mention of his poor surroundings with that of the vavassor's air of thoughtful preoccupation. It is this riddle that draws Erec, the element seemingly out of place in the tableau before him, an image of reserve, of standing back from the general hubbub. Given what we find out later about his fortunes (ll. 509–17), we would be justified in reading Enide's father's attitude as a protest, a refusal to participate further in either collective labour or joy. Indeed, now the general tenor of the opening description of life in Laluth becomes readily understandable: the colourful cavalcade of tasks Chrétien describes (ll. 348–60) stands in contrast to the monotonous, wearing menial labour passed over in silence when he introduces Enide and her mother (ll. 397–400). The work of courtly accomplishment, revolving around the fruits of collective endeavour and the bestowal of largesse and gifts, appears as a cycle of reciprocity in which Enide's family pointedly do not participate.[5] Thereby hangs something of a history, several histories in fact.

Beauty('s) Troubling History: Enide with Philomena

French literature has a long tradition of cautionary and mock-cautionary tales of of either the dangers facing either young women outwith the control of their menfolk or those abandoned and alone in the world. Voltaire's creation, Cunégonde, for example, speaks of herself as having been 'violée autant qu'on peut l'être', a grotesque elevation of the act of rape from a singular attack that puts in question her future worth in the sort of aristocratic alliance looked for by her snobbish brother to a darkly subversive apogee of violation as brutal routine transforming her from the analogue of the 'tender Helen' of the *Roman de Brut* to that of the old nurse, ancestor of Cunégonde's companion, 'La Vieille'.[6] The threat also hangs over Diderot's creation, Suzanne Simonin, the pitiable heroine of his experimental sentimentalist joke novel, *La Religieuse*, a topos then taken to extremes in the heroine's fate in the Marquis de Sade's *Justine ou les malheurs de la vertu*, who, in a sign of the unthinkable horrors to be heaped on her, rather than simply being raped, is sodomised, beaten and forced to perform oral sex in the first attack on her by the monks.[7]

Such accounts are the descendants of older narratives examining the dangers facing daughters in their first step out into the world or the risky business of using them as collateral – indeed, all the works cited above deal prominently with the matter of marriagibility, whether positively or negatively. A key ancestor here is Ovid's tale of Philomena, daughter of King Pandion of Athens, given into the care of her Thracian brother-in-law, Tereus, so that she might be taken to visit her sister Procne (*Metamorphoses*, book 6). However, Tereus proves false and imprisons and rapes Philomena, cutting out her tongue so that she cannot denounce him for his crime. Chrétien's translation and reworking of the story survives in manuscripts of the verse *Ovide moralisé*.[8] Reading this tale in parallel with Enide's betrothal to Erec and departure from Laluth provides us with a range of reflections on the risks inherent in compacting marriages in societies where kin groups knew many cautionary tales about the dangers of trusting suitors too easily and where women marrying into communities far from home found themselves faced with suspicion and hostility. In that respect, the Philomena narrative appears as the counter-pole to those that presented brides acquired through exogamous exchange as primary agents of treachery, a key example being the scheming, adulterous Eufeme from *Le Roman de Silence*, or Arthur's unnamed queen in Marie de France's *Lanval*, both devoid of the capacity for remorse demonstrated by the Guinevere of *La Mort le roi Artu*.

However, Chrétien's vision is not simply one of geographical difference: these stories of marriage are also tales of cultural interaction between cultures 'living in different centuries', as Chakrabarty puts it. Thus, if Enide's story is a version of the Philomena story that turned out well, it is also a successful microcosmic completion of a larger process of *translatio*. Chrétien makes of Ovid's tale a snapshot of history pointing in the direction of the courtly accomplishments of the Middle Ages: Philomena – the equal of Appolonius and Tristan (ll. 174–87) – is tragically silenced by the barbarous Tereüs, representative of a barbaric primitivism in thrall to its own desires. However, at the same time, Chrétien positions the despotically sovereign rule of Love as the apogee of courtly modernity. In all this debate, *Erec et Enide* also seems out of time, with no instances of

Love as a personification occurring, a detail that for Duggan strengthens the argument for a later dating for Chrétien's lyric and Ovidian poems.[9] By contrast, I will argue that the close parallels between *Erec et Enide* and *Philomena* on the one hand and, on the other, between the adaptation and his lyric poetry point to Erec's arrival in Laluth as a key jigsaw-piece in Chrétien's amorous history.

Although apparently different in their visions of the control of women in domestic space, both narratives are linked by their interest in the piquancy of the first view of the beloved, caught unguarded in a glimpse that holds the promise of greater intimacy to come. Thus Enide's torn white shift offers tantalising hints of what might otherwise be left to the imagination:[10]

> La dame s'en est fors issue,
> Et sa fille qui fu vestue
> D'une chemise par panz lee,
> Delïee, blanche et ridee.
> Un blanc chainse ot vestu desus,
> N'avoit robe ne moins ne plus,
> Mais tant estoit li chainses viez
> Que as coutes estoit perciez.
> Povre estoit la robe defors,
> Mes desoz estoit beax li cors. (ll. 401–10)

> The lady came out as did her daughter, who was dressed in a flowing shift of white cloth, white and pleated. Over it, she wore a white tunic and nothing else. The tunic was so terribly old that it was worn through at the elbows. But wrapped in rags as she was, underneath them her body was lovely.

If time seemed to catch its breath with Erec's arrival on stage, that sense is redoubled here with Chrétien's extensive celebration of Enide's beauty (ll. 411–41), whose quasi-divine origins as the handiwork of Nature mark an irruption of the eternal in the present. In *Philomena*, a similar scene greets Tereüs arriving at Pandion's palace:

> A tant est d'une chambre issue
> Philomena eschevelee.
> Ne sanbloit pas nonain velee,
> Car grant mervoille iert a retreire

> Son jant cors et son cler viaire,
> Que ne poïst ce croi sofire
> A totes ses granz biautez dire
> Li sans ne la langue Platon. (*Philomena*, ll. 129–31)

> At that moment, Philomena, her hair unpinned, came out of one of the chambers of the palace. She did not look like any nun in her veil, for it would be a marvel to tell of her fair body or radiant face. I do not believe that the wisdom or eloquence /language of Plato could suffice to fully describe her great beauty.

The power of beauty Philomena's beauty is then paralleled by her historically precocious wisdom and accomplishments.[11] Chrétien's elaboration of exactly how beautiful Enide was suceeds where the tongue and mind of Plato would have failed with regard to Philomena. The subaltern can apparently speak better than the master. However, Chrétien's celebration of her beauty and intelligence sounds a warning note through his evocation of her untied tresses. As Noëlle Lévy-Gires comments:

> On le sait, la chevelure est très tôt apparue comme un des attributs majeurs de la féminité impure. Parce qu'elle encadre et enlumine le visage, parce qu'elle est proche des yeux, mais surtout parce qu'elle est perçue comme élément originel, naturel, sauvage, elle fascine et obsède. [...] Eve, la première Marie-Madeleine, les sirènes, les figures de la Luxure ont en commun leurs longs cheveux déployés, qui semblent relever de la même symbolique que la nudité: les premières représentations de la Luxure montrent la femme dans sa corruption originelle, nue, les cheveux flottants, le plus souvent mordu par un serpent ou un crapaud.[12]

In this respect, Philomena is caught up in a history that brackets and predates her own intentions: for all she may appear as a prodigy of her time, her hair – as visual marker of the taint of original sin – has a life and history of its own, speaking louder than her good sense and wisdom. Seemingly granted the licence that might be accorded such a precocious flower of a distinctly modern vernacular subjectivity, Chrétien's comment highlights the continuing need for her to remain subject to *chastoiement*, to paternal constraint and tutelage.

It is in the matter of paternal authority that the key difference between the two pictures emerges. Philomena is presented as an artful young woman whom Tereüs persuades to take an active role in seconding him in negotiations with her father, Pandion, in seeking his permission to have her accompany him back to Thrace (*Philomena*, ll. 275-91). Although the spectacle of the mourning, grief-stricken Pandion letting his daughter go allows Tereus a witness to the gentle side of the paternal Law that perhaps ought to have sufficed as a reminder of the dictates of *pietas*, his effacement from Tereüs's world-view following their departure from Athens leaves the unfortunate young woman to her fate. In this world, paternal authority can only return in the obscene spectral guise of the superego Law, the *Nom / Non-du-Père*: in Ovid, *nefas* and *scelus*, profanation and betrayal will out, rousing the vengeful forces of the supernatural world. The life given to the voices of Ovid's victims is embodied in Philomena's twitching severed tongue, an 'organ without a body' crawling back towards her in a sign that her denunciation cannot be silenced, even by the most brutal act:

> radix micat ultima linguae
> ipsa iacet terraeque tremens inmurmurat atrae
> utque salire solet mutilatae cauda colubrae
> palpitat et moriens dominae vestigia quaerit.
> (*Metamorphoses*, book 6, ll. 557–60)

The mangled root quivers, while the severed tongue lies palpitating on the dark earth, faintly murmuring; and, as the severed tail of a mutilated snake is wont to writhe, it twitches and, dying, seeks its mistress.

Seemingly less lurid, Chrétien's version makes no mention of the severed tongue crawling back, and there is no sign of the avenging forces to which it calls. In his vision of Antiquity, for all paganism ('paiennime', l. 228) – the rule of a law that is not one – is initially associated with the impieties of Thrace, Chrétien's vision is of a world where all roads lead to hell: Progné's sacrifice to Pluto (ll. 978–1060) anticipates the impious killing of Itys and in spite of her good intentions ultimately binds her to the service of the god and lord of hell ('deus qui d'anfer est roi et sire', l. 1052). As we then pass through the accounts of Philomena's suicidal despair, Tereüs' unquenchable lust (ll. 1061–69), Progné's unnatural infanticide (ll. 1296–1332) and Tereüs's shamelessness at everything except not being able to avenge his son (ll. 1423–27), Chrétien paints us a picture of a universe constrained by no law. Philomena's *entrée en scène* stops time and history, but not, ultimately, in a good way: the promise of modernity she seems to embody unleashes the violence and night of primitive, atavistic forces.

In *Erec et Enide*, history looks rather different even if time stands still, with Erec taken aback by Enide's beauty:

> Erec d'autre part s'esbahi,
> Quant en li si grant biauté vit. (ll. 448–9)
>
> Erec, seeing such dazzling beauty, was overwhelmed.

Amplifying this moment of shock and awe, Chrétien's excursus-description of Nature's marvelling at her own handiwork (ll. 414–20) represents an irruption of the cosmically eternal into the present. Indeed, the attempts to replicate that singular event that is the first sight of our heroine is not merely the spawning of 500 lesser beauties – coincidentally the female complement of Arthur's court (l. 50) – but also an attempted recreation of that effect, that spellbinding moment. Although Enide is to be found in impoverished circumstances, the account of Nature indicates the moment of encounter is overlaid with the same Boethian finery that would clothe and provide the programme for a ceremonial entry. The resources mobilised for Katherine of Aragon's *adventus* into London in 1501 for her marriage to Henry VII's son Arthur – a moment meticulously designed as a 'stellar apotheosis' with strong Macrobian and Boethian colourings – are gamely conjured here in rhetorical form in Chrétien's impromptu royal rhetorical fireworks.[13] What emerges then is a certain *sprezzatura*, a certain creative, improvisatory *bricolage* in the wake of the shattered design of what should perhaps have been Erec and the Queen's handmaiden's entry into Arthur's court, an entry likely to have been embellished and embroidered in similarly fine rhetorical style.

This brings us to the question of what voices are mobilised in the text at this point. Enide's father speaks on her behalf, leading to comments in some quarters that no regard is paid to her wishes.[14] However, the textual backdrop complicates the picture. For one, as Peggy McCracken argues, Chrétien's treatment of female silence offers a mirror image of Lavine's vociferousness on the subject of her arranged marriage to Turnus in the *Roman d'Eneas* (see, for example ll. 8327–54).[15] The contrast with Ovid's tale may well strengthen such a weave. The tragic difference is that Erec's negotiations with Enide's father give a more prominent role to paternal insight and design, with Enide's father's schooling of his daughter to silence appears as a mark of concern for her safety. Philomena's father, by contrast, does not keep his daughter 'like a (veiled) nun' and his intervention trusts to pathetic appeal (ll. 556–74) to a plausible criminal swept away by a chance encounter that fans his impious desires. Yet both works owe their debt to the ravishment of desire.[16] The difference is that the risk taken by Enide's father appears more knowing. The joy Enide's father expresses in describing his daughter (ll. 537–46), strongly reminiscent of Pandion's (*Philomena*, ll. 339–80), could be taken at face value, but it may function as a calculated appeal on the part of someone prepared to stake all in spite of the warnings from history telling him of the risk inherent in such a gamble. And yet, for all Enide's father closes the moment down, another voice, the narrator's, brings an element of celebration and colour to proceedings.

For all Enide's father strikes a pose rather different from Pandion's sentimentally impotent concern, this is not to say that his household is free of potentially irresponsible flirtation. His affectation of idleness – lounging at the doorstep of his house while his wife and daughter work – frames a question designed to tease the interest of the right passing stranger. Indeed, further intimations that the world of Laluth is a less innocent, more calculating place than Athens follow. Part of the bait tendered in exploratory role-play is the potentially disturbing fulsomeness of the vavassor's praise of Enide as sole source of his 'deduit' and 'plesir' (ll. 541–6), comments that have raised more than one critical eyebrow. As Bezzola comments, 'on comprend l'orgueil d'un père plein d'affection pour son enfant, mais ces [...] vers [...] dépassent de loin le langage d'un père et rejoignent

177

celui de l'amant'.[17] Bezzola's remark may not just be an anachronistic misunderstanding of the conventions of the sometimes strangely effusive, often urgently bodily, nature of medieval protestations of apparently 'platonic' love and regard. Where in *Philomena* it was Tereüs who had no regard for the paternal Law, we have here the figure of Pandion speaking in echo of the impious desires and designs of his son-in-law.

Chrétien's densely-woven appropriation of Ovid seems not merely an ornament addressed to an external audience: to the right internal reader it offers a puzzle pointing to what lies beneath the surface of the internal politics of Laluth and to the connection between two separate facts: Enide's father has fallen on hard times through debts accrued in war and has refused offers of suitors looking to secure her hand. If the Count had had a role in the marriage offers made to Enide's father while failing to reward his follower for service in past wars, then he is guilty of trying to profit doubly from the labours of his vassal kinsman. As with *Philomena*, we have a character assimilable to Tereüs in that he seemingly wants two goods for the price of one: his service and his daughter. In response, Enide's father makes it clear through his actions that he would rather subject his daughter to forced labour and even give her to the first passing stranger with a semi-plausible story to tell rather than hand her over to a relative who had shown such slight regard for her interests and who seems only interested to have her at as cheap a price as possible. Thus, where *Philomena* appears as a document of the dangers of exogamy, *Erec et Enide's* version of the schema exposes the ugly face of endogamy.[18] Indeed, we arguably see a move from the supreme theft of *jouissance* that is the failure to respect the incest prohibition – allegations of incest or sodomy being stock themes in neighbour defamation – to an almost contrary position where it becomes clear Enide's father is driven by a desire to uphold paternal proprieties even at the price of willingly recreating Ovid's nightmarish scenario.

'L'Amour en... *paiennime*':
Courtly Love in Space and Time

To render love as an irruption into time rendered in terms of allusions to prexisting traditions in which past moments seem to live again can blend uneasily into visions either of a loss of personal or cultural identity, or for that matter, demonic possession. What works for accounts of relations between individuals, also holds for relations also between cultures. Especially troubling for the vernacular Middle Ages is the striking double character of Chrétien's use of the Ovidian material as a story both paradigmatically 'barbarous' in the events it narrates and yet also 'civilised' in its poetic virtuosity. In that sense, his treatment of Philomena contrasts directly with Chaucer's in the *Legend of Good Women* (ll. 2228–393), the latter censoring his source so as not to pass on what the 'venym of so long ago' (l. 2241). This stance would seem little different from the attitude evinced by earlier medieval commentators on Ovid's pernicious influence were it not for Philomena's spectral presence in *Troilus and Criseyde*, where Chaucer's reprise of Ovid's descriptions of Tereus as taloned eagle (*Metamorphoses*, book 6, ll. 516–18) and his violated victim as a trembling dove bloodied from the grip of cruel claws (*Metamorphoses*, book 6, ll. 527–30) creates a disturbing background flitter in the declarations of Chaucer's lovers, especially the comparison of the shy but rhapsodically entranced Criseyde to the 'newly startled nightingale' (*Troilus and Criseyde*, III, ll. 1233–46), the creature into which Philomena transforms.

Thus if Chrétien suggests Erec's and Enide's beauty has the power to make time stand still, then what this raises beyond any modern understanding of the cliché is the possibility of doorways being opened. In this world, comparisons and allusions do not merely suggest similarity, but rather reach across time to other places and moments. This is especially important in traditions also influenced by the matter of Troy, where the influence of the eternal gods is likewise direct and determining in shaping the human present, and where past time can also reach into the present in resurgences of savage energy, such as Aeneas's killing of Turnus, a raw act of vengeance sparked by Aeneas's glimpse of a sword-belt looted from his fallen comrade, Pallas (*Aeneid*, book 12, ll. 938–52), driving him to a merciless act rippling with what Lee Patterson describes as the 'regressive pull of a primitive and barbaric past [that] is felt frequently throughout the *Aeneid*'.[19] However, Chrétien's vision of the past cannot then be seen as a simple image of a barbarian world, but rather of one that is already living in several centuries at once, thanks to the cultural oppositions that structure and divide one civilisation from another. This division is then compounded by the fact that civilisations can then be internally divided, a case in point being the tribal / provincialised world of the Greek city-states. Here, Chrétien's opposition between the cities of Athens and Thrace is cast in terms of a savage pagan past and a more genteel present assimilated to the ultimate beneficiary of the shifts of *translatio* through his favourable comparison of Philomena to Tristan and Appolonius. As prologue to Chrétien's horrific account of Philomena's rape and mutilation, he offers the following damning comment on Tereüs's desire for his sister-in-law:

> Por ce, s'ele iert sa suer germaine
> N'estoit mie amors vilaine,
> Car uns lor deus que il avoient
> Selonc la loi que il tenoient
> Establi qu'il feïssent tuit
> Lor volanté et lor deduit.
> Tel loi lor avoit cil escrite
> Que quanqu'il lor plest ne delite
> Pooit chascuns feire sanz crime,
> Itel loi tenoit paiennime.
> Por ce se poïst cil deffandre,
> S'il fust qui l'an vosist reprandre
> De ce qu'il li plesoit a feire
> Ne devoit nus a mal retreire.
> Mes or leissons lor loi ester.
> Qui porroit Amors contrester
> Que trestot son voloir ne face? (Chrétien, *Philomena*, ll. 219-33)

Just because she [Philomena] was his [=Tereüs's] sister germane didn't mean that there was anything ignoble or vile about his love, for one of the gods they

> had, according to the [law /covenant /religion] they followed had laid down that they should all do whatever they wished and pleased. Such a law had he written for them, that they could do whatever they pleased or desired without any crime. Such was the law of pagan peoples. For that reason, [Tereüs] could defend himself were there anyone who wished to reproach him concerning what it pleased him to do – no one should think he had done ill by it. But now let us leave their law be. Who could argue against Love, such that he does not fully and entirely carry out his will? (trans. mine)

Chrétien's recasting of Ovid offers an account of a world before the universality of Law: the Thracians recognise neither the incest taboo nor any logical extension of it and act instead only in accordance with their own desire.[20] In a skilful use of irony, Chrétien's statement poses as self-contradictory for effect: his indictment of Thracian depravity is doubled by his sardonic concession that the 'law' of their religion dictates they should act on their impulses – a neatly barbed anticipation of François Rabelais's abbey of Theleme, with its motto 'fais que voudras'. To take Chrétien's acceptance of Tereüs's defence at face value constitutes a stupidity akin to the latter's belief he had been granted *carte blanche* to do as he wished with his wife's sister. Of course, such a construction of civilisation before the Law appears quite paradoxical: the refutation of the possibility of crime by the Thracian gods either marks them as living in a Freudian 'primal horde' or as having been granted a holiday from an already-existing history whose existence only '*one* of their gods' (l. 221) chose to deny. In short, Chrétien's ironies target both the 'gods' that grant such a licence and the credulous *vilains* who accept it as *bona fide* exemption from even the most basic civilising principles. Thus, the logic of his condemnation of pagan Antiquity lies in the parallel it posits between pre-Christian belief in the past and heresy or other deviance in the present: pagans, ancient or modern, are happy to be deluded by deceiving spirits. Such an argument not merely recalls early expressions of scepticism regarding the power of evil such as that of Augustine but also from Chrétien's contemporaries, such as John of Salisbury:[21]

> The evil spirit, with God's permission, inflicts the excesses of his malice on certain people in such a way that they suffer in the spirit things which they erroneously [mendacissime] and wretchedly believe they experience in the

> flesh. It is in this sense that they claim that a *noctiluca* [a creature identical in other works with Diana] or Herodias or a witch-ruler of the night convokes nocturnal assemblies at which they feast and riot and carry out other rites where some are punished and others rewarded according to their merits.[22] [...] Who could be so blind as not to see in all this a pure manifestation of the wickedness created by sporting demons. Indeed, it is obvious from this that it is only poor old women and the simple-minded kinds of men who enter into such credences. (*Policraticus*, book 2, chapter 17)[23]

Following Augustine, John goes on to argue that the remedy for such delusion is rational examination: communities that believe in such powers are simply allowing the work of darkness ('opera tenebrarum') to continue.[24] Indeed, while Chrétien's extensive evocations of omens, demonic presence and pagan practice in *Philomena* (see ll. 27–31; ll. 1010–61) may reflect a fascinated exoticism, it is arguable that his descriptions of self-subordination to demonic power, epitomised in the barbaric cannibal holocaust that engulfs representatives of both Athens and Thrace, highlight the dangers posed by the hold of demonic forces on imaginations whether past or present, the possibility that the willing and gullible in either age might foolishly agree to surrender their will so that the 'works of darkness' might prevail. But then, adding to the paradoxes, the narrator then flashes forward, back to a universalised 'present' ruled by another incarnation of the law of love, a will to which all enlightened courtly moderns must seemingly bow. Having started out his speech with outraged sarcasm, ostensibly endorsing Tereüs's monstrous act, Chrétien then wrong-foots the reader at the end, leaving it unclear as to whether the modernity in thrall to the law of love is 'Thracian' or 'Athenian'. What this may reflect more widely is a response to the 'moral panic' attaching to Ovid's work, Chrétien slyly ridiculing the chain of reasoning that to translate such work and write about *fin'amor* will lead to the collapse of history, end the rule of Law and so usher in an age of unbridled fornication and incest.[25] As Scots say, 'Aye, right'.

Chrétien's *Philomena* is part of a more general questioning of the temporal and cultural location of courtly love that extends across his work both in verse narrative and in lyric and to destabilise oppositions between past and present, self and other. This vision of love as a challenge to the progress of the rational in history appears in

Chrétien's other works, where the law of love and the lord of love base their rule in fear, as we can see from the byzantinely flavoured *Cligés*:

> Serjanz qui son seignor ne doute
> Ne doit remanoir en sa route
> Ne ne doit faire son servise.
> Seignor ne crient qui ne le prise,
> Et qui ne le prise ne l'a chier. (ll. 3827–81)

> A servant who does not fear his master should not stay in his company or serve him. You fear your master only if you respect him, and you respect him only if you hold him dear.

Here, love overthrows any idea of feudal reciprocity, Interestingly, this comment appears not in a discourse on political structures per se, but rather in a discourse on the rules governing the court of love ('les coustumes et l'usage / De sa cort', *Cligés*, ll. 3813–14), juxtaposing homosocial political allegiance between 'serjanz' and 'sire' with the erotic bonds of *fin'amor* between Cligés and his 'amie'. And yet, 'custom' and 'use' scarcely sound the most imperialistic of legal terms, especially when associated with the topical elements of the kind Chrétien applies. Courts, like those of Arthur and of Love, seem to be places one attends out of a desire to distinguish oneself, which means that the acceptance of their laws is a free and conscious choice, rather than a universalising rule of law imposed on a wider territory. However, this is not to say that the regulation of sexual and other mores is simply left to willing subordination, although it is often presented as a matter of territory.

Love's troubling history also figures in Chrétien's lyric poetry. If Chrétien's locating of pagan hedonism in relation to medieval modernity provides no clear indication of how far 'we' are from the ancient, lawless 'them', his lyric production, poems dated to the early 1170's, paints the psychic life of the age of *courtoisie* as a 'modernity' counterintuitively transcending the simple zero-sums of feudal reciprocity:[26]

> Nuls s'il n'est courtois et sages
> Ne puet d'amors rien aprendre;

> Mais tels en est li usages,
> Dont nulz ne se seit deffendre,
> Q'ele vuet l'entree vandre.
> Et quels est li passages?
> Raison li convient despandre
> Et mettre mesure en gages. (Chrétien, 'Amors tençon et bataille', ll. 17–24)
>
> No one, if he is not wise and courtly can learn anything [from /of] love. But such is the custom from which none can defend himself, that love sets the entry tariff. And what is the price of passage? You must [spend /put aside] reason and pawn restraint. (trans. mine)

The vision of love here is as an irrational, irresistible force, a tyrannical lawless law demanding quasi-feudal subjection on the part of the subordinate but offering no assurance of corresponding recompense. But then, is courtly modernity 'after' feudalism in the sense that it is its successor, or is it 'before' it insofar as Love's service reduces us to the status of the barely human Thracians? Are we becoming more human or less? In 'Amors tençon et bataille', cited above, Chrétien sees love as the province of the courtly and the wise who must nonetheless put aside reason and restraint. Except that this is not to do full justice to the curious formulations he uses. 'Raison li convient despandre' (l. 24) seems to mean that reason has to be *dispensed with*, except that we also have the sense of *despendre* as 'spend'. Thus rationality appears as a currency to be expended, or at least handed over. To whom, and for what? Similarly, if moderation is to be 'pawned' (l. 23), then who profits from the exchange? Such formulations seems familiar enough in Lacanian terms in that what seems to be being implied is a surrendering of both the principals and principles that are rationality and moderation from which some sort of surplus accrues. The logic of this is the counterintuitively spiralling returns of a perverse *plus-de-jouir*, an economic exchange in which, even though the fate of this surplus seems in doubt, still admits of a greater discursive proliferation.

This fascination with the power of *fin'amor* as the signature of a seemingly neo-barbaric modernity to collapse historical difference is also illustrated in Chrétien's, 'D'Amors qui m'a tolu a moi':[27]

> D'Amors qui m'a tolu a moi
> N'a soi ne me veut retenir,
> Me plaing ensi, qu'adés otroi
> Que de moi face son plesir.
> Et si ne me repuis tenir
> Que ne m'en plaigne, et di por quoi:
> Car ceus qui la traïssent voi
> Souvent a lor joie venire
> Et g'i fail par moi bon foi.

Of Love, who has taken me from myself and yet does not want to keep me as a retainer I complain thus: I henceforth consent that she do as she wish with me. And yet I can't keep from complaining, and I will say why. For I see those who betray her often achieve the joy they seek while I fail by my good faith. (trans. mine)

Even though 'Chrétien' complains of Love's despotic power that leaves him not his own man, but rather an unvalued retainer, he then paradoxically exempts Love of any responsibility for his plight (ll. 1–4). But, then again, he reasserts his complaint as a codicil of greater length than his opening proposition (ll. 5–9). Chrétien's adds interest to the topos of self-pity by a recurrent return to paradoxical formulations whose clear subtext is a questioning of the nature and economics of reciprocity in either politics or pleasure. This is especially apparent in the subsequent stanza, where he asserts his debt to Love:

> Mon cuer, qui siens est, li envoi;
> Mes de noient la cuit servir
> Se ce li rent que je li doi.

My heart, which is hers, I send to her, but I do not think I serve her at all if I only give her what I owe her. (trans. mine)

Again, we see an economic paradox: the lover hands over a heart which is *already* hers, apparently as her due. Except that at this point he chooses to highlight the fundamental problem of love service: mere reciprocity is not service. Paradoxically, love's true vassal is always Love's abject servant.

As part of his engagement with questions of suspension and desire, Chrétien's vision of counterintuitive libidinal economics also encompasses a commitment to the experience of the 'thin time' or *carestia* ('chier tans', l. 42) that must not be a deterrent to the courtly lover:

> Ja, mon los, plenté n'ameras,
> Ne pour chier tans ne t'esmaier
> Biens adoucist par delaier,
> Et, quant plus desiré l'auras,
> Plus t'en ert douls a l'essaier.

> Never do I advise that you love plenty, nor will you be dismayed by time of want. A good thing is sweeter for the delay and, when you have desired it more, it will be all the sweeter to try it. (trans. mine)

Seebass-Linggi argues that 'D'Amors', conventionally datable to just after *Erec et Enide*, provides an explicit summation of the earlier poem's underlying programme.[28] However, whereas the lyric offers a reflection on patience in love whose 'narrative frame' is missing, the *carestia* that will follow Enide's revelations in the bedchamber is an interpolated part of an ongoing history – not exactly an instance of the traditional troubadour and *trouvère* themes of service without reward and love from afar, but rather what will be the interruption of a period of sexual *plenté* providing a perverse *re*schooling in desire curbed.

In short, taking these various texts together presents us with a plural and highly mobile vision of historical difference in which seemingly fundamental differences are subjected to reshaping forces, and in which the affective and the political seem interchangeable. With that in mind, we return from the wider world of Enide's spell to the narrower focus of Laluth. Three, two, one... Back in the room.

Acquiring Enide: A Fair Face on Ugly Business

There are reasons why Enide's father might decide to trust Erec more than Pandion should have trusted Tereüs. The recognition of possibilities and qualities rather than individuals is clearly what distinguishes Erec and the vavasour from the world of Laluth, in which Yder is acclaimed as a known individual and the present incumbent rather than in any genuinely abstracting acknowledgment of his excellence. Indeed, the entire play of events leading up to the Sparrow-Hawk contest is based on the contrast between individual embodiment on the one hand and collectivity or generality on the other, as can be seen from the description of Enide as the peerless creation Nature was unable to replicate (ll. 411–23) and the father's discourse on the themes of fortune and poverty (ll. 509–46) in which he himself serves as exemplar.

Paradoxically, if both Erec and Tereüs experience a similar moment in the first encounter with their significant others, it is what Erec reveals in his speech as opposed to what Tereüs conceals that makes him seem like a safer bet. Erec gives some acknowledgement of what he saw, where Tereüs does not, flagging up the issue of matters that should be under paternal control. However, there is still a risk in his gambit: Erec's inquiry concerning the poverty of Enide's dress could be seen as insensitive. After all, this is the attire in which the Count's niece sees it as shameful that Enide should be led away (ll. 1360–74). However, what is clearly established prior to this is that her attire, like the vavassor's thoughtful demeanour, is designed to provoke questions. Asking the right one requires both understanding and daring, since to see the inequality is to wish to right it.

That 'beauty' serves as guarantee and word to the wise in this exchange had already been carefully emphasised by the vavassor's repeated reference to Enide by the affectionate honorifics 'bele douce fille' (l. 451) and 'bele fille chiere' (l. 470), both of which introduce sets of instructions concerning the ritualised show of respect due to a guest and hint that her 'beauty' may well inhere not just in her Nature-given appearance. Indeed, the first demonstration of Enide's acquired performative *biauté* is for her to attend to Erec's horse (ll. 451–8). Chrétien joins in with the general atmosphere of punctiliousness by carefully emphasising the fact that Enide carries her father's orders out to the letter (ll. 459–69) and then shows her guest due hospitality according to the dictates of courtesy (ll. 470–3). The responses of both Enide's father's and Enide herself mark them out as able to respond *isnelement* in social situations of this kind, demonstrating an understanding of how things should proceed. The fact that there is no gap in understanding makes for an exemplary performance of what is effectively a palace staff in miniature, with Enide decorously filling the office of chief equerry, allowing business to be conducted rapidly:[29]

> 'Dites moi, *beax ostes*', fait il,
> 'De tant povre robe et si *vil*
> Por qu'est vostre fille atornee,
> Qui tant par est *bele* et *sennee*?'
> '*Beax amis*, fait li vavasors,
> Povretez fait mal a plusors,
> Et autretel fait ele moi.
> Mout me poise, quant je la voi
> Atornee si povrement,
> Mais n'ai pooir que je l'ament.' (ll. 505–14, my emphasis)

> 'Tell me, good host', he said, 'Why is your daughter, so lovely and so full of good sense, dressed in such a poor and unseemly dress?' 'Good friend', said the vavassor, 'poverty injures many men, and I am one of them. It grieves me when I see my daughter so poorly dressed, yet I am powerless to make things better.'

Erec signals to his host at the start of the key interaction that stands at the centre of the evening's festivities that the entire exchange will be carried out according to the dictates of *biauté*, even where it comes to the discussion of *vilenie*. His discreet but telling praise of the daughter, moving from his honouring of the father to the dress to Enide's beauty and wisdom, is carefully sequenced and framed, the limits of the social theatre that will unfold are clearly marked. Indeed, the fact that there is no real danger is apparent from the very initial formulation, both parties carefully seeding key terms in the manner of tentative, coded hints to one another: Erec's sympathetic reference to his 'fair host' ('beax ostes', l. 505) already implies a respect for the status and reputation of the *domus*. To begin thus indicates that, in spite of the need to mention certain painful facts, this game will be played in accordance with the dictates of *biauté* and that, although the vavassor finds himself in a subordinate position and required to speak of his own destitution, his lack of 'pooir' (l. 514), there is no reason to fear any actual shame.[30] Accordingly, Erec's coding seeks to elicit an answer that should demonstrate such honour, beauty and sense that will redound to the speaker's credit. Seizing the occasion, the vavassor's language at this point amounts to a challenge to the social order he sees around him and which allows such injustice as he experiences to persist.

Chrétien has already hinted that the vavassor is far from misguided to expect that Erec will feel his sense of slight and neglect as keenly as he does, given that both of them have been referred to by the ambiguous designation 'ostes', having the sense of both 'guest' ('A son oste grant honor fait', l. 396) and 'host' (see l. 461, l. 482 and l. 505, cited above). The narrator's delight in playing on the ambiguity of this term is then made further apparent in the density of his echoing of it in the derived noun 'ostel' (l. 392) and the forms of the verb *oster*, 'to remove' (l. 455, l. 461), the later particularly foregrounded in the couplet 'Le frain et la sele li oste. / Or a li chevax mout bon oste.' ('She took off its saddle and bridle. Now the horse was in excellent hands', ll. 461–2). Thus, the host becomes someone who divests his guest of his burdens, while the guest becomes the person who takes from the host what is offered to him. What the return for this will be remains to be seen, but the cycle of gift and counter-gift is clearly about to snowball given the lively sympathy and command of conventions that makes the two men equals in this exchange. Repetition and word play underscore how the two of them effectively become of one mind on this subject beginning with the cue provided in Enide's father's thoughtfulness, an invitation to reflect on the scene Erec encounters that the young man takes up in the blink of an eye.

If the initial scene with Erec, Guinevere and the first *pucele* in the forest had all the appearances of a languid play of puns, promise, looks and possible desires, now things move along rather more smartly. Erec and Enide's father engage in a game in which each one cues the other to take the next step. If we compare these two negotiation scenes further, we can also see the second as answering the first in that its apparent privacy addresses public questions. The shared status of the young man and the young woman were the guarantee that all could then proceed according to the dictates of desire – under the voyeuristically watchful eye of the Queen, that is. Here, however, a negotiation is concluded with little reference to Enide's wishes. However, what the parallelism and contrast between the two moments gives us to understand is that there is no such scene without some at least implicit parental consent, without which the first *pucele* would have had no sanction for following her heart in the forest. That scene seemed set to promise much, but could not deliver without a change of location. It is in this regard that Erec's apparently precipitate offer of marriage is of primary importance. Peter Noble comments that Erec 'did not need to offer marriage, so quickly at any rate, to secure Enide as his *amie*, although he does know that marriage is certainly what he intends for his daughter'.[31] Of course, the speed of the offer can be read as a further nod to the Philomena tale in that it is precisely the offer that Tereüs could not make and that it indeed provides the public, avowable counterpart of the scandalous secret of the Thracian's quasi-incestuous desires. But, then again, what we also know of that narrative is that Tereüs's marriage to Progné was accompanied by the most sinister portents (*Philomena*, ll. 15–34).

It is precisely because of this emphasis on protocol and performance that Enide's reaction to the arrangement concluded between Erec and her father stresses something other than personal desire:

> Grant joie font tuit par leanz:
> Mout en est li peres joianz,
> Et la mere plore de joie,
> La pucele sist tote coie,
> Mais mout estoit joianz et lie
> De ce que li ert outroïe,
> Por ce que prouz ert et cortois,
> Et bien savoit qu'il seroit rois.
> Et ele meïsme honoree
> Riche roÿne coronee. (ll. 681–90)

> The entire household is overjoyed. The father is as pleased as can be, and the mother weeps for joy. The maiden herself is quite quiet, but delighted and happy at what has been granted her, because he was valiant and noble and she knew he would be king and she honoured and crowned as queen.

This air of quiet calculation has caused a certain amount of critical consternation, as can be seen from Peter Noble's comment: 'Enide and her mother are both delighted at the news, but Enide's reaction is quite materialistic.'[32] Enide's reaction here is perhaps not quite the girlish enthusiasm some might expect, but this is not just a matter of shyness and inexperience. Read against Philomena's charming, cheerful spontaneity, the fact that Enide sees a future based on a judgement of the person she observes is significant: that vision places her squarely in the public sphere rather than raped, mutilated, imprisoned in a dungeon and given out for dead. What Noble sees as materialism could also read as Enide sharing or at least not contesting her father's shrewd hunch about Erec, his immediate appearance, manner and bearing tokens of an acquired knowledge and performative command that make a king. In that respect, Enide's reaction is not just a daydream: it is also a judgement based on her wisdom and intuition as her father's daughter, as someone who may have learned from his qualities, to judge from his praise of her gifts, meaning assumptions about her gendering as naïve or submissively feminine rather than clerkly or even valiant may be misplaced.[33] After all, the prehistory Chrétien sketches for Enide is of a young woman brought up around and in court circles, who has seen a fair amount of business conducted, some of which – the marriage proposals her father has received – concerns her directly. The fact that Chrétien does not mention beauty directly is telling at this point: he arguably thereby paints a picture of Enide's thought processes as governed not by desire, but by a shrewdness evident in her appreciation of Erec as someone whose appearance, bearing and *savoir faire* equip him to play a major role in court circles.

Enide's silence during these negotiations has been read as reflective of a social conservatism part of which is the 'endorsement of marriage practices that promote dynastic alliances', as McCracken puts it.[34] Chrétien's emphasis on acquired political savvy may modify

191

critical assessments centring on the 'innate' qualities of Chrétien's characters, on intuition and 'latent' *savoir*.[35] Just as Erec has been at court three years, Enide too has served her apprenticeship of quiet, thoughtful observation. The accent is on nurture rather than nature, with Chrétien highlighting the place of performance in public life and courtly self-fashioning, the modification of instinct through reflection and extensive observation. Topsfield's strongly polarised picture of Chrétien's political geography renders all the examples that Laluth has to offer bad ones. However, that assumption, based on the premise that the town's dominant elite is characterised by an *orgueil* expressed through the inappropriate use of force, is placed in doubt through the Queen's maiden's actions in the encounter in the forest. Indeed, her ill-thought-out act is precisely an example of the 'neighbourly appropriation' commented on by Žižek (see above) standing in counterpoint to Yder's mangled *courtoisie*. Chrétien's problematisation of rigid moral categories – binary oppositions of self and other, good and evil – continues in Erec's adventures in Laluth. Indeed, what we might well intuit without undue violence is a sense of Enide's complicity analogous to that which Freud enjoined Dora – a later but also apparently helpless object in negotiations about marriage exchange – to examine. Enide may not be as beautiful a soul as we might think or the narrator and her father's descriptions might lead us to believe at first sight.

Enide thus finds herself in a rather different situation from the other *puceles* we have encountered so far in that she appears to be the object of what transpires, rather than the subject. Nonetheless, such details as her admiration of Erec paint a picture of someone more than capable of understanding and manipulating the social milieu from the position in which she will find herself. Her action at that moment is then less the mark of inexperience than an assured demonstration of the tact and discretion necessary to the sort of royal demeanour described by Clifford Geertz:

> In struggling to characterise the king's role [...] the phrase that comes immediately to mind is T. S. Eliot's 'still point of the turning world'; for, insofar as he was an actor in court ceremonies, his job was to project an enormous calm at the centre of an enormous activity by becoming palpably immobile.[36]

Enide's stillness continues her concealment of the wisdom for which her father praises her. The lesson here then is the exercise of judgement, especially with respect to social performance. As we shall see, this emphasis on elegant social performance as a combination of both *biauté* and *prouesse* that crossed and problematises gender oppositions, prefigures issues that will be explored in the scenes to follow.

'The World of Boxing': The Sparrow-Hawk Revived

> La vertu du catch, c'est d'être un spectacle excessif. On trouve là une emphase qui devait être celle des théâtres antiques. [...] Le catch participe à la nature des grands spectacles solaires, théâtre grec et courses de taureaux: ici et là, une lumière sans ombre élabore une émotion sans repli. [...] Bien sûr, il existe un faux catche qui se joue à grands frais avec les apparences inutiles d'un sport régulier: cela n'a aucun intérêt.[37]

> [Le public] sait que la boxe est un sport janséniste, fondé sur la démonstration d'une excellence: on peut parier sur l'issue d'un combat de boxe: au catch, cela n'aurait pas de sens. [...] L'avenir rationnel du combat n'intéresse pas l'amateur de catch, alors qu'au contraire un match de boxe implique toujours une science du futur.[38]

To cast Huizinga's pessimistic views in terms of Barthes's essay on wrestling, the medieval tournament was more catch than boxing, more theatre than science or art of war. This is not to say a tourney that was more *le catch* than *la boxe* would be devoid of meaning, of course, even though, as Barthes puts it, the grammar of wrestling fragments into discrete moments of spectacular excess where boxing appears as a 'rational' accumulation. However, it would be wrong to assimilate the tournament to one rather than the other: instead it combines boxing's 'science du futur' with an element of spectacle that is partly festive, partly judicial. On the side of science, we have an element of technical appreciation in which the language of fencing (*escremie*), the secret dark art of medieval combat, seems to feature more often in more intricately described combat scenes from the mid to late twelfth century onwards.[39] On the side of spectacle, the tourney combat is the not-so-distant cousin of the ordeal, in which the victor becomes the agent of a spectacular justice, the representative of higher powers of this world and the next. However, a theme central to Barthes's essay, and equally central to Chrétien's evocation is the behaviour of the public, caught uncertainly between rational appreciation and emotional involvement. For now, Yder's approach to the sparrow hawk belongs more to the world of wrestling, although this is not to say that the audience of townspeople, the *gent*, will remain fixed in either identity or opinions. Making a quieter entry, Erec has already arrived and is standing off to the side.

>Toutes les *genz* le conoissoient,
>Tuit le conjoient et convoient.
>Aprés lui ot grant bruit de *gent*:
>Li chevalier et li serjant.
>Et les dames corrent aprés
>Et les puceles a eslés.
>Li chevaliers va devant toz,
>O lui sa pucele et ses goz.
>Mout chevauche orgoillousement
>Vers l'esprevier isnelement.
>Mais en tor avoit si grant presse
>De la villainne *gent* engresse
>Que l'en n'i pooit atochier
>Ne de nule part aprochier.
>Li cuens est venuz en la place,
>As *vilains* vient, si les menace.
>Une verge tient en sa main:
>Arriers se traient *li vilain*. (ll. 787–804)

They all knew who he was and crowded around him joyfully to escort him. A great press of people followed him in a hubbub, with knights and men-at-arms and running after him ladies and maidens, as fast as they could go. The knight rode on ahead of them, maiden and dwarf beside him. Full of pride, he rode straight towards the sparrow hawk, but around it there was such a throng of common-folk that he couldn't get near it on any side. Then the Count came along and made straight for the commoners and threatened them, holding a baton in his hand. The commoners drew back.

Chrétien's description makes much of the emotive and demonstrative aspects of public occasion, the increasing animation of the crowd set against the stern, lordly demeanour of the nobles instrumental in staging this display. At this point, we might wonder about the precise content of *orgoil*. Obviously, the term's most common associations are negative, denoting overweening pride or arrogance, in contrast with the more ambiguous, but generally more positive, *fierté*. However, that said, context is all: *orgoil* is not without its neutral or even positive connotations.[40] The adjective *orgoilleus* in particular is attested in the sense of 'swift' when applied to horses, rivers and so on ('li cheval sunt orguillus et curant', *Roland*, l. 3966), while both battles and warriors can be positively described as *orgoilleus* in the sense of energetic or valiant. The question is then one of perspective. Chrétien cuts between Yder riding 'orgoillousement' towards the Sparrow-Hawk and a larger description of what seems to be an increasingly lively, potentially unruly throng who seem not 'know their place', that is to say, where to put themselves in the collective choreography. The question is then whether Yder's orgoil is an undifferentiating reaction to the crowd or to the 'vilainne gent engresse' (l. 798) which may or may not include the 'chevaliers', 'dames' and 'puceles' mentioned just before. Here the question is of emotional territory: is *orgoil* any less appropriate a terrain for a knight than 'joy' is for a *vilain*, given that the entire crowd lays claim to the latter (l. 788)? In that regard, we can see the position of the spectators and the conflicting perspectives on their place and motivations as a source of quiet anxiety, the collective hubbub here perceived through Erec's sense of offence as a 'theft of enjoyment' from the court of Arthur.

Laluth is not uncommonly taken to be associated largely with an inelegant show of brute force that attracts critical censure of all manifestations of violence. For example, Topsfield criticises the Count for threatening the crowd with a baton ('verge', l. 803), although this arguably overlooks some of the ambiguities in Chrétien's presentation of the scene.[41] Viewed negatively, the Count's show of force here might indeed indicate either that he is incapable of managing such an event without recourse to excessive force or that he faces a crowd incapable of behaving in a fitting manner. Moreover, by

195

acting as crowd control for Yder, the Count assimilates himself to the dwarf – although this is to assume that dwarves are invariably and inherently poisonous, a view that will be tested later with the appearance of Guivret. That said, it is not to be taken for granted that the Count is being quite as uncourtly as Topsfield concludes and the scene takes on something of a different cast if we reflect on analogous gestures in other manifestations of court spectacle and scenes of 'crowd control'. For one, the use of batons can denote laudable restraint, such as in the Béroul *Tristan*, where the hero's attendant, Governal, uses one to strike down the leper Ivain (ll. 1260–1) to whose company Mark has ignominiously gifted Iseut as a concubine, while Béroul praises Tristan as courtly for not drowning him, which he claims happens in some competitor versions (ll. 1265–70).[42] Although it is clear that the Count and Yder are less on the side of the angels than Arthur's court, Chrétien may therefore be setting a scene in which we are tempted to read 'the opposition' more harshly than we might in a narrative in which the narrator likewise stands back from the frame, his perspective not so far removed from Erec's and designed to amplify the latter's solitary, discordant presence through echo of his point of view. However, another possibility is that the gestures and attitudes of both the Count and Yder partake of the exaggerated pantomime of public spectacle, the implicit boast attendant on any public appearance of a high-status individual. If the Count and the dwarf appear as front-line guardians, keeping the crowd back from Yder who in turn guards the Sparrow-Hawk as central focus of the custom, part of their function is to amplify the effect of its agalmic kernel.

For all this reading of the Count and the crowd might sound like some fashionably perverse relativist apologetic for a community subjected to critical opprobrium, a reading thus far removed from any sensible moral 'realism', there is a serious point here with considerable bearing on the perspectives of a courtly circles who might have been the audience for Chrétien's poem. The emotional process of cultural interaction in these circumstances would have been complex and intense. As we know from work in the sociology and psychology of conflict resolution, diplomatic negotiations require the management, interrogation and modification of what might seem like the most native and visceral impulses. In that sense, the African expression, 'of course they are our enemies, we marry them', covers a considerable distance in a short space – perhaps inviting us to gloss over some of the bumpier midway ground without due imaginative consideration for the feel of those particular shoes, the shocks and clashes. If Chrétien melts perspectives and sympathies here, then this is part of the imaginative remodelling of the emotional journey Erec's arrival here requires him to undertake, moving from the position of outraged foe to skilful but forceful emissary to affiliation to the family through marriage. Erec's experience of Yder's acutely provoking 'orgoil' encapsulates the estranging effect of competing and evolving claims in the context of a diplomatic process whose horizon simultaneously encompasses both past hatreds and future loves: the defeated Yder will reappear later at Erec's coronation as a prominent member of his household; the Count of Laluth will not.

Chrétien's narrative thus becomes a liminal 'dreaming', a sort of pupal state in which different impulses coexist. After all, Laluth's apparent absence of decorum mostly manifests itself in the greater numbers and diversity of the audience. Arthur seems able to invite a better class of person who only manifest 'esfroi' when he directly provokes them. Fundamentally, the question can then be seen as one of enjoyment: the spectacle of Laluth passionately engaged is 'ugly' insofar as it is observed from outside. Although the appearance of absolute difference between festivities at Laluth and at the court of Arthur can be rooted in the social diversity highlighted in the description of Laluth, the play of difference becomes harder to sustain with Yder, whose apparently negative qualities may be a product of his place in the social theatre of the tourney. Thus, *orgoil* might not exclusively designate Yder's disposition here as opposed to the adoption of a specific role. Of course, part of Chrétien's suggestion may well be that Yder is too absorbed in his 'pride', this may mean he has forgotten Erec or omitted to bear in mind the possible intersubjective dimension created by the tournament. From this vantage point, Erec, too, has his own perspective on Yder's *orgoil*. Again, the knight's pride is not necessarily a defining quality but rather manifest in him being too quick and too direct (*isnel*) in his approach to his prize. He is 'orgoilleux' in the measure that his direct approach to the prize shows he does not reckon on the possibility of a presence such as Erec's. But then equally, it becomes the very character of his provocation, and one which would have not had the same force if he had merely ridden towards the sparrow hawk *mout fierement* or *par grant fierté*. Thus, although near-synonyms, the differences of nuance and point of view these qualifiers imply is crucial. After all, Yder's casting as the *chevalier orgoilleux* (l. 795) is at least in part a product of Erec's point of view, part of a world where the clock is ticking and where Erec must act 'isnelement' in due obedience to the Queen's original instructions if he is to fulfil his boast. The crude pantomime labels of the stock figures of adventure tales are here arguably being fleshed out with a more nuanced consideration of role and function in court spectacle. But then Erec does not have as pivotal a role in the organisation of the proceedings: he simply makes his way to the centre of the Sparrow-Hawk contest and takes up an appropriate place to one side ('Illuec de l'une part s'esturent / Ou le chevalier atendoient', ll. 776–7).

That both parties have a role to play can be seen from the opening of proceedings in the form of a lengthy exchange of threat and insult between the two contenders. The shifting mood and dynamics appears as part of a carefully orchestrated music, beginning with Yder's *piano* instruction 'en paiz' (l. 806) to his maiden that she should step forward to take the hawk. At this, Erec runs to prevent the maiden from taking the hawk in an emphatic *contredit* whose sudden irruptive force echoes the shifts in language and gesture of the encounter in the forest. Not that all the players necessarily snap into place: as Jean Frappier puts it, the repetition of Erec's instruction ('"Bele", fait il, "avant venez! [...] Damoisele, avant vos traiez!"', ll. 827–30) could indicate that the inexperienced Enide misses her cue and has to be told twice.[43] However, although this could be an error, it may also mark a deliberately suspenseful delay, the absence of perfect, clockwork *entente* marking Erec's solitary, insistent agency, his control of *cadence* in a tournament whose prize, as Deborah Nelson points out, appears as a symbol of solitude.[44] Erec's role thus highlights the dramatic function of the stranger, forcing the crowd to realise through Enide's hesitation that no one is exactly privy to his designs or the truth of his desire. What it may also indicate is that

Yder, as the sitting champion and object of universal acclaim in the place, has less dramatic claim to the sparrow hawk than he does. But then, just as there seem to be layers within the topography of the custom (the Count, Yder and then the hawk), so there are layers in its understanding that are then subject to ironic reversal. If the contest is in effect a mirror in which the knight identifies with the singularity of the hawk, then the approach to the mirror places the protagonist further away from it more profoundly in the visual field of the reflection where the person closer to it appears more prominently in the foreground.

Interestingly, for Erec to name the bird as the specific object of his quest ('Uns chevaliers sui d'autre terre. /Cest esprevier sui venuz querre.', ll. 843–4) either reads as a lie or a coded utterance seizing on and appropriating the prize now as metonym for *his* quest, object for object-cause. Accordingly, Erec's participation here appears as a sort of 'Trojan Horse' virus, smuggling in another purpose under a guise of conformity to local protocols. That said, his appearance does show a deference to form: at the very least he has no wish to stop the tournament being a good show. Yder's motivations are rather harder to read. After all, as the sitting tenant of the contest, where no contender has presented themselves for the past few years, he might be taken to be both expecting and not expecting a challenge to his reign. Either way, either out of genuine hostility or a sense of theatrics, he gamely rises to the occasion, self-consciously presenting himself as a romance hero on a journey.[45]

In more than one sense, it seems as if Erec arrived in the nick of time. After all, as a local festival, the Sparrow-Hawk contest was arguably not engaging in sufficient publicity, having seemingly, at a mere day's ride from Arthur's court, dropped off the radar of events in the local area. In that regard, there was seemingly every danger of it slipping from something exceptional into a regular calendar fixture of no special interest, lapsing from its place in mythical time to an ordered regularity. As for the crowd, this is presumably precisely what they came for, two knights exchanging harsh words and getting ready to rumble. Of course, Erec for his part does not break with the framing device of the event: there is nothing to indicate that he could not simply have entered the arena as acting royal champion and challenged Yder directly to combat on the basis of the insult done to the Queen and her maiden. However, this would have left us with something of a quandary: supposing Yder had not remembered the event or had simply apologised and offered amends as indeed he subsequently did, there would in effect have been no fight. In a sense then, what we can see here is a negotiation with an ethics of intention influenced by the thought of Peter Abelard attested elsewhere in texts of the period, notably the *Tristan*, as particularly highlighted by Tony Hunt. The shift here is from an emphasis on effect to a greater prominence of intent.[46] At some level, to judge from his later surrender to Erec, Yder clearly intended no wrong to the party in the forest, a potential *escondit* that could have left any challenge issued by Erec bogged down in legal arguments of a kind not likely to prove very interesting for the crowd. Thus, by conforming to the custom of the place, Erec in effect adds capital to the local system even as it is clear from his actions he is seeking redress. However, what he also achieves by his obedience to local custom is a neat circumvention of the question of whether the damage done to the royal party was *wilful* or not. Rather, what matters now is the orchestrating force of his will. The sense that Yder has been manoeuvred is clearly apparent from Erec's grim satisfaction: 'I have never *wanted* anything more' ('onques plus nule rien ne *vox*' l. 861, my emphasis).

Erec's revitalisation of the Sparrow-Hawk custom, or rather the sense of spectacle that seemed to have become rather depleted over the years provides a reflection on the relation of Chretien's poem to earlier tradition. Just as the 'Lais de l'épervier' versions I–III are presumably after all quite short and of no particular interest, so the reworking that provides the 'mout bele conjunture' paradoxically renews the *esfroi* of this event. Indeed this reflection on antecedent tradition is part of Erec's behaviour: just as the hunt for the White Stag is arguably presented as a cliché, so Chrétien's treatment of the contest is of a spectacle potentially devoid of any real life and now waiting to be revivified in the manner of Arthur's court. In short, the Sparrow-Hawk contest was a scene in search of an author. Similarly, at a performative level, the scene both invites us to be blinded by the spectacle of violence and haughty pride and yet also to consider their place as strategic interventions in a wider play of forces. This double aspect to the scene is emphasised in Erec's response to Yder's threats, dismissing them, 'tot par mesure vos dot' (l. 857), is translated by Fritz as 'I fear you but very little' ('je ne vous redoute que bien peu'). However, this misses a key step in Erec's logic. 'Tot par mesure' indicates, 'I fear you no more than is appropriate'. What is implied by the echo then of his earlier uses of the verb *doter* ('Le chevalier armé dotoie', l. 240), is that he no longer fears him as he did, that 'fear' amounting to a shrewd tactical assessment of the threat he poses, first in an unfair contest, now in a fair one. He thus marks himself out as someone who understands the production of effect and his own place in the drama that is to unfold. That understanding is apparent in his choice of terms and their own micro-history. The insulting sting in the conclusion to Erec's speech here thus picks up and resolves his earlier comment to Guinevere, marking both his self-mastery through his own courage and of the narrative he constructs starting from that boast. More than this, it also contains a strong hint as to his identity. Erec is hinting that there is more than one theatrical perspective at work here: Laluth's own local show is caught in an interlace with his dramatically loaded reprise of key terms in the Arthurian narrative that began back in the forest, cutting across the romance of *Erec et la pucele*.

If Yder's pride was the first part of the work's interrogation of the moral limits of social performance, the duel that follows Erec's challenge tests those boundaries further still. Fundamental ambiguities emerge in the description of the two knights attacking each other 'felonessement' ('Felonessement s'entressaient', l. 878), a term attested as having more negative associations and usages – potentially pertaining to felony as lawless, treacherous savagery – than positive ones, but of which both Carroll and Fritz give more neutral translations ('with great fierceness', 'cruellement'). Of course, this is the term that will then later render the manner in which Fortuna casts down Arthur, at begging the question of whether the laws of the universe can ever be properly said to have such a savage edge. The extent to which the combat wears its participants down, such that they have to pause for rest after several hours of intense fighting is taken by Seebass-Linggi as a potentially ironic reflection on the convention of heroic indefatigability.[47] However, although there is clearly an

201

elelment of distance from the conventions of epic, Seebass-Linggi's sense of the hauberks of legend not living up to their reputation here is perhaps not the most probable reading. As David Edge and John Miles Paddock comment, 'mail is not a rigid defence and, although it will stop a cut, the force of a blow is transferred directly through it, causing injuries of a type known as blunt trauma, that is broken bones and haemorrhaging'.[48] The sum of the violence Erec and Yder visit upon each other is written on their bodies if not in all its sharp detail, then at least in crushing, mangling impressions that leave them sore and weary.

The extent to which Erec's actions sow a salutary 'esfroi' among the citizens of Laluth, then another aspect is the calm they damage elsewhere. For all Enide might have appeared as preternaturally detached in her consideration of Erec's marriage offer, the tourney forces her to contemplate the nature of the compact she has entered into. As Peter Noble comments, it is during the combat that we see the first mentions of Enide's and Erec's feelings for one another, the former anxious to the point of tears (ll. 891–4), the latter inspired by her concern (ll. 907–12).[49] Thus their regard for one another is formed in a moment of *esfroi* of various flavours, echoing the turbulent confusion of the hunt for the White Stag.

Chrétien highlights the moral ambiguity inherent in the use of force and in the manipulation of feelings, the rational calculation of effect in the irrational domain of 'outrage'. Most problematically, Erec is driven by anger in the battle, the emotion reviving him after he has rested for a moment ('ses mautalanz li renovele', l. 925), at which point he addresses his opponent 'par ire' (l. 926). Medieval commentators insist a good deal on distinctions between just and sinful anger, a debate that clearly informs Chrétien's presentation of Erec's resentment as legitimate in cause and pursuit.[50] What is perhaps easy to overlook at this point is that Erec is no anonymous *juvenis* walking the line between, as Bernard of Clairvaux would put it, *militia* (chivalry) and *malitia* (malice), but rather a young king in training.[51] These shows of emotion, carefully evaluated in Chrétien's casuistry of anger, can be read as reflecting a more general movement to restrain violence in tournament contexts without these events devolving into a pantomime anticipatory of Huizinga's vision of the 'waning' Middle

Ages. So much is also reflected in Chrétien's comment that the pair 'de rien nule ne se faignent' (l. 883): this is no mere show. The total nature of the conflict is also apparent in the wounds Erec receives, notably the cut to his flank that precedes his defeat of Yder:

> Bien dut illuec estre afolez:
> Sor la hanche li est colez
> Jusqu'a la char li aciers froiz,
> Diex le gari a cele foiz:
> Se li cops ne tornast defors,
> Trenchié l'eüst parmi le cors. (ll. 945–50)

> Erec could have been badly injured: he felt the cold steel cut right to the flesh of his thigh. But God protected him, that time: had the blade not been deflected outward, he would have been sliced right through.

It is this moment that then inspires Erec to rally and strike his opponent down with three mighty blows, arguably a more neatly choreographed climax than found in the *chansons de geste* thought to have much influenced Chrétien.[52] In the extreme physical theatre the poem proposes, it is only at this point that Erec can truly take his revenge having felt the cold touch of steel on his bare skin. This, short of permanent physical harm, is as far as the game can go against Erec. As the chronicler, Roger of Hoveden comments in justification of the tourneying of Henry II's sons, 'he is not fit for battle who has never seen his own blood flow, who has not heard his teeth crunch under the blow of an opponent, or felt the full weight of his adversary upon him'.[53] Symbolically, and indeed actually, Erec has probably gone as far in training as he can.

Although the tournament constitutes the last word in extreme physical theatre, the motivation here is perhaps not equal on both sides: Yder is simply defending his title whereas Erec is fighting in the name of a wrong done to him and to the Queen. Erec's opponent is therefore not aware at this point that the contest has been transformed into a judicial combat. As Keen points out, it was far from uncommon for tournaments to become occasions for score-settling.[54] However, this imbalance of the passions between the two participants overthrows the symmetry and equality apparent in the even matching of the opponents and the *tac-au-tac* swapping of blows and the identical attitudes of the two women weeping and praying for them. Indeed the imbalance is literalised not only in Yder's staggering and then fall (l. 982), but also mathematically in the rein of blows Erec unleashes just prior to that final defeat:

> Chascuns dou sanc grant masse pert
> Mout afoibloient ambedui,
> Cil fiert Erec, et Erec lui;
> Tel cop a delivre li done
> Sor le hiaume que tot l'estone.
> Fiert et refiert tot a bandon,
> Trois cops li done en un randon,
> Li hiaumes escartele toz,
> Tranche la coife de desoz.
> Jusqu'au test l'espee n'areste,
> Un os li tranche de la teste. (ll. 970–80)

> Both were bleeding badly and growing very weak. He struck Erec and Erec him, landing such a blow square on Yder's helmet that he quite stunned him. Erec struck at him freely again and again, three blows in quick succession, breaking the helmet apart and slicing through the coif beneath. The sword went all the way to his skull, cutting away part of his skull.

From the shared loss of blood and weakening, the reciprocal exchange of blows we modulate into a unilateral sequence of moves from Erec: first *one* blow ('tel cop', l. 973), then *two* in the form of the blow and its viciously effective redoubling ('fiert et refiert', l. 975) to *three* (l. 976), to then the *quartering* of the helmet (l. 977).[55] The neatness of sequencing and the playful manipulation of different principles of pattern and structure make Chrétien's protestations of the dullness of formulaically constructed combats in *Le Conte du graal* perfectly understandable. The lack of suppleness in texts such as the *Chanson de Roland* is made glaring by Erec's sudden break of cadence and the accumulation that denotes his rapid capitalisation on a momentary advantage.[56] What had seemed the limit of theatre at one point, the bite of cold steel in Erec's very flesh, is now spectacularly upstaged by the violence Erec demonstrates, beating Yder down in a hail of blows, the last of which pierces his skull – albeit without touching the brain (ll. 980–1). The limits of combat written on the body in an absolute show of brinksmanship provide a final guarantee of authenticity.

However, Erec goes one step further. His actions seemingly purely mechanical and his thoughts entirely centred on the shame he suffered in the forest (l. 989–91), he removes Yder's helmet with a view to decapitating him (ll. 985–7). Unlike in the exchange with the vavassor, no mutual agreement as to the safety protocols of ritual appears to obtain, Erec's fury seeming to echo episodes such as Aeneas's killing of Turnus, 'inflamed by fury and wrath' ('furiis accensus et ira', book 12, l. 946) at the sight of Pallas's sword belt, taken from the latter's body and fatefully given to Turnus. However, although this history impinges in *Erec et Enide*, the world has moved on. Yder seeks to understand the rationale behind Erec's seemingly monstrous intentions, realising he must be guilty of some great wrong. Likewise, if Erec's challenge is fought out of 'hatred', it is nonetheless the reaction to a specific 'outrage' (l. 989), it still recognises rules of engagement, Erec's respect for Yder's appeal making it clear he is driven by something other than the overmastering rage denounced as not merely *ira*, but *malitia*.[57] Rather, Erec's experience of his own 'hatred' is a formal structure in which he is sufficiently implicated for it to spur him to greater effort, but from which he is sufficiently detached to acknowledge when honour has been satisfied: he does nothing merely 'by instinct'. In that sense, although a highly dramatic backdrop for any duel, the killing of Turnus owes its striking charge to the fact it is an extreme exception rather than a rule in matters of chivalric combat. In not merely accepting Yder's surrender but also providing for his social advancement, moving him from a comital to a royal retinue, Erec shows himself a consummate chivalric modernist in the mode of Geoffrey le Bel (see chapter epigraph).

This sense of chivalry as 'a different century' is apparent at other levels in Chrétien's text, and it is at this point that we might distinguish other modes of aristocratic performance and will that make themselves felt in the scene. In this regard we return to Koziol's assertion that conflict and diplomatic interaction in the Angevin territories in the tenth to twelfth centuries reflected a weave of different political cultures and ritual practices, the very texture of interesting times:

> The power of the seigneurial families in western France was [...] augmented by
> the unusual belligerence and expansionism of the counts. Why the counts
> should have been so embroiled in warfare is difficult to explain. Perhaps the
> contiguity of so many political entities led to friction, particularly on their
> edges, where castellans were easily pried from their loyalties. Whatever the
> reasons, from the last decade of the tenth century through the second third of
> the twelfth century, the border regions of these counties were scenes of intrigue,
> invasion and rebellion.[58]

Although Yder is the first representative of Laluth we meet in the forest, the influence of the Count of Laluth – keen to affirm and indeed extend his prestige through display – is implicit in the actions of his agent. However, the fact that the Count's party encounters a *royal* one indicates that his 'local' jockeying for prestige may have lured him out onto a terrain where he is out of his social and political league. Yet, although the Count might have associations with a 'former' age of territorial friction and dispute, he is not a creature entirely out of time: the Sparrow-Hawk contest is clearly part of a 'culture war' rather than a war per se.

Such an intersection of performance and territoriality has both positive and negative effects. For all the Count may appear little better than a thug, his joyously ebullient people, celebrated in the description of bustle and activity accompanying Erec's arrival in the town, are no more stable. Just prior to this, 'li pueples' (l. 751) had whisperingly acclaimed Erec as the one who could claim the prize, in full accordance with *la règle du jeu* ('par droit' l. 757) and foreshadowing Erec's speech justifying Enide's superior claim to the sparrow-hawk ('bien est *droiz* que voz l'aiez', l. 829, my emphasis). From this body social fit to pronounce in matters of 'custom', the picture changes and atomises into that of a milling throng, the vibrant vision of the socially plural multitude of *gens* (l. 787, l. 789), giving way to that of a now loathsome 'villainne gent engresse' (l. 798), and, finally, 'li vilain', driven back by the Count's intervention (l. 802, l. 804). This is the crowd contemplated from up close, revealing itself as an object of ambivalence at best, as taking on some of the character of a Boschian grotesque in a way that stands at odds with its apparent shows of fair-mindedness.[59] It may be that there is some criticism here of the Count and of Laluth as a whole that they do not know how to organise a collective according to the dictates of *biauté*, his treatment of the vilified crowd generating its ugliness and informing Yder's seemingly undiscriminating view of a world peopled by nothing but *vilains*. And yet we have to ask whether the turbulence of the crowd at Laluth is necessarily so different from that of the body of knights, ladies and other courtiers – set to turn ugly at a certain moment – that Arthur contemplates 'a la parsome' (ll. 2008–09), 'all together' at the end of the hunt.

What seems like Yder's anti-social absorption in his role can also be seen as a trace of the 'comital hardness' organising the space of Laluth. Yet, interestingly, it is precisely Yder's 'local' blindness to how events here are being shaped from elsewhere that saves him, not recognising Erec because the armour disguises him, and because the dwarf's assaults were already part of the narrative of *Yder and the Sparrow-Hawk*. However, the problem here is that Guinevere, the maiden and Erec were thereby in effect assimilated to the 'vilains' later driven back by the Count, already confused with the crowd when there was no crowd. That is Yder's real crime. And yet clearly, as we can see from Guinevere's reaction, Yder is devoid neither of sense nor sense of show, his wandering in the woods – as I commented earlier – bears little relation to the ambuscades staged by the robber-knights later, but rather, on his way to a tournament already in character, contributes to a piece of court spectacle.[60] Thus, although apparently negative, his behaviour is in its way still a forceful gift to the social sphere and part of the economy of *pris*, even if the praise of the collective is only his for want of a more worthy focus.

In that sense, Erec's actions target a historical split: the values of chivalry transform Yder from being simply and directly one of the Count's retainers, relocating him to a 'border' status from which position he can be 'head-hunted' away like some sort of roving castellan. The 'thickness' of this social space can also be seen in the literary oppositions that weave their allusive threads through it. Although the nub of the Sparrow-Hawk combat may be seen as climactically 'Virgilian' in character, the extent to which Erec arrives in Laluth from another place or even *time* – just as Yder's party blundered profaningly, in 'untimely' fashion, into a space irradiated by understandings and a play of gazes left unspoken, all hidden to the internal audiences not in the know – can be characterised as 'Ovidian' in its complex interlacing of different worlds and ages.[61] This dialogue between closure and resonance is apparent in narratorial comments elsewhere in the poem that certain episodes constitute *lais* in themselves, notably the 'Lai de Joie' (l. 6180), reminiscent of the effect derived by Ovid from both interlaced narratives and braided, competing desires, both divine and human. Likewise, Yder's *conte d'aventure*, a closed work blind to any 'extra-textual' dimension and carrying within it an edge of territoriality symptomatic of behaviours and displays centring on the Count, suddenly encounters the tale of seduction that was *Erec et la pucele*, a story centred on the Queen.

If comital power – invested in but also dissimulated and transformed by its mediators – is one of the determining forces in the actions of agents simultaneously participating in a plurality of value systems, then Erec's behaviour is similarly duplicitous. Unlike in the chanson de geste, with its scrupulous detailing of the ritual of combat by ordeal and its concern with the niceties of wording in both accusation and denial, Erec does not disrupt proceedings by openly declaring Yder's *forfait* or revealing himself as seeking redress for the wrongs done against the Queen, her handmaiden or himself. This occlusion of his jurisdiction will be mirrored later in his refusal to take the dress: on both occasions Erec shows a respect for the laws of the place, concerned not to present himself or others in the guise of someone not invited, not part of the local picture. Yet, if there is a careful deference to the rules of place is counterbalanced by an interest in the role of excess and transgression. For one, no one ever defeated Yder by simply playing their part in the tournament, the involvement of another community with its own history and agenda providing the key, the element of revenge in Erec's victory, as we are reminded (ll. 917–20) an 'excess' over the closed economy of the Sparrow-Hawk custom to answer that of Yder's intrusion into the private world of Guinevere and her party.

Merely to see Chrétien's presentation of Laluth as indicating a lack of moderation on their part is to miss the moral ambiguity implied, and indeed the progression of values. What Chrétien could be suggesting is that Yder and Erec are alike in that they are both capable of functioning as focuses of court spectacle. The question of what use is then made of that ability and influence is then a separate one. In that sense, we could see Chrétien as ostensibly elaborating a position not far removed from that of Machiavelli's 'and there is nothing in the world but ordinary people', except that what is then implied is that the ruler must combine on the one hand, power and a sense of courtly theatrics with, on the other, purpose and a sense of moral values. If Erec stopped at this stage in his political education, then, although able, he would be as hollow an individual as Yder. Where the elite defaults on its moral obligations, everyone loses out and the entire status system collapses. The theatre must have a *sens*, a purpose, the promise of an 'avenir rationnel'. As Barthes points out, the rhetorical structure of 'le monde où l'on catche' is not a 'mout bele conjunture'. Although Köhler presents the two visions of custom in the 'premiers vers' as fundamentally contrasting, it is arguable that the differences are more of perspective.[62]

As with Arthur's court, the Sparrow-Hawk custom seems to contradict 'common sense' in that both target the stable order that had obtained and both share an element of show in their violence. The Count's seemingly despotic threatening of the crowd functions as pantomime prelude to Yder's challenge, both gestures setting out the lines not to be crossed as part of the drama. Indeed, the contrast with Morholt invoked in Chrétien's description of the events following the combat is telling, possibly even ironic. Both a giant demanding human tribute and yet, at the same time, kinsman of Iseut, Morholt appears as a quasi-tyrannical creature devoid of any sense of justice and in part the ambassadorial representative of the Irish kings, maintaining their right to demand tribute. Although Yder appears as the monster, Erec, too, can be assimilated to Morholt, forcibly re-establishing Laluth's tributary subservience to Arthur's court. In Geoffrey, the legitimacy of Arthur's territorial claims is recurringly contrasted with the claims of giants, the latter appearing in caricatural form, hinting at grotesque, cannibalistic sacrifice. However, as commentators have noted, this does not mean that King and giants are without likeness.[63] And, likewise, neither man here is exactly a monster. Although he appears as the military wing of the Count's domination, Yder's 'concession

209

speech' (ll. 1046–58) reveals a clear sense of obligation and diplomacy, even if our reassessment of his character is troubled by Chrétien's introductory nudge to bear in mind that the fine words are after all extorted by force ('Lors li dit cil, *ou vuille ou non*', l. 1045, my emphasis), but then, for now, the appearance is enough: 'fake it until you can make it [to court]'. Thus, while one might argue his defeat breaks the spell of pride that held him prisoner, a reading potentially in keeping with the events of the Joy of the Court, the self-consciously performative dimension in his actions mitigates against seeing his actions as dictated by a quasi-magical entrapment, a total involvement in his own brutality. Rather what emerges is a performative engagement in the game that arguably has no less right or reason to colonise the outside world of the forest than the hunt of the White Stag. Of course, another possible sense of the contrast with Morholt is as a rather less serious assessment: as with the passing evocation of Turnus and Aeneas, Tristan's victory over the bogey-man giant might serve as no more than a mythical, and possibly cliché, benchmark of crowd excitement in the world of the tourney.

Notes

1   Köhler, 'Le Rôle de la coutume dans les romans de Chrétien de Troyes', *Romania*, 81 (1960), 386–97. Köhler argues that while customs such as the hunt are an obligation on Arthur, the Sparrow-Hawk contest appears as a source of discord which is resolved by the intervention of a representative of Arthur's court. On custom, see also Philippe Ménard, 'Réflexions sur les coutumes dans les romans arthuriens', in *Por le soie amisté. Essays in Honour of Norris J. Lacy*, ed. by Keith Busby and Catherine M. Jones (Amsterdam: Rodopi, 2000), 357–70 On the episode, see also Paule Le Rider, 'L'Episode de l'épervier dans *Erec et Enide*', *Romania*, 116:3–4 (1998), 368–93.
2   On which, see Koziol, pp. 241–88.
3   On these conflicts see Kimberly A. LoPrete, 'Le Conflit plantagenêt-capétien vu des frontières', in *Capétiens et Plantagenêts: confrontations et héritages*, ed. by Martin Aurell and Noël-Yves Tonnerre, Histoires de Famille: La Parenté au Moyen Age, 4 (Turnhout: Brepols, 2006), pp. 359–75.

4 Köhler, *L'Aventure chevaleresque*, p. 203.
5 On Enide's humble origins, see especially Köhler, *L'Aventure chevaleresque*, pp. 84–9.
6 On rape in the *Brut*, see Gravdal, *Ravishing Maidens*, pp. 42–5 and Cohen, *Of Giants*, pp. 37–9.
7 Sade, *Justine ou les malheurs de la vertu*, in *Oeuvres complètes* (Paris: Cercle du livre précieux, 1966), III, pp. 11–345 at pp. 168–72.
8 For text and translation, see Pochothèque edition, pp. 1225–67. For studies, see E. Hoepffner, 'La *Philomena* de Chrétien de Troyes', *Romania*, 57 (1931), 13–74; Glyn Burgess, 'The Theme of Beauty in Chrétien's *Philomena* and *Erec et Enide*', in *An Arthurian Tapestry: Essays in Memory of Lewis Thorpe*, ed. by K. Varty (Glasgow: University of Glasgow French Department, 1981), pp. 114–28; Gravdal, *Ravishing Maidens*, pp. 61–4; Burns, *Bodytalk*, pp. 115–50; James-Raoul, notably pp. 229–31 and pp. 240–4.
9 Duggan, *The Romances of Chrétien de Troyes*, p. 156.
10 On which, see Gravdal, *Ravishing Maidens*, pp. 58–60.
11 On Philomena's beauty and accomplishments, see Burns, *Bodytalk*, pp. 118–24.
12 Noëlle Lévy-Gires, 'Se coiffer au Moyen Age ou l'impossible pudeur', in *La Chevelure dans la littérature et l'art du Moyen Age*, ed. by Chantal Connochie-Bourgne, Senefiance, 50 (Aix-en-Provence: Publications de Université de Provence, 2004), pp. 279–90, here at pp. 279–80. On Enide's dress see also Roger Middleton, 'Enide's See-Through Dress', *Arthurian Studies in Honour of P. J. C. Field*, ed. by Bonnie Wheeler, Arthurian Studies, 57 (Cambridge: Brewer, 2004), 143–63.
13 On Katherine's entry into London, see Kipling, pp. 209–21.
14 See for example, Burns, *Bodytalk*, p. 158 and note 11; Noble, *Love and Marriage*, pp. 12–14.
15 Peggy McCracken, 'Silence and the Courtly Wife: Chrétien de Troyes's *Erec et Enide*', *Arthurian Yearbook*, 3 (1993), 107–26, p. 107.
16 The connection here between *Erec et Enide* and the Ovidian tradition seems more strongly foregrounded here than the contrast Raymond Cormier notes between the encounter between Erec and Enide on the one hand and Lavine and Eneas on the other (Cormier, p. 88).
17 Bezzola, pp. 106–07.
18 On endogamy and exogamy in Chrétien from this point of view, see Duggan, *The Romances of Chrétien de Troyes*, pp. 89–92.
19 Patterson, *Negotiating the Past*, p. 164.
20 On this passage see especially Gravdal, *Ravishing Maidens*, pp. 62–3.
21 On Augustine on demonic power, see notably G. R. Evans, *Augustine on Evil* (Cambridge: Cambridge University Press, 1990), pp. 98–111.
22 On the *noctiluca*, see Alan C. Kors and Edward Peters (eds), *Witchcraft in Europe, 1100–1700: A Documentary History* (London: Dent, 1973), p. 37 and note 1.

23 For edition, see John of Salisbury, *Policraticus*, ed. by K. B. Keats-Rohan, Corpus Christianorum Continuatio Medievalis, 118 (Turnhout: Brepols, 1993).
24 'Si vero quisquam eorum qui hac illusione laborant ab aliquo constanter et ex signis aliquibus arguatur, ex quo quis in luce arguitur, cessant opera tenebrarum. Huius autem pestis cura efficacissima est ut fidem qui amplexus his mendaciis subtrahat mentis auditum et nequaquam respiciat ad huiusmodi vanitates et insanias falsas.' (*Policraticus*, book 2 chapter 17).
25 On cultural anxieties regarding Ovid's work in the Middle Ages, see Simpson, *Fantasy, Identity and Misrecognition*, pp. 133–90.
26 On the dating of Chrétien's lyric poetry, see Duggan, *The Romances of Chrétien de Troyes*, pp. 24–5 and p. 156. For a study of Chrétien's lyric poetry, see Marie-Claire Zai, *Les Chansons courtoises de Chrétien de Troyes*, Europaïsche Hochschulschriften, 13:27 (Bern: Peter Lang, 1974).
27 For commentary on 'D'Amors qui m'a tolu a moi' and its relation to Chrétien's other work, see Alfredo Roncaglia, 'Carestia', *Cultura Neolatina*, 18 (1958), 121–37; Topsfield, pp. 67–9; Seebass-Linggi, pp. 218–47 and, on the potion imagery, Gaunt, *Love and Death*, pp. 129–37.
28 Seebass-Linggi, p. 222.
29 On the possible Celtic roots of Enide's association with horses, see Duggan, *The Romances of Chrétien de Troyes*, pp. 214–16.
30 Obviously, this is then a much more domesticated version of the opening scenario of *Le Chevalier au lion*, in which the revelation of his cousin's shame is the cause of Yvain's first act of folly, namely the solitary departure from court that foreshadows his actual madness later.
31 Noble, *Love and Marriage*, p.13.
32 See Noble, *Love and Marriage*, p. 13 and, *contra*, Seebass-Linggi, p. 139.
33 In that regard, I would take issue with readings such as Firestone's: 'Clearly, [Enide] knows nothing of the fickleness of fortune. The condition of the family is not the result of bad luck, but is only reasonable in view of her father's rank or behaviour' (p. 79). On Chrétien's construction of Enide's background, education and gendering, see S. L. Clark and Julian N. Wasserman, 'Language, Silence and Wisdom in Chrétien's *Erec et Enide*', *Michigan Academician*, 9 (1976), 285–98; Grace M. Armstrong, 'Enide and Fenice: Chrétien de Troyes's Clerkly Heroines', in *Papers on Romance Literary Relations: The Creation of Female Voices by Male Writers in Romance Literatures*, ed. by Martha O'Nan, Charity Cannon Willard (Brockport: State University of New York College, 1987), pp. 1–8; Erin Murray, 'The Masculinisation of Enide's Voice: An Ambiguous Portrayal of the Heroine', *Romance Languages Annual*, 8 (1996), 79–83; Margaret Jewett Burland, 'Chrétien's Enide: Heroine or Female Hero?', in *On Arthurian Women: Essays in Memory of Maureen Fries*, ed. by Bonnie Wheeler and Fiona Tolhurst (Dallas, TX: Scriptorium, 2001), pp. 167–86
34 McCracken, 'Silence and the Courtly Wife', p. 107.
35 For example, Topsfield, p. 36.

36 Geertz, *Negara*, p. 130.
37 Roland Barthes, 'Le Monde où l'on catche', in *Mythologies*, Points (Paris: Seuil, 1971), pp. 13–24, here at p. 13.
38 Barthes, 'Le Monde où l'on catche', p. 14.
39 Views in medieval French texts seem divided between technical appreciation and suspicion of the kind later to be voiced more uproariously by Mercutio in his lambasting of Tybalt (*Romeo and Juliet*, act 2, scene 4). Notably, Renart's expertise in fencing, prominently mentioned in the narrative of the judicial duel between him and Isengrin (Br. VI, ll. 829–46 and ll. 1135–42), is presented as part of the fox's generally sly and cynical approach to legal procedure.
40 See Glyn Burgess, '*Orgueil* and *fierté* in Twelfth-Century French', *Zeitschrift für Romanische Philologie*, 89 (1973), 103–22.
41 Topsfield, p. 37.
42 For edition, see Daniel Lacroix and Philippe Walter (eds and trans.), *Tristan et Iseut: les poèmes françaises, la saga norroise*, Lettres Gothiques (Paris: Livre de Poche, 1989).
43 See Jean Frappier, 'La Brisure du couplet dans *Erec et Enide*', *Romania*, 86 (1965), 1–21, p. 20. This detail of course has its later echo in Enide's tardy arrival at the coronation, forcing Arthur to send Gauvain for her (ll. 6802–06). One possibility here is that in the latter instance, Enide is marking her special status by delaying her arrival, even as Erec marked his at court by asking Arthur to bring forward the date of the wedding (ll. 1911–18) and then sent his squire to chide her for tarrying before their departure on the quest from Carnant (ll. 2660–75).
44 Deborah Nelson, 'The Role of Animals in *Erec et Enide*', *Romance Quarterly*, 35:1 (1988), 31–8, at pp. 32–3.
45 As Sarah Kay points out (*The Chansons de geste in the Age of Romance: Political Fictions* (Oxford: Clarendon, 1995), p. 50), the object of the romance quest is often left mysteriously unspecified or as a cipher. However, here Chrétien seems to foreground the motif as a narrative cliché.
46 Tony Hunt, 'Abelardian Ethics and Béroul's *Tristan*', *Romania*, 98 (1977), 501–40.
47 Seebass-Linggi, pp. 44–52.
48 David Edge and John Miles Paddock, *Arms and Armour of the Medieval Knight* (London: Defoe, 1988), p. 57.
49 Noble, *Love and Marriage*, p. 14.
50 See discussion in chapter 1, above.
51 On *militia* and *malitia*, see Tony Hunt, *Chrétien de Troyes: 'Yvain'*, Critical Guides to French Texts (London: Grant and Cutler, 1986), pp. 37–51 and Kaeuper, *Chivalry and Violence*, pp. 64–88.
52 For example, even extended combats in the later rhymed versions of the *Chanson de Roland* have opponents mechanically swapping blows in a rhythm

little different from the shorter confrontations a prominent feature of the first encounter with the Saracen army and the Frankish rearguard.
53 Roger of Hoveden, *Chronica*, ed. by W. Stubbs (London: Rolls Society, 1885), II, pp. 166–7 (translation cited from Maurice Keen, *Chivalry* (New Haven and London: Yale University Press, 1984), p. 88).
54 Keen, *Chivalry*, pp. 85–7.
55 To redouble or to reprise is to strike two blows without the opponent responding in between. In modern foil fencing, redoubling is largely eliminated as an inelegant and marginal possibility by the formalising principles of 'time' and 'right of way' (Fr. *priorité*), according to which once an attack has either been parried or has simply discontinued, the opponent has a right to respond in a new phase. This reflects the general philosophy of foil as a training weapon whose discipline appears as a structured rhetoric of *dit* and *contredit*. The same does not apply with regard to the heavier weapon known as the *épée*, where the target area is the entire body (rather than just the torso as in foil, or the upper body in sabre fencing), and where the scoring system (clearly derived from training for a 'first blood' duelling system) recognises absolute rather than formal notions of 'time' (the attack that lands first scores, unlike in foil, where the attack that has right of way scores). In effect, however, the formalised economy of all the weapon disciplines in modern fencing gives no space to accumulation, largely redundant in a system where creating and then pressing an advantage has no real rationale.
56 'Cadence' as a fencing term refers to the rhythm of a sequence of movements in a given attack. Part of the psychological aspect of the sport is then to unsettle an opponent by breaking their rhythm or to establish cadence and use it to deceive the opponent.
57 Hunt, *Yvain*, pp. 37–51.
58 Koziol, p. 252.
59 Bosch in that regard combines precisely the concern with differentiation by dress as indicative of status and function with the further individualisation through the elaboration of a range of facial types that is both more varied in terms of precise detail but then as or even more restricted in terms of its basic themes (noses, chins, expressions).
60 After all, what would have been entirely unthinkable would have been the scene in which Erec met an unarmoured Yder, who cheerfully accepted to have him accompany them, only then to stop just before Laluth and say 'Sorry! I've just got to put my armour on and get into character. Would you mind awfully following behind us and looking as if you've got a grudge against me? Thanks. There's a reception afterwards – do come along.'
61 On overlapping and intersecting temporalities, see Cohen, 'Introduction: Midcolonial', pp. 1–3.
62 Köhler, 'Le Rôle de la coutume', p. 389.
63 Cohen, *Of Giants*, p. 80–4.

Companho, farai un vers covinen
Et aura'i mais de foudatz no'i a de sen
Et er toz mesclatz d'amor e de joi e de joven

E tenhatz lo per vilain, qui no l'enten
Qu'ins en son cor voluntiers res non l'apren
Greu partir si fai d'amor qui la trob' a son talen.

Dos cavals ai a ma selha, ben e gen;
Bon son ez ardit per almas e valen;
Ma no'ls puesc tener amdos, que l'uns l'autre no consen.

Si'ls pogues adomesgar a mon talen
Ja no volgr' aillors mudar mon garnimen,
Que meils for' encavalguatz de nuill hom en mon viven.

La uns fo dels montanhiers lo plus corren,
Mas aitan fer' estranhez' ha longuamen
Ez es tan fers e salvatges, que del bailar si defen.

L'autre fo noiritz sa jos, pres Cofolen;
Ez anc n'on vis belazor, mon essien;
Aquest non er ja camjatz, ni por or ni por argen.
    (William IX, 'Companho, farai un vers covinen', ll. 1–19)

My friends, I'll make a seemly poem and there'll be in it more folly than there's sense, and it will be all mingled with love and joy and youth. And consider him a serf who doesn't understand it or in his heart learns it not willingly; it's hard to part from love for one who finds it to his liking. I have two horses to my saddle, right and properly; good they are and skilled in war, and valiant. But I cannot keep them both, for one can't abide the other. If I could break them in to my desire, I would never wish to change my gear elsewhere, for I'd be better mounted than any living man. One was the swiftest of those from the mountains, but for long it's shown such wild restiveness – it's so wild and shy that it refuses to be groomed. The other was reared down here, by Confolens, and you never saw one more handsome; to my mind; this one will not be changed for either gold or silver. (trans. after Press)

Chapter Four
'Just Right for a Maiden':
Approaches to Marriage at Court

Having examined the confrontation between Arthur's court and the world of Laluth, an encounter that might be more a matter of conflicting desires converging in a single space rather than black-and-white moral antitheses, we move now to the events leading up to the celebration of Erec and Enide's wedding. In a sense, this narrative arc, this 'phrase' opened at the very beginning of the poem and only now moves towards its resolution. The history here is a complex one with various possible competitors emerging. However, what we will see in this chapter is that that sense of finality and seeming naturalness had been subject to various challenges and disruptions from the outset.

From where we are on a road caught between one place and various possible destinations, we might consider the following possibilities. Suppose Arthur had had Erec's marriage in mind all along. Thus, the announcement of the hunt would then have been a staged final item remaining on the court's agenda to provide a backdrop for the betrothal of Erec and the unnamed king's daughter who would have just then reappeared at court from stage left. Given the emphasis on Erec's 'beauty' and the 'love' he has earned at court, it is not unreasonable to assume the announcement of his forthcoming marriage might well have created sufficient 'feel-good factor' to provide a resolution to Arthur's scheme. A 'happy ending' of this kind might well have carried the day – especially if certain key courtiers just happened to 'fall in' behind the decision, a likely candidate here being Gauvain, whose prominent displeasure at the original announcement now positions him as a convenient focal point of collective feeling. Arthur's production of the new couple would then have allowed (or prompted) his nephew to recognise with a delighted spontaneity (or, as with Yder, at least its appearance) the fittingness of it all and so carry with him a court looking to him for a cue. As for the wedding, it might have taken place as late as the following Christmas or as early as the feast of St John. It would have been as if it had been planned all along.

But something went wrong. Although the arrival of Yder could have provided a chance for Erec's possible intended to distinguish herself, the moment misfires to the point of derailing any 'unofficialised' plans. If the Arthurian court had been depending on the appearance of an improvised solution before, that commitment to *sprezzatura* returns to haunt them as they wait anxiously for what will unfold. In the meantime, Erec's progress, having now derailed Yder's acclamation as the Sparrow-hawk Champion, will itself be subject to attempts at sabotage appearing in the most paradoxical of guises.

Of course, the phrase of my argument here cuts across the structural divide that is Erec's return to court with Enide, bringing together things that seemed separate and opposed. This is of course deliberate. The point is to illustrate the similarity in tactics and the shared worlds of value and allusion that underpin even the most tense encounters along the way, the manners in which these histories are then resolved into unions of friendship and cooperation reshaping and dissolving the contours and divides of the world in which the various players move. In short, these histories – in which Erec has, or *will* have, a friend called Yder and a beloved kinsman who is the Count of Laluth – will all be rationalised for the best. In its possible echoes of Chrétien's treatment of the Philomena story, Laluth might appear as a version of Thrace against Arthur's Athens, but that opposition is only temporary. The picture Chrétien paints is of an evolving history of court societies constantly reshaping the cultural geographies which provide their backdrop. What seemed like conflict is recoded as pre-wedding carnival, a suspension extended to encompass various elements that will appear in retrospect as a lewd and jocular play that provides the collective *Vorlust* preceding the wedding night itself.

On Palfreys and Horse-Trading

Cited at the beginning of this chapter, the poem, 'Companho, farai un vers covinen', attributed to William IX, grandfather of Eleanor of Aquitaine, is read as being less about a choice of horse than between 'Lady Agnes' and 'Lady Arsen' (l. 24), painting a picture of a lively, not to say lewd, court culture in which the lord appeals to his companions in a spirit clearly unbridled by moderation, testing the limits of what can be said in the public sphere regarding matters of love. The poem presents us with a robust and volatile interplay of wills and desires, an interlocking structure of related, but assymmetrical, demands and counter-demands. For all that one mistress is presented as fiery and proud, the other is no more willing to compromise. For all one is incomparably, almost abstractly beautiful, the other – a sort of *farouche* Atalanta figure – seemingly unattainable in her own way.[1]

However ostensibly unhallowed and undomesticatable the triangle he presents, William's poem paints an interesting picture of marital politics at court. What are we to understand from his designation of one mistress as a wild creature from the mountains? Does this description mark her as simply foreign to the Poitevin court or of less noble extraction than her rival? Such figures fit with the image of the foreign bride as both an object of desire and a source of danger, whether in the form of Guinevere and her negative antitypes to be found in *Lanval* or *Le Roman de Silence*, or in the form of the adulteress-magician Iseut or that ultimate conquest of the feminine wild, the 'Saracen Princess' (Orable, Nicolette and so forth).[2] Against this, we have the image of a more familiar 'girl-next-door', lacking the rough edges of the lady of the mountains.

The opposition seemingly presents not much more than a medieval version of what Balzac was to recast in the nineteenth century as the image of woman as 'a work in two volumes', a justification of metropolitan masculine adventurism. However, what R. Howard Bloch terms the 'biopolitics of lineage' here are more complex.[3] In this scenario, the 'wild woman' figures the alluring strangeness of custom and aspect attaching to a neighbour culture less immediately domesticatable, less familiar (in all, and perhaps especially its oldest senses) to the host court than the untradeable 'beauty' of the object of endogamous desire. What this bears witness to is a culture of ambivalence with regard to the marriage market, an economy in which communities, nervous at the possible outcomes, are happy to gain but unwilling to give up commodified female beauty.

William's presentation of the two female figures, more or less explicitly outspoken in the defence of their desire and prerogatives provides an insight into the history of women's status and agency at court. It may seem as if the 'rugby club' atmosphere the poem seems to posit is simply a manner of laughing two woman down by shaming them in front of a crowd whose metaphorical descendants are the ignoble rapist horde following Harpin de la Montagne in *Le Chevalier au lion*. We could also see echoes of more comic scenarios, such as the humiliation visited on the Countess in *Le Chevalier qui fist parler les cons*, a woman seeking to maintain control over her body in a social economy regulated by coarse misogynistic ridicule. However, in this irresolvable conflict, William is similarly explicit in presenting his will as unable to prevail against theirs even as it is unable to bring him to a choice between them.

Part of the lesson of Chrétien's text lies in the use by both male and female courtiers made of force, whether at a physical or discursive level. What the premiers vers demonstrates is that shows of force is do not always lead to untrammelled physical conflict, as is apparent from episodes such as Arthur's pronouncement and the Queen's maid's attempt to push past the dwarf. In that sense, the combat with Yder consummates possibilities the text has merely flirted with up until that point, Erec seeking satisfaction from his man and forcing him to recognise the claims of the social theatre of Cardigan rather than those of Laluth, which had initially and unknowingly asserted its priority through Yder's appearance in full arms at a point where everyone else was dressed for another occasion.

However, Yder's defeat does not put an end to violent interaction in Laluth. The war continues by other means. Erec's refusal of hospitality following the tournament reminds us that the fact he did not make himself known to the Count on arrival in Laluth was a snub, thus effectively already a hostile act, a *laidure* compounded after his victory over Yder. Indeed, the climax of the combat with Yder is the phased *redoublement* of his blows is mirrored in the sequence of rebuffs inflicted on the Count in a campaign more sustained than the actual combat with his champion, whom Erec subsequently poaches for his own household, as we see from Yder's place in the coronation ceremony (l. 6811), an occasion the Count just happens not to attend. As part of this rocky relationship, problems threaten to re-emerge as negotiations founder over the question of the dress. Erec offers no justification for his refusal of the offer or any suggestion as to what he would deem more fitting. But then, as we know from the foregoing scene, it is partly his role as the Sparrow-Hawk champion to appear mysteriously intransigent, and he here maintains that line with determination, seemingly manifesting the 'Real' of a fundamental conflict merely mimed in the show tournament.

As per Elias's account of the civilising process, court conversation here thus appears as a key element in a 'war by other means'.[4] It is left to the Count's niece – like Gauvain with Arthur, displaced by Erec's 'parole' (l. 1355) – to assess what damage accrues from this gesture, her comment to her uncle stressing the shame that will be his (ll. 1355–64). Her brief response maps the social terrain neatly: referring to both men as 'sire' (l. 1360; l. 1362), she moves to block, interposing herself between them so as to draw a line in the sand. In answer, and without seeming reference outside the circle to see whether his suggestion meets with Erec's approval, the Count instructs her to give Enide her best dress (ll. 1365–8). Faced in turn with a 'parole' (l. 1369) he does not like, Erec leaves them no room for manoeuvre: not waiting for anything to be relayed via the niece, he effectively 'breaks time', pointedly cutting across the discursive and social space of their exchange to warn the Count against pursuing this line any further (ll. 1370–4), a thinly-veiled squash of a kind best avoided unless very sure of one's ground.[5] However, countering very much *du tac au tac*, the niece's unfazed retort (ll. 1376–98), especially its opening – with a steely 'Ohi!' prominently positioned at the first line end – leaves us wondering for a microsecond what this clearly formidable young woman's next move will be before she leads us surefootedly to the description of the palfrey, of which more presently.

For Erec, the subtext of this scene is supplied by his earlier remarks to Enide's parents, detailing the gifts of furs and clothes he intends to give to them. However, the gifting is not just material, but also symbolic: in referring to Enide's mother is 'his dear lady' ('la moie chiere dame', l. 1342), he credits her with a title used of no less a person than the Queen but a few lines later ('ma dame', l. 1346), doubling his material largesse with a compensatory soft-soaping of the vavassor and his wife, his account of the castles that will be theirs and his use of honorifics making it clear what their new or renewed status will be in this other place. The values of kin and court are thus brought into clear parallel, Erec painting thereby a brief picture of Cardigan as both larger stage and familiar mirror of their own household, a new world in which he will serve as their guide. Accordingly, when Enide's cousin flags up the potential disgrace for her uncle, Erec's stern refusal gains in force from his mention of Guinevere as 'the Queen' (l. 1374), a reference to higher authority that checks Count and niece. The suggestion seems to be that those of Laluth will have to tailor their words and gifts to a new situation where there is now no space to make last-minute amends for previous neglect.[6]

However, although the court of Laluth may have been shown up by the rapid evolution of events, the test is how rapidly a circle reacts and adapts to new contingencies without adopting the posture of a society disgraced and defeated, looking to make appropriate gestures, but still not abandoning the possibility that it might reassert itself or turn the situation to its advantage. In this context, the niece's description of the palfrey is of capital importance:

> 'Li oisel qui volent par l'air
> Ne vont plus tost dou palefroi;
> Et si n'est pas de grant esfroi:
> Tex est con a pucele estuet,
> Uns enfes chevauchier le puet,
> Qu'il n'est ombrages ne restis,
> Ne mort, ne fiert, ne n'est ragis.
> Qui moillor quiert, ne set qu'il vuet.' (ll. 1388–95)

> 'No bird flying through the air can go as fast as that palfrey. No one ever saw it bolt or rear; a child can ride it. He's just right for a maiden: he is neither skittish nor stubborn, and never bites, lashes out or gets in a temper. Whoever seeks a better one does not know what he wants.'

The amends to be made here lies in conveying Enide to court in the most fitting manner, and the resolution of the dispute can be seen silently reflected in Erec's reported vociferous praise of the horse (ll. 1413–15). A difficult negotiation has been concluded, with the Count's niece offering a brief allegory of the settling of any dispute between the various parties, ending without violence or umbrage. This is not the part of the negotiations that should be 'de grant esfroi' (l. 1390):

> 'Qui le chevauche, ne s'en duet,
> Ainz va plus aise et plus soëf
> Que s'il estoit en une nef.' (ll. 1396–8)

> 'Riding him is no discomfort for anyone – you'll go along as easily as if you were in a boat.'

Actual praise for the palfrey is merely the surface message, the animal becoming a metaphor for negotiations that should proceed or at least end as smoothly as it ambles. Mention of the ship merely puts the icing on the cake: taken with the reference to Morholt that follows the end of the duel between Yder and Erec, the obvious intertext is again the *Tristan*, making for both a flattering comparison and effectively a blessing of the relationship. Erec and Enide's journey together will proceed more smoothly – and enjoy better sanction – than that of their literary prototypes returning by sea, their *mal de mer* being the bittersweet taste of illicit and unavowable love, to Mark's court.[7] However, this lulling motion contains the possibility of leading the rider in unexpected directions more to do with the undercurrents and bestial motions that are the seamier side of court life. Just as Yder is not – either in terms of family connection or manner – 'like' Morholt, so the references to the Tristan material may in effect constitute a red herring. The clue here may be affiliation: the Morholt–Iseut connection keeps that narrative 'in the family' in one way where Chrétien's revisioning of the connection looks to other kinships. Indeed, the question arises as to whether Chrétien sees the 'Tristan problem' as meriting any more serious treatment than the 'Celtic' motifs critics such as Luttrell and Frappier have seen him as lampooning. What may be more entertaining is whether the audience is being invited to see the niece's *Tristan* reference as alluding to a common language and history of courtly *faits divers*, in which the ill-fated couple exist in Erec and Laluth's life-world, or whether the niece is referring to the Tristan legend as a 'text-world', marking her cultural savvy through the spice of literary allusion. The ambiguity breaks the time of the text, smoothly folding the worlds of internal and external audiences into one another.

Thus, a note of impishness is introduced by the gender-bending of the rider, who, via the intermediary of the 'enfes' (l. 1392), is no longer just limited to being a 'pucele' (l. 1391), now becomes an indefinite 'qui' (l. 1396), a move that parallels the ambiguity of 'qui moillor quiert', noted above. It also strategically inverts all the key terms of Isidore's description of the warhorse, the niece's description mirroring the behavioural ideal for the individual or kind of person it is intended to carry in the same way that the *destrier* represents the virile passions of the knight it carries. Her description of the palfrey reflects her own balancing of the various possible qualities that are 'right for a maiden': neither prone to bad temper nor easily frightened. However, although Bezzola argues that the palfrey can be seen as a symbol of Enide's purity and the nature of the union between the two, there is perhaps more here than meets the eye: the image implied of Enide as demure and self-effacing is in itself not so innocent.[8]

It is when we consider this passage in the light of literary circles and controversies associated with the court of Henry II that a further layer of complexity emerges. A feisty young woman might well express such thoughts, but where would she get them from? The niece's comparison of one horse with another of a different colour, proceding by a systematic negation of the characteristics of the *destrier* (derived presumably from Isidore), might put us in mind of another comparison of two horses, namely that framed by William IX, cited above. Re-reading the scene in the light of this tale of two temperaments, the Count's niece could be taken to be implying a number of possible things.

One clue as to what any possible reference to William here might mean can be taken from a later use of horse imagery in a later lyric by Raimon de Miraval (1191–1229), 'Ben aia-l messagiers' (Song 32 in Topsfield's edition).[9]

> Qe-ill fui al prim destriers
> Et apres palafres,
> Mas er creis tant l'arnes
> Que trop peza-l dobliers;
> E puois ades baissa-l logiers
> E-m sembla que l'afanz cregues,
> No m'aura mais ab si per servidor
> E lais me Deus mon miells trobar aillor. (ll. 41–8)
>
> For first I was her warhorse and then her palfrey, but now the harness is getting too heavy and, since I earn less and less while it seems my trouble only grows, she will have me no longer as her servant. May God let me find better elsewhere. (translation after Topsfield)

Here, Raimon's presentation of himself as having slipped down the ladder from 'stallion' to 'palfrey' implies a position where either his lady has assumed a dominant role in the relationship, or she has acquired a new 'destrier' and so displaced the poet from *a-* to *b-* male, a change that would find support in his listing of epic heroes in the preceding stanza, the message then being that things are getting awkward because there are too many men in Raimon's world and his standing is being placed in question. One message here is then clearly social: although palfreys are a standard mode of transportation for ladies, they are also the second-class citizens of the horse world. After all, William was choosing between two *cavals*. Message: Enide is not the same class of creature as some other people in the room.

Describing the palfrey as a mount becoming to someone like Enide could also read as a coded sexual flattery of Erec or disparagement of her, on top of which we might see a slur on Erec's sexual continence through an implied invitation to share in and thereby pass judgement on Enide. Quiet, submissive and docile, the palfrey is *a similar kind of ride to Enide*. Readers of Jane Austen might detect a note of condescension here: Enide, clearly already

225

adept in horse care, is being presented with the equestrian equivalent of an adorable little runabout, a gift suitable for 'people like her' because it's all a wee slip of a girl can handle. Indeed, the niece may be suggesting Erec might wish to consider a second mount with a view either to choosing between the two of them or – through a replay of William's potentially despotic insistence in the fourth stanza that he is unwilling to transfer his 'garnimen' (l. 11), his *equipment* (in various senses), from these two – keeping them both. The niece may moreover be implying that if Erec is the sort of person likely to take a mistress, the docile character imputed to his current choice may drive him to it sooner rather than later. Is this then an insult indicating that Erec – neither a child nor a palfrey – might prefer something a little less tame? Is the niece – in a foreshadowing of the scene from the comic romance *Le Chevalier à l'épée* where Gauvain is forced into offering his new bride the choice of whether to stay with him or take another lover – implying that she might be a more 'valiant' palfreywoman, should he change his mind and decide, like Michel de Montaigne in his essay on conversation, that he prefers a certain amount of scratching and biting? In suggesting herself as a candidate, a potential royal mistress and rival to Enide's queen, or perhaps a willing version of Philomena, she displaces her seemingly less verbally dextrous kinswoman into the second chair role of the rival Procne while 'silencing' her like Philomena through her show of assurance and experience.

Another potential problem appears in the comment 'a child could ride her' (l. 1392): what does the Count's niece know? What have the 'children' been up to before Erec came along? Does the strange history of Laluth include a suppressed tale of experimental heterosexual contact between youngsters (which, as Jane Gilbert comments, is the object of the Emir's queered voyeuristic fascination at his discovery of the lovers in *Floire et Blanchefleur*), a tale thus not included in the 'official' narrative of the marriage transaction?[10] Is there more to the comparison with Iseut than meets the eye? Is Erec about to be revealed as even more undiscriminating than Marc in that it is not simply an exchange of apparently unique but basically interchangeable *puceles* he does not notice, but, more glaringly, the fact that his bride, as in *Trubert's* game of musical beds, is simply not intact, her hymen as *depecié* as his own face? After all, it is not as if these sorts of allegations were not used to queer the pitch in medieval marriage negotiations, the rumours of scandal associated with Eleanor being a case in point.

Indeed, although Raimon compares himself to a palfrey, *Erec et Enide's* earlier possible echoes of the slandering of Eneas, we should not assume the only possible scandal relates to *heterosexual* desire. Rather, another possible 'shadow' here might lie in the sort of scene presented at the end of *Trubert*, our hero, disguised as his sister, now maid of the Duke's daughter, who now finds herself embracing and caressing a person she takes to be of her own sex. *Trubert's* commentary on the cultural invisibility of female same-sex relations is highlighted by its repeated narratorial comment possibly parodying Chrétien's insistence on Arthur's freedom from base or lecherous intent in kissing Enide ('Roseite la [=Trubert] tint enbracie / N'i entent point de vilenie', ll. 2477–8; 'Roseite entre ses mains le [vit] prent / Nule mauvestié n'i entent', ll. 2497–8). This then appears as a more jocularly collusive version of Queen Victoria's fabled refusal to proscribe lesbian acts on the grounds that she did not believe such things to exist. Again, read against the scene in *Trubert*, what we might have is a nod back to a history that court culture otherwise presents as being without consequences and without afterlife, now mobilised here for the purposes of slandering Enide. The niece's sense and strong character are clearly signalled through the description of her as 'mout prouz, mout sage et mout vaillanz' (l. 1350), terms which can be understood in gender-neutral terms such as 'very prudent, sensible and worthy' (Carroll), 'a brave and noble girl, courteous and wise' (Raffel) or 'fort généreuse, fort sage et fort valeureuse' (Fritz). However, the young woman might be like – or perhaps not so like – Nicolette, gender-bendingly referred to as 'li preus, li sage' (*Aucassin et Nicolette*, § 37), her readiness and capacity for 'action' not without subtexts. As Gaunt emphasises in his reading of *Le Chevalier à l'épée*, 'preux' can also have 'overtly sexual' senses, the young woman presented in terms no different from those in which Enide admired Erec.[11] Thus, the Count's niece may even be positioning herself as the possessor of a knowledge emanating from the 'closet' of the female

227

household in which she seemingly appears as equinely aggressive or even 'butch' in relation to Enide's palfreyesque 'femme'.

In short, Erec seems to have stumbled into a place and a history where he can have his choice of skeletons from the closet, seemingly confirming the worst suspicions one might have about the ways of (other) courts. However, there are other possibilities here. If Yder really is assimilable to Morholt in this world then the Count's niece could be seen as 'unselfconsciously' presenting the sexual politics of court of Laluth as something rather akin to those of William's Poitiers, with herself conforming to lyric caricature of the *domna*'s sexual desire as threateningly animal.[12] However, it is also possible to see the niece as acting as a literary subject in her own right, a court poet whose sly evocation of lyric's misogynistic 'vision of savage alterity' may also be part of a highly ironic, multi-layered play with the topos of the 'foreign' or 'provincial' court as locus of untamed animal desire. In so doing she offers Erec the opportunity to step into the literary minefield she has created and potentially show himself up in turn as a bumpkin. In short, Erec's canny manipulation of the public text of Laluthian ceremony in the Sparrow-Hawk contest might just have been beginner's luck – time for round 2… Where *Philomena* presented a bogey-man vision of demonic shadows flitting about Tereüs's palace, the niece's suggestions place Erec in a position assimilable to Tereüs, the intertext of William's poem begging the question of whether this other new arrival shows any appetite for duality. Again the question is whether such shadows are part of some portentously looming backdrop or the young lady is just enjoying the chance to toy with and measure herself against some competition from out of town.

Whatever the niece's knowledge or the relations of her words to their subtexts, she seems firmly in the saddle when it comes to teasing Erec. Indeed, the negotiations concerning Enide's apparel are more or less entirely a test of the skills of the two younger interlocutors, with the Count sidelined after his initial offer of the dresses and with the sparky conversation between the two young courtiers appearing as an echo of Philomena's undaunted questioning of Tereüs. Her *prouesse* is thus manifested in her undaunted and yet diplomatic response to Erec's refusal, a display of discursive force that marks her out as more accomplished in this domain than both Enide and that other *pucele*, the Queen's maiden, showed herself in the encounter with Yder. This feisty young woman's carefully-weighed defiance of Erec makes it quite clear that this is the last reasonable offer on the table. The line 'qui moillor quiert' (l. 1395) does not necessarily just refer definitely to the palfrey, but also indefinitely: 'whoever seeks *better* [by way of a proposal] does not know what he wants'. A 'diplomatic' reading would thus argue that, in spite of the palpable edge, discussions are moving in the right direction, with the opening of Erec's response, 'ma douce amie' (l. 1399) indicating that the forcefulness of her interventions has been appreciated. In thus not entailing any disgrace for those around her – unlike Guinevere's maiden's show of 'despit' – the niece's quick thinking and well judged response saves face (or, rather, 'onor' and 'droiture') for the Count, who is thus not required to appease Erec personally. This is one possible explanation for why the *pucele* is referred to as 'prouz': she succeeds in enhancing the collective 'beauty' of the event by smoothing over a potentially 'ugly' moment. This absence of speech foreshadows the narratorial treatment of Erec's own comments on the palfrey, which are only reported. The issue is put to bed and left in the stable, as can be seen from the narratorial comment that follows: 'At that they took their leave, having had a merry time that night.' ('A tant se departirent tuit, /Grant joie orent fait cele nuit', ll. 1419–20). Not the entire picture, but a deftly tactful minute of a not entirely easy meeting. 'Joy' here proceeds from the successful resolution of potential conflicts and impasses, as the result of a workable settling of issues. Against this, the 'perverse' reading would see something rather different in the scene. In addition to their deliberate neglect of Enide, in order to drive down her 'bride-price' (possibly with a view to removing her as potential competition for another of her kinswomen) the Count's family have now staged a brazen attempt to hijack and derail the marriage negotiations between Erec and the vavassor, reasserting the primacy of their branch of the family even to the point of putting forward the Count's own… niece. Not daughter, though. Does this simply mean that there is no daughter or that she was not even deemed worth bringing into play for such an apparently minor matter as this unknown journeyman and that a sacrifice of a lesser piece was

229

considered sufficient? Indeed, the logic of the gift of the dress tends in precisely that direction: from the position he arrogates for himself as Laluth's principal marriage broker, what the Count does in asking his niece to give Enide her best dress is to substitute Enide for herself, pretending to the outside world that the clan had always seen these two young women as being of equal status and worth in the marriage market.

In response to either of these scenarios, Erec's strategy seems to be the same. Focus on the horse. His unreported but ecphrastic praise of the palfrey – a narratorial 'whatever!' foreshadowing Shakespeare's dismissive 'Indeed, my lord, it is a most absolute and excellent horse' (*Henry V*, act 3, scene 7), possibly readable as a self-caricature as a slow-witted and superficial aristocrat – defuses the situation by affecting to ignore or miss most of the subtexts, whether spiky or seductive. In this what we have is an inversion, in Chrétien's earliest and what is sometimes presented as straightest romance, of the possibility discerned by Roberta Krueger for contestatory reading. Marginal figures such as dwarves and women appear as the narrative focus for dissonant understandings of scenes. This is certainly the case. However, the possible casting of Erec as *deliberately slow* brings to the fore the utility of misrecognition and disavowal in the multi-layered discourses of courtly interaction. Another reflection, however, lies in the direction of the possible echo of scandals associated with Eleanor's line. In possibly invoking William IX's deliberately scandalous outing of himself as the adulterous focus of courtly discourses of sexual excess in the context of a passage presenting the quasi-Thracian sexual deregulation associated with the court of Laluth, Chrétien potentially throws down a gauntlet to the *losengiers*. His textual genealogy of court scandal, ostentatiously projecting onto the Laluthian Other the vices associated with Poitiers and then Aquitaine, undercuts any attempt to secure a vision of courtly identity and propriety based on a distinction between the 'beauty' that is the sexual politics of the Athenian/Arthurian self and the 'ugliness' of those of its Laluthian/Thracian neighbour. The 'dépécié' face of the avenging Erec, ready to attack his opponent as 'felenessement' as may be required to get the job done, shows resistance to either domestication or disingenuous othering. Moreover, his invocation of this family history sets itself in parallel with the larger history of medieval debate about and critique of courtly morals. Unlike the dwarf's lash, the generation long tradition of slander may, in Chrétien's forceful facing down, have lost its sting.

'Le Monde où l'on [baise]': Kiss, Marriage, Tournament

> When we kiss, we devour the object by caressing it; we eat it, in a sense, but sustain its presence.[13]

> Quant li rois ot que a toz plaist,
> Or ne laira que ne la baist:
> Vers li se trait, et si l'acole.
> La pucele ne fu pas fole,
> Bien vost que li rois la beisast;
> Vilainne fust si l'en pesast. (ll. 1825–30)

> When the king heard that it pleased everyone, he was determined to kiss her: he turned towards her and embraced her. The maiden was no silly girl: she wanted the king to kiss her, and would have been uncourtly had she been diffident.

The climax of the 'premerains vers' is Arthur's declaration that he will kiss Enide and so consummate the hunt of the White Stag. This is done in the name of his father and by will not to break with his traditions. However, the problem with Uther Pendragon is that he is either – depending on your point of view – a usurper or, less negatively put, at least not part of a long dynastic succession of kings. In that sense, there is a profound tension between the apparent setting out of a political stall Arthur engages in and the actual story of his line. What Chrétien can be seen to be doing here is exploiting that tension and playing on the short duration of the Arthurian dream.

The kiss also puts a seal on the acclamation of her beauty. Kathryn Gravdal does not comment on this specific episode, however, her comment made elsewhere in her examination, 'rarely has sexual

231

assault looked so endearing' certainly applies, although her reading perhaps stops short of exploring some of the wider ramifications.[14] Arthur here subjects Enide to attentions it would be inappropriate for any of his courtiers to bestow, and which he could arguably not bestow on any other lady at court. In that respect, what we have here is almost an inversion of the primal myth of the savage horde: the horde transforms itself into civilised society by granting the king the right to enjoy women it itself does not get to enjoy. If we look at the lexical fields represented here, then what is taking place is clear. Enide's appearance at court has many aspects in common with violent sexual assault, such as the forced kiss in the early part of the *Conte du graal* (ll. 657–90). Certainly, her reaction to the courtiers gives a sense of her reading of their desiring gaze:

> Quant la bele pucele estrange
> Vit toz ces chevaliers en range,
> Qui l'esgardoient a estal,
> Son chief encline contre val;
> Vergoingne en ot, ne fu merveille,
> La face l'en devint vermeille,
> Mais la honte se li avint
> Que plus bele asez en devint.
> Quant li rois la vit vergoignier,
> Ne se vost de li esloignier;
> Par la main doucement l'a prise,
> Delez lui l'a a destre assise.
> De la senestre part s'asist
> La roÿne, qui au roi dist:
> 'Sire, si con je cuit et croi,
> Bien doit venir a cort de roi
> Qui par ses armes puet conquerre
> Si bele fame en autre terre.
> Bien fesoit Erec a atendre;
> Or poez vos le baisier prandre
> De la plus bele de la cort.' (ll. 1747–67)

When the beautiful stranger, the maiden saw all the knights gathered and staring straight at her, she bowed her head. She was embarrassed, and no wonder. Her face flushed red, but modesty suited her so well she became even more beautiful. When the King saw that she was embarrassed, he did not want to leave her on her own, but took her gently by the hand and seated her beside him on his right. At his left the Queen took her seat and said to the King: 'My Lord, I do believe anyone should be welcome at court who can win such a lady by deeds of arms in other lands. It was a good idea to wait for Erec: now you can take the kiss from the fairest one at court.'

The ghost of Philomena hovers uneasily in the background of this situation. Enide's shame, like Philomena's eloquence is powerless to regulate desire. Indeed, just as both her appearance and her speech only ever seem to serve to drive Tereüs to worse excesses – first rape, and then mutilation rather than the death Philomena hoped for as a release from further shameful assaults – so Enide's blushes only seems to make matters worse (ll. 1752–3). Arthur's reaction is similarly ambiguous: it is far from clear from the formulation of ll. 1755–6 whether his motivation for not being able to stay away from the embarrassed Enide is protective sympathy or desire. Furthermore, his positioning of her at his right hand, through its displacement of the Queen, hints at not just the narrative of Griseldis, but also Philomena's outraged argument that Tereüs's desires would make her a 'rival' to her sister Progné (ll. 784–8). However, crucially, the king's motivation does appear to be sympathy, and his desire does, to judge from the Queen's accord, appear to be to assert the place of the newcomer at court. Even the savage barbarians of Thrace, such as Tereüs, having no other law than their pleasure, seem concerned to keep up appearances to the extent that they conceal their adulteries from the light of day. As Gravdal points out, rape tends to be something that happens off-stage in Chrétien – with the exception of Philomena, perhaps.[15] It is therefore unlikely that a Christian king would show himself such a monster as to give in to such desires under the horrified eyes of his assembled courtiers. But then, Guinevere's speech does not seem to put much of a better gloss on the situation. After all her praise of Erec as a who can 'conquer' a woman of such beauty (l. 1763), elliptically omits the tale of propriety and negotiation for something that sounds like a revival of the 'Custom of Logres' as described by the Lovesome Damsel in *Le Chevalier de la charrette* (ll. 1302–16), another repudiated past in which 'Chrétien offers the audience the contemplation of a world in which rape is a male right'.[16] But then again, the appearance of shockingness is all, with any leering

233

designs on the part of the courtiers faced down by displays that hint at worse. Just as Erec reassured Enide's father by falling in step with his strategy of 'going public', so Arthur and Guinevere stage a 'double ravishment' to protect courtly propriety. Of course, the person who is really displaced is the *pucele* left by the wayside in the forest, Guinevere's comment on the wisdom and judgement manifest in Erec's patience (l. 1765) seeming to implicitly praise Erec for not taking the first available maiden.

The details of Arthur's performance in the kiss itself thus serve to reinforce the shock value inherent to their pantomime strategy: like (but unlike) Tereüs, he is presented as not being about to take no for an answer, as we can see from 'or ne laira que ne la baist', while the verb indicating the embrace (*acoler*) is commonly used in descriptions of sexual contact. We also know from Chrétien's other romances that the kiss has a key place in narratives of forced intercourse: 'a woman who offers her mouth will give the rest easily' ('Feme qui sa boche abandone /Le soreplus de legier done.' *Le Conte du graal*, ll. 3545–6).[17] In that sense, what are we being invited to look at? Are we to understand that this is the final phase in an extended courtly narrative of abduction, with the kiss as the climax of Erec's victory at Laluth, marking his bringing home of the other trophy, or is this some sublimated version of *ius primae noctis*, with Arthur allowed to grope and smooch with another man's woman in front of the entire court? Possibly, but probably not. What the charitable reading invites us to entertain at this point is that the King 'wants' Enide in the same way that Guinevere 'wants' Yder.

What we have here in the different phases of the hunt of the White Stag are instances of both parties deploying behaviour associated with the consolidation, affirmation and signalling of diplomatic and social bonds. The strength of those bonds is then emphasised by their investment with a certain erotic charge. In that respect, Chrétien casts the future that awaits the Arthurian realm as a sort of confusion: Guinevere will forget herself in her dealings with Lancelot and allow 'vilenie' to cloud the picture. At this point, however, things have not taken their negative turn and so Chrétien paints an image of the social scene as necessarily underpinned and indeed owing its 'liveliness' to a certain investment of feeling, whether erotic or aggressive. From the point of view of the kiss and its more general relation to the political economy subtending Arthur's charismatic reign, we see what Adam Phillips describes as the simultaneous and contradictory elements of consumption and preservation inherent in the gesture, as is made apparent by Chrétien's insistence on both the king's insistence and his restraint. Phillips' comment highlights the relation of the kiss not so much to sexual desire, but to a more general issue of Arthur's reign as a denial of cannibalistic impulses characteristic of the giants he displaces, with the King's orchestration of the scene as a mark of the work involved in the domestication of ravishing, devouring energies that both sustain and threaten his rule.

Another way of looking at this scene would be to argue that Chrétien's exploration of the vocabulary of sexual contact is part of a wider exploration of the place of both violence and sexuality as images of risk and uncertainty in the political. Enide understands the situation and submits herself to the king's attentions. In a sense, Chrétien's exploitation of the limited lexical field indicates that there are only so many words for this sort of business, and so sometimes those words have to have other senses. It is then the boundary lines between those other meanings that is the subject of policing rather than the presence of the words themselves. 'Vilenie' is not then an absolute presence, but rather a sense, a misunderstanding, a cast of mind.

A further question hangs over this episode in the narrative. It is at this point that Arthur presents his much commented discourse on the rights and duties of kings and on the nature of royal authority (ll. 1776–1816).[18] If Enide is perhaps not the partner originally intended for Erec, is this nonetheless the speech Arthur would have given in any event? After all, even though it is not actually scripted by palace spin-doctors, Arthur's address is the summing up (the *parsome*) of the order of business of his plenary court. Of course, that said, that this speech now appears as the conclusion of a ritual turned genuinely dangerous conveniently adds to its charge and urgency, the sense of it as part of 'actually occurring history'. In that sense, the fact that things turned out differently from how they were intended contradicts his statement 'I am a king and must never lie' ('je sui rois, ne doi pas mentir' l. 1789):

> 'Ceste est et de cors et de vis,
> Et de quant qu'estuet a pucele,
> La plus gentis et la plus bele
> Qui soit jusque la, ce me semble,
> Ou li ciels et la terre assemble.' (ll. 1778–82)

> 'In body, face and in everything else that pertains to a maiden, this is the noblest, most beautiful creature from here to where the earth touches the sky.'

Would Arthur have said the same of the king's daughter? If so, now that we know about Enide, it would have been a manifest lie sprung from a mix of parochial ignorance and undiscriminating expediency. However, does not the fact Arthur says so now of Enide in effect make a lie of what the account of Nature marvelling at her own handiwork suggests is a valid statement? To now proclaim Enide the fairest from here to the ends of the earth is to claim knowledge of a geography clearly insufficiently unexplored at the point when the plan was conceived. In short, the 'beauty' that Arthur evokes here as a vehicle for his own boundless authority – which assertion was the whole point of convening the court – was always the product of a usurping will to power. Thus, the fraud that is Arthur's positioning of his usurper father, Uther Pendragon (l. 1807) as fount of customary practice and basis of his legitimacy is echoed in the improvisatory substitution of one *pucele* for another. Iseut? Brangane? Whoever. As Machiavelli said, 'people are always persuaded by the outcome of a thing, and [from here to where the earth meets the sky] there is nothing but ordinary people'.

Lèse-Majesté, Lèse-Pucelage: Royal Marriage and its Grievances

Although the kiss foreshadows Erec's wedding night with its description of Enide's defloration, Chrétien's narrative does not proceed directly to that end, perversely emphasising instead the patience that is the subordination of nature to culture in ceremonial proceedings: 'Bien fesoit Erec a atendre' (l. 1765). Where Tereüs only waited as long as was strategically necessary, Erec's passion – although not feigned – is offset by the regulated purity of his love for her, 'sanz vilenie, /Sanz mauvestié et sanz folage' (ll. 1834–5), the Philomena story reasserting itself again in his clear obedience to the paternalistic claims of the Law. Thus it is no coincidence that Erec's first thought when he sees Arthur take the kiss is of his agreement with Enide's father (ll. 1841–6): Enide may be an object of desire in her own right, but she is also 'between men', a token of patriarchally-regulated exchange and bonding. Indeed, from that point of view it is unclear which man Arthur is acting after in his bestowal of the kiss. Here again we might think of how the scene might have played itself out with a different young woman taking the role. Arthur's kissing of the king's daughter would have mirrored the encounter in the forest, a moment seethingly pregnant, underwritten by glimmerings of raw animal desire rather than – with the young woman's father absent and Arthur's attention elsewhere – paternal authority. Arthur's kiss would then have been a signal to the courtiers: any appearance of *lecherie* in the earlier proceedings was only that. The kiss would then have been Arthur's mime of, on the one hand, Erec's submission to the law and, on the other, on behalf of her father, with Arthur acting *per procurationem*, not as some shady court pimp but as a political equal in carefully-agreed plenipotentiary representation. What Erec's 'spontaneous' thought reveals is that nothing about the regulatory framework has changed with the switch of partners.

All aspects of the ceremonial calendar of the wedding, including the conveying of Enide's parents to the Arthurian court spring from his determination not to break with the covenant of the Law: 'Covent mentir ne li voloit' (l. 1846). However, if restraint is part of pleasure, restraint that might be indicative of mere compliant apathy appears as the contrary evil. Accordingly, Erec's eagerness for the wedding night is the driving force in the collective arrangement:

> Ne tarda gaires ci aprés,
> Que li termes en fu mout pres,
> Que ses noces faire devoit;
> Li atendres mout li grevoit:
> Ne vost plus tarder ne atendre
> Au roi en ala congié prendre,
> Que a sa cort, ne li grevast,
> Ses noces faire li lessast. (ll. 1911–18)

> It was not long after this that the date arrived that had been set for Erec's marriage. Waiting was weighing on him, and he did not want to delay any more. He came to ask the King's permission, if it did not displease him, for the marriage to be performed at his court.

Chrétien's practice of accumulation and repetition paints a very particular picture of the relation between individual desire and political obligation. It is interesting, following on from the speech made by Arthur at the conclusion of the hunt for the White Stag, that Erec should effectively invert the path taken by his royal patron and mentor: we move from the modality of right and due ('devoit', l. 1913) to individual will or desire ('ne vost plus', l. 1915).[19] Linking these two phases is the single verb *grever*, used to describe both Erec's impatience ('Li atendres mout li grevoit', l. 1914) and also due deference to Arthur as king ('ne li grevast', l. 1917). Erec's wish that the wedding be moved forward, takes due account of whether such a change of date would step on the royal toes by interfering either with Arthur's overall timetable (Camelot appearing here in the guise of heavily-booked conference-centre) or any specific arrangements he might already have in hand. In that regard, *grever* designates potential damage that to Arthur's reputation through disruption of his stage management of the theatre of court.

Fortunately, individual and collective considerations can be reconciled at this point: for all Erec's desire obtrudes, it is accommodated, subsumed in and possibly even energising the royal *ban*:

> Li rois le don li outroia,
> Et par son roiaume envoia
> Toz les rois et les contes querre,
> Ceus qui de lui tenoient terre,
> Que nul tant hardi n'i eüst
> Qu'a la Pentecoste n'i fust.
> N'i a nul qui remenoir ost,
> Que a la cort ne veingne tost,
> Des que li rois les ot mandez. (ll. 1919–27)

> The King gave his consent and sent for all the kings, dukes and counts who held land from him, declaring that none should be so bold as to be absent at Pentecost. None dared stay behind, and each came quickly to court when he received the King's summons.

The insistent nature of Arthur's summons doubles that of Erec's desire, a pairing which locates some of the force of royal utterances in individual wishes. Thus, running somewhat contrary to the theory of the king's two bodies expounded by John of Salisbury, where the key is a separation out the public and private wills (the latter abnegated in favour of a mimesis of divine authority), here the power of a public utterance derives first and foremost from the insistence of individual desire (*privata voluntas*).[20] This is made emphatically apparent not so much in the announcement of Erec's wedding as the replay of Arthur's assertion of authority in the kiss, but, crucially, in the bringing forward of the ceremony. However, this pandering to Erec's particular interest through manipulation of the time of the ritual calendar for the royal wedding is not simply a concession to an individual, but rather serves as a reaffirming reminder of Arthur's more general officialisation strategy of asserting the particularity of royal will, a reiteration designed (in terms of Strohm's discussion of English coronation ritual as 'legible practice') to make his practice more 'readable' to his subjects and perhaps also to suggest that Erec as future king should be expected to have licence to do the same in other circumstances.

A panoply of public celebration and intervention mediates the shift from court to chamber. The prominent, intrusive, and – indeed – pruriently voyeuristic presence of the agents of social regulation reminds us that this step must be carefully negotiated precisely because there is a certain necessary violence that founds the whole enterprise, leaving it rippling with double meanings, such as in the idea that the King gives Erec 'the gift', indicating both a culture of exchange that is here ghosted by lyric discourse of *le don* as physical consummation. The scene is part of a 'pervert art' precisely because, following the Law, people have to be taught how to desire. Indeed, this lesson extends to the very 'ends' of desire, even the 'other country' of the *soreplus* – a moment not 'outside' the bedroom scene, but rather a necessary prelude to it, marking the beginning of the elaborate collective foreplay that prepares the bride for the event itself. It is in this spirit that we come to *that* moment:

> Et l'amors qui iert entr'aux deus,
> Fist la pucele plus hardie:
> De rien ne s'est acohardie,
> Tot soffri, que que li grevast. (ll. 2098–101)

> The love between them made the maiden more bold. She was not afraid of anything, but endured all, though it pained her.

The private business of the chamber, even when unobserved, complies scrupulously with the economy of surveillance that is the sexual grammar of courtly love, great emphasis being placed on the kissing. However, the sexual act itself is given comparatively little space, emphasising the narratable and therefore public face of Erec and Enide's 'private moment'. What the 'soreplus', the 'natural' (if there is such a thing) enjoyment of Enide's body, betokens is thus necessary but only allotted the minimal space Chrétien, otherwise noted as painter of titillating pictures, decrees for it. Indeed, what we see here is such a thorough permeation and encoding of the 'natural' by the 'cultural' that its texture is entirely transformed and subsumed, creating a realm of the perverse that problematically regulates and stimulates both Erec's sexual desire and Arthur's will to rule.

The complexity of such explorations of the limits and boundaries of culture and nature are further complicated by Chrétien's emphasis on the historicisation of the Law at both collective and individual levels, mirroring our own critical anxieties about the interpretation of cultures. As Kathleen Biddick observes, the 'making visible' of categories such as women and boundaries is one of the most problematic tasks for historians dealing with medieval cultures.[21] This question can clearly be viewed in terms of the dominant-subaltern paradigm's interrogation of who gets to 'speak' and the extent to which different academic discourses, especially historiographies, silence or traduce what is said. As one of the principal – but not the only – objects of the scopic drive in Chrétien's text, Enide's body's place in the wedding ceremony appears as an allegory of the issues Biddick raises, a medieval counter-interrogation of our own disciplinary concerns. In narrating the sexual act in the way it does, and in emphasising the role of decorum and witness, Chrétien arguably seeks to make *almost* everything publicly visible or sayable. However, this nuptial visualisation is contradicted by the fact that Chrétien's rhetoric also 'clothes' the nakedness of its construction of the natural in the ritualised acculturations of the perverse.

In minimising the terrain of the *soreplus* as he does, Chrétien reduces what can be said to be 'outside' the text of culture, even if the precise boundary, the 'event horizon', shrouded in the mist of the anxious passionate disturbance that is *esfroi*, remains impossible to locate. The remainder or the limit is then in-folded and hidden in the place both he and the *Roman de la rose* construct as the last redout to be breached in their campaign of deferral. Yet this domain of 'nature' is walled on both sides, before and after, by Chrétien's depiction of the public reception of the ritualised sexual act. Thus, although the next morning she rises to be publicly acknowledged as 'a new-made dame' ('dame novele', l. 2104), what is not being said is that Enide is 'known': 'dame' is no less fallible a public label than that applied to the 'pucele' who is presumably not one we meet later in the Joy of the Court. Insofar as her will remains emphasised in terms of what she consents to endure, she retains subjective status: as with Arthur's shattering fall from Fortune's wheel, there is no fading 'retreat of the body into death' that would simply make her an 'object' of the scopic drive.[22] Thus, Chrétien posits a meeting of the 'inside' and 'outside' of culture *somewhere* out of sight in Enide's vaginal accommodation of Erec's and her own *esfroi*. The limit and *limen* of culture resists visualisation, although we still sense it is out there as a source of anxiety.

This question of the relation between the audible and the visualisable brings us back to the question of *la jouissance equine* and its 'noisiness': Enide here is silent but seen. Chrétien assures us of the decorum of the wedding night, but the scenario of 'becoming palfrey' described earlier returns here. If, as Jane Burns argues, narratorial silencing is a key weapon in Chrétien's censoring misogyny, then there is no reason not to assume that some subversive sound (rather than *parole* on this occasion) from Enide's 'disruptive mouth' is being passed over. However, given that all we are told about her experience is that she endured all however it *hurt* her, it is not to be assumed that any such sound was one of pleasure. Enide's moment is thus far from recuperable as some ancestor of Emma Bovary's orchestral orgasm on the forest floor, no 'hiatus of the ego' in waves of thrill but rather a maintenance of lucid subjectivity under the offence of pain that may have more to say about the potentially nightmarish extremes that hover in the background of Enide's resistance of Oringle than any vision of pleasure (see chapter eight below).

Is what is seen there 'to be read' or does it 'speak' to us? To what extent are we limited by thinking of the place of subaltern categories in cultural practice as 'legible' as opposed to not so much 'writable' ('scriptible') in the sense Roland Barthes gives that term in *Le Plaisir du texte*, as *writing*.[23] In that sense, we pass from a cultural performance predicated on the uncritical reading of conventions to a performance that, however seemingly 'silent' in its acquiescence to subaltern status, nonetheless acts as a writing. Indeed, to reduce Enide's place here to mere silence might be to miss some the force of Chrétien's parallel emphasis on what might have aggrieved her and what might have aggrieved Arthur. Both are 'consensual' acts, but we should not assume that only one is, as Chakrabarty puts it, 'backed up by an army'.[24] We can see this question recur in the portrait of Guivret's sisters, the two young women doctors: 'en eles n'ot que ensoignier' (l. 5214). In maidens there are lessons that are the product of their internalisation of cultural capital rather than some sort of fetishistically appropriable naturalised agalmic secret to be known and taken through the penetrative agency of defloration. For Chrétien to have translated into some sort of disambiguating sign of the presence of that strange sound and its meaning would have been to have traduced the question it asks and overshadowed Enide's tutelary assertion of will. Moreover, given the proliferation of subtexts derived from earlier romance material, although the wedding may read as a sort of festive plenitude that suggestively underpins the couple's experience of what Foucault described as 'perverse implantation', the accent in other regards seems to be the policing and reduction of other, far more lurid possibilities. Indeed, after all his preliminary narrative teasing, Chrétien's account of culture's regulatory perversity offers a straightforward nuptial *jouissance* that seemingly writes out the seeds of all the possible subversive or troubling echoes and anxieties sown earlier. In spite of the messy patch created by the meeting of the 'natural' and the 'cultural', the new couple go to sleep both as good little consenting heterosexuals and as representatives of two separate kingdoms brought together for the purposes of diplomatic negotiation.

Of course, the deliberateness of the narrative leading up to the wedding night contrasts rather with the bright, splendid but somehow breezier narrative of the tournament.[25] Alfred Adler follows Walter Nitze in suggesting that '[Erec's] performance in the tournament after his wedding places him clearly as a beginner. [...] The threefold victory at the tournament is the ceremony of initiation for the courtly lover'.[26] However, Erec is hardly some new arrival impressing his fair lady with a show of excellence, but rather a member of the Round Table of some considerable standing and connection as well as someone more than capable of manipulating the theatre of tournament. If this event crowns Erec's initial triumph over the court and his self-subordination to its 'pervert economy', then one question that needs perhaps to be asked is why he (or Chrétien) makes it look quite so easy. After all, we move from a conflict in which it required most of a day for Erec to best Yder to dispatching several kings in a few lines (ll. 2168–91), and then, without Chrétien going into many – or, indeed, any – details, outstripping the first day's achievements on the second (ll. 2249–58). Part of the sense here lies in the place of the tournament in collective life. After all, the wedding, which provides the impetus in the calendar of festivities is in a sense the focus of the proceedings. Gauvain and his opposite numbers effectively play secondary fiddle and allow Erec his moment on the stage. Nothing turns too ugly here. We are not in the same world as Marie de France's *Chaitivel*, for example, in which hecatombal destruction of the suitors brings the courtly idyll uncomfortably face-to-face with its underpinning risks.[27] In fact, everything here speaks of a sort of breezy, festive efficiency of which Erec is the primary exponent. The point is precisely not to lay the host's brains bare. What this section then reveals is the extent to which Erec's intervention at Laluth was excessive, even if that excess was not without its satisfactions, whether for participant or audience. Of course, had the question of Erec's *los* and *pris* been settled once and for all, there would be no need for any future demonstration. The work of spectacle would be at an end. The future is not 'rational' in that it does not simply admit of such convenient QED's: Chrétien's comparisons of Erec to Absalom, Solomon and Alexander (ll. 2262–6), the mark of him as a fulfilment of historical promise one might think would have been enough for most audiences, do not seem to linger too long in the minds of the people of Carnant, after all.[28] But then, if such comparisons had been made with regard to the Young King early on in his career, there are reasons to think courtiers might not remember them with pleasure afterward, Chrétien's evocation of Absalom seeming especially sinister when set alongside Walter Map's comment on Henry's rebellion and subsequent death in 1183:

> His Absalom ['Absalon suus'] had stirred up all Aquitaine and Burgundy, and many of the French, against our lord his father, and all of them of Maine and Anjou and the Bretons; and of those who were on our side, the more part fell away to him. [...] And when the power of all the world was flocking to Absalom, he took an oath against his father at Martel, and on that same day was smitten with the hammer ['martellum'] of death by the all-righteous avenging hand, he was not, and riot was turned to quiet, and so the world was at rest when Python perished. (*The Courtier's Trifles*, dist. 4, § 1).

As I argued earlier, given that we cannot really be sure of the date of Chrétien's text, we cannot then really know what the relation is between his mention of Absalom and Walter's: depending on that date, the picture painted in *Erec* could be either glorificatory or portentous. It may have been both depending on when it was read and reread. What such a shift might indicate that in effect there is no hope of permanence in the language of comparison and typological assimilation: the poetry of Lucan, for example, appears as a catalogue of 'misreadings', in that moments so often yield a future that is the grotesquely ironic contrary of their immediate and apparent promise. Viewed retrospectively, the present rarely – if ever – 'speaks' to the future in sympathetic concord: the time is always 'out of joint'. So is there a measure in which the 'ordinary people' would always necessarily fail to understand the role of the tournament? Does this then mean that their apparent satisfaction at what they see is at some level 'feigned' or false because it is impermanent? Of course, there is a sense in which we are dealing more with appetite than rationality: the grammar of spectacle partakes more of the parataxis Barthes sees in wrestling than of boxing's articulation of 'un avenir rationnel'. Consequently, the resurgence of appetite manifested in complaints about Erec's lack of chivalric activity after the tournament is inevitable. Indeed, although the courtiers speak of him as being excessive in his desires and Enide as having put a spell on him, their complaints reveal that the agalmic magic of their all-possessing enjoyment of him has been interrupted. All this in spite of the fact that the economic rationale of the situation should be perfectly apparent: although Erec may not go to tournaments, he nonetheless continues to equip his followers in exemplary feudal manner such that they may go out and distinguish themselves, thereby contributing to the economy of renown. However, the persistence of public demand in the the symbolic diminution imputed to Erec appears as a reminder of desire's excess over need. Of course, their desire here is not expressed in heteroerotic terms, unless lord and vassal are construed as being of different genders. Nonetheless, as Chrétien's lyric production also makes clear, feudalism is insufficient as a distributive rationale for the libidinal economy. As in the atomised world of wrestling, seduction, the renewal of the libidinal covenant, will have to happen all over again.

* * *

Although views of the encounter between Erec and the clan of Laluth have often presented the two worlds as a simple binary opposition, there is much to suggest that the picture is more complex, Chrétien's vision of that encounter questioning both the perception of contrast and opposition and its place in the evolving temporal scheme of the diplomatic encounter. Further problems are raised by Chrétien's vision of the place of activity and passivity, speech and silence: just as Erec's apprenticeship at court seems to consist of observation and reflection followed by action, so Enide may be doing more than languish in silence at this stage. For a start, simply by doing nothing, she either avoids traps into which various sisters-under-the-skin and competitors fell (the Queen's handmaiden, Philomena) or profits more with less effort (the Count's niece). Of the three, two are 'lost to history' in different senses: Philomena, callously disfigured and silenced, disappears in the remote past, while the Queen's handmaiden is lost to this history at least, disappearing without further trace. As for Enide's cousin, time will tell, but the contrast between Enide's and Philomena's households may suggest Fortune does not always favour the most active participant.

Once the opposition between the two courts is settled through the defeat of Yder and the successful conclusion of negotiations with the Count, what remains is a court that had simply been forgotten in terms of its feudal allegiances. After all, it would be hard to damn Laluth, as Topsfield does, as the kingdom of 'non-*savoir*' and then correspondingly praise an Arthurian court that seemed to be ignorant of a substantial court collective that, although only a day's ride distant and bound to them both by allegiance and blood, did not seem either to figure on its political map or to be noticed when it did not respond to Arthur's *ban*.[29] Chrétien's narrative in the *premiers vers* thus has to be understood as a rather ironic reflection on the process of 'othering' observed in other works. Laluth, through the role of the Count's niece in the negotiations, seems in its own way to respond to the caricature that is implicitly painted of it by Erec's intervention. Yder is no Morholt; the palfrey is not a ship; there is no love potion. Here again the question of what is family and what is familiar remains fundamental: Morholt may be Iseut's kinsman, but Yder is not Enide's. Chrétien's vision of Tristan's return with Iseut from Ireland thus points to a more complex picture of diplomatic alliance. Although Laluth and Enide's family continue as actors on the stage, Iseut's family appears somewhat as a disposable 'back-story', a 'premerains vers' having little organic connection with the main action constituted by the adultery. Are we really to believe that once Iseut is transported to Cornwall, her marriage to Mark ends the war with the Irish and leaves her isolated in the manner of a Procne simply forgotten by her family, thus ending any cultural interaction between two kingdoms now separated in a sort of mutual oblivion? By contrast, *Erec et Enide's* sense of a continuing story, a more elaborate and enduring diplomatic 'conjunture' posits the Tristan as offering too simplistic an account of the relation between self and neighbour. In the next chapter, we will see how that problem of the relation to the neighbour and his enjoyment takes on nightmarishly troubling dimensions.

Notes

1   Atalanta appears twice in Ovid's *Metamorphoses*, taking a key role in the hunt of the boar sent by Diana to wreak vengeance on Calydon (book 8, ll. 260–546), and then in book 10 in the narrative of her race against Hippomenes (ll. 560–707), both episodes associating her with a beauty only courted at the price of divine displeasure.
2   See Jacqueline de Weever, *Sheba's Daughters: Whitening and Demonizing the Saracen Woman in Medieval French Epic*, Garland Reference Library of the Humanities, 2077 (New York and London: Garland, 1998), passim.
3   See Bloch, *Etymologies and Genealogies*, pp. 71–5.
4   Elias, *The Civilising Process*, p. 387–414.
5   To *break time* in fencing is to introduce 'a pause […] into an action […] normally performed in one movement', thereby interrupting the *cadence* or 'rhythm in which a sequence of movements is made'. On 'cutting' in face-to-

face interaction, see Erving Goffman, *Behaviour in Public Places: Notes on the Social Organisation of Gatherings* (New York: Free Press, 1966), pp. 114–16.
6 See Burgess, *Erec et Enide*, p. 31.
7 The sense of closure here with respect to the problems raised by the *Tristan* can appear potentially rather pat, making of *Erec et Enide* a somewhat facile, self-contained response to the legend. This apparent simplicity then contrasts with what Matilda Bruckner sees as the extensive, multifaceted response articulated over his middle romances (on which, see Bruckner, *Shaping Romance: Interpretation, Truth and Closure in Twelfth-Century Fictions, Middle Ages* (Philadelphia: University of Pennsylvania Press, 1993), pp. 90–104).
8 Bezzola, pp. 123–4.
9 For edition and translation, see Leslie Topsfield (ed. and trans.), *Les Poésies du troubadour Raimon de Miraval*, Les Classiques d'Oc (Paris: Nizet, 1971), pp. 272–8. See Sarah Kay, *Subjectivity in Troubadour Poetry*, Cambridge Studies in French, 31 (Cambridge: Cambridge University Press, 1990), p. 98, note 30 at p. 238.
10 See Jane Gilbert, ' "Boys Will Be... What?" Gender, Sexuality and Childhood in *Floire et Blancheflor* and *Floris et Lyriope*', *Exemplaria*, 9:1 (1997), 40–61.
11 Gaunt, *Gender and Genre*, pp. 117–8.
12 See Huchet, *Amour discourtois*, pp. 72–3 and Kay, *Subjectivity in Troubadour Poetry*, p. 98.
13 Adam Philips, *On Kissing, Tickling and Being Bored* (London: Faber and Faber, 1993), p. 103.
14 Gravdal, *Ravishing Maidens*, p. 51 (à propos of Perceval's forced kiss).
15 Gravdal, *Ravishing Maidens*, p. 46 and pp. 61–3.
16 Gravdal, *Ravishing Maidens*, pp. 66–7.
17 On which, see Gravdal, *Ravishing Maidens*, p. 52.
18 See notably Maddox, *Arthurian Romances*, pp. 25–32.
19 Maddox, *Arthurian Romances*, pp. 26–30.
20 Kantorowicz, p. 95–7.
21 See Biddick, *The Shock of Medievalism*, pp. 136–41.
22 On the vagina and the scopic drive, see Luce Irigaray, *Speculum of the Other Woman*, trans. by Gillian C. Gill (Ithaca NY: Cornell University Press, 1985), pp. 13–129. The notion of the body as transcending the limits of the pleasure principle by offering a fantasy of persisting 'beyond the retreat into death' is central to Lacan's discussions of masochism (see Evans, *Introductory Dictionary*, p. 168).
23 See Roland Barthes, *Le Plaisir du texte*, Points (Paris: Seuil, 1973), p. 82.
24 Chakrabarty, *Provincialising Europe*, p. 43 (cited above).
25 On the tournament see in particular Seebass-Linggi, pp. 60–8.
26 Adler, p. 918, following Nitze, *Lancelot and Guenevere: A Study on the Origin of Courtly Love* (Chicago: University of Chicago Press, 1930), p. 81 and p. 97.
27 Burgess, *Erec et Enide*, p. 44.

28 On the comparisons and their potential ambiguities see W. Ziltener, *Chrétien und die 'Aeneis': eine Untersuchung des Einflusses von Virgil auf Chrétien von Troyes* (Graz: Böhlaus, 1957), p. 785; Peter Haidu, 1969), pp. 115–17; Peter W. Hurst, 'The Encyclopaedic Tradition, the Cosmological Epic and the Validation of the Medieval Romance', *Comparative Criticism*, 1 (1979), 53–71, at p. 60; Roger Dragonetti, *La Vie de la lettre au Moyen Age ('Le Conte du graal')* (Paris: Seuil, 1980), pp. 101–07 (on Alexander); Allard, pp. 48–52, and also Seebass-Linggi, pp. 63–6 and pp. 150–2.
29 On geography and kinship in this section, see Joan Brumlik, 'Kinship and Kingship in Chrétien's *Erec*', *Romance Philology*, 47 (1993), 177–92 and Duggan, *Romances*, pp. 59–64.

MARK ANTONY
Tend me to-night;
May be it is the period of your duty:
Haply you shall not see me more; or if,
A mangled shadow: perchance to-morrow
You'll serve another master. I look on you
As one that takes his leave. [...]

DOMITIUS ENOBARBUS
What mean you, sir,
To give them this discomfort? Look, they weep;
And I, an ass, am onion-eyed: for shame,
Transform us not to women.

MARK ANTONY
Ho, ho, ho!
Now the witch take me, if I meant it thus!
Grace grow where those drops fall!
My hearty friends,
You take me in too dolorous a sense;
For I spake to you for your comfort; did desire you
To burn this night with torches: know, my hearts,
I hope well of to-morrow; and will lead you
Where rather I'll expect victorious life
Than death and honour.
                (Shakespeare, *Antony and Cleopatra*, act 4, scene 1)

Nullus unquam meruit iras quas non posset primis placare lacrimis, nil concupivit quod non paucis extorquere blandiciis, quippe qui quemvis hominem contra seipsum optinebat, quia contra conscienciam et fidem Deo derelicto. (*The Courtier's Trifles*, dist. 4, § 2, pp. 282–3 in edition)

He [the Young King] never provoked anger which he was not able to pacify with the first tear he shed; never set his heart on anything that he could not extort with a little coaxing: he was one who could win over any man against his will, forsaking God and going against conscience and faith.

Chapter Five
'Misfortune Brought You There':
History (and Geography) in the *Boudoir*

> The great adventure of chivalric romance is the adventure of becoming what (and who) you think you can be, of transforming the *awareness* of an inner self into an *actuality* which impresses on the external world the fact of a personal, self-chosen destiny and therefore of an inner-determined identity.[1]

If, as Robert Hanning, Sarah Kay and others have commented, the central trope of chivalric romance is so often the quest or journey, this still begs the question of what journeys are and where they happen, as is illustrated by Erec's decision to depart from his father's court with no destination specified.[2] After all, every other journey in Chrétien's romances seems to be undertaken with some clear goal in mind. Alexander and Cligés both present 'mission statements' of what they intend to achieve; Calogrenant is driven by curiosity, Yvain by revenge; Lancelot wishes to rescue the Queen; Perceval wishes to become a knight. Erec, by contrast, simply sets out and insists. The nature of the difference between the journeys in *Cligés* on the one hand and in *Erec et Enide* on the other can be illustrated through their echoes of the journey of Aeneas. Where in the *Aeneid* the crossing of the Mediterranean had been partly flight and partly the fulfilment of a destiny, in *Cligés* those crossings are now executed in good order with relatively smooth sailing on relatively calm seas. This situation reflects Chrétien's prefatory reflections on the nature of the historical dialectic that has bestowed divine favour and excellence on the kingdoms of Europe. It also marks a difference from in the mixed reactions to the character of Eneas, a figure of uncertain character and reputation, subject both to praise and vituperation, favour and persecution. In that sense, Eneas – a character not merely buffeted by but infected with Junoian instabilities to a point that he is as much her mirror as her enemy – appears as a vehicle in which the fundamental 'scandalousness' of history is unveiled. Against this, *Cligés* can be seen as a reflection on the varying accounts of whether the world stage provides a sympathetic accommodation for Priam's son, a backdrop of fitting grandeur rather than scornful derision. This debate then continues with Gauvain's experiences in the burlesque *Chevalier à l'épée*, where, rather than accommodating his assertion of virile agency, the world seems to titter at him through the perplexing visions with which he is presented, the plunging blade he must repeatedly dodge while endeavouring to consummate his relationship with the lady in the castle's magical trap bed threatening to pin him from behind much like the male partner Eneas would have allegedly sought to attract by pimping his wife's favours.

Sex and sexuality are a major part of the problem here: if Aeneas passes from Creusa to Dido to Lavinia without his morals or orientation being much impugned, the *Eneas* sees his 'unmooring' from Troy as source of a much wider 'gender trouble' manifest in slanders and retributory deaths of 'deviant' figures such as Euralyus or Camille.[3] In that sense, we are in effect to understand that Eneas's first marriage is little different from Dido's Carthage: both constructs appear as historical precocities whose shaky ground has simply been disavowed.[4] Accordingly, the journey in the *Roman d'Eneas* marks less a suspension of sexual activity than of sexual *identity*, a cultural 'dream-time' threatened with being overwhelmed by a lurid range of medieval fantasy projections onto the ancient past.[5]

In that sense, one way of understanding the space opened in both individual romance journeys – and, more broadly, in the wider narrative of *translatio* – is in effect caught between neurosis and psychosis.[6] For Lacan, the distinction here is that the neurotic subject believes he inhabits language, while the psychotic believes language inhabits or possesses him.[7] In their representation of hallucination, romance texts bears witness to the fear of subjectivity being overwhelmed by language as the domain in which fantasy is generated, a theme recurring even in such late 'romance' works as Arthur Schnitzler's *Traumnovelle*, the source for Stanley Kubrick's film *Eyes Wide Shut*, which reads as an exploration of the subject's war against the hallucinatory, 'psychotic' dimension of fantasy life. Here, the journey constitutes an assertion of subjective status where otherwise the Subject might be 'fucked with' by the fantasy netherworld, much as Freud's original psychotic, Paul Schreber, believed God was trying to have sex with him. In that sense, Hanning's vision of romance as a (neurotic) assertion of subjective mastery then does not account for the intrusion of compulsion to repeat manifested by various works, or their clear anxieties about the relation between subjectivity and fantasy.[8]

As with *Eyes Wide Shut*, Erec and Enide's quest appears as a suspension of sexual activity in the private realm. However, unlike the spectacular violence of the various tournaments, the violence of the quest is positioned between private and public: if a knight falls in the woods, does it make a sound when no one is there to applaud or be deterred? Thus, although the couple's self-imposed *carestia* might be thought to transpose the stolen *jouissance* of the royal boudoir back into the display culture of the public sphere, it instead marks another kind of withdrawal, this time in displeasure or anger – as rendered by the French verb, *bouder* ('to sulk', 'to withdraw').[9] Erec's refusal to provide unmediated access to the spectacle the collective desires forms a subversive reflection of a scenario in Sade's *Philosophie dans le boudoir*: the arch-libertine Dolmancé asks leave to withdraw to a side room (thus, a boudoir within the boudoir) to engage in a practice so abhorrent – to judge from the reaction of his libertine fellows to his whispered revelations – it cannot happen 'on stage', but rather must remain the secret, debasing kernel of his deregulated impulses.[10] What differentiates the two figures is Erec's refusal to disclose that kernel: by refusing to discuss his intentions and withdrawing to the forest, Erec lays claim to a space beyond both collective regard and the Law in which, as he gives them to understand, something monstrous will happen. Moreover, different from the 'masochistic' strategy adopted by Arthur, Erec's withdrawal manifests a sadistic dimension through his refusal to enter into any 'contract' with the court, a progression mirroring Lacan's vision of sadism as a second-generation product derived from a 'dénégation' of masochism.[11]

Chrétien's exploration of the limits of endurance in the quest hovers between waking and the lurid dream of the encounters that follow. Although marked initially by a sovereign will, the world around them will prove a strange place in which the sleep of *carestia* – like that of reason – brings forth monsters. Indeed, the contrast between Enide's enforced insomnia and Erec's brute exhaustion creates a space in which anxiety's wakefulness stands at a distance from the pattern of fight-sleep-eat, the appearance of Erec as a machine provoking trouble in others. While *Eyes Wide Shut* gives colour and texture to what Lacan terms 'émoi', the troubling of motion characteristic of anxiety, Hanning (see above) suggests that romance – whose conventions the film parodies – acts to throw off any such sense of *empêchement*. Herein lies some of the sense of the anamorphic encounter: the relation of permanent tension between the object and the rest of the picture means our eyes cannot be entirely or unequivocally open to its 'true' form. The approach to this truth proceeds stepwise, with the first meeting with Enide offering a vision of unparalleled beauty, with the knights of Arthur's court readily able to agree she is indeed the 'parsome' of Nature's achievement. However, as we know from the traditions of courtly love, beauty is rarely such a simple thing, and this chapter will explore how, starting from Enide's revelation of her knowledge of the rumours concerning Erec's *recreantise*, the text offers a series of uncomfortable visions. These are haunted not merely by death, but, more problematically, by the living, 'undead' presence of undomesticatable desires and wishes to which the eyes of have to remain 'wide shut'.

Considerable space has been devoted to the question of Enide's appearance and body: most suggestively, Kathryn Gravdal sees female beauty as a spur to desire and sexual violence in Chrétien's romances, while Jane Burns shows how Enide's beauty is part of an occlusion of the founding of romance discourse in prurient desire for and objectification of the female body.[12] As Chrétien emphasises, for all Erec looks at her (ll. 1482–93), Enide looks at him just as much ('Mais ne regardoit mie mains /La demoisele le vassal', ll. 1494–5), a symmetry reinforced in Erec's father's first meeting with his son's new bride, at which point he could not tell which of the two pleased him more' ('Ne set li quelx d'aux mieuz li plaise', l. 2356). While voyeuristic elements in Chrétien's text clearly point to an intensity of libidinal investment in the feminine, to see his assertions of gender-blindness as no more than *mauvaise foi* risks underplaying the roles not only of male beauty but also beauty's non-embodied, performative dimension.[13] Although in romance – not unlike cinema – it can seem axiomatic that 'men act and women appear', we should not forget that 'acts' have an element of appearance and appearance can be an act.

'Chivalry Roused as if from a Slumber'

> When, as often happens, brother Quintus, I think over and recall the days of old, those men always seem to me to have been singularly happy who, with the State at her best, and while enjoying high distinctions and the fame of their achievements, were able to maintain such a course of life that they could either engage in activity that involved no risk or enjoy a dignified repose. And time was when I used to imagine that I, too, should come to be entitled, with well-nigh universal approval, to some opportunity of leisure and of directing my mind to the sublime pursuits beloved of us both, […] The hopes born of my thoughts and plans have been cheated, alike by the disastrous times of public peril and by my manifold misfortunes. (Cicero, *On the Orator*, book 1, § 3)
>
> The more beautiful the boy, the less likely he is to survive.[14]
>
> In this pitiable and care-ridden court I languish, renouncing my own pleasure to please others. While there are very few who can help one, it is in the power of anyone to injure; unless I have singly appeased the whole body, I am nowhere. If I take the place of a worthy man so as to become enviable, they will backbite me, and say my supporters are taken in by appearances. Is any simple? He is called a fool. Peaceable? He is a sluggard. Silent? A villain. Well-spoken? An actor. Good-natured? A flatterer. Over-anxious? Covetous.[…] Compassionate? Slack. Rich? A miser. Says his prayers? A hypocrite. (Map, *The Courtier's Trifles*, dist. 4, chapter 13, p. 373 in edition)

Cicero's comments in *On the Orator* bear witness to the impact of the crisis of the Roman Republic resulting from the resurgence of tyrannical and imperial ambition, disturbing an order and prosperity born of generations of devotion to civic ideals. This is then the image of Rome rocked to its foundations in a civil upheaval contemplated in the long view. Although the political economy of Arthurian romance operates in a less predictable environment, Cicero's return to public life and Erec's rousing from his *recreantise* have notable points of contact. Both moments are marked by an assertion of values through the means of performance and spectacle. However, both moments share their anxieties. Nervous about the consequences of practice, Cicero presents himself as a 'theoretician', the treatise he produces following his 'recall' to civic duty a reflection on the orator's social responsibilities. By contrast, Erec's performance appears as practice seemingly devoid of regulating theory, a headlong course made no more reassuring by the fact that it seems no more unsparing of the feelings and safety of others than it is of himself.

Although less attention has been paid to Erec's charms than to Enide's, critics tending to concentrate on the cult of *prouesse* in male identity formation, the male body was also an object of contemplation, its capacity to 'ravish' central to court society, with Erec's role-model, Arthur, as dependent as his ladies on his capacity to beguile and to fascinate, relations between vassal and lord determined by the latter's seductive capacities. An analogue can be found in the description of the young Parzival, who only knows his name to be 'beau fils' (*Parzival*, book 4, § 140, l. 6): that beauty that marks him out as destined to hold sway in the public domain is squandered through a mother's love that seeks to protect him from his knightly identity and calling. Obviously, just as charismatic kingship struggles to balance limited supply and irrational demand, the economy of beauty in appearance and action presents considerable problems. In that regard, the episodes that follow Erec's return to his father's court bear witness to the anxieties attendant on the *jouissance* of royal performance and presence. This goes in parallel with the alleged *recreantise* that accompanies his seeming subservience to his new love object, Enide: 'Mes tant l'ama Erec d'amors, / Que d'armes mais ne li chaloit' (ll. 2430–1).[15] Unconstrained by any sense of moderation, Erec's dalliance with Enide represents the absolute rule of pleasure, a Thracian surrender to the demands of appetite and to her seductive powers that are, as Burgess notes, the flip-side of the virtues Chrétien ascribes to her immediately before (ll. 2397–429).[16] Of course, much of the problem is to do with youth and beauty: Cicero speaks as an older man withdrawing from public duty to pursue a life of the mind.

By contrast, the young – but, at 25 or 26, now not so young – Erec withdraws from the public sphere of the court to pursue that of the body. Yet both scenarios raise the question of desire even though its expression differs radically in the two cases. Balancing between personal desire and philosophical principle, Cicero's interlocutors seek to convince and sway their beloved master to turn his attention to them.

Where Cicero's followers might legitimately call on him to share his wisdom with them either for their profit or as counsel in times of trouble, Erec's followers seem more irrational: after all, their material needs are met and their lord's *largesse* allows them to attend tournaments in fine style (ll. 2446–54). Thus their criticisms might at least in part be motivated by jealous resentment at the withdrawal of his presence.[17] But then, given that, as Lacan points out, it is the remaining surplus of *demand* over the satisfaction of *need*, desire, the condition of the subject, is never exactly rational.[18] The contrast of Erec's youth with Cicero's age and experience thus points to the permanence of trouble and anxiety, the idea that freedom from it, the possibility of some 'holiday from history', is no more than an illusion. Indeed, the entire episode appears as testimony the enduring 'undead' life of psychic forces. Enide's guilt-filled reaction to the rumours of Erec's *recreantise* bear witness to the excess and irrationality power fundamental to the Law, while her desiring contemplation of his body, encompassing both memory and the persistence of desire, gives weight and poignancy to her mournful reflections. The question here is the rational foundation of her feelings: is she confessing to or denying her place in the narrative as a desiring Subject? After all, the impossible utterance would be a queen's confession before the court that her sexual appetite had indeed led her to detain her lord excessively. While the suspicion might well be that such is precisely one of the seamy undersides on which court life is predicated and while it might be voiced through the unofficial, contestatory discourses of rumour and criticism resumed under the heading of *losengerie*, such a view cannot be acknowledged officially. In the work attributed to Chrétien, the nearest we come to such a revelatory moment is in Guinevere's sudden appearance in *Le Chevalier au lion*, where, having exhausted the King (ll. 49–52), she surprises the circle of knights, her appetite for new matter seemingly unabated. However, although the courtiers are clearly shocked to the point that they forget the dictates of decorum (ll. 64–85), the intrusive presence of the Queen's body offering a grim foreshadowing flash of events to follow, their reaction stems more from what is suggested than what is stated.

But then, the sin in some explicit acknowledgement of royal excess might arguably be less against propriety than expediency. Scandal thus offers a potential strategic advantage to those high-status individuals able to unbalance court life, something Enide arguably fails to grasp and manipulate. Her mortification is an unwilling concession that her desires have a role, and yet it is also excessive insofar as she fails to consider the irrationalities of her accusers. Arguably quite out of step with its cause, her reaction reflects the indifference of the superego Law, the overwhelming ripple effect of her interpellation needing time to be accommodated or yield strategic insight.[19] In the meantime, not yet a sufficiently savvy player to meet the accusations with some sort of courtly 'Che vuoi?' – the Lacanian question that throws back the burden of an utterance on the speaker him/herself ('You're saying this to me, but what are you really saying?') – what we have is a *folie* of pure panic as she scrabbles for a frame in which to accommodate the impact of her actions:[20]

> Tel duel en ot et tel pesance
> Qu'il li avint par mescheance
> Que ele dist une parole
> Dont ele se tint puis por fole,
> Mais ele n'i pensoit nul mal.
> Son seignor a mont et a val
> Commença tant a esgarder,
> Le cors bien fait et le vis cler,
> Et plore de si grant ravine
> Que chiesent desor la poitrine
> Son seignor les lermes de lui,
> Et dist: 'Lasse, con mar m'esmui
> De mon païs! Que ving ça querre?
> Bien me devroit sorbir la terre,
> Quant toz li mieudres chevaliers,
> Li plus hardiz et li plus fiers,
> Li plus beax et li plus cortois,

Qui onques fust ne cuens ne rois,
A de tout en tout relinquie
Por moi tote chevalerie.
Donques l'ai je honi por voir;
Nel vousisse por nul avoir.'
Lors li a dit: '[Tant] mar i fus!'
A tant se tait, se ne dit plus. (ll. 2481–504)

She felt such pain and sorrow that, as luck would have it, she made a remark for which she later counted herself foolish, though she intended no harm by it. She began to study her husband from head to foot, looking at his handsome body and fair face, and suddenly wept such a flood of tears that, some of them fell on his chest. 'Wretch', she said, unhappy me! Was it for this I left my home? Let the earth open and swallow me down, for the very best of knights – the boldest and the bravest, the most loyal, the most courteous that was ever count or king – has turned his back on chivalry because of me. Clearly I have brought shame on him, though I would not have wished it for anything.' Then she said to him: 'What great misfortune brought you there!' With that, she fell silent and said no more.

In this scenario, the confusions Enide brings to the table are of paramount importance. Her thought processes condense and are born out of tensions between public censure (ll. 2455–64) and private experience (ll. 2471–2). Her contemplation of Erec combines and blurs her erotic investment in the object of desire, the disavowed history of her seduction repudiated in its necessary excess and fascination. The past tense here is key: 'lor lit / Ou eü orent maint delit' (ll. 2471–2, my emphasis). The erotic spell seems to be temporarily broken or lifted much as the Béroul *Tristan* posits a moment of clarity that is the wearing off of the potion (*Tristan*, ll. 2147–220). But here we have not so much the breaking of a spell as the high point of a tension between contradictory forces. The gossip about Erec's *recreantise* does not simply put an end to their idyll then and there, but rather seeps in from outside into Enide's awareness and so builds as a pressure that calls for something to happen.

Those mixed thoughts find their focus in her contemplation of Erec, both present to her and yet at the same time lost in that her articulation addresses the 'public' face most threatened by the apparent damage to his reputation. In that respect, the male body stands opposed to that of the monster or giant, whose gross and exaggerated physicality is so often the mark of a moral monstrosity that commonly finds its censure in combat and defeat.[21] However, if the character of the loathly body of the monster is that it can appear as the support or juncture of contradictory features, the same is true of beauty, whose appearance of presence gains from the simultaneous perspective of its loss. Erec's body thus appears, as Germaine Greer puts it, as an 'icon of male vulnerability'.[22] Enide's contemplation of the sleeping Erec can be read as a foreshadowing of his death and of her despair over the vision of the body on the bier in the court of Oringle, a double vision suggesting that Erec belongs to the set of living things as opposed to those things that are dead. However, in other regards, as future king and embodiment of the law (*lex animata*) Erec is also of necessity partially 'dead'. What the scene reveals is that Erec himself is subject to a degree of anamorphic distortion of the kind seen in Holbein's *The Ambassadors*: in effect, he is the skull, both alive and dead at the same time, the thing both unreadable because apparently out-of-place and yet fundamental to the sense of the image.[23] Alan of Lille offers a similar vision of temporal anamorphosis in his description of Hymenaeus, simultaneously young and old:

> As he seemed subject to the laws of no age, he was now blooming in the spring of youth, now a countenance of maturer years proclaimed his seriousness, now his face gave the impression of being ploughed by the furrows of old age.[24]

Similarly collapsing different times into a single vision, Enide's reflection also illuminates the libidinal basis of charismatic power mimed in her earlier striptease appearance before the court, but here now twisted in a manner that the object that appears dead to her his also still sexually attractive. Thus the pathos of the scene depends at least in part on a stain of tittilation. Of course, all such flashes are fleeting, a momentary vision of apparently incompatible elements caught in the play of apparently irresolvable perspectives.

Interestingly, the narratorial comment that Enide 'meant no harm', perhaps reflective of Abelardian concerns with intention rather than action, places her reaction to the guilt weighing on her ('pesance') beyond that sort of question. The question that then remains is the content of the term 'fole', here perhaps analoguous to Lucan's comment on the bloody prelude necessary to the re-establishment of order under Nero: 'if the Fates could find no other way /[...] then we have no complaint'. In short, her reaction is 'irrational' from various points of view, in that she takes on herself a burden of affect she had no real need to own. Thus, reference to her seeming *folie* indicates that, even in retrospect, her actions here have no rational sense. Then again, although what Chrétien's comment also indicates is a regard for Enide's opinion and evolving judgement we will see reflected later, we cannot actually be sure he gives us to understand this is in fact the 'final sum', *la parsome*, of her subsequent reflections on the matter, and indeed Chrétien seems to signal fairly clearly that only so much evidence is forthcoming (l. 2504). That said, we are at least reassured that Enide's capacity for reflection marks her as something other than the female equivalent of the tyrannical giant, a creature whose subservience to appetite admits of no such self-scrutiny. In Lacanian terms, what we in effect have is an image of the 'barred Subject' ($): Enide's sense of interdiction – although irrational in that it is founded in the tyranny of the Law – is nonetheless the mark of her subjection to the attractions and anxieties (*esfroi*) of desire ($◊a). However, the determining influence of other scenes hints at problems less easily resolved. One resonance here may come from the *Roman d'Eneas*: Enide's desire may have a human dimension, but then, even though it was forced on her by divine agency, so did Dido's. Against that, we might see her lament at ever having left her country as an echo of generations of reflection on the travels of Aeneas, not least Augustine's Virgilian regrets at his decision to leave his home and set out for Italy. All of these archetypes carry with them a range of perspectives in which the question of the ultimate sense of an action set against the questions that hang on its motivation loom large, part of a troubling backdrop of *émoi* contextualising Enide's own reflections in a larger history of anxiety.

Enide's experience of regret and loss condenses into the lament for Erec's beauty and, most specifically, in the nub of the *parole* that sprouts as a coda to the end of her speech: 'Con mar i fus' (l. 2503) as it appears in Fritz's edition, emended from 'Tant mar' in Ms. B on the basis of a comparison with Ms. P as well as with other versions, such as the Guiot copy, B. N. fonds fr. 794. Given that this seems to be one of the central problems in the speech, not least since Erec seizes on it in his questioning (l. 2517), it is interesting to see the degree of variation in *what* she actually said recorded across the manuscripts of the work. As Fritz points out in his introduction to his edition, one of the shifts in the perception of the transmission of these works is the reassessment of the place of the Guiot copy. Following on from earlier cautions regarding an over-emphasis on that manuscript such as that offered by Tony Hunt, Fritz presents this version, taken as the basis for Mario Roques' earlier CFMA edition, as the eccentric rather than the flagship of the tradition:[25]

> La qualité de la copie de Guiot pour *Erec*, et, à degrés divers, pour les autres romans de Chrétien, résiderait moins dans la qualité de son modèle ou dans une proximité plus grande avec l'original que dans la qualité de ses réfections: Guiot s'était suffisamment imprégné de l'art de Chrétien de Troyes pour refaire 'du Chrétien de Troyes' lorsqu'un vers de son modèle était corrompu ou qu'un passage du romancier lui semblait obscur.[26]

Crucially, Guiot's reading of Enide's lament 'con mar fus' (Roques, l. 2503) is that also of the other manuscripts grouped together with Fritz's base, B. N. fonds fr. 1376 (cp. Fritz's apparatus at l. 2503), although not that of 1376 itself. Thus, all these versions omit the pronoun *i*, an oddity given that in the Guiot copy and the other versions it still features in Erec's questioning ('por qu'avez dit que mar i fui?', Roques, l. 2517).[27] Erec's hearing, although he was half-asleep, seems to be sharper than that of some of the scribes. However, for all Fritz argues against Guiot's pervasive influence on our view of Chrétien, he is effectively prepared to accept that version as determining in the matter of the 'tant' / 'con' variance. The justification is quite simple of course: 'con mar' provides a key echo both within Enide's speech here (cp. l. 2492) and her later lament in the forest (l. 4631). What are the senses of these differences?

If the pronoun *i* is omitted in Enide's lament, then what she says is simply a lament for Erec. Her sin is that she speaks of him as if the concerns of his courtiers regarding the fading of his chivalric energies were justified and that his renown, and he himself were already 'dead' (socially, that is). Fonds fr. 1376's reading places the accent rather differently. In having Erec lament that he ever came there, which is to say to her country of Laluth, she offers a counterpoint to her regrets at having left her land ('con mar m'esmui / De mon païs', ll. 2492–3). As with Chrétien's casting of the journeys that led to Tereüs's encounter with Philomena, the lament is thus for the *fatalité* of the fortuitous encounter – as Humphrey Bogart was to put it rather later: 'Of all the gin joints, in all the towns, in all the world, she had to walk into mine'.[28] The 'tant' / 'con' variation raises other questions, some that can be framed in terms of the different origins of the two words: O.Fr. *tant* derives straightforwardly from Latin *tantum* ('so much', 'so'); whereas O.Fr. *con* /*come*, although derived from Latin *cum* ('with'), also covers the semantic terrain of Latin *quam* and *quantum* ('*how* much').[29] Although, given the sheer range of its functions, *come* is obviously not invariably a interrogative marker, its use in this context does raise at least the ghost of the question: *how* great a misfortune, exactly? By contrast, *tant* is potentially slightly more emphatic: 'it was *such* a great misfortune that brought you there'. Thus, varying the formula she uses at other points, the Enide in fonds fr. 1376 states her claim to insight slightly more conclusively than her sisters in other versions of the text. Moreover, the reading in fonds fr. 1376 for the opening of Enide's lament is 'tant mar i vi', which, as Fritz rightly points out, is incomprehensible given the line that follows. However, there is a suggestion that the scribe might have been thinking of Enide's key speech as hinging on a repetition of *Tant mar... Tant mar*, even if he could not contrive an intelligible latter part of the line for the first occurrence. Of course, Erec's response to her speech in Ms. B indicates that such a difference may not be that significant: he clearly hears the 'i' but the 'tant' disappears ('por qu'avez dit que mar i fui', l. 2517) – whereas *que con** would put two conjunctions together in a barbarous pairing, *que tant mar i fui* is at least syntactically possible, albeit hypermetric in the immediate context. Although the weight of the tradition seems to be against fonds fr. 1376's rendering of this line, we might consider the ways in which 'tant mar' might be justified as *lectio difficilior*. The particle appears frequently in expressions of duration and result, such as *tant (…) que* ('until') or *tant con* ('as long as'), or of degree, such as *tant par* ('so'

263

+adj.), the first 1,000 lines of Chrétien's text alone yielding a very large number of occurrences in a work that seems obsessed with duration (e.g. 'Tant con durra crestïentez', l. 25), with waiting for a moment (e.g. Erec's 'Tant que je puisse armes trover', l. 257) or with the impact of sustained or intense forces ([...] tant nos conbatrons andui / Qu'il me conquerra ou je lui', ll. 263–4). Enide's words here could therefore be taken as echo of a more general concern with the results of pursuing particular courses of action, with the limits of human striving and agency in history. Erec's arrival at Laluth was after all the product of a persistence whose ends now seem clear to his wife.

Until... A small word, possibly but an important one, potentially carrying a note of menace.[30] Until what? Until, in the end..., or to put it together in Chrétien's terms, *tant qu'a la parsome*.... Again, what? Death? Ruin? However, the 'final sum' ('parsome') that is the ultimate sense of Enide's transformations and peregrinations is a matter for later, rendering precipitate any claim to understanding voiced in her regrets and uncertainties here. Faced like the external audience with a prosopopaeic riddle, she knows no more about herself than Chrétien gives us to know about Erec, whose motives – as Chrétien carefully and teasingly emphasises later (ll. 6470–4, cited above) – are a matter for him to know and others to wonder about. Depending on whether the narrator is regarded as withholding the cause of Erec's departure as a source of shame or merely sparing his audience the repetition, his comment here is open to a variety of understandings, Erec's rebuke to Enide targetting the presumption that his courtiers have definitive insight into what *moves* him, whether in terms of movement, motivation or emotion, all crucially collapsed together in the uses of *movoir* and *esmovoir*. For the courtiers to have this knowledge is for the exorbitant life of his royal desires to be understood, domesticated and deprived of the enigma that gives it its charismatic power.[31]

Erec's terroristic action thus targets their claim to knowledge of the economy of movement in his singular trajectory. As Lacan comments, 'beware understanding!' The problem is that the role Enide takes on, her 'symbolic mandate', appears as a mistake both on her part and on that of Erec's followers. But then identification is always misidentification: as Žižek points out, the Subject's response to the 'Che vuoi?' of the Other is 'Why am I what you're telling me that I am?', or, in more condensed form, simply 'Why me?', the resistance that accompanies the process of Mary the whore interpellated into Mary the Saint, Christ the man into the Saviour.[32] Similarly, Enide's 'hystericisation' by the interpellatory force of the court's view of her as a seducing Eve – an accusation whose weight she both feels and contests – is coextensive with her 'interpellation into' a new role over the course of Chrétien's narrative: her resistance to the court's slander and to her mandate are one and the same. Moreover, the echo of the *Roman d'Eneas* suggests that the outcome is rarely simply a sanitised, redeemed figure (such as Mary): as we will see, even late on in Chrétien's text, Enide is uncertainly distinguished from or assimilated to Dido, 'whore' *malgré elle* of the *translatio* narrative, through the carvings on the saddle given her by Guivret. In that sense, what we have is 'Eve interpellated into Eve', the paradoxical relation of change and identity affirming the radically scandalous nature of the mandate that locates her in a central role in the libidinal economy of the court. This paradoxical assertion of difference and no difference echoes or anticipates devices such as Alain of Lille's evocation of the anamorphic *émoi* of the ageless figure of Hymenaeus. Thus, the two readings of Enide's lament – 'con mar fus' and 'con mar *i* fus' – do finally meet up, a convergence perhaps hinted at in uses of the *mar fus /fust* formula in subsequent laments and warnings. The readings attested in the other versions thus do attest to an understanding of one aspect of what is at stake here. However, there is more than one perspective at play in the scene.

Thus, in a narrative that hinges so much on the ways in which what people think they know or think to achieve (both rendered by the verb *cuidier*), telling your opponent what they will regret is a dangerous move.[33] Erec's next step is then to unleash a storm of fearful confusion, demonstrating his capacity to keep both friend and foe alike utterly off-balance. Shifting gear into an aggressively forensic rhetoric designed to extort an understanding of her motivations while keeping her uncertain regarding his, Erec's sudden, desk-lamp-in-the-face sowing of fear and confusion forms a two-pronged attack, mixing perplexing inscrutability and frightening, insistent precision –

in which, like Valmont's pressing of Mme de Volanges, she is allowed no room for manoeuvre or temporisation – follows with giddying speed.[34] What Enide blurred in her lament he means to tease apart with all the determination of the author of the *Varrine Orations*. Although the rapidity of Erec's reaction has been taken as indicative of his wounded pride, another possibility is to see the scene is as part of a Ciceronian reflection on public duty: when, as Cicero asks in the opening to *On the Orator*, do you ever get to retire from activity? After all, the picture that Chrétien paints of his relation to his followers in the run-up to the crisis itself presents him as a generous lord who has endured a certain amount of personal danger to arrive at a point where he is able to foster and encourage his underlings. In that sense, Chrétien's vision of the public sphere, informed by Augustinian and Boethian reflections on the role of Fortuna in the narrative of *translatio studii* and *imperii*, is one of permanent crisis. In this world, the conditions of public life do not allow for the 'retirement' of which Cicero speaks so longingly. Erec's awakening here thus appears less as an entirely extraordinary event than as the necessary discomfort attendant on what it is tempting to refer to as a permanently 'new normal' order of business. In that sense, Chrétien's presentation of charismatic authority appears not just as the mark of a society bent on melancholy, pagan self-destruction, but rather represents the most beautiful realisation of what is otherwise a crudely ugly game of historical forces. In this, Enide herself was the instigator. In response to her 'mar [i] fus', Erec's reproach is in part an affirmation that there may well come a time and a place for such talk, but not today. On the other hand, another reading would be to argue that Enide opens up the bedchamber and makes a certain kind of kingship possible with the king as object of all sorts of discursive combinations, confusions and mismatches, whether as living embodiment of a cult of the ancestor or as exemplar.

Such confluences and confusion seem almost magical in nature. And yet, in echo of her arming of Erec at Laluth (ll. 709–19) – where neither charm nor incantation ('charaie', l. 710) were used, Enide alludes to and perhaps implicitly ridicules rumours of magical or sexual wiles on her part ('si vos ai lacié et pris', l. 2559).[35] This denial places Enide in uncertain relation to Chrétien's other charmer,

Fenice's nurse Thessala in *Cligés*, who vaunts her mastery of various magics, including 'charaies' (*Cligés*, l. 3010). Whether she will or no, Enide is at the centre of a spell that conjures and binds together life and death, loss and desire in a conjuncture that marks Erec's resurgence as absolute figure of the law in a doubled moment that ties the here-and-now of the bedchamber and the castle of the Count of Limors together in uncanny bilocation. Indeed, the very bedchamber setting underscores an intimate relation not only between seemingly separate discursive domains but also separate times, bound together by the force of Law. The (unpleasant) surprise is crucial, the rude awakening – as Žižek puts it with reference to the unexpected success of war crimes trials in Croatia – heralding Carnant's 'rediscovery of itself as a state ruled by law'.[36] As Žižek points out, this rediscovery is a resurrection, the Law returning in its 'undead' guise. This dimension appears most directly in Chrétien, with Erec witchily reaching out in cruel willingness to exploit his position, twisting and pulling at the threads that bind him to his subjects.[37] Jane Burns observes that any assertion of equality or bond on Chrétien's part only really seems to obtain between men, measuring themselves against one another in combat scenes that show a passionate intensity not mirrored in relations between the sexes.[38] However, the pivotal scene in the bedchamber shows Enide acceding to a new status as social player through the baptism of a 'live-fire' exercise in which the uncertainty as to whether Erec is genuinely angry with her or not is part of the game.

If, as Adler among others would argue, Erec's thought is to restore the fear that is the ultimate basis of his sovereign authority, then Enide's part in the court drama acted out in the chamber is to experience that emotion without any appearance of feigning and to respond to it.[39] This she does, although her initial gambits appear a less than polished performance according to the dictates of *savoir*. In tactical terms, the field is his. Erec harries Enide, systematically breaking down her first clumsy defences and temporisations in a manner emphasised by Chrétien's practice of suppressing narratorial cues as to the identity of the speaker and splitting the two lines of particular couplets between the protagonists.[40] Allowing herself to be caught using 'songe' (l. 2531) as the rhyme for the first line of a couplet would then appear the most elementary error in such a fencing match or chess game, with Erec then able to supply the 'moon–June' response of 'Or me servez vos de mençonges!' (l. 2532), and then redouble with the variation 'apertement vos oï mentir' (l. 2533). Through this stinging and wearing down, he forces her to show her mettle in an avowal of remarkable pace, courage, eloquence and clarity (ll. 2536–71). In its elegant chaining separate phases of her argument neatly together, her speech recalls the organisation of court interventions such as Thierry's intervention on behalf of the beleaguered Charles in the Oxford *Roland* (ed. by Short, ll. 3824–36). However, where it differs from that moment is in its dose of tough love: rather than flying straight and level in her response, Enide shifts ground, only giving comparatively brief space to relaying the courtiers' criticisms (ll. 2536–51), moving instead to a consideration of how it impacts on her, first via a signal of sympathy for his position (ll. 2552–4) to complaint that the blame falls on her (ll. 2555–61), a far cry from Erec's former care not to damage Arthur's standing. The climax of her speech falls at the end of this section, with Enide calling for a renegotiation of the relation between the public and private sphere:

'Blasmee en sui, ce poise moi,
Et dïent tuit raison por qoi,
Que si vos ai lacié et pris
Que tot en perdez vostre pris,
Ne ne querez a el entendre.
Autre consoil vos convient prendre,
Que vos puissiez ceste blame esteindre
Et vostre premier los ateindre.' (ll. 2557–64)

'For this they lay the blame on me, which is hard to bear. And they all talk about why this has happened, saying that I have you so bound and ensnared that you have lost your reputation and have no wish to think of anything else. You must take counsel anew so that you can efface this slander and restore the renown of your early days.'

The doorway between the two moments is the ambiguous *entendre* which, following on from the previous context has the sense of 'think of', 'turn one's attention / mind to', but, in anticipation of

l. 2562's reference to 'other counsel' takes on more the sense of listening or giving heed to. What is then unclear in Enide's speech is how this evocation positions him, her or them: Enide could be indicating that Erec must stop keeping *his own* counsel on how he should best spend his time, or that he should distance himself from *her*, now tarred as having monopolised access to him, or – if the complainers are Erec's former inner circle – he should look for better advisers than this crowd of envious, short-memoried tittle-tattlers. The Boethian overtones are quite clear: if Erec is charged with having turned in on himself and his worldly desires, then Enide is in no mind to be cast as his *meretricula*, his 'little slut', but rather claims her rightful public role as a *familiaris*, a valued participant in the business of the household, the equal of any manly companion he would find at Carnant. After that, only the loose ends of why she was weeping remain to be tied up, Enide passing to the revelation that Erec was less half-asleep than he perhaps thought: this is far from being the first time she has been driven to tears (l. 2567), and that ongoing pressure has temporarily undermined her habitual capacity for self-control ('Tel pesance orendroit en oi, / Que garde prendre ne me soi', ll. 2569–70).

In its combination of pathos, sternness and adroit footwork, one might have thought there would really be no answer to such a speech. But then, that would have forced Erec's hand and left him no room for manoeuvre. Therefore, logically, we might expect Enide to expect him to do something else. But then, 'something else' would be the thing most expected, which means that – in a logic of double-, possibly even triple-bluff – the least-expected course of action would be to say your wife was right and then profit from the surprise-effect to proceed from there. That this is the effect is apparent from Enide's psychological collapse: if this young woman had been believed to have tied her man up in knots, now she comes dramatically 'unstrung', her silent, anguished perplexity followed by vituperative recriminations against herself (ll. 2580–606) sign of someone far from sure of the impact of the formidable hand she has just played. In contrast to Erec's later interventions, one of Enide's finer moments passes without approbative comment from the narrator, the only reaction being Erec's. The audience is thereby left to ponder what the outcome of the exchange actually was: did Erec concede defeat in the bout or profit from the momentum of her attack to disarm her? Exacerbated by the absence of narratorial cues, the fact that Erec's response leaves Enide so uncertain puts the poem's external audiences equally 'on the back foot'. However, in this they are at least a step ahead of the internal audience of Erec's court, who do not know at this point what is about to hit them.

As with Arthur, any acknowledgment on Erec's part of the weight of the criticisms voiced to him by Enide has to be reconciled with safeguarding his personal authority in a political climate shaped not by the consideration of weighty matters of state but by the sniping of bored household *familiares*. There are rational answers to the points they raise. For example, against the criticism that Erec takes less part in tournaments, patronage of a large group of well-equipped retainers seems a legitimate and effective enough means of advertising one's wealth and status. Moreover, to attribute any *recreantise* to some uxorious obsession sounds like petty jealousy. Discontent among the ranks in the *chansons de geste* usually stems from more substantial grievances or omissions than this. Although laxity may well be an issue, it is nonetheless tempting, given that the *sensus communus* has been wide of the mark in the understanding of court matters on at least three occasions – Gauvain's reaction to the call for the hunt, Laluth's acclamation of Yder, the offer of the dress – to ask what the critics have missed. However, this is not tantamount to arguing we are intended to see Erec as not having erred in any regard. Indeed, when Erec says the courtiers were within their right to criticise him (ll. 2572–3), it is tempting to assume on the basis of what follows that the criticism is received with something other than equanimity.[41] However, the idea that his actions are in part motivated by revenge is not necessarily incompatible with cold calculation the effect of his words in what is then the counterintuitive business of manipulating the public sphere.

In a work that is both obscure by dint of its remoteness from us and also clearly deliberately obscure, Erec's furious departure from court raises many questions.[42] However, one point that has perhaps been overlooked is its formality. In sending word to Enide via his squire, Erec re-emphasises the division between the King's and

Queen's households that structured the drama of the Hunt: the regulatory governance of the palace is being restored. Chrétien's presentation of the manner in which Erec holds those around him at a distance, keeping them from any secure insight into his motivations through division and misdirection, appears as a masterclass in manipulation. Thus, Erec's targeting of his wife keeps her distress front and centre as a prelude to his next moves, separating her off before seemingly bringing his own house down in a few swift strokes. As an object of pathos, Enide offers a microcosmic spectacle of internal division that announces itself benignly enough in the repartition of function in the noble household, with characters previously functionally invisible returning to the stage as live presences. Internally divided in her own confusion, she paradoxically divides and affirms the order of the palace through the activity she generates around her, asking one of her maids to summon one of her squires (ll. 2612–13) so she can instruct him to saddle her palfrey (ll. 2614–19). The apparent redundancy of having the maid fetch the squire so that he can be told what to do maximises the audience rather than simply dissipating the energy along the chain of command, her adherence to etiquette and procedure as part of a gradual mobilisation of the palace staff reinforcing the ripples spreading out from their epicentre. However, a further pebble is about to be tossed into the pool. Erec, simultaneously silently withdrawn and publicly visible, calls another squire to bring both his arms and the Limoges rug to a high gallery (ll. 2620–5).[43] His activity then continues unexplained, any direct speech on Erec's part replaced by the description of his marvellous hauberk (ll. 2635–48). If the palfrey at Laluth was the vehicle and basis for the complex interactions and histories that made up the diplomatic process, Erec's shining mail, the focus of the astonished gaze of the collective, speaks its own volumes:

> Li serjant et li chevalier
> Se prenent tuit a mervoillier
> Por qoi armer il se fesoit,
> Mais nuns demander ne l'osoit. (ll. 2649–52)

> All his men-at-arms and knights fell to marvelling and wondering why he was having himself armed, but no one dared ask why.

271

Men-at-arms and knights... The tremor transmits itself across the web of court society. Whatever Erec is thinking, something is communicating itself quite effectively. The next phase is to summon Enide. As with Guinevere's earlier instructions to her maid, the squire's carrying out of his lord's instructions (ll. 2671–5) shows a confidence that contrasts sharply with Enide's alarm and uncertainty. While Enide – a queen's household of one – is on the back foot both in terms of experience and means, Erec's squire – invested with a quasi-plenipotentiary rhetorical licence – has freedom to use his lady (verbally) more or less as he wishes. The echoes and subtexts here are of course disturbing in the extreme, an echo being Harpin's threats to give a young noblewoman up to his followers – in this case in the most grotesque of gang rapes (*Le Chevalier au lion*, ll. 3867–70). However, instead the image of internal conflict focuses briefly on the enjoyment Chrétien imputes to the squire, given to act in a spectacle he himself witnesses that is both a 'holiday from' the normal order in which he is able to be impertinent to someone greatly his superior and an affirmation of a 'new normal'.[44] In that sense, although the reactions of the courtiers as a body will highlight their collective distress, here we have a vision of the quasi-carnivalesque *jouissance* of internal conflict. And yet, at the same time we have a further internal fracture, this time within Erec's household: although Erec tells his underling *how* to deliver the message (ll. 2661–7), he does not explain to him *why*. In that sense, the squire's position effectively appears as an 'idiotic', 'bureaucratic' enjoyment in which the perverse Subject is absolved of uncertainty and responsibility by the fact that 'the System possesse[s] (or pretend[s] to possess) an answer'.[45]

Although Enide's distress at Erec's harsh, impatient but unfathomable instructions is considerable, she rapidly controls herself (ll. 2676–80). Her obligation to pattern her behaviour according to the dictates of courtly decorum in a situation she does not understand is central to Erec's manipulation of collective emotion. If the squires, men-at-arms and knights mentioned earlier represented the clatter of a few pebbles dislodged here and there, it is Enide's progress across the courtyard – miming a cheery demeanour (ll. 2679–80) where only moments before she had been seen weeping and wailing (ll. 2669–70) – that now releases the full avalanche at the collective level.

Previously isolated, she is now followed by Erec's father (ll. 2681–2), bringing behind him the entire court, all now ready to go wherever Erec might wish to lead (ll. 2683–7). Where the collective opinion might previously have been that Enide was to blame for Erec's *recreantise*, the absence of any discernable shared purpose between a father – previously seen to embrace his new daughter-in-law as if she were his own offspring (ll. 2354–6) – and his son sows the seeds of more general confusion:

> De plorer tenir ne se puet
> Li rois, quant de son fil depart.
> Les genz replorent d'autre part,
> Dames et chevalier ploroient,
> Por li mout grant duel demenoient:
> N'i a un soul qui duel ne face,
> Maint se pasmerent en la place.
> Plorant le baisent et acolent,
> A pou que de duel ne s'afolent.
> Ne cuit que plus grant duel ne feïssent,
> Se mort ou navré le veïssent.
> Lors dist Erec por reconfort
> A touz: 'Por qoi plorez si fort?
> Je ne sui pris ne mahaigniez,
> En cest duel rien ne gaaingniez.
> Se je m'en vois, je revenrai
> Quant Deu plaira et je porrai.
> Toz et totes vos commant gié
> A Deu, si me donez congié
> Car trop me faites demorer.
> Ice que je vos voi plorer,
> Me fait grant duel et grant ennui.'
> A Deu les commande, et il lui.
> Departi sont a quelque poinne. (ll. 2738–61)

The King could not keep from weeping at being parted from his son. The entire court shed tears with him. Ladies and knights wept and showed great sorrow on his account. There was no one who was not grief-stricken. Many fainted and fell to the ground. In tears, they kissed and embraced him, nigh sick and mad with grief. I do not believe they could have shown greater sorrow if they had seen him dead or mortally wounded. To comfort them he said: 'Why such tears? I am neither wounded or taken prisoner. Your sorrow avails you not at all. If I am leaving now, I shall return when God allows it and when I can. I

273

commend you to Him one and all, and ask that you give me your leave, for you detain me excessively and it is sad and wearisome to see you weep so.' He commended them to God and they did him. At that, they parted in great despondency.

Erec's speech dramatically splits its audience, with his father as direct addressee and the other courtiers as an internal 'third party'. Such a division carries with it various ironies: although it is entirely proper that Erec would demand *congé* or formal leave from his father as king, he would not ask the same of his feudal subordinates. However, in a not-so-subtle advertisement for the power of court poetry to act as a supplementary redout and butress of the royal will, if Erec is divided from his household at this point, he appears hand-in-glove with his narrator. Thus, in a text where Chrétien is very careful to remind us where he spares us unnecessary repetition (ll. 5563–71, ll. 5574–5, ll. 5727–30, ll. 5879–85, ll. 6475–87), the wide-eyed innocence of his passing comment that he would be surprised if they made more of a commotion if Erec were actually dead – a thread taken up immediately by Erec himself – appears as deliberately collusive cruelty at the expense of the court as internal audience.[46] After all, these were exactly the same mob who not a couple of hundred lines previously had been tattling among themselves about the decline in their young lord's *los* and *pris*, voices multiplied through the doubling of narrator's listing of 'bernages', 'chevaliers' and 'sergenz' (ll. 2455–60) in Enide's reporting of their gossiping back to her husband, her alternative version of the 'long and the short and the tall' of the land cast in terms of hair and complexion ('li noir et li blonc et li ros' l. 2541).

Erec's dialogue with Lac makes plain the 'final destination' of both of them, both here accepting – whether they will they or not, as the narrator put it of Yder ('vuille ou non', l. 1045) – their mandate as what Lacan refers to as the 'Imaginary Father', that is to say the (debased) manifestation of the paternal Law. As Lacan points out, this figure can appear in a variety of guises, benevolently as the kind, caring, but impotent father (thus, the figure of Pandion) or *in malo* as the 'father-enjoyment' (*le père jouissance*), the obscene head of the primal horde (thus, giants or tyrants as figures of the child-devouring

Saturn). The division of generations in the house of Carnant reflects that division of function, the royal line staging its own two-pronged attack on the collective. Erec in effect appears here as his 'dead' royal self, his persecution of the court through emotional blackmail aiming at the masochistic release of its anxieties. The haunting of this moment by future deaths is made plain in the hammering accumulation of terms such as *duel* and *plorer*, anticipating the insistent, panicky repetition of *fuir* in the aftermath of the killing of Oringle of Limors (ll. 4863–79), Erec already speaking from his bier. What is not knowable here is how conscious a piece of political theatre we are looking at in a situation far less readable than that at Arthur's court, where the Queen seems perfectly capable of following unspoken cues or of asking the perfect question at the perfect time in order to allow her husband to best give them the benefit of his wisdom. Though internally frantic, Enide's self-possession allows her gamely to put on a brave face (ll. 2676–80) while she waits for some signal as to what her lord's intentions are. The most dramatic part is played by Erec's father, any sense this scene might simply be contrived swept away by the intensity of a despair compelling by dint of the possibility – or, from our external perspective, fact – that he will not see his son again.

The collective gaze of the court having been drawn in by the lines of a pattern of movement, to those of the closest blood ties, a move that drives from the minds of the courtiers any reflections on the evils of exogamy focalised on Enide as internal other or even witch. Obviously, his father's show of grief and foreboding may also function as another nod to Chrétien's *Philomena*, the scenario inverted, with Lac as Pandion, Erec as Philomena and Enide as Tereüs: a father weeps for a son taken from him by the excessive desires of a daughter-in-law.[47] Erec's feelings for his father will always now be a private matter, as we will see when Erec officiates in the arrangements for Lac's funeral, presenting the formal, public version of mourning while concealing his private grief (ll. 6512–19). The joke will rebound on Erec, his sense of bereavement dissimulated later in obedience to a decorum reminiscent of the cold comfort dispensed to figures such as the grieving Charlemagne (*La Chanson de Roland*, ed. by Short, ll. 2945–50). For the time being, however, the cruel edge of Erec's humour is emphatically turned against his courtiers, mocking those who presumably undermined his reputation and torturing them with the prospect of a genuine loss that will not merely return to haunt him with Lac's death, but also is his fate. In that regard, what we have here is a situation where the king's Symbolic mandate appears as something 'in him more than himself', taking the form of an agency to which he is either blind or which follows him as an unseen *doppelgänger*, the figure of *das Nächste*, the object-cause of a desire he is not given to articulate in its full and final sense, but whose spectral glimmer he nonetheless intuits.

In that sense, although not the all-out bloodbath common to representations of intergenerational hostility in the chansons de geste, what this scene suggests is that Erec's succession to the throne of Carnant is perhaps less entirely 'effortless' than Sarah Kay's comparison of succession and intergenerational conflict in the two genres paints it.[48] If Lac is like Pandion in this scene, then are we to understand he also resembles him in that grief at the loss of his son – whose fate is as unknown to his household in Carnant as Philomena's is to her father – shortens his days, 'dispatch[ing him] to Hades before his time' ('Hic dolor ante diem longaeque extrema senectae / Tempora Tartareus Pandiona misit ad umbras', *Metamorphoses*, book 6, ll. 675–6)?[49] Indeed, it could be argued that Erec's removal of himself from the court of Carnant for the remainder of his father's life ambiguously affirms both the order of succession and yet the non-coexistence of the two generations of the royal line – a separating out of the community that suggests more serious underlying conflict.[50] Here some of the sense of either cruelty or foreboding comes from Erec's the narratorial comment on Erec's response to Lac's entreaties:

> Erec respont *a la parsome*,
> Et se li dit tot a devise
> Coment il a sa voie emprise:
> 'Sire', fait il, 'n'en puet *el estre*.' (ll. 2712–15, my emphasis)

> At length, Erec replied, telling him why he was making this journey: 'My lord', he said, 'I have no other choice.'

What the use of *parsome* here may indicate is that Erec's response comes at the end of Lac's desperate efforts to persuade him. Taken with the other occurrences of the term, this acquires a fateful resonance. Lac can struggle all that he might, but *a la parsome*, things will not be any different: the cosmic forces – with which Erec allies himself by means of his stony *it cannot be otherwise* ('n'en puet el estre') – will take their course.[51]

Chrétien's evocation of the collective trauma occasioned by Erec's decision to withdraw from (*bouder*) the palace of Carnant might have resonated eerily with audiences who were witness to the conflict between Henry II and his sons, especially the rebellion of Henry the Young King. This episode is recounted with singular poignancy and bitterness by Walter Map, notably in the kernel of his lament and condemnation: 'the son of our King Henry who, God be thanked, is matched by none today' ('nostri filius Henrici regis, cui nemo (Deo gracias!) hodie par est', dist. 4, chapter 1, pp. 278–9 in edition). This cruel, suffusing presence perhaps explains other details of the scene, such as the leopard-motif rug (ll. 2630–1) on which Erec arms himself. Opinions on its cultural significance vary: Bezzola sees this is as a symbolic reclaiming of chivalric virility, while Duggan emphasises its heraldic connections with the kings of England, noting that the same animal appears with the 'cocadrille' on the thrones presented to Erec in the coronation scene (ll. 6720–1).[52] However, the animal's symbolism is ambiguous: although associated in texts such as the *Chanson de Roland* with laudable ferocity, as Burgess and Allard point out, it can also embody a cruelty that compares unfavourably to the noble character of the lion.[53] This inferiority to the lion also manifests in accounts of its origins, Hugh of St Victor presenting the creature as the product of adultery between the lioness and the panther.[54] Assimilated to the failure of the king of beasts to keep his household in order, whether polluted by the *luxuria* of the lioness or with the leopard's cruelty a debasement of the coin of leonine justice, Erec appears to advertise his failings as springing from either want or subversion of paternal principle. In so doing, he cuts himself off from his father doubly, not only in his refusal to listen to him and remain at court but also in suggesting that his shortcomings are indicative of some taint of 'illegitimacy', whether actual or symbolic, a self-indicting gesture that confronts his courtiers with a new domestic scandal capable of destabilising their existence as a community united around the house of Carnant.[55]

In keeping with Chrétien's vision of romance as a prosopopaeic riddle, we are left unable to tell whether Erec's actions are a product of strategic 'engineering' or the tactical 'mackling' of *bricolage*. Fracture and disarray are part of the armoury. Thus, although Enide's part in this scene is not quite note-perfect in some passages, her dismay is arguably precisely the effect required for Erec's purposes. Likewise, if Chrétien's vision of the public sphere suggests the king can never be right all the time, his exploration also shows how error can be reappropriated to keep the body social off balance and under control, royal *faux pas* becoming feints that draw the adversary into over-committing themselves by speaking or acting too hastily. Such an unstable world seems to admit of few 'neat' solutions: if any 'revival of custom' is necessarily irruptive and 'out of joint', there is no reckoning when would be the right time to disturb the peace of the court. In that regard, it seems as if either side can engage in disruptive behaviour: if Arthur relaunches the hunt against his courtiers, it is Erec's followers who seem to initiate the call for renewal. But then if Arthur's action is arguably 'proactively' pre-emptive in character, does this mean Erec's action necessarily appears as merely 'reactive'?

To decide one way or the other in this matter would be to assume Arthur acted from a more secure estimation of the court's 'attention span' than Erec, but then, equally, the actions of both seem dictated by a proto-Machiavellian logic of not giving their publics what they think they want – that way lies bankruptcy and exhaustion. Indeed, the contrast between Erec's achievements in the tournament at Edinburgh – culminating in the hyperbolic hailing of him as new Absalom, Solomon and Alexander (ll. 2259–66) all rolled into one – and his subsequent lapse seems to suggest the boom-bust economy of chivalric fame works by the short shelf-life of extremes rather than by managed and moderate means. In a world of spectacle where 'you're either [extremely] hot or you're not', the remedies for error are no more simple: Erec cannot simply apologise and promise to do better in future. Rather, the restoration of social cohesion begins with him terrorising his men in a spectacular demonstration all the more effective for being utterly unsparing – whether of Enide, his father or himself.

In that sense the 'forfait' Erec refers to in his later reconciliation speech (ll. 4914–25) following Oringle's death and their escape from Limors could lie in Enide's failure to bring the court gossip to his attention sooner, or, more crucially, in her attentiveness to him as an object of desire. Here the comparison with the Middle Welsh *Geraint* is revealing: Geraint immediately suspects that the reason for Enid's remark is that she desires another. However, in Chrétien's version we learn nothing of Erec's thoughts, and certainly have not reason to assume jealousy, desire is part of the problem. In both works the heroine's behaviour appears as something analoguous to the image of the Hitchcockian heroine looking away over the shoulder of the leading man as she is embraced by him – either because her heart is divided or because she has some guilty secret. Erec's reaction is then predicated on the fact that Enide has shown herself 'not all' in relation to him, an interruption that then has to be appropriated and turned to his advantage. In that regard, what we can see here is that the problem is one of the distinction between love and desire. 'Love' is characterised by Lacan as a state of fusion with the object, echoing the descriptions found in versions of the Tristan story where the couple appear as a single object united in symbiosis, such as the hazel and honeysuckle in Marie's *Chevrefeuille* (ed. by Harf-Lancener, ll. 68–76).[56] Desire, by contrast, marks a distance, a space never simply private, but rather predicated on the intersection of multiple looks. Enide's lament therefore introduces an obstacle, another object into the libidinal circuit of their mutual regard, revealing a certain truth about the the play of desires underpinning the political situation of the court. Such a dynamic is then fundamentally unstable. As with the motivation for the hunt of the White Stag, is there too much or too little consensus, too much or too little fascination? Thus, Erec seizes the moment provided by Enide's and the court's either excessive or insufficient regard for him. In this situation, both he and Enide were always going to be 'in trouble', so the only question is what the best way is to be in it.

'Dead Man Riding': Out of Carnant... into History

> [He willingly underwent] every danger and refus[ed] no toil. Now, at his love of danger his men were not astonished, knowing his ambition, but that he should undergo toils beyond his body's apparent power of endurance amazed them, because he was of spare [build] and had a soft and white skin, suffered from distemper in the head and was subject to epileptic fits, a trouble which first attacked him, we are told, in Corduba. Nevertheless, he did not make his feeble health an exuse for soft living, but rather his military service a cure for his feeble health, since by wearisome journeys, simple diet, continuously sleeping in the open air and enduring hardships, he fought off his trouble and kept his body strong against its attacks. Most of his sleep he got in [chariots] or litters, making his rest conducive to action.
> (Plutarch, *Life of Caesar*, § 17, para. 1)[57]

If Arthur appears as a figure of mystery modelled on the puzzle of Caesar, then the same can be said for Erec, whose death in the version of the *Roman d'Erec en prose* contained in B. N. fonds fr. 112 reflects some of the same problems.[58] Having killed his sister and not only received the hermit's prophecy of his death but also the curses of the three huntresses he encounters at the Fountain of the Virgin, Erec jousts with Sagremor, whom he unhorses. He then engages with Yvain of the white hands, an encounter which leaves the latter mortally and Erec seriously wounded. Finding the body of Yvain, Gauvain swears vengeance, tracks Erec and challenges him, refusing to give up the fight even when he learns his identity. After a long, indecisive combat, Gauvain is forced into the disloyal recourse of killing Erec's horse under him. Erec rebukes Gauvain:

> 'Certes, messire Gauvain, or ay je y veu ung rain de couardise et de mauvaistié, qui mon cheval m'avés occis. Or ne pourriez vous mie dire, quant vous me verrés mort, que vous m'ayés occis, mais la deffaulte de mon cheval. Or ne me chault il mais qu'il adviengne de moy, car je en ay eu l'onneur jusques icy, et vous la honte.' (ed. by Pickford, p. 207)

> 'Certainly, my lord Gauvain, now I have seen something born of cowardice and evil, for you have killed my horse. Now you may not say when you see me dead that you killed me, but rather that it was the fall of my horse. Now I do not care

what happens to me from here on in, for I have won honour from this combat up until now and you have had the shame.' (trans. mine)

The context of this version of the Erec, a prelude to *La Mort le roi Artu*, makes plain the cultural history underpinning this moment: in a reversal of the civilising process, Gauvain kills Erec because he has no answer for him, appearing here as a degenerate figure, no more capable of distinguishing himself in conversation than on the field of combat, his values seemingly more akin to those of the robber knights Erec faces in Chrétien's text. Troubled by anger, guilt and fear at the fact that the wounded Erec is able to press him so hard, Gauvain has no answer, and instead runs his opponent down with his horse, causing Erec to faint with pain and knocking the sword from his hand. What follows is not pleasant:

> Messire Gauvain sault jus du cheval quant il le voit gesir en tel maniere, et vient, et lui soubzlieve le pan du haubert, et ly boute l'espee ou corps; et cil s'estent, et se commence a debatre com cil qui la mort angoissoit durement. Quant messire Gauvain voit que c'estoit chose oultree de luy, il en est moult liez, car bien s'en est vengiés, ce luy estoit advis. Si remet s'espee ou fuerre, et vient a son cheval, si monte, et s'en vait grant erre tout ung autre chemin, qu'il ne vouldroit en nulle maniere qu'il fust aparceuz de cestui fait, qu'il scet vraiement qu'il en seroit blasmé de tous ceulx qui parler en orroient. Si laisse Eret gisant a terre en tel guise com je vos conte, et cuide bien qu'il soit ja mors; mais non estoit encores, ains a tout son memoire, aussi bien com il ot oncques, mais il n'a tant de povoir qu'il se remue ains gist adens. Mais de tant luy est il bien avenu que si le corps est assez martirés, et playés, et navrés, toutesvoyes a il le cuer si parfaictement a son Sauveur qu'il ne le puet oblier, ains laisse toutes autres choses pour la remembrence de luy. (ed. by Pickford, pp. 207–08)

> My lord Gauvain jumps down from the horse when see sees him lying thus, and comes to him, lifts the flap of his hauberk and drives the sword into his body. And Erec falls back and begins to thrash about like a man whom death is tormenting greatly. When my lord Gauvain sees Erec is done for, he is delighted, for he is well avenged of him – so he thinks. He puts his sword back in the scabbard, returns to his horse, mounts and rides off at great pace along another path altogether, for he would not want it known he was involved in this business, for he is entirely certain he would be blamed by all who heard about it. And so he leaves Erec lying on the ground as you have heard, believing him already dead. But Erec was not yet dead, having still full command of his memory as well as ever, although he cannot move, but rather lies there. But,

fortunately for him, even if his body is so martyred, wounded and mangled, yet still his heart is so perfectly given over to his Saviour that he does not forget Him, but gives up all other thoughts for memory of Him. (trans. mine)

The answer this passage makes to the entire Arthurian tradition lies in its cold, mechanical realism. Gauvain's cravenly murderous thrust, leadenly rendered by the verb *bouter*, utterly devoid of any technical brilliance – such as that which marked the combat between Yder and Erec in its initial stages – negates a poetry of combative motion carrying in it an equivocation about the finality of death.[59] But then, of course, that crudeness of gesture was always present: Chrétien's Erec, having pushed Yder over ('Erec le *boute* /Et cil chiet', ll. 983–4) and wrenched off his protecting mail (l. 987), seemed no less ready to put him to an ugly death.

Thus it is that, although Erec is not dead yet, it is arguable that what is reflected in later prose tradition is the sense that Erec in particular even here was haunted by some future doom. However, it is also arguable that Chrétien's vision of his place is already as a nexus of certain unfolding strands and questions. The parallels between the three figures, Caesar, Arthur and Erec, are suggestively filled out in the prose account of Erec's mangling, the knight imitating not only Arthur in his lucidity following his fall and mortal, treacherous wounding at the hands of the disloyal Gauvain, here implicitly assimilated the band of conspirators, but also the passionate, 'bodily' Caesar as bloody, twitching mass ('et se commence a debatre', p. 208). Just as Caesar's murder unleashes a wave of feuds and vendettas, so the discovery of Erec's body threatens to sow strife among the knights of the Round Table. Erec's companion Meraugis sees Gauvain's brother, Gaheriet, leave the scene and makes to go after him to avenge Erec, only to be stopped by Hector, who points out that Gaheriet is as aggrieved by the spectacle as Meraugis, making Gauvain's great disloyalty an individual matter rather than grounds for clan warfare (p. 213). Accordingly, Arthur, who 'loved all the knights of the Round Table as if they were begotten of his own flesh and blood' ('qui tant aymoit les compaignons de la Table Ronde, com s'il les eust tous engendrés de sa char', p. 214), curses Gauvain and his family and strips him of his place at the Round Table (p. 217). If we locate the *Roman d'Erec* in its context as a prelude to *La Mort le roi Artu*, then Gauvain's treachery here foreshadows the questions hanging over his conduct in the opening sections of that text, with Gauvain rumoured to be and revealed as responsible for the death of over half the 32 companions missing from the Grail quest party, notably King Bademagu (*La Mort le roi Artu*, § 2–4).

This sense of the kingdom of Logres as bound into a Lucanian vision of history is replicated elsewhere, as can be seen in the *Roman de Perceforest*, which extends the process to the point of inverting the genealogical relation between Roman archetype and Arthurian reperformance. Here the assassination of Caesar, the fruit of labyrinthine patterns of feuding and exile in the Northern kingdoms, appears as revenge for an *inimicitia* in which British noble houses are not simply descendants or distant witnesses but prime movers: the Queen of Scotland orders her grandson to kill Julius with the spearhead that killed his father. Indeed, the fateful styluses with which Caesar is struck are made from that same weapon.[60] In that regard, the Lucanian overtones of Arthurian history are revealed as part of the more general repositioning of 'the North' from marginal frontier to part of the historical, political and cultural centre.[61]

If the forces evoked in view of Erec's future seem implacable and ineluctable, this is clearly not a cause for Arthur's court to abandon hope. Even as Gauvain is revealed as an assassin of members of his own house, Arthur immediately 'ordered a tournament to be announced at Winchester, because he nevertheless did not want his companions to cease wearing arms' (*La Mort le roi Artu*, § 3). His show of defiance has a Don Giovanni-esque aspect: although they have seen an instance of how the call of *armes et amours* will lead to their destruction, Arthur's followers still embrace the defining activities of chivalry. It is therefore no coincidence that the King's announcement is followed immediately by the revelation that, in spite of having renounced Guinevere, Lancelot's return to court leads him to fall back into his adulterous relation with her (*La Mort le roi Artu*, § 4). Such a juxtaposition tars the two dimensions of chivalric life with the same morbidly addictive taint, revealing a principle turned cancerous. While it may be that wherever doom threatens, defiance

283

prevails, that same vital spark carries with it its undomesticatable 'undead' aspect, metastasising in new betrayals, new murders.

From the perspective of Chrétien's first romance, such a vision is of course a long way down the road, although the germ of it is perhaps already present in Erec's warning to Enide against disobeying his instructions. While his words appear lapidary, there are hints not everything he says should be taken at face value:

> 'Et gardez ne soiez tant ose,
> Se vos veez aucune chose,
> Que vos me dïez ce ne qoi.' (ll. 2765–7)

> 'And be careful that you are not so bold as to dare say a word if you see anything amiss.'

'Do not be so bold as to...' – surely a red rag to any creature of a certain temperament. As Burgess notes, uses of *oser* and its related adjectives often mark lines not to be crossed except in a spirit of daring that is the necessary component of chivalric valour. If Erec then refers to her as 'Dame' in this phase of the narrative, one possible implication is that what is being emphasised is her new symbolic mandate, not so much as a creature subject to her husband's control as someone mandated to trouble, ostensibly told to obey but also, codedly, to *disobey* in the manner of one fitted for forceful action in public life. However, at this point, Enide seems silenced and reduced to the margins. If this quiet young woman had attracted any suspicion of being a mutterer of charms, now she is reduced to muttering plain and simple in the form of her laments to herself, notably the soliloquy-cum-*aria* introduced by the proverbial 'tant grate chievre que mal gist' (l. 2584, then ll. 2585–606 for the speech itself) along with the first of her interior monologues on the road (ll. 2778–90) and during the first night of the quest (ll. 3104–14).[62] If her father had praised her earlier for her wisdom (ll. 537–40), then we see here some of its stock-in-trade, her emphasis on the workings of Fortune cut from the same cloth as her father's comments on the relation between poverty and individual worth (ll. 510–11). If her lament over Erec in the bedchamber condenses earlier impressions and reflections, producing the emotional equivalent of a 'Big Bang', then these later speeches can be seen as elements in a '(re-)expanding universe' in which they swirl along with other materials. While the astrophysical metaphors may seem extraneous, in the intellectual context in which Chrétien's first romance was written, the theme of the rise and fall of individual fortunes as an expression of the gravitational rhythms of the cosmos would have been ready-to-hand. The Boethian underpinnings in Enide's various laments, exploded out from the central speech and scattered in her worrying at them in repetitions and variations, are, in their content, central to the problems of understanding. And yet there is still a problem of perspective in that their fundamental theme is uncertainty, which means Erec's earlier question remains central: 'why did you say misfortune brought me there?' (l. 2517). Although Enide of course had already answered him in specific terms (l. 2571), his question still points to the open-endedness of any dialogue on this subject, the permanent lack of assurance as to definitive understanding. Thus, Enide's worryings are not devoid of sense, but rather appear as fragmentary motifs in a larger music of foreboding ready to recondense around some node as yet unseen even as material objects, such as Erec's sword, are glimpsed at various moments, their perspectivally-allotted trajectory having reached its vanishing point. As we can see from the far future of fonds fr. 112, that moment may be uglier than could ever have been foreseen.

'If This be a Man'/ Knaves... or Fools?: The Robber Knights

> To these [...] men of the 24th Marine Expeditionary Unit, the desert in its entirety is a blue void. [...]There is a third man in the fox-hole, an unseen man, the enemy. He does not summon fear, but anxiety. Where is he? Show your face. Come out and fight. The more he does not appear, the more the marines think of him. The purpose of the sentry is to protect the camp. So, it is almost perverse to wish for an attack. But the wish is there nevertheless. A marine wants to earn his keep. Without an adversary, he is nothing but a man sitting in a hole in the road between nowhere and nowhere.[63]

The king reigns only by virtue of his future death' is but one of the wonderful *sententiae* coined by René Girard.[64] Yet that death, although foretold, is deferred, meaning that if it is not the king's day to die, then it is probably someone else's. In *Erec et Enide*, the fact that it is not yet Erec's time, the coming of that 'parsome' which will make vain all his earthly strivings is made apparent in the variations of detail Chrétien rings, his endless, almost obsessive detailing of the combats, the individuals involved and their horses. As Jean-Paul Allard emphasises, the exuberant energy of the death of the robber knights is the very texture and exercise of sovereign power.[65]

The encounter with the three knights begins to unfold the range of political technologies Erec will bring to bear. As Claudia Seebass-Linggi has commented, the combat scenes in this work seem to owe much to the formulaic repertory of the *chanson de geste*.[66] However, what is rather different from the massed battle scenes of the *Chanson de Roland*, which seem mainly structured around sequences of individual encounters, is the sense of a single figure gathering pace and not allowing his opponents room to manoeuvre or collect themselves. Conveniently, in a short encounter not unlike the laisses devoted to Roncevaux, the first victim simply misses his mark and is killed by a lance thrust (ll. 2855–70). Not before two things have been emphasised though: Erec is marked out as someone who demonstrates knowledge ('Erec [...] / Qui bien le *sot* droit envahir', ll. 2860–1, my emphasis) and also the passionate commitment of his hatred ('Sor l'escu fiert par tel *haïr*, / Que d'un chief en l'autre le fent', ll. 2862–3, my emphasis). After this, Erec flashes past and continues the sequence with a minimal variation in that the next knight's lance breaks and he is only described as wounded by Erec's attack, albeit seriously (l. 2883). The flight of the third gives us a clue however as to the widening remit of Erec's political grasp, in that he attempts to take refuge in the forest, taking himself out of the realm of the law into that of the outlaw ('En la forest cort recet prendre', l. 2888). However, Erec denounces this strategy as ineffective, his refusal of the brigand's right to disengage affirming a claim to jurisdiction beyond the immediate field of the personal combat. Erec's threat to strike the knight as he flees (l. 2893) clearly marks the would-be robber as subject to a one-man hue-and-cry in which normal judicial protection is no longer extended to him. Indeed, his addressing of the fleeing knight as 'vassal' serve as a reminder of the chivalric code which the robber has abandoned, first by giving himself up to a life of crime and secondly by revealing himself as a coward. Indeed, Erec's justificatory comment 'so that I do not strike you down while you are fleeing' ('Que je ne vos fiere en fuiant', l. 2893) offers a choice: be struck down from behind or from the front. In the first capacity, the robber may be a creature of the forest, but, as a fleeing outlaw, he has no rightful refuge there; in the second, as a knight, he may not quit the field in such a manner without dishonour.[67] Of course, this is not the first disconcerting element: Chrétien's reassurance that the three will not attack together out of deference to 'custom' (ll. 2822–6) has been taken as ironic.[68] Another possible reading here is that the robber knights, a less effective army than they might have ostensibly appeared, thereby manifest a residual sense of civilisation: it is the remainder of 'honour among thieves' that will be their undoing and the sign of their degenerate status as the ignoble 'neighbour knight', whose obedience to code is merely a mocking mime. Again, the problem could either be internal to the thoughts of the characters or one of the narrative grammar of the text. In the latter case, Chrétien could be offering a jocular treatment of the conventions of the *chanson de geste*, in which massed battles are for the most part broken down into individual encounters.[69] In the former case, that grammar is posited as internalised by the robber knights in the form of a code or received wisdom regarding chivalric performance, leaving them as caught in an outdated or degenerate pantomime of *chanson de geste*, with the single combat maintaining and reinforcing the group's internal hierarchy, allowing them to create a narrative and a history of themselves. Boasting is the error in that regard, committing them to a syntax of heroic narrative out of keeping with real-world practicalities. This problem of integrating the individual heroic performance into collective activity is neatly illustrated in Takeshi Kitano's (dir.) film *Zatoichi* (2003) where a group of *ronin*, standing shoulder-to-shoulder, prepare to attack the hero – one of them drawing his sword in a flamboyant gesture, only to accidentally slash the arm of his left-hand neighbour.

Given that his actions during the combat had been characterised as born of such an extreme and 'excessive' emotional state as hatred, Erec's attitude after the combats points rather to an emphasis on economy. The first knight receives minimal attention in the space of the text. The second is then described as wounded but posing not so much further threat, but rather no further drain on his energies ('Cil ne le fera plus *lasser*', l. 2882). This mood of disengagement is emphasised in the overall narratorial comment, 'De ces trois n'a il mais regart' (l. 2900). In that sense, the encounter demonstrates a range of contrasting features in which royal engagement is marked by intensity but not unnecessary expenditure. The all-encompassing ambition that underlies this lesson is hinted at through the minimal differentiation of the robber knights. As with the palfrey, it is the horses that are the clue to the basic logic of the narrative: just as the knights are only differentiated with respect to their desires, it is in the description of the three horses 'one white like milk, the second black and not ugly, the third was all dappled' (ll. 2906–09) that we see an encapsulation of the total horizon laid out, harking back to Enide's earlier description of Erec's subjects and critics as 'li noir et li blanc et li ros', his victory here thus, as Bezzola points out, a symbolic assertion of his will.[70]

In the encounter with the five robber knights following immediately after, this wider dimension of social organisation. Here the minimal variety allowed for in the earlier combat – leaving us with one dead, one wounded and one unhorsed (ll. 2901–03) – is now amplified through a broader palette of possibilities. The knights divide among themselves the spoils. As at the royal court, a balance is struck between the imperiousness of desire and the concessions made to guarantee collective unity. Thus, more lyric *miles amoris* (so, rapist) than epic hero, the first knight claims he will take the maiden or die trying (l. 2941–2).[71] The remainder divide up the horses between them, crucially marking themselves as content with their lots, this especially emphasised in the case of the second brigand, who asks for no greater share of the haul than the dappled horse ('que plus ne quiert / De trestot le gaaing avoir', ll. 2944–5). The fifth brings up the rear, laying claim to Erec's war-horse and armour, paying due regard to procedure continues in his formal request to be granted the honour of the first blow:

> Et li quinz ne fu pas coharz
> Qu'il dist qu'il avroit le destrier
> Et les armes au chevalier.
> Soul a seul les voloit conquerre,
> Et si l'iroit premiers requerre
> Se il le congié l'en donoient. (ll. 2948–53)
>
> And the fifth was no coward, boasting he would have the war-horse and the arms of the knight. He wanted to win them in single combat and so asked leave to go out to join with him in battle first if they would allow it.

Of course, one possible reading of this passage is as a parody of the seeking of leave to strike the first blow as seen in texts such as the Oxford *Roland* (see ll. 860–73), a resonance that would mark it out as a moment of some dramatic irony, with the robber knight appearing as a home-grown version of a pagan champion hubristically setting himself up for the inevitable fall.[72] There are of course more serious implications in that the robbers appear as a structured community aping the niceties of chivalric society. Then again, we can also see them as presenting a more 'balanced' and consensual image of court life than at the apparently more modern Carnant.

Erec's response to the threat is to pretend to be unaware of it: 'Erec le vit et semblant fist /Qu'encor garde ne s'en preïst' (ll. 2957–8), a dissimulation of response that then produces a clear and dramatic reaction from Enide, who, in contrast both to the 'uncowardly' fifth knight and her unflappable husband, experiences a profound sense of alarm she neither controls nor conceals:

> Quant Enide les a veüz,
> Toz li sans li est esmeüz
> Grant paor ot et grant esmai. (ll. 2959–61)
>
> The moment Enide saw them, her blood went racing – she was most frightened and alarmed.

The moment of panic is followed by an internal monologue – or perhaps internal *committee*, in parallel to the knights – during which she decides to warn her husband in spite of the risk to herself (ll. 2962–78). There is something of a paradox here: for all that Chrétien has her translate her narrated experience into direct discourse using the same terms in which that experience is described ('mout m'esmai', l. 2983), the fact that her utterance follows on from a carefully weighed decision in which she entertains the worst case scenario ('Il m'ocira. Assez m'ocie!' l. 2977) introduces an inevitable gap between experience and expression. This is no longer the rendering of emotion pure and simple, but rather its expression for the purpose of persuasion, with Enide starting from a position of terror and moving very rapidly into a position of self-mastery, learning to observe and report in the stress of a combat situation. Indeed, this focus on the gaze being redirected arguably fits with the focus of a scene in which the principal combatants are actually minor players, with Erec concentrating more on Enide than the robber knights, his seeming lack of regard for them a clue as to the real addressee of this particular piece of theatre. Again, this scene can be read as a version of the Eneas scenario, albeit here in an inverted form, the man is looking to attract a third party, but remaining more interested in the woman.

The combat scenes follow as further methodical display, with the first attacker – last to speak up in the division of spoils – struck down and injured, the next one killed outright, the third crushed and drowned when Erec throws his horse down on top of him at a ford (moral: whatever you may read in romances, don't joust at fords). As in the brutal hyper-realism of films like *Saving Private Ryan*, where the narrative presents the audience with a catalogue of death in war (wounds to the liver, lungs, throat; death by gunshot wounds versus as opposed to by higher calibre weapons; death by misadventure and errors, such as failing to throw a bomb in time) we are presented with a thesaurus clearly intended to outshine the relatively limited formulaic repertory of the *chanson de geste*, perhaps mirroring the attention to detail of the saint's life.[73] In that regard, the violence done to the knights is at once generic and yet distinct in nature, particularised into a grammar of pain: lances pierce chests or throats, or enter bodies – whether to the depth of a foot-and-a-half or three quarters their length; shoulders are smashed by a lance or severed by a sword; the spine can be shattered at the neck or further down. As with science-fiction visions of pitiless robot killers or Orientalist fictions of the man-machine that is the samurai warrior, the knowledge of anatomy here seems designed to make Erec a more effective – and more fascinating – killing machine as he passes his tests in the jousts almost in the manner of a series of martial arts *kata* or set pieces.

In a sense, the 'shock and awe' of this scene which causes the two remaining brigands to flee lies in its speed and variety, as well as in its capacity to deprive the enemy of the capacity for reflective action. Erec's pursuit here follows on from the premise established in the earlier encounter in that now he does not even warn the fleeing knights, but rather simply attacks. The grammar of his dispatch of the fourth brigand is particularly interesting in that it is the unfortunate's foolish, not impossibly *involuntary*, impulse. It is the fact this combatant sits up again that puts him in harm's way and costs him his life ('Cil releva, si fist que fox', l. 3051), a savage flurry of blows from Erec severing his shoulder (ll. 3052–5). As R. Howard Bloch argues, following Tony Hunt's work on Abelardian influences in Béroul, Béroul's presentation of Mark's decision to spare Tristan and Iseut when they are discovered in the forest (*Tristan*, ll. 2001–38) may reflect Abelard's opening up of a more difficult ethical terrain in which the invisibilies of intuited intention take primacy over action in judgements regarding sin.[74] By contrast, here Erec asserts what seems like a more savagely authoritarian stance that manifests a mime of distinctly un-Arthurian tyrannical *jouissance* by paying no regard to such niceties. This display, which one might read as an abridged quartering, forces the fifth knight for his part into a desperate, terrified demonstration of his surrender, whose frantic bricolage ('Tel paor a, *ne set que face*', l. 3060, my emphasis) contrasts sharply with both Erec's implacable focus and, finally, lack of regard as he simply takes his lance (ll. 3068–70). In any 'Hollywood' version, the character would probably fall full-length in a dead faint at this point.

Herein lies some of the sense behind the minimal show of self-mastery evident in the preliminary discussions between the five knights: the subordination of desire and the mastery of fear apparent in their bravado and courtesy to one another is stripped away in that they exhibit the self-mastery that is Erec's skill in combat and are indeed deprived of the capacity to act rationally or for effect. Crucially, although Enide appears as the first one stricken with fear, her process is the reverse, as she moves from the terrified contemplation of two sources of mortal peril to a settled course of action, carried out whether it pleases her lord or not. In terms of her positioning, however, Enide appears as the mediator of that sense of fear in that she is the first one to experience what is then experienced more widely. Her increasing self-mastery in the scene, achieved through an internalised dialogue, hints at what is to come in that she will move from being a foil to Erec to someone increasingly capable of acting manipulatively in her own right. Some hint of this is given in the unwise boasting of the first knight, who claimed he would take 'la pucele' (l. 2942) or die trying: given that that label had already been applied to individuals of differing fortunes and abilities, and is furthermore applied erroneously here, the suggestion is perhaps that Erec was not the only one they underestimated.

Enide's schooling in manipulation and control continues with Erec's instruction that she should lead the horses (ll. 2912–17), an instruction that various critics have seen as a reduction to a servile role reminiscent of her humble beginnings.[75] That there is some larger significance is apparent in the contrast between the palfrey, which the Count's niece vaunted as easy to handle and so the appropriate mount for a 'pucele' (ll. 1392), and the eight war-horses, which pose rather more of a challenge, presumably since they show all the temper the lighter mount does not: as Isidore says, they do bite and lash out with their hooves. In this therefore we have some of the significance of the skills Enide showed as a squire in her father's household and then of the gender specific nature of the training hinted at in the Count's niece's gift. What this seemed to imply was the circumscribing of Enide's future role. Furthermore, this sequence of events seems to mark out further the contrast between Enide and Philomena, the latter presented as schooled in the rather more noble art of hunting, and in her mastery of a range of distinct activities and species. Here, however, the horses operate not merely as a metonymic figure of the knights that ride them, Erec having disposed of the parts that would be too unruly for the purposes of the present exercise, but also as an image of the control of the passions. The fact that Enide then ends up leading a number of horses now identifying the schooling she receives as in the management and control of the irrationalities of collective emotion. Of course, that her actions here function as metaphor is entirely in keeping with the status of her character as something between an actual person and a quasi-allegorical figure of sovereignty, as highlighted in the interpretation of the tale's Celtic analogues.[76] However, that status is dusted of its mythical baggage through the possible Boethian overtones: having presented herself as desiring to resemble Philosophy rather than the Muses, Enide finds herself under stern tutelage.

Another aspect to this scene is the perverse subtext of the overall process. Erec set out from Carnant with Enide riding before her valiant husband and his lance in *grant esfroi*. Seeing this pair in their procession, a number of knights, *mout esfreez*, charged towards them one after the other. The question of the Eneas subtext to the earlier scene sows something rather strange here: borne before her husband and offered up – as Kathryn Gravdal notes – to tempt the desires of other men, Enide finds herself in a revised version of Lavine's mother's vision of her daughter in a man–man–woman sandwich.[77] Instead – in a copulation no more acceptable to Alan of Lille – Chrétien's subtending fantasy formulation runs man–woman–man, Enide experiencing what de Sade's Chevalier de Mirvel described as 'les plaisirs de l'entre-deux'.[78] However, although the *ménage à trois* (or is that *Troyes*?) is clearly flagged in the work's relation to the anterior tradition, merely to see in it an act of sodomy is to miss the point, Chrétien in effect taking issue with those who would dismiss vernacular fiction as nothing more than an obscenely perverse and nugatory pornography. To see no more than a version of Eneas's (alleged) misdeeds is to miss the political will brought to bear on those subjects drawn in by their own 'lecherie', and yet caught in a seeming inversion of the court-other opposition, Erec appearing as a figure of a new breed of cruelty and corruption in contrast to the robber-knight 'traditionalists', here appearing in the form of old-school 'ordinary, decent criminals' still remembering enough of the *Roland* to make them a danger to themselves. That said, the sexual subtext hints at a point of view in the scene that is as Frappier put it, 'résolu à jouer à tout ou rien'.[79] That willingness may return to haunt him, however…

Notes

1 Hanning, *Individual*, p. 4 (original emphasis). For discussion, see Crane, pp. 125–39 and notes 56–60.
2 Kay, *The Chansons de geste in the Age of Romance*, p. 49–51.
3 On which see Gaunt, *Gender and Genre*, pp. 75–85 and William J. Burgwinkle, 'Knighting the Classical Hero: Homo/Hetero Affectivity in *Eneas*', *Exemplaria*, 5:1 (1993), pp. 1–43.
4 Dido's citadel is initially presented as the very epitome of modernity in antiquity, although it is then revealed that it is imperilled partly through the origins of the city in her tricking of ? by means of the ox-hide ruse and partly quite simply because she is a woman.
5 My reading here has been influenced by readings of Stanley Kubrick's last film, *Eyes Wide Shut* (1999), based on Arthur Schnitzler's *Traumnovelle* (Berlin: Fischer, 1926), a narrative that offers what amounts to a parody romance by way of exploratory parable of the anxieties gnawing at contemporary bourgeois sexuality. On *Eyes Wide Shut*, see Žižek, *How to Read Lacan*, pp. 40–60 (chapter: 'From *che vuoi?* to Fantasy: Lacan with *Eyes Wide Shut*').
6 Žižek's reading of the end of *Eyes Wide Shut* is especially significant in this regard: 'Kidman – upon ascertaining that now they are fully awake, back into the day [...] – tells [Cruise] they must do something as soon as possible. "What?" he asks, and her answer is: "Fuck". End of the film, the final credits roll. The nature of the *passage à l'acte* ("passage to the act") as the false exit, the way of avoiding confronting the horror of the phantasmatic netherworld, was never so bluntly stated in a film: far from providing them with a real-life bodily satisfaction that will supersede empty fantasising, the passage to the act is presented as a stopgap, as a desperate preventative measure aimed at keeping at bay the spectral netherworld of fantasies. It is as if her message is "let's fuck right now, and then we can stifle our teeming fantasies before they overwhelm us again".' (Žižek, *How to Read Lacan*, p. 59). On Schreber's account and on psychosis, see Freud, 'Psycho-Analytic Notes on an Autobiographical Account of a Case of Paranoia (Dementia Paranoides)', in *The Standard Edition of the Complete Psychological Works of Sigmund Freud (Volume XII)*, ed. and trans. by James Strachey and others (London: Hogarth, 1956), pp. 3–38, *Le Séminaire de Jacques Lacan (livre III): les psychoses (1955–6)*, ed. by Jacques-Alain Miller, Le Champ Freudien (Paris: Seuil, 1981). For a brief account of Lacan's discussion, see Evans, *Introductory Dictionary*, pp. 154–7. On Schreber's delusions and their relation to fantasy, see also Žižek, *Plague of Fantasies*, pp. 71–81.
7 'Si le névrosé habite le langage, le psychotique est habité, possédé, par le langage.' (Lacan, *Le Séminaire III*, p. 285).

8 See Fradenburg, *City, Marriage, Tournament*, pp. 192–224. On hallucination in the prose *Didot Perceval*, see Michael Darin Amey, *Pursuing an Elusive Ideal: Masculinity in the Grail Legends*, University of Glasgow, unpublished doctoral dissertation, 2004.
9 According to *Le Robert*, *boudoir* and *bouder* are first attested in the fourteenth century.
10 Sade, *La Philosophie dans le boudoir*, in *Oeuvres complètes* (Paris: Circle du Livre Précieux, 1966), III, pp. 349–549, at p. 532.
11 Lacan, *Le Séminaire XI*, pp. 169.
12 Burns, *Bodytalk*, p. 165–9.
13 On Erec's beauty in this regard, see Jeanne A. Nightingale, 'Erec in the Mirror: The Feminization of the Self and the Re-Invention of the Chivalric Hero in Chrétien's First Romance', in *Arthurian Romance and Gender/ Masculin/ Féminin dans le roman arthurien médiéval/Geschlechterrollen im mittelalterlichen Artusroman*, ed. by Friedrich Wolfzettel (Amsterdam: Rodopi, 1995), pp. 130–46.
14 Germaine Greer, *The Boy* (London: Thames and Hudson, 2003), p. 197.
15 On this episode, see in particular Seebass-Linggi, pp. 210–28, who stresses how little Erec's behaviour has in common with the posture of the *fin'amant* (on which see also pp. 180–1). See also M. B. Ogle, 'The Sloth of Erec', *Romanic Review*, 9 (1918), 1–20; Adler, 'Sovereignty', pp. 924–9; Douglas Kelly, 'La Forme et le sens de la quête dans l'*Erec et Enide* de Chrétien de Troyes', *Romania*, 92 (1971), 326–58; Plummer, pp. 382–5; Penny Sullivan, 'The Education of the Heroine in Chrétien's *Erec et Enide*', *Neophilologus*, 69:3 (1985), 321–31, at pp. 323–4 as well as Nancy Bradley-Cromey, 'The 'Recreantise' Episode in Chretien's *Erec et Enide*', in *The Study of Chivalry: Resources and Approaches*, ed. by Howell Chickering and Thomas H. Seiler (Kalamazoo: Medieval Institute, 1988), pp. 449–71.
16 A problem noted by various critics. See, for example, Burgess, *Erec et Enide*, pp. 47–8.
17 Burgess, *Erec et Enide*, p. 48.
18 See Evans, *Introductory Dictionary*, pp. 34–5.
19 In that sense, Enide's reaction appears as an 'Answer of the Real': Erec's reaction is the event that leads her to identify herself as 'radically responsible' for what has happened. As Žižek comments, insofar as the answer of the Real has a determining, interpellating effect on the subject, it can be seen as a form of 'successful misunderstanding' (see Žižek, *Looking Awry: An Introduction to Jacques Lacan Through Popular Culture*, October (Cambridge MA and London: MIT Press, 1992), pp. 29–30). This motif of misinterpretation can be seen as a recurring device in Chrétien's poem (see, in particular, Joan Tasker Grimbert, 'Misrepresentation and Misconception in Chrétien de Troyes: Nonverbal and Verbal Semiotics in *Erec et Enide* and *Perceval*', in *Sign, Sentence, Discourse: Language in Medieval Thought and Literature*, ed. by

Julian N. Wasserman and Lois Roney (Syracuse: Syracuse University Press, 1989), pp. 50–79). See also Castellani, 'La "Parole" d'Enide', passim.

20 See Žižek, *Sublime Object*, pp. 110–29. As Žižek points out, the question of desire arises in the gap between an utterance framing a *demand* and its unstated illocutionary force.

21 See, for example, Cohen, *Of Giants*, pp. 38–9 and discussion above.

22 See Greer, pp. 195–217.

23 On anamorphosis, see discussion in introduction, above.

24 'Qui nullius aetatis legi videretur obnoxious, nunc enim juventutis vere pubescebat, nunc maturioris aevi facies seria loquebatur, nunc vultus senectutis sulcis videbatur arari.' (Alan of Lille, *De Planctu Naturae*, in *Patrologia Latina*, 210, cols 431–82, here at col. 471. For translation, see *Plaint of Nature*, p. 196.

25 See Hunt, 'Chrestien de Troyes: The Textual Problem', notably pp. 258–60.

26 Fritz, introduction, pp. 58–9 in the collected edition. On this passage, see also E. S. Sheldon, 'Why Does Erec Treat Enide So Harshly?', *Romanic Review*, 5 (1914), 115–26.

27 Interestingly, as evidence of a certain critical penchant for the *mar fus* reading, Duggan (*Romances*, pp. 104–05) glosses the 'mar i fus' reading, translating it as 'too bad for you that you were there', only then to render the same phrase in her later lament for him as if it were the 'mar fus' reading (see pp. 96–7). Topsfield (p. 27) likewise cites the line as 'mar i fus' but translates it as 'how cruel was your fate'.

28 *Casablanca*, dir. Michael Curtiz (1942).

29 See Töbler and Lommatzsch, II, cols 592–602.

30 One might think of Carol Shields' novel, *Unless* (London and New York: Fourth Estate, 2003), structured by chapter titles consisting of small words and fragments taken out of syntactic context (e.g. 'Wherein', 'Here's', 'Thereof', 'Thus', 'Whence', 'Beginning with', 'Already').

31 Obviously this line of argument goes against readings such as that of Allard, who sees Erec's *recreantise* following his return to Carnant as a mark of his potential unworthiness as a successor to Lac (see Allard, pp. 52–60).

32 Accordingly, in *Casablanca*, dir. Michael Curtiz (1942), Ilsa (played by Lauren Bacall) hovers ambiguously between debasement as adulterous *femme fatale* and redemptive purity, the latter role accepted only at the price of regretful renunciation.

33 For uses of *cuidier*, see Töbler and Lommatzsch, II, cols 1128–31.

34 Laclos, *Les Liaisons dangereuses*, letter 125 (see *Oeuvres complètes*, ed. by Laurent Versini, La Pléiade (Paris: Gallimard, 1979), pp. 287–95 at p. 293).

35 Here we have another example of Chrétien's flirting with past and non-Christian cultures, his narratorial assurance that no charms were used in Enide's arming of Erec before the tournament at Laluth ('N'i ot fait charaie ne charme', l. 710) drawing on the 'suspicions' that might attach to Enide's role in a

description that nonetheless focuses significantly on the tying of laces (l. 711; l. 714) and thongs (l. 712). The reference here underscores the parallelism between verbal charm and material objects, whether in the form of knot-bundles or curse amulets bearing symbols or even the text of the spell. On evidence of binding spells in Antiquity, see John C. Gager, *Curse Tablets and Binding Spells from the Ancient World* (Oxford: Oxford University Press, 1992). Although there are survivals of both pre-Christian and post-conversion charms in the European vernaculars (notably in Old High German and also in English traditions), the evidence from pre-modern French sources is patchy (see Owen Davies, 'French Charmers and Their Healing Charms', in *Charms and Charming in Europe*, ed. by Julian Roper (Basingstoke and New York: Palgrave MacMillan, 2004), pp. 91–112). Of course, the problem here is that the presentation of Enide moves between different gendered provinces of labour: the idea that Enide might have magical powers manifest in knot-tying is then rather contradicted by the masculine and public nature of her contribution to Erec's arming, handling armour and shield, belting on his sword (l. 718) and then *commanding* Erec's horse be brought to him (ll. 719–20), where it had previously seemed she was the most junior in a very reduced household. All of these gestures mark an expansionist mode as Enide's behaviour crosses status and gender boundaries, taking her from de facto stable boy to squire.

36 Žižek, 'What Lies Beneath', *Guardian Review*, May 1st, 2004, p. 7. Žižek is commenting here on Croatian judge Irka Saric's indictment of general Mirko Norac and his followers for crimes against the Serbian people, a case that received little public or official support because it was thought likely to threaten the civil peace by provoking the nationalist Right. His description of Saric as an 'ethical hero' (ibid.) is a clear reference to Lacan's commentary on Sophocles' *Antigone* in *Le Séminaire VII*.

37 This effective 'transfer' of Enide's (non-)witchery into Erec appears analogous to the developing climate of persecution in the early Modern period. As Robin Briggs argues, the witchcraft crazes of this period can be seen as the substitution of one 'web of power', namely the emergent sovereign states, denying their inability to provide for centralised control by targetting – and supplanting – another in the form of witch-covens and conspiracies (*Witches and Neighbours: The Social and Cultural Context of European Witchcraft*, rev. edn (Oxford: Blackwell, 2002), pp. 276–320).

38 Burns, *Bodytalk*, pp. 168–9.

39 Adler, p. 925.

40 On the 'theatrical effect' of breaking couplets in this dialogue, see Frappier, 'La Brisure', pp. 8–9.

41 A modern analogue in the history of *ira regis* can perhaps be found in former UK Prime Minister John Major cursing his colleagues – as he believed, out of earshot – with a satisfyingly vehement '*Bastards!*'.

42 On this scene and its interpretations, see Seebass-Linggi, pp. 35–52.

43 On Erec's arming here, see in particular Castellani, 'La Description du héros masculin', pp. 111–13.
44 On the place of such motifs as verbal insult and gestural familiarity in carnival, see notably Mikhail Bakhtin, *Rabelais and his World*, trans. by Hélène Iswolsky (Bloomington: Indiana University Press, 1984), pp. 197–277. However, see also Žižek, *Metastases of Enjoyment*, pp. 54–7.
45 Žižek, *Metastases of Enjoyment*, p. 64.
46 A recurring protestation Paris seems to have found somewhat irritating (p. 154 and note 6).
47 In *Philomena*, by contrast, this binary opposition is not replicated in human form. Rather the 'return' of the father as persecutory figure in contrast with the benevolent Pandion takes the form of idolatory, notably the figure of Pluto.
48 Kay, *The Chansons de geste in the Age of Romance*, p. 95.
49 Chrétien's *Philomena* adaptation closes with his account of the transformation of the two sisters and Tereüs, but makes no mention of Pandion's subsequent fate.
50 Chrétien's dissimulation of the strongly oedipal dimension of the relation between Erec and Lac is apparent in R. Howard Bloch's reading of the Joy of the Court (*Etymologies and Genealogies*, pp. 189–90): 'Like the hero, Maboagrains has been given overly to sexual desire and as a result finds himself trapped in a senseless obligation to action. Erec's conquest of his alter ego – first with speech (entreaty) and then by arms – represents an assimilation of both sides of a newly integrated persona which prepares the way for his own succession [...]. For the synthesis of both poles of this psychological dilemma, which coincides with the death of the father, is again duplicated in the fusion of discursive modes: the hero who accedes to the paternal function becomes at the same time the father of the text.' (p. 189).
51 Of course, in Lacanian terms, such a use of cosmic forces as pretext for the evil one does is redolent of Superego cruelty. If Chrétien's presentation of Erec and Lac here does show some reflection of relations between Henry II and his sons, their actions as carried out in the name of higher forces, then the perspective is distinctly jaundiced.
52 See Bezzola, p. 147 and Duggan, *The Romances of Chrétien de Troyes*, p. 11 as well as Philippe Walter, 'Erec et le cocadrille: note de philologie et de folklore médiéval', *Zeitschrift für Romanische Philologie*, 115:1 (1999), 56–64.
53 Burgess, *Erec et Enide*, p. 54; Allard, pp. 62–5.
54 Burgess, *Erec et Enide*, p. 55.
55 A variant form of this symbolic illegitimacy can be seen in Guerri's insulting of Raoul as a 'bastard' through his dispossession by Louis (*Raoul de Cambrai*, ed. by Sarah Kay, trans. by William Kibler, Lettres Gothiques (Paris: Livre de Poche, 1996), l. 486)
56 Marie de France, *Lais*, ed. and trans. by Laurence Harf-Lancener Lettres Gothiques (Paris: Livre de Poche, 1990).

57 John of Salisbury comments approvingly on accounts of Caesar's willingness to endure hardship (see *Policraticus*, book 4, chapter 3 and book 5, chapter 8).
58 On Erec in the *Roman d'Erec*, see Anne Berthelot, 'La Carrière avortée du "chevalier qui jamais ne mentit"', in *Erec ou l'ouverture du monde Arthurien: actes du colloque du Centre d'Etudes Médiévales de l'Université de Picardie-Jules Verne, Amiens 16–17 janvier 1993*, ed. by Danielle Buschinger and Wolfgang Spiewok, WODAN, 18 (Greifswald: Reineke, 1993), pp. 2–9 and Friedrich Wolfzettel, 'Le *Roman d'Erec* en prose du XIIIe siècle: Un Anti-Erec et Enide?', in *The Legacy of Chrétien de Troyes*, ed. by Norris J. Lacy, Douglas Kelly and Keith Busby, 2 vols (Amsterdam: Rodopi, 1988), II, pp. 215–28.
59 On this episode, see Charles Brucker, 'Gauvain et la mort dans le roman en prose: Erec', *Revue des Langues Romanes*, 87:1 (1983), 89–103.
60 On conflict in the *Perceforest*, see especially Sylvia Huot, 'Cultural Conflict as Anamorphosis: Conceptual Spaces and Visual Fields in the *Roman de Perceforest*', *Romance Studies*, 22:3 (2004), 185–95.
61 On which, see notably Suzanne Conklin Akbari, 'From Due East to True North: Orientalism and Orientation', in *The Postcolonial Middle Ages*, pp. 19–34.
62 'Crucial to both the operation and the preservation of the *secret* was that they should not be clearly pronounced but rather muttered or murmured'. (Davies, p. 94, original emphasis). On muttering and charms, see also Jacques Cheyronnaud, 'Quand marmotter, c'est prier…', in *Panseurs de douleurs: les medicines populaires*, ed. by François Loux (Paris: Autrement, 1992), pp. 195–9.
63 *The New York Times*, April 12th, 2003. Cited from Salecl, *On Anxiety*, p. 16.
64 Girard, *Violence and the Sacred*, p. 107.
65 See Allard, pp. 67–71.
66 On the robber knights, see Seebass-Linggi, pp. 68–83.
67 See Seebass-Linggi, p. 75.
68 See Gaston Paris, Review of Foerster (ed.), *Erec und Enide*, *Romania*, 20 (1891), 148–66, p. 159 note 4; Dembowski (ed.), *Erec et Enide*, p. 1091 and Seebass-Linggi, pp. 76–7.
69 See, for example, the Oxford version of the *Chanson de Roland*, ll. 1188–2114.
70 Bezzola, p. 162.
71 See Seebass-Linggi, pp. 79, note 48.
72 Seebass-Linggi, pp. 79–80.
73 Seebass-Linggi takes this 'raw' quality as part of the scene's 'epic colouring' (p. 81). Steven Spielberg (dir.), *Saving Private Ryan* (1998).
74 Bloch, *Etymologies and Genealogies*, pp. 182–6. On Abelard, see Hunt, 'Abelardian Ethics'.
75 Topsfield, p. 39.
76 On which see, among others, Joan Brumlik, 'Chrétien's Enide: Wife, Mistress and Metaphor', *Romance Quarterly*, 35:4 (1988), 401–14 and, for an overview

of discussion regarding the possible Celtic sources and Enide as a sovereignty figure, see Duggan, *Romances*, pp. 212–13.
77   Gravdal, *Ravishing Maidens*, p. 55.
78   Sade, *La Philosophie dans le boudoir*, p. 476.
79   Frappier, *Chrétien de Troyes*, p. 87.

MINSTREL [singing]:
He was not in the least bit scared to be mashed into a pulp.
Or to have his eyes gouged out and his elbows broken.
To have his kneecaps split and his body burned away,
And his limbs all hacked and mangled, Brave Sir Robin.
His head smashed in
And his heart cut out
And his liver removed
And his bowels unplugged
And his nostrils ripped
And his bottom burnt off
And his penis spl…
ROBIN [interrupting]: That's… that's enough music for now, lads!
Looks like there's dirty work afoot. (*Monty Python and the Holy Grail*)

Chapter Six
'If You Don't Do What [We] Do, Why Are You [Here]?': Queering the Quest

'Si ea quae sunt curiae non agis, quid in curia quaeris?'[1]

'If you don't do what courtiers do, why are you at court?'

'I am cock-crazy', my landlord, a quite ordinary *afficionado* by Balinese standards, used to moan as he went to move another cage, give another bath or conduct another feeding. 'We're all cock-crazy.'[2]

Courtly ways are strange in many senses: the above quotation from Gerald of Wales's *Life of Geoffrey, Archbishop of York* is the response given to a new arrival shocked to find same-sex relations the rule rather than the exception at Geoffrey's court. Such tales of sexual deviance form one of the most common expressions of the foreignness of curial culture. However, encounters with the strange ways of other cultures can also reflect back troublingly on the exploring self, we can see from Clifford Geertz's account in his essay 'Deep Play' of the role of cock-fighting in his initiation into Balinese village society, an involvment that leaves his ethnographical narrative troubled through what Kathleen Biddick sees as its uneasy mix of collusion with and parody of 'the conventions of the hypermasculine genre'.[3] Where Erec's assertion of chivalric prowess seemed unproblematic in the encounter with the robber knights, we now move to a series of adventures whose political and desiring foundations are rather less intuitively rational, rather less *familiar*. Indeed, it is on account of this fundamental difference that the chapter break falls at the end of the first day of the quest. With Erec having acquired a number of horses, we move into the next phase of his 'reconquest' of reputation in the irrational economy of chivalric renown (*los*) and Enide's crash-course schooling in the arts of power and manipulation at court. What this chapter then examines is *Erec et Enide's* vision of the nature and origin of romance's libidinal geography in an uncanny conarrative infolding of both strange and native ways. In their own ways, the segments of the second to fourth days of the quest permute the Enean tableau of men, women and horses. Galoain stands at the centre of a hypervirilist court society seething with turbulent attractions that focus initially on Erec to be displaced onto Enide as the object of a violent, transgressive adulterous desire finally embodied in his unarmed, headlong charge. Guivret – pound-for-pound the biggest noise on a horse the Arthurian world has ever seen – represents the untamed dynamism of both chivalry and the wild borderland, energies that surge in quest of a possibility of expenditure only to be parodied in Kay's 'joy ride' on Gauvain's horse, 'le Gringalet', preceding Erec's arrival in the royal camp. All these moments offer their own libidinal puzzles that are only then resolved in the encounter with the giants and their captive, Cadoc of Tabriol, tied to a pack nag and led away to a shameful fate at their hands – perhaps not even then.

Count Galoain: Stealing (a Man's) Beauty

> Il n'y a rien qui enlaidisse certains Courtisans comme la présence du Prince; à peine les puis-je reconnaître à leurs visages, leurs traits sont altérés, et leur contenance est avilie: les gends fiers et superbes sont les plus défaits, car ils y perdent plus du leur.[4]

Even if his performance here is not quite as breezily carefree as at Danebroc, with eight opponents dispatched in just slightly more than twice the space (ll. 2791–3073) devoted to the combat with Yder (ll. 862–992), Erec's defeat of the robber knights epitomises swift, vicious efficiency. This questioning about the investment of energy is also evident in the 'scorn and slight regard' (*Henry V*, act 2, scene 4)

Erec shows those opponents no longer in a position to do him harm: the efforts they have shown have earned them less than nothing. However, although the terror Erec inspires in his opponents and his quasi-Foucauldian rationale of denying them refuge in the forest locate his deeds in the public sphere, we are faced with something of the judicial and political equivalent of the old chestnut of whether a tree falling in a deserted forest really makes a sound if there is no one to hear it. Moreover, the problem of managing the conquered horses underscores the inherently laborious nature of man-on-man violence, and so, from the pure economy of virile energy that is the combat, we move to the lumpy world of commodities. This encumbering is, however, mostly passed on to Enide, who must learn to lead the restive, fiery beasts, animals full of far greater 'esfroi' than her palfrey.

If, as Cohen reminds us, it takes one horse to make a knight, eight extra do not necessarily create a creature nine times more useful, an economic truth shaping Erec's tactics in the joust at Danebroc, where he does not pause to collect the horses of his defeated opponents, but rather leaving them and concentrating on demonstrating his worth (ll. 2211–14) – the symbolic capital of kudos being more useful after a certain point than the merely material. But then, even that vein only admitted of so much mining, with Chrétien passing rapidly over the tournament's second day. Accordingly, the second day of the quest shows a shift from conquest as wearying linear accumulation to a more dynamically exponential economy of renown and beauty. Such a move is of course fundamental to the spectacular and suggestive poetics of romance, as is clear from Chrétien's earlier reduction of the train of knights present at Arthur's court to a dustily perfunctory *et cetera* ('Les autres vos dirai sanz nombre / Por ce que li nombrers m'encombre', ll. 1699–1700).

That violence is not the only mode of conquest available to Erec on his travels through the forest is clear from the arrival of the squire. Here it is Erec's generosity that bears fruit far beyond the immediate value of the commodities involved, reminding us there is at least one other use for horses.[5] Of course, Erec is not (yet) in the situation summmed up in the much-postcarded Amerindian saying, 'when the last tree has died and the last fish has been poisoned, we will realise

305

we cannot eat money'. Then again, even in such dire circumstances as the siege of Montauban, the sons of Aymes did not eat Bayard – only his blood, which they drained to make sausages (*Renaut de Montauban*, ed. by Thomas, ll. 12129–41).[6] Indeed, as Joyce Salisbury and Cohen point out, the eating of horsemeat was forbidden by the Church, even if the clergy, while finding the practice repugnant, also in effect seem to have conceded that such an interdiction was practically unenforceable.[7] Although deer are the time-honoured prey of aristocratic hunts, eating horses would thus appear as some sort of grotesque autophagia.[8] Besides, just as there were no butchers in the *Roman de Thèbes*, there are none here. Chrétien thus saves us the scene of one of his heroes gnawing the raw flesh of some hapless quadruped for *Le Chevalier au lion* (and even there it is a stag rather than a horse). Fortunately so: had Galoain's squire come upon Erec and Enide, fed up waiting for their picnic delivery and now snacking on rump of warhorse instead, he might have turned back in disgust.

Although such a scene might seem far-fetched, it would be no more than the dietary equivalent of the 'raw' (or should that be 'cooked'?) violence we have just witnessed, and thus raises the question of the relation of cultures to their 'obscene subtexts'. Erec is both like and yet differentiated from the cannibalistic tyrant giants of Geoffrey of Monmouth: although we have seen him 'butcher' people, this is not to devour them. The underlying 'rawness' of its 'cooked' acts reminds us that the absolute rule of law is in itself a memory or mime of savage despotism. The problem with the courtly milieu, however, is that it seems to problematise that sense of difference. In the same sense, the party of Erec and Enide, plus eight extra horses is a memory both of the violence we have seen here and of transgressive or violent sexual acts from other texts. The parallel with the *Roman d'Eneas* is to some extent exact: Erec *did* use Enide to attract other men, he was happy to 'trot along behind', he is not interested in 'poil de conin' (at the moment) and he did 'engage' with a plurality of partners. However, all of these similarities are simultaneously differences: Erec and Enide are still good courtly heterosexuals on a picnic, not tyrant monsters engaged in some depraved, quasi-cannibalistic, gang-bestial amplification or foreshadowing of Manet's *Déjeuner sur l'herbe*. And, even if they had been, we can find an example of the salvaging of civilised face in matters of dietary transgression in *Richard Coer de Lyon's* invented narrative of the King's unwitting cannibalism. To cure the King's fever, the royal cook prepares a broth of roast Saracen flesh instead of the pork he asked for. When it is revealed to Richard what he has eaten, his reaction is unexpectedly one of delight, the King saying his army will never want for food if Saracens are so delicious.[9] Either Erec, or perhaps Enide, who – as we will see from the sharp inventiveness ('grant voidie', l. 3973) she will display in the later encounter with Kay – is always up for a joke, might well have managed a similarly disarming witticism (*facetia*) as evidence of her courtly humour (*lepor* or *hilaritas* – for discussion see introduction above).

Fortunately, Erec and Enide are saved from such extremities by the timely arrival of Galoain's squire.[10] Although it might seem extravagant to repay the offer of a relatively small amount of food with a fine horse, Erec's situation invites us to consider how much a string of them is worth if you have nothing to eat. However, with the arrival of the squire, we move seamlessly into a world of commodities and foodstuffs exchanged, cooked, processed and refined. Wine (as we know from Barthes) is one of the most culturally 'cooked' of distillations, after which we have the fine-milled white bread-cakes (from *terre gaste* to *terre gastel*...), and the 'gras fromages de gaÿn' (l. 3124), the *foie gras* of soft cheeses.[11] As a UK supermarket slogan puts it, 'taste the difference'. Moreover, all of this is served on fine linen and with beautiful drinking cups (ll. 3148–50).

In its details, the scene fast-forwards through the cultural anthropology Chrétien will elaborate further in *Le Chevalier au lion*, the picture in *Erec et Enide* forming a striking contrast to Yvain's progression from raw meat to coarse, low-quality bread and water to cooked but unseasoned meat – all consumed without preparation or ceremony – finally to the exchange of meat for good quality loaves (see *Le Chevalier au lion*, ll. 2824–84). The comparison of course reveals the ellipsis or acceleration in Chrétien's earlier text: Yvain's progress from an economic 'degree zero' is more painfully linear, whereas Erec and Enide do not merely avoid eating raw meat, they jump directly to the cheese, bypassing the main course. Another aspect missing from the scene in the later poem is the dimension of speech: instead of the crude, silent exchanges between madman and hermit, predicated on objects and the most basic necessities of life, we move to a world of consideration, politeness, good intention and decorum. The squire demonstrates the capacity for quick-witted improvisation and good heart of the ideal courtier ('Puis s'apensa de grant franchise' l. 3137), and shows himself selflessly disinterested in material gain ('rien ne vos quier ne demant', l. 3147) as well as well-schooled in serving elegantly at table ('de beau servise' l. 3161). Thus, whereas the scene in *Le Chevalier au lion* was predicated on the barriers to any extensive mutual understanding – except insofar as Yvain is susceptible to what Jeffrey Cohen would see as a quasi-reoedipalisation as the hermit's pseudo-dog, this grouping operates on the basis of apparently like minds and conditionings.[12]

The weight both scenes place on the nature-culture divide makes it clear that more than mere physical nourishment is at stake. Rather, in Lacanian terms, we move between two worlds: that of *manque-à-avoir* (lack of having), the world of material need and demand, versus the world of desire, regard and esteem, referred to as *manque-à-être* ('want of being' or 'want-to-be').[13] What Chrétien and Lacan seem to agree on at that point is that desire may be the thing that makes us what we are, but it also makes life difficult. *Manque-à-avoir* is, given the means, a comparatively simple world of quid-pro-quo exchanges: Yvain may not be capable of sophisticated interaction with or understanding of the hermit, but – as with Lacan's dog, Justine – he never mistakes his benefactor for anyone else. By contrast, as we will see, the economics of *manque-à-être* are rather more complex, although out in the forest the exchange of esteem seems to be flowing nicely for the moment. The formality and good organisation shown by the squire and pages, the latter deferentially taking over the care of the horses (ll. 3163–4), stands as a testimony to civilised values subjected to an earlier, barbarous neighbour-parody in the robbers' mock-courtly division of the spoils expected from their attacks on a seemingly easy target. Indeed, the squire is not so much repaid for goods as rewarded for performance ('son *servise* pas ne pert', l. 3176, my emphasis). A relatively small bill, but a big tip. But then, it was abundantly clear – from the entry in procession with the pages, to the manner in which he addresses Erec and the care he lavishes on the pair – that this scene was all about added value.

However, for all the appearance of sincerity and spontaneity, the encounter between Erec's party and that of the squire presents us with two sets of Janus-faces: like some court poet well-versed in the classical canon and the arts and ethics of *bene dicere* finding himself in the employ of a treacherous tyrant, as Galoain's subaltern he cannot reliably speak or answer for the truth of what are not actually matters of *his* intention. Chrétien's sequencing of prior events, evidenced in the potentially puzzling accumulation of horses, places a brutal crime just off-stage and out of sight, the present moment also putting a fair face on a potentially ugly domestic history. For his side, on the other hand, the squire may insist on his sincerity ('nou di pas por vos losengier', l. 3146), but his position as both the man and acceptable public face of Galoain makes him a liar.[14]

The emphasis on beauty and largesse in this scene is indeed deceptive, with the Count keeping his economy on a tighter rein. The economic foundation of this kingdom, ruled by a 'want of beauty' ('want' here in the sense of both appreciative desire and hungry lack) is apparent from the initial posture of Galoain and his three knights, leaning at a window looking out (ll. 3210–11), a pose no different from Arthur's courtiers, who spend much of their time doing the same (see ll. 1517–19).[15] However, the different tenor of Galoain's grasping visuality is apparent from the speed with which he notices a fine, new horse his squire clearly did not get from him (ll. 3212–16). The crucial difference between the two places lies in the subsequent turn of events and the irruption here of the 'lecherie' the Arthurian court manages to keep in check. What is then generated from the encounter becomes apparent in the squire's conversation with his lord, Count Galoain, to whom he remarks that he has met the most beautiful man he has ever seen (l. 3223). Fortunately, either the effect of the charismatic seduction is sufficiently apparent that the squire's audacity is lost here in the reflected glow, or Galoain is sufficiently Arthurian in that his reaction to wonder is a desire to see it similar to Arthur's response to the 'nouvelle' of the fountain (*Le Chevalier au lion*, ll. 659–74) – rather than shoot the messenger who brings the news his lord has made second place at most: 'Je cuit et croi / Que il n'est pas plus beax de moi' (ll. 3227–8).[16] Still clearly ravished by his encounter, the squire replies:

> 'Par foi, sire', fait li sergenz,
> 'Vos estes assez beax et genz;
> N'a chevalier en cest païs,
> Qui de la terre soit naïs
> Que plus beax ne soiez de lui.
> Mais bien os dire de cestui
> Qu'il est plus beax de vos assez,
> Se dou haubert ne fust quassez
> Et camoisiez et debatuz.
> Qu'en la forest s'est combatuz
> Touz seus contre huit chevaliers,
> S'en amene les huit destriers.' (ll. 3229–40)

> 'On my word, sir', said the squire, 'you are very handsome and fine. There is no knight born of the earth who is better looking than you; but I dare say this one would be far handsomer than you if he weren't exhausted by his hauberk, and battered and bruised. In the forest he did battle all alone against eight knights and has brought back all their chargers.'

'Mirror, mirror on the wall…'. It seems only someone quite mad or quite in love would respond as the squire does. Even a magical mirror will lie to save itself (maybe *only* magical mirrors can truly lie), but then mirrors do not fall in love.[17] Crucially, such is the effect of Erec's beauty is that the squire even deploys the affirmatory formula 'bien os dire' – *I dare say*.[18] In that sense, the shape of the trial to come is already clear: Erec will be challenged at the level of his seductive power, with the Count here showing the vanity that will motivate his attempt to steal Enide, a theft both blurring and interrogating the categories of *avoir* and *être*. *Avoir* in that it is a matter of possessing Enide as commodified chattel and *être* in that what seduced Galoain is what one might term a *plus d'être*, a surplus of being reflected in the repletion of the beguiled and rewarded squire. Thus, what will enrage Galoain later is precisely Enide's failure to return his regard for her. It is furthermore no coincidence that Erec refuses any possibility of the Count paying his lodging expenses for him: ' "Assez ai", dist il, "a despendre, / N'ai mestier d'*autrui avoir* prendre"' (ll. 3277–8, my emphasis). Perhaps, but what is happening to *autrui estre*? Galoain clearly perceives Erec's influence as a threat to his sense of his own unrivalled, unstolen beauty. His anxiety is not necessarily misplaced in a text that returns recurrently to 'being' as a substance, or at least a substantive, describing one of its 'beautiful people', the Queen's maid, as being 'de grant estre' (l. 144) and with various characters at key moments asking after the 'estre', the status and identity, of those they encounter (e.g. l. 2415, l. 3864, l. 4083, l. 4482, l. 6023).

Of course, one way of understanding what is at work here is that we are to understand either the Count or the text itself as finding the implications of these effusions and exchanges too troubling for further pursuit. Just as Stephen Jaeger sees medieval sources as presenting the history of courtly love as a perversion of the language of bonding, so the text, having let them speak at length of whatever Chrétien shuffles past us under the police blanket of 'Mout parolent de mainte chose' (l. 3279), turns its attention to Enide as conveniently paradigmatic addressee of all turbulent and contradictory discourses about desire.[19] Galoain's axiomatic assertion that 'a woman only becomes prouder when one begs and flatters her' ('Bien est voirs que fame s'orguille, / Quant on plus la prie et losenge', ll. 3346–7) hints at an economy of *être* out of balance: like the superego taxman, the more tribute you pay the Lady, the more she demands.

Galoain's lack of existential largesse was always present in germ, the new horse and the sense of delight radiated by the young squire sufficient to set off a pathological snowball effect. This fragile psychic economy stands in sharp contrast to the fact that, as the squire observes, Erec's beauty is only temporarily diminished (as back in Laluth) by the bruises and injuries he bears from his combats in the forest (ll. 3235–7). But then, Erec's effect on the squire – speaking with the flowing generosity of one transfixed – began with the intuitably finite formality and decorum of polite but not obtrusive or over-familiar service at table only to proceed troublingly to open the agalmic joy within the squire, giving Galoain a vision of *courtoisie's* seemingly boundless charismatic largesse revealed in a jealous interception of a rapt gaze directed at once elsewhere and nowhere. Not only did the squire give Erec the food and wine, the *avoir* (already infused with *être* by its manufacture), intended for the Count, he also gave himself more completely than he seemingly ever had to Galoain.

We are as perhaps as close as could be here to a homosocial equivalent of Žižek's examination of the traumatic fantasy of a partner's infidelity ('Why did she have to lick him right *there*? Why did she have to spread her legs *so wide*?').[20] But then, to say 'homosocial' is to imply that there is no erotic dimension to the relation between Erec and Galoain or between any of the other men on the scene at this point. For a start, we know that the language, ritual and affectivity of *amicitia*, of male bonding in diplomatic relations, was not unlike that of marriage, much as the relation of the soul as bride to Christ made gender inversion and erotic intensity a staple of male spiritual writing and accounts of experience.[21] However, medieval sources seem to both to queeringly explore those bonds and to police them for any hint of homoerotic 'lecherie'.[22]

Interestingly, although part of his nonchalant but deliberate show of unpossessiveness, Erec is notably quiet or at least under-reported in this section.[23] Just as Enide seemed to take little part in the marriage negotiations being concluded on her behalf in Laluth, so Erec now has no more than two short speeches (ll. 3277–8 and ll. 3302–05): in the first he refuses Oringle's offer of payment for his lodgings; in the second he freely gives him permission to go sit and speak with Enide. In that sense, like Freud's Dora, his complicity in how he is to be bought and sold in this scene may repay further examination. Moreover, his manner with the Count indicates an absence of affective investment, a carefreeness that manifests as benevolent but potentially provoking *suffisance*.[24] There is everything in that rapt proximity to *objet a* to enflame a man such as the Count. And yet, for all Erec's ravishing beauty is the focus for the intense relations Galoain sees around Erec, Chrétien allows our errant knight to efface himself from the picture and melt into its *arrière plan*. One approach is to argue that Galoain's attachment to Erec and his experience of *amor de loin* occasioned first by the description provided by the squire and later by his contemplation of Enide (ll. 3280–7) signal a free-floating affect of the kind that can only lead to trouble. Galoain's fury is that of a man spurned, but the *indirectness* of his reaction, the displacement of his 'hainamoration' onto Enide, is an inversion of that of the Queen in *Lanval*, who springs immediately to accusing Lanval of sodomy when he rejects her (*Lanval*, ll. 279–88). In the midst of the confusion,

Galoain manifests his excessive libidinal energies through a 'straight' confession of adulterous and murderous desire in a terroristic assertion of the legitimacy of his investments, be it in terms of same-sex or heterosexual relations.

Once again, I would argue that the figure of Philomena hovers in the background. Clearly, in spite of the squire's 'Athenian' hospitality we are, in terms of Lucan's 'knowledge of the law of proper measure', somewhere more like Thrace. Indeed, Galoain's quite sociopathic show of friendly concern and his willingness to play along with the illusions of polite sociability assimilate him to the figure of Tereus in that the latter also only conformed to the decorum of Athenian society as long as he deemed expedient. In similar wise, Galoain waits until he is out of Erec's hearing and then proceeds to make his overtures to Enide, believing that he has already won and that the prize only remains to be taken by persuasion or force declaring himself ready to kill Erec regardless of any consideration of right or wrong (ll. 3353–5). Of course, although the more obvious archetypes here are Paris and Helen, it is nonetheless instructive to read this scene against Chrétien's reworking of the Philomena story. If Galoain is Tereüs, then Erec is Pandion, trusting to the conventional civilities that should make a collective existence free of *vilenie* possible. He allows Enide out of his immediate purview and control, trusting to others to see to her safety insofar as all that is addressed in the interaction between himself and Galoain is the question of whether there need be any cause for concern between the two men. This time around, his sleep and her wakefulness appear as the live version of the situation 'rehearsed' in the forest, where Enide, under the pressure of Erec's stern interdictions, taxed herself with her lack of faith in her husband. This time around, she finds herself keeping watch with a view to two cares, balancing her assessment of her husband's exhaustion against the contrary force of Galoain's unsleeping desires, dangerously encouraged by her own words, which could well incite him to kill Erec and leave her with little legal defence in any ensuing abduction or forced sexual congress.

In that sense, for all the scene between Erec, Enide and Galoain is predicated on private conversations, passions and understandings, the rhetorical models and values brought into play are those of the public sphere, as is clear from the mix of erotic and feudal language Burgess notes in the exchanges between Enide and Galoain, and especially highlighted in his potentially duplicitously coded use of the term 'service'.[25] Indeed, so much was foreshadowed by the vanity and lack of self-control Galoain initially displayed in his jealousy of Erec's charismatic influence on the squire. His outrage at seeing one of his subjects appear subject to a seductive force emanating from elsewhere or, as Lacan puts it, 'not all' in relation to him – a ravished Ganymede to Erec's Jove.[26]

In keeping with Ciceronian concerns regarding the effect of the orator's persuasive force over the passions of the mob, Enide's beauty, a force operating outwith the controlling stricture of rational or paternalistic authority, has inflamed the passions of her public to a dangerous degree. Enide walks the tightrope of misleading her audience and encouraging its transgressive desires through contrary assurances of her own willingness to break with the regulatory structures that position her. Obviously, the negotiations between Enide and the Count appear as a model of the slippery nature of courtly desire and the counterintuitive ways in which the passions excited by the royal couple have to be handled. Enide moves rapidly from a situation in which she has appeared uncomfortable with her mandate as object of courtly regard, to a period of apparent quiescence in which things seemed calm enough. Now she finds herself the object of violent overtures in which she defeats Galoain by pretending to embody his fervid misogynistic portrait of the proud woman. As in Alfred Hitchcock's vision in *Vertigo* of Judy Barton counterfeiting the cool, unattainable Madeleine Elster, Enide – as Seebass-Linggi shows in detail – takes on the language and guise of the lyric *domna* and, in that dressing-up, reveals a dangerous truth: she *is* the Lady.[27] In Hitchcock's film, Judy Barton pays the inevitable price for having appropriated the beauty of *l'entre-deux-morts*, the space between the two deaths, while Enide's fate appears in the form of the deadly trap she sets herself. From another perspective, however, Enide's deception reminds us why Philomena fails to persuade Tereüs: since he is a monster, her evocation of morality and authority, a mirror to his monstrous desire, is more likely to enrage than to tame him. Her fate is therefore a version of Antigone's, her insistence on absolute standards driving him to crime. In comparison, Enide meets Galoain something more like half-way, presenting her concerns as personal rather than abstract and moral. Indeed, her throw-and-roll manoeuvre goes far enough to tie the knot through her insistence on assurances from his side, reversing the position and speaking transgressively from a place of apparently naked desire that mirrors his own expression of urgency. When Erec's courtiers claimed that Enide had enlaced and caught their lord (l. 2559), they may not have expected to find her so adept in the ensnaring art of seduction. Galoain's will to fight without armour is therefore in part a product of Enide's power to unveil, although it can also be seen as a continuation of Erec's seduction of the squire, a desire to match the beauty of his male competitor. In that regard, Erec's arms are not merely a mark of his compliance with chivalric strictures on health and safety. Rather, this 'armour of an alienating identity' (to quote Cohen quoting Lacan) functions as the minimal distance necessary, the absence of a complete investment of the self in conflict. Compared to Galoain's 'loud and noisy' effusion, Erec in armour appears closed as a silencing domestication of passionate *esfroi*.

Crucially, the resolution of the scene comes not with Galoain's death but with his instruction to his men is that they should not pursue Erec any further (ll. 3631–52). There is no particular reason that Erec might not have killed him in the attack: there is no mention of him making any concession to the unarmoured Galoain as he will shortly with Keu (ll. 4040–3), and indeed, the Count's powerful attack asks no quarter. Fortunately, Erec's good hauberk protects him, although perhaps not as well as the triple-worked coat (l. 3685) Guivret is about to don in the next encounter. Evidence that he has received the regard he desires from Erec and can now return it without any sense of it impinging on his own beauty. Interesting the pose in which he is returned to the castle is the dead echo of that of his seneschal, the latter carried on his upturned shield (ll. 3654–5) as if a tomb effigy. Galoain is thus located in regard to two kinds of male fixity that domesticate the question of male beauty. The first is his specular relation to the dead object that is the seneschal, a companionship that is the narrative echo of his earlier place in a brethren of desiring men symbolised by his position among the three followers staring out the window alongside him. Nonetheless, the Count seems to be vouchsafed an Arthurian lesson in the knowledge of the law of limits: as in *La Mort's* vision of the King's dream, he is given to understand the nature of his passions in his fall. For a knight whose passions were seemingly as unregulatedly polymorphous as those of the giants defeated by Arthur, this is clearly something of a privilege, but it then does raise the question of the potential for an uncanny queering in the encounter between King and Giant, the former being allowed to disavow the strangeness of his libidinal foundation through the censure of the latter.[28] One interesting comparison here is with later representations of the figure of Galehaut, 'son of the beautiful giantess', who, initially a threat to Arthur's kingdom, becomes fascinated and seduced by the achievements and beauty of Lancelot. As Gaunt comments, Galehaut's selfless passion in his position between Lancelot and Guinevere as a third party contrasts tellingly with the possessiveness of the Queen.[29] In this scenario, we can see Galoain's encounter, with his final renunciation of the pursuit of Erec as a reassertion of the ethical dimension of his desire in a scene that has moved through a number of displacements. There seems to be a similar move here: Erec's wounding of Galoain stems the latter's turbulent drive and causes him to leave off the pursuit of Erec on his *straight* path through the dark forest of chivalric gendering ('Parmi la forest a droiture / S'en va poignant grant aleüre' ll. 3615–16). Galoain's reward is to still the mob of his followers through the persuasive force of his speech (ll. 3631–52), emanating from a body whose beauty lies now not in its forceful compelling power but in the pathos of its broken wounding, reflecting his acknowledgement of a shameful, *vilain* excess. In that sense, the Count himself appears as a puzzle: he begins by seeming drawn to and jealous of Erec's beauty but then transfers his attentions to Enide. This of course can be seen as an illustration of the 'ugliness' of the neighbour, manifested in contradiction and obscenity. Yet, set against this, Enide's performance appears as a daring, potentially high-risk imitation of the lyric *domna*, a strategy that would leave her with no room for manoeuvre if anything were to go awry. However, this operation of displacement seems to mark a strategy of glossing over potentially inconvenient libidinal subtexts, since what is notable about Galoain's court is the absence of women and the emphasis on men looking at men as objects of desire and envy. In that sense, the image of Galoain's court fits with other homophobic characterisations of the milieu in medieval sources as a place in which practices other than sodomy appear outlandish and exceptional.

'Get in ma' [maisnie]': The Domestication of Chivalric Energy

> FAT BASTARD (to Mini-Me): That looks like a baby. [...] I'm bigger than you and higher up the food chain. GET IN MA' BELLY![30]

In *Austin Powers: The Spy Who Shagged Me* – the second of Mike Myers' parodic mirrorings of 007's compensatory fantasy defence of British influence and relevance in Cold and post-Cold War world affairs – the villainous Dr Evil (played by Myers) creates a homucular clone of himself known as 'Mini-Me'. This creature, combining aspects of child, pet and object of desire, rapidly supplants Dr Evil's biological son in his affections and, as an object of the supervillain's 'unnatural' mad-scientist libidinality, functions as a permanent reminder of the obscene underside of power. Mini-Me also exerts a considerable fascination over another of Dr Evil's alter egos, a grotesquely fat-suited and lascivious caricature Scot known as 'Fat Bastard' (also played by Myers) whose refusal to be a mere obedient minion in Dr Evil's plans is manifested both in his exaggeratedly coarse manners and in his recurrent bargaining with the would-be criminal mastermind. His main avowed goal here is to eat Mini-Me in a cannibal version of a suckling-pig roast. In so doing, Fat Bastard manifests a tyrannical *jouissance* apparently lacking in the perverse order of Dr Evil's organisation – a world of technocratic neutrality spiced with neat uniforms, committee meetings and (possibly de-caffeinated) coffee from Starbucks, and thus in danger in the absence of its animating genius of becoming merely... a modestly successful

317

global corporation. Thus, the second film's presents us with the return and revival of Dr Evil and Mini-Me, shaking his enterprise out of its regulated accommodations with global affairs and reminded of its roots in deranged megalomaniacal appetite.[31] In these narratives, the dwarf functions as a guarantee of the intransigent, transgressive persistence of a desire that seeks to incorporate him by the most embarrassing means possible, whether, in the case of Dr Evil, through the discursive kiss (or devouring?) of singing karaoke versions of love songs to him or, in the case of Dr Evil's alter ego, Fat Bastard, eating him.

The question of why tyrants want to eat dwarves thus appears as a version of Jean Baudrillard's reflections on the 'fate' of evil and energy in an increasingly entropic modernity.[32] In a manner seemingly prescient of Baudrillard's reflections on the subject, Chrétien's heroes seem the very embodiment of extraordinary vigour. Much as his poetics aims at condensation rather than unnecessary amplification or repetition, so it follows that characters of small stature can be seen as concentrations rather than truncations. As the narrator points out, Guivret may be small of stature, but every aspect of him bespeaks the furious energy that drives him.[33] This interior world translates out into the great warhorse he rides, the heavy lance and the saddle bow carved with lions. His horse is so entirely expressive of this internal foment that it crushes the pebbles beneath its hooves finer than a mill grinds grain (ll. 3702–06). His entire purpose seems to be to exhaust this fearsome drive:

> [...] veü a devant ses lices
> Un chevalier armé passer
> A cui se vuet d'armes *lasser*,
> Ou il a lui se *lassera*
> Tant que toz recreanz sera. (ll. 3686–90, my emphasis)

> He had seen an armed knight pass in front of his lists and wanted to test his mettle against him until he was exhausted, or until the other had worn himself out and declared himself defeated.

In a seeming exorcism of the troubling same-sex desires haunting the encounter with Galoain. Guivret sees Erec from the window and, once again, one knight is seized with the imperious desire to measure himself against another – a potentially tall order for a dwarf. However, herein lies the key difference between this and the scene between Galoain and Erec: Guivret is secure in his sense of energetic brio whereas Galoain experienced Erec's charismatic energy as a threat or source of anxiety, even when mediated to him by echo and reflection through the objects it touched before reaching him.[34] The fresh, energetic power of Guivret's presence is made apparent in Enide's reaction, as the terrifying 'noise et l'effroi' (l. 3711) of his approach fill her with fear such that she thinks she would faint (ll. 3712–13), her blood runs cold (ll. 3714–15) and her face turns deathly pale (ll. 3716–17). She hesitates greatly, her tongue tied with fear, needing a lengthy conversation with herself before she screws up her courage to speak (ll. 3722–60). Caught between Erec and the approaching devil-on-horseback that is Guivret, Enide thus manifests an extreme of *esfroi*.

Yet for all Guivret appears as the very embodiment of *esfroi* and indeed the evidence of its efficacy, the effect he produces being out of all proportion to his size, the scene is not without its comic dimensions. After all, Chrétien's romance was composed only a few years before the putative date of composition of the episode of the *Roman de Renart* known as 'Le Siège de Maupertuis', in which the numerous kin of Pelé the Rat, murdered by the fox, bring their thunderous complaint to court with a noise that shakes the world (ed. by Dufournet, ll. 2121–2).[35] However, the comic overtones of some part of it, which make Enide's reaction look disproportionate are counterbalanced by the seriousness of the threat he poses. What we are prepared for is a combat where shields and mail are of little protective value and the two fighters hack at each other causing serious injury of a kind we have not seen Erec sustain before. In that sense, there are two possibilities. One is that the scene is misjudged in that it presents Enide in a ridiculous light, especially given her recent experience and the perfunctory narratorial *blah* in which Erec's chastisement of her is reported ('Ele li dit; cil la menace', l. 3761). Another is that the potential comic overtones are indeed present, but the audience is effectively being misdirected to see the risk posed as less than it seems to Enide, who emerges justified given that the wounds Erec carries away from this fight represent the major proportion of the harm done to him. It should also be born in mind that contempt was the attitude of the king's daughter who unwisely assumed Yder's miniature companion was worthy of nothing more. Yet, that said, the spectre of the *Eneas* appears again, albeit in a sublimated form, with Erec the object of Guivret's boundless passion, manifest in the unnatural commotion and furor he makes in the saddle. In that sense, it could be argued that part of Enide's terror at this point may stem from the fact that Guivret's ferocious approach to Erec cuts her out of the strategy of weakening seduction previously used against Galoain. The source of real fear at this point is that such an emphatically hypermasculine approach carries with it an implicit threat to heterosexual relations at court foreshadowed in the picture of Galoain's troubled and turbulent libido. Her fear is thus that of being reduced to a redundant witness of man-on-man action.[36]

The question is how the machine that has been set in train can be safely brought to a halt. The hint is precisely in the energetic motif Chrétien introduces:

> En quatre lieux sont embatues
> Les espees jusqu'as chars nues:
> Forment afeblissent et lassent.
> Se les espees lor durassent
> Ambedeus longuement entieres,
> Ja ne s'en traïssent arrieres,
> Ne la bataille ne fenist
> Tant que l'un morir covenist. (ll. 3795–802)

> In four places their swords struck right into naked flesh. So weak and tired did they grow that. If their swords remained whole much longer, they would not have drawn back and the battle would not have ended until one of them was killed.

Indeed, at no point does there appear to be any prospect of give in the machine, an unbridled destructive engagement reflected in Enide's complete distraction to the point of madness, a show whose pathos would have moved all but the most *fel* (ll. 3803–10). Crucially again, Enide appears as the intermediary frame or internal spectator fundamental to the setting of tone for both internal and external audiences. As with Guivret's approach, Chrétien suggests the audience should take its cue from her reactions – as the key witness to Erec's deeds of prowess – rather than its own impulses.

Conveniently, implacable as the war machine might appear, Chrétien's none too subtle hint announces the forthcoming resolution: the dwarf shatters his sword against Erec's shield (ll. 3822–5), casts the remaining part away in fury (ll. 3827–8), only to find himself defenceless and forced to ask for mercy (ll. 3837–42).[37] Again, the question of authenticity is paramount: Erec compels the disarmed Guivret by threat of further attack – and therefore presumably death – to acknowledge his defeat not merely by admitting Erec has conquered him but also by revealing his name (ll. 3856–69). Crucially, here Erec is apparently prepared to run the risk of being labelled 'fel' and 'fiers' (l. 3838), thus both criminal and discourteous, by showing himself ready to kill an unarmed opponent if the latter will not bow to every detail of his terms. In short, what we reach here is the collapse of the fight as controlled dialogue in the reciprocal fury of the participants marked by their refusal and acceptance of limits. Guivret's breaking and discarding his sword out of 'mautalent' (l. 3828) – a far more spectacular show than Yder's simple surrendering of his weapon (l. 999) – marks the limit of the chivalric value system. The rage that is both a flaw and yet a mark of his sincerity marks him as a worthy opponent. His sheer dynamite fury exceeds the very capacity of physical instruments to mediate it, a convenient paradox that thus simultaneously contains and celebrates his power, marking an absolute limit position that leaves him safely impotent in his heroic potency.[38] The language of the exchange is also defiant, and foregrounds the control that both characters lay claim to over the world around them. In both cases, the protagonists stress the extent of their territories. The terms Guivret uses are particularly interesting:

> 'Je sui de ceste terre rois,
> Mi home lige sont Irois,
> N'i a nul ne soit mes rentiz.
> Et j'ai non Guivrez li Petiz;
> Assez sui riches et poissanz,
> Qu'en ceste terre, de toz sanz,
> N'a baron qui a moi marchisse,

> Qui de mon commandement isse
> Et mon plesir ne face tot.
> Je n'ai voisin qui ne me dot,
> Tant se face orgoillox ne cointes.' (ll. 3861-71)

> 'I am king of this land, and the men who owe me tribute and loyalty are Irish. My name is Guivret the Little. I am rich and powerful in abundance. In every direction there is no baron whose land borders on mine who does not obey me and do exactly as I wish. All my neighbours fear me, no matter how proud they are or how brave.'

What Guivret presents here is a paradigmatic lesson in political authority that is nonetheless not that of an absolutist state. His power over those at a distance, apparent to Enide in the terrifying noise of his horse's hooves, is such that he can dominate 'the Irish', here functioning as an indomitable, quasi-barbaric other.[39] As Fritz points out, the geography of this scene seems somewhat fantastical, in that Erec has clearly not left Britain.[40] However, the relation can cut two ways here: either Guivret is so feared, he can dominate others at the most extreme distance, which is to say a land separated from his territory by the sea, or that the territory he dominates are parts of Wales *controlled* by marauding Irishmen, present here as invading feudal lords in keeping with the narratives of migration and conquest associated with the Scythians, invoked as the nomadic ancestors of the Irish and Scots. Interestingly, Guivret thereby effectively appears as the agent of Tristan, the link between two seemingly separate textual universes. Indeed, Guivret's ongoing war with or domination of the fighting Irish appears as a coda to the questions raised about the relation between Yder and Morholt. This ongoing conflict raises the question of how definitive Tristan's two great successes – first, in the killing of Morholt and second that of the dragon – actually were in the censuring and conjuration of the energetic imbalance that marks them as a tyrannically predatory nation. Another possibility, of course, is that the story of *Erec et Enide* is a parallel fictional reality in which Tristan's conquest never in fact happened, but rather only appears in the manner of a tapestry backdrop.

What then emerges from this is an image of a social order that cannot become a settled diplomatic relation. Guivret appears required to subdue his neighbours through the continuous exercise of terror, even though they yield no quarter and continue to present themselves as aggressive and indomitable to him and to each other. This is a wild frontier that remains fundamentally wild, boiling with turbulent energies and potentially highly flattering as a reflection on the conquering Erec or in the context of Norman expeditions to Ireland, such as Henry's landing at Waterford in 1171.[41] Guivret's strategy is an embodied one: as a dwarf keeping the daily comings and goings in his territory under close, personal surveillance, he appears as a figure of intensive political *micro*-management of the kind practiced very ineffectively by the robber knights. However, in that we are given to understand that, one way or another, the terroristic energy that drives him has communicated itself effectively to a wider audience, his activity has impressive scope and efficiency at a macro level. Indeed, his embodiment can be read another way: that is to say he appears as the paradigmatic example of how the private body of the king both energises and yet is also dwarfed by the power and achievements, the renown that should be expected of him. This quintessential show of force stands is presented as the origin of the economy of renown seen elsewhere in the text. Enide's father may have heard of Erec and have been impressed (ll. 670–1), but people hear Guivret and go out of their minds with fear. In those circumstances, it is understandable that the thing that would cause him to hesistate, thereby eliciting renewed threats from Erec which finally result in him being 'esmaiez' (l. 3853), is the prospect of being incorporated into Erec's household: Guivret's is the energy that would precisely resist domestication. Erec's wording of his request is crucial here:

> Erec respont: 'Quant tu me pries,
> Outreement vuil que tu dies
> Se tu es outrez et conquis.
> Plus ne seras par moi requis,
> Se tu te mez en ma menaie.' (ll. 3843–7)

> Erec replies, 'Since you beseech me, I want you to admit in clear terms whether you are beaten and defeated. [I shall attack you no more /will ask no more of you] if you surrender yourself and become part of my household.'

323

Erec's approach to the dwarf emphasises everything that might have been overshadowed in the latter's egregious, dramatically ecphrastic display of might and will. First of all he acknowledges his request for mercy, but makes its granting conditional on further concessions beyond that. There is a precise technical question here: is Guivret formally admitting defeat in clear and unambiguous terms that will not permit him to renew hostilities? The concern here is not unlike that shown in literary representations of judicial ordeals, where the wording of the oath is of paramount importance in that it can allow the accused – as is the case with Iseut's oath before Mark and Arthur – to weasel their way out of the charges levelled against them. However, the legalistic neutrality barely conceals the assertion of will founded in military might. Guivret is asked to make his admission 'outreement' (l. 3844), which means both as a clarifying supplement to the wording he first offers, but, in a second sense made apparent by the next line, also *as a man defeated* ('outrez', l. 3485). It is understandable then that Guivret would not miss the excessive, *outré* quality of the request, and which Erec, arguably mockingly, presents as but a small concession. This double quality continues with his use of the verb *requerre* (l. 3846), which Fritz renders as 'ask' ('je ne t'en demanderai pas plus'), but which clearly also carries the sense of its many uses in the work so far as 'attack'. This combination of formal *courtoisie* and terroristic aggressivity presents the necessarily double character of diplomatic language, asserting the force that underpins the niceties of discourse in the royal household. The centrality of this event can also be seen from its exceptional nature: previously, Yder was effectively forced to become a hostage of Arthur's court. With Guivret, Erec now demands surrender to him, not to another: thus, where the terms presented to Yder constituted an assertion of values, Erec's treatment of Guivret appears as an assertion of will in which – as is then clear from the speech that follows – he may admit of only Arthur as a superior (ll. 3874–83).

The 'outdoor' part of the business concluded, we move to the domestic scene. Note now that Guivret speaks of a 'recet' (l. 3895) or refuge of the kind sought by one of the robber knights: Guivret's territory appears as a solid military and legal structure in comparison to the unsubstantiated territorialisation characteristic of the outlaw.

Crucially although Guivret's show of largesse is clearly at one level a generous offer of hospitality, also envisages the peripatetic court as an occupying force subordinating the lord who receives it: 'Ja tant n'i voudroiz demorer / Que desor moi ne soiez sire' (ll. 3892–3), the first line not so far removed from a boast that might greet a besieging army, except that the conclusion is rather different. A proud boast it remains, though: neither the material demands of lavish hospitality nor the symbolic concessions made to the victor would diminish or drain Guivret's resources. In response, Erec's response to his offer now appears as a genuinely minor request: rather than accept the challenge to eat Guivret out of house, home and patience, he only asks him to keep an ear out for any news of himself in danger and come with aid as needed ('se [...] / [...] la novele a vos venoit / Que j'eüsse mestier d'ahie', ll. 3903–05). Where Guivret's domination through his terrifying noise was emphasised, now it is to his corresponding capacity to listen to the world's rumour that Erec appeals. The scene of the binding of wounds that follows can be read as a metonymic representation of relations between high-status figures in time of peace. In its language of love, care and private friendship, this scene seems to constrain any propensity towards a 'leakiness' of the chivalric passions through its remodulation from the vision of beauty as object of desire towards its repositioning in a tragic perspective. What should move Guivret to action in future is not desire, whose ends, as with Galoain seem rather harder to tie up in their intensities and flows, but pathos in the contemplation of him as both the vulnerable object he sees before him and the mortal object he may hear of later. This endless passionate aliveness to possible loss thus replaces its eroticised manifestation in the potentially endless pursuit by Galoain and his enflamed entourage. Herein lies the sense of the apparent gratuity Burgess detects in the scene, a sense also reflected in the reference to his 'mautalant' (l. 3828), which Burgess sees as reflective of a flaw in his character.[42] This seems a misreading on two counts. First, Guivret's anger was directed at his broken sword, thus an inanimate object rather than a person. Second, to criticise Guivret on the one hand for his bellicosity and then for 'fear of death' in a joust whose purpose was to test his mettle seems unfair.[43] However, where Burgess may be right is in smelling a disavowed *jouissant* rat in

325

all this free-floating affect. Without proper relations to channel and domesticate them, Guivret's energies are potentially as dangerous as Galoain's, offering a riddle to which we have not yet seen the solution.

Arthurian Camping: Kay's 'Joy-Ride' with Gauvain

> Doctor: I have you in my eye, sir.
> George III: No, I have *you* in my eye.[44]

In a pair of scenes that end with the problem of chivalric libido tied up in more-or-less the right way for now, Erec has escaped one encounter practically unscathed in spite of having being called upon to face down a hundred foes, while Enide has had reason to fear for her future reputation and survival. The potential comic elements of these scenes (Galoain's initial show of vanity, Guivret's stature), juxtaposed with clear and serious threats. All of this has been negotiated at no more than the price of the wounds Erec has received. However, although the introduction of the dwarf might seem a potentially comic signal, we have not yet seen the serious issues raised in Erec's encounters with his two opponents treated in burlesque mode. It is in this spirit now of a holiday from knotty negotiations of the laws of chivalric desire that we come into the encounter with Kay and the court.[45]

In contrast to the strange or frightening passions of the knights Erec has met previously, Kay presents himself in rather more ludic fashion – even if his theft of Gauvain's horse foreshadows his foolhardy determination to be granted the boon of defending the Queen from Meleagant in *Le Chevalier de la charrette*. Yet for now, Kay appears as nothing more harmful than a cheery buffoon – a clown version of Richard II's champion, John Dymmock – who cannot help galloping off on Gauvain's fiery, feisty mount, 'le gringalet', waiting saddled and bridled in front of the court. Although effectively opportunistic theft, there seems something jockishly harmless in Kay's actions. The terms used indicating throughout a light-hearted play with the proprieties of court life: Kay explicitly acts out of high spirits ('por envoiseüre' l. 3956). In cheeky echo of the concerns of Gauvain or Arthur with good order at court, he pauses to see if his actions elicit any *contredit* from a non-existent gallery ('Prist le cheval et monta sus, / C'onques ne li contredist nuns', ll. 3957–8). What is signalled through this opening is a scene in which serious considerations will be temporarily suspended in a sort of Arthurian carnavalesque. Of course, thanks to Jeffrey Cohen, it is impossible not to read this scene without wondering about the nature of its libidinal investments: Kay borrows Gauvain's horse and rides off in what Isidore of Seville would describe as *great high spirits*. Nykrog for one sees the scene as clearly humorous, with Kay, seemingly envious of the status of other knights at court, here the butt of Chrétien's jokes.[46] A further dramatic irony appears in this scene's burlesque of the encounter with Guivret: Kay is in a sense 'dwarfed' by his place in Gauvain's shadow, the lesser courtier then appropriating a place in Gauvain's saddle much to his own delight. In that sense, after Eneas, Kay rides after (or behind) Gauvain.

Given Chrétien's earlier nods to questions of equine temperament and sexuality, one might well wonder what is going on in the seneschal's appropriation of another man's widely-admired means of bestial movement.[47] Indeed, there is a sense that perhaps Kay – not as smart or anxious a soul as Jean-Paul Sartre, the latter famously troubled by the idea of being caught in embarrassingly voyeuristic, possibly masturbatory situations – does not understand the nature of the encounter between himself and our favourite law-abiding couple. After all, we are not so far here from the world of *Berangier au long cul*, in which a man is shamed when he is caught by his wife beating his own equipment in the forest.[48] 'Doing a bit of a Gauvain' – we might wonder which bit – , Kay seems to have gone a step further and is performing the same trick with someone else's. No wonder Enide is as amused as Philippe Pot catching Philip 'at it'. There also seems to be something of a rehabilitation of *avoir* in this scene as well, although, as Shakespeare's King Lear comments, 'Our basest beggars are in the poorest things superfluous' (act 2 scene 4): mere possession is a trifle compared to the questions of respect and status bound up with being, which is why this scene is a joke. Erec recognises 'le seneschal / et les armes et le cheval' (ll. 3965–6), Chrétien's run over onto the next line possibly indicating an amused recognition that this 'conjunture' does not actually go together.[49]

The playfulness is rendered all the more touching by Enide's gesture, covering her face 'as if to guard from the heat and dust' (l. 3977), but in fact out of the impishness of 'grant voidie' (l. 3973), a cunning less to do with the high-risk self-preservatory savvy she has shown before now and will again than with her spontaneous joining in with a shared joke. The minimal signal that this apparent terror of the forest is no more than a sham, comes from her. Erec and she may not be seeing eye-to-eye at the moment, but this does not mean that they do not share a common insider culture, combining understanding of the structuring propriety of ritual with a knowledge of the excess over the system founded in the exceptional status of key personalities (the King, the Court Idiot...) into a ludic embroidering of the legible practices of court life. Indeed, the clear sense of this scene here is of Erec and Enide re-enacting the encounter in the forest between the Queen's party and Yder's. Minus the dwarf of course, but that role can always be filled by Kay, whose *fanfaron* pretensions to glory and status always trip him up. Such discreet gestures and observations frame a scene that then functions as confirmation of much of the queering play that has gone before: Kay wishes to imitate or be 'after' Gauvain. In that sense, Gauvain – object of a seemingly more than potentially queerable homosocial admiration – finds himself problematically (although for now absently) caught as middle term in the relation of Kay mounted on le Gringalet. The scene thus appears as the ludic apogee of the sequence of allusions to the perverse Enean triangle. It is not the last version of this scene we will see, however.

Just as the maiden chose to proceed by the risky road of force, so the seneschal seizes Erec's reins without prior warning or greeting (l. 3981), and thus laying claim to a victory he has not earned in such a breaking of the rules that could only be permitted in a court fool or someone singularly favoured (in various senses – the priapic imagery often associated with jesters and their kin is clearly a mark of their pseudo-precedence). These are the sorts of faux pas that can only be accommodated at the price of violence... or humour. And indeed, the exchange proceeds between the two parties (with Enide quietly off at the side playing the role of Aloof Maiden) continues with Erec again in an ostensibly straight role: whatever nods we receive concerning Enide's actions, there are no narratorial cues that her husband is treating this encounter as a joke, his poker face uncrackable. Yet, as with his remarks to Yder, there is a code here. While he responds to Kay's taunts like-for-like (as is apparent from the echoing uses of 'fox' (l. 3986) and 'folie' (l. 4011; l. 4023)), he also acknowledges the Seneschal's fair speaking and hospitality ('Vos dites bien' l. 4005). However, Erec's assertion of outraged surprise – 'touz seürs estre cuidoie, / Vers vos de rien ne me gardoie' (ll. 4027–8) – is clearly starting to smack of tongue-in-cheek pantomime collusion. Impetuous, stationed out front and sufficiently unaware of manners and convention to avoid a conflict, Kay, appears as the perfect 'fall-guy' here. However, we are perhaps invited to wonder whether Erec could even have been retained at all without the promise of some sort of violent encounter, real or ludic.

The second stage in the encounter is Gauvain, who engages in what appears as downright deception, causing Erec to waver from his path. What could not be managed by the forceful (but non-serious) seizing of Erec's reins can be 'euphemised' in another way in order to make its actual effect possible. In that sense, this part of the scene renews the interrogation of legible and non-legible practice in court ritual. Besides, in effect it is a matter of the nature of his mission that Erec has to be tricked. The sincerity of his quest is indeed guaranteed by the fact that it cannot be stopped in any other way. Where Gauvain had apparently failed with Arthur, here he is given to suceed most elegantly. Never did anyone profit so much from the apparent theft of their horse. Of course this use of trickery as a means of providing limits for chivalric activity was already apparent in the preceding episode's trick of fate. The accumulation of terms relating to joy in this part of the episode are in a way the main meal for which the encounter with Kay was the appetiser, in French the *amuse-gueule*. Indeed, this general sense of amusement is then amplified through the adroit and elegant manipulation of ritual to produce the most satisfying result. Just as Erec gave virtually no hint of his true intentions to Kay and seemingly lied in his protest that the seneschal had caught him unawares, so we are invited to take his protestations to Gauvain as apparently sincere. In effect, the more he protests, the more we may be required to understand his words as coded praise of Gauvain for following the hint he offered earlier: send someone who can make this look like a trick. In effect, this is the ludic echo of Enide's instruction to the Count: 'take me by force' ('Si me fetes a force prendre' l. 3385). There the suggestion was that Galoain satisfy Enide's will by contriving the appearance of her abduction through the extreme theatricality of the murder of her husband and, potentially, the act of rape that would be the negation of any future protest on her part if the game went wrong. In such a scenario, there would have been no 'safety word' to put the brakes on sadistic *jouissance*.

Thus, on a superficial level, Gauvain's overtures to Enide are potentially suspect in the manner of Galoain's, but show neither the mark or source of the passionate deregulation of 'esfroi'. However, the difference here lies in the knowledge of personality. Where Galoain's echo of Tereüs's minimal conformity to the formality of moral norms gave us the picture of a classic divorce between seeming and substance, our knowledge of Gauvain brings us back into a world where the play of signs operates against a reassuring backdrop of trust. Not every conversation involving either illusion and trickery or the appearance of breaking with the conventions of polite conversation has to be as stressfully crucial as either Erec's negotiations with Enide's father or Enide's deception of Galoain. This does not imply that the encounter with Keu was entirely nugatory, of course: the seneschal's obtrusive 'felenie' answers Enide's 'voidie', guaranteeing that this was something more complex and entertaining than a simple mock joust.

On the other hand, for all the appearance of genteel amusement, for all the absence of the 'esfroi' of genuine strife, for all the ludic re-echoing of what twistings and subcurrents of desire Erec might have missed or ignored in the forest, a spectral Real haunts the scene in the presence of the mortal drive wracking Erec's shattered body, driving his great horseback adventure and sowing confusion in the order that subtends the elegant ambiguities of court performance. Here, Erec's determination appears as an excess, the use of Morgane's magical salve to treat him indicating the inhuman exorbitance of his motion, its foreshadowing of more catastrophic destruction and loss to come. This sense is all the more powerful for the fact it is initially denied: Gauvain says he would have wept on seeing Erec but for the fact he was so overjoyed to see him (ll. 4178–82).[50] Most importantly, we have further 'reaction shots' of Arthur, sighing deeply (l. 4212), shaking his head (l. 4241) and showing concern, both through his choice of foods for the evening feast (ll. 4256–64) and through his orders that Erec be put to bed separately (ll. 4266–8). Against these wills, Erec's however remains emphatic, restated through a sequence of careful positioned, courteous but insistently worded speeches, on his arrival at Arthur's tent (ll. 4234–40), following the King's attempt to persuade him to stay at court (ll. 4250–2) and again on departure (ll. 4293–5). Beginning, middle and end. What had thus been silently dissimulated as the subtext of all subtexts in the various exchanges is Erec's perilous condition. In spite of this, the joy of the court persists in uneasy mix with their 'esfroi' regarding Erec's condition. In that sense, Erec has mastered the emotional dynamic that seemed to have got out of joint at his own court: where the mood of that court appeared as an unstable bipolarity, lurching between giddy celebration and sour ingratitude, here two contradictory states, joy and grief coexist in the same moment. Of course, sustaining the power of that pathos and delight is a mortal business that can only be prolonged by the unnatural magical means of Morgane's precious unguent (ll. 4213–24).

In the film, *The Madness of King George*, we are presented with a vision of the King's body and the body politic apparently out of order and temper. However, there is a potential for misrecognition here. The King's condition is manifest both in his apparent insanity and also in the discoloration of his urine, which turns purple. Therein lies the sense of the symptom: for all that the quintessential sign of porphyria, the *purpleness* that gives the condition its name, is the mark of the disease, it is also at the same time the mark of his royal condition. George is so through-and-through a King he pisses royal purple. In that sense, what the film affirms is not so much a restoration of the monarchy as the passing of certain styles of royal government: George's concluding comments on the future of English kingship are ambiguous, poised between progressive accommodation of the changing *Zeitgeist* and coded assertion of continuing absolutism. Most notably, George brusquely dismisses the doctor who had so often found himself at loggerheads with the royal will. As in the film, so in the romance, we have the question of the regulation and rational accommodation of the King's passions remaining a matter of uncertainty and trust in a political economy where the King's condition must remain defiantly pathological and excessive, forcing the court to constantly run to catch up with the king or displace itself to encompass him.[51] Once again, we are drawn back to the image of the Holbein skull, the motion of the court forced to describe a path on which it contemplates and reflects on its relation to an object where there is no 'right' perspective.

Getting Medieval on his *roncin*: Cadoc of Tabriol

BUTCH: What now? So, are we cool?
MARSELLUS: What now? Well, let me tell you what now. I'm gonna call a coupl'a pipe-hittin' niggers who'll go to work on the homes here with a pair of pliers and a blowtorch. [to Zed] Hear me talkin' boy? I ain't through with you by a damn sight. I'm gonna get medieval on your ass.
BUTCH: I mean what now between me and you?
MARSELLUS: Oh, *that* 'What now?'. Well, let me tell you what now between me an' you. There is no me and you. Not no more.
BUTCH: So we're cool?
MARSELLUS: Yeah, man, we're cool. Two things I ask: don't tell nobody about this. This shit's between me and you and the soon-to-be-livin'-the-rest-of-his-short-ass-life-in-agonising-pain Mr Rapist here. It ain't nobody else's business. Two: leave town. Tonight. Right now. And when you're gone, you stay gone. Your LA privileges are used up. Deal?
BUTCH: Deal.
The two men shake hands, then hug one another.[52]

The sodomitical violence in this scene is different from any other violence in the film and it calls for a different remedy: it is ritualised sexual torture, it is dark and perverse and it must be met by a personal vengeance that is itself ritualised, torturous, dark and perverse.[53]

The above scene from Quentin Tarantino's *Pulp Fiction* contains one of its most frequently cited lines, the cultural afterlife of which attracted the attention of medievalists, notably Carolyn Dinshaw.[54] What Dinshaw highlights is the extent to which the scene's seeming assertion of straight sexual identity – founded in the violent punishment of 'deviants' who dare act out in literal form what the film's hypermasculine heroes, notably Butch, only touch on in either jest or insult – is queered by its compulsive fascination with anal-sadistic interactions running the gamut from pain to pleasure.[55] Moreover, that transgressive pleasure has then to be demarcated from the violence the characters in such a hypervirilist, 'hard-boiled' universe regularly inflict on one another, 'perverse' sadism distinguished from the things 'a man's gotta do'.[56] As Dinshaw points out, the conclusion of Tarantino's film, tying together the interlaced, crosscut narrative strands, shows Butch and his French *amie*, Fabian, 'roaring away on the Harley owned by the homo whose medieval torture is being planned – white hypermasculine Butch, drawing on the sexually powerful look of a macho gay man, but whose ass, we know for sure now, is straight, male, modern'.[57] Were this scene to 'get medieval', Butch's assertion of his masculinity would see him mounted as a knight on a *destrier*, rather than some lesser mount, whether palfrey or pack-horse, as indeed Erec is still having left Arthur's camp, where he encountered Kay mounted on his ill-gotten medieval equivalent of not merely some standard-range Harley-Davidson, but indeed a hot-rod, 'custom shop' version in the form of Gauvain's horse, Le Gringalet. From there, we move to a scene featuring another 'inappropriate' pairing of horse and man in the form of Cadoc of Tabriol mounted on a sumpter nag ('roncin') and being led away by two giants clearly about to 'get medieval' on him.

From the pathos of Erec's encounter with the court, where Erec's unsparingness of himself appears as a lack of a certain sympathy with the position of the moved and concerned Arthur, we move out again into the forest and into scenes in which Erec will be moved by the plight of others. Obviously, this is the first time we have heard an actual distress call (ll. 4304–10), which in effect opens the space to multiple re-experiences, multiple 'reaction shots' of the same situation: we hear the scream, we hear the maiden's account (ll. 4334–

333

51) and then we see Erec see Cadoc being led shamefully naked, tied bare-back to a horse (ll. 4379–98).[58] Cadoc's position is a spectacle of pathos, but, given the encounters we have already seen, the spectacle of a naked torture victim in a forest seems to offer a summary of some of the encounters already witnessed in which there was something either disturbingly or ridiculously 'naked' about the nature of the desires of characters such as Galoain and Kay. Thus, having encountered two unusual libidinal organisations in the forest, first Galoain and then Kay, we move into a scene in which men are once again surprised doing something shameful that reflects back on the construction of chivalric masculinity. Of course, part of the answer here is that he is opposing the rule of law to the rule of force. The emphasis on will is apparent in the formal use of language right through this scene. Erec challenges the giants much more explicitly and in due legal form than any of his previous opponents (ll. 4401–12). Where we might have expected to see him attack on the basis that these creatures are clearly cruel monsters, he first makes legal objection to their behaviour based on the evidence he sees before him. Rather than simply rushing into action (a restraint Allard sees him as having learned from the example of Guivret's rash aggressivity), he explains to them his perception of the facts of the case.[59] Unexpectedly, although brusque in manner, the giants frame their answer in similarly legal terms (ll. 4413–16). Their response is in effect a targeting of Erec's perception of the nature of the judicial spectacle they have created where Cadoc is treated 'as a thief' ('comme larron', l. 4403). Cadoc is an 'outlaw' of the law of their land, but this does not mean he can be claimed by any other version of the law that happens along, the giants arguing that Erec's concerns overstep legal bounds into a terrain over which, as far as their will is concerned, Erec has no jurisdiction: 'A vos que tient?' (l. 4413). This is the vision of a land before the advent of a universalist 'Age of Chivalry', a land that still belongs to giants. However, given that the scene is staged 'after Arthur' – in that it follows on from his foundational gestures of decapitation and symbolic tyrannicide – , it can also be seen as positing the intrusion into the present of an 'old law', a space of differing temporality that is the inverted image of the medieval present's intrusion into the barbaric past as narrated in *Philomena*.

The importance of this scene lies in Chrétien's continuing exploration of the libidinal foundation common to will, desire and Law. As with other entries, spectators not privy to the entire story struggle to understand a disturbing spectacle. In this scene, jurisdictions questionable and certain shadow the scene: as Per Nykrog comments, the giants appear as demonic figures seizing a man's soul.[60] Do they have some sort of claim over him? After all, in saints' lives and chansons de geste, only the guilty are given up to diabolical torment. Against this, Chrétien paints a less assured picture: in *Le Chevalier de la charrette*, Lancelot will be asked to take the life of a defeated opponent on the mere assurance that he has merited such a fate (ll. 2779–939), while Erec's far future in the prose tradition paints him as massacrer of his own innocent sister, compelled not by the assertion of her guilt but by a casual promise. Such scenes are thus part of romance's interrogation of the chivalric code as manifestation of the Law, an investigation of an obscene underside dissimulated in other genres. In that regard, what this scene reveals is the contradictory nature of trouble, an alternation between play and intransigence made apparent in Erec's encounter first with Kay and then the court, Erec ultimately unmoved by Arthur's attempts to persuade him to remain for his own sake. In that sense, the previous scene unveils the truth hidden in Erec's departure from Carnant: the object of his demonstrations was not Enide, the robber knights or anyone else but Erec as tyrant over himself. From there, however, we now move into an episode in which the Law of will is queeringly affirmed through the spectacle of gigantist sadism.

However, to say that giants occupy a space 'before' the Law is not to say that the libidinal life of their power is entirely deregulated. Rather, the giants are the incarnation of the perverse neutrality of the Law insofar as it applies to the notion of consent. What we have seen in Chrétien's narrative so far is that not only is there no encounter without some element of violence or grievance, but, moreover, 'there is no consensual encounter'. That is to say that individual subjectivities remain 'without immixture' at the level of will. This separateness will be particularly important for my reading of the Augustinian poetics of Enide's contemplation of suicide and then her attempt to provoke the irrational and wilful Oringle.

Foreshadowing Enide's later flirtations with the pathos inherent in the performance of martyrdom, the vision of Cadoc bound to a horse and scourged reflects scenes of hagiographical torture, such as those of St Margaret or St George, the victims seated astride wooden horses ('cheval-fust'), blades or sharp planks, not uncommonly with weights tied to their feet.[61] As Sarah Kay comments, such scenes have a clear sexual dimension, albeit closeted, that would tend to suggest a sexual dimension to Cadoc's abduction. However, Chrétien's extensive flirtation with horsemanship as a metaphor for sexually perverse acts and his accumulated nods to traditions of sexual slander 'outs' that aspect in a way that the scene that follows will confirm, just supposing we missed the point here. Indeed, the lurid erotic investment becomes a sort of textual over-performance, a hypermimesis that not merely opens the door on the sado-masochistic hagiographical closet, but, through its braiding with the Eneas, unveils the fundamentally sadistic character of the original sodomitical triangle described by Lavine's mother (not to mention the hag's own disavowed enjoyment in elaborating it). In its viciously sadistic parody of the earlier scene of the encounter between Erec, the Queen, the maiden and the two horses, it furthermore also exposes the perverse libidinal underside of the courtly scenario. The ghost of the *Roman d'Eneas* returns here once more, with the giants as the monstrous, sadistic exaggeration of the sodomitical triangle outlined by Lavine's mother, with Cadoc occupying the position of her daughter and the giants as the figure of Eneas and his male partner, presented in an interchangeable sameness. The indifference of the giants to the claims of law is then partly the mark of their status as the antecedent occupants of the land before the institution of the laws of chivalry, but also that of the sadist to 'tout le reste', a position most apparent in that of Cadoc's *amie*, reduced to the status of remainder, irrelevant except as reminscence of the 'original' Enean tableau.

In that regard, Cadoc's fate can be read as a reflection of the role of sexual violence in intercultural conflict. In his body, chivalric modernity is made gigantism's 'bitch'. Indeed, part of the mechanism for this can be seen to work through the dual generic resonances of the scene. With his flesh opened down to the bone (ll. 4389–90) in an obscene gash through which both tormentors work their pleasure on their chosen victim, Cadoc speaks of the life being 'ravished from his body' ('la vie / Qui ja me fust dou cors ravie', ll. 4481–2). Such a remark connects this episode with a number of tales that associate giant abduction with sexual violence towards women, as seen not only in Geoffrey of Monmouth but also in *Le Chevalier au lion* in which the giant Harpin, having already humiliated the father by killing two of his sons in front of him – an impotence that strikes at the cohesion of the family group – now threatens to give the castellan's daughter to his followers (*Le Chevalier au lion*, ll. 3866–71).[62]

How is Cadoc like Helena? Given the context of Arthur's career, we are invited to suppose that the next step will be – either actually or symbolically – the sadistic, bare-back gang rape of Cadoc, split and torn apart like Hoel's daughter. However, where Geoffrey has Helena simply die of fright, Wace subjects both her and the audience to the gruesome, pornographic excess of her crushing.[63] Chrétien seems to be implying that the possible narration of Cadoc's fate may go further still in pushing back the bounds of decency. Moreover, as with Enide's silence on her wedding night, Helena is not given to speak, thereby eliminating any possibility that her words might betray any shaming and denied enjoyment of the kind Augustine suspected was the true reason for Lucretia's suicide.[64] By contrast, Cadoc's words carry the possible double sense of pain and of *jouissance* pushed to its very limits. Such a tricksy extortion of an involuntary avowal is then the precise point of the giants' war on chivalry's self-disciplining renunciations in its aim to produce a culturally accommodatable and regulated version of the hyper-masculine. Thus, the description of Cadoc's humiliation points to another form of unmanning, namely criminal status, a point Erec repeats in his challenge (l. 4403, l. 4406). For the giants, Cadoc's 'outlawing' transforms him into the medieval equivalent of the abject creature known in British prison slang as a *nonce*, the unmanned target of a revenging assertion against the Law taking the form of a hypocritically obscene caricature of law, and indeed the scapegoat whose maltreatment marks what Žižek would term 'a holiday from the Law'.[65] However, Žižek's comments here deal with mere humans rather than the perverse designs of monsters, designs which might well have wider implications. It can be argued that in the history Chrétien elaborates what the giants attempt is to

337

undo the shift marked by Arthur's affirmation and conclusion of the project of expropriation that begins with the arrival of Brutus. As we saw with *Philomena* and his lyric poetry, Chrétien's history both of culture and desire is of something fragmented and multi-locational, a continuum in which any seemingly univocal sense of direction is always open to undoing. If one version of the March of History is encapsulated in the Dadaist dictum, *ceci tuera cela*, then *cela* is back, and in Arthur's lifetime. In its potentially cataclysmic implications for chivalry's attempt to ally itself with the regulatory force of the Law, the giants' intentions are both *unseeable* in their shaming, debasing intent and *unthinkable* for the unsettling ambiguities they open up. Thus it is that Erec's strike at them – in both cases attacking the head (ll. 4440–3 and ll. 4464–5) – targets precisely the question of a knowledge he wishes to and indeed must not simply deny but consign to the beyond of the limit of death. As Maximilien Robespierre was to comment later on the rights and wrongs of trying Louis, 'we do not execute kings: we drop them back into the void'.[66] So here it is with giants.

Contemporary awareness that Chrétien's scene is emblematic of a larger collective and historical conflict can be seen in the illuminations associated with the scene in fonds fr. 24403 (fol. 155): here the illuminator shows not simply Erec but a group of *five* knights attacking two giants clad in armour and armed with clubs. In its relation to the episode in Chrétien's romance, it is as if the larger group of robber knights decided to spare Erec the trouble and take care of these creatures who give ordinary, decent criminals a bad name. However, although the composition thereby appears a misreading of Chrétien's text, it also echoes illuminations associated with the other texts in the collection, notably the illustration at fol. 47, which shows the giant Robastre, clad in chainmail and wielding a club, helping Garin in a battle with his enemy, Gaufroi. In presenting the giants as wearing armour, the illustrator of fonds fr. 24403 does not entirely fly in the face of artistic convention: other codices show giants armoured like humans, only larger.[67] In that regard, what we have is a sort of inverted history: whereas humanised giants fight alongside knights against other knights in *Garin de Monglane*, *Erec et Enide* asserts what seems like a more 'proper' historical order: knights vs. giants. However, the co-existence of the two illustrations in the same codex relativises what might seem as the Arthurian narrative of giant-slaying's counterpointing of the larger narrative of *translatio imperii*, suggesting that, as in the epic of revolt and elsewhere, old enemies can find themselves fighting side-by-side. Against this, textual descriptions of giants in works such as Geoffrey's *History of the Kings of Britain* or Wace's *Brut* make much of their monstrous and unkempt appearance, clad in coarse clothing, dirty and, in the case of the giant of Mont-Saint-Michel, smeared with blood. Nor are there any human figures in such a state in fonds fr. 24403 which has no figure identifiable with Cadoc visible in the illumination. In emphasising the chivalric appearance of the giants, the illuminator uses the hypermasculinist epic flavour of the codex to play down or disavow the inhumanity of their designs.

Although there is evidence to suggest illuminators sought to clear up Chrétien's scene, this is not simply amount to them betraying their author through their visual translations. Indeed, it can be argued the illuminator takes his cue from Erec's behaviour, in itself a policing akin to the reassertion of virile solidarity in the silencing of the scandalous history of the sodomitic attack perpetrated on Marsellus in *Pulp Fiction*. Having killed the giants, Erec looses Cadoc's bonds, dresses him and remounts him on his horse (ll. 4472–5). Cadoc shows himself abjectly, effusively grateful in a speech in which he addresses his saviour as *tu* throughout (ll. 4477–90). The sense that a line has perhaps been crossed here is apparent from Erec's *vos*-form response, in which he refuses both Cadoc's discursive intimacy and his offer of service, declaring instead he will restore him to his 'amie' (ll. 4494–507). Cadoc, perhaps somewhat rebuffed and resuming the guise of polite court formality once more, answers Erec as *vos* in his second speech (ll. 4508–17). However, Erec's comment is perhaps not as extreme as the translations of 'Amis, vostre servise / Ne vuil je pas ainsi avoir.' (ll. 4494–5) given in Fritz's edition ('Je n'ai que faire de votre service'), or Carroll's version ('Friend, I do not want service from you.') would make it appear. What initially appears as a dusty rejection is in fact an opening gambit to Erec's instruction that Cadoc should find Arthur and present himself at court (ll. 4518–39). The key here is the 'ainsi', the force of which has to be taken as 'as you offer it

339

in these terms'. Likewise, his refusal to reveal his name is reinforced by a seemingly blunt insistence that Cadoc desist from further questioning ('ja plus n'en parlez', l. 4519), an interdiction that mirrors both his earlier command to Enide and Arthur's refusal to Gauvain. Again, the key follows in his teasing follow-up to his initial curiosity-sparking 'ainsi': 'but if you want to find out...' ('Mais se vos savoir le volez', l. 4520). In that sense, the combat with its prior negotiation was prelude to this discussion: Erec engages in polite, formal discussion with the giants so that he can be rude to the knight, refusing his service as he offers it and withholding his name from him. In a sense, Erec answers to Cadoc mirror the absolutist language of the giants, except that where the giants' use of legal formulae offered no room for negotiation whereas Erec's apparently uncourtly refusal tantalisingly reveals a way forward.

Thus, Erec refuses Cadoc's offering of submission to him as 'his man' and instead emphasises the reciprocal nature of the service Cadoc can perform for him by going to Arthur's camp and publicly proclaiming his account of events in the forest. There will be nothing here that remains in the S&M closet. Given that Chrétien's work elsewhere places great emphasis on the excessive and tyrannical nature of the law of love, of the necessity of subjection, it is perhaps surprising that at this point we should have a return to the feudal values of reciprocity he positions as the 'before' of the interpellative power of *amour courtois*. However, herein we can see evidence of Chrétien's policing of the potentially problematic language of virile subjection to a perversely sadistic will. Love may get medieval on your ass, packhorse, palfrey or steed, but there are limits beyond which Chrétien is apparently reluctant to go.

It is this affirmation of masculine integrity that explains the role of conflict and non-satisfaction in Erec's negotiations with the rescued knight. Cadoc's case raises the problem of the ritual uncleanness of the sexually transgressing and transgressed, the handling of which was regulated in medieval law regarding acts of sexual violence or other culturally taboo contact, whether rape, bestiality or sodomy.[68] However, Cadoc's status is made problematic by the fact that his position was neither deserved or desired, even if at some level a 'yes' was extorted or posited by the positioning of this scene as a sadistic burlesque and unmasking of courtly mores. Thus, Erec's almost entirely unexplained refusal of Cadoc's offer of service constitutes a degree zero in the cultural prophylaxis providing limits in negotiations between men. Moreover, although Cadoc seems in no state to offer anything useful, the emphasis on his power to help Erec curatively emphasises his status as Subject. The same applies to the maiden who initially approached Erec, offering herself to him as his 'ancele' (ll. 4361–5) in return to for his aid. There are terms here that may promise too much for comfort on both parts, and it is therefore of capital importance that the solution to Erec's intransigence is one that has to be elaborated in common between Cadoc and his *amie*. However, there is still a slight subversion of gender roles in that it is the maid who frames the offers made in the central part of these negotiations:

> Cele respont par grant savoir:
> 'Sire, bien nos devez avoir
> Andeus conquis, et moi et lui;
> Vostre devons estre ambedui
> Por vos servir et honorer.
> Mais qui porroit guierredoner
> Ceste deserte neis demie?' (ll. 4557–63)

> She answered him very wisely: 'My lord, you have conquered us both, myself and him. Our duty can only now be to serve and honour you. But who could repay even half of what you have done for us?'

Again, as in Erec's father's reception of the happy couple, we have an emphasis on symmetry. Why is this a response 'par grant savoir'? In part because she understands the nature of the gift made to both of them, a gift of which any given individual could only repay half in a way that indicated *thus far and no further*. This sense of formal limit is also apparent in Erec's argument to her that, his service having been to her in the main, she should recognise her own equal part in the situation. These niceties may well reflect a determination to turn a blind eye to some of the potentially disquieting resonances: with the grotesque sexualised attack on Cadoc forming the apogee in a sequence of variations on the Enean threesome, the woman is relegated to horrified spectator, her cries appearing as the most extreme version of the noise Enide may or may not have made on her wedding night. What we are invited to consider however is that such is the debasement to which the system of chivalric masculinity and its various metaphors (love, service) has been subjected that what need to be asserted at this point are the limits and boundaries that shape that society. The eyes must remain 'wide shut' to the grotesque sadistic interrogation of chivalric sexuality. Of course, if Erec had been asked whether he had noted any of these queering undercurrents, we would almost certainly have to content ourselves with the answer that he had never seen or thought a thing, that the rescue was in that sense simply a gratuitous act.[69] Yet at the same time its vision is of something beyond the limits of what can be contemplated. Offering what seems the final, most apocalyptic replay of the *Eneas* scenario and placed the other side of the encounter with the court groups, the three preceding encounters now emerge in retrospect clustered together as a series of episodes libidinally haunted by the obscenity of a scenario that presents the Arthurian world with the sum of all its fears and disavowed enjoyments. However, this does not mean that the full implications of Erec's encounter with the giants are spelt out even here. Rather – as we will see later – that element of textual *jouissance* is perversely deferred.

Crucially, Erec's treatment of Cadoc after his rescue emphasises a hygienic protocol deployed against the potential troubling sexual subtexts in the language of courtly service reactivated by the traumatic scene and which must now be silenced once more. This moment brings us back to Geertz's account 'of cocks and men' mentioned at the opening of the chapter. As Kathleen Biddick comments:

> The rhetoric of the concluding section of Geertz's 'Deep Play' restores good homosocial order. Geertz writes of *ethnography* as 'penetrating a literary text' [p. 448]. It says 'something of something'. He insists that the saying something of something should be said to *somebody* [p. 453], but he never broaches the question of who that somebody might be, whether he or she would give permission to be penetrated, and where. Where would such conversation occur, who would participate and how would the participants wish to embody a conarration?[70]

Although Chrétien's account of the encounter between Erec and the giants ostensibly seeks to drop their sadistic tyranny 'back into the void', through revisiting the founding Arthurian tableau of giant-slaying it also questions the construction of otherness that scene inaugurates in its underlying assertion that what defines humanity is that it sees no *jouissance* in giants penetrating people. In that regard, Arthur's giant-killing founds and articulates an ethnography – a 'what we do and why we are here' – that emphatically displaces and relegates the giant to the wild frontier. Indeed, it is at precisely this point that the Arthurian project highlights what is at stake in ethnography: not the history of 'peoples' (i.e. the ethnographer's others), but of 'The People' qua self, the construction and writing of the history of the centre. However, at this point, one might cite Biddick's sardonic presentation of Geertz's ethnographic construction:

> Conventions of the hypermasculine genre work to contain its intense homoerotic charge safely within the orbit of the homosocial. Closeted as such, the convention can then mobilise the sexuality of power to 'fix' its mobility – cocks in the centre, women, children and unfit men to the margins.[71]

In the same way, Erec seeks to put a certain vision of masculinity back in the centre of the chivalric world view by refusing any conarrative possibility that through Cadoc's experience of the gigantist 'script' written on his receiving body, courtly deference can become the mark of an 'unfit man', indeed to affirm that there was never even a ghost of a chance that the cocks – or, here, horses – left that centre. After all, Erec's careful handling of the interaction with both Cadoc and his *amie* afterwards can be see as an attempt to police the way in which the discourse of courtly service might appear thereafter as a 'conarration' between penetrating and receiving participants, its 'embodiment' not any regulated becoming-animal hybrid of horse and man in the form of an idealised chivalry but rather some perversely polymorphous, three-way human-animal-monster 'sport' (the term used to translate Alan of Lille's 'jocus' – 'hybrid' / 'joke'). In that sense, the conditions of 'saying something of something […] to somebody' in the form of a renarration at court of what Erec did appear strictly limited. To revisit the script of the Arthurian hypermasculinist gesture is to open the door to trouble whether Erec wills it or not.

If Erec's quest began with a savage assertion of royal authority that does not recognise bounds or limits (the distinction between the field of combat and refuge, or that between voluntary and involuntary act), then the episodes that follow point to further blurring of boundaries in the different cultures and communities with which, through his Enean riding of Enide, he enters into contact. In that sense, just as the seemingly invisible facial wound was the mark of a *laidure* that brought him into negotiation with the ugly history of Laluth, it is here the ugly ghost of an insistent, sadistic *jouissance* that proves troubling to the worlds through which he passes, interrogating Lucan's vision of the knowledge of proper measure of the law ('nosse modum juris'), and finding that the space of desire before the Law is a more anxiously murky picture than the stark vision of republican Stoics might suggest. What those limits are will soon be subjected to further, far more intense testing as both characters look beyond the limits of their own lives. Death is often presented as polite, but that does not mean there is any refusing his invitation. Likewise, what the sequence of scenes in this part of the quest problematises is the question of the 'yes' to fantasy, the problem of limit and refusal, the question of what gifts and invitations can and cannot be refused and of whether – as Jacques Derrida remarks – an invitation or gift that does not admit of the possibility of refusal or countergift is not genuinely an invitation. Indeed, as Žižek observes, cases such as Haneke's *Piano Teacher* emphasise that the subject may well recoil in horror when the manifestation of fantasy breaches the fantasy frame and enters the world.[72] Against this, feminist concerns regarding Lacanian fantasy's *fatalité* rightly identify the potential for an abusive and coercive victimisation through tropes such as Freud's exploration of Dora's disavowed or unwitting complicity. But then, the risk attaching to *jouissance* is that, as the beyond of pleasure and its accommodations, the Law does not seem to distinguish between desire's prayer and the destructive opening of the self to absolute destitution and abjection as the support of the Other's enjoyment. This is perhaps one of the senses of Lacan's phrase 'le sadique ne voit que *tout le reste*', that the sadistic regard of the Law is blind to distinctions regarding who gets whose *jouissance*. In response to this, as Erec's refusals, silences and insistences make plain, sometimes the Subject may also, for his part, have to appear a bit blind. The problem here is precisely that hightlighted by Simon Gaunt: in effect the entire Arthurian tradition seems to collapse into perversely ludic hilarity, with texts like *Le Chevalier de la charrette* and *Le Chevalier à l'épée* full of jokes at the expense of their heroes. Gauvain in particular is ridiculed through his participation in scenes of a kind he never heard of or imagined: sex in a mechanical trap bed, where he consummates his relationship with his new *amie* while trying to avoid being stabbed himself; suffering from the 'corte joie' (*Le Chevalier à l'épée*, l. 1091) that could either indicate underwhelming equipment or twitchy precocity; swinger-style exchanges with other knights making indecent proposals; riding small horses that collapse under him. In this context, where Gauvain is either the great courtly hero or sexual clown, critics – even the laudably *pervers* Jeffrey Cohen – seem to see or rely on Chrétien's earliest composition as unironic and 'consensual'. But then again, our own critical *méconnaissance*, our blindness may also present its own insight and knowledge of the limits and anxieties attendant on life before the law of the perverse. In the midst of this anxious world, 'bravely bold Sir [Erec] rides forth from Camelot' (or some other silly place), like Monty Python's fearful Sir Robin, bedevilled by a perversely taunting theme that is the knowledge of his own anxious refusal to contemplate objects of *esfroi*. As the song proceeds, the minstrel (a scampering Neil Innes) elaborates with a glee worthy of medieval hagiography the tortures not feared by his great lord, accumulating a list of parts that turns increasingly… strange. In a similar way, brave sir Erec's quest, while elaborating a catalogue of cruelties in an apparently less ludic manner, has nonetheless drawn out some of the seamier undercurrents in the communities he has passed through. Only his sadistic insistence saves him from the debasing, disavowed masochistic dimension of what he sees with his eyes wide shut.

Notes

1. Gerald of Wales, *De Vita Galfredi Archiepiscopi Eboracensis*, in *Giraldi Cambrensi Opera*, ed. by James F. Dimock, 8 vols (London: Rolls Series, 1868), IV, pp. 357–431, at p. 423, trans. cited from Burgwinkle, *Sodomy*, p. 83. For discussion of Gerald of Wales, see Burgwinkle, *Sodomy*, pp. 82–4.
2. Clifford Geertz, 'Deep Play: Notes on the Balinese Cock-Fight', in *The Interpretation of Culture: Selected Essays* (New York: Basic, 1973), pp. 412–53, at p. 419. For discussion, see Biddick, *The Shock of Medievalism*, pp. 85–90.
3. Biddick, *The Shock of Medievalism*, p. 87.
4. La Bruyère, p. 321.
5. As Seebass-Linggi comments, given that the couple now find themselves overburdened with the beasts, Erec's gift to the squire, thus ridding himself to advantage of what would be a burden were a quick get-away required, is not an entirely selfless act (p. 132).
6. '*Renaut de Montauban*': *édition critique du manuscrit Douce*, ed. by Jacques Thomas, Textes Littéraires Français (Geneva: Droz, 1989).
7. Salisbury, *The Beast Within*, pp. 55–7 and pp. 87–8.
8. Cohen, *Medieval Identity Machines*, pp. 47–9.
9. On Richard's alleged cannibalism, see Geraldine Heng, 'The Romance of England: *Richard Coer de Lyon*, Saracens, Jews and the Politics of Race and Nation', in *The Postcolonial Middle Ages*, ed. by Cohen, The New Middle Ages (Basingstoke and New York: MacMillan, 2000), pp. 135–71 and Michael Uebel, *Ecstatic Transformation: On the Uses of Alterity in the Middle Ages*, The New Middle Ages (London: Palgrave MacMillan, 2005), pp. 44–51.
10. On the squire, see notably Allard, pp. 72–8, who sees him as symbolic of Erec's mastery of the values of the Indo-European 'third function' (material provisions and reproduction). Allard's reading here fits well to my mind with the fact that precisely what is *not* served is meat gained through the royal / chivalric (thus both first and/or second function) domain of the hunt.
11. On wine, see Roland Barthes, 'Le Vin et le lait', in *Mythologies*, pp. 74–7. *Fromage de gain* or 'harvest cheese' is typically made from milk from animals grazed on new spring grass and aged for the summer.
12. On dogs as 'oedipal' creatures, see Cohen, *Of Giants*, pp. 129–30. On Yvain's madness, see Sylvia Huot, *Madness in Old French Literature: Identities Found and Lost* (Oxford: Oxford University Press, 2003), pp. 29–31.
13. On lack, see Evans, *Introductory Dictionary*, pp. 95–6.
14. See Burgess, *Erec et Enide*, p. 61.
15. On Galoain, see notably Allard, pp. 78–90 and Seebass-Linggi, pp. 83–92.
16. Bender highlights the passage but offers no comment on its undercurrents (see pp. 44–5).

17 The point of the various narratives that centre on royal vanity if this kind is that the person asking the question claims to want to know the truth but actually desires to be flattered. What the versions of the Sleeping Beauty narrative do not then consider, and which the parody fairy tale *Shrek* does, is the idea that the magical device learns to lie, in that it qualifies its truthful response to the vain and tyrannical lord Farqhuad with the cavaeat that he is not the fairest king of all 'because – technically speaking – you're not a king'.

18 One possible reading here would then be to see the squire as a potential potentially placing him in the position of Antigone, who, to follow Lacan's reading, gives voice to the rationality that is the horrific beauty of *atè*, the beyond of the order of the polis, irrationally regardless of the consequences of that act for her. On this, see Lacan, *Le Séminaire VII*, pp. 285–333.

19 Jaeger, *Ennobling Love*, p. 184–97. On Enide's role in this scene see also McCracken, 'Silence and the Courtly Wife', pp. 116–20.

20 Žižek, *The Plague of Fantasies*, p. 1.

21 See Bynum, *Jesus as Mother*, pp. 110–69 and Jaeger, *Ennobling Love*, pp. 124–7.

22 This echoes intriguingly Žižek's comments on the gesture of censorship as inherently perverse (see *The Plague of Fantasies*, pp. 179–82).

23 On Erec and the type of the 'jalos', see Seebass-Linggi, pp. 213–15.

24 Not unlike the position of the Minister commented on in Lacan's Seminar on Edgar Allen Poe's *The Purloined Letter* (see 'Le Séminaire sur *La Lettre volée*' in *Ecrits*, pp. 11–61, at p. 35).

25 See Burgess, *Erec et Enide*, pp. 62–4 and Seebass-Linggi, pp. 208–13.

26 In the scenario that Lacan describes as typical of the construction of *jouissance féminine*, the masculine subject's vision of an object's troubling remainder of resistance to or exemption from (its status as 'not-all' in relation to) its/ his power to fascinate, neatly illustrated by the cinematic cliché of the *femme fatale* kissing the hero while her gaze appears directed elsewhere, as with Judy Barton's (played by Kim Novak) kissing Scotty in the second section of Alfred Hitchcock's *Vertigo* (on which, see Žižek, *The Fragile Absolute*, p. 145).

27 Seebass-Linggi, pp. 211–13.

28 See Cohen, *Of Giants*, pp. 60–1, but, against this, Eagleton, *Sweet Violence*, p. 164. The difference between the two positions can be explained by the specificity of what Eagleton sees as the function of Imaginary identification in tragic discourse.

29 Gaunt, *Love and Death*, p. 202.

30 *Austin Powers: International Man of Mystery*, dir. Jay Roach (1997).

31 *Austin Powers: The Spy who Shagged Me*, dir. Jay Roach (1999).

32 Jean Baudrillard, *The Transparency of Evil*, trans. by James Benedict (New York and London: Verso, 1993), pp. 81–8 and pp. 101–05.

33 On Guivret, see, among others, Allard, pp. 91–8 and Seebass-Linggi, pp. 92–6.

34 In which regard, see Patterson's brief but suggestive reading of the Guivret episode (*Negotiating the Past*, p. 190).
35 See Simpson, *Animal Body*, pp. 197–9.
36 For this latter point, I am grateful to Eilidh MacDonald.
37 On this scene, see Kaeuper, *Chivalry and Violence*, pp. 216–17. Kaeuper's reading is interesting on the subject of aggression, although his comments on the possible 'Freudian' resonances of the bonding between the two characters symbolised in the cutting of the shirt tails to make bandages (p. 217), is doubtless jocular in nature. If anything, Guivret's gesture here recalls the actions of St Martin, the resonance here thus being of fraternal love founded on an absolute commitment to the law of charity.
38 In that respect, Guivret can be seen as a pantomime figure not unlike 'Puss in Boots', the cat assassin character in *Shrek 2*, a figure whose bristling implacable feline rage is further spiced by his voicing by Antonio Banderas, thus signalling Puss as a parodic combination of two roles played by Banderas: Zorro in Martin Campbell's (dir.) *The Mask of Zorro* (1998)and the last two of Robert Rodriguez's (dir.) *Once Upon a Time in Mexico* trilogy films: *El Mariachi* (1992), *Desperado* (1995) and *Once Upon a Time in Mexico* (2003). Puss's implacable ferocity is thus both partly animal and partly stereotypical Latin temperament, manifest in his apparently paradoxical wildness and yet total submission to an honour code. However, a sudden camera pull-back during his ambushing of the central characters comically reveals his diminutive stature, a debunking move that initiates his domestication and assimilation to the mock-heroic group.
39 Note that in this respect the tale situates itself again 'after' the Tristan legend. The fundamental political relation there is the defeat of the Irish, as alluded to earlier in the reference to the giant knight Morholt, the figure sent to demand tribute each year, but finally defeated by Tristan.
40 See l. 3682, note.
41 See Duggan, *The Romances of Chrétien de Troyes*, p. 11.
42 Burgess, *Erec et Enide*, p. 67.
43 As Paris points out, the motivation is nothing more than 'pur amour de la joute' (p. 161).
44 *The Madness of King George*, dir. Nicholas Hynter (1994).
45 See Seebass-Linggi, pp. 97–105.
46 Per Nykrog, *Chrétien de Troyes: romancier discutable*, Publications Romanes et Françaises, 213 (Geneva: Droz, 1996), p. 69.
47 Not that le Gringalet's name is without its problems. As Paris points out, the name may indicate that Gauvain's horse may if anything be light to the point of somewhat scrawny (pp. 149–50 and note 3 on p. 150). Thus, if there are any underlying games being played here, then Chrétien's implications may be more in line with the mocking humour of *Le Chevalier à l'épée* than at first seems.
48 For edition, see *Fabliaux érotiques*, pp. 241–61.

49 Also noted by Seebass-Linggi, pp. 100–01.
50 On the accumulation of references to Erec's physical state and the court's reaction, see Seebass-Linggi, pp. 103–05.
51 In that respect, I would disagree slightly with the accounts given by Burgess and Topsfield of this episode's place in the work's overall structure. Burgess sees the preceding episodes as marked both by self-vindication, notably the encounters with the robber knights, and by an indifference to the needs and interests of others chiefly expressed through his treatment of Enide (See Burgess, *Erec et Enide*, p. 69). Topsfield sees the scene as a continuation of Erec's 'quest of self-discovery and expansion' (p. 33). However, we can also see the encounters with the robber knights and also this scene as connected by a demonstrative assertion. In that sense, Erec's first encounters capture the energy of his initial impulse in a manner that is then recovered and reasserted here after the uncertainties created by the encounters with Galoain and Guivret, both of whom appear as 'obstacles' much in the same way that Erec complains of the interference of Arthur's camp.
52 Quentin Tarantino, *Pulp Fiction* (London and Boston: Faber and Faber, 1994), p. 131.
53 Dinshaw, p. 184.
54 On Tarantino, see Dinshaw, pp. 183–206.
55 See especially Dinshaw's comments on the monologue in the flashback scene in *Pulp Fiction* in which Captain Koons (played by Christopher Walken) hands to Butch as a young boy the watch that had belonged to his grandfather and father, a *patrimoine* both they and Koons had been constrained to hide in their rectums in various prison-camps in various wars (Dinshaw, pp. 186–88).
56 Dinshaw, p. 187.
57 Dinshaw, p. 186.
58 On this episode, see notably, Köhler, *L'Aventure chevaleresque*, pp. 140–1; Seebass-Linggi, pp. 106–16 and Ian R. Campbell, 'An Act of Mercy: The Cadoc Episode in Hartmann von Aue's Erec', *Monatshefte fur Deutschen Unterricht, Deutsche Sprache und Literatur*, 88:1 (1996), 4–16.
59 Allard, p. 98.
60 Nykrog, p. 70.
61 On the 'cheval-fust', see Kay, 'The Sublime Body', pp. 11–15.
62 See Žižek, *Plague of Fantasies*, pp. 215–6 and *Metastases of Enjoyment*, pp. 73–4: 'the raping of a girl (or a boy for that matter) in the presence of her father, forced to witness the affair [...] is bound to set in motion the vicious cycle of guilt. The rape thus entails, besides the girl's physical and psychic suffering, the disintegration of the entire familial socio-symbolic network.' (*Metastases of Enjoyment*, p. 74).
63 See Cohen, *Of Giants*, pp. 37–9 (on Geoffrey's version of the scene) and pp. 70–1 (on Wace) as well as Gravdal, *Ravishing Maidens*, pp. 42–8.

64 For edition and translation see *The City of God Against the Pagans*, ed. and trans. by G. P. Goold and G. E. McCracken, 7 vols, Loeb Classical Library, 411–18 (Cambridge, MA and London: Heinemann, 1957 [1981 printing]) and *Concerning the City of God Against the Pagans*, trans. by Henry Bettenson (Harmondsworth: Penguin, 1984). On Augustine's treatment of the case of Lucretia in *City of God*, see particularly the discussion of Enide's attempted suicide below.

65 See the OED entry: '1984 *Police Review* 18 May 975:3 *Nonce*, prison term for a child molester. The very bottom of the prison pecking order, the "nonce" is usually segregated from ordinary prisoners at all times for his own protection. Originally derived from "nancy-boy".' An alternative explanation for the origin of the term is from an acronymic annotation of prison records indicating the prisoner should be segregated: 'not on normal courtyard exercise'.

66 See Žižek, 'Robespierre or the "Divine Violence" of Terror', in *Virtue and Terror*, ed. by Jean Ducange, trans. by John Howe, Revolutions (London and New York: Verso: 2007), pp. vii–xxxix.

67 A notable case in point is the illuminations from the Hainault chronicle, or the illuminations of Arthur and his giant foe in matching suits of black-painted plate armour (See illustrations to Cohen, *Of Giants*).

68 On penance and other isolatory practices with regard to charges of sodomy and other proscribed practices, see Brundage, pp. 212–14 and Mark D. Jordan, *The Invention of Sodomy in Christian Theology* (Chicago and London: University of Chicago Press, 1997), pp. 29–66.

69 On gift and gratuity in *Erec et Enide*, see Seebass-Linggi, pp. 134–6.

70 Biddick, *The Shock of Medievalism*, p. 88, original emphasis.

71 Biddick, *The Shock of Medievalism*, p. 88.

72 Žižek, *Welcome to the Desert of the Real*, pp. 20–1.

Carmina qui quondam studio florente peregi
Flebilis heu maestos cogor inire modos.
Ecce mihi lacerae dictant scribenda camenae
Et veris elegi fletibus ora rigant.
Has saltem nullus potuit pervincere terror
Ne nostrum comites prosequerentur iter. [...]
Mors hominum felix quae se nec dulcibus annis
Inserit et maestis saepe vocata venit.
Eheu quam surda miseros avertitur aure
Et flentis oculos claudere saeva negat.
(Boethius, *Consolation of Philosophy*, book 1, metre 1, ll. 1–16)

Verses I made once glowing with content; tearful, alas, sad songs I must now begin. See how the Muses grieftorn bid me write and with unfeigned tears these elegies drench my face. But them at least my fear that friends might tread my path, companions still, could not keep silent. [...] Death, if he come, not in the years of sweetness, but often called to those who want to end their misery, is welcome. Alas, my cries he does not hear; cruel, he will not close my weeping eyes.

When she saw that the Muses of poetry were present by my couch giving words to my lamenting [toro fletibusque meis uerba dictantes], she was stirred a while; her eyes flashed fiercely, and said she, 'Who has suffered these seducing mummers [has scenicas meretriculas] to approach this sick man? Never do they support those in sorrow by any healing remedies, but rather do ever foster the sorrow by poisonous sweets. These are they who stifle the fruit-bearing harvest of reason with the barren briars of the passions: they free not the minds of men from disease, but accustom them thereto. I would think it less grievous if your allurements drew away from me some uninitiated man, as happens in the vulgar herd. In such an one my labours would be naught harmed, but this man has been nourished in the lore of Eleatics and Academics; and to him have ye reached? Away with you, Sirens, seductive unto destruction! leave him to my Muses to be cared for and to be healed.' (Boethius, book 1, prose 1)

Chapter Seven
'As If You Were My Secretary':
Scripting Enide's Histories

In the previous chapter we dealt with those parts of *Erec et Enide* that seemed to target the limits of human experience at least in terms of what is avowable and permissible. The various adventures of the quest that seem to target the question of desire point to a *jouissance* beyond the Law whose confusions and anxieties Chrétien either passes over in silence (Galoain) or forestalls and effectively erases. Thus Erec both kills the giants and refuses offers of service from Cadoc and his *amie* that carry with them troubling echoes of a masochistic subjection. Accordingly, this chapter reads those sections of the narrative that then probe at the beyond of experience with regard both to Enide and Erec. Here the Boethian frame of Chrétien's story looms increasingly large. If the arc of Arthurian narrative offers an exemplary vision of the relation of the human world to Fortuna, it follows that its lesson is not merely the intellectual understanding of historical mechanisms but also their internalisation, a schooling of the passions in light of experience advocated by Augustine and, perhaps most compellingly for medieval audiences, Boethius. In the *Consolation of Philosophy* the narrator progresses from despair to an active and engaged understanding of his fate transcending the passivity that would be mere fatalistic resignation. In Chrétien's text, we see the central characters interrogate that limit through manipulations of effect that not only reflect Patristic teaching but which also reach out daringly to occupy positions beyond the measure of the law.

'Le Monde où l'on [pleure]': Enide's Lament

CLEOPATRA
No more, but e'en a woman, and commanded
By such poor passion as the maid that milks
And does the meanest chares. It were for me
To throw my sceptre at the injurious gods;
To tell them that this world did equal theirs
Till they had stol'n our jewel. All's but naught;
Patience is scottish, and impatience does
Become a dog that's mad: then is it sin
To rush into the secret house of death,
Ere death dare come to us? [...]
Good sirs, take heart:
We'll bury him; and then, what's brave, what's noble,
Let's do it after the high Roman fashion,
And make death proud to take us.
              (*Antony and Cleopatra*, act 4, scene 15)

Dripping his life's blood as he goes, Erec's return to Enide's hiding place reads as an imitation of Cadoc. However, in Erec's case, this haemorraghing, as with the slow drain of charismatic seduction, is concealed from sight. Where before Enide had looked down at Erec as if he were a tomb effigy, now she sees an apparently living man dead on his feet, the shock of his collapse thus also the tragic, poignant recollision of those two temporal perspectives. Just as Roland's soul departs the field of Rencesvals the line before Charlemagne arrives (*La Chanson de Roland*, ll. 2397–8), Enide bears horrified witness to the apparently final exhaustion of Erec's animate energy in a heart-rending variation on Henri Bergson's vision of the mechanical in the human. But then we already knew this was the moment to which we were tending: 'mar i fus' – 'alas that you came to *this*'. Not that that knowledge is now any comfort: where Erec's *motion* seems to be ceasing, Enide's *emotions* are mobilised in all their unremitting, undammable energy. Alternating a series of apostrophes – addressed to God (l. 4612), herself (l. 4617), Erec (l. 4631), God again (l. 4649) and then, indirectly, His great follower, Death (l. 4650 onwards) –

with ever-renewing tears in a shuddering, wracking outpouring of grief, her ground-zero mourning of Erec an unendurable series of shockwaves hitting her in the relentless equivalent of a phased bombardment.

The test is then courage under fire, whether in extreme circumstances people will recall past lessons or fall into indisciplined panic of the kind manifested by one of the unfortunate robber knights. Thus, although Enide's tearing at 'sa tendre face' (l. 4611) may be part of a gestural repertoire of lament as an object of pathos – just as we will see again in the description of Laudine's grief for Esclados in *Le Chevalier au lion*. However, that word can also have less positive senses, as we can see from Charlemagne's awkward dismissal of Ganelon's plea that the emperor should look after the interests of his son Baldwin in the event of his death ('trop avez tendre coer', *La Chanson de Roland*, l. 317). Even in the smallest details, Chrétien's evocation in this scene paints an ambiguous picture of the irrational force of the emotions. Enide's staggering, grieving, fainting progress may recall that of Roland's last moments, but, unlike him, she does not seem to be giving serious thought to the good of her soul. When Roland looked on Durendal for the last time, he did nothing more dangerous than worry for its future (*La Chanson de Roland*, ll. 2297–354). When Enide looks on Erec's sword, her thoughts tend somewhere far darker.

One key tension in the bedroom scene lay in its mingling of the retrospection of lament and the futurity of still-live desire, a warping, anamorphic tension that echoes Arthur's earlier relaunch of the hunt. Both interrupt a potentially destructive relations between court and king, beloved and lover. Accordingly, one possibility based on the foreshadowings we have seen is that Chrétien views the road that brings us here as a rhetorical education, a schooling in the public business of the court, the Imaginary colonisation of the natural by the cultural. Where their wedding night had presented us with the intrusion of socialising agencies into the most intimate of bodily experiences, Enide now draws on her acquired command of the ethics of *bien dire* to master herself and rally those forces she might most usefully wish to have under her command in this worst moment:

> 'He!' dist ele, 'con mar i fus,
> Sire, cui pareilz n'estoit nus!
> En toi s'estoit Beautez miree,
> Proece s'i iere esprovee,
> Savoirs t'avoit son cuer doné,
> Largece t'avoit coroné,
> Cele sanz cui nuns n'a grant pris.' (ll. 4631–7)

> 'Alas! Misfortune brought you here! My lord, none was your equal! You were the living image of Beauty, Valour tested itself in you, Wisdom had given his heart to you, Generosity – without whom no one can have great renown – had crowned you.'

In the forest again, we find ourselves faced once more with a moment that, as in earlier scenes, straddles and challenges public / private binaries. Where this lesson may eventually tend can be seen in Erec's decorous and obedient concealment of his own private grief in the public mourning for his father (see conclusion below). However, for now we have a seemingly sharper test, in the absence of an actual public presence to buttress any internalised sense of *devoir*, and with the promise of reconciliation glimpsed moments before cruelly snatched away. Enide's self-mastery at this point, delivering what is effectively the first reading of Erec's funeral oration, would in Boethian terms constitute a truly heroic act.[1]

If Enide had erred before by speaking of Erec either as if he were dead or should never have come to Laluth, then this is not because such a thought might never have its moment even if its occurrence was out of time then. Here, however, the once extraneous element comes to assume its place in and organise the discursive field, the 'mar i fus' repeated verbatim in her apostrophe to Erec (l. 4631). Ostensibly formal in more than one regard, Enide's grieving is structured according to the protocols of a public rhetoric exemplified in Laudine's lament for Esclados, the young woman marshalling her resources not merely in tribute to the dead man but also in *psychomachia*, in internal war against her own despair.

First we have the assertion of Erec's incomparability, although what Enide does not mention is that the mirror she holds up to him is herself, the only person who could pay fitting tribute and endure standing at the focal point of this spectacle. What she has implicitly understood is Erec's lesson: the thing that would here produce the greatest effect on the public would be for her to stand sufficiently unmoved, even as he himself invited the court of Carnant to reflect on and endure the prospect of his certain destruction. Qualities pass in poignant review, beginning with his beauty, the first thing we ever knew of him. Enide's qualification to speak here makes for an intriguing *mise en abîme*, in that the woman first known to us as Nature's finest handiwork now stands back as the painter who reflects on Erec's relation to the allegorical figure. Her abnegation reflects the parallel between Chrétien's tale and one of its most important sources and models, the patience of Griselda. What Enide is required not merely to endure but to celebrate at the very moment of his death is Erec's relation to these other women. Decorum requires she position herself, like Guinevere, at his left hand where they sit at his right, or, to put it in terms of another model, as Brangane to their Iseut, as the moon compared to the full light of the sun.[2] Her abnegation of self as she rhetorically yields the floor, is obviously touching, and yet that distancing move is the very thing that makes it possible for her to function as the artist and architect of the public text.

Crucially, the language of Enide's lament blurs the boundary between 'private' (affective) and 'public' (ceremonial) relations. If Wisdom had, in effect, 'fallen in love with' Erec, and Beauty had 'admired' him, then this seems – at least on the surface – to avoid the mire of sentimentality denounced by Philosophy in her scolding of the narrator and those 'hysterical sluts', the Muses, at the opening of *Consolation of Philosophy* (book 1, prose 1). Largesse had *crowned* him. The 'marriage' Enide oversees – whose model is clearly then the post-Boethian tradition of philosophical allegory, exemplified in such contemporary works as the *Marriage of Mercury and Philology* or the *Metamorphosis Golye Episcopi* – is clearly a political one, its oratory played out in the public theatre of the court.[3]

The intertextual parallel with Boethius's text, where the appropriate handling of grief through the disciplines of rhetoric and philosophy is a key theme, is exact and illuminating. What is apparent in that context is that the business of rhetoric is to lead one away from grief to consolation. However, the dual focus on Enide's quasi-Boethian words and her disconsolate, despairing actions raises a question: does her use of personification allegory reflect Philosophy's healing *carmen* or the poetry of the theatrical Muses? Taking her words on their own, Enide's invocation of the allegorical virtues seemingly tends in exactly the opposite direction of the presence of the Muses at the opening of Boethius's work. Yet it is more reminiscent in spirit of book 1, metre 1 (cited above) than book 1, prose 1. Her separation from Erec by means of their introduction and her self-effacing before the mirror would be part of what might appear as the 'stern talking-to' from Philosophy. Thus Enide's speaking might move from the figures of the interior monologues of the crisis and quest, soliloquies voiced to no-one in particular, to a public speech counterpointed by unspoken messages she directs to herself. Enide would then be mistress of herself, having internalised the lessons of consolation to the point of being able to perform an 'official' lament for her husband. This, in a sense, was the test foreshadowed in the encounter with Yder the forest. How do we respond when the unforeseen or even the unthinkable happens?

Of course, the figures she mentions might and might not lead her to salvation. After all, it is certainly no coincidence that Enide's praise focuses so prominently on *largesse* as a sine qua non, its unstintingness manifest in the giving of the self to the court fundamental to charismatic authority and with Erec here lamented as a martyr to the claims of lordly duty. The emphasis on the refusal of counter-gifts and service following the rescue of Cadoc, the Christ-like figure beaten like a thief and led away to a nameless end in the guise of a criminal, appears then as a foreshadowing of Erec's death. However, if such a gifting of the self is part of the vain business of the court, is it so clear, as Machiavelli asked, whether that self-sacrifice is a good or not? Such an ambiguity also mirrored in the vision of Erec's apparently dead body, the 'cadaver' positioned as a tutelary Other observing the courtly Subject as in Sarah Kay's reading of *Le Chevalier au lion*. The eyeless look of the dead functions as the prime manifestation of the traumatically reproachful gaze founded in the vision of death, one of the most uncanny revisionings of the question of desire's asymmetry: 'you do not look at me from where I look at you'. The dead body looks back from its own place. However, the fact that Enide draws the sword implies that these are precisely the lessons that have not been learned and internalised to the point of self-mastery.[4]

If Enide's lament is to be taken as an interpolated short-form performance, then in Boethian terms, its suicidal despair marks her as *dictated to* ('ecce mihi [...] dictant', book 1, metre 1, l. 3) by the Muses, rather than heeding the true script of philosophy, standing in mistaken relation to her textual antecedents the active mastery of which might lead her to spiritual if not physical salvation. However, her passionate *esfroi* – unlike the self-control she showed on her wedding night – marks a surrender of her will. This vision of the relation to Philosophy in Boethius reappears in work influenced by him, such as Alan of Lille's *Plaint of Nature*, where Natura describes the narrator's relation to her being 'as if you were my *familiaris* and my secretary' ('tecum quasi cum familiari et secretario meo', metre 8, ll. 103–04). This fleshing out of Boethius's use of the verb *dictare* marks a shift, with Alan's narrator appearing, as Michael Cherniss observes, 'more reporter than consolee', called upon to follow his mistress's dictation not merely in dutiful passivity but with active understanding.[5] Part of this revision lies in its gendering. The pathos of Philosophy's laments for the Boethius-narrator in book 1, prose 2 is bolstered by the quasi-maternal narrative of his education, from its 'first milk' ('nostro quondam lacte nutritus') to the 'solid food' of learning that nurtured his 'manly soul' ('nostris educatus alimentis in virilis animi robur evaseras'), man and master of the world he surveys (book 1, metre 2). By contrast, Alan's relation to Natura is emphatically predicated on his virile performance – whether sexual or intellectual / writerly. Moreover, and crucially, the relation is cast in court terms, with Alan's narrator, *secretarius* and *familiaris*, a key privy member of Natura's household. In this role, he is called upon to follow the 'true script of Venus', avoiding the sophistries and solecisms of sodomy and perversity. Whatever form the exile might take – whether actual banishment, or, more generally, the estrangement from the divine that is mortal, physical existence – a relation of proximity and, indeed, privileged intimacy mark the enduring nature of his understanding. By contrast, to lapse into despair – and so become 'secretary' to those hysterical sluts, the Muses, rather than assert one's will in order to the emanuensis and *familiaris* of Philosophy – is to accept both distance and subordinate status.

In short, what kind of script is Enide's history? At this stage, it seems hard to tell. Profoundly ambiguous, her reminiscences and fearful misrememberings bear witness to an anxiety of influence attaching to Roman educational traditions, their counsels of Stoicism seemingly ready to overbalance into despair. A glimmer of that is apparent in Enide's anticipation of the sorts of topoi later rehearsed by Shakespeare (see epigraph above):

> 'Mout m'a la Morz en grant despit,
> Quant ele ocire ne me daigne.
> Moi meïsme estuet que je praigne
> Le venjance de mon forfait.
> Ainsi morrai, mal gré en ait
> La Morz qui ne me vuet aidier.
> Ne puis morir por sohaidier,
> Ne riens ne me vaudroit complainte:
> L'espee que mes sire a ceinte
> Par raison doit sa mort vengier.
> Ja n'en serai mes en dangier,
> N'en proiere ne en sohait.'
> L'espee fors dou fuerre trait,
> Si la comence a regarder. (ll. 4652–65)

> 'Death scorns me much when she does not deign to kill me. I myself will have to take revenge for my crime. I'll die, and Death can lump it, for she will not help me. If I cannot die for wishing it, then it serves no purpose to make complaint. The sword my lord belted on should by rights avenge his death. And then I'll be in no one's power, nor have need to beg with wishes and prayers.' She drew out his sword and stared at it.

Enide may have been good with horses, but no female character picked up a sword yet. Indeed, that object – all Erec carried with him in the encounter with the Queen (ll. 103–04) and which he used even when he borrowed Enide's father's armour (ll. 625–6) – assumes a sinister place now as the instrument of her self-destruction. The instrument, trembling with the spectral life of drive, gives physical form to a steely thought relentlessly pursued: Enide's sustained conceit of assembling the various allegorical women in her court continues with the addition of the last 'ele', Death (l. 4653).

Just as the scene forms part of a tradition of Christian critique of Stoicism as a philosophical cloak for the irrationalities of despair, so it echoes other possible subtexts. A key instance is Dido's lament in the *Roman d'Eneas*, where, having stabbed herself with the departed hero's sword, the unfortunate queen breathes her last over her departed lover's clothes:

> 'Mar vis onques ces garnemens.
> Ils me furent commencens
> De mort et de destruction.' (ll. 2128–30)

> 'Alas that I ever saw these pieces of equipment. They were the beginning of my death and destruction.' (trans. mine)

Dido's complaint here evokes the uncanny power of objects, their sinister subjectivity in history's anamorphic collapse into the obscenity of revealed sense. Loss and sexual desire collide in the same moment and perspective as she contemplates the equipment – O.Fr. 'garnemens' carries the same potential ambiguity as its Occitan cognate 'garnimen', used punningly in William IX's 'Farai un vers' – of a man no longer there.

Enide finds herself likewise caught between warring temporalities. Just as she had paused in contemplation of Erec lying in their bed, so now she gazes in fascination at the weapon before her, another instrument to be mastered. In that regard, her moment here reads as the collapse of two others, this time external to the poem: Roland's contemplation of and lament for Durendal (*La Chanson de Roland*, ed. by Short, ll. 2327–54) and Aude's instant, instrumentless death (ll. 3705–22). If, as Seebass-Linggi argues, Chrétien can be read as taking an ironic distance with regard to epic conventions, notably indefatigability, here he targets another, perhaps rather more sharply. To have Enide protest that no one ever died by wishing it cuts back at the noble convention of the sudden death from grief, Aude being one of the better-known examples. However, given the previous scene, we might think of another, namely Geoffrey and Wace's accounts of

Helena. In Geoffrey's version, the pure girl dies of fright before the giant of Mont-Saint-Michel can work his will on her:

> 'O infelix homo, quod infortunium te in hunc locum subvectat? O innerabiles mortis penas passuere! Miseret me tui, miseret, quia tam detestabile monstrum florem iuventutis tue in hac nocte consumet. Aderit ille sceleratissimus invisi nominis gigas qui neptim ducis quam modo hic intumelavi et me illius altricem in hunc montem advexit, qui inaudito mortis genere te absque conctamine afficiet. Proh tristia fata: serenissima alumpna receptor infra tenerrimum pectus timore dum eam nefandus ille amplecteretur vitam diuturniori luce dignam finivit. Ut igitur illam que erat michi alter spiritus, [...] fedo coitu suo deturpare nequivit, detestanda venere succensus michi [...] vim et violentiam ingessit.' (ed. by Wright, pp. 117–18).

> 'O unfortunate man, what misfortune brought you to this place? I pity you for you are about to suffer death by the most unspeakable tortures. This very night a foul monster will destroy the flower of your youth. The most odious of giants will come here. Cursed be his name! It is he who carried the Duke's niece off to this mountain. I have just buried her in this very spot. With her he brought me, her nurse. Without a moment's hesitation, he will destroy you too by some unheard-of form of death. How hideous the fate of my fairest nursling was! When this foul being took her in his arms, fear flooded her tender breast and so she ended a life worthy of a longer span. Since he was unable to befoul with his filthy lust this child who was my sister soul, [...] in the madness of his bestial desire he raped me, against my will.' (*History of the Kings of Britain*, § 165, trans. by Thorpe, p. 238)

The nurse's account of Helena's end presents her sublimely vanished, her life leaving her just as her body is spirited from the stage, decently hidden in the earth from any perverse contemplation. However the tyrannical power of the giant's lust remains and indeed extends to new conquest, the nurse's warning adumbrating the obscene, Sadean *jouissance* of Arthur's possible 'unheard-of' fate, the loss of the flower of his youth ('florem iuventutis tue') in sexualised parallel to that of the monster's most recent victim and as product of the frustration of his desire to defile the young woman. In short, the intertexts of this scene flesh out the possibilities that haunted Erec's vision of Cadoc's shameful fate. Interestingly, Geoffrey casts the nurse's appeal as what seems like a plausible antecedent of Chrétien's 'mar i fus': 'quod infortunium te in hunc locum subvectat?' rendered rather differently in Wace as 'Quel mesaventure te meine?' (l. 11383). As noted, Wace's account is less euphemistic: Helen is raped to death (ll. 11407–10), the agency of the giant's act in her destruction nakedly apparent. In the tension between the two versions of Helen's fate is answered by other narratives that explore the topos of sublime will. A frustrated version of Helen and Aude, poor, damned Dido *thought* to die of grief ('Doncques *cuida* de duel morir', *Roman d'Eneas*, l. 2095, my emphasis) but, victim of the internal tyranny of her raging passions, had to make her *quietus* with her own hand instead. The *double entente* of that last sentence is no accident. The fact that she spends herself on the clothes Eneas leaves behind bears witness to a parallel between suicide and masturbation, both cast as tyrannical overthrowings of rationality. In contrast, Erec's death is revealed as both a tragic version of the fate potentially awaiting the young Arthur, with Erec now seemingly appearing as the flower of his youth destroyed, a life 'worthy of a longer span' cut short. However, what also glimmers behind it is the glimmering of a sexualised shame, the disavowed *jouissance* of the spectacle of a victim, male or female, mastered and – as Wace makes clear – defiled in death: 'the giant shamefully slew my love' ('m'amur / Ad li gaianz a hunte ocise', ll. 11414–15).

Thus Chrétien's vision of Enide's attempted suicide weaves together various models to mock as a deluded fancy the convention of the heroine's pure death: the will and the passions have only so much control over the body. Enide's reading of epic thus espouses a path of Stoic *virtus* by supplying, in her mime of Roland's last contemplation of Durendal, the object and the agency that was missing from the scene of Aude's death, indeed, the possibility it specifically refused. In that sense, we arrive at the end of nightmare and at the moment of 'passage à l'acte' in the form of suicide.[6] In rejecting the tyranny of another's brutal power over her body and in refusing the impotent *émoi* of begging and wishing, Enide toys with the one message that, as Lacan puts it, will arrive at its destination. Chrétien makes the road a plausible one, implicitly negating other fictions that might provide some fantasy resolution to the potential vision of Job's suffering, what Žižek sees as the fundamental fantasy, the troubling object of anxious collective surplus enjoyment: 'somewhere a woman is being tortured-coïted'.⁷ The shocked modernity of the central Middle Ages is faced with the agonising real of its own relation to suffering and to enjoyment. The intertexts of this scene thus provide a uneasy recursive vision of what it was we did not want to look too closely at in the encounter with Cadoc and the giants, the possibility of a knight being, as Žižek puts it, 'tortured-coïted' in place of a woman, as the support of a sadistic drive that the institutions of culture seek to accommodate through the management of structures of perversion and the regulation of object-relations, making pleasure out of whatever might otherwise aggrieve and pain us.

And yet, fortunately, in this anxious vision we have yet another of Chrétien's foldings of narrative logic as Enide pauses to remember her pain:

> Dex la fist un pou retarder,
> Qui ploins est de misericorde
> Qu'endementres qu'ele recorde
> Son duel et sa mesaventure,
> A tant ez vos grant aleüre
> Un conte a grant chevalerie,
> Qui de mout loing avoit oïe
> La dame a haute voiz crïer. (ll. 4666–73)

> But God in his mercy made her linger a little, kept her still. As she was recalling her sorrow and misfortune, there came galloping a count with a host of knights, who from afar had heard the lady crying out.

Oringle of Limors may not be Charlemagne, but, although far inferior to his ancestors in knowledge of the limits of his power, he is still useful in the time given him by Enide's 'recording' of the grief and misfortune that drives her to suicidal despair. Just as Guivret's self-defeating fury at his broken sword was the *deus ex machina* that allowed the apparently fatal combat between him and Erec to be resolved, so here Enide's 'parole', now tending towards the worst end to which foolish speech might lead one, unexpectedly serves a salutary persuasive function.

Willing Death: Enide, Lucretia and Oringle of Limors

> If you look at the matter more closely, you will scarcely call it greatness of soul, which prompts a man to kill himself rather than bear up against some hardships of fortune, or sins in which he is not implicated. Is it not rather proof of a feeble mind, to be unable to bear either the pains of bodily servitude or the foolish opinion of the vulgar [stultam vulgi opinionem]? And is not that to be pronounced the greater mind, which rather faces than flees the ills of life, and which, in comparison of the light and purity of conscience, holds in small esteem the judgment of men, and specially of the vulgar, which is frequently involved in a mist of error [humanum iudicium maximeque vulgare, quod plerumque caligine erroris involvitur [...] contemnere]? (Augustine, *City of God*, book 1, chapter 22)

Although her lament for her apparently dead husband is in some regards the high point of Enide's assimilation of the rhetoric of traditions of personification allegory, if not their consolatory message and spirit, it is not the most dramatic public use she will make of the lessons she has learned.

Ostensibly, Enide wishes to see Erec rise from his bier. However, there is another way of understanding her speech here, which is as a form of the suicide she attempted earlier but from which she was prevented by the intervention of the Count. Parallels with the unspoken message can be seen in slightly later works such as the prayers and wishes voiced by Aude in the rhymed Paris version of the *Chanson de Roland*. Her grieving wish for the consolation of hearing Olivier speak ('Que Oliviers me die son talent', *Paris Roland*, l. 5694) translates in the work into her wish to die, which is then granted.[8] Her goal is then to use her rhetorical skills even further to provoke the Count into killing her, the ultimate abnegation of herself, and the assertion of her self-mastery as the mirroring of his absolute lack of that same quality, manifested in his subservience to his own sexual desire, his self-serving cruelty and his loss of face in front of his followers. This act would then have the effect of becoming the ultimate capping of Erec's own reinvention and reassertion of his charismatic authority in the killing of the robber knights and the acquisition and distribution of horses. Enide, if successful in her goal would then construct herself as the object not of Oringle's desire but of the court's in the form of the lady they never had. Central to this is the implicit subtext of her own address to the Count, the use of the form *tu* (ll. 4838–46) appearing not as one of the 'private' relation as husband and wife, but rather contempt. He is the *vilain* and she the *courtois*. However, her potential death here is set against the other possible fate, a living death in which, like Philomena, she is imprisoned in the sepulchral silence of a lost castle in the forest, in the midst of a people whose lord knows no law other than his own pleasure.

In addition to his possible assimilation to Tereus the Thracian abductor, various readings of *Erec et Enide* have considered Oringle of Limors as an antitype of Erec. His brutalisation of Enide stands as a figure of everything Erec is not. In that sense, his killing appears as the final conjuration of the negative aspects of the relationship as revealed in the quest. In Cohen's terms, the killing of Oringle marks Erec's self-disciplining, the definitive disavowal of what he has been, prior to the test of the Joy. However, the episode also marks the end of Enide's political apprenticeship. Of course the destruction of his court begins with the introduction of Enide. Her refusal to eat and then her railing against the count after he strikes her, addressing him as a social inferior, effectively deposes him from his place at the centre of that court circle, and thus form the initial moves that then call down the mere final gesture that is Erec's strike at him. As is the case with the giants encountered just prior to this, she finds herself faced with a lord who pays the most barbaric of lip-service to the rights and dues of aristocratic society. His attempts to console her prove a parody of what should be the disinterested attempt to move someone through consolatory rhetoric, demonstrating his failure to internalise the wider lesson of its language. Oringle's vicious, self-interested wheedling contrasts sharply with the reservations of his followers who judge her grief understandable and supported by a clear moral consensus (ll. 4823–30) and his unilateral assertion of passionate urgency (ll. 4831–3), the undomesticated cousin of the desire that drove Erec to bring forward the wedding. It is at this point that we see the key difference from earlier episodes in that previously there had been no actual audience who could have acted as chorus to the actions of the principal characters, their various assertions made in a moral vacuum the most salient example of which was the indifference of the giants to the claims of law. In contrast to their articulation of the claims of time, the Count presents the terroristic presentness of will.

Enide's course of action here represents a desperate, improvisatory embrace of the opportunity to hand. Chrétien presents us with the prospect of Enide about to kill herself in despair. It might indeed be thought that the deus ex machina appearance of the Count would then have put that mortal peril once and for all. However, one reading of the scene is that his arrival merely defers the problem, substituting what only seems a more acceptable alternative. In addition to the model of Dido's suicide, we might also consider Sextus Superbus's violation of Lucretia and her subsequent suicide. The tale was handed down through both Livy and Ovid, and was taken up by Augustine in *City of God* (book 1, chapter 19).[9] Here it appears as the starting point for an extensive reflection on heroic status accorded in Roman history to various notable suicides. The foundation of Augustine's argument – expanding on Jesus's comment recounted in Matthew 15:17–21 that it is only our evil thoughts that defile us, not actions visited on us – is that the criminal will of the violator cannot sully the will of the chaste victim:[10]

> Not more happily than truly did a declaimer say of this sad occurrence: 'Here was a marvel: there were two, and only one committed adultery.' Most forcibly and truly spoken. For this declaimer, seeing in the union of the two bodies the foul lust [iniquistissimam cupiditatem] of the one, and the chaste will [castissimam voluntatem] of the other, and giving heed not to the contact of the bodily members, but to the wide diversity of their souls, says: 'There were two, but the adultery was committed only by one.' (*City of God*, book 1, chapter 19)[11]

Through his privileging of the intactness of the will, Augustine presents suicide as a non-solution, an unnecessary despair that highlights paganism's misunderstanding of the relation between act, guilt and repentance possibly indicative of shame at some 'secret consent' on the part of the victim (*City of God*, book 1, chapter 19). From here, he targets Lucretia's motivation as both unknowable and shameful, arguing that although we cannot reconstruct her motivation, one possibility is that she killed herself at the shame of some pleasure she took in the act forced upon her:

> She herself alone knows her reason; but what if she was betrayed by the pleasure of the act, and gave some consent [sua libidine inlecta consentit] to Sextus, though so violently abusing her, and then was so affected with remorse, that she thought death alone could expiate her sin? Even though this were the case, she ought still to have held her hand from suicide, if she could with her false gods have accomplished a fruitful repentance. (*City of God*, book 1, chapter 19).

The central point here is Augustine's insistence on the absolute and permanent separateness of wills in any act that may seem conjoint. However, permanent as that possibility may seem, there exists also the equally ineradicable possibility of the body's disobedience to the chaste will, which he takes as the major pagan argument in defence of suicide, namely to prevent any risk of a self-betrayal too shameful to contemplate. Against this, Augustine continues to stress that, from a Christian point of view, suicide is simply a misplaced and excessive response:

> But far be it from the mind of a Christian confiding in God, and resting in the hope of His aid; far be it, I say, from such a mind to yield a shameful consent to pleasures of the flesh, howsoever presented. And if that lustful disobedience [illa concupiscentialis inoboedientia], which still dwells in our mortal members, follows its own law irrespective of our will [praeter nostrae voluntatis legem quasi lege sua movetur], surely its motions in the body of one who rebels against them are as blameless as its motions in the body of one who sleeps. (*City of God*, book 1, chapter 25)

As much as to say that an act not consented to is nothing and, moreover, no act that can be consented to – by the 'will' or by the 'body' – cannot be repented of in this life. What Augustine's argument makes apparent however is that there is a key shift from the pantheon of the heroes of pagan Rome to those of Christianity: for him the paradigm is unequivocally Job rather than Cato and Lucretia (*City of God*, book 1, chapter 24). In fact, his argument against Cato's suicide as the act of 'a feeble rather than a strong mind' is that it does not go far enough: in accordance with the principles underpinning his decision to take his own life, namely his refusal to submit to Caesar, he should have killed his son as well (*City of God*, book 1, chapter 23).

However, insofar as his vision of subjectivity and consent takes little account of gender, Augustine was not interested in the legal ramifications of rape in the same way as medieval jurists were. As Kathryn Gravdal points out, later medieval legislation seemed to give little regard to the consent of the woman as opposed to forestalling any possible conflict between families that might result from incidents of abduction and forced intercourse.[12] If the wrong incurred through sexual violation was regarded as remediable by an offer of marriage, then any negotiations between the offender and the family of the victim would probably envisage the public honour of those parties rather than take account of the wishes of or the wrong done to the woman. Although by forcibly marrying Enide and then threatening to rape her, Oringle incurs the displeasure of his courtiers, the potential future consequences might not be that severe. After all, Chrétien presents his followers as offering no objection to the marriage per se. Indeed, the fact they send for the chaplain ('*Cil ont* le chapelain mandé', l. 4761, my emphasis), implies an acceptance of arguments he offered in the hastily-convened privy council ('Endementres li cuens conseille / A ses barons priveement', ll. 4744–5). Rather, their objection is to the count's insistence that Enide share his board (and therefore implicitly bed) so shortly after the death of her husband. For all their defence of her rights might make them appear the surrogates of her kin at this point, if the Count did rape her, the marriage – although forced – and its seemingly generous terms would supply a remedy to that wrong. Thus, although Enide's resistance puts the crowd on her side for now, Chrétien arguably suggests it is not to be assumed that their defence of her would continue to coincide with her view of her rights and status. A marriage ceremony is in effect the cultural 'cooking' of a woman, an objectifying similitude echoed in such places as Hamlet's description of his mother's bereavement and indecently rapid remarriage, where the 'funeral baked funeral meats [which] did coldly furnish forth the marriage tables' (*Hamlet*, act 1, scene 2). Given that at Oringle's 'wedding feast' the leftovers from

Erec's wake do not require so much as a brief zap in the microwave, Enide's 'yea' or 'nay' might not matter that much. But then, the accumulated references to *voloir* and *vuel* in the description of the Count's treatment of her, while stressing his disregard of her wishes or consent – whether generally in the matter of being happy (l. 4776–807), but also specifically in getting married (ll. 4764–7), sitting down (ll. 4780–81), eating (l. 4807) or engaging in sexual activity (ll. 4831–3) – also point in the direction of more than one possible resurgence.

Enide's provocation of the Count thus addresses the 'death' of various wills: the absence of any defence from her husband or kin, the contrived circumventing of her own right to object, and the future possibility of her own de facto 'consent' founded in the (Augustinian) consideration that whatever might be forced on her, she could later be argued to have enjoyed, however 'latently'. However, the 'liveness' of her will at this point remains problematic: even if Enide could be posited as seeking to avoid any possibility of taking pleasure with her new husband, such resistance as she might be expected to offer would presumably not extend to her possibly knowing contrivance of her own death by driving her new 'husband' to such a frenzy that he kills her.[13] The act would remain culpable insofar as it could be presented as tantamount to suicide. Thus, although it might appear logical that Chrétien should save his heroine from suicide in the forest, the peril either to her life or to her soul is merely in abeyance. Augustine may censure suicide, but he does not discuss examples of those who willingly and deliberately sought to bring about their death by other hands. In that regard, it would have been interesting to see Augustine's opinion on Philomena and Procne's revenge against and provocation of Tereus.

The case Augustine does comment on in his discussion of suicide is that of the defeated Roman general, Marcus Regulus. Following his capture by the Carthaginians, Marcus was allowed to return to Rome to negotiate with the Senate for his own release. However, having exhorted the senators not to accept the Carthaginian terms, obedient to his oath, Marcus returned to Carthage and voluntarily delivered himself to certain death at the hands of his captors:

> Having such a contempt of life, and preferring to end it by whatever torments excited enemies [cum saevientibus hostibus] might contrive, rather than terminate it by his own hand, he could not more distinctly have declared how great a crime he judged suicide to be. Having such a contempt of life, and preferring to end it by whatever torments excited enemies might contrive, rather than terminate it by his own hand, he could not more distinctly have declared how great a crime he judged suicide to be. (*City of God*, book 1, chapter 24)

If such is Augustine's view of Marcus Regulus's case, then an Augustinian gloss of Enide's attempt to provoke the Count would target the immixture and conflict of different wills and different kinds of will in a constellation where there might be less will than at first appears: 'Here was a marvel: there were two, and only one committed adultery'. The argument about the inviolability of the individual will applies again: Enide has a right to say no to her new husband, even if such refusal may offend him. However, by the same argument that a victim of rape is not sullied by the perpetrator's lust, so the Count's enraged reaction – Augustine's 'enemy savagery' – is an individual one undetermined by her intransigence. In short, if we follow Augustine's line of thought with regard to Lucretia, no compelling determining relation can be adduced between the apparent provocation and the act that is claimed as the reaction following from it. Enide's attempt to provoke the count escapes any definitive determination of its rights and wrongs based on patristic tradition. If the absence of adulterous will, or rather the mastery of the law of the body by the chaste will is an example of the mortification of the flesh, then the question is rather how many versions of 'will' subtend this scene. After all, Enide has no wish to betray her apparently 'late' husband, and she seems to have no will to commit the culpable act of suicide in the way that she clearly manifested earlier: she constructs an exculpatory fiction at least no more specious than the Count's. As for Oringle, insofar as he manifests a private will that is not the universal one of collective consent, and which also appears as the tyranny of the 'law of the body' against the rational will, then again we have arguably either less volition or more sources of it than meets the eye. Meanwhile, the apparently dead Erec seemingly exerts no will whatsoever. Unless one were to see the presence of his body at the feast as a foreshadowing of the picture painted in *Le Chevalier au lion*, where the agency of Esclados's corpse, its wounds reopening and bleeding, drives the court to seek his killer (ll. 1178–85), illustrating that not all apparently inanimate objects are devoid of something approximable to volition.[14]

That Enide's manipulation of Oringle amounts to a 'return' of her will is apparent from the apparently slender means at her disposal and the considerable effect with which she deploys them. Faced with his final warning following her apparently nonsensical refusal to eat unless she sees Erec do the same, Enide simply does not care or deign to reply ('Cele mot ne li *vost* respondre', l. 4818, my emphasis).[15] That not all silences are the same is apparent from John Plummer's observation of the parallels between this scene and Enide's tense negotiations with Galoain: 'Enide refuses, even in the face of death, Oringle's offer of (again) wealth and power, when, as with Erec, silence would have guaranteed a kind of prosperous peace'.[16] Where the action previously had centred around the shocking and excessive effects of *la parole*, Oringle likewise countering Enide's protestations by asserting that they are nonsensical (ll. 4786–817), thus effectively consigning her to the subaltern 'silence' of the unintelligible or disregarded. Thus we have Enide's will manifest in a brief and crushing silence, a daring tactical move not unlike some apparently unguarded defensive posture used to taunt or provoke a rash and unschooled adversary into committing himself to a too-hasty attack. The difference between the situation here and the earlier conversation in the chamber at Carnant is that Enide now appears to be more than able to capitalise on a position that might otherwise place her on the back foot. In response to the Count's intemperate, heavy-handed attack, her cry of outrage turns his courtiers against him at one neat stroke (ll. 4823–30). The Count compounds his error by railing against them in the manner of Charlemagne: there is no Thierry to help him here. Besides, where Oringle's response to their reproach indicates that he will affirm his power by working his 'pleasure' ('si ferai de li mon plesir', l. 4833), his debased will on the body of *la condamnée*, Charlemagne did not reveal himself as a tyrant by proposing to put Ganelon to death in spite of the advice of his counsellors. This position, which presents in the poorest possible light what Alfred Adler describes as 'economically determined marriages of brutal convenience', then seems rather different from what McCracken presents as her seeming earlier endorsement of something like the same model with her silent consent to her father's disposing of her as he saw fit.[17] Fighting on two fronts, Oringle finds Enide unable to contain her rage, and yet this time the understatement lies not in her silence but in a silencing in the form of the narrator's reporting of her oath (l. 4835). The Count strikes again, this time faced with the humiliation of her contempt-filled *tutoiement* (ll. 4838–46), Enide presenting herself in part as a potential martyr deriding her pagan tormenters. However, the other strand to her attack is to be found in her comment 'Assez me bat, assez me fier' (l. 4841). The violence she inflicted on herself in the forest is no conventional gestural of mourning: here the spectre of the most extreme of self-violence, her narrowly averted suicide, reappears. Simone de Beauvoir comments in *The Second Sex* that female suicide is not uncommonly represented as a dissolution of the self (drowning or poison) rather than a violent ending by the woman's own hands.[18] Against that preconception and against the Count, Enide reminds those around her of her record of virile determination. For Duggan, the fact that 'Chrétien never refers to suicide as a sinful or reprehensible act is a remarkable token that his primary values are profane'.[19] While I would broadly agree, it is arguable that Enide's failure to learn from Boethius's example and the progression from a model of suicide in despair to an 'unwilled' self-destruction reminiscent of Marcus Regulus's make fully apparent the serious implications of her actions here. In that sense, as Marie-Nöelle Lefay-Toury observes, Enide's temptation to take her own life may be brief relative to the representations in Chrétien's other romances, but the scene is not 'superfluous' as she puts it, supplying her provocation Oringle with its troubling, profane edge.[20] Unlike the possibly humorous treatment of the attempted suicides of the lovers in *Le Chevalier de la charrette*, Chrétien does not trivialise either Enide's gesture or its potential consequences.[21] In that sense, what we have here is a reversal of the quest motif: whereas Erec and Enide seemed initially faced with disturbing images of unregulated *jouissance*, here the scenario is in effect reversed with Enide's performance appearing as a problematic condensation of exemplars drawn from other periods.

Erec's Will: The Spectral Way of the Samurai

> Il est évident que l'Erec du roman en prose a une conception excessive sinon maladive du code chevaleresque. Le but de l'auteur en exposant ces incidents macabres [i.e. the killing of his sister] est, comme l'ont déjà dit C. Pickford and F. Wolfzettel, de faire 'une critique romancée d'un code d'honneur inadéquat'.[22]

> Even if one's head were to be suddenly cut off, he should be able to do one more action with certainty. The last moments of Nitta Yoshisada are proof of this. Had his spirit been weak, he would have fallen the moment his head was severed. Recently, there is the example of Ōno Dōken. These actions occurred because of simple determination. With martial valour, if one becomes like a revengeful ghost and shows great determination, though his head is cut off, he should not die.[23]

Erec's revival does little to deproblematise the situation of the 'immixtion des volontés' at the court of Limors.[24] Very little is said about his will at this point, which would seem consistent with Chrétien's presentation of bodies in dire states of fear or other physical or emotional duress as being marked by a fading or negation of subjective volition. Whether the fourth of the five robber knights sitting up again in his saddle after Erec had first attacked him could be described as a voluntary or involuntary reaction, it was interpreted as sufficient reason to make an example of him to his remaining comrade-in-arms. In the same way, Erec's striking down of the Count appears both over and under-determined. Chrétien accumulates the reactions that drive him: fearful amazement (l. 4850), sorrow and anger (l. 4852), rage engendering courage (l. 4856) and, finally, love (l. 4857). Yet for all this happens under the seeming sign of passionate determination (again, the movement is made 'isnelement' l. 4855), it is also devoid of the signs of regulated, deliberate action in that it is also 'sanz desfiance et sanz parole' (l. 4861). But then, of course, no warning was required since he and Enide were already at blows, and for any concerned as to the rights and wrongs of her tag-team partner joining the fray in light of Chrétien's earlier explanation that the 'custom of the time' regarded as treachery simultaneous attacks by more than one knight against a single opponent (ll. 2822–6), Enide, although 'combat active' in some sense, is still not technically a knight. But then again, a question also hangs over the hiatus of Erec's chivalric will and activity: are knights who are dead or sleeping still knights? Erec's rise from the dead in this regard can arguably be seen as an early continental predecessor of the dynamic poses of effigies on twelfth-century English aristocratic tombs. As Rachel Dressler comments of such medieval representations of the (not so) dead warrior, 'his youthful, vigorous stone body appears to resist decay and to claim the perfection of resurrection. His dynamic pose proclaims that all those gifts of youth, vigour, perfection and courage are placed in the service of Christ. All earthly failures or inadequacies are obliterated in the resurrection body.'[25]

Just as in *Vertigo's* braided substitutions and impersonations, or indeed the spectacle of Enide taking on the guise of the scheming feudal *femme fatale* she had previously rejected, so this scene revolves around a motif of trading places in the dance of Death. Erec's blow merely cleans up a remainder from the operation that has already taken place. Enide's quasi-suicidal brinkswomanship in effect draws out and stages the Count's intransigent refusal to give up on his desire, whether in terms of the stricture expressed against it or in terms of his moderating the violence of its expression. Having thus placed himself in the monstrous mirror of the beauty attaching to those who occupy the brief space 'between the two deaths' – as with the passing and purloining of curse-parchments in M. R. James's horror tale, 'Casting the Runes' – the clock allotting him his 'time allowed' is set in motion.[26]

Of course, this is not to say that the scene entirely resolves the question of who is 'alive' and who is 'dead'. Indeed, the simultaneous presence and absence of will in Erec's dead-handed blow unifies the court in absolute and unholy terror. Where previous parts of the scene had been characterised by an almost unbearable collision of contradictory or undecidable states of will, the resolution of the scene is into the dominant mode of terror as Erec disperses the court of Limors to the four winds. Thus, although the ostensible contrast is between Erec and the Count insofar as Enide's first husband is the one who is alive and the Count the one who is dead. (Riddle: how do you lose your second husband before you lose your first?) However, if we undo the opposition and look again at the extent to which the king is already necessarily a dead man, then we see something about the nature of sovereignty that has been articulated over the course of the work. Erec appears as the dead man in the respect that all his 'natural'/private reactions have been mortified. He always already understood this in a sense: the decision not to take the dress from the Count of Laluth appears as a refusal of what one might think of as the instinctive thing to do, the acceptance of the initial act of favour. However, it must be remembered that Erec's refusal, although unexplained, shows an awareness of the potential consequences of such a gift. It could be disastrous to bring Enide fully clothed into court as a trophy wife when in fact the entire resolution of the hunt of the White Stag depends on her acceptance by all the other knights at court. In that sense, Erec becomes the creature who has mastered his own body to the point of destroying it. He goes out to present the courtiers with a vision of what it is they apparently want, and yet which also fills them with grief and horror. In that respect Erec appears as a version of the 'man of steel', the *Staline*, the believer.[27]

Thus, the killing of Oringle appears as the culmination in a process of silent self-mortification of desire and flesh designed to produce Erec in the undead spectral form of the 'devil', the living effigy who slides quietly from the bier to strike at the head and disperse the court of Limors to the four winds. This gesture that then answers Arthur's potentially disastrous decision to hunt the White Stag. The lesson of both these moments is that the body social is ultimately the king's to destroy. What is remarkable about this moment is the extent to which it stages itself as comedy. Readings of this scene have highlighted the break of this moment from the seriousness of the preceding narrative, and yet it can be argued that the comic moment here functions precisely as a key narratorial collusion with the terroristic speech act, emphasising Erec's mastery of intervention at its most spectral and 'out of joint'.

Inevitably, the creation of that open space through the agency of the 'revenging ghost' provides the place for an interlude of reconciliation that mirrors in microcosm Arthur's brief stay atop the wheel. In that sense, the instability of Arthur's position explains the inscrutability of Erec's pardoning of Enide, the blindness or clarity of this denial or acknowledgment of his own guilt. Arthur, like Erec, is unreadable, and perhaps therefore writeable. This suspension of the normal order is also apparent in the almost magical removal of the court, the cast of thousands disappearing in the manner of a Broadway musical cast making their exit as the set is spirited away. All that is left is the leading couple and one dramatically convenient horse, just in time to be reunited in a (slightly bloodied) moonlight idyll.

The persistence and insistence of Erec's will, evident in his sheer endurance in Chrétien's poem, and carried to its obscene limit in the *Roman d'Erec*, can be seen as presenting a chivalric version of Jim Jarmusch's 1999 film, *Ghost Dog: The Way of the Samurai*. Here, the central character (played by Forrest Whitaker), a hit-man working for an aging circle of sub-Mafiosi mobsters, styles himself as a samurai retainer, whose loyalty stems from the fact that one of the gang saved his life when he was a teenager. While the strict rules governing Ghost Dog's performative evocation make him a useful resource, they also ultimately lead him to massacre the entire gang over a point of honour (they killed his collection of pigeons). The only one he spares is his boss, whom he eventually tricks into killing him, again out of obedience to 'the code': as a 'retainer', his life belongs to his 'lord', who is thus the only one who can 'rightfully' put a stop to the cycle of vendetta. The problem with the Ghost Dog character, like Erec in the prose romance, is whether his actions are categorisable as excessive. Obviously, one reading of the film is to see in it a lesson in Imaginary identification as misreading or misrecognition, in the manner of Jaroslav Hašek's 'good soldier Schweik', a figure who basically brings the system into crisis by his punctilious, literal-minded obedience.[28] However, what all this figures exemplify is the inherent excessiveness manifest in codified systems, their dimension of 'superego evil' signalled by the almost mechanical recurrence of the trope of 'killing in the name of…'.[29] If Erec's actions in Chrétien's poem show this 'excess' in bud (flowering fully in his idiotically bureaucratic execution of his sister in the later prose version), this is not to say that we should only read the evolution of his character from the verse to the prose texts solely as a developmental process, however. Rather, that obscene truth is already present. Erec's intransigence in Chrétien's poem is plainly marked, revealed in his 'pardoning' of Enide. After all, if we are to read his treatment of her as a punishment of his courtiers at Laluth, a sadistic performance whose effects on both her and him aim at eliciting their anxiety, that is to say the disavowed *jouissance* inherent in the Girardian trope of the 'king's future death', then her role is effectively to be subjected to the equivalent of a Stalinist 'show trial'.[30] Her 'forfait' – the rights and wrongs of which are, as various critics have highlighted, clearly debatable – functions as a convenient fiction Erec chooses to discard when he feels his point has been sufficiently proved and when this phase of the narrative seems to have arrived at a satisfactory conclusion.[31] After all, the process here is little different from that seen in his speech to Guinevere before pursuing Yder: narrative 'conjunture' is all. In that regard, the appearance of arbitrariness precisely raises the point of the king as the embodiment of the law in John of Salisbury's *Policraticus*. Royal *voluntas* is here affirmed to the point of narrative and bodily exhaustion potentially compounded by the open secret that all the time Erec was reduced, as Bill Burgwinkle puts it, to acting as little better than a bully.[32] To that charge we might add fraud: as with Arthur's address to the court at the conclusion of the hunt of the White Stag, was this speech something planned at the outset? In that sense, what we have is only apparently a 'private' moment, the presence of the term *forfait* highlighting – possibly even jokily – the public dimension of even the most intimate aspects of their relationship. However, just as with the vanitas motifs laid out in the bric-à-brac on Holbein's table, or as part of the tension between engineered set-piece and adaptive improvisation, Erec's 'pardon' is perhaps precipitate as reassurance. What this may signal, in contrast to the couple's departure from Carnant, is a closer allying of the narratorial point of view with that of Enide: Erec now speaks too soon. We are not out of the woods yet. There is more than one person involved in the scene and more than one view of the situation to be considered. For Enide, the testing is far from over.

Guivret and the Law of 'Friendly Fire'

While the encounter with the Count of Limors may well underscore the 'undead' drive characteristic of charismatic despotism, this does not mean Erec is any steadier on his feet. Obvious point here is the ride away from the court. Erec appears again in the guise of the living man walking, but in that regard we have already seen the dead man walking and that element remains in him now. Chrétien's handling of this theme revolves around a continuation of the black humour we had seen at the court of Limors: Erec fell from his horse once before in a moment of tragedy, a more poignant replaying of the tragedy of Roncevaux in that where Charles arrives just as Roland's soul departs, so Enide sees her husband fall from his horse, witnessing the very moment of his death, the impossibility of their being reunited. Here now we see a back to front version of the Roland tragedy as Guivret strikes Erec down unawares, blinded by the darkness.[33] Just when we thought Erec was back in the saddle, he keels over again.

A clue to the likely sequence of developments is Guivret's off-stage reaction to the 'military intelligence' he receives in the form of the mini-romance of the grieving Enide:

> Mout est tost alee novele,
> Que rien nule n'est si isnele
> Ceste novele estoit alee
> A Guivret le petit contee,
> C'uns chevaliers d'armes navrez
> Iert morz en la forest trovez,
> O lui une dame tant bele
> Qu'Iseuz semblast estre s'ancele;
> Si fesoit duel mout merveillous.
> Trovez les avoit ambedous
> Li cuens Oringles de Limors,
> S'en avoit fait porter le cors,
> Et la dame esposer voloit,
> Mais ele li contredisoit.
> Quant Guivrez la parole oï,
> De rien nule ne s'esjoï,
> Qu'erramment d'Erec li sovint.

> En cuer et en penser li vint
> Que il ira la dame querre,
> Et le cors fera metre en terre
> A grant honor, se ce est il. (ll. 4933–53)

> The news travelled quickly for nothing else is so swift. It had already reached Guivret: it was recounted to him that a knight wounded in combat had been found dead in the forest, and with him a lady of such beauty that you would have thought Iseut her chambermaid. Count Oringle of Limors had found them both, had had the body borne away and he desired to marry the lady, but she refused him. When Guivret heard the news, he was not at all happy, for he promptly thought of Erec. Both reason and emotion led him to seek the lady and to wish to bury the body if it turned out to be Erec.

Crucial here is the comparative anonymity of Erec, simply referred to as the wounded knight, as opposed to Guivret's overriding concern with Enide, this especially noteworthy in that she had played such an apparently minor role in their initial encounter. In that sense, Enide's *los* in this scene appears as a mirror of her beauty outshining Iseut to the point the latter finds herself taking the reduced role of Brangane (or, arguably, Erec as Procne, in that he is the object of the original bond between the two houses, to Enide's Philomena). Somehow, the 'tapestry' of military intelligence or rumour was smuggled out of Limors. Also of importance is the mention of the *contredit*, mention of which appears as the last element in the narrative. This short passage can in that respect be taken as yet another *mise en abyme* of Chrétien's examination of structure and closure. The mini-tale ends with a open-ended, dramatically compelling response: 'mais ele li *contredisoit*' (l. 4946, my emphasis), the imperfect making it clear that the *contredit* here takes the form of a refusal of forced marriage and, implicitly, sexual violation. As this 'novele' casts it, even if she dies by provoking him to kill her, she *will still be refusing him.* Her indominatable resistance to Oringles echoes the position of Chrétien the poet who presents his overall project as a similarly open-ended one, with his prologue casting his literary fame as an ongoing and exemplary *contredit* both to learned pagan antiquity and to vulgar vernacular tale-telling on the other.

In that sense, this section of the narrative, as a lead-up to the Joy of the Court, celebrates and foregrounds Enide's discursive mastery as a combative persistence that can even potentially incorporate her own physical death. Unlike Philomena, whose tale Chrétien translates, she can be mastered neither through rape or silencing violence. Erec's instructions to Enide now appear as a repeat of those given prior to the commencement of the quest. The difference here is the wear and tear on the body emphasised both through his own remarks and the narratorial comment on the unfair nature of the encounter between him and Guivret. The rhythms of injury and rehabilitation appear as a writing on the body that echoes and counterpoints the more general treatment of vicissitude in the work. Tales of injury and wounding constantly appear framed by other stories. The first phase of the quest ends just after the first encounter with Guivret, Erec finding Arthur's camp and allowing himself only the briefest of respites. The fact then that Chrétien chooses to emphasise the idea of a physical cycle at this point is clearly central, fitting partly with Philippe Walter's comments on the centrality of festivals, seasons and other temporal cycles in the poem. More crucially, it serves as a reminder of the role of the contingent in the cycles that constitute the poem. What we have here is less the self-begetting violence of *Raoul de Cambrai* than a series of self-contained pathologies or pathographies whose intersections appears as an immixtion des sujets where each radically demarcated individual history has its own waxing and waning, its own alternations of rest and motion, healing and harm. This makes for a more organic, less programmatic vision of pattern. The stars may not determine the lives of individual people in the manner of a governing pattern (this being Augustine's objection to astrology in his *City of God*), but their cosmic model of cyclicity does offer a point of departure for considering other interweavings of trajectories. Guivret's tale moves in less grand sweeps as he returns to the stage somewhat recovered from the previous encounter the previous day, even if the only real advantage he has is that provided by a greater amount of rest and food.

Erec's warning as they hear the approach of Guivret's entourage not only echoes the injunction to Enide at the start of the quest but also constitutes a 'second take' of the scenario whose first traumatic (but felicitously instructive) rehearsal was Erec's collapse and her abduction by Oringle. Just as she was instructed to keep silent, so she is now ordered to stay out of the way. The dangers of such a situation are made amply clear from the fact that Enide has as much to fear from her friends as from her enemies, but then, in a situation in which she has effectively acted as a Trojan horse bringing Oringle's killer into Limors, those two categories can scarcely be distinguished. This sense of the 'fog of war' (and rumour) surrounding Limors then focalises in the pint-size powerhouse that is Guivret. Passionately and impetuously concerned for his friend to the point of being unable to recognise him, the dwarf – as Nykrog aptly puts it – is unlikely to do anything more reflective than 'charge first and ask questions later'.[34] Unexpectedly, however, such headlong momentum – as an unhorsed jouster in the film *A Knight's Tale* put it, 'he has no style, but then neither has an anvil' – then finds its answer in Enide's desperate, last-ditch deployment of her powers:

> Quant son seignor a terre voit,
> Morte cuide estre et malbaillie:
> Fors est de la haie saillie
> Et cort por aidier son seignor.
> S'onques ot duel, or ot greignor.
> Vers Guivret vint, si le saisist
> Par la reinne, puis si li dist:
> 'Chevaliers, maudiz soies tu!
> Un home foible et sanz vertu,
> Doillant et pres navré a mort,
> As envahi a si grant tort
> Que tu ne sez dire por qoi.
> Se ci n'eüst ore que toi,
> Que sous fusses et sanz ahie,
> Mar fust faite ceste envahie,
> Mais que mes sire fust haitiez.
> Or soies frans et afaitiez,
> Se laisse ester par ta franchise
> Ceste bataille qu'as emprise.' (ll. 5016–34)

Enide [...] thought herself dead and done for when she saw her lord upon the ground; she leapt out from the hedge and ran to help her lord. If she had felt grief before, now it was greater. She moved towards Guivret, seized his reins, and said to him: 'Cursed be you, knight, for you have attacked a man who is alone and powerless, in pain and near death from his wounds, so wrongfully that you cannot account for it! If no one but you were here now, and you were alone without help, this attack would be ill made, provided that my lord was in good health. Now be generous and noble, and in generosity abandon this combat that you have begun.'

Enide's badgering accumulation of man- (or, rather, horse-) handling, curses, veiled threats and appeals to the better nature of this unknown assailant land like the redoubled blows with which she had seen her husband subdue or dispatch his opponents. She also repeats the *mar fus(t)* motif that played such a significant role in the pivotal bedroom scene, except that here it appears as part of a warning of what would have happened if Erec had been in better form. Such moves signal her mastery of the rhetoric of lament with this key formula used as a weapon in a now formidable discursive armoury. Enide thus succeeds where the maiden in the forest failed, her show of physical intimidation followed up without pause or respite in an effective show of force. Crucially, her brief concessions regarding Erec's physically weakened state, which take a back seat to her belabouring heaping of judicial and moral language as she pours shame and scorn upon the bemused Sir Shortstop, go together with her appeal to his noble nature. However, this does not merely represent a blindness to the possible implications of her situation or a lighter variation on what had gone before in the encounter with the count of Limors. Rather, what we see here is a version of the reasoning Augustine presents in his discussion of Marcus Regulus: Enide's appreciation of the possible mortal danger she is in is clear enough (l. 5017), but her invocation of the values of *franchise* mark a refusal to simply be cowed by the suspicion that she is merely at the mercy of a savage enemy. Interestingly, her rebuke that the assailant 'does not know' (l. 5027) why he has done what he has done leaves the door open that the act is the product of the law of the body rather than rational in nature.

This scene also sees the final, successful reworking of the 'maiden meets dwarf' motif. Enide's use of verbal force, clearly apparent in her use of the *tu* form so wounding to the count of Limors, meets with no response from its target, who admits his wrong. Interestingly, this detail seems incidental to the thrust of the narrative. Crucially, Enide changes back from *tu* to *vous* once she has asserted her position. At this point, the conflict is resolved. Faced with Enide's dunning tirade, Guivret – perhaps contrary to expectations – concedes

383

her superiority and her right. Significantly, Enide changes from 'tu' back to 'vous' in the encounter with Guivret, deploying a show of outraged scorn for effect but then withdrawing it when placated. We might well expect a scene of reconciliation. However, the detail of Guivret's textbook offer of reassurance and apology is more complex, as he launches into a mixture of lament and self-exculpation. Guivret offers similarly, Enide now standing by as a judge of the rights and wrongs of the case he expounds in his defence:

> 'Certes, se mout ne vos amasse,
> Ja voir ne m'en fusse entremis.
> Je sui Guivrez, li vostre amis;
> Mais se je vos ai fait ennui
> Por ce que je ne vos connui,
> Pardoner bien le me devez.' (ll. 5076–81)

> 'Be assured that if I did not greatly love you I should never have been concerned with this. I am your friend Guivret, and if I caused you harm because I did not recognise you, you must indeed forgive me.'

Guivret is certainly no craven, concluding his speech to the apparently unconscious or even, in Enide's words, mortally wounded knight with a clear statement that he has complied with the demands of law and duty and so fully discharged his responsibilities to the man he acknowledges as his lord: 'Pardoner bien me le devez' (l. 5081). If, as Seebass-Linggi comments, Chrétien here reflects the influence of the chanson de geste and particulary the *Chanson de Roland*, there may even be an element of intentionally comic parody, a slightly bungled mime of Oliver's mistaken striking at Roland, only with a heightened element of black humour as the offending party here offers a slightly more aggressive defence of his position in the speech to his comrade. Indeed, if, as Allard comments, 'acceptant la leçon méritée que lui a value sa folle bravoure, [Erec] jugera qu'il n'est plus contraire à son honneur et à sa valeur de ne pas refuser l'hospitalité du Petit Roi', a formulation that makes plain this scene's coda-like comic doubling of the equivocations about what Erec consented to or was tricked by in his earlier encounter with Kay and then Gauvain.[35]

What emerges in this scene is the interrelated pairing of consolatory discourse on the one hand and that of the assertion of legal rights on the other. Consolation becomes a reminder of the limits of the human condition, an acknowledgement of frailty combined with a dose of 'tough love' that then mirrors the sincere, but limitedly concessive admission of wrong Guivret offers. Moreover, Guivret's lament has a certain amount of comic interest in that it places him in a parody of Enide's position with her as the observer. We now have Enide as the audience for and judge of another's rhetorical performance. This is a constellation that we will see repeated in the latter part of the tale, with the stakes progressively raised. Indeed, the gradual promotion of Enide into increasingly 'managerial' roles follows almost immediately with her assessment of the medical care provided by Guivret's two sisters. In that sense, this scene prepares us for a change from the previous pattern in which she was increasingly called on to intervene directly in high-risk situations, making fine judgements about the weight and effectiveness of her actions.

Cura (passionium) regis: Erec, Enide and her Maidens

> ZOOT: Oh, come come, you must try to rest! Doctor Piglet, Doctor Winston, practice your art.
> PIGLET: Try to relax. [Undoes Galahad's belt and lifts his surcoat.]
> GALAHAD: Are you sure that's necessary?
> PIGLET: We must examine you.
> GALAHAD: There's nothing wrong with *that*!
> PIGLET: Please – we are doctors. (Monty Python and the Holy Grail)

Et Guivrez li redist aprés:
'Sire, j'ai un chastel ci pres,
Qui mout siet bien et en sain leu.
Por vostre aise et por vostre preu
Vos i voudrai demain mener;
S'i ferons voz plaies sener.
J'ai deus serors gentes et gaies,

Qui mout sevent de garir plaies;
Celes vos garront bien et tost.' (ll. 5097–105)

And Guivret replied: 'My lord, I have a castle nearby, nicely situated in a fine location. For your comfort and benefit let me take you there tomorrow, so we can have your wounds taken care of. My two gracious and cheerful sisters will cure you speedily and well.'

Although the excerpt cited from *Monty Python and the Holy Grail* is more comic in tone than the section of *Erec et Enide* dealing with Erec's convalescence (Erec is more in need of actual medical attention than Galahad, for a start), there are genuine parallels between the two. The *Python* representation arguably draws on Arthurian traditions of castles inhabited by women of the fairy otherworld who could misuse their powers to cure the body, acting instead to snare the senses and bend the will of those who strayed into their hands to their own designs. However, the question underlying both 'early' and 'late' versions of the scene target the same problem: who is to be trusted with the care of the knightly body, its appetites and passions?

It is therefore crucial that the care of Erec's body is seen to be a matter of concord between the three main players. Guivret's politeness stresses the harmonious relations between the three of them. Erec agrees to Guivret's suggestion that they pitch camp for the night (l. 5111). Enide's response is more nuanced: although pleased and reassured by the lodgings Guivret is able to contrive in the field (l. 5122), she reserves for herself the right to tend first to his wounds ('autrui n'i lessa tochier', l. 5127), an assertion that is clearly allowed by Erec, who finds nothing to criticise in her care of him (ll. 5128–9), and by Guivret, whose solicitude only to adds to the joyful harmony of the situation ('Guivrez *qui mout le conjot*', l. 5131, my emphasis) in which Enide is greatly pleased with everything he does (ll. 5153–4). This mood continues with Guivret's careful cajoling of Erec to eat, emphasising the small amounts he should consume versus the great benefit that such an action will accrue not merely to him but also to those around him (ll. 5144–51). Erec's consent to be governed is apparent in the tempering of his impulses, notably the fact that he *dared* drink but little ('car il n'osa', l. 5159). Just as the economy of terroristic violence in the quest started from a small cast and first principles, so the economy of care in this section proceeds by the same steps. Indeed, the regime of care seems divided into days much in the same way as might be a tourney, festival or other court occasion. It is therefore not yet the time for the new 'puceles' to present themselves: these will be assigned their place when the royal party reach Guivret's castle.

Interestingly, the next day's journey brings the reappearance of a rhyme we have seen before:

> Enide ont baillie une mure,
> Car perdu ot son palefroi;
> Mais ne fu pas en grant esfroi,
> N'onques n'i pensa par semblant.
> Bele mule ot et bien amblant,
> Qui a grant aise la porta.
> Et ce mout la reconforta,
> Qu'Erec ne s'esmaioit de rien,
> Ainz lor disoit qu'il garroit bien. (ll. 5168–76)

> To Enide, who had lost her gentle palfrey, they lent a mule. However, she did not seem not greatly troubled by this and apparently never gave it a thought. The mule was fine and sure-footed and carried her very comfortably. And it also comforted her greatly that Erec was not at all troubled, saying he would make a good recovery.

As before, where the palfrey was an object that provided a means to address other issues through diplomatic circumlocution, so here we are given to understand that there is more here than meets the eye, as is apparent from the slight shift from the description given by the count's niece earlier in which the palfrey was suitable for a maiden because it was not 'de grant esfroi' (l. 1391). Here, by contrast, that quality is now explicity transferred to Enide. The drift of the lines that follow on from Enide's lack of concern at the loss of her original palfrey make it clear that her main attention is focused on something else, the 'ce' in l. 5174 referring both forwards and backwards. Another way of resuming the strange logic the translation smooths over slightly, Enide is reassured by the mule she has received *because* her husband says he does not feel worried about his prospects for

387

recovery. Importantly, Enide is here being looked at from the outside for the signs she herself gives, with our sense of her assessment of the situation apparent from her engagement in the interactions with those around here: she is acceding to the status of a courtly player who is able to both control and dissimulate her feelings as required, who speaks through the codes and conventions of her milieu and whose role is to be seen and be wondered about.

Once we arrive at the castle, both Enide and Guivret are able to step back from their directly interventionist roles, and the duty of care is relinquished to Guivret's two sisters. Although they are referred to several times as 'serors' (l. 5181, l. 5187), at the last mentions of them during Erec's convalescence they are referred to as 'puceles' (l. 5210, l. 5288, l. 5293), assimilating them to the various maidens we have met so far. The equally matched and skilled 'pucele' sisters mirror the oppositional relationship of the two maids that subtended the opening part of the narrative, providing a vision of the symbolic reconciliation of one of the work's major oppositional relationships that hints at what is to follow. The shift in terms of reference also marks the stay at the castle as a return to the courtly milieu as a place regulated by closely observed distinctions of status. Of course, as we know from Chrétien's comments on the morning after the wedding feast, Enide is no longer a 'pucele' but rather a 'dame' (l. 2104). It is therefore legitimate that she delegate activity to her social juniors and also ensure that it is carried out to her satisfaction, as she indeed does, noted as being constantly present at Erec's side:

> Mais, qui qu'alast et enz et fors,
> Toz jorz estoit devant son cors
> Enide, cui plus en tenoit. (ll. 5199–201)
>
> > But, whoever else went in or out, Enide – to whom it mattered most – was at his side every day.

Another suggestion is that it is made clear that Enide is to be kept at a slight distance from Erec for other reasons. The intensive management of Erec's regime also requires that his passions be kept under control. What clearly restores Enide's happiness in the subsequent description of Erec's return to health is the resumption of marital relations, described at length in what, as the climax of the period of convalescence (ll. 5228–51). Crucially, the impatience that is apparent is really Enide's, a subtending tremor also signalled in the fact that she is the one who is kept away from his bed during the brief sojourn with Arthur earlier in the quest (ll. 4265–8). This therefore becomes the narrative of her impatience and desire as opposed to his. Whereas before the wedding, propriety is on the side of Arthur and Enide and desire on Erec's, in that it is he who brings the wedding forward, here it is Enide who is being kept from her partner. This positioning of Enide as a desiring subject goes hand in hand with the quest's positioning of her as a rhetorical subject and Erec's equal in terms of her manipulation of the public sphere through the master and performance of emotion. Desire is at the foundation of what she does, but it is the modulation of that impulse that provides public life with its texture.

In addition to the reparation of the young king's body, we also have a normalisation of the microcosmic court order. The focus on sincere attention to courtly nicety evident in Guivret's courteous solicitude emphasises the consolidation of personal and diplomatic relations between the three of them. Moreover, the description of Erec and Enide's pleasures – whose withdrawal from the careful rhythms of day-by-day curative routine into the *feutré*, breathy murmur of the secluded chamber reads like a medieval romance version of Serge Gainsbourg and Jane Birkin's controversial 1974 hit, 'Je t'aime' – is shown to remodulate sweetly back into the more socially oriented themes of the work, being followed directly by the affirmation of the bonds of friendship that tie them to Guivret ('Si ont Guivret congié rové, / Cui mout orent ami trové', ll. 5253–4) and their decision to return to court.

The relations between the three parties, given equal emphasis, mark the stress that Chrétien places on all three as active participants on the courtly stage. What is also important is that we see Enide judging Guivret's behaviour. Her position here as a subject in her own right, viewed as someone whom Chrétien suggests is a figure whose satisfaction is of sufficient importance to require noting, emphasises a salutory shift in the balance of power. Just as Erec has been challenged by the brutal testing of both body and resolve and having risen to that challenge, so the traumatic effect of the preceding episodes on Enide necessitates its own period of care. Crucially though, in both cases, the acquisition of experience marked into the body does not simply imply a return to the status quo, but rather appears as the assimilation and consolidation of growth. Powers and techniques have been tested, and the body social as a whole must settle into the new state of affairs.

The allusions to the narrative of Troy in the description of Enide's new saddle hints at another resolution of a problem posed by classical antiquity.[36] Having now appeared as a modern version of the Philomena tale gone aright, and indeed having managed to present a courtly answer to the problem of Lucretia, Enide now appears as a version of Lavine, finally sure not only of her place in her beloved's affections but also in her capacity to assert her place in the political economy. Just as the summarised narrative of Eneas's travels presents us with a picture of deception and suicide, of an Eneas whose mobility is associated with slipperiness and unmanliness so those issues are laid to rest. Where the narrative of Eneas locates women for the main as objects of conquest and deception, Chrétien's presentation of Enide describes a possible space for aristocratic women as desiring and willing Subjects rather than as the objects of divine interference in the matter of the passions, the competing *esfrois* of Juno and Venus providing the shape and texture of Roman history. However, this is not to say that all is now the plenitude of promise fulfilled: the courtly art of perverse deferral still has a place. The description of the palfrey and its equipment reflects the savouring of gift and artefact, in that it is almost fifty lines that pass from the first mention of the animal (l. 5308) to the formal act of gifting ('Li palefroiz li fu bailliez', l. 5349), a perhaps now entirely sincere version of the delight Erec showed in the horse first presented to Enide at the court of Laluth, the gift here accepted under rather more difficult and less entirely cordial circumstances.

This sense of Enide's actions denoting a 'transcendence' of the role she had previously played and a reflection back on the learning process she has been involved in is also symbolised in Guivret's two sisters, mirrors of the two *puceles* Enide implicitly but effectively bested in the forest and at Laluth. However, the presence of two maidens here has less of the oppositional quality and points rather more in the direction of a symbolic reconciliation. Erec's departure from court marks the reassertion of royal will against the regime of care: Erec orders that everything necessary be made ready for him to set out at dawn. Again, as before, we have the emphasis on immediate action, and, where he has now rested for some time, the insistence on movement is once again apparent, with Erec voicing his intention not to break his journey until he finds Arthur (ll. 5270–4). This impatience is also apparent in Enide ('Ja ne cuide veoir cele ore / Enide qu'il soient monté', ll. 5306–07), her haste here contrasting then with the description of the gentle amble of her new palfrey that follows immediately after (l. 5309–10). Similarly, the description of the party, with many hounds and hawks (ll. 5354–8), makes it clear they are setting out as a hunt party rather than as a military expedition, as might have been expected from the manner of their arrival at Guivret's castle. Not that this means the spectre of passionate *esfroi* has been entirely laid to rest. Indeed, the description of the saddle presents us with an oddly-accented narrative of settlement:

> La sele fu d'autre meniere,
> Coverte d'une porpre chiere.
> Li arçon estoient d'yvoire,
> S'i fu entaillie l'estoire,
> Coment Eneas vint de Troie,
> Coment a Cartage a grant joie
> Dido en son lit le reçut,
> Coment Eneas la deçut,
> Coment ele por lui s'ocist,
> Coment Eneas puis conquist
> Laurente et tote Lombardie
> Et Lavine, qui fu s'amie. (ll. 5327–38)

> The saddle was completely different, covered with expensive silk. The saddle bows were of ivory, and carved on them was the story of how Eneas came from Troy, how in Carthage Dido joyfully received him into her bed, how Eneas betrayed her, how she killed herself on account of him, and how Eneas later went on to conquer Laurentum, all of Lombardy and his fair friend Lavine.

As with the crisis scene in the bedroom, the differences between readings in this version and that of the Guiot copy and related

391

manuscipts change the sense of the passage in crucial ways. In the Guiot copy, which has 'Dont il fu rois tote sa vie' as the equivalent here of l. 5338, Lavine goes problematically unmentioned. As Joseph Wittig comments, there are clear differences in emphasis between the visions of the Aeneas narrative as found in Virgil and in Chrétien's possible intermediary sources, such as the commentaries on the *Aeneid* of Fulgentius and Bernardus Silvestris, differences which lead to a rather different vision of the place of Dido.[37] As Wittig points out, these commentaries transform Aeneas into a sort of Everyman, presenting his journey as an allegory of maturation and dalliance in Cathage in particular as the age of lust or desire ('libido' in Bernardus's text) rather than maturity characterised by his less self-indulgent relationship with Lavinia.[38] However, although this means that in Virgil's poem, 'Dido is simply abandoned, dead and largely forgotten', Enide shows a continuity with herself, a sort of moral resurrection denied the Queen of Carthage, the latter only to be encountered as a silent, fleeing ghost in the underworld.[39]

In B. N. fr. 1376, by contrast, Lavine is not omitted, Eneas's narrative thereby inflected as one of military and amorous contrast rather than a progression from wandering and passionate turbulence to the settled proprieties of kingship in his mature years. The fact that the saddle is of carved ivory, the same material as the thrones to be described in the coronation, accounces this object as being of a key foundational importance. Interestingly, what one might expect instead of what we see, namely the tale of Eneas and Dido, is the tale of Eneas and Lavine. In that sense, what the saddle does is take what appears from the point of view of the *Roman d'Eneas* the central *méconnaissance* of the Trojan narrative and to found medieval modernity on the very forces of desire that destroyed two kingdoms. The question is then effectively one of how one should 'mount' a 'palfrey'. And, clearly, the *Roman d'Eneas* has much to say about the proprieties and improprieties of its hero's *grande chevauchée*, of who, what and how he rode. Key here is Dido's tale, which sows trouble for Eneas in Italy, the skeleton – or perhaps, ghostly shade – in his closet that forms a central, organising trope for all the sexual slanders that follow. But then, as the mention of his kingship makes clear, to mention his deception of her is effectively then to repeat a criticism that is, in the long view (*a la parsome*), irrelevant. Indeed, the scene of Enide mounted on the palfrey speaks of an incorporation into her 'becoming animal' of the turbulent forces associated with what Lee Patterson refers to as 'the old Dido', the key confluence of the influences of her patron Juno and of Venus, whose agency places the Queen of Carthage in such *esfroi*.[40] Adding to this sense is the parallel Burgess notes between the description of Enide's new palfrey (ll. 5311–21) and that of Camille's extravangantly pied mount in the *Roman d'Eneas* (ll. 4049–68), this 'horse of another colour', to quote the *Wizard of Oz*, a reflection of her sexually exotic status.[41] Enide's mount is more restrained: black and white with the single dividing line of green down the forehead (ll. 5319–21), a detail Bezzola sees as symbolic of hope and new life, or which Ruth Firestone presents as the line of Enide's new path, one in which she will exemplify Boethius's exhortation (*Consolation of Philosophy*, book 4, metre 7, ll. 20–1) to neither 'despair at adversity nor be corrupted by pleasure, but occupy [the middle ground of courage] "firmis medium viribus"' in a virtuous, 'manly' style that would then resolve the earlier problems Chrétien highlighted in his description of the Count of Laluth's niece as 'mout prouz, mout sage et mout vaillanz' (l. 1350).[42] The fact that Chrétien in effect passes over Lavine not once but twice suggests various possibilities. The first, and more socially conservative, is that the missing term is Enide herself as the new Lavine, with Chrétien's presentation of Dido and Camille suggesting, as with Pandion's failure to curb and protect Philomena, they are simply women given too much licence. In this reading, as Burgess puts it, Enide's former self appears as a figure of the 'naïve, carnal love' associated with Dido.[43] Such an interpretation would fit with the readings offered by Fulgentius and Bernardus Silvestris of Aeneas's career as a process of maturation.[44]

However, just as Virgil's successors seemed uncomfortable with his seeming domestication of history's 'Junoian' dimension, so a resolution of the possibilities of *esfroi* here might be premature and even dangerous. B. N. fr. 1376 does not entirely domesticate either Lavine or Enide: for all the one-line mention distinguishes the former from Dido's more colourful history, Eneas's ultimate union thus cast in this vignette as a resolving coda to the troubles elaborated in earlier sections of the narrative, she is nonetheless still referred to as 'amie', still offering the potential for some element of Junoian trouble.[45] Thus an alternative reading might highlight the scandalous assertion inherent in Enide's transcendence of Eneas's two significant post-Trojan women. Her symbolic mounting of the two of them places her as Lavine 'riding' both Camille (horse) and Dido (saddle), just as Eneas appears riding Lavine and then his male lover in the slander Lavine's mother paints of him. Thus, Enide's assertion of her position is not simply the docility of the palfrey but rather one of hyper-virile, even perverse activity. However, unlike the boorish Kay, who seems to overlook the comic potential latent in his appropriation of Gauvain's position, Enide's control of *esfroi*, the shock effects of sense and subtext, marks her as more the master here. Moreover, insofar as this writing of history inherent in Enide's new horsewomanliness retains a scandalous dimension, an allusion to archetypes that do not sit quite as comfortably in the saddle, so Chrétien does not simply leave us with a docile pair of good little heterosexuals but rather twin embodiments of the acculturated perverse. As with Arthur's apparent blunder, Erec's scar or Holbein's skull, the most uncomfortable aspect is placed in plain view, challenging all *contredit* and facing down all those who would mock or criticise.

Notes

1   On Enide's lament, see, among others, Alan Press, 'Death and Lament in Chrétien de Troyes's Romances: The Dialectic of Rhetoric and Reason', *Forum for Modern Language Studies*, 23:1 (1987), 11–20 and Virginie Greene, 'Le Deuil, mode d'emploi, dans deux romans de Chrétien de Troyes', *French Studies*, 52:3 (1998), 257–78. Firestone's comment that '[Enide's] decision to join Erec in death by means of his sword reveals that she has overcome contempt for adversity which she cannot bear: she knows that she can neither live nor die without him' (p. 95) I find cryptic on various fronts. For one, it seems to suggest some endorsement on Chrétien's part of Enide's 'Stoic' reaction to Erec's apparent death, whereas I would argue the poem sets itself very much against any such perspective.

2   See Gottfried von Strassburg, *Tristan*, trans. by A. T. Hatto, rev. edn (Harmondsworth: Penguin, 1967), pp. 185–8.
3   On the *Metamorphosis*, see Peter Dronke, *Abelard and Heloise in Medieval Testimonies*, W. P. Ker Lecture, 26 (Glasgow: University of Glasgow Press, 1976), pp. 16–18.
4   On Enide's attempted suicide and its cultural and theological background, see Marie-Noëlle Lefay-Toury, *La Tentation du suicide dans le roman français du XIIe siècle* (Paris: Champion, 1979), pp. 92–140 and Duggan, *The Romances of Chrétien de Troyes*, pp. 151–3. More generally, see Nicole Gonthier, *Le Châtiment du crime au Moyen Age: XIIe–XVIe siècles* (Rennes: Presses Universitaires de Rennes, 1998), as well as Alexander Murray, *Suicide in the Middle Ages: 1) The Violent Against Themselves* (Oxford: Oxford University Press, 1998) and *Suicide in the Middle Ages: 2 The Curse of Self-Murder* (Oxford: Oxford University Press, 2000).
5   Cherniss, p. 59.
6   On suicide as *passage à l'acte*, see Lacan, *Le Séminaire X*, pp. 119–53 and Žižek, *Enjoy Your Symptom!*, pp. 43–6.
7   Žižek, *Metastases of Enjoyment*, p. 75.
8   For edition, see *The Song of Roland: The French Corpus*, ed. by Joseph J. Duggan and others, 3 vols (Turnhout: Brepols, 2005). For discussion, see Simpson, *Fantasy, Identity and Misrescognition*, pp. 29–53.
9   On Lucretia and Cato and Marcus Regulus, see Murray, *Suicide in the Middle Ages: 2*, pp. 136–44, on the opposition between Stoic suicide and the example of Marcus Regulus in Augustine, see pp. 114–20.
10 Murray, *Suicide in the Middle Ages: 2*, p. 398.
11 For text, see Augustine, *The City of God Against the Pagans*, ed. and trans. by G. P. Goold and G. E. McCracken, 7 vols, Loeb Classical Library, 411–18 (Cambridge, MA and London: Heinemann, 1957 [1981 printing]). However, as a translation I prefer *Concerning the City of God Against the Pagans*, trans. by Henry Bettenson (Harmondsworth: Penguin, 1984).
12 Gravdal, *Ravishing Maidens*, pp. 9–10.
13 On resistance, see Kenneth Varty, 'The Giving and Withholding of Consent in Late Twelfth-Century Literature', *Reading Medieval Studies*, 12 (1986), 27–49, at pp. 35–6.
14 On which, see Kay, *Courtly Contradictions*, pp. 264–75.
15 On Enide's silence in this scene, see McCracken, 'Silence and the Courtly Wife', pp. 120–21.
16 Plummer, p. 389.
17 Adler, p. 929 and McCracken, 'Silence and the Courtly Wife', pp. 108–11.
18 'There is a way out that is open to the woman who has reached the end of her resistance – it is suicide. But it seems less often resorted to by women than by men. Here the statistics are very ambiguous. Successful suicides are much more common in men than in women, but attempts to end their lives are commoner in

the latter. This may be so because women are more likely to be satisfied with play-acting: they *pretend* self-destruction more often than they really *want* it. It is also in part because the usual brutal methods are repellent: women almost never use cold steel or firearms. They are much more likely to drown themselves, like Ophelia, attesting to the affinity of woman with water, where, in the still darkness, it seems that life might find passive dissolution.' (de Beauvoir, *The Second Sex*, p. 621, original emphasis)

19 Duggan, *The Romances of Chrétien de Troyes*, p. 152.

20 Lefay-Toury argues that the gesture of attempted suicide is 'superfluous' in the sense that Enide's cries in the forest would have attracted Oringle in any event, just as her outburst at Limors would have woken Erec (pp. 94–5).

21 On the comic potential of the suicide in the *Charrette*, see notably Gaunt, *Love and Death*, pp. 123–5.

22 Seebass-Linggi, pp. 32–3.

23 Yamamoto Tsunetomo, *Hagakure: The Book of the Samurai*, ed. and trans. by William Scott Wilson (Tokyo and London: Kodansha International, 2000), p. 74.

24 On Erec and the killing of Oringle, see Allard, pp. 100–04; Seebass-Linggi, pp. 116–8.

25 Rachel Ann Dressler, *Of Armour and Men in Medieval England: The Chivalric Rhetoric of Three English Knights' Effigies* (Aldershot and Burlington VT: Ashgate, 2004), p. 75.

26 M. R. James, 'Casting the Runes', in *Collected Ghost Stories*, Wordsworth Classics (Ware: Wordsworth: 1992), pp. 235–67.

27 On Stalin, see Žižek, *Sublime Object of Ideology*, p. 108 and *Plague of Fantasies*, pp. 58–60.

28 See Žižek, *Plague of Fantasies*, pp. 21–3.

29 See Žižek, *Welcome to the Desert of the Real*, pp. 86–90.

30 See, for example, Köhler, *L'Aventure chevaleresque*, pp. 167–9

31 See, for example, Jean-Charles Huchet's comments: 'La parole envolée d'Enide dévoilait une carence masculine; l'empêcher équivalait à donner la preuve par les armes qu'elle était fallacieuse et à la convertir en parole d'amour. Le roman de Chrétien révèle qu'on ne saurait contraindre une parole féminine; aussi faut-il apprendre à l'approprier, fût-ce contre soi, ou à n'y lire que ce qui s'avère conforme à l'orgueil masculin.' (*Littérature médiévale et psychanalyse: pour une clinique littéraire*, Ecriture (Paris: Presses Universitaires de France, 1990), p. 133). See also Adler, p. 945; Burns, *Bodytalk*, pp. 182–4 and Seebass-Linggi, pp. 123–4.

32 Burgwinkle, *Sodomy*, p. 168.

33 See Seebass-Linggi, pp. 118–27.

34 Nykrog, pp. 72–3.

35 Allard, p. 104.

36 On the saddle and the palfrey, see Patterson, *Negotiating the Past*, pp. 190–5. Burgess, *Erec et Enide*, p. 79 and Wittig, who sees in the detailing of the saddle bows a strong parallelism between the careers of Erec and Aeneas. See also Nelson, 'Animals', p. 35.
37 Wittig, pp. 240–8.
38 On Dido, Bernardus comments as follows: 'Increpat Mercurius Eneam oratione alicuius censoris. Discedit a Didone et devescit scilicet a libidine. Dido deserta emoritur et in cineres excocta demigrat', Bernardus Silvestris, *The Commentaries on the First Six Books of Virgil's 'Aeneid' Commonly Attributed to Bernardus Silvestris*, ed. by Julian Ward Jones and Elizabeth Frances Jones (Lincoln N and London: University of Nebraska Press, 1977), p. 25.
39 Wittig, p. 251.
40 Patterson, *Negotiating the Past*, p. 194.
41 Burgess, *Erec et Enide*, pp. 77–80. On Camille, see in particular Huchet, *Le Roman médiéval*, pp. 60–80.
42 Bezzola, p. 196.
43 Burgess, *Erec et Enide*, pp. 77–80.
44 See references to Wittig above.
45 On which see notably, Barbara Nelson Sargent-Baur, Erec's Enide: "sa fame ou s'amie"?', *Romance Philology*, 33 (1979), 373–87, p. 385.

Chapter Eight
Illusions and Consolations: Joys of the Court

Don Giovanni in Brandigan: Erec and Evrain

> Don Giovanni: Ho fermo il cuore in petto: Non ho timor: verrò!
> (*Don Giovanni*, act 2, scene 19)
>
> 'My heart is firm in my breast. I am not afraid. I will see.'

The 'Joy of the Court' has had something of a varied critical history since Gaston Paris's lengthy dismissal of it in his review of Foerster's edition.[1] However, Paris's spluttering incredulity at what he takes as Chrétien's gross literary vandalism is countered by voices offering a more positive appreciation of its place in Chrétien's composition can be found from early on, a neat summation of which position is John Plummer's remark that the 'episode reinforces the lessons of *Erec et Enide* both large and small'.[2] In light of what we have seen so far, another reading might present it as a continuing interrogation of the boundary between pleasure and enjoyment in a scene that is presented as an embarrassment of courtly riches, both material and discursive.

If one of the problems Chrétien seems to be treating in his poems is the notion of continuity and foundation in the narrative of *translatio imperii* – a debate which, as Sarah Spence argues, sets the hopes for stability in Virgil and Vitruvius against the instability and uncertainty of Ovid and Augustine – we might well look to the details of the countryside around Brandigan. As Chrétien notes, the castle is cut off from the rest of the world by a raging torrent:

> [...] vienent devant les bretesches
> D'un chastel fort et riche et bel,
> Tout clos en tor de mur novel;

> Et par desoz a la roonde
> Corroit un eve mout parfonde,
> Lee et bruiant come tempeste. (ll. 5362–7)
>
> They found themselves in front of a beautiful castle surrounded by fine, new-made walls. And around their base ran a deep stream, rapid and loud, rumbling like a storm.

Commentators have emphasised the troubling dimension of the water: as Gérard Chandès remarks, 'les eaux violentes [...] toutes marquent une situation d'angoisse'.[3] One subtext here might well be the isolation of the island on which Tristan fights his duel with Morholt. However, there are other possibilities: as Burgess notes, the mention of storms recalls the weather that forced Dido and Eneas to take shelter in a cave (*Roman d'Eneas*, ll. 1506–09).[4] However, the two scenarios differ crucially, the foundation of the two citadels, Carthage and Brandigan, giving the cue. In the *Roman d'Eneas*, as in the *Aeneid*, Carthage is built on trickery: Dido asks for only so much land as can be encompassed by a single ox hide.[5] She then cuts the hide into fine thongs that then enable her to mark out a huge area. However, this deceptiveness returns to haunt her, her position as lord the lie at the heart of her city's seeming stability. Similarly, Aeneas's sojourn in Carthage is marked by impermanence and is indeed the product of turbulence, the 'tempeste' a destablising instrument of divine will rather than a feature integrated into the landscape as at Brandigan. This detail then points to the character of Brandigan as not entirely Vitruvian in conception, but rather having seemingly successfully incorporated a Junoian element into its structure. This is clearly apparent in Guivret's account of the origin of the castle: the torrent offers sufficient protection that the walls are in effect redundant (ll. 5400–06).

A key issue here is Erec's evident fascination ('Erec en l'esgarder s'areste', l. 5368) with a spectacle so strongly assimilated to Carthage, and thus seeming to mark a symbolic reversion vis-à-vis his archetype's career, forsaking the Lavine at his side for some new Dido. In that sense, we are required to seek some other explanation for his entrancement. Or are we? One possibility is that the roles of Eneas and Dido are here taken by Maboagrain and his *amie*. However, the anxiety sown in the party by Erec's rapt contemplation of this seemingly fateful object of desire hints at a permanence of *esfroi*, the enduring possibility of a 'return to Carthage', even if only as a mark of the absolute singularity of his royal will. It is here that the place of Guivret as interlocutor becomes vital, with Enide – logically enough – silent at this point because she is not privy to the relevant information. The openings of his two speeches attempting to persuade Erec not to seek the joy suspend his name. In l. 5418, Guivret is simply 'this one' / 'he' ('cil'), a reprise of the start of the previous speech ('cil cui mout grevoit' l. 5411). By suppressing his name, Chrétien accents Guivret's function, not as one aggrieved and moved by Erec's intrusion on to his lands or by his own 'mautalant', but by concern for his friend's safety. Correspondingly, Erec's utterances and his desires emphasise both distance from but also fellow-feeling for those around him, his testing of those ties once more placing a burden of anxiety on them even as this is offset by a greater show of sympathy than previously:

> 'Sire nel tenez mie a jeus,
> Que ja par moi ne le savroiz
> De ci que creanté m'avroiz,
> Par l'amor que m'avez promise,
> Que par vos ne sera requise
> L'aventure dont nuns s'estort
> Qu'il n'i reçoive ou honte ou mort.'
> Or ot Erec ce que lui siet.
> Guivret prie que ne li griet. (ll. 5432–40)

> 'Don't think I'm joking, my lord: indeed, whatever I know you'll never learn it from me unless, in the name of the love you've pledged me, you swear you won't attempt to seek the adventure from which no one escapes without shame or death.' Now Erec had heard what he wanted to hear and begs Guivret not to be aggrieved.

Although only reported, Erec's speech reflects back Guivret's reactions, compensating his grievance through entreaty (the verb *prier*). However, equally prominent is Erec's visceral reaction to what he is told. In a condensation of the irony of the Joy, what sits with him best is shame and death, although interestingly Guivret's expression

401

appears as a version of the highway robber's stock phrase, 'Your money or your life', where what is proposed is not a choice between *either* money *or* life, but rather a demand for either one or *both*. As Lacan comments, this 'false choice' can be seen as a model of the obscenity of the Law. But then Guivret himself offers a deceptive impression: the glaring reverse psychology of his request that Erec should not press him for further information demonstrates the difficulty inherent in caring for the royal passions.

Both Erec's reactions and Guivret's counsel have their counter-intuitive dimensions, a mode also apparent in Guivret's account of Evrain:

> 'Alons i; nostre ostex est pris,
> Que nuns chevaliers de haut pris,
> Ce ai oï dire et conter,
> Ne puet en cest chastel entrer
> Por ce que herbergier i vuille,
> Que li rois Evrains ne recuille.
> Tant est gentis et frains li rois
> Qu'il a fait banc a ses borjois
> Si chier con chascuns a son cors
> Que proudons qui viegne defors
> En lor maisons ostel ne truisse,
> Por ce que il meïsmes puisse
> Touz les proudomes honorer
> Qui leanz voudront demorer.' (ll. 5471–84)

> 'Let's go. Our lodgings are arranged, for no knight of high standing – so I have heard tell – can enter this town in search of hospitality without being welcomed by king Evrain. The king is so noble and gracious that he has made a proclamation to his burghers that, if they value their lives, no nobleman who comes from outside must find lodging in their houses. Honouring men of valour is a charge the King takes on himself.'

Guivret's account of Evrain's custom mirrors the paradox central to the Joy.[6] It is Evrain's *franchise* that instructs him to kill any bourgeois who takes in a knight of renown. The apparent contradiction here between courtly qualities and absolute and savage justice has been arguably seen before at the Sparrow-Hawk contest. We remember that there the Count threatened those members of the populace who obstructed Yder's procession to the centre of the arena.

A witness to Brandigan's spectacular power, Chrétien's cornucopian accumulation is likewise a mark of seduction. In a visual equivalent of the torrent surrounding the citadel, its sensory overload threatens to sweep away the *conjunture* of the poem by detaining both narrator and audience in nugatory delights compared to the pleasures that are to come:

> Mais por qoi vos deviseroie
> Les pointures, les draps de soie,
> Dont la chambre estoit embelie?
> Le tens gasteroie en folie;
> Mais je ne le vuil pas gaster,
> Ainçois me vuil un po haster,
> Car qui tost vait la droite voie
> Passe celui qui se desvoie;
> Por ce ne m'i vuil arester. (ll. 5563–71)

> But why should I tell you in great detail all about the paintings and silken drapery with which the chamber was so beautifully decorated? Why waste time on foolish matters when instead I wish to hurry on a bit, for the man who goes quickly by the straight road passes the man who strays from the path. Therefore I do not wish to linger.

Chrétien's apparently sensible hastening past possible distracting 'folie' can also be read as a paradoxical assertion characteristic of the conflict at the heart of courtly poetics. He does not want to give into the *jouissance* of that temptation too soon (we must wait for the coronation and the description of the robe), and yet he also wants to speed things up a bit. The analogy between the libidinal and poetic economies he sketches is evident from the detail devoted to the question of the relation between 'soreplus' (as the pleasure that defies narrative convention) and the pleasures of seduction.

That 'bel semblant', while evident of a mastery of self, is of course at the same time dependent on a degree of violence, a pathological unbalancing of the passions. After all, the hunt that accompanies Erec can be read as a spectacular display of courtly *oisiveté*, but it also appears as the rehabilitatory coda to a period of treatment and convalescence in which the young king's appetites and desires have been carefully managed. Indeed, Guivret continues in role of care as in feudal duty earlier and also in mode of medical management. He is given the care of the king's body. The idea that emerges from the pairing of the detail of his control of Erec's diet during his period of recuperation, avoiding spice and richness, is that Erec's condition as charismatic leader is, in a sense, permanently pathological. Here is a dish that must be kept from him at all costs: some tales cannot be told without them having an effect. The entire subsequent setting as presented in Chrétien's version makes that spectacular dimension of the feast abundantly apparent. We move from a meal with Evrain to the orchard, containing all the riches nature can offer to the raw and unappetising sight of the severed heads. Note that the conclusion of the narrative thereafter will focus on descriptions of food and feasting. The question then emerges of what it is the king can eat or should eat. After all, the royal diet is a major thematic concern in the wider Arthurian narrative, the king here being the creature who must refuse certain foods lest he be tarred with the cannibalistic enjoyment that is the mark of the tyrant.

In that sense, Guivret's actions indicate that, by his assessment, the joy is something Erec should have no stomach for. Its language should have no savour for him, and yet, where the irony of the joy is repugnant to the populace, it is apparently sweet to Erec. Again, we must bear in mind the dimension of royal spectacle here. All foods presented in ceremonial setting at the court, whether they be destined for the monarch's plate or for other mouths, are, in a sense, always a tribute to the king. He devours them with his eyes if not otherwise, a consideration especially apparent in a culture where visual adornment and flavouring went hand in hand in an almost synaesthetically interchangeable manner: a leek pie with a gilt crust might be relatively bland in taste, but the decoration is the visual mark of its 'richness' as a dish. Erec insists in a manner that makes it plain that this scene is not a straightforward affirmation of harmony and balance attained through his quest, as Allard argues.[7]

Erec's beauty is a source of fascination and pathos to the good people of Brandigan. But that quality is in part dependent on his defiance of their perspective. Against the 'fog' of discord that keeps the Joy as an object of mystery, he refuses to see anything but good in the marvel. From the perspective of all those around him, this looks like a suicidal delusion. The young king's reading in good of the 'joie' mirrors Chrétien's reading in bono of the Arthurian legend, boldly refusing to be cowed by its tragic dimension. It is this refusal to be cowed by the reflection on Fortune, this fundamental defiance that endows Erec's 'contenance' with its consuming beauty of charisma, the mark of someone who has taken the extraordinary step that positions them 'between the two deaths', outside the normal order of social structure and yet still alive:

> Dïent en haut: 'Dex te desfende,
> Chevaliers, de mesaventure,
> Que mout es beax a desmesure;
> Et mout fait ta beautez a plaindre,
> Que demain la verrons estaindre.
> A demain est ta morz venue,
> Demain morras sanz atendue,
> Se Dex ne te garde et desfent.'
> Erec ot bien et si entent
> Qu'en dit de lui parmi la vile,
> Que plus le plaignent de deus mile,
> Mais riens ne l'en puet esmaier.
> Outre s'en va sanz delaier,
> Saluant debonairement
> Touz et toutes communement.
> Et tuit et toutes le salüent,
> Et li plusor d'angoisse süent,
> Qui plus dotent que il ne fait
> Et de sa honte et de son lait.
> Soul de veoir sa contenance,
> Sa grant beauté et sa semblance,
> A si les cuers de toz a lui,
> Que tuit redoutent son anui,
> Chevalier, dames et puceles. (ll. 5510–33)

Then they said aloud so Erec could hear: 'May God protect you and keep you from harm, knight. You are as handsome a man as can be, and so we mourn your beauty, for tomorrow we'll see its light extinguished! Tomorrow will your death come, tomorrow you'll die without delay, unless God protect and defend you.' Erec heard them clearly and understood what they were saying all across town: more than two thousand pitied him but nothing could daunt him. Onward he went without tarrying, greeting one and all in fine style, and they in turn greeted him. Many sweated with anguish, fearing to see him dead or dishonoured more than he did himself. The sight of his bearing, his great beauty, and his appearance alone had so won him the hearts of all that everyone – knights, ladies and maidens alike – dreaded the misfortune that would befall him.

The nature of Erec's performance is apparent from the detachment of his passions: his absence of fear (l. 5521) and relaxed, debonair demeanour (l. 5523) clearly emphasised. The laments they pronounce over Erec, whose countenance is a source of joy that seduces, excites and mesmerises the crowd, are intensely expressive of a consuming desire for the royal presence, and an anxious, almost morbid fear of its loss.

The sheer intensity of the crowd's desire is apparent from the accumulation of opposites in the collective discourse: they speak of Erec's beauty (l. 5530), but, in their distraction, see it here as little more than the presage of his 'lait' (l. 5528), the ugly, ignoble fate that awaits him. As we approach the joy, popular rumour, condenses into a contradictory weave of its acclamatory concern and apparent vulgar stupidity, stating and mis-stating the nature of the Joy. Not only can joy not be misery, a person cannot die *tomorrow without delay* ('demain sanz atendue' l. 5516) otherwise that would be now, a logical contradiction announced in the previous line's curious use of tense – 'a demain *est* ta morz *venue*' (l. 5515): literally 'your death *has come* tomorrow' – in which the present is simply swallowed in ellipsis. In that regard, the Joy appears as a perfect example of the gravitational effect of desire before the fantasy screen, collapsing oppositions, whether logical or temporal, so that the object can radiate its condensed power of singular fascination.

Chrétien presents rumour and collective utterance as having a life of their own fundamental to the texture of aristocratic society. What is revealed by this collective fervour is the sense of Erec's action, bringing another object – himself – into the fantasy space surrounding and emanating from the joy. His serene demeanour and purposeful approach demonstrate both an innate and performative mastery of contradictions in his manipulation of the crowd and in his capacity to provide a still, yet dynamic quilting point for their emotional investments in what appears as a symphonic sweep and progression in orchestration of emotion. Yet there is also a necessary element of contestation and resistance there: their fears may see him already hence from the confines of this world are counterbalanced by a motion that, to their horror seems driven from another source, animated by another energy: 'outre s'en va sanz delaier' (l. 5522). Interestingly, insofar as the populace of Brandigan curse the name of joy, they are not merely caught in its gravitational field but also appear as the generators of it. This fantasmatic quality will be given solid form in the wall of air surrounding the orchard, bearing witness to Chrétien's dual vision of the power of (collective) *parole* to both distance the subject from the object of desire and to draw him closer to it. Indeed, this scene explains some of the brief nods to the power of rumour that have peppered the work at key points, from Erec's renown that had reached Enide's father (ll. 670–3) to the rumblings of discontent regarding his alleged *recreantise* (ll. 2455–8), to the news that reaches Guivret of the perils faced by Enide (ll. 4933–49).

Erec's serenity at this point stands in instructive contrast to the show of insistence both to Guivret and, subsequently, to Evrain. It is this involvement that marks him as likewise caught in the web of desire. The excessive nature of Erec's desire for the joy provides the marker of what Lacan would refer to as his 'not-all' status in relation to the crowd, the assurance that there is another fantasy dimension at play in this situation in which he is entirely caught up: the enthralling power of the object-cause, *das Nächste*. Where they see only his death, he sees a source of seductive power. Yet again, in spite of the grip it seemingly exerts on the irrationality of the passions, his relation to the joy appears as one of understanding. The king's visual ingestion of the spectacle is thus a necessary part of his charismatic domination of court life, the necessary supplement that is the guarantee of courtly taste. This leads us into a paradox. After all, the idea of having 'eyes bigger than one's stomach' is a common expression of the excess of visual over physical appetite. Fair enough, except that the royal stomach and its appetites must be carefully managed for the good of the body politic. In that sense, the king's visual tyranny, the demand for an excess of riches in spectacle and appearance becomes the

407

guarantee of the authenticity of court life: its spectacular dimension is the response to a rapacious demand orchestrated from the centre. The fact that the Real of appetite must always be feared is the price to pay for the thing that then gives the collective endeavour its own spice.

This emphasis on desire's disturbance of the regular appetites is dramatised by the Joy's creation of an awkward moment at the dinner table. Both the narrator and Erec leave off from the details of Evrain's lavish hospitality, the former cutting short both his description of the chamber Evrain prepares for the couple (ll. 5563–71) and that of the meal (ll. 5580–2), while Erec interrupts the feasting, plunging first into a show of thoughtful preoccupation with the Joy (ll. 5586–8) and then to speaking of it (ll. 5589–99). Yet, for all Erec's obvious preoccupation and then raising of the uncomfortable, elephant-in-the-room subject are clearly out of keeping with the festivities, his insistence is not received as some churlish interruption or gaffe, as can be seen in the carefully mixed reception given to his inquiry. The fact that Evrain is described as encouraging Erec's 'parole' ('Li rois Evrains l'a maintenue', l. 5590) and his polite opening formula 'beax amis' (l. 5601) both signal that the game is being played with due and satisfactory respect for form, in spite of the stern warnings and sharp instructions that follow ('Parler vos oi de grant oiseuse', l. 5601; 'N'en parlez plus, taisez vos en!' l. 5610). In that sense, there is both feigning here and non-feigning: Evrain is giving Erec a genuine warning founded in previous experience, but that caution, even in its absolutely emphatic terms, is also part and parcel of the events that are to follow. In that sense, the 'no' is not entirely a 'no'. Rather, from beginning to end, Evrain's actions are part of a carefully and well-practiced show of honour for his guest, from the king's acknowledgement of Erec's fitness as a courtly player to carefully stressed avoidance of 'traïson' and 'mesprison' (ll. 5631–2) through his giving of the warning. Evrain thus does Erec the honour of showing that all the demands of custom have been satisfied in exact and punctilious compliance with the last letter of the law.

Evrain's speech crowns the collective performance of the townspeople with their obsessive and repeated assertions of fear and desire and indeed reveals the logic of the intense play of emotional and temporal perspectives. In that regard, the spatial layout of

Brandigan seems to display a collapsing of time in that both feared and desired futures saturate and distort the present to the point of fracture and nonesensicality. Not all productions go so far in their demonstration of conflict and dissonance of course: for example, the January illumination of the *Très Riches Heures*, which depicts a scene of feasting in a room decorated with tapestries depicting a battle. However, the exploration of intense perspectival contradiction marks a number of medieval and early modern mixed media installations. Again, one need only think of *The Ambassadors*: the parallel between painting and text is that both organise gaze and anamorphosis as part of a specific structuring of particular public spaces. Holbein's painting reflects and shapes patterns of movement in the space before it, the *conjuncture* of its visual field supplied by the viewer's progress, articulating the discursive content of its *sens*. Chrétien is also alive to these questions of perspective, whether spatial or temporal, as we can see from his comments on Arthur's contemplation of his court. Both Arthur's contemplation of the court and Erec's contemplation of the joy are thus counterpointed by the *parsome* that is the certainty that death, if nothing else, will cast them down from the top of Fortune's wheel. Erec is drawn by the joy, that word apparently out of joint, whose seductive power seems to lie as much in its capacity to distort the present as in its promise of possible resolution. And yet there is the insistence of the present will, the assertion that now is the time. Never after all, has Erec been so articulate about the object of his desire as he is at this point where he himself remarks that '*Des ore* est tens / Que je die quanque je pens' (ll. 5591–2) – '*now* is it high time I tell you what I have in mind'. By contrast, he does not speak of his fascination with Enide, but rather experiences it silently as thought during their ride back from Laluth to the court (ll. 1482–93). This assertion of will – like Chrétien's opening boast 'Des or comencerai l'estoire / Que toujours mais iert mais en memoire', ll. 23–4) – does not simply lay claim to the passing present moment. Rather it announces its *extensio*, its claim to more than the share of time that is its uttering: not simply 'ore', but 'des ore' – the first element having the sense of 'from' or 'as of'.

Chrétien's exploration of the perspectival problem encompasses the intersubjective clash of different experiences and desires intruding into the same space and time. After all, from another point of view, everything that has happened so far has prepared Erec for this moment in its echoing and fulfilment of the promise of the 'premerains vers'. The play of contrasts is carefully woven, but we are also invited to read it as one that is felt and experienced by the characters, not only to see but to posit a mindfulness of the contrast between Erec then and Erec now, giving us a sense of the road subjectively travelled. This is especially apparent in the comparison as well as contrast between Erec and Yder that makes of this a far grander and more compelling version of the Sparrow-Hawk tournament, whose tired, eventless repetitions – Yder had won it *uncontested* twice in a row (ll. 595–6) – pale before the singularity of this moment. This paradoxical quality is apparent in the arms he receives from Evrain (ll. 5676–82), his acceptance simultaneously indicative not only of his willingness to play the role required by the custom of the place, but also – through its recall of the borrowing of those of Enide's father (ll. 612–34) and his turn away from the arms he wore during the quest – of a resonance in terms of his personal itinerary pointing forward to the role he will play as 'still centre' in the turning world of the coronation. Thus, like and unlike the question of the dress, Erec's acceptance of the new equipment is then not merely based on practical considerations, as Chrétien's description underlines, it is also, to judge from the terms of that same description, determined by on aesthetic ones.

As we move on, the intensity of the ironies and riddles start to reach breaking point, with cracks showing in the very fabric of the narrative:

> Li rois, qui lez lui est a destre,
> Li dit trestot et se li conte:
> 'Amis,' fait il, 'savez que monte
> Ceste chose que ci veez?
> Mout en devez estre esfreez,
> Se vos point amez vostre cors,
> Car cil seus pex qui est defors,
> Ou vos veez ce cor pendu,
> A mout longuement atendu,
> Mais nos ne savons pas bien cui,
> Se il atent vos ou autrui.

> *Garde, ta teste* n'i soit mise,
> Car li pex siet en la devise.
>
> Bien vos en avoie garni
> Ainçois que vos venissiez ci.' (ll. 5782–96, my emphasis)
>
> The King, riding beside him at his right hand, told him everything and said: 'Friend, do you understand the meaning of this thing you see here? Be very afraid if you value your life, for this one stake set apart, where only that horn hangs, has for a long time been waiting for a knight. Who, we don't know. You or someone else. Beware lest your head be placed there, for the stake is set up for that purpose. I gave you fair warning before you came here.'

As I commented earlier, one way of understanding Erec's motivation for setting out on the quest was as a response to Enide's speaking of him as if he were already dead, as if he had already *come to that place*, an address that then made problematic the use of informal and intimate forms of address in the rest of the work. Consequently, as we approach the joy, it is to an extent unsurprising that Erec finds himself addressed in different voices. Although Evrain, even in his strongest admonishments, keeps entirely to the *vous* form characteristic of polite courtly interaction, the intemperate, passionate effusion of the collective is rendered in a number of speeches addressing him as *tu* (ll. 5697–700, ll. 5708–13). Given that Evrain has shown an uncommon degree of self-mastery, blending stern warning with joyful hospitality, the sudden shift in his address leaps out in striking contrast to the rest of the speech around it, as if in a different voice. One objection to reading much into this detail might be the hypermetrism that would be created by the use of *vostre*, but the attention paid to code-switching prior to this argues against a simple glitch. The effect is a sudden flash of the intimacy of threat and insult in midst of courtly discourse that gives a sense of the disturbing strangeness of the scene Evrain describes with Erec's destiny, a brief fracturing wrinkle that brings into focus the more general anamorphic distortion of the discursive field surrounding the joy.

Of course, such a prospect is not likely to intimidate our hero, who shows his mastery of these strategies by his immediate appropriation of them. Erec's account of his own possible future death seems designed to present all the more strikingly the picture Enide paints for herself in her mind's eye, with Erec arguably seeking to flesh out that apprehensive vision in even more horrifying detail than she herself imagines, while at the same time demonstrating his undaunted equanimity.

'Douce dame, encor ne savez
Que ce sera, ne je nel sai;
De neant estes en esmai.
Mais sachiez bien certainnement:
S'en moi n'avoit de hardement
Que tant con vostre amors me baille,
Ne doteroie je sanz faille
Cors a cors nul rien vivant.
Se fais que fox que je me vant,
Mais je nou di por nul orguil,
Fors tant que conforter vos vuil.
Confortez vos, laissiez ester!
Je ne puis mais ci arester,
Ne vos n'iroiz plus avec moi,
Car avant mener ne vos doi,
Si con li rois l'a comandé.' (ll. 5844–59)

'Gentle lady, you don't know this will come to be, nor do I. You are frightened for nothing. Know for a truth that, had I only so much courage as comes from your love, I would not fear to face hand-to-hand any man alive. I may be a fool to make such a boast, but I do not say so out of pride, but rather only to comfort you. Be of good cheer and let it be. I can stay no longer, and you may go no further with me, for the King has commanded me not to take you past this point.'

Erec's self-possession is manifest in his ability to distance himself from his own deliberately audacious claims regarding his and Enide's feelings, highlighting the effect of her love on his courage as well as his deference to the custom of the Joy that does not allow him to take her any further. But then of course, his progress at this point reflects the nature of the Joy as an object of terror: its effects are felt at a distance, but the actual spectacle is hidden from sight, gaining in its imaginative recastings whether by the townspeople or by Erec himself.

A Big Teaser's Vile Deliverance: The Festive Erotology of the Arena

> Got a good reason
> For taking the easy way out. [...]
> She's a big teaser:
> She took me half the way there. [...]
> She was a day tripper –
> One way ticket, yeah!
> It took me so long,
> But I found out. (The Beatles, 'Day Tripper')
>
> Maximus (bellowing to the crowd): 'Are you not entertained?'[8]

Even if, as we are assured, the Joy is no mere show tournament, then one might perhaps still be forgiven for sensing an element of pantomime exaggeration in Maboagrain's bellowed threats to Erec (ll. 5899–906). Just as with Clint Eastwood's laconic screen persona in the early 'spaghetti Westerns', the original script pared back to the spare style that became his trademark, Erec is allowed a dramatic pause in which to look the big bully up – for Allard, the very embodiment of the capacity for violence inherent in the second function body of warriors – and down (ll. 5906–10) and then ask him why he is making all that noise (ll. 5911–26).[9] Although the aesthetic of the Eastwood Westerns, the poetry of the lawless, inbred grime of one-horse towns, is very different from the bright splendours of courtly romance, Chrétien's approach shows parallels, albeit here in a step back from the consuming din of *copia dicendi*. In so doing, he reminds us of a basic fact: by this stage, we have seen a lot of *words*, the audience pummelled and punch-drunk from their accumulated evocative power. And yet, we are also conscious of having been spared a few, Chrétien clearly flagging the further distractions with which he could have belaboured us. In this dramatic pause, no one makes a move until Erec answers Maboagrain ('Li uns vers l'autre ne se mut, / Tant qu'Erec respondu li ot', ll. 5909–10).

Although the display of heads at the centre of the Joy appears as the mark of the monstrous, exorbitant nature of this spectacle, Maboagrain – laconically content in his own way to let the spectacle do the talking – does not threaten Erec with a shameful beheading or anything else so apparently outside the system of values we have seen presented up until now. His warning comment, 'This very day you will pay most dearly for your foolishness, I swear by my head' ('Vos comperroiz encui mout chier / Vostre folie, par ma teste.' ll. 5904–05), can be read as a grim joke hinting at both the rules of the game and the fate potentially facing Erec, but it is not the full and explicit description of the horrors that lie in wait given by King Evrain the previous night. Indeed, Maboagrain's second warning is conventionally formalistic: 'Be sure you'll get a fight, for I challenge and defy you' ('Sachiez, bataille ne vos faut, / Car je vos requier et desfi.' ll. 5928–9). Thus, there is a sense that the more that we approach the violence that lies at the heart of the Joy, the more it is mediated and trammelled by the invisible walls that are the ground rules of chivalric combat. Indeed, Maboagrain issues his challenges in a way that signals arguably greater regard for and submission to the formal niceties than manifested by the giants abducting Cadoc. This paradoxical concurrence of total commitment and theatricality is further emphasised in the combat with Maboagrain by the fact that, once the warning has been given, it is then left to the narrator to provide the sort of commentary that denotes the unstinting nature of the combat. Their reins are not held in check (l. 5931), and the lances are not slender, but thick and well-planed (ll. 5932–3).

Everything seems to augur well for a spectacular and decisive combat. Yet, perhaps not unpredictably given the grand single combats we have seen so far, the duel ends in exhaustion rather than death, albeit this time more extreme than we saw in the combat with Yder. Once again, as with the initial phase of the duel with Yder and the later combat with Guivret, we have a paradoxical assertion and guarantee of its authenticity through its lasting until the opponents can no longer strike effectively:

> Ne plus ne se püent pener
> D'aux empirier ne d'aux grever,

> Que il se poinnent et travaillent. [...]
> Mout sont doillant et mout sont las.
> Neporquant ne recroient pas,
> Ainçois s'esforcent miauz et miauz.
> La suors lor troble les iauz,
> Et li sans qui avec degoute,
> Si que par pou ne voient goute;
> Et bien sovent lor cops perdoient
> Si comme cil qui pas ne voient
> Lor espees sor aus conduire.
> Ne se püent mais gaires nuire
> Li uns vers l'autre; neporquant
> Ne recroient ne tant ne quant,
> Que trestoz lor pooirs ne facent.
> Por ce que li huil lor esfacent
> Si que tot perdent lor veoir,
> Laissent jus lor escuz cheoir,
> S'entraerdent par grant ire. (ll. 5961–87)

They did everything they could to hurt and harm one another. [...] Weary and in pain, they did not give up. They struggled on, pushing themselves harder and harder, even though they could barely see for the sweat and blood dripping down in their eyes. Often their blows swung wide, for they could hardly see to guide their swords at each other. And still they did not give up a jot, but tried as hard as they might. Their eyes failing, they fought on blindly, letting their shields fall and seizing each other with great fury.

Interestingly, although their shields suffer the usual damage in the early phases of the fight, being hacked and broken apart, they are not discarded and here appear in the last movements as emblematic of their weaponry. Camouflaged as a poetic variation on the fates of the various weapons up to this point, Chrétien's account of the final phase here conveniently glosses over what becomes of Erec's and Maboagrain's swords. This unexplained disappearance or fading contrasts tellingly with the dramatic breaking that ended the first encounter with Guivret, the last pitched single combat with another knight preceding the Joy episode. Here, by contrast, the struggle degrades into a blind, fumbling tactility. Their shields discarded, they grapple in a manner paradoxically both ineffectual and satisfying in terms of both honour and the drama at hand, their struggle a version of the martyrdom of epic heroes such as Oliver, the pathos of whose final moments is rendered more acute by his blind striking at Roland (*La Chanson de Roland*, ll. 1989–2009). The disappearance of the swords here denotes a general exhaustion of means, the mark of a commitment to totality fulfilled in keeping with a culture in which appearing to surrender too readily was cause for shame and could indeed give rise to accusations of treachery.[10] However, the fact that their shields seem to have survived until this stage (somewhat exceptionally in terms of typical romance presentations of sustained combat) also hints at another dimension, the shield appearing as a sort of veil, an obscuring of identity that is the last thing then to be torn aside in preparation for the emergence of new identities in the form of Maboagrain as a creature of the public sphere as well as that of Erec as king.

Thus, although Erec pulls off Maboagrain's helmet and forces him to bend down in preparation for his decapitation (ll. 5994–7), not only are the swords temporarily out of the picture, but also the defeated knight is unable to maintain the posture of the victim and simply collapses face down on the ground (ll. 5998–9). This momentary stay of execution briefly forestalling what seems like the inevitable climax a little more, further action is delayed by Maboagrain's speech, which conveniently is extracted under a sort of compulsion ('Li convient dire et outroier', l. 6001) and 'with great reluctance' ('que que il li doie *grever*', l. 6000, my emphasis). The recurrence of the key verb *grever* assimilates this quasi-consensual relation to that between Erec and Arthur and then... Erec and Enide on their wedding night. Circumstances are stronger than the defeated Maboagrain, who has to know whether his opponent really is simply the best, better than all the rest:

> 'Et mout voudroie par proiere,
> S'estre puet en nule meniere,
> Que je vostre droit non seüsse,
> Por ce que confort en eüsse.
> Se mieudres de moi m'a conquis,
> Liez en serai, jel vos plevis;
> Mais se il m'est si encontré
> Que pires de moi m'ait outré,
> De ce doi je grant duel avoir.' (ll. 6007–15)

'And I would greatly like, if I may ask, and were it at all possible, that I might know your name, for I may take some comfort from it. I swear to you, if a better man has beaten me, I will be glad. But it it turns out that I have been beaten by a lesser man, then I will have cause for great sorrow.'

Obedient to the order of ceremonies as per the sudden *tutoiement* of Evrain's warning (ll. 5697–700; ll. 5708–13), Erec's response is seemingly both comforting and threatening, reprising both that form of address and his earlier opening to his initial response to Maboagrain's threats before the combat – 'Friend,…':

'Amis, vuet tu mon non savoir?
Fait Erec. 'Et jel te dirai,
Ja ainz d'ici ne partirai,
Mais ce iert par tel convenant,
Que tu me diras maintenant
Por qoi tu es en cest jardin.
Savoir en vuil tote la fin,
Quex est tes nons et quel la Joie,
Car mout me tarde que j'en oie
La verité de tot en tot.' (ll. 6016–25)

'My friend, so you want to know my name?' Said Erec. 'And indeed I will well you it before I leave this place, although on condition you tell me now what you are doing in this garden. I want to know the story from beginning to end – what your name is, what the Joy is – for I am impatient to hear the truth of it all.'

Conveniently, although it might seem that the logical climax to the Joy would be for Erec to behead Maboagrain, everything leads away from such a vision, centring on other possible climaxes such as Erec's naming of himself and the amplification of that gesture in the souding of the horn.[11] The first deliverance having been the Maboagrain's collapse, we move to his concession speech in which he does not beg for his life in so many words, as Erec mentioned as the final disgrace that might await him ('Qu'il m'estovera merci atendre /Et deprïer, estre mon vuel', ll. 5840–1), but rather asks who has defeated him, a fitting end at the hands of a worthy adversary seeming sufficient consolation ('confort', l. 6010). In that regard, Maboagrain shows himself rhetorically more *adroit* than Yder, forced to call stop in rather less elegant terms and luckier than

Turnus, whose appeal in the *Aeneid* had Aeneas almost swayed until the latter saw Pallas's sword belt (*Aeneid*, book 12, ll. 938–52), or, in the *Roman d'Eneas*, ring (ll. 9818–56). That the climax here is at some level patterned after the *Roman d'Eneas* is apparent from the reaction of the crowd to Eneas's killing of Turnus. Whereas the reaction to Turnus's thigh being pierced by Eneas's lance is undifferentiated in terms of party ('la gent et les barons / [...] forment s'en escrïerent', ll. 9812–13), the reaction to Eneas's killing of a man who had just begged him for mercy and offered all reasonable terms, renouncing any claim either to Lavine or Latium, divides the crowd quite emphatically:

> Mout i ot noise merveilleuse
> La gent de Troye en fu joieuse
> Et cil dolant de l'autre part. (ll. 9857–9)

> The noise and hubbub was astounding: the Trojans were overjoyed, while those on the other side were sorrowful. (trans. mine)

In that sense, much as the negotiations over Enide can be read as a version of *Philomena* that turned out happily, so again here we have a seeming 'rectification' of an ancient source, although crucially on the part of both players. Unlike Maboagrain, Turnus is afraid ('Turnus le vit qui paor ot', l. 9817), a detail possibly suggesting that, although abjectly cowed now, Turnus – like the defeated Saracens in the Oxford *Roland* – may prove untrustworthy later. Eneas's apparently barbaric act is thus arguably somewhat redeemed by its prevention of further bloodshed. However, rather than being dismayed, Maboagrain is *won* by his opponent's performance. Thus, the gigantist gestures of the *Roman d'Eneas* – Turnus's throwing of the great rock (ll. 9796–806) or Eneas's mighty strides towards his defeated foe ('Avant ala tout son grant pas', ll. 9817) – are reappropriated and domesticated here as part of a tournament aesthetic. Thus, the fact that the inevitable might perhaps not be so inevitable is then also apparent from Erec's response, answering Maboagrain's question with another question of his own and thereby indicating what he sees as the dramatic finale of the Joy: not death, but revealed knowledge (as opposed to *Le Chevalier de la charrette's* conclusion of beheading and concealed knowledge). As we pass from there into Maboagrain's lengthy explanation of how he came to find himself in the orchard, the possibility that there might be another killing recedes, especially as the big knight – having taken over the role of master of ceremonies from Evrain – works his way round seamlessly to the end ('la fin') that is not his death but his liberation through the sounding of the horn (ll. 6136–47). Erec falls in line with the local strategy of teasing the crowd and avoiding the appearance of a 'vilainne [...] delivrance'. Thus, although the traumatic spectacle of shameful, mangling death looms large in the tales told of the Joy and indeed in the initial accounts and vision of it, the possibility of the traumatic Thing, the – 'snuff-movie money-shot' – happening centre-stage before our eyes seems to recede from the very moment we pass from dialogue and description to the combat itself. What we see from a distance is the obscene irony of the Joy as lamented by the townsfolk. What we find at 'ground zero' is a conventional duel in which the possibility of death re-elides at the shift back from description into dialogue.

In short, what Chrétien targets in this scene as at Laluth and Danebroc is the extent to which entertainments of this kind, the 'conflictus Gallicus' or 'Gallic battle' (as tourneys were referred to in non-French sources in the period), is the line that made them, as Maurice Keen puts it, 'only just distinguishable from real battle'.[12] If, as Sandra Hindman argues, *Erec et Enide* was received at least in some quarters as a text that looks towards the conventions of epic as the 'real thing', then Erec's combat with Maboagrain provides a central show-down between two modes of knighthood, one 'romance', the other 'epic':

> Though their skills are closely matched, Erec and Mabonagrain stand in sharp contrast as warriors. Mabonagrain's military aptitude finds its expression only in ritualised combat, since he is confined by his lover to an enchanted garden. Erec's skill as a warrior, however, has been tried in a setting outside the court, the forest fraught with unpredictable dangers, and, unlike Mabonagrain, he has demonstrated that his lover need not impede his military performance. In a curious turnabout, this episode casts Erec as a brave warrior from epic and Mabonagrain as a fickle hero from romance.[13]

However, from my discussion above, it could equally well be argued that there is much that also suggests a view of Erec as one perfectly capable of reading and enacting the conventions of romance, even to the point of miming the bravery of some of the genre's most fearsome heroes... or villains ('Se fust Thiebauz li Esclavons / Ou Opiniax ou Fernaguz', ll. 5770–1).[14] In that sense, what would *not* be needed would be a less comic version of Aucassin's participation in the 'war' scene in Torelore, a burlesque food-fight ended by real violence as the young male lead butchers a large number of the participants (*Aucassin et Nicolette*, § 32). Indeed, that is not what the spectators get: although blond-haired Aucassin bears the Arabic name, it is Erec who is able to pick up on his host's cues to play Saladin in a sure-footed display of courtly *savoir*. In that sense, another way to look at Hindman's reading on the basis of the illustrations in fonds fr. 24403 is that just as the codex's contextualisation of *Erec et Enide* polices and contains the poem's queerer possibilities, so Hindman closes down what we might see as the Joy's exposure of the 'erotology' of the arena, its strangenesses, whether sexual or ethnic. For a start, Chrétien's narratorial comment that the scene of the stakes would be enough to scare Thiebaut, Opinel or Fernagu, seems to imply that there is something singularly barbaric about the horrors of the orchard. Moreover, although it is Chrétien the narrator speaking here, the narrative point of view seems to reinforce Evrain's warnings, enhancing the atmosphere generated by the local guide. Indeed, what the comparison implies is that from the point of view of the townsfolk, the ideal participant condenses a seemingly contradictory range of qualities: while Erec is praised and lamented for extensively for his beauty (ll. 5708–13), the outsider also ideally arrives in the guise of a savagely exotic enemy, thus a twelfth-century anticipation of *Pulp Fiction's* fetishisation of hypermasculine gangster stylings generally – and specifically those of the supremely 'badass' black crimelord Marsellus, epitomised in his threat to 'get medieval' (see discussion above). And, not merely do the crowd at Brandigan seem fickle in their desire for an ideal knight who condenses every hero in one, they are unable to face up to the sadistic truth of their own desires as realised in the obscene spectacle of the Joy. In that sense, to quote Lacan, what we have here is an example of the sender's receiving his /

her message back 'in inverted form'.[15] Still, that said, once an audience has watched as many chivalric snuff-movies as there are stakes in the orchard, and realised this isn't what they wanted in order to be truly, finally entertained, where do you go then?

Obviously, actual violence is and is not like 'sexual' desire. However, the questions of how and whether one can really 'go all the way' in courtly spectacle are no less apparent in the account Maboagrain gives of his relationship with the maiden, a tale that raises interesting questions about the relation between perception and identity. When Erec entered the orchard, we are told he saw a 'pucele' (l. 5875). However, such perceptions have been wrong before, as was the case with the first of the five robber knights who laid claim to the 'maiden' they saw heading in their direction (ll. 2941–2).[16] Erec's first sight of the 'amie' also stands at odds with Maboagrain's assertion that he loved the maid 'sans rien laissier' (l. 6053). Although this testimony, that 'nothing was omitted', seems to indicate that the 'sorplus' of consummation did in fact take place, the 'amie' still keeps the name of 'pucele'. It therefore seems to matter little whether she actually is a virgin or just 'like' one. As we know from earlier, clothes and other apparel may be stolen and apparently noble people may harbour ignoble desires, so exterior appearance is no safe guide. But then, this play between appearance and reality as a source of dramatic satisfaction also figured in the approach to the Joy when Erec was described as 'looking very like' a count or king ('*Bien resembloit* as hernois /Que li sire estoit cuens ou rois', ll. 5537–8, my emphasis).

What may underpin this apparent indeterminacy is the public nature of sexual conquest that was made apparent in the wedding ceremony, with Guinevere and other representatives of the court in attendance up until more or less the last minute and public acclamation of Enide's new status appearing first thing the following day. What Chrétien thereby presents is a vision rather at odds with the emphasis on intact maidenly status seen in other works, such as the Tristan legend, where Iseut's loss of virginity has to be concealed by the substitution of her maid Brangane. Accordingly, either Chrétien's apparently rigid system of designations is not what it appears, or Erec's initial error is indicative of an overriding assumption sustained and affirmed as part either of social nicety or, quite simply, theatre.

According to this logic, actual *jouissance* does not lie in the private act of coupling or killing but rather in its public celebration. It is thus conventional that women participants as objects of potential desire are or at least pass for 'maidens', although this no more guarantees they are such any more than were the 'maids' who appeared in Shakespeare's original productions of his plays, a polite fiction only unmasked in comic tales such as *Le Mantel mautaillé*.[17] What is not visible does not necessarily have to have happened. Of course, we might also detect an ironic, even mischievously vengeful, echo of the Count's niece's implied slander of Enide. Where the former had implied that more might be known about Enide than was consonant with her status as 'pucele', now the latter's potential disgrace is airbrushed from the picture. This is not the last polite fiction that we will see maintained with regard to Enide's family.

There is of course an aspect to the *pucele's* ambiguous status that reflects her place in an orchard which can be entered but from which nothing can be removed. This magical character seems to affirm the values of an officially regulated aristocratic sexual politics, but so as to allow transgressive desires little of the disruptive power associated with them in moral and satirical commentary. Indeed, here, instead of threatening the system, illicit sexual activity can do nothing against it and is simply written out, the 'maiden' magically trapped in physical stasis. Thus the orchard appears as not so much a place of sensual abandonment as a refusal of history. This position is then the height of perversity, part of a system in which the object of desire can be approached in different ways, whether through the 'official' version that is the ceremony of marriage or through the elevation of unconsummated desire that is the courtly cult of the beloved lady. In that sense, one way of reaching the orchard is as a failed version of the vaginal 'infolding' of the divide between the natural and the cultural in the wedding ceremony described earlier, the limit now externalised in the wall of air that divides the cultural world of Brandigan from the natural garden it keeps within its bounds. To resolve this paradox, it was necessary for a knight, valiant and transfixed by desire, to approach the bloody rose.

However, for all the parodic elements, as the townspeople remind us, this is no laughing matter. In that regard, the orchard appears as a ceremony gone wrong, a festive *vacance* that has in effect deformed the social construction of space and time. In their cursing of the Joy, the townspeople point us in the direction of what might seem like a barbarous psychoanalytical reading but one that is entirely licenced by Chrétien's presentation of the relation between sexual activity and other activities that can become the focus of public spectacle. After all the underpinning notion is that courtly love is predicated on desire for and impossibility of the act. Against this, Chrétien's description of the pleasures enjoyed by Erec and Enide after Erec's return to health is one of an unnumbered sequence of acts in which the dialogue between 'joie et [...] deduit' (l. 5231) and 'soreplus' is, implicitly, repeated over and over again:

> Li uns encontre l'autre tance
> Coment li puisse mieuz plaisir;
> Dou soreplus me doi taisir. (ll. 5246-8)

> Each of them sought to outdo the other in giving pleasure. I'm not permitted to say more.

Such a narration entails an inevitable lie on Chrétien's part, and indeed the economy of sensual pleasure he implies is fundamentally ambiguous. Indeed, to have told us more about either the act or their fecundity in invention would have turned the scene into a *fabliau*. Thus, the fact that he is quiet about the 'soreplus' functions as a signal: this thing he is not allowed to speak about did happen, and, indeed, given the tenor of the rest of his description, probably several times. However, actually counting the occurrences would be inappropriate – that way lies the world of *Trubert*, with the Duke's wife suddenly obsessed with keeping a tally of her husband's performances (ll. 688–703). Besides, Chrétien seems to imply, such an enumeration misses the point, and herein lies the sense of the ambiguity: if what the use of the term 'soreplus' indicates is that 'joie', 'deduit' and 'plaisir' are not synonymous with penetration and intercourse to climax, then there was also a good deal of foreplay too, the teasingness of which is rendered in Chrétien's use of the verb *tancer*, meaning 'to compete with', 'to strive' and 'to argue with'. However, if those terms are synonyms, then he has given us a language that encompasses both the representability and transgressively shocking unrepresentability of the act, a language that simultaneously affirms and resists the laws of literary *bienséance*.

Chrétien's perverse-yet-fulfilling literary strategies contrast sharply with the impasse of Brandigan's collective frustration, the scene permeated by a festive *Vorlust* to the point that it becomes a nightmarish ordeal. Of course, this does not mean that Brandigan is not enjoyable in its own way, much as in the same way Laluth was not a realm of absolute alien evil. Chrétien is indeed sufficiently caught up in the panoply that he has to tear himself away from getting lost in the heat of his description of tapestries that, although not the main attraction, are clearly 'to die for'. As Žižek points out, it is far from uncommon for fetishists to enjoy their symptom well enough that they have no wish to seek a 'cure'. But then this is the problem: if every version of pleasure is synonymous with all the others, there is no way out. 'D'amors ne sai nule issue', to quote Chrétien's lyric. Trapped in the frisson of anxiety, the people of Brandigan act as guardians of a ritual that has failed to discharge itself, and indeed has failed to end so many times that they no longer entirely know who or what they are waiting for. Their *Vorlust* has become a nightmarish suspension. Indeed, Evrain does not think Erec will find his way out of this puzzle either:

> 'Ne cuit que ja mes en issiez,
> Ne soiez morz et detranchiez,
> Car nos en savons ja bien tant
> Que li pex vostre teste atant.
> Se ce avient qu'ele i soit mise,
> Si con chose li est promise
> Des lors que il i fu fichiez,
> Uns autre pex sera dreciez
> Aprés celui, qui atendra
> Tant que ne sai qui revendra.
> Dou cor ne vos dirai je plus,
> Mais onques sonner nou pot nus.' (ll. 5797–808)

'I doubt you'll ever get out before you end up dead and dismembered. And since you now know, this stake awaits your head, and if it comes to be set there, as was predicted as soon as the stake was put in place, another will be planted after this one, which will wait until someone else, God alone knows who, comes along. Of the horn I shall tell you nothing save that no one has ever been able to sound it.'

Of course, Evrain's own strategies are no less dishonest than Chrétien's: he *does* proceed immediately after this to tell Erec what would happen if someone succeeded in blowing the horn.

Maboagrain's place in this erotic ritual is no less unsatisfactory. His bloody reign of terror as champion of the Joy attests to the contradictory nature of chivalric behaviour: protocols were felt to obtain, but, as the twelfth century drew to a close, the frequency of laments regarding loss of life among the noble *milites* suggests more than some conventional deploration of the barbarity of the present.[18] It is this seemingly irrational coexistence of impulses to both mercy and brutality the Joy of the court reflects. Unlike the repeated non-event presided over by Yder and the Count of Laluth, the body-count at Brandigan offers the vision of a tournament in no danger of collapsing into empty show, but which has clearly passed beyond the bounds of 'le plaisir'. And yet the audience cannot tear itself away, revealing the contradiction underpinning its desires, torn between horror and a bloodlust they seek to disavow, a problem that had niggled at Western societies even from before Augustine's tale of his friend Alypius in the *Confessions* painted a picture of a Christian world trying to wean itself from the guilty pleasures of the arena.[19] The underlying problem is neatly summed up by another 'big guy' in the arena: Maximus, the central character in Ridley Scott's film *Gladiator*. Emerging from the tunnel of a provincial amphitheatre, he proceeds to dispatch five opponents in an exemplary display of swiftly brutal, bone-crunching efficiency, the combat over in less than a minute. The audience's *angoisse* is palpable: are they horrified by the reality of this violence or dissatisfied because it did not draw out the spectacle sufficiently? In response, Maximus throws back the negative question, 'Are you not entertained?', challenging the crowd to traverse the fantasy of the grotesque play-act mime it presumably expected and assume the truth of its desire. Likewise, Maboagrain plays his role at the bloodily immediate and yet apparently unapproachable centre of the stage, giving the crowd the apparently interminable spectacle they are not sure they want. What Maximus's question highlights is the problematic relation between violence and sexual activity: the one is and is not like the other. Only fantasy orchestrates violence into an erotic grammar: its raw stuff, actual combat, works according to a more clipped, less demonstrative syntax. At this point in Ridley Scott's narrative, Maximus is chiefly driven by the statement 'revenge is a dish best served cold', and is not interested in providing spectacle properly 'cooked' the crowd wants.

Back at the provincial amphitheatre of Brandigan, the erotological problem of the arena is similarly apparent, although the sexual dimension is more directly to the fore: just as the crowd cannot derive (or perhaps better, in the words of the Rolling Stones, 'can't get no') satisfaction, Maboagrain presents himself as unable to obtain the *soreplus* of the scene from his lady, and so is waiting for a man to provide the solution, the 'deliverance', the *don de merci*, he does not think will ever come:

> 'Des que je soi le bien en li,
> En la rien que je ai plus chiere,
> N'en dui faire semblant ne chiere
> Que nule rien me despleüst,
> Que, s'ele s'en aperceüst,
> Tost retraisist a li son cuer;
> Et je nou vousisse a nule fuer
> Por rien que ce deüst avenir.
> Ainz me cuida retenir
> Ma damoisele a lonc sejor.
> Ne cuidoit pas que a nul jor
> Deüst en cest vergier entrer
> Vasaux qui me deüst outrer.
> Por ce me cuida a delivre
> Toz les jors que j'eüsse a vivre
> Avec li tenir en prison.
> Et je feïsse mesprison,
> Se de rien nule me fainsisse,
> Que trestoz ceus ne conqueïsse
> Envers cui j'eüsse puissance:
> Vilainne fust la deliverance.' (ll. 6074–94)

'Once I knew the good in her, the person I held most dear, what choice did I have? I could not have shown my displeasure, for, if she had noticed, I would have lost her love for ever, and I did not wish that at any price, no matter what the consequences. That is how my lady thought to keep me in here all these years, not thinking any knight would ever come along who could best me. Thus she easily thought to keep me all the days of my life imprisoned with her. And how wrong I would have been to hold back and feign not to be able defeat any I could overpower: such an escape would have been ignoble.'

One remarkable thing about this speech is the reporting and summarising of the lady's position: Maboagrain takes the law of her love as absolute, not questioning its dictates at any level. His killing of all his competitors is then the mark of a wholehearted commitment to his oath that reduces him to the status of instrument, perversely, consensually bound without exception and to the letter. From a 'theological' point of view, this could well be read as Christian allegory of the relation between the 'Old Law' and the 'New', with Maboagrain caught in the power of a letter that kills rather than a spirit that vivifies. However, the 'pagan' dimension is more apparent in Chrétien's presentation, Maboagrain demonstrating the necessarily absolute submission of the knight to the law of chivalry, a law of desire in which there is no golden mean, with his unfeigned commitment demonstrated through his killing of the other knights.

And yet, in a neatly vicious circle, the sheer mutton-headed stupidity of Maboagrain's reasoning is the guarantee of a sort of innocence. If he could not spare any of his opponents and maintain he had acted in full accordance with the dictates of his beloved, he cannot logically extend the same mercy to his opponents as Erec did at Laluth, and is thus obliged not merely to kill them, but also to butcher them and display their heads. Thus, his actions are less a product of the hot impulse of raw 'hatred' than of a coldly neutral logic of entailment. Obviously, what we have here is an example of what Lacan refers to as the obscene tyranny of the superego here made evident in Maboagrain's emphasis on the function of the intentions and thoughts he attributes to her, highlighted by the insistent repetition of the verb *cuidier* (l. 6082, l. 6084, l. 6087), a normally pejorative term associated with the thought processes of the proud and the ill-intentioned. Of course, this position does rather make Maboagrain either a medieval cousin of figures such as the 'good soldier Schweik', in danger of looking rather less like a heroic lover than a (literally) bloody-minded, hidebound court bureaucrat caught up in a monstrous version of the 'idiotic' enjoyment of his task we saw in the person of Erec's squire at Carnant or a theme-park employee deriving a perverse thrill from being 'in character'.

In that sense, Maboagrain and his lady appear, as many critics have noted, as a version of Erec and Enide, albeit lacking the same breadth of behavioural and emotional repertoire. Tellingly, the giant knight's capacity to analyse the casuistry of his situation stands in counterpoint to his powerlessness to do anything to free himself from his unwise promise. However, simply to relegate the lady to the status of monster is to miss the function of this extreme commitment which operates as a subtext in the versions of chivalry as lived by both Erec and Arthur. To reject Maboagrain as nothing more than an excessively extreme version of chivalry is to misconstrue the strong connection that ties him into chivalric society, a connection directly apparent from his revelation that he had spent time at the court of Erec's father (ll. 6032–3). Maboagrain thus appears in the form of an uncanny vision whose similarity cannot be entirely or definitively disavowed, a troubling double that reveals the terroristic extremity that lies at the heart of the chivalric ideal, to be revealed ultimately in Erec's beheading of his own sister in the later prose reworking. Thus, although it can be presented as a scathing parody of the teachings of Andreas Capellanus, Maboagrain's relationship with his lady is in this respect arguably not so unlike the relationships of understanding (*consensus*) that exist between Arthur and Guinevere on the one hand and Erec and Enide on the other. All three are predicated on a shared training towards intuitive understanding of each another's thought processes, the ability to work both separately and yet in harmony. This bond is then subjected to the most extreme of tests in the requirement of Maboagrain's absolute contractual obedience to his lady's commands.

To then say that the lady has simply exercised an inappropriate influence in the manner of that attributed to Enide – rumoured to have 'enlaced' her lord, entrapping him by a not dissimilar magic – is to miss the wider question of what binds a society together. After all, although Maboagrain is isolated by an invisible wall, his narrative also reveals his permanent awareness of the expectations of that wider audience. Were he wrong simply to obey his lady's command and remain with her in the orchard, then one must also wonder at the nature of a society content to fall in line with and support such thoughtless obedience. Thus, the existence of Brandigan as 'tourist attraction' and the collusion of its townspeople in its drama speaks of a society entirely loyal to its lord and lady, even to the point of endorsing a spectacle of senseless, murderous brutality. From that perspective, there is little to choose between the court that submits itself to the logic of the Joy on the one hand and one that submits itself to the equally senseless and potentially destructive hunt for the White Stag on the other.

Consequently, Brandigan reveals the obscene superego dimension of social cohesion that extends beyond the immediate community to ensnare new arrivals, the other knights who embarked on the same quest seemingly unable to extricate themselves short of losing their lives. After all, Maboagrain's insistence that he could not 'take the easy way out', be delivered from the orchard in any manner that might be construed as 'vilainne' (l. 6094), suggests that he might also not unreasonably expect the same extreme fate. It also suggests a similar confluence of different themes to that found in courtly complaints such as the Beatles's song 'Day Tripper'. Does the 'easy way out' denote a decision to end the relationship in a manner that might otherwise be concluded as *lâche*, an admission of suicidal despair at its apparent impasse, or, more lewdly, a lack of satisfaction justifying recourse to masturbation: 'she's a big teaser – she took me half the way there'? In that sense, following on from my earlier discussion, the song could also pass as a soundtrack to Dido's suicide in the *Roman d'Eneas*, which forms an early statement of the same traditions of orthodox sexual regulation also informing the Catholic culture of postwar Liverpool: masturbation is a form of (spiritual) suicide.[20] All are possible here: Maboagrain's implied reasoning might reflect a conviction he could not allow himself to be killed without committing de facto suicide, and indeed – unlike the case of Marcus Regulus discussed above – in such a potentially trivial context, he might have been right. Similarly, no grounds would seemingly have justified his breaking of the formally-binding device of the 'parole'.

The impossibility of deliverance or issue transforms the relation between Maboagrain and his 'amie' into a *rapport sexuel qui n'en est pas un*, a state of permanent frustration unassuaged even though their relationship is seemingly fully consummated. The deadlock is neatly engineered: although the 'amie' is thereby in effect positioned as a 'teaser', Maboagrain's refusal to employ any counter-ruse, any 'vile deliverance' in the form of some sort of improper or 'sodomitical' attempt to break out of the seeming libidinal impasse upholds the letter of its perverse law. Indeed, the scenario here appears as a murderous version of the tableau originally hinted at in the encounter in the forest: like Eneas, Maboagrain uses his 'pucele', that is to say the spectacle of her as yet unconquered desirability, to lure passing knights into a bloody, paroxysmic forerunner of the entrapments that recur throughout Sade's *La Philosophie dans le boudoir*.[21] Yet, however viciously, extravagantly sadistic it might seem, the spectacle of an unmarried couple – one of whom may have made at least an implicit boast about her fiery desires and appetites – engaging in sexual relations in the midst of a gory mire of flowers and severed heads is still 'before the Law', still not *jouissance*. In short, harking back to Freud's earlier theories of anxiety, this is the ultimate vision of *angoisse*. This emphasis on the libidinal haunting of scenes in Chrétien's romance may well explain some of the work's comic dimension. In implying Erec supplied him with a satisfaction he never could have obtained from any other man or woman, the gratefully exhausted Maboagrain is able to resolve, or at least stage the appearance of resolving, the erotic and violent impulses underpinning courtly love. Finally here there is the 'falling' of the object Lacan associates with detumescence, albeit here not experienced as the sum of all anxiety ('le sommet de l'angoisse') but rather as orchestrated now into a series of expanding waves that will engulf and release the rest of Brandigan from the *déplaisir* of an overextended *Vorlust*.[22]

While this might sound all a bit far-fetched, it should be born in mind that other medieval sources speak of men 'exhausted but not satisfied' by the company they keep with one another. As Bill Burgwinkle points out, Richard of Devizes, writing in the mid-1190s, was to use precisely these terms to describe the intensity of affection in which Richard the Lionheart and Philippe Auguste, en route to the Holy Land in 1190, parted following this their last meeting on good terms before the English king's rejection of Philippe's sister Aelis, to whom he had been betrothed since the age of four.[23] Richard of Devizes's comment just happens to be an echo of Juvenal's description in his sixth satire of the insatiable wife of emperor Claudius being carried back from her nightly exertions in the whorehouse, 'and with her [vulva / clitoris] still rigid, and exhausted by men but unsatisfied, she went sorrowfully away' ('adhuc ardens rigidae tentingine volvae / Et lassata viris necdum satiata recessit', ll. 129–30).[24] Although Juvenal's language is explicit as to the nature of Claudius's wife's physical state, appetites and sensations, we cannot assume this implies the same of Richard and Philippe, however. As Burgwinkle comments:

> If Devizes did mean to imply a sexual interlude between the kings, then it is interesting to note that Richard's role in the rest of the account is in no way tainted with suggestions of femininity, lasciviousness or decadence, characteristics that generally accompany any suggestion of sexual activity between men in the early twelfth-century chronicles of John of Salisbury, Orderic Vitalis and Walter Map.[25]

Indeed, as Burgwinkle goes on to point out, it is precisely Richard of Devizes's narrative that contains the first references to Richard as a 'lion'. However, this is not to say that Devizes's account is not without its dose of trouble. As Burgwinkle also remarks, an echo of Juvenal's description can be seen in the *Roman d'Eneas* in Tarcon's coarsely misogynistic mockery of Camille, promising her that she would be 'tired but not satisfied' ('Vos en porriez estre lassee, / Mais ne seriez mie saoulee', ll. 7171–2) if she gave up her rough armour and weapons and allowed herself to be used by him and his companions.

The *Roman d'Eneas*'s presentation of Camille positions her as a key intermediary figure between Juvenal and Richard of Devizes, reminding us of the wider context of Richard's allusion. Juvenal's description of Claudius's wife in satire six follows directly on from the tale of 'Eppia the senator's wife [who] ran off with a gladiator

431

[*ludus*]' ('Nupta senatori comitata est Eppia ludum', l. 83 – see ll. 82–113 for the narrative as a whole). Juvenal's picture here is of a woman taken out of the privileged context in which she was brought up and transformed into a 'she-gladiator' ('Quid vidit propter quod *ludia* dici / Sustinuit?', ll. 103–04: 'What did she see in him to allow herself to be called a "She-Gladiator"?'), forced to rough it on the ship that bore her away from her homeland, vomiting on her new husband (ll. 100–01) and eventually adapting sufficiently to the sea-life to hang around the sailors, in whose company 'she delights in hauling at hard ropes' (ll. 101–02). Juvenal's segue into the narrative of Claudius's wife – 'Do the doings of Eppia affect you? Then look at those who rival the gods and hear what Claudius endured.' (ll. 114–16) – is the key, highlighting the transgression of social and gender roles in both cases. Where Eppia transgressed her womanly role through desertion and abandonment of noble ways in favour of an obscenely ludic mime of the low milieu of the arena, so Claudius's wife echoes and outstrips Eppia by becoming a quasi-gladiatorial champion of the brothel, retiring undefeated at the end of each night, her deregulated lusts compromising not one household but an entire edifice of Roman family values. Tarcon's insulting of Camille as a 'she-gladiator' thus pulls together Juvenal's two portraits, denigrating the Amazon as an Eppia-figure and then compounding the insult by offering to restore her to some sort of 'true' nature as a figure of Claudius's wife.

This linking of narratives in Juvenal seems to set a pattern. In the same way, Richard of Devizes's account of King Richard centres on an exaggerated heroic masculinity:

> The king of England set up camp outside the city, because the king of France had already been received in the palace of Tancred, the king of Sicily, within the walls. On the same day, the king of France, when he learned of the arrival of his companion and brother, flew to meet him, and gestures, between embraces and kisses, could not sufficiently express how much they delighted in each other [nec potuit inter amplexus et oscula gesticulatio satis exprimere quantum eorum uterque gauderet ex altero]. The armies refreshed themselves with mutual applause and conversation, just as if among so many thousands of men there were only one heart and one soul [non aliter quam si tot milibus hominum esset cor unum et anima una]. The holiday was spent in such pleasures, and the kings, tired but still not satiated [regibus lassatis nondum satiatis], separated and everyone returned to his quarters.[26]

Richard's account of the meeting of the kings locates their particular effusions in the context of a hypermasculinist chivalric amphitheatre in which mutual admiration bolsters self-esteem, the audience of men reflecting each member back at double the size, to paraphrase Simone de Beauvoir. The armies, like the kings, are united in regard for each other, meaning any suggestion of an 'unnaturally' close affection between Richard the Lionheart and Philippe is displaced onto the collective. If anything happened, it was only down to the collective madness of the locker-room hothouse. The queering note perhaps only comes with the Juvenal reference, and I would argue that, rather than a straightforward slander of King Richard, Richard of Devizes move is perhaps rather more akin to Carolyn Dinshaw's reading of *Pulp Fiction*: it presents a jubilant picture of hypervirilist sociality and then drops in the detail that points to its disavowed libidinal subtexts. What the *Roman d'Eneas* adds to the picture is its reflection on the question of perceived overperformance: Tarcon's sleazy taunting of Camille implies through its nod to Juvenal's mirroring that to be a she-gladiator is to be a whore *in denial*. In the same way, Richard of Devizes comment may be less a statement than a question: what are all these devastatingly butch guys not saying?

Datable to midway between the *Roman d'Eneas* and Richard of Devizes's account of the two kings, *Erec et Enide* lies in its possible echoing of Juvenal but in a manner that displaces its various deregulations onto other actors, the satire shadowing and mocking Chrétien's tableau much as we have already seen with the use of Lavine's mother's slander as a backdrop haunting and queering other episodes in the romance. Just as the mark of Claudius's wife's insatiable appetite is embodied in her ever-rigid *volva*, her genitals a grotesque mime of gladiatorial virility, so the stakes of the joy ordeal present themselves as a mock-phallic parody of an insatiable appetite for sexualised destruction. No matter how many men come along, another stake always rises up erect, waiting for the next victim or customer for the Joy. Thus, the point is that the stakes are precisely not 'phallic' per se, but rather 'vulval' or 'clitoral' echoes of a libidinal excess othered and disavowed as feminine: the Joy thus appears as a forerunner of Hélène Cixous's vision of the 'Medusa', the polymorphous, threatening sea-creature, the Deleuzian 'organ without

433

a body' that forms the centre of her counter-phallic allegory *Le Rire de la méduse*.[27] Accordingly, Erec and Maboagrain's extreme exhaustion and yet also regard for one another appears as an echo of Claudius's wife's throbbing, inexhaustible arousal. And yet, that very provision of a referential backdrop points to a further disavowal: if there is anything gay detectable in this scene, it must be a woman's fault. Of course. It always is. Indeed, the political lesson here may be quite simply Roman in its inspiration: Maboagrain appears as a sort of Claudius figure against Erec, his rule transformed into a grotesque parody of right and justice through the impulses of his *amie*. Having mastered his own uxoriousness, Erec's victory in the Joy then tames all the most luridly base manifestation of the libidinal underside of the *res publica*. Then again, the possible divisions in Richard of Devizes's readership (those in on the Juvenal reference and willing to entertain what it may imply versus those who are not and would rather not) may also appear in Chrétien: what appears as a life-or-death encounter in the midst of an emergent vernacular tradition trying to take itself seriously and affirm its non-sublaternity still appears mocked and interrogated by an antecedent literary tradition, its affirmation of chivalric virtue and virility still the echo of a painted, imperial whore, its centrepiece an echo of a satirist's lewd reference to the trouble under her toga. Then again, Chrétien's gesture could also be seen as a trivialising mockery of the problems highlighted in Juvenal. Rather than us being left with an unadulteratedly epic finale, Chrétien's allusion to satirical views – whose prosopopoeic project is to illuminate all that is venal or ridiculous and expose it to laughter – remind us that the *gravitas* of classical sources should not prove too daunting to the ages that follow.

The subterfuges here also explain the convenient logic of the Joy by which, paradoxically, Yder was able to appeal to Erec on the grounds that to kill him would be 'trop grant vilenie' (l. 998), and that Guivret made a similar plea (ll. 3837–42). Are we then to understand that all the previous opponents were incapable of framing the same kind of argument which, if deployed, would surely have forced a truce between the combatants if the true end were to avoid the appearance of *vilenie*? In that respect, it is hard to judge what is more horrific: the spectacle of the deaths of Erec's predecessors as brutal, hot-blooded savagery, or as a mute, frozen compliance with the rules that apparently dictated their fate. In Lacanian terms, Maboagrain's punctilious compliance with the Joy thus appears as a delusive lure (*le leurre*): just as in the Augustinian 'two wills' model of rape underpinning Enide's thoughts of suicide, the entailment dictating his actions is an entirely separate structure of will from the other formality of the appeal for mercy. Accordingly, the unthinking obedience of knights who went as lambs to the slaughter when a simple appeal to the rules of fair play should have saved their lives appears as the most grotesque of misunderstandings. Would Augustine have expected the example of Marcus Regulus to have such an obscenely trivial afterlife? But then, the death of the other knights is the mark of Maboagrain's authenticity and the source of his effective disinculpation: he presumably expected no more quarter than he gave. The other victims suffer as the martyrs to the 'esfroi' that sustains the Joy of the Court, becoming the necessary price and guarantee of its truth. In that regard, Maboagrain's rational participation is bureaucratically offloaded onto Evrain, whose alternation between courteous hospitality and innumerable warnings appear as a medieval version of the computer software designed to assist suicide in terminally-ill patients, the person plugged into the mechanism required at multiple points to indicate their rational and informed consent by clicking 'continue'. In that sense, the Joy may offer a chivalric system in which all possibilities of appeal are in effect 'front-loaded'. Thus, Evrain appears as a version of Albert Camus's Caligula, who, at the close of a meeting with a group of senators, warns them to leave the room by the left-hand corridor: in the right-hand one he has stationed soldiers with orders to kill anyone who passes.[28] Both Brandigan and Camus's play highlight the contradictory vision of the cleanly, clinically mechanistic as perversely, dirtily obscene: no formal structure can rule out the possibility of appeal without becoming culpably, tyrannically inhuman.

Enide and the Importance of Being Earnest

> How is it that they [the astrologers] have never been able to explain why, in the life of twins, in their actions, in their experiences, their professions, their accomplishments, their positions – in all the other circumstances of human life, and, even in death itself, there is often found such diversity that in those respects many strangers show more resemblance to them than they show to one another, even though the smallest possible interval separated their births and though they were conceived at the same moment, by a single act of intercourse? (Augustine, *City of God*, book 5, chapter 1)

Although they are from the same place and same family, Enide and the Count's niece in the orchard are not the same person.[29] Indeed, neither are the 'Count's niece' from the negotiation scene at Laluth and the one here. However, the typological assimilation of one actress to another under the heading of 'pucele' and as part of the horizontal weave of the Count's marriageable kinswomen is central to Chrétien's examination of vicissitude in social fortunes. One maiden in a forest called upon to act misjudged her moment and brought shame on the knight who accompanied her. Another who spoke out forcefully and conducted herself well on another occasion was not ultimately the one who brought her family the greatest renown.

Jane Burns presents the latter sections of Chrétien's poem as characterised by an increasing suppression of Enide's perspective and a corresponding editorialising in Erec's versions of events, all of which she regards as evidence of the work's oppressive gender asymmetry. I would agree that there are some key elisions in terms of what Enide is given to say, but I would see their sense rather differently. Accordingly, what I would propose here is that the narrator's presentation of Enide's prologue to the romance of her and Erec's adventures is her contribution to the reassertion of the fortunes of her family, including those kin who had allowed her to languish as a poor relation. In constructing the speech she makes to her cousin, Enide pulls together a number of strands that do not entirely sit well together, but not necessarily because she is protecting Erec's vanity. Rather, what we see is a subtle mix of comfort and carefully veiled rebuke, all bound together by Enide's insistence on the truth and legitimacy of what she says, its accordance with *droiture*.

Obviously, her cousin's narrative (ll. 6265–85), with its emphasis on private promise ('La feïsmes noz covenanz / Entre nos deus, tex con nos sist', ll. 6268–9) and individual desire ('Lui demora et moi fu tart / Que je m'en venisse avec lui.' ll. 6276–7), is what Enide inverts in her tale of public ceremony and honours.[30]

> 'Voir vos ai dit; or me redites,
> Ensi con je vos ai conté,
> De vostre ami la verité,
> Par quel aventure il vos a.'
> 'Bele cousine, il m'esposa
> Si que mes pere bien le sot
> Et ma mere grant joie en ot.
> Tuit le sorent et lié en furent
> Nostre parent, si con il durent.
> Liez en fu mes oncles li cuens […]' (ll. 6282–91)

> 'I've told you the truth; now tell me, exactly as I've told you, just how it happened that your lover chanced to have you.' 'My dear cousin, he married me with my father's full consent, and my mother was overjoyed. All of our relatives knew of it and rejoiced as they ought. The Count, my uncle, was delighted.'

Just as Enide a mere few weeks earlier made the school error of finishing a speech in the first line of a couplet with the rhyme word 'songe', so her cousin lays herself open with her invitation to *redire* what she has just said. Just as *contredire* has a range of possible senses, so the semantic field of *redire* runs from repetition to imitation, echo, to possibly even parody. Enide obliges and produces what – in an age influenced by Jane Austen's vignettes of the crass, drawing-room insensitivities of which kin and visitors alike are capable– could well read as a piece of jaw-droppingly smug cattiness, setting her legitimate, and now rather more successful, career to the tune of her cousin's disgrace such that the Old French equivalent of a prefatory 'Unlike you,…' although not present, is strongly suggested. However, if there is a twist to the knife here, the inspiration is probably Boethian, the model being Philosophy's only slightly sugared course in tough love.

Yet the inversion is not as total as it might appear. For a start, Enide effectively dissimulates in her 'public' narrative of *devoir* all extremes of emotional state, from fear and anxiety to the pressing character of individual desire, the imperative that drove Erec to bring forward the date of the wedding and Enide to yearn for him during his convalescence, the same desiring insistence that is then the ultimate foundation of Arthur's assertion of legitimacy following the hunt of the White Stag. Moreover, the goal is not to administer a vengeful put-down but to affirm family unity in a way that will bring the greatest benefit to all. Accordingly, the person who is let off lightest – if anyone – is her uncle the Count of Laluth, a character whom one might have thought gone from the stage (not unlike Enide's long-suffering palfrey lost at Limors (ll. 5169–70). Indeed, *lïece* is a strikingly generous and imaginative way of describing his immediate and spontaneous reaction. Enide's description of the Count's 'delight' (l. 6291) tactfully passes over both his faux pas regarding the dress and the fact that he was also the ungrateful cheapskate who quite possibly overlooked her father's service and certainly left her to languish in the poverty from which, as she herself remarks, Erec rescued her (l. 6303). But then, what is paramount here is clearly the overall effect and force of what she says, the principal goal of which is comforting and consoling her kinswoman (ll. 6325–7). The central drama here is then the fact that the fortunes of Laluth prosper through the ascendance of another branch of the same family drawing the rest of the clan along with it when their fortunes had otherwise been in danger of stagnating in their own small, inward-looking pond. By contrast, Enide's consolatory fiction embraces a bigger picture, with the promise of establishing or re-establishing the clan of Laluth at the Arthurian court, as can be seen from her tactful inclusion of her uncle, the Count in her speech, his 'delight' Enide's retroactive assertion on his behalf of his place at the bargaining table. In a sense, then, it may be that if Enide omits elements from the tale of Erec's arrival in Laluth it is not with a view to sparing him. Burns comments that Enide's narrative undermines Erec's concealment of the events surrounding his discomfiture in the forest at the outset of the tale.[31]

However, one might well also argue that her version serves her persuasive purpose by making it clear to her cousin that shame is part of public life, something that can be faced down and integrated into texture of the public text in the manner of the open secret symbolised in Erec's marred beauty:

> 'Onques encor ne me soi faindre
> De lui amer, ne je ne doi.
> Dont n'est mes sires filz de roi?
> Dont ne me prist il povre et nue?
> Par lui m'est tex honors venue
> Qu'ainz a nule desconsoillie
> Ne fu si grant aparoillie.
> Et, s'il vos plait, je vos dirai,
> Si que de rien ne mentirai,
> Coment je ving a tel hautece;
> Ja dou dire ne m'iert parece.' (ll. 6300–10)

> 'I could never be fainthearted in my love for him, nor should I be. For indeed, is my lord not the son of a king? Did he not take me when I was poor and naked?'[32] Through him, I have received such honour, more than was never bestowed on any poor, unprotected creature. And, if you like, I shall tell you without the ghost of a lie of my rise to these heights. That is a tale I shall never tire of telling.'

Given what we have seen so far in the performance of 'unfeigned' hostility and love, it is now unsurprising that Enide lays such stress on the absence of empty show in her love of her lord. What is not rendered by Carroll's translation is the tense of the modal verb *devoir*, which does more than gloss over whether there was any need for deceit in the past. Rather, what we have is a profession of political faith directly echoing Arthur's speech at the end of the hunt of the White Stag ('Je sui rois, *ne doi pas* mentir', l. 1789, my emphasis). What Enide says is that it would be a derogation from Arthurian ideals for her to feign – or, at least, to be caught doing so. Indeed, the political art she has learned depends precisely on her ability to maintain an appearance of earnest truthfulness, both she and he boldly dissimulating and yet revealing in code the dependency of regulatory constructions of duty on the imperious turbulence of desire and will.

Indeed, it is precisely the element of audacity necessary for persuasion that is paramount. Enide's account of her rise to such heights as she has attained ('tele hautece', l. 6309) mirrors her earlier abject lament for herself, brought low, as she said, by a pride that had raised her up too high ('trop m'a orgueuz sozlevee', ll. 2602). By contrast, now we have a queen proclaiming her position at the top of Fortune's wheel. The most negative view of this speech taken out of context would be that Enide is now utterly blind to her own hubris and entirely caught up in the glory of things mutable. However, the context requires that we take account of its shows: Enide dissimulates what we know to be her own clear knowledge and experience of the vicissitudes of human existence in order to present a theologically brave face to her downcast interlocutor. In short, as per Erec's speech to her before he entered the orchard (ll. 5826–59), she follows him where he told her she should not venture, albeit rhetorically in that the effect of her speech is the main point: 'I do not say so out of pride, but rather only to comfort you' (ll. 5853–4, cited above). The tailoring of tale to listener lies in its restoration of fortunes. Enide's *redit* presents her cousin with a bigger picture than the view from the tender trap of the orchard would have afforded her: be of good cheer – we won.

The centrality of this act of consolation is apparent from the manner in which Enide is received and congratulated by the male characters who run to meet her. In this, Chrétien pays careful attention to the cousin's joy and then Maboagrain's, who rejoices more than the others. Now their behaviour has a public stage, Enide's demonstration of her rhetorical savvy in consoling the other maiden paving the way for a reintegration of the errant couple into the various communities of which they are part. Thus, the joy closes on an act of *prouesse* that is hers rather than Erec's. After all, it can also be argued that the tale is then of her usurpation of Erec's possible betrothal to a king's daughter. This is then the story of how she nearly was not found. In that respect it is tempting to ask out of the Arthurian court and that of Laluth who precisely assimilated whom? In the same way, Enide's apparent passivity is set against the less successful activity of the two other maidens and the Queen, their manipulations effectively playing into what emerged as Enide's or her father's hands.

From that point of view, the situation at the end of the narrative reflects the inscrutable workings of Fortune, undoing and inverting power relations in a way that makes the cases of even the closest kin, the most apparently generically interchangeable of court players utterly distinct in the patterns traced by their progress through the world. In that sense, as we move into the latter phases of the narrative, we see the strands of Chrétien's reflection on fortune being braided together. In his narrative of differentiation, he highlights both the complexities that must be acknowledged by any attempt to account for human striving and the apparently senseless defiance of universal forces, all that is done being done as a *contredit* against Fortuna. But then, just because Fortune is to be reckoned with should not mean she is to be taken as the ultimate arbiter. As Augustine comments, Fortune stands against all, but fortunes vary:

> What is the point of worshipping her if she is so blind that she blunders into people at random, so that she often passes by her worshippers and attaches herself to those who disregard her? (*City of God*, book 4, chapter 19, at p. 157)

Here, then, the opposition between fortune and will becomes paramount. As Augustine comments slightly later in book 5 of *City of God*: 'our wills are ours and its is our wills that affect all that we do by willing, and which would not have happened if we had not willed' (book 5, chapter 10, at p. 195), a position very little removed from that outlined by the more scandalous Machiavelli. In a sense, what Chrétien can be seen as warning against implicitly is a sort of melancholic pagan appropriation of the Arthurian legend, of one that would encourage a resignation to fate that could border on a culpable apathy, more assimilable to an idolatrous worship of Fortuna than to an acknowledgement of the limits of mortal striving and the transitoriness of earthly achievements. Fortuna does not negate the exercise of free will. What Chrétien in effect highlights is the caution that to be excessively cowed by her is to fall into a form of heretical determinism, a recurrent question throughout *City of God*.

The chief subject of this chapter was the roads down which certain words may lead us. Enide's 'parole' seemingly brought us to a place where Enide, lost in grief and rage, picked up Erec's sword, an instrument with no less a guiding role than the rhetorical devices she arrayed in a *mout male conjunture* leading her down the dark road her thoughts travelled in that brief time before she was saved. Yet, the absolute, self-destructive insistence of that logic was precisely fundamental to the role she takes at Limors, Chrétien flirting dangerously with the bringing together of cases Augustine deemed safest considered separately. In the meantime, Erec's progress is evidence of what seems like a temporary grace, a moral and physical luck that allows him not merely to travel but also return. In that sense, his near-physical destruction counterpoints Enide's near moral one. And yet, as with the uneasy proximities seen in Laluth, it cannot be argued that either extremist stance is without its useful effect. While the Joy of the Court has sometimes been dismissed as a disturbance of the structure and economy of Chrétien's text, my reading here emphasises the significance of the distortions and imbalances that are arguably an intentional aspect of its exorbitance. Its ambiguity provides a reflection of the nature of the will and energy that originally drove Erec to leave the court. Indeed, it is highly significant that Chrétien presents Erec's decision to face the challenge as an assertion of personal desire on the part of one who up until now says he has kept silent, his part in the collective theatre here being to emphasise the fascination exerted by this most horrifically improper and barbarous of spectacles. Once again, for all the stakes at the centre of the orchard appear as the most awful of visions, its formality counterpoints the brutality of Maboagrain's bloody harvest of heads. And indeed, Erec is surprisingly quick to pardon the knight, freeing him from his oath through his victory over him. The question then here arises as to why the pardon is given, why this scene has no consequences for a man who otherwise appears as a gigantist murderer. Yet, moreover, the scene swiftly changes into that of rejoicing. Part of the lesson here is that Brandigan appears as yet another setting entirely committed to the ideology of spectacle, this time even to the point of nonsensicality and savage waste of life. As part of that focus on the most apparently improbably rapid swings of fortune, from defeat to rejoicing, from malediction to embracing, what then emerges as arguably the pivot of this section is Enide's consolation of Maboagrain's 'amie' through the carefully woven narrative she spins of her own adventures. Indeed, it is this event, the marker of Enide's definitive mastery of the ethos of theatre and effect that truly unleashes the Joy. However, other, harder lessons follow after the giddy whirl of this part of Chrétien's coda.

Notes

1   Paris, pp. 152–7. On the episode, see also Frappier, pp. 89–95; Luttrell, pp. 196–225; Maria Luisa Meneghetti, ' "Joie de la Cort": Intégration individuelle et métaphore sociale dans *Erec et Enide*', *Cahiers de Civilisation Médiévale*, 19 (1976), 371–9; W. A. Nitze, 'Erec and the Joy of the Court', *Speculum*, 29:4 (1954), 691–701; Nykrog, pp. 74–7; Plummer, pp. 391–3; Margueritte S. Murphy, 'The Allegory of "Joie" in Chrétien's *Erec et Enide*', in *Allegory, Myth, and Symbol*, ed. by, Morton W. Bloomfield (Cambridge MA: Harvard University Press, 1981); Sara Sturm-Maddox, '*Hortus non Conclusus*: Critics and the *Joie de la Cort*', *Oeuvres et Critiques*, 5:2 (1980–1981), 61–71 and her 'The *Joie de la cort*: Thematic Unity in Chrétien's *Erec et Enide*', *Romania*, 103 (1982), 513–28 as well as Cristina Noacco, 'La Dialectique du don dans la quête de la Joie d'*Erec et Enide*', in *Guerres, voyages et quêtes au Moyen Age. Mélanges offerts à Jean-Claude Faucon*, ed. by Alain Labbe, Daniel W. Lacroix and Danielle Queruel, Colloques, Congrès et Conférences sur le Moyen Age, 2 (Paris: Champion, 2000), 299–311.

2   Plummer, p, 391.

3   Gérard Chandès, 'Recherches sur l'imagerie des eaux dans l'oeuvre de Chrétien de Troyes', *Cahiers de Civilisation Médiévale*, 19 (1976), 151–64, at p. 159.

4   Burgess, *Erec et Enide*, pp. 81–2.

5   On Dido's ruse, see Huchet, *Le Roman médiéval*, pp. 116–18.

6   On Evrain, see in particular, Köhler, *L'Aventure chevaleresque*, pp. 150–1. Köhler points out that there is a potential contradiction in the idea that Evrain opens his welcome to all *prodomes*, a danger of the violence it unleashes spiralling out of control. In that sense, Erec, who just happens to be a king's son, appears as an answer to the custom of the Joy just as Enide appears as an answer to the custom of the White Stag. As Köhler puts it, 'le danger se trouve conjuré par le fait que le prodome reste d'origine chevaleresque' (p. 151).

7   See Allard, pp. 106–07.

8   *Gladiator*, dir. Ridley Scott (2000).

9   Allard, p. 109.

10   On which, see Matthew Strickland, *War and Chivalry: The Conduct and Perception of War in England and Normandy, 1066-1217*, Cambridge Studies

in Medieval Life and Thought (Cambridge: Cambridge University Press, 1996), pp. 224–9.

11 On naming in Arthurian Romance, see in particular Carlos F. C. Carreto, 'Au Seuil d'une poétique du pouvoir: manipulation du nom et (en)jeux de la narration dans le roman arthurien en vers', in *The Propagation of Power in the Medieval West: Selected Proceedings of the International Conference, Groningen 20–3 November 1996*, ed. by Martin Gosman, Arjo Vanderjagt, Jan Veenstra, Mediaevalia Groningana, 23 (Groningen: Forsten, 1988), pp. 249–63.

12 Keen, *Chivalry*, p. 85.

13 Hindman, p. 133.

14 Hindman has it that it is Erec who compares himself to Thiebaut, Ospinel and Fernagu, although in fonds fr. 1376 the passage in question is clearly a narratorial intervention.

15 For an illustration and exploration of Lacan's dictum, see notably Žižek's comments on Alfred Hitchock's film *Rope* (1948). Here two students conspire to strangle one of their friends in apparent realisation of the sub- / pseudo-Nietzschean teachings of their college professors (played by James Stewart). When faced with what they have done and the leader's account of their rationale, the professor refuses to own any connection with their actions.

16 Interestingly the first of the group of three robber knights to comment on Enide remarks that he does not know if she is a 'dame' or a 'pucele' (ll. 2803–05).

17 For edition, see Philip E. Bennett (ed.), *'Mantel' et 'cor': deux lais du XIIe siècle*, Textes Littéraires (Exeter: University of Exeter, 1976). For comment, see R. Howard Bloch, *The Scandal of the Fabliaux* (Chicago and London: University of Chicago Press, 1986), pp. 22–58.

18 Strickland, *War and Chivalry*, pp. 164–9.

19 On Alypius, see Augustine, *Confessions*, book 6, chapter 8.

20 Although penalties for masturbation in ecclesiastical sources from the central Middle Ages are comparatively light (see Brundage, pp. 212–13), as Brundage notes, Paul is severe on the subject (see 1 Corinthians 6: 9–10), arguing that those who engage in the sin 'were unworthy of God's kingdom' (Brundage, p. 60).

21 Thus, just as Gaunt (*Love and Death*, pp. 213–15) sees the episode he cites from the *Cent-Vingt Journées de Sodome* as informed by the conventions of the 'coeur mangé' narrative, so we have in the use of the secret entrances and other rooms of the *boudoir* a version of the unmapped space of forest adventure.

22 On the relation between 'la détumescence', orgasm and anxiety, see Lacan, *Le Séminaire X*, pp. 185–98.

23 See Burgwinkle, *Sodomy*, pp. 76–8.

24 For edition and translation, see *Juvenal and Persius*, ed. and trans. by G. G. Ramsay, Loeb Classical Library, rev. edn (London and Cambridge MA: Heinemann, 1940). Ramsay's translation of these verses is, however, rather more

euphemistic ('and, with passion raging still hot within her […]'), so my rendering here is based on Burgwinkle's translation.
25 Burgwinkle, *Sodomy*, pp. 77–8.
26 Richard of Devizes, *The Chronicle of Richard of Devizes of the Time of King Richard the First*, ed. and trans. by John T. Appleby (London and New York: Thomas Nelson, 1963), pp. 16–17.
27 Hélène Cixous, 'Le Rire de la méduse', *L'Arc*, 61 (1975), .39–54
28 'En sortant, prenez le couloir de gauche. Dans celui de droite, j'ai posté des gardes pour vous assassiner.' (Albert Camus, *Caligula: version de 1941 suivi de la poétique du premier Caligula*, ed. by A. James Arnold, NRF: Cahiers Albert Camus, 4 (Paris: Gallimard, 1984), act 3, scene 2 (p. 77).
29 On Enide's cousin, see J. V. McMahon, 'Enite's Relatives: The Girl in the Garden', *Modern Language Notes*, 85 (1970), 367–72.
30 On this speech see also McCracken, 'Silence and the Courtly Wife', pp. 122–3.
31 Burns, *Bodytalk*, p. 162–5.
32 Cp. Carroll's rather flat rendering in the Penguin translation: 'My lord is in every way the son of a king, yet he took me when I was poor and naked.'

All things have their season, and in their times all things pass under heaven. A time to be born and a time to die. A time to plant, and a time to pluck up that which is planted. A time to kill, and a time to heal. A time to destroy, and a time to build. A time to weep, and a time to laugh. A time to mourn, and a time to dance. A time to scatter stones, and a time to gather. A time to embrace, and a time to be far from embraces. (Ecclesiastes 3: 1–5)

As Baldwin V of Hainault prepared to die, all the religious relics of the region were gathered together as for a public peace assembly and all his vassals were summoned to swear on those relics to maintain the peace. More intimate was the final agony, which took place in the chamber. A poem composed in honour of William the Marshal of England, who died in 1219, gives one of the most detailed accounts we have from this period of the death of a prince. [...] Night and day people watched over him, as he gradually rid himself of all his possessions. Once he had relinquished the patrimony (which was not his, but which had merely been given to him to hold in his lifetime), he disposed of all his personal belongings: money, jewels clothing. He had paid all his debts and begged pardon of all those he had wronged in his life. He turned his thoughts to his soul and confessed his sins. [...] The next day, at noon, he bade farewell – this time in private – to his wife and knights: 'I pledge you do God. I am no more. I can defend myself against death no longer.' He thus departed the group whose leader he had been; divesting himself, he transferred his power to God. For the first time since birth, he was alone. (Georges Duby and Philippe Ariès (eds), *A History of Private Life: II – Revelations of the Medieval World*, trans. by Arthur Goldhammer (Cambridge MA and London: Belknap and Harvard University Press, 1988), pp. 82–3)

ELIZABETH II (to Tony Blair): You won't always be popular. (*The Queen*, dir. Stephen Frears (2006))

Conclusion
Arts of Spinning and Dazzling:
The Coronation

Where Chrétien had previously focused on time standing still (or nearly), in the wake of the Joy of the Court and Erec's return to Arthur, time seems to speed up as events accumulate in the shadow of the lengthily-narrated but comparatively brief weeks that constitute Erec's period of testing. Yet even though the wheel of cosmic forces seems to pick up its pace again, we are reminded that the medieval vision of Fortune does not place everyone on the same cycle, but that rather the cosmos is made up of an interweaving of individual rises and falls, the interplay of vicissitudes giving history its distinctive detailed braiding. Arthur and Erec preside over the reassertion of the noble status of Enide's fortunes. Erec's father dies and Erec is crowned king. The frantic whirl of the Joy sets the scene for what is to follow in the latter part of the narrative, readable as a reflection on the problem of the discourse of *consolatio*. The Joy of the court relies on an inherently unstable and ironic situation that forces its witnesses into a rhetoric of paradox. It is then no coincidence that the section following continues this interweave of crucial questions of loss and desire, joy and sorrow. Both Erec and Enide will be called on after here to dissimulate their feelings as part of the constraints of the emotional theatre of public life: Enide in her delight over the restoration of the fortunes of her parents, Erec at of the death of his father. The two moments precede the coronation, offering a contrasting set of examples that in combination sketch out the arc of Fortune's wheel with Enide's father once cast down and now rising again set in contrast to Erec's father facing the fate of all mortals. Each of these events is in its own way a foreshadowing of Arthur's fate, which is then part of their place in the moment Chrétien opens up in the overall history of the great king's reign. However, what also has to be understood here is the extent to which these fates then hang over both Erec, whom we have seen near death, and Enide, whom we have seen close to being deprived of the protection his presence affords. Motifs of consolation and lament are repeatedly rehearsed in the preceding episodes, from Enide's lament for Erec's apparently definitive loss of reputation to the *planctus* she pronounces over him following his faint prior to the encounter with the Count of Limors.

The 'Joy' appears as a section in which the relation between private emotion and its public expression appears to be tested to breaking point, the condensed time-frame of the narrative drawing together in close proximity the exuberance of joy and celebration with the harsh tests of bereavement and grief. In that sense it appears as a rehearsal of the limits of consolation in face of the uncertain future that hangs over all the characters: the ending can be read as foreshadowing Erec's death in old age or as part of the cataclysm that will engulf Arthur's realm. Enide is similarly faced with the prospect of losing not merely her husband but also her own parents. We are arguably even left to wonder whether one of the possible futures adumbrated in the narrative of Enide's marriage and sexual awakening in which 'she was not afraid of anything; she endured all, whatever the cost' ('De rien ne s'est acohardie, / Tot soffri, que que li grevast', l. 2100–01), and in which there is more talk of 'delit' than procreation, might not hint at her own 'high-risk enterprises', the dangers she will face and the possibilities of her own fate, such as death in childbirth.

Such reflections on the inescapable prospect of loss make of Erec and Arthur's triumphs at the end a beguiling assertion of values driven by things even as fragile and questionable as whims and desires, their power deriving from the weightless gravitas of their defiance in the face of the forces that will inevitably destroy them. In that sense, the assertion of the power of theatricality appears as a defence of the exemplary power of all striving in the face of the ephemerality of all human achievement. This sense of the joy and frailty of existence hangs over the remainder of the text, with individuals and families moving in differing but complimentary rhythms first hinted at in the gaps in age and experience between the otherwise mirroring pair of Erec and Enide.

As for the House of Erec, Erec tarries at court until his father dies. This could be presented as the redouble of his earlier *recreantise*, as indeed it is in the Welsh version. However, another reading might highlight the obvious political benefit in the massive show of royal favour accorded to Erec by Arthur. If Erec cannot remain at his father's court without attracting negative attention, then the best thing is for his courtiers to miss him in the way that medieval kingship seems a mourning for the passing of Arthur. What is implied is that Erec perhaps best serves the prestige of kingship in his father's realm by not being there, not because he is disliked, but rather because his stay at Arthur's court amounts to an absolutely emphatic consecration, realised in the messianic moment of the Nativity coronation, which presents him as the double of Arthur and Charlemagne. The sense of cosmic wheels turning is also apparent in the change of family fortunes in the House of Laluth. That a new star finds itself in the ascendant is made emphatically clear by the exchange between Arthur and Erec on the arrival of Enide's mother and father at the coronation, a moment that effectively writes out the dishonour done to them through their loss in status.[1]

The text's emphasis on the power of the king's will either to rewrite history or shape the public sphere is also then apparent in Erec's reaction to the death of his father.[2]

> Erec en pesa plus assez
> Qu'il n'en mostra semblant as genz;
> Mais duelx de roi n'est mie genz,
> N'a roi n'avient qu'il face duel. (ll. 6516–19)
>
> Erec was saddened far more than he showed outwardly, but grieving is unseemly in a king and it is not fitting for him to make woe.

The choice of verb is all: not merely *convenir*, whose sense in Old French survives, but rather *avenir*. This verb carries both the same sense as *convenir* – *avenant*, 'seemly' – while – in parallel to the noun *aventure* – conveying the notion of a happening visited on the person. Unrestrained shows of grief in kings is unfitting to the point that it should not happen, so they do not grieve in public more than is appropriate to the demands of ceremony. Erec's schooling of his passions in the lead-up to the consummation of his marriage to Enide was the pleasurable reverse to this particular coin. As Enide, worthy daughter of Philosophy, could tell him on the basis of knowledge hard-won from her darkest experience, all displays of royal emotion are calculated.

Erec's commitment to the Law expresses in the hard school that is the giving of self to royal duty is then mirrored in his receiving his lands back from Arthur in fief (ll. 6536–7). This symbolic divesting of himself is then repeated and underscored in the considerable largesse he displays following the funeral rites, making Erec the symbolic double of his dead father, much as in the description of the ideal self-divesting practiced by Baldwin and William prior to their deaths. It is again mirrored in Erec's praise of Enide's father (ll. 6597–601), who gave up everything he had to him without listening to the advice of his *familiares* ('Sanz los et sanz conseil d'autrui', l. 6601). This emphasis on the unspoken basis of his judgement then mirrors the absence of justification from all the main male characters, but also crucially presents the pattern for courtly behaviour, which it is that it is occasionally without resort to counsel. All three patriarchs – Arthur, Erec and Liconal – are linked by their capacity for acting against the collective.

Chrétien's emphasis on the irrationality of royal expenditure of all kinds, energetic, passionate or material is particularly highlighted at this point, his praise of Arthur highlighting not the authority of settled custom, but rather his audacity:

> Ne tant n'ossassent pas despendre
> Entre Cesar et Alixandre
> Con a la ot cort despendu. (ll. 6675–7)

> Nor did Caesar and Alexander between them dare expend as much as was spent at the court.

The currency basis of this perhaps less than prudent fiscal policy is the 'esterlin', coin of the realm since the time of Merlin, a blithe mention hinting at uneasy connections between magic, coining and legitimacies of all kind, whether authority or birth.[3] More than a passing whiff of wonder, the name of Merlin takes its place in a dialogue with the classical models of excellence in daring Chrétien invokes at this point. This is a bold strategy. After all, it was

Merlin's intervention that legendarily made Arthur's conception possible. Given that coining is a common image in medieval writings for fatherhood, this reference could then well mean that the esterlin is identifiable with Arthur himself as the bastard coinage of Uther Pendragon. Part of the combination of the classical points of reference is then to place the new coinage in the context of a new genealogy that is capable of asserting its own legitimacy even where its illegitimacy is most advertised, in keeping with Seebass-Linggi's questioning of Peter Dembowski's comment that 'Jules César et surtout Alexandre le grand étaient traditionellement considérés comme des modèles de générosité'.[4] However, Dembowski's point is not entirely a misreading, classical accounts of Caesar's life highlighting if not generosity then certainly a capacity for daring acts of profligacy (see chapter 1). Likewise, Alexander's largesse was not selflessly gratuitous, but rather strategic and calculating in line with a reputation for treacherous gift-giving stereotypically associated with the Greeks epitomised in the Trojan horse: 'timeo Danaos et dona ferentis' ('I fear the Greeks and the gifts they bring', *Aeneid*, book 2, l. 49).[5] What makes all of this possible then is the daring, the assertion of value and authority in the face of the depredations of time and tide. Furthermore, it also places the notion of economy in the frame of terroristic insistence of authority: the common coin is the common coin, its appearance and value, the worth that is carried by the face it bears, underpinned by a magic glamour of cruelty and violence, the presence of the coin the stamp of that original violence foundational to Arthurian polity. This free circulation of Arthurian currency then mirrors and outdoes the small-time shenanigans of the robber knights Erec dispatches, surpassing them as the supreme appropriative force of the realm. Gifting and money economy are thus connected by the paradoxically bare-faced dissimulation of the unilateralism that drives them.

What Chrétien's ending presents is then a discursive economy in potentially runaway proliferation, where Arthur is able once again to sate the audience in an orgy of largesse where before his actions were seemingly driven by a concern with the limits of his political economy. The emphasis on number and increase appears as the symphonic orchestration of the new economy we saw Erec build in the quest. In that respect, Chrétien's avoidance of and much advertised impatience with renarration does not so much amount to a silencing of voice, but rather shows that the telling of it is snowballing exponentially. Comments about time are capital here. From the four days of the quest we move to the days and weeks of joy that follow on from its completion. The single driven act in a sense seems to devour time in the respect that it can energise it and justify the mood of the collective without apparent danger of the exhaustion of charisma manifested in the accusations of *recreantise*. We can also see this in the gifts made by Arthur: the thrones and sceptres and cloaks. Crucially, the crowns are items from the treasury, whereas the robes are made to measure with an iconographical programme in mind. Somewhere between these two versions of invention, whether in the form of finding or composition, there appears the work of something like providence, except that it looks more like improvisation, bricolage rather than engineering. After all, it is the robe that provides the external appearance of order, the enclosing script.

Again here, we have the clash of the fairy culture of the matter of Britain on the one hand with the legacy of Antiquity on the other. In spite of the apparent difficulties and contradictions latent in the project, the reconciliation between these two apparently heterogeneous elements lies in the fact that they are both pagan, albeit in different ways. Although the cloak represents the division of the quadrivium, there are reasons to suspect whether the schema is intended as a serious programmatic description.[6] Although foundational to medieval educational structures, these are knowledges that stand apart the historical economy of salvation, subject by dint of their dependence on pagan antiquity to a similar suspicion to that which attached to dialectic. Indeed, the ordering of them is in some regards a cause for concern. After all, 'Astronomy' appears here less in the guise of the study of the cosmos than astrological divination of a kind emphatically denounced in the Christian tradition by no less a figure than Augustine.[7] Indeed, Augustine specifically denies that the stars can be used to tell the future in the way Chrétien describes:

> Those who suppose that the stars decide, quite apart from the will of God, how we shall act and what blessings we shall enjoy or what disasters we shall suffer,

are to be refused any hearing whatsoever, not only from those who hold the true religion but even from those choose to be worshippers of Gods of any sort.[8]

Were this report on the condition of knowledge not ambiguous enough, then after it we have the mention of the thread of the robe made from the fur of 'unes contrefaites bestes' (l. 6787), the 'barbïolete' (l. 6793). Again, given that one of the more famous 'contrefaite beste' is that arch-deceiver Renart the fox, the most celebrated vernacular tales of whose antics date from this period, are we really intended to take this account as unproblematic?[9] Against this it can be argued that astrology was a subject of some interest to Christian thinkers in the twelfth century, commentators at this point being curious rather than simply content to toe the Augustinian line.[10] That said, it is clear that astrology and divination were also subject of considerable concerns for writers in the twelfth century, John of Salisbury devoting considerable space in book 2 of the *Policraticus* to an attack on the fashion for such 'trifles' at the court of Henry II.[11] As Carey points out, the subtitle of John's treatise (*De Nugiis Curialium et Vestigiis Philosophorum*) is telling in this regard: *Of the Frivolities of Courtiers and the Footprints of Philosophers*. Here is precisely a vision of subaltern culture: a fashion- and spin-driven court modernity producing a tattered, half-remembered, intellectually-flawed text of the kind deplored by Philosophy in Boethius's *Consolation* (book 1, prose 2).

Once again, however, from Chrétien's perspective, we are looking back over something of a gap: John's account of the court of Henry in the *Policraticus* was written in about 1159. It is therefore not impossible that Chrétien's view might be somewhat detached. With this possibility in mind, we might take a closer look at the terms of his account of this potentially most despicable and damnable of arts:

> La quarte, qui aprés ovra
> A mout bone ovre recovra,
> Car la moillor des arz i mist:
> D'Astronomie s'entremist
> Cele qui fait tante merveille,
> Qui as estoiles se conseille
> Et a la lune et au soloil.

> En autre leu ne prent consoil
> De rien qui a faire li soit.
> Cil la consoillent bien a droit
> De tot ce qu'ele lor enquiert,
> Et quanque fu, et quanque iert,
> Li font certeinnement savoir
> Sanz mentir et sanz decevoir. (ll. 6769–82)

> The fourth one, who came after, made a most excellent piece of work. She took as her subject the highest of the arts: she concerned herself with Astronomy, who works many a wonder and takes counsel from the stars, the moon and sun. Nowhere else does she seek advice about anything she needs to do. These counsel her as is right about whatever she asks of them. Through them she can know for certain whatever was or will be, without lying or deceit.

The rehabilitation of star-gazing as part of a meditation on pattern and order sanctioned by Boethian and Macrobian traditions suggests something of a revival in the economy of political knowledge. However, the other key detail, and one consonant with the vision of royal government we have seen to far is the observation that Astronomy takes no other counsel except from herself ('*se* conseille', l. 6774, my emphasis) or from the stars, moon and sun – *and from nowhere else about anything* (ll. 6776–7).[12] The emphasis is significant in that its forceful insistence goes hand-in-hand with an act of rhetorical legerdemain, misdirecting the 'vilains', the 'gent esbahie' who would look to the occulting of knowledge as seductive in itself and so be deceived by the appearance rather than the reality. To look to the stars is to look to an object to be interpreted. The fact that they cannot speak themselves then robs them of the power to deceive and lie. The implicit lesson could then be said to be not one of trusting to the art of prognostication as a means of strategically manipulating and mystifying the *gent*, while not allowing oneself to be swayed by those who might lie and deceive, a good general dictum, but also a resonance especially interesting with regard to possible later datings of Chrétien's text where, for example, such a comment might chime with young Henry's reputation for taking advice from bad counsellors.[13] Both voices and threads layer and interweave here, Chrétien reading a fictional tapestry woven by a third party who happens to be a fairy. Thus magic, too, becomes part of the glamour of grammar, with the distancing effect of successive layers of irony woven into the narrator's comments. Of course, if Chrétien's narrative has sketched a path from isolation to integration, as critics have argued, this passage undercuts that tendency, foregrounding in the weave and weft of Chrétien's construction of ideal kingship the necessity for a certain detachment.[14] There is of course nothing especially shocking here: Charlemagne after all had been presented as slightly aloof from his prelapsarian circle of counsellors in the Oxford *Roland*, as long to think and slow to pronounce ('De sa parole ne fut mie hastifs: / Sa custume est qu'il parole a leisir', ll. 140–1). However, whereas the Emperor's reserve is presented in terms of a sensible caution, a weighing of the advantages and disadvantages, the position presented in *Erec et Enide* owes more to prognostication and spin, revealing an anxiety about the nature of political knowledge that might be viewed from a number of points of view and which can just as well be deployed as a smokescreen to give licence to the exercise of the royal will as it can to reflect on the pros and cons of particular courses in the sagely reflective milieu of a Boethian cosmos.

Chrétien's description thus reads as an assertion of the cultural independence of a medieval Christian modernity in whose view to be entirely and unconditionally in thrall to the ancients is tantamount to believing in divination, to fall prey to the letter rather than heed to the spirit. However, it does not challenge the place of deception and the role of appearance in a public sphere whose barbarous modernity and foregrounding of the surface and the fictional is in fact its concealed and dissimulated promise of salvation. The duty of the Christian ruler is thus to deceive where it is expedient to do so. To emphasise the function of the coronation as the supreme affirmation of pure catch spectacle, and to argue from there that Chrétien's presentation of the event is in some respects ironic is not necessarily to read it as a denunciation of Arthur or indeed Henry. If these events do indeed reflect Henry's coronation then the possibility is that Chrétien is suggesting that 'regime change' marks not only an absolute historical break, but also a radical epistemological one. Rather than appearing as a sort of capitulation to the inimitability of the past, it reflects back on the antique and biblical models to which the Middle Ages looks for authority to show that in themselves they offer no ultimate guarantees.

If Solomon and Alexander – standing metonymically for the Antique and Old Testament traditions – were as known for their vices as for their virtues, then the advantage lies with the moderns rather than the ancients. There was never anything but daring bricolage. Of course, the charge of Machiavellian cynicism could be countered: following Tony Hunt we might assume some sort of Abelardian inflection wherein the purity of intent is all. If the king's will is good then all will be well. However, this still, small voice is fairly carefully concealed amidst the vastly effusive panoply and spectacle of the coronation as public theatre. The despoiling of Pharaoh's treasure house – to invoke a commonly cited justification for the Christian use of ancient sources – merely provides the means for the exercise of persuading and beguiling that is the public theatre of largesse.

In that sense, the robe is not unreminiscent of the knowledge that seems to be implied by such artefacts as the Bronze Age 'hats' made of beaten gold showing the moon in the phases of the 'Metonic cycle', mapping the relation between lunar and solar years. This vision of time may have served to mark the wearer as lord over past and future, as given insight into the cosmic cycles in a manner that would both allow him both to guide his followers in hunting and cultivation, but also quite possibly mystify them through his access to occult knowledge.[15] In the same way, Chrétien's carefully-advertised debt to Macrobius highlights the potential amorality of 'description', the elaboration and interpretation of underlying significance that sanctions his lavish construction of the surface appearance of things: all material culture here is in effect sublated or translated into the rationale of an eternity beyond the transactions of a history whose goalposts are thus his to move. Accordingly, the radiance of the crowns is apparently purged of its radioactive danger, any troubling sense of excess lost for now in the flash-bomb effect of the royal fireworks. In awing the public through the spectacular agency of the coronation, any problems dogging the Arthurian construction of a charismatic theatre state are conjured, if only for a while. Thus, the 'doing a bit of a…' central to the exercise of the royal passions now appears as a source of manageably compelling *esfroi*, strategically manipulated through a 'science de l'avenir' whose power derives from the contained use of such singular, explosive moments of ekphrasis as well as from the structures and rhythms that fascinated medieval political cosmology. As part of a libidinal economy of kingship, such a bag full of the perverse tricks pleasure plays with the Law of *jouissance*, in the exploitation of the dark arts of an absolutist terror.

Although critics have emphasised Enide's effacement in the latter sections of the narrative, it is also arguable that her role here reflects the restricted 'elbow room' available to individuals in collective ritual. Just as she was unable to give full force of her joy on seeing her parents again, so here her capacity to test the frame of ceremony is constrained. That element of individual agency is not absent though, as we can see from a key moment of court theatre:

> Enide n'estoit pas encor
> Ou palais venue a cele hore.
> Quant li rois voit qu'ele demore,
> Gauvain comande tost aler
> Li et la roïne amener.
> Gauvains i cort, ne fu pas lenz,
> O lui li rois Cadovalenz
> Et li larges rois de Galvoie.
> Guivrez li Petiz les convoie,
> Et aprés Ydiers, li filz Nut.
> Des autres barons i corrut
> Tant por les deus dames conduire,
> Bien poïssent un ost destruire,
> Que pres en i ot d'un millier. (ll. 6802–15)

> And still Enide had not yet come to the palace; seeing she was late, the King instructed Gawain to go and lead her there at once. Gawain hurried to obey, taking with him King Carduant and the generous king of Galway. Guivret the dwarf escorted them, followed by Yder, King Nut's son. And other barons quickly joined them to escort the ladies: there were more than a thousand – enough good knights to conquer an army!

What has to be born in mind here is the order in which things appear in the description of the coronation. Once we settle down to the menu of joys awaiting the young king, we start with the description of the thrones (ll. 6705–21) followed by that of the robe (ll. 6728–801) and then the revelation Enide is not yet at the palace. However, that they precede Enide does not imply they take precedence over her. Rather,

457

the descriptions only run on so long because the Young Queen is not yet at the palace. At this point hierarchies and decorum are suspended: Gauvain is ordered to fetch her, and, quite unlike the Queen's handmaiden, he sets off hot-foot. Moreover, in a replay of the frantic dispersal of the court of Limors, we have a vision of a vast throng of courtiers scrambling after him. That Chrétien wishes us to reflect on the disturbance of order here relative to the unfolding history we have seen up until now is apparent from two of the characters in this cast of nigh a thousand: Guivret and Ydier. The order here both repeats and reverses that seen in the initial encounter in the forest: although Guivret's position is as escort, as with Ydier's original dwarf, Ydier is 'after' Guivret in that he follows him as a subordinate in the pecking order. That said, Ydier is present not as prisoner or servant but rather as member of the court and, indeed, as one of Erec's own *familiares* such that the ordering here is not simply an external perspective and matter of dramatic irony but even a 'family joke' whose sense is not lost 'internally' to the world of the text. Enide plays her part in this show by delaying her entry onto the scene, her prominence signalled by the fact that Guinevere appears as her follower. The difference from that of her and Erec's departure from Carnant at the start of the quest now some three or more years previously is that Arthur's dispatching of the courtiers reflects her licence to manipulate the time of court ceremony, to 'speak' in its history through precisely her silence and absence.

In this regard, Enide's gesture here contrasts sharply with some earlier accounts that would present her as more demurely silent. A key instance here is a passage that does not appears in fonds fr. 1376 or indeed in the 'Guiot copy', B. N. fonds fr. 794, but rather only in Ms. A (Chantilly, Condé 472), recounting another ceremony, namely Enide's gifting of an altar cloth presented to her by Guinevere, who had come by the artefact by more suspect means:

> Jesu et la virge Marie
> Par boene devocion prie
> Que an lor vie lor donast
> Oir qui aprés ax heritast.
> Puis a ofert desor l'autel
> Un paisle vert, nus ne vit tel

> Et une grant chasuble ovree;
> Tote a fin or brosdee,
> Et ce fu veritez prove
> Que l'uevre en fist Morgue la fee
> El val Perilleus, ou estoit;
> Grant entente mis i avoit.
> D'or fu de soie d'Aumarie
> La fee fet ne l'avoit mie
> A oes chasuble por chanter,
> Mes son ami la volt doner
> Por feire riche vestemant,
> Car a mervoille ert avenant;
> Ganievre, par engin molt grant,
> La fame Artus le roi puissant,
> L'ot par l'empereor Gassa;
> Une chasuble feite en a,
> Si l'ot maint jor en sa chapele
> Por ce que boene estoit et bele;
> Quant Enide de li torna,
> Cele chasuble li dona;
> Qui la verité an diroit,
> Plus de cent mars d'argent valoit. (ed. by Roques, ll. 2348–76)

> She most devoutly prayed to Jesus and the Virgin Mary, that during her life and her husband's, they might be given an heir. And then as an offering, she gave a wonderfully woven green silk cloth and a priestly cloak, covered with filigreed gold, made by all her skill and care by Morgana le Fay at her home in the Valley of Danger. The silk was from Spain, and surely Morgana had never made the cloak for use in church, but let one of her lovers have it because it was richly elegant. Guinevere, mighty King Arthur's wife, had deceived the emperor Gassa and gotten it and had it used to celebrate mass in her chapel because it was lovely. And when Enide had left her, the Queen had it made a gift for Erec's wife. It was said to be worth a hundred ounces of silver. (trans. by Raffel)

The authenticity of this passage is a matter of some debate: Alexandre Micha sees it as an interpolation in the manner of Chrétien, while Roques does not exclude the possibility of it being a subsequent addition of Chrétien's contained in a now-lost ancestor of the *b*-group manuscripts.[16] Yet it merits further consideration in that its account of a unique artefact makes explicit a number of interesting questions subtending other manuscript versions about the basis and propriety of female royal power. Enide, in the only mention of the subject I am aware of in the various manuscript versions of Chrétien's romance, prays for an heir to be born during both her and Erec's lifetimes (ll. 2340–1). In contrast with Enide's pious obedience, Morgane's gift to her 'ami' has a clearly profane motivation, while Guinevere's trickery of Gassa is haunted by the spectre of her sexual allure, both visions of how the characteristic appropriative mode of vernacular subalternity is little better than whorehouse theft. However, in contrast, Enide's docility reduces the claim of the subaltern to speech still further. In this historical logic, women seem damned (memorially) if they do and damned if they don't.

In desiring the child not be left fatherless, Enide distinguishes her and Erec's hoped-for progeny from figures both internal and external to the poem. Externally, the most notable example is Perceval, initially nameless as 'li filz a la veve dame' (*Le Conte du graal*, l. 72). Internally, we might look to figures such as one of Erec's opponents in the tournament at Edinburgh: Rindurant, 'son of the old woman of Tergallo' or 'of the widow of Tergallo' ('Rinduranz [...] / filz la Vielle de Tergallo' ed. Fritz, ll. 2178–9).[17] This knight cuts an isolated figure in a vision of lineages such as the Scottish king, Aguisel, and his sons, Cadret and Coi (ed. by Fritz, ll. 1966–8), or of old men such as 'Quarron, the old king of Ariel' who, although childless, is able to muster a redoubtable retinue of Methusalans, the youngest seven score years in age (ed. by Fritz, ll. 1981–4). Such a varied listing bears witness to a sort of descriptive *émoi*, effectively an collectively embodied anxiety contrasting with other more successful affirmations of line.

Ms. A's emphasis on piety and genealogical continuation thus contrasts strikingly with the improprieties associated with the acquisition of an artefact that owes its existence to the lustful Morgane and its transmission to Guinevere's deception of Gassa. In the text's order of ceremonies, the interpolating mention of Arthur *between* the Queen and the other emperor is interesting, the naming of her husband and the seeming assurance of a match between his *puissance* and her 'engin' ostensibly offsetting any intimation that her success might have owed anything to the illegitimate use of her seductive wiles. Moreover, any scandal in its history is counterbalanced by the overall arc of the narrative – if problematically. If Morgane intends it specifically not for hallowed ends but as a gift for her lover, then Guinevere thwarts her rival in the manner of Christendom's mission of 'despoiling Pharaoh', being absolved of guilt and, crucially, debt through divinely-sanctioned 'Manifest Destiny'. Whereas Chrétien might have spared a thought as to whether the maker of the saddle was ever paid, here it was right to steal the product of Morgane's 'grant entente'. However, Guinevere's 'entente' is far from clear: although she then places the cloth in her chapel, this is not from explicitly charitable intentions but 'because it was lovely' (l. 2372). The cloth then passes from Guinevere, the childless adultress, to Enide, who gifts it to a chapel associated with her husband's family in a prayer for the continuation of his line.[18] Thus, just as the saddle depicts the history of Eneas and Dido, so this description has its place in a complex reflection on history, genealogy and desire. Its story is one of a domestication of female impropriety, whether in the form of adulterous desire, deception or the failure to provide legitimate continuators to a noble line. The generations of this romance thus gradually undo the consequences of a fall associated with signification qua the expression of thought and intention, now turned back to some hoped-for stability in continuation and language.[19] As commentary on the relation between female agency and royal power, the history of the cloth is freighted with a range of distinctly uncomfortable resonances.[20] After all, one person Enide implicitly least wants her son to resemble is Arthur, born never to know his father Uther Pendragon and to have his paternity remain a matter of question.[21] The contrast between saddle and cloth raises questions about the relation between history, ethics, legitimacy and desire, questions that hinge on whether the debts and investments associated with these artefacts were properly settled. However, they also raise the importance of a certain gratuity. Just as the maker of the saddle invested his 'entente', so did Morgane. What moved Arthur's sister seems of little concern to Guinevere and scarcely appears to undermine the sincerity of Enide's wish. The presence of both object and description in Ms. A thus raises an intriguing question as to how the different manuscript versions understand the role of Enide. One reading of Condé 472 is to see its presentation of the coronation as crowning and fulfilling its earlier promise of consensual female subordination to patriarchy's will manifest in concerns with legitimate and stable continuation. Against this, it is arguable that the version in fonds fr. 1376 posits a more open and subversive futurity, allowing Enide the 'elbow-room' to stretch and pull at the ceremonial time of History.

Indeed, in the absence of such a passage, what fonds fr. 1376 seems to suggest is that the issue of elbow-room applies on both sides of the gender divide. After all, it can also be argued that Arthur himself has relatively little space for manoeuvre in the music of ceremony, as we can seen from his part in greeting Enide's parents on their entry into Nantes:

> Erec nule rien ne l'en cele:
> 'Sire', fait il, 'de ceste dame
> Vos di qu'ele est mere ma fame.
> 'Sa mere est ele?' 'Voire, sire.'
> 'Certes dont vos sai je bien dire
> Que mout doit estre bele et gente
> La flors qui naist de si bele ente,
> Et li fruiz mieudres qu'en i quiaut,
> Car qui de bon ist, soëf iaut.
> Bele est Enide, et bele doit
> Estre par raison et par droit,
> Que bele dame est mout sa mere.
> Bel chevalier a en son pere.
> De nule rien ne les forligne,
> Car mout retrait bien et religne
> A ambedeus de mainte chose.' (ll. 6604–19)

Erec concealed nothing from him: 'My lord, this lady, I tell you, is my wife's mother.' 'Her mother, is she?' 'Indeed, my lord' 'Then certainly I see that a flower sprung from such a plant so lovely must itself be beautiful and noble, and the fruit one plucks from it better still, for whatever comes of good stock spreads a sweet perfume. Enide is fair, as by reason and right she should be for her mother is a most fair lady. A fair knight she has in her father. In no aspect is she false to her line, for she resembles both of them in many regards.'

Here, the careful answerings and repetitions in his praise of Enide and her family (ll. 6608–19) are redolent of an 'officialised' praise poetry destined for public consumption, even as the attitudes and gestures that mark the entry of the young couple and the elders into the city belong to the conventional dance of social theatre. For all the reflection on beauty and for all the poetic language, what we have here is also hard-nosed business. In emphasising their aristocratic 'beauty', a praise extended both to Enide's mother and father following Erec's praise of Enide's father's generosity exercised 'sans los et sanz conseil d'autrui' (l. 6601). In that sense, Arthur's words are a response to what he sees and hears, to the evidence of appearances and actions. Crucially, in their slow and careful elaboration, his remarks here – with their emphasis on 'raison' and 'droit' (l. 6614), the use of sententiae (l. 6612), the repeated use of *car* marking a concern with demonstration (l. 6612, l. 6618) and its accumulated modal verbs (l. 6609, l. 6613) – recall his statement at the conclusion of the hunt of the White Stag, although perhaps now less subtended by intimations of improvisatory slight-of-hand. Behind the florid embellishment, his speech thus constitutes a renewal of the family's royal charter, Arthur following Erec's cue that Enide's father acted without prompting or advice from anyone else (l. 6601) – certainly not the Count – and repositioning this apparently minor scion of the house of Laluth now at the centre of a history underpinned by the 'naturalised' laws of beauty and *pietas* embodied in the minimal chain of the two generations standing before him.

In that sense, Arthur's gesture here explains the potential fraudulence of his own earlier statement, his own potentially problematic allusion to Uther Pendragon: assertions of principle are always to some extent abstracted from their 'genealogical' context. The history created reaches back into the past from the present to found its legitmacy. After all, nobody had mentioned that Enide's mother was 'beautiful' up until now: even the seemingly self-evident requires articulation, the apparently natural requires construction and construal. The potential drawback that is the irruptive nature of such a gesture is here bypassed in the affirmation of natural law apparent in the relation between mother and daughter, fruit and flower. (Indeed, were a later dating for the poem to be accepted as defensible, such might also be apparent in the possible similarities between the description of Enide's father and Alan of Lille's portrait of the handsome Hymenaeus.) These creatures are not the product of a metonymic chain but rather imprint themselves from eternity into the present.

The potential implications of Arthur's language here are radical indeed, announcing a divorce from custom and genealogy in their 'literal' sense: the language of political knowledge here – echoing the robe's allegorical presentation – is simultaneously ancient and modern, drawing on the authority of classical learning for its *gravitas* while at the same time refusing to be caught in the potential straitjacket of legitimising strategies dependent on any 'narrow' understanding of genealogy. Of course, while the positive presentation of this is that the substance of Arthur's discourse stems from principle, it might be objected that to sideline actual lineal descent or continuity of practice in favour of such a 'bloodless' allegorical or typological model of genealogy is to create a structure that can be manipulated entirely ad lib. Does this make the once-and-future king a cynical artist of spin playing fast and loose with the foundations of aristocratic legitimacy? Well, yes. But should we be surprised? After all, for all the positive metaphysical connotations of light, all we have to do is look to the description of the crowns, resplendent with their radiant carbuncle stones:

> Maintenant commande fors traire
> Deus corones de son tresor,
> Toutes massises de fin or.
> Des qu'il l'ot commandé et dit,
> Les corones sanz nul respit
> Li furent devant aportees,
> D'escharboncles enluminees,
> Que quatre en avoit en chascune.
> Nule rien n'est clartez de lune
> A la clarté que toz li mendre
> Des escharboncles poïst rendre.
> Por les clartez qu'eles rendoient,
> Tuit cil qui ou palais estoient,
> Si tres durement s'esbahirent
> Que de piece gote ne virent;
> Et nes li rois s'en esbahi,
> Et neporquant mout s'esjoï,
> Quant si les vit cleres et beles. (ll. 6828–45)

> And then he ordered his servants to take two heavy crowns of gold from his treasure chests. As soon as he had spoken and given his commands, the crowns were brought before him forthwith, studded with shining rubies so that each one had four of them. The moon's light is as nothing that even the least of the rubies gave forth. Because of the brilliance they gave out, those who were in the palace were so dazzled that for a time they could see nothing – even the King himself was dazzled, and yet at the same time delighted to see them so bright and beautiful.

The removal of the crowns from the royal treasury appears as the climax of a planned event. Unlike the robe and those other elements already in place before this gesture or before Enide's arrival, here the work of production – in the sense of fetching – is part of the suspense. The radiance emanating from the crowns also raises questions, the dazzling effect not expressed as a physical impairment but rather in terms of fear and awe. Moreover, Arthur's participation in the general confusion may have an element of genuine anxiety, it is also mixed with joy. Even at this stage in the poem, Chrétien offers no simple presentation of what the experience of individual or collective *esfroi* actually feels like.

For all the implications of Arthur's words and actions are radical, at the same time they are also designed to demonstrate a magisterial sense of due form, key here being Chrétien's comment on the end of his speech: 'Ci se taist li rois et repose, /Si lor comande que il sieent' ('The King said no more and took his ease, commanding them that they should sit', ll. 6620–1). Here, rather than offering any sort of disruptive *parole* that would be the mark of him doing a bit of an Arthur, the King instead removes himself from the world of official discourse, Chrétien marking the distinction between what is said to be heard by the wider audience on the one hand and his relaying of stage directions to Enide and her family on the other. In that sense, what we have here is rather reminiscent of a violinist leading an ensemble: after playing a brief flourish, he/she returns to directing the other players. Indeed, that Arthur 'rests' at this point is less to do with actual repose than with his relinquishing the leading role for a few bars only then to take it up again in the descriptions of his generosity both to his barons and the population at large. Again, though, the musical analogy is both illuminating and misleading: that Arthur recedes into reported speech does not mean he actually falls silent even if his invitation and instructions to Enide's family are less to the fore in the music of court spectacle. By publicly marking both his own rest and his concern to put the newly arrivals at their ease, he doubles his words with a range of more 'tacit' signals. Speech and silence are thus abstracted from their common sense oppositionality and recontextualised in the 'language' of performance. And yet, from another point of view, is this really 'speech' in the sense in which Chrétien uses the term 'parole', chiefly associated in this poem with utterances that are out of place or troubling? The decorum Arthur shows here contrasts sharply with the announcement of the hunt of the White Stag or Enide's lament for Erec.

In all of this, the question of fate offers a way round the sense that the court is all fake, all emotional manipulation and show: Erec, Arthur and Enide may be at least minimally 'detached' from the events around them, but this is compensated for by their total implication in the fatal and fateful movement of Fortune's wheel. Their play with the push-and-pull of *émoi* and *esfroi* that keep their underlings on the back foot not merely has its price, but indeed their leverage may even derive from it. However, to push too hard is still to court disaster. Thus, I began my reading of *Erec et Enide* here with the vision of what may have been the social death of a princess: the discomfiture of an unnamed 'king's daughter' as possible pretender to Erec's hand, savagely lashed as she reached out to grasp the opportunities before her. However, for all she disappears downcast early on in Chrétien's narrative, she is less unlike those figures around her who prosper more in Fortune's favour. That said, what she does seemingly fail to do is to position herself as enough of an object of pathos for the unfolding trajectory of the narrative to carry her to the 'hautece' enjoyed by Enide, the latter having lived the object lesson of seeing her own fortunes rise, fall and rise again with remarkable speed. What comes after the coronation and her vision of her immediate family restored in their standing following the damage done by the callous indifference and self-interested intrigues of her own kin is not known, the subsequent prose tradition dramatically divided as to both her destiny and that of her husband.

Such a deconstruction of the emotional rollercoaster focalised in royal ceremony and ritual reflects back on our own contemporary anxieties about the place of *esfroi* in collective life. Appeals to medieval excess are often read as the response of a bewildered modernity that believes itself starved of 'authentic' participatory experience. At the funeral of Diana, Princess of Wales in 1997 – in a burst of noisy *esfroi* that would probably have surprised medieval courtiers very little indeed – hecklers called upon the frigidly impassive Elizabeth II: 'Show us you care, Ma'am!'. This seeming 'failure' in the performance of royal passions, the absence of dramatically satisfactory cues, opposed the (fantasised) openness of the 'People's Princess' to the remoter emotional styles – often characterised as 'professionalism' – of the House of Windsor. This moment was taken up as symptomatic of more general tensions between rational and irrational forces in Western societies. In an alienated climate of 'history without actual events', apathy and cynical detachment are deplored as the dominant condition, responsible for phenomena ranging from the 'democratic deficit' blamed on the phoniness of uncharismatic mainstream politicians, to the rise of both extremist and from single-issue politics to reality television. Of course, to invoke Žižek's recurring 'Coca-Cola' comparison, this begs the question of how and whether the apparent appetite for a 'caffeinated', 'non-diet' experience can be pandered to safely or, indeed, rationally.[22] The the 2006 cinematic prosopopoeia/biography of Elizabeth II, *The Queen*, looks back to the election victory that brought the British Labour party to power in 1997, the monarch turning to the recently elected Prime Minister, Tony Blair, with the quasi-Delphic warning cited above: 'you won't always be popular'. As much as to say that in an era of media saturation, one reading of the actions of this Elizabethan court is to see it as having decided on the 'patrimonial' view that charismatic government is not rational, that it only offers a future in fantasy. By contrast, Mr Blair, New Labour's arch-courtier, was seemingly happy to 'reign by virtue of his future death'. Danger has its useful effects, but as Arthur's hunt for the White Stag shows, it is still danger.

What *Erec et Enide* highlights is that any look back to past cultures is unlikely to provide us with clearer, more innocent or emphatic histories of spectacle. Royal theatre always depended on showmanship. But then, even the most rational and terroristic institutions have found themselves attacked for not offering enough semblance, Napoleon's argument for overthrowing the *Directoire* – the governing council of the young Republic – being that it had 'ni coeur, ni âme, *ni illusion*'.[23] That the about-to-be emperor affirms the power of illusion – rather than rationalistic engagement seems a return to the despotism of the monarchy. However, it can also be read as a defence of the principles underpinning the Terror and an acknowledgement of the fundamentally divided nature of the French Republican project, where anxieties about the power of rhetoric to stir collective passions were manifested most notably apparent in the silencing of the feared demagogue Georges Danton. Such anxieties persist in debate about the nature of ironic (or 'post-ironic'?) uses of quasi-Fascistic spectacle.[24] The concern here, as with Cicero and Augustine is that the power unleashed by such rhetoric has a destructive potential to disturb the rational life of the polis. The lesson of *Erec et Enide* is that the absence of that danger leaves political knowledge bloodless. But then equally, to return to the example of Philippe Pot's teasing cited at the outset, the notion that such apparently absolutist claims were ever any more than bluff and brinksmanship would only seem credible to someone doing a bit of an Arthur.

Notes

1 See Brumlik, 'Kinship and Kingship', pp. 188–9.
2 See Plummer, pp. 393–4.
3 See Duggan, *Romances*, p. 201.
4 See Dembowski (ed.), *Erec et Enide*, p. 1110 and Seebass-Linggi, pp. 152–3 and note 155.
5 See Dragonetti, p. 113 and Seebass-Linggi, p. 154.
6 The cloaks have attracted a massive amount of critical comment. See, in addition to the relevant sections in the various commentaries, among others, Thomas Elwood Hart, 'Chrestien, Macrobius and Chartrean Science: The

Allegorical Robe as Symbol of Textual Design in the Old French *Erec*', *Mediaeval Studies*, 43 (1981), 250–97; Marie-Madeleine Castellani, 'Mythe et représentation du monde: la robe d'Erec dans *Erec et Enide* de Chrétien de Troyes', *Uranie*, 1 (1992), 101–19.
7   Augustine, *City of God*, book 5, chapter 1.
8   Augustine, *City of God*, book 5, chapter 1 (pp. 180–1 in Bettenson's translation).
9   See of course Burgess and John L. Curry, ' "Si ont berbïoletes non" (*Erec et Enide*, 1. 6793)', *French Studies*, 43:2 (1989), 129–39 and Burgess and Curry, 'Berbiolete and dindialos: Animal Magic in Some Twelfth-Century Garments', *Medium Aevum*, 60:1 (1991), 84–92.
10 See Wetherbee, p. 14. For more detailed accounts of the debates regarding astrology and astronomy in the early and central Middle Ages, see S. J. Tester, *A History of Western Astrology* (Woodbridge: Boydell, 1987), pp. 98–204, Hilary M. Carey, *Courting Disaster: Astrology at the English Court and University in the Later Middle Ages* (London: MacMillan, 1994), especially pp. 25–36, and Laura Ackerman Smoller, *History, Prophecy and the Stars: The Christian Astrology of Pierre d'Ailly, 1350–1420* (Princeton: Princeton University Press, 1994), pp. 25–32.
11 On John of Salisbury, see Carey, pp. 28–30.
12 An interesting example of critical impasse about this passage can be found in Plummer's brief comment towards the end of his article (p. 394), citing the same passage and then proceeding to offer no detailed comment on it in a manner redolent of a small can of worms being left carefully unopened.
13 See above.
14 See, for example, Plummer, pp. 385–6.
15 Four of these have been found at sites in Switzerland, Germany and France. The earliest example dates from 1300 BCE.
16 Roques, *Erec et Enide*, p. xlix and Micha.
17 Raffel glosses Rindurant / Randuraz as a widow's son (see p. 68) although the manuscripts give her only as 'old woman'. Given the emphasis on paternity in the lists preceding both the wedding and in the preparations for the tournament, it seems a reasonable supposition that any knight mentioned only as his mother's son might have lost a father.
18 On Guinevere's barrenness and adultery, see especially McCracken, *The Romance of Adultery: Queenship and Sexual Transgression in Old French Literature*, The Middle Ages (Philadelphia: University of Pennsylvania Press, 1998), pp. 25–31
19 See R. Howard Bloch, *Medieval Misogyny*, especially pp. 13–47 and Margharita, p. 144.
20 Here I am influenced by Roberta Krueger's discussion of Benoît's 'dedication' to the 'riche dame de riche rei' (*Roman de Troie*, here at l. 13468 – see ll. 13457–70 for the full passage), not uncommonly interpreted as Eleanor of

Aquitaine (*Women Readers and the Ideology of Gender in Old French Verse Romance*, Cambridge Studies in French, 43 (Cambridge: Cambridge University Press, 1993), pp. 3–7). As Krueger points out, 'read in context [...] the passage works as much to undermine female authority as to acknowledge a powerful patron' (p. 4).

21   On the thorny question of Arthur's paternity and legitimacy and differing representations of Arthur's conception and birth, see Rosemary Morris, *The Character of King Arthur in Medieval Literature*, Arthurian Studies, 4 (Woodbridge: Brewer, 1985), pp. 24–35.

22   Žižek returns frequently to Coke as emblematic of the 'sublime object' /vanishing signifier, the thing that has no positive identity of its own but is rather more the focus for discourses. Of course, the development of the corporation's latest product, 'Coke Zero', a version of Diet Coke intended to appeal to a male market, marks what seems like the ultimate fulfilment of the inverse logic of affirmation founded in absence: what more dynamic a vision of the 'it' Coke famously is could there be than the defiant proclamation of an absolute void? The disturbing dimension here is that 'Coke Zero' presumably acquired some of its marketable currency from the phrase 'Ground Zero'. Interestingly, part of the plans for the site include a memorial to the *absence* of the approximately 2800 victims of the WTC attacks.

23   On which, see variously Žižek, *Welcome to the Desert of the Real*, pp. 5–32, The Puppet and the Dwarf, pp. 35–57 and his introduction to *Virtue and Terror*.

24   See Žižek, *Metastases of Enjoyment*, pp. 71–2.

Bibliography

Editions and Translations of Chrétien de Troyes

Cline, Ruth Harwood (trans.), *'Erec et Enide' by Chrétien de Troyes* (Athens GA and London: University of Georgia Press, 2000)

Fritz, Jean-Marie (ed. and trans.), *Chrétien de Troyes, 'Erec et Enide': édition critique d'après le manuscrit B.N. fr.1376*, Lettres Gothiques (Paris: Livre de Poche, 1992) reprinted in *Chrétien de Troyes: Romans*, La Pochothèque (Paris: Livre de Poche, 1994)

Dembowksi, Peter (ed.), *Erec et Enide*, La Pléiade (Paris: Gallimard, 1994)

Dorothy Gilbert (trans.), *Chrétien de Troyes: 'Erec et Enide'* (Berkeley and Oxford: University of California Press, 1992)

Foerster, Wendelin (ed.), *Kristian von Troyes, 'Erec und Enide'*, rev. edn (Halle: Niemeyer, 1934)

Kibler, William W. and Carleton W. Carroll (eds and trans.), *Chrétien de Troyes, Arthurian Romances* (London: Penguin, 1991)

Raffel, Burton (trans.), *Erec et Enide, Chrétien de Troyes* (Newhaven Conn.: Yale University Press, 1997)

Roques, Mario (ed.), *Les Romans de Chrétien de Troyes édités d'après la copie de Guiot (Bibl. Nat. fr. 794): 'Erec et Enide'*, CFMA (Paris: Champion, 1981)

Prose Reworkings of *Erec et Enide*

Pickford, Cedric (ed.), *'Erec': roman arthurien en prose publié d'après le ms. fr. 112 de la Bibliothèque Nationale*, Textes Littéraires Français, 524, rev. edn (Geneva: Droz, 1968)

Timelli, Maria Colombo (ed.), *L'Histoire d'Erec en prose: roman du 15e siècle*, Textes Littéraires Français, 524 (Geneva: Droz, 2000)

Research Bibliographies: Chrétien de Troyes

Kelly, Douglas (ed.), *Chrétien de Troyes: An Analytic Bibliography*, Research Bibliographies and Checklists, 17 (London: Grant and Cutler, 1976)

Kelly and others (eds), *Chrétien de Troyes: An Analytic Bibliography (Supplement 1)*, Research Bibliographies and Checklists, New Series 3 (London: Grant and Cutler, 2002)

Other Primary Sources

Albertus Magnus, 'Quaestiones de Animalibus', in *Alberti Magni Opera Omnia: 'De Nature et Origine Animae', 'De Principiis Motu Processivi', 'Quaestiones de Animalibus'*, ed. by E. Filthaut, (Aschendorff: Westphalian Monastery, 1955)

Aimon de Varennes, *'Florimont': ein altfranzösicher abenteurroman*, Gesellschaft für romanische Literatur, 48 (Göttingen: Gesellschaft für romanische Literatur; Halle: Niemeyer, 1933)

Alcuin, *Liber de virtutibus et vitiis*, in *Patrologia Latina*, 101, cols 613–38

Alan of Lille, *De Planctu Naturae*, in *Patrologia Latina*, 210, cols 431–82

——, *The Plaint of Nature*, trans. by James J. Sheridan, Medieval Sources in Translation, 26 (Toronto: Pontifical Institute of Mediaeval Studies, 1980)

Andreas Capellanus, *The Art of Courtly Love*, trans. by John J. Parry, Records of Western Civilisation (New York: Columbia University Press, 1959)

Aristotle, *'De Motu Animalium': Text with Translation, Commentary and Interpretative Essays*, ed. and trans. by Martha Craven Nussbaum (Princeton: Princeton University Press, 1978)

Augustine of Hippo, *Against Julian*, trans. by M. Schumacher, The Fathers of the Church, 35 (New York: Catholic University of America Press, 1979)

——, *Confessions*, ed. by E. Capps and others, trans. William Watts, Loeb Classical Library, 2 vols (New York and London: Heinemann, 1922)

——, *The City of God Against the Pagans*, ed. and trans. by G. P. Goold and G. E. McCracken, 7 vols, Loeb Classical Library, 411–18 (Cambridge, MA and London: Heinemann, 1957 [1981 printing])

——, *Concerning the City of God Against the Pagans*, trans. by Henry Bettenson (Harmondsworth: Penguin, 1984)

——, *Aurelii Augustini: 'De Doctrina Christiana, 'De Vera Religione'*, Corpus Christianorm Series Latina, 32 (Turnhout: Brepols, 1962)

——, *On Christian Doctrine*, trans. by D. W. Robertson Jr (New York: Liberal Arts Press, 1958)
Bernardus Silvestris, *The Commentaries on the First Six Books of Virgil's 'Aeneid' Commonly Attributed to Bernardus Silvestris*, ed. by Julian Ward Jones and Elizabeth Frances Jones (Lincoln N and London: University of Nebraska Press, 1977)
——, *Commentary on the First Six Books of Virgil's 'Aeneid'*, ed. and trans. by Earl G. Schreiber and Thomas E. Maresca (Lincoln N and London: University of Nebraska Press, 1979)
Boethius, *The Theological Tractates and the Consolation of Philosophy*, ed. by E. H. Warmington, trans. by H. F. Stewart, E. K. Rand and S. J. Tester, The Loeb Classical Library, 74 (Cambridge MA: Heinemann, 1973)
——, *The Consolation of Philosophy*, trans. by V. E. Watts (London: Penguin, 1969)
La Bruyère, Jean de, *Les Caractères de Théophraste traduits du grec avec les caractères ou les moeurs de ce siècle*, ed. by Marc Escola (Paris: Honoré Champion, 1999)
Burgess, Glyn S. and Anne Elizabeth Cobby (eds and trans), *'The Pilgrimage of Charlemagne' and 'Aucassin and Nicolette'*, ed. and trans. by, Garland Library of Medieval Literature, 47 (New York: Garland, 1987)
Chaucer, Geoffrey, *The Riverside Chaucer*, ed. by Larry D. Benson et al., rev. edn (Boston: Houghton Mifflin, 1987)
Cicero, *De Oratore*, ed. by T. E. Page and others, trans. by E. W. Sutton and H. Rackham, Loeb Classical Library (New York and London: Heinemann, 1942)
——, *De Officiis*, ed. by T. E. Page and others, trans. by Walter Miller, Loeb Classical Library (New York and London: Heinemann, 1913)
Dufournet, Jean (ed. and trans.), *Le Roman de Renart*, 2 vols (Paris: Flammarion, 1985)
Li Fet des Romains, ed. by L.-F. Flutre and K Sneyders de Vogel, 2 vols (Paris and Groningen: Droz and Wolters, 1938)
Gaston Phébus, *The Hunting Book of Gaston Phébus (Manuscrit français 616, Paris, Bibliothèque Nationale)*, ed. by Marcel Thomas, François Avril and Wilhelm Schlag, Manuscripts in Miniature, 3 (London: Harvey Miller, 1998)
Geoffrey of Monmouth, *Historia Regum Britannie: Bern, Burgerbibliothek, Ms. 568*, ed. by Neil Wright, The Historia Regum Britannie of Geoffrey of Monmouth, 1 (Woodbridge: Brewer, 1985)
——, *The History of the Kings of Britain*, trans. by Lewis Thorpe (London: Penguin, 1966)
——, *Geoffrey de Monmouth: 'Histoire des rois de Bretagne'*, trans. by Laurence Mathey-Maille (Paris: Belles Lettres, 1992)
Georges Chastellain, *Oeuvres*, ed. by Kervyn de Lettenhove, 8 vols (Brussels: Heussner, 1863–1866)
Gerald of Wales, *De Vita Galfredi Archiepiscopi Eboracensis*, in *Giraldi Cambrensi Opera*, ed. by James F. Dimock, 8 vols (London: Rolls Series, 1868)

Gottfried von Strassburg, *Tristan*, trans. by A. T. Hatto, rev. edn (Harmondsworth: Penguin, 1967)

Guillaume de Lorris and Jean de Meun, *Le Roman de la rose*, ed. and trans. by Arman Strubel, Lettres Gothiques (Paris Livre de Poche, 1992)

Le Cycle du Guillaume d'Orange, ed. by Dominique Boutet and others, Lettres Gothiques (Paris: Livre de Poche, 1996)

Hincmar of Rheims, 'Quierzy, Nov. 858', in *Concilia Aevi Carolini DCCCXLIII–DCCCLIX*, ed. by Wilfried Hartmann, Monumenta Germaniae Historica: Concilia, 3 (Hanover: Hahn, 1984), pp. 403–27

——, *De Ordine Palatii*, ed. by T. Gross and R. Scheiffer, Monumenta Germaniae Historica: Fontes Iuris Germanici Antiqui, 3 (Hanover: Hahn, 1980)

——, *On The Governance of the Palace*, in *The History of Feudalism*, ed. and trans. by David Herlihy, The Documentary History of Western Civilisation (London: MacMillan, 1970), pp. 208–27

Isidore of Seville, *Isidori Hispalensis Episcopi Etymologiarum sive Originum Libri XX*, ed. by W. M. Lindsay, Scriptorum Classicorum Bibliotheca Oxoniensis, 2 vols (Oxford: Clarendon, 1911)

James, M. R., *Collected Ghost Stories*, Wordsworth Classics (Ware: Wordsworth: 1992)

Jenkins, T. A. (ed.), *Eructavit: An Old French Metrical Paraphrase of Psalm XLIV* (Dresden: Niemeyer, 1909)

John of Salisbury, *Policraticus*, ed. by K. B. Keats-Rohan, Corpus Christianorum Continuatio Medievalis, 118 (Turnhout: Brepols, 1993)

Laclos, Choderlos de, *Oeuvres complètes*, ed. by Laurent Versini, La Pléiade (Paris: Gallimard, 1979)

Lacroix, Daniel and Philippe Walter (eds and trans.), *Tristan et Iseut: les poèmes françaises, la saga norroise*, Lettres Gothiques (Paris: Livre de Poche, 1989)

Lucan, *The Civil War*, ed. and trans. by G. P. Goold and J. D. Duff, Loeb Classical Library, 220 (Cambridge, MA and London: 1988)

——, *Civil War*, trans. by Susan H. Braund, World's Classics (Oxford: Oxford University Press, 1992)

Machiavelli, Niccolò, *The Prince*, trans. by Peter Bondella and Mark Musa, World's Classics (Oxford: Oxford University Press, 1984)

'Mantel' et 'cor': deux lais du XIIe siècle, ed. by Philip E. Bennett, Textes Littéraires, 16 (Exeter: University of Exeter, 1976)

Marie de France, *Lais de Marie de France*, ed. and trans. by Laurence Harf-Lancener Lettres Gothiques (Paris: Livre de Poche, 1990)

Martin, Ernest (ed.), *Le Roman de Renart*, 3 vols (Strasbourg: Trübner; Paris: Leroux, 1882–1887 [reprinted New York and London: de Gruyter, 1973])

La Mort le roi Artu, ed. by Jean Frappier, Textes Littéraires Français, 3rd edn (Geneva: Droz, 1964)

——, *The Death of King Arthur*, trans. by James Cable (Harmondsworth: Penguin, 1971)

Nelson, Jan A. and Emanuel Mickel Jr. (eds), *The Old French Crusade Cycle 1: 'La Naissance du Chevalier au cygne'* (Alabama: University of Alabama Press, 1977)

Ovid, *Metamorphoses*, ed. and trans. by Frank Justus Miller and G. P. Goold, Loeb Classical Library, 42–43, rev. edn, 2 vols (Cambridge, MA and London: 1977)

Ovide moralisé: poème du commencement du quatorzième siècle, ed. by C. de Boer, Verhandlingen der koniklijke Akademie van Wetenschapen te Amsterdam afdeeling Letterkunde, n.s. 15 (Amsterdam: Johannes Müller, 1915)

Owen, D. D. R. and Ronald C. Johnston (eds), *Two Old French Gawain Romances* (Edinburgh: Edinburgh University Press, 1972)

Pálsson, Herman (trans.), *Hrafnkel's Saga and Other Stories* (Harmondsworth: Penguin, 1970)

Peter of Blois, *Dialogus inter regem Henricum secundum et abbatem Bonevallis*, ed. by R. B. C. Huygens, *Revue Bénédictine*, 68 (1958), 87–112

Plutarch, *Lives: Demosthenes and Cicero, Alexander and Caesar*, ed. by E. H. Warmington et al., trans. by Bernadotte Perrin, Loeb Classical Library (Cambridge MA and London: Heinemann, 1917 [1967 printing])

Press, Alan R. (ed. and trans.), *Anthology of Troubadour Lyric Poetry*, Edinburgh Bilingual Library, 3 (Edinburgh: Edinburgh University Press, 1971)

Raoul de Cambrai, ed. by Sarah Kay, trans. by William Kibler, Lettres Gothiques (Paris: Livre de Poche, 1996)

'Renaut de Montauban': édition critique du manuscrit Douce, ed. by Jacques Thomas, Textes Littéraires Français (Geneva: Droz, 1989)

Robespierre, Maximilien, *Virtue and Terror*, ed. by Slavoj Žižek and Jean Ducange, trans. by John Howe, Revolutions (London and New York: Verso, 2007)

Roger of Hoveden, *Chronica*, ed. by W. Stubbs, Rolls Society: Chronicles and Memorials of Great Britain and Ireland during the Middle Ages, 4 vols (London: Longman, 1865–1871)

La Chanson de Roland, ed. and trans. by Ian Short, Lettres Gothiques, rev. edn (Paris: Livre de Poche, 1990)

The Song of Roland: The French Corpus, ed. by Joseph J. Duggan and others, 3 vols (Turnhout: Brepols, 2005)

Le Roman de Jules César, ed. by Olivier Collet, Textes Littéraires Français, 426 (Geneva: Droz, 1993).

Le Roman d'Eneas, ed. and trans. by A. Petit, Lettres Gothiques (Paris: Livre de Poche, 1997)

Rosenberg, Samuel N. and Hans Tischler (eds and trans), *'Chanter m'estuet': Songs of the Trouvères* (London and Boston: Faber and Faber, 1981)

Rossi, Luciano and Richard Straub (ed. and trans.), *Fabliaux érotiques: textes de jongleurs des XIIe et XIIIe siècles*, Lettres Gothiques (Paris: Livre de Poche, 1992)

Sade, Sade, *Justine ou les malheurs de la vertu*, in *Oeuvres complètes* (Paris: Cercle du Livre Précieux, 1966), III, pp. 11–345

── , *La Philosophie dans le boudoir*, in *Oeuvres complètes* (Paris: Cercle du Livre Précieux, 1966), III, pp. 349–549

Schnitzler, Arthur, *Traumnovelle* (Berlin: Fischer, 1926)

Shields, Carol, *Unless* (London and New York: Fifth Estate, 2003)

Sigebert of Gembloux, *Sigeberts von Gembloux Passio Sanctae Luciae Virginis und Passio Sanctorum Thebeorum*, ed. by Ernst Dümmler, Akademie der Wissenschaften, Berlin, Philologische-Historiche kleine Abhandlungen, 1 (Berlin, 1893)

Suetonius, *Lives of the Caesars*, ed. by T. E. Page et al., trans. by J. C. Rolfe, Loeb Classical Library, 2 vols (Cambridge MA and London: Heinemann, 1954)

Tarantino, Quentin, *Pulp Fiction* (London and Boston: Faber and Faber, 1994)

Tsunetomo, Yamamoto, *Hagakure: The Book of the Samurai*, ed. and trans. by William Scott Wilson (Tokyo and London: Kodansha International, 2000)

Quintilian, *The Orator's Education*, ed. and trans. by Donald A. Russell, 5 vols, Loeb Classical Library, 124–7 and 494 (Cambridge MA and London: Heinemann, 2001)

Virgil, *Eclogues, Georgics, Aeneid*, ed. by Jeffrey Henderson, trans. by H. Rushton Fairclough and G. P. Goold, 2 vols, Loeb Classical Library, 63–4, rev. edn (Cambridge MA and London: Heinemann, 1999)

Wace, Robert, *Wace's 'Roman de Brut': A History of the British (Text and Translation)*, ed. and trans. by Judith Weiss, Exeter Medieval Texts and Studies, rev. edn (Exeter: University of Exeter 2002)

Walter Map, *The Courtier's Trifles*, ed. and trans. by M. R. James; revised by C. N. L. Brooke and R. A. B. Mynors, Oxford Medieval Texts (Oxford: Clarendon, 1983)

Whitman, Walt, *Leaves of Grass, Authoritative Texts, Prefaces, Whitman on his Art Criticism*, ed. by Sculley Bradley and Harold W. Blodgett (New York and London: Norton, 1973)

William IX, *Guglielmo IX d'Aquitainia: Poesie*, ed. and trans. by Nicolò Pasero (Modena: Mucchi, 1973)

William of Newburgh, *The History of William of Newburgh*, ed. and trans. by Joseph Stevenson (London, 1856 [repr. Felinfach: Llanerch, 1996])

Wolfram von Eschenbach, *Parzival*, ed. by Gottfried Weber (Darmstadt: Wissenschaftliche: Buchgesellschaft, 1963)

── , *Parzival*, trans. by A. T. Hatto (Harmondsworth, Penguin, 1980)

Wright, Neil (ed. and trans.), *Gesta Regum Britannie*, The Historia Regum Britannie of Geoffrey of Monmouth, 5 (Woodbridge: Brewer, 1991)

Secondary Sources

Accarie, Maurice, 'Faux mariage et vrai mariage dans les romans de Chrétien de Troyes', in *Hommage à Jean Onimus*, ed. by J.-B. Guiran, Annales de la Faculte´ des Lettres et Sciences Humaines de Nice, 38 (Paris: Belles-Lettres, 1979), pp. 25–35

Adams, Alison, 'Destiny, Love and the Cultivation of Suspense: The *Roman d'Eneas* and Aimon de Varennes's *Florimont*', *Reading Medieval Studies*, 5 (1979), 57–69

Adler, Alfred, 'Sovereignty as the Principle of Unity in Chrétien's *Erec*' *Publications of the Modern Language Association*, 60 (1945), 917–36

Agamben, Giorgio, *Homo Sacer: Sovereign Power and Bare Life*, trans. by Daniel Heller-Roazen, Meridian: Crossing Aesthetics (Stanford: Stanford University Press, 1998)

Ainsworth, Peter, 'Legendary History: *Historia* and *Fabula*', in *Historiography in the Middle Ages*, ed. by Deborah Mauskopf Deliyannis (Leiden and Boston: Brill, 2003), pp. 387–416

Akbari, Suzanne Conklin, 'From Due East to True North: Orientalism and Orientation', in *The Postcolonial Middle Ages*, ed. by Cohen, The New Middle Ages (Basingstoke and New York: Palgrave MacMillan, 2000), pp. 19–34

Airlie, Stuart, The Middle Ages in the Cinema', in *The Medieval World*, ed. by Linehan and Nelson, pp. 163–83

Albu, Emily, *The Normans in their Histories: Propaganda, Myth and Subversion* (Woodbridge: Boydell, 2001)

Allard, Jean-Paul, *L'Initiation royale d'Erec, le chevalier*, Etudes Indo-Européennes, 1 (Milan: Archè, 1987)

Althoff, Gerd, '*Ira Regis*: Prolegomena to a History of Royal Anger', in *Anger's Pasts: The Social Uses of an Emotion in the Middle Ages* ed. by Barbara H. Rosenwein (Ithaca and London: Cornell University Press, 1998), pp. 59–74

Amey, Michael Darin, *Pursuing an Elusive Ideal: Masculinity in the Grail Legends*, University of Glasgow, unpublished doctoral dissertation, 2004

Amin, Shahid, 'Ghandi as Mahatma: Gorakhpur District, Eastern UP, 1921-1922', *Subaltern Studies*, 3 (1984), 1–61

Amos, Mark Addison, ' "For Manners Make Man": Bourdieu, de Certeau and the Common Appropriation of Noble Manners in the *Book of Courtesy*', in *Medieval Conduct*, ed. by Kathleen Ashley and Robert L. A. Clark, Medieval Cultures, 29 (Minneapolis and London: University of Minnesota Press, 2001), pp. 23–48

Amtower, Laurel, 'Courtly Code and Conjointure: The Rhetoric of Identity in *Erec et Enide*', *Neophilologus*, 77:2 (1993), 179–89

Angeli, Giovanna, *L'Eneas' e i primi romanzi volgari* (Milan: Riccardo Riccardi, 1971)

Archambault, Paul J. 'Erec's Search for a New Language: Chrétien and Twelfth-Century Science', *Symposium*, 35:1 (1981), 3–17

Arditi, Jorge, *A Genealogy of Manners: Transformations of Social Relations in France and England from the Fourteenth to the Eighteenth Century* (Chicago and London: University of Chicago Press, 1998)

Armstrong, Grace M., 'Enide and Fenice: Chrétien de Troyes's Clerkly Heroines', in *Papers on Romance Literary Relations: The Creation of Female Voices by Male Writers in Romance Literatures*, ed. by Martha O'Nan, Charity Cannon Willard (Brockport: State University of New York College, 1987), pp. 1–8

— —, 'Women of Power: Chrétien de Troyes's Female Clerks', in *Women in French Literature*, ed. by Michael Guggenheim and Henri Peyre (Saratoga, CA: Anma Libri, 1988), pp. 29–46

— —, 'Enide and Solomon's Wife: Figures of Romance *Sapientia*', *French Forum*, 14 supp. 1 (1989), 401–418

— —, 'Recent Gender Benders', *Women in French Studies*, 6 (1998), 114–26

Aronstein, Susan, 'When Arthur Held Court in Caer Llion: Love, Marriage, and the Politics of Centralization in *Gereint* and *Owein*', *Viator*, 25 (1994), 215–28

Artin, Tom, *The Allegory of Adventure: Reading Chrétien's 'Erec' and 'Yvain'* (London and Lewisburg PA: Bucknell University Press, 1974)

Ashe, Geoffrey, *From Caesar to Arthur* (London: Collins, 1960)

Astell, Ann W., *Job, Boethius and Epic Truth* (Ithaca and London: Cornell University Press, 1994)

Auerbach, Eric, *Literary Language and its Public in Late Latin Antiquity and the Middle Ages*, trans. by Ralph Mannheim (London: Routledge and Kegan Paul, 1965)

Baldwin, John, *The Language of Sex: Five Voices from Northern France around 1200* (Chicago and London: University of Chicago Press, 1994)

Alain, *Ethics: An Essay on the Understanding of Evil*, Wo Es War (London and New York: Verso, 2000)

Barber, Richard, Barber, *Henry Plantagenet* (Ipswich: Boydell, 1964 [2001 reprint])

— —, *The Knight and Chivalry*, rev. edn (Woodbridge: Boydell, 2000)

— —, 'Eleanor of Aquitaine and the Media', in *The World of Eleanor of Aquitaine: Literature and Society in Southern France between the Eleventh and Thirteenth Centuries*, ed. by Marcus Bull and Catherine Léglu (Woodbridge: Boydell, 2005), pp. 13–27

Barthes, Roland, *Mythologies*, Points (Paris: Seuil, 1971)

— —, *Le Plaisir du texte*, Points (Paris: Seuil, 1973)

Barton, Richard E., ' "Zealous Anger" and the Renegotiation of Aristocratic Relationships in Eleventh- and Twelfth-Century France', in *Anger's Pasts: The Social Uses of an Emotion in the Middle Ages* ed. by Barbara H. Rosenwein (Ithaca and London: Cornell University Press, 1998), pp. 153–70

Bartosz, Antoni, 'Fonction du geste dans un texte romanesque médiéval: remarques sur la gestualité dans la première partie d'*Erec*', *Romania*, 111:3–4 (1990), 346–60

Baswell, Christopher, *Virgil in Medieval England: Figuring the 'Aeneid' from the Twelfth Century to Chaucer*, Cambridge Studies in Medieval Literature, 24 (Cambridge: Cambridge University Press, 1995)

Bataille, Georges, 'La Littérature française du Moyen Age: la morale chevaleresque et la passion', *Critique*, 5 (1949), 585–601

Bates, David, Julia Crick and Sarah Hamilton, 'Introduction', in *Writing Medieval Biography, 750–1250: Essays in Honour of Professor Frank Barlow* (Woodbridge: Boydell, 2006), pp. 1–13

Baudrillard, Jean, *The Transparency of Evil*, trans. by James Benedict (New York and London: Verso, 1993)

——, *The Spirit of Terrorism*, trans. by Chris Turner (London and New York: Verso, 2003)

——, *The Gulf War Did Not Take Place*, trans. by Paul Patton (London: Power, 2004)

Beauvoir, Simone de, *The Second Sex*, trans. by H. M. Parshley (London: Vintage, 1997)

Bendelow, Gillian and Simon J. Williams, *Emotions in Social Life: Critical Themes and Contemporary Issues* (London and New York: Routledge, 1998)

Bender, Karl-Heinz, 'L'Essor des motifs du plus beau chevalier et de la plus belle dame dans le premier roman courtois', in in *Lebendige Romania: Festschrift für Hans-Wilhelm Klein*, ed. by A. Barrera-Vidal and others, Göppinger Akademische Beiträge, 88 (Göppingen: Kümmerle, 1976), pp. 35–46

——, 'Beauté, marriage, amour: la genèse du premier roman courtois', in *Amour, mariage et transgressions au Moyen Age: actes du colloque des 24, 25, 26 et 27 mars 1983, Université de Picardie, Centre d'Etudes Médiévales*, Göppinger Arbeiten zur Germanistik, 420 (Göppingen: Kümmerle, 1984), pp. 173–83

Benton, John F., 'The Court of Champagne as a Literary Centre', *Speculum*, 39 (1961), 551-91

——, *Culture, Power and Personality in Medieval France*, ed. by T. N. Bisson (London: , 1991)

Berthelot, Anne, 'La Carrière avortée du "chevalier qui jamais ne mentit"', in in *Erec ou l'ouverture du monde Arthurien: Actes du colloque du Centre d'Etudes Médiévales de l'Université de Picardie-Jules Verne, Amiens 16–17 janvier 1993*, ed. by Danielle Buschinger and Wolfgang Spiewok, WODAN, 18 (Greifswald: Reineke, 1993), pp. 2–9

Bezzola, Reto, *Le Sens de l'aventure et de l'amour: Chrétien de Troyes* (Paris: La Jeune Parque, 1947)

Bhabha, Homi K., *The Location of Culture* (London and New York: Routledge, 1994)

Biddick, Kathleen, 'Bede's Blush: Postcards from Bali, Bombay, Palo Alto', in *The Past and the Future of Medieval Studies,* ed. by John van Engen, Notre Dame

Conferences in Medieval Studies, 4 (Notre Dame and London: University of Notre Dame Press, 1994), pp. 16–44
——, *The Shock of Medievalism* (Durham NC and London: Duke University Press, 1998)
——, 'Coming Out of Exile: Dante on the Orient Express', in *The Postcolonial Middle Ages*, ed. by Cohen, The New Middle Ages (Basingstoke and New York: Palgrave MacMillan, 2000), pp. 35–52
Blaess, Madeleine, 'The Public and Private Face of King Arthur's Court in the Works of Chrétien de Troyes', in *Chrétien de Troyes and the Troubadours: Essays in Memory of Leslie Topsfield*, ed. by Peter S. Noble and Linda M. Patterson (Cambridge: St Catherine's College, 1984), pp. 238–48
Bloch, Marc, *Feudal Society*, trans. by L. A. Manyon (Chicago: University of Chicago Press, 1961)
——, *The Royal Touch: Sacred Monarchy and Scrofula in England and France*, trans. by J. E. Anderson (London: Routledge and Kegan Paul, 1973)
Bloch, O. and W. von Wartburg, *Dictionnaire étymologique de la langue française*, rev. edn (Paris: Presses Universitaires de France, 1991)
Bloch, R. Howard, *Etymologies and Genealogies: A Literary Anthropology of the French Middle Ages* (Berkeley and London: University of California Press, 1983)
——, *The Scandal of the Fabliaux* (Chicago and London: University of Chicago Press, 1986)
——, *Medieval Misogyny and the Invention of Western Romantic Love* (Chicago and London: University of Chicago Press, 1991)
Bloom, Harold, *The Anxiety of Influence: A Theory of Poetry*, rev. edn (Oxford: Oxford University Press, 1997)
Blumenfeld-Kosinski, Renate, *Reading Myth: Classical Mythology and its Interpretations in Medieval French Literature*, Figurae: Reading Medieval Culture (Stanford: Stanford University Press, 1997)
Bogdanow, Fanni, 'The Tradition of the Troubadour Lyrics and the Treatment of the Love Theme in Chrétien de Troyes's *Erec et Enide*', in *Court and Poet: Selected Proceedings of the Third Congress of the International Courtly Literature Society*, ed. by Glyn S. Burgess, A. D. Deyermond, W. H. Jackson, A. D. Mills and P. T. Ricketts (Liverpool: Cairns, 1980), pp. 79–92
Boitani, Piero, *The Tragic and the Sublime in Medieval Literature* (Cambridge: Cambridge University Press, 1989)
Bossy, Michel-André 'The Elaboration of Female Narrative Functions in *Erec et Enide*', in *Courtly Literature: Culture and Context*, ed. by Keith Busby and Erik Kooper (Amsterdam: Benjamins, 1990), pp. 23–38
Bourdieu, Pierre, *Outline of a Theory of Practice*, trans. by Richard Nice (Cambridge: Polity, 1977)
——, *Distinction: A Social Critique of the Judgement of Taste*, trans. by Richard Nice (London and New York: Routledge, 1986)

— —, *The Logic of Practice*, trans. by Richard Nice (Stanford: Stanford University Press, 1990)
Bowie, Malcolm, *Psychoanalysis and the Future of Theory*, The Bucknell Lectures in Literary Theory, 9 (Oxford: Blackwell, 1993)
Bradley-Cromey, Nancy, 'The 'Recreantise' Episode in Chretien's *Erec et Enide*', in *The Study of Chivalry: Resources and Approaches*, ed. by Howell Chickering and Thomas H. Seiler (Kalamazoo: Medieval Institute, 1988), pp. 449–71
Brand, Wolfgang, *Chrétien de Troyes: zur Dichtungstechnik seiner Romane*, Freiburger Schriften zur romanischen Philologie, 19 (Munich: Fink, 1972)
Brennan, Teresa, *The Transmission of Affect* (Ithaca and London: Cornell University Press, 2004)
Briggs, Robin, *Witches and Neighbours: The Social and Cultural Context of European Witchcraft*, rev. edn (Oxford: Blackwell, 2002)
Broadhurst, Karen M., 'Henry II of England and Eleanor of Aquitaine: Patrons of Literature in French?', *Viator*, 27 (1996), 53–84
Brogyanyi, Gabriel J., 'Motivation in *Erec et Enide*: An Interpretation of the Romance', *Kentucky Romance Quarterly*, 19 (1972), 407–31
Brooke, Christopher, *The Medieval Idea of Marriage* (Oxford: Oxford University Press, 1991)
Brucker, Charles, 'Gauvain et la mort dans le roman en prose: Erec', *Revue des Langues Romanes*, 87:1 (1983), 89–103
Bruckner, Matilda Tomaryn, *Narrative Invention in Twelfth-Century Romance: The Convention of Hospitality (1160–1200)*, French Forum Monographs (Lexington KY: French Forum, 1980)
— —, *Shaping Romance: Interpretation, Truth and Closure in Twelfth-Century Fictions*, Middle Ages (Philadelphia: University of Pennsylvania Press, 1993)
Brumlik, Joan, 'Chrétien's Enide: Wife, Mistress and Metaphor', *Romance Quarterly*, 35:4 (1988), 401–14
— —, 'The Knight, the Lady, and the Dwarf in Chrétien's *Erec*', *Quondam et Futurus*, 2:2 (1992), 54–72
— —, 'Kinship and Kingship in Chrétien's *Erec*', *Romance Philology*, 47 (1993), 177–92
Brundage, James A., *Law, Sex and Christian Society in Medieval Europe* (Chicago and London: University of Chicago Press, 1987)
Bryson, Anna, *From Courtesy to Civility: Changing Codes of Conduct in Early Modern England* (Oxford: Clarendon, 1998)
Buc, Philippe, 'Political Rituals and Political Imagination in the Medieval West from the Fourth Century to the Eleventh', in *The Medieval World*, ed. by Linehan and Nelson, pp. 189–213
— —, *The Dangers of Ritual: Between Early Medieval Texts and Social Scientific Theory* (Princeton: Princeton University Press, 2001)
Buckbee, Edward J., '*Erec et Enide*', in *The Romances of Chrétien de Troyes: A Symposium*, ed. by Douglas Kelly (Lexington, KY: French Forum, 1985)

Bührer-Thierry, Geneviève, ' "Just Anger" or "Vengeful Anger"? The Punishment of Blinding in the Medieval West', in *Anger's Pasts: The Social Uses of an Emotion in the Middle Ages* ed. by Barbara H. Rosenwein (Ithaca and London: Cornell University Press, 1998), pp. 75–91

Bull, Marcus, *Thinking Medieval: An Introduction to the Study of the Middle Ages* (Basingstoke and New York: Palgrave MacMillan, 2005)

Burger, Glenn and Steven F. Kruger, 'Introduction', in *Queering the Middle Ages*, ed. by Burger and Kruger, Medieval Cultures, 27 (Minneapolis and London: University of Minnesota Press, 2001), pp. xi–xxiii

Burgess, Glyn S., '*Orgueil* and *fierté* in Twelfth-Century French', *Zeitschrift für Romanische Philologie*, 89 (1973), 103–22

——, *Chrétien de Troyes: 'Erec et Enide'*, Critical Guides to French Texts (London: Grant and Cutler, 1984)

——, 'The Theme of Beauty in Chrétien's *Philomena* and *Erec et Enide*', in *An Arthurian Tapestry: Essays in Memory of Lewis Thorpe*, ed. by K. Varty (Glasgow: French Department of the University of Glasgow), pp. 114–28

Burgess, Glyn S. and Curry, John L. ' "Si ont berbïoletes non" (*Erec et Enide*, l. 6739)', *French Studies*, 43:2 (1989), 129–39

——, 'Berbiolete and dindialos: Animal Magic in Some Twelfth-Century Garments', *Medium Aevum*, 60:1 (1991), 84–92

Burgwinkle, William J., 'Knighting the Classical Hero: Homo/Hetero Affectivity in *Eneas*', *Exemplaria*, 5:1 (1993), pp. 1–43

——, *Sodomy, Masculinity and Law in Medieval Literature: France and England, 1050-1230*, Cambridge Studies in Medieval Literature (Cambridge: Cambridge University Press, 2003)

Burkart, Lucas, 'Au seuil d'une poétique du pouvoir: manipulation du nom et (en)jeux de la nomination dans le roman arthurien en vers', in *The Propagation of Power in the Medieval West*, ed. by Martin Gosman, Arjo Vanderjagt and Jan Veenstra (Groningen: Forsten, 1997),

Burland, Margaret Jewett, 'Chrétien's Enide: Heroine or Female Hero?', in *On Arthurian Women: Essays in Memory of Maureen Fries*, ed. by Bonnie Wheeler and Fiona Tolhurst (Dallas, TX: Scriptorium, 2001), pp. 167–86

Burns, E. Jane, *Bodytalk: When Women Speak in Old French Literature*, The Middle Ages (Philadelphia: University of Philadelphia Press, 1993)

——, *Courtly Love Undressed: Reading Through Clothes in Medieval French Culture*, The Middle Ages (Philadelphia: University of Pennsylvania Press, 2002)

Burrell, Margaret, 'The Specular Heroine: Self-Creation versus Silence in *Le Pèlerinage de Charlemagne* and *Erec et Enide*', *Parergon*, 15:1 (1997), 83–99

Burrichter, Brigitte, *Wahrheit und Fiktion: der Status der Fiktionalität in der Artusliteratur des 12. Jahrhunderts*, Beihefte zu Poetica, 21 (Munich: Fink, 1996)

——, 'Ici fenist li premiers vers' (*Erec et Enide*), Noch einmal zur Zweiteilung des Chrétienschen Artusromans', in *Erzählstrukturen der Artusliteratur: For-*

schungsgeschichte und neue Ansätze, ed. by Friedrich Wolfzettel and Peter Ihring (Tübingen: Niemeyer, 1999), pp. 87–98

Busby, Keith, *Gauvain in Old French Literature*, Degré Second, 2 (Amsterdam: Rodopi, 1980)

Busby, Keith et al. (eds), *Les Manuscrits de /The Manuscripts of Chrétien de Troyes*, 2 vols (Amsterdam: Rodopi, 1993)

Butler, Judith, *Gender Trouble: Feminism and the Subversion of Identity*, Thinking Gender (New York and London: Routledge, 1990)

——, *The Psychic Life of Power: Theories in Subjection* (Stanford, CA: Stanford University Press, 1997)

Bynum, Caroline Walker, *Jesus as Mother: Studies in the Spirituality of the High Middle Ages* (Berkeley and London: University of California Press, 1982)

——, *Fragmentation and Redemption: Essays on Gender and the Human Body in Medieval Religion* (New York and London: Zone, 1992)

Camille, Michael, *Image on the Edge: the Margins of Medieval Art* (London: Reaktion, 1992)

Campbell, Ian R., 'An Act of Mercy: The Cadoc Episode in Hartmann von Aue's *Erec*', *Monatshefte fur Deutschen Unterricht, Deutsche Sprache und Literatur*, 88:1 (1996), 4–16

Caputo, John D., *The Prayers and Tears of Jacques Derrida: Religion without Religion* (Bloomington and Indianapolis: Indiana University Press, 1997)

Carey, Hilary M., *Courting Disaster: Astrology at the English Court and University in the Later Middle Ages* (London: MacMillan, 1994)

Carreto, Carlos F. C., 'Au Seuil d'une poétique du pouvoir: manipulation du nom et (en)jeux de la narration dans le roman arthurien en vers', in *The Propagation of Power in the Medieval West: Selected Proceedings of the International Conference, Groningen 20–23 November 1996*, ed. by Martin Gosman, Arjo Vanderjagt, Jan Veenstra, Mediaevalia Groningana, 23 (Groningen: Forsten, 1988), pp. 249–63

Carey, Stephen Mark, *Medieval Literary Consciousness and Narrative Innovation in Wolfram von Eschenbach's 'Parzival'*, Dissertation Abstracts International, Section A: The Humanities and Social Sciences 62:1 (2001 July), p. 162–63

Carroll, Carleton W., 'A Reappraisal of the Relationship between Two Manuscripts of *Erec et Enide*', *Nottingham French Studies*, 30:2 (1991), 34–42

——, 'Un Fragment inédit d'*Erec et Enide* et sa place dans la tradition manuscrite', *Scriptorium*, 46:2 (1992), 242–50

——, 'Quelques observations sur les reflets de la cour d'Henri II dans l'oeuvre de Chrétien de Troyes', *Cahiers de Civilisation Médiévale*, 37 (1994), 33–9

——, 'Text and Image: The Case of *Erec et Enide*', in *Word and Image in Arthurian Literature*, ed. by Keith Busby, (New York: Garland, 1996), pp. 58–78

——, 'The Knights of the Round Table in the Manuscripts of *Erec et Enide*', in *Por le soie amisté. Essays in Honour of Norris J. Lacy*, ed. by Keith Busby and Catherine M. Jones (Amsterdam: Rodopi, 2000), pp. 117–27

Carruthers, Mary, *The Book of Memory: A Study in Medieval Culture*, Cambridge Studies in Medieval Literature, 10 (Cambridge: Cambridge University Press, 1990)

Castellani, A., 'La "Parole" d'Enide', *Cultura Neolatina*, 18 (1958), 139–49

Castellani, Marie-Madeleine, 'Mythe et représentation du monde: la robe d'Erec dans *Erec et Enide* de Chrétien de Troyes', *Uranie*, 1 (1992), 101–19

— —, 'La Description du héros masculin dans *Erec et Enide* de Chrétien de Troyes', in *La Description au Moyen Age: Actes du colloque du Centre d'Etudes Médiévales et Dialectales de l'Université de Lille III*, ed. by Aimé Petit, Bien Dire et Bien Aprandre, 11 (Lille: Centre de Gestion de L'Edition Scientifique, 1993), pp. 105–17

Castleden, Rodney, *King Arthur: The Truth Behind the Legend* (London and New York: Routledge, 2003)

Chakrabarty, Dipesh, *Provincialising Europe: Postcolonial Thought and Historical Difference* (Princeton and Oxford: Princeton University Press, 2000)

Chandès, Gérard, 'Recherches sur l'imagerie des eaux dans l'oeuvre de Chrétien de Troyes', *Cahiers de Civilisation Médiévale*, 19 (1976), 151–64

— —, *Le Serpent, la femme et l'épée: recherches sur l'imagination symbolique d'un romancier médiéval: Chrétien de Troyes*, Faux Titre, 27 (Amsterdam: Rodopi, 1986)

Chênerie, Marie-Luce, *Le Chevalier errant dans les romans arthuriens en vers des XIIe et XIIIe sìecles*, Publications Romanes et Françaises, 172 (Geneva: Droz, 1986)

Cherniss, Michael D., *Boethian Apocalypse: Studies in Middle English Vision Poetry* (Norman, Oklahoma: Pilgrim, 1987)

Cheyronnaud, Jacques, 'Quand marmotter, c'est prier...', in *Panseurs de douleurs: les medicines populaires*, ed. by François Loux (Paris: Autrement, 1992), pp. 195–9

Clark, S. L. and Julian N. Wasserman, 'Language, Silence and Wisdom in Chrétien's *Erec et Enide*', *Michigan Academician*, 9 (1976), 285–98

Clemente, Linda M., *Ekphrasis in Medieval French Romance 1150–1210*, American University Studies Series II: Romance Languages and Literatures, 166 (New York and Bern: Peter Lang, 1992)

Coghlan, Maura, The Flaws in Enide's Character: A Study of Chrétien de Troyes's *Erec*', *Reading Medieval Studies*, 5 (1979), 21–37

Cohen, Jeffrey Jerome (ed.), *Monster Theory: Reading Culture*, Visible Evidence (Minnesota: University of Minnesota Press, 1996)

— —, 'The Armour of an Alienating Identity', *Arthuriana*, 6:4 (1996), 1–24

— —, *Of Giants: Sex, Monsters and the Middle Ages*, Medieval Cultures, 17 (Minneapolis and London: University of Minnesota Press, 1999)

— — 'Introduction: Midcolonial', in *The Postcolonial Middle Ages*, ed. by Cohen, The New Middle Ages (Basingstoke and New York: Palgrave MacMillan, 2000), pp. 1–17

——, *Medieval Identity Machines*, Medieval Cultures, 35 (Minneapolis and London: University of Minnesota Press, 2003)

Colby, Alice M., *The Portrait in Twelfth Century French Literature: An Example of the Stylistic Originality of Chrétien de Troyes* (Geneva: Droz, 1965)

Colish, Marcia L., *The Stoic Tradition from Antiquity to the Early Middle Ages: 2) Stoicism in Christian Latin Thought Through the Sixth Century*, rev. edn (Leiden and New York: Brill, 1990)

Collins, Frank, 'A Semiotic Approach to Chrétien de Troyes's *Erec et Enide*', *Interpretations*, 15:2 (1984), 25–31

Colombo Timelli, Maria, 'Entre histoire et compte: De l'*Erec* de Chrétien de Troyes à la prose du XVe siècle', *Lettres Romanes* (1997), 23–30

Cook, R. G., 'The Structure of Romance in Chrétien's *Erec and Yvain*', *Modern Philology*, 71 (1973), 128–43

Cormeau, Christoph, 'Fortuna und andere Mächte im Artusroman', in *Fortuna*, ed. by Walter Haug and Burghart Wachinger (Tübingen: Niemeyer, 1995), pp. 23–33

Cormier, Raymond J., 'Remarques sur le *Roman d'Eneas* et l'*Erec et Enide*', *Revue des Langues Romanes*, 82 (1976), 85–97

Courcelle, Pierre, *La 'Consolation de Philosophie' dans la tradition littéraire: antécédents et postériorité de Boèce* (Paris: Etudes Augustiniennes, 1967)

Crane, Susan D., *The Performance of Self: Ritual, Clothing and Identity During the Hundred Years War*, The Middle Ages (Philadelphia: University of Pennsylvania Press, 2002)

Croizy-Naquet, Catherine, *Ecrire l'histoire romaine au début du XIIIe siècle*, Nouvelle Bibliothèque du Moyen Age, 53 (Paris: Honoré Champion, 1999)

Cropp, Glynnis M., 'Count Galoain's Courting of Enide', *Parergon*, 3 (1985), 53–62

Curtius, Ernst Robert, *European Literature and the Latin Middle Ages*, trans. by Willard R. Trask (London: Routledge and Kegan Paul, 1979)

Darrah, John, *Paganism in Arthurian Romance* (Boydell: Woodbridge, 1994)

Davies, Owen, 'French Charmers and Their Healing Charms', in *Charms and Charming in Europe*, ed. by Julian Roper (Basingstoke and New York: Palgrave MacMillan, 2004), pp. 91–112

Davis, R. H. C., *The Medieval Warhorse* (London: Thames and Hudson, 1989)

Delbouille, Maurice, 'Le *Draco Normannicus*, source d'*Erec et Enide*', in *Mélanges Pierre le Gentil* (Paris: SEDES, 1973), pp. 181–98

Deleuze, Gilles, *Masochism: On Coldness and Cruelty with 'Venus in Furs'*, trans. by Jean McNeil (New York: Zone, 1991)

——, *The Fold: Leibniz and the Baroque*, ed. and trans. by Tom Conley (London and New York, Continuum, 2006)

Dembowski, Peter F., 'De nouveau: Erec et Enide, Chrétien et Guiot', in *Et c'est la fin pour quoy sommes ensemble: Hommage à Jean Dufournet professeur à la Sorbonne Nouvelle: Littérature, histoire et langue du Moyen Age*, ed. by Jean-Claude Aubailly, Emmanuèle Baumgartner, Francis Dubost, Liliane Dulac, Marcel Faure, and René Martin, 3 vols (Paris: Champion, 1993), I, pp. 409–17

——, 'Textual and Other Problems of the Epilogue of *Erec et Enide*', in *Conjunctures*, ed. by Keith Busby and Norris J. Lacy (Amsterdam: Rodopi, 1994), pp. 113-27
Derrida, Jacques, *La Dissémination* (Paris: Seuil, 1972)
——, *Of Grammatology*, trans. by Gayatri Spivak (Baltimore and London: Johns Hopkins University Press, 1976)
——, *Given Time 1: Counterfeit Money*, trans. by Peggy Kamuf (Chicago and London: University of Chicago Press, 1992)
——, 'Before the Law', in *Acts of Literature*, ed. by Derek Attridge (London and New York: Routledge, 1992), pp. 181-220
——, *Specters of Marx: The State of the Debt, The Work of Mourning and the New International*, trans. by Peggy Kamuf (New York and London: Routledge, 1994)
——, *Force de loi*, La Philosophie en effet (Paris: Galilée, 1994)
——, *The Gift of Death*, trans. by David Wills (Chicago and London: University of Chicago Press, 1995)
——, *Monolinguisme de l'autre ou la prothèse d'origine*, Incises (Paris: Galilée, 1996)
Dinshaw, Carolyn, *Getting Medieval: Sexualities and Communities, Pre- and Postmodern* (Durham NC and London: Duke University Press, 1999)
Docherty, Thomas, *Reading (Absent) Character: Towards a Theory of Characterisation in Fiction* (Oxford: Clarendon, 1988)
Doel, Fran, Geoff Doel and Terry Lloyd, *Worlds of Arthur: King Arthur in History Legend and Culture* (Stroud: Tempus, 1998)
Dolar, Mladen, 'Hitchcock's Objects' in *Everything You Wanted to Know About Lacan But Were Afraid to Ask Hitchcock*, ed. by Slavoj Žižek (London and New York: Verso, 1992), pp. 31-46
Douglas, Mary, *Risk and Blame: Essays in Cultural Theory* (London and New York: Routledge, 1994)
Dragonetti, Roger, *La Vie de la lettre au Moyen Age ('Le Conte du graal')* (Paris: Seuil, 1980)
Dressler, Rachel Ann, *Of Armour and Men in Medieval England: The Chivalric Rhetoric of Three English Knights' Effigies* (Aldershot and Burlington VT: Ashgate, 2004)
Dronke, Peter, *Abelard and Heloise in Medieval Testimonies*, W. P. Ker Lecture, 26 (Glasgow: University of Glasgow Press, 1976)
Duby, Georges, *Love and Marriage in the Middle Ages*, trans. by Jane Dunnett and others (Chicago: University of Chicago Press, 1994)
Duby, Georges and Philippe Ariès (eds), *A History of Private Life: II – Revelations of the Medieval World*, trans. by Arthur Goldhammer (Cambridge MA and London: Belknap and Harvard University Press, 1988)
Duggan, Joseph J., *The Romances of Chrétien de Troyes* (New Haven CT: Yale University Press, 2001)

Dulac, Liliane, 'Peut-on comprendre les relations entre Erec et Enide?', *Le Moyen Age*, 100:1 (1994), 37–50
Eagleton, Terry, *Sweet Violence: The Idea of the Tragic* (Oxford: Blackwell 2003)
——, *Holy Terror* (Oxford: Oxford University Press, 2005)
Edge, David and John Miles Paddock, *Arms and Armour of the Medieval Knight* (London: Defoe, 1988)
Elias, Norbert, *The Court Society*, trans. by Edmond Jephcott (Oxford: Blackwell, 1983)
——, *The Civilising Process: Sociogenetic and Psychogenetic Investigations*, trans. by Edmund Jephcott, ed. by Eric Dunning, Johan Goudsblom and Stephen Mennell, rev. edn (Oxford and Malden, MA: Blackwell, 2000)
Epstein, David F., *Personal Enmity in Roman Politics 218–43 BC* (London and New York: Croon Helm, 1987)
Eskenazi, A., '*Cheval* et *destrier* dans les romans de Chrétien de Troyes', *Revue de linguistique romane*, 53 (1989), 397–433
Evans, Dylan, *An Introductory Dictionary of Lacanian Psychoanalysis* (London and New York: Routledge, 1996)
——, *Emotion: The Science of Sentiment* (Oxford: Oxford University Press, 2001)
Evans, Michael, *The Death of Kings: Royal Deaths in Medieval England* (London and New York: Hambledon and London, 2003)
Evergates, Theodore, 'Louis VII and the Counts of Champagne', in *The Second Crusade and the Cistercians*, ed. by Michael Gervers (New York: St Martins, 1992), pp. 109–17
Farrier, Susan E., '*Erex Saga* and the Reshaping of Chrétien's *Erec et Enide*', *Arthurian Interpretations*, 4:2 (1990), 1–11
Fenster, Thelma, 'Christine at Carnant: Reading Christine de Pizan Reading Chrétien de Troyes's *Erec et Enide*', in *Christine de Pizan 2000: Studies of Christine de Pizan in Honour of Angus J. Kennedy*, ed. by John Campbell and Nadia Margolis (Amsterdam: Rodopi, 2000), pp. 135–48
Ferlampin-Acher, Christine, 'Merveilleux et comique dans les romans arthuriens français (XIIe–XVe siècles)', in *Arthurian Literature, 19: Comedy in Arthurian Literature*, ed. by Keith Busby and Roger Dalrymple (Cambridge: Brewer, 2003), 17–47
Fink, Bruce, *The Lacanian Subject: Between Language and Jouissance* (Princeton: Princeton University Press, 1995)
Firestone, Ruth H., 'Chrétien's Enide, Hartmann's Enide et Boethii *Philosophiae Consolatio*', *Amsterdamer Beiträge zur alteren Germanistik*, 26 (1987), 69–106
Fisher, Rodney, 'Räuber, Riesen und die Stimme der Vernunft in Hartmanns und Chrétiens Erec', *Deutsche Vierteljahrsschrift fur Literaturwissenschaft und Geistesgeschichte*, 60:3 (1986 Sept.), 353–74
Fleckenstein, J., 'Die Struktur des Hofes Karls des Grossen im Spiegel von Hincmars *De Ordine Palatii*', *Zeitschrift des Aachener Geschichtsvereins*, 83 (1976), 5–22

Fleischmann, Suzanne, 'On the Representation of History and Fiction in the Middle Ages', *History and Theory*, 22:3 (1983), 278–310

Florence, Melanie J., 'Description as Intertextual Reference: Chrétien's *Yvain* and Hartmann's *Iwein*', *Forum for Modern Language Studies*, 29:1 (1993), 1–17

Foucault, Michel, *The History of Sexuality: An Introduction*, trans. by Robert Hurley (London: Penguin, 1990)

Foulon, Charles, 'Le Rôle de Gauvain dans *Erec et Enide*', *Annales de Bretagne*, 45 (1958), 147–58

——, 'Les Vavasseurs dans les romans de Chrétien de Troyes', in *An Arthurian Tapestry: Essays in Memory of Lewis Thorpe*, ed. by K. Varty (Glasgow: French Department of the University of Glasgow), pp. 101–13

Fourquet, Jean, 'L'Episode de la Joie de la Cour dans l'*Erec* de Chrétien de Troyes: sa signification pour l'histoire littéraire médiévale', in *Erec ou l'ouverture du monde Arthurien: Actes du colloque du Centre d'Etudes Médiévales de l'Université de Picardie-Jules Verne, Amiens 16–17 janvier 1993*, ed. by Danielle Buschinger and Wolfgang Spiewok, WODAN, 18 (Greifswald: Reineke, 1993), pp. 43–50

Fourrier, Anthime, *Le Courant réaliste dans le roman courtois en France au Moyen Age*, 2 vols (Paris: Nizet, 1960)

Fradenburg, L. O. Aranye, *City, Marriage, Tournament: Arts of Rule in Late Medieval Scotland* (Madison, W: University of Wisconsin Press, 1991)

——, 'The Love of Thy Neighbour', in *Constructing Medieval Sexuality*, ed. by Karma Lochrie and others, Medieval Cultures, 11 (Minneapolis and London: University of Minnesota Press, 1997), pp. 135–57)

——, *Sacrifice Your Love: Psychoanalysis, Historicism, Chaucer*, Medieval Cultures, 31 (Minneapolis and London: University of Minnesota Press, 2002)

Frappier, Jean, 'Virgile, source de Chrétien de Troyes?', *Romance Philology*, 13 (1959), 50–58

——, *Chrétien de Troyes*, Connaissance des Lettres, rev. edn (Paris: Hatier, 1968)

——, 'La Brisure du couplet dans *Erec et Enide*', *Romania*, 86 (1965), 1–21

——, 'Sur la versification de Chrétien de Troyes: l'enjambement dans *Erec et Enide*', *Research Studies*, 32 (1964), 41–49

——, 'Pour le commentaire d'*Erec et Enide*: notes de lecture', *Marche Romane*, 20 (1970), 15–30

——, *Etude sur 'La Mort le roi Artu'*, Publications Romanes et Françaises, 70, rev. edn (Geneva: Droz, 1972)

Freeman, Michelle A., *The Poetics of 'Translatio studii' and 'Conjointure': Chrétien de Troyes's 'Cligés'*, French Forum Monographs, 12 (Lexington: French Forum, 1979)

Freud, Sigmund, 'Psycho-Analytic Notes on an Autobiographical Account of a Case of Paranoia (Dementia Paranoides)', in *The Standard Edition of the Complete Psychological Works of Sigmund Freud (Volume XII)*, ed. and trans. by James Strachey et al. (London: Hogarth, 1958), pp. 3–82

——, 'The Economic Problem of Masochism', in *On Metapsychology*, ed. by Angela Richards, trans. by James Strachey, Penguin Freud Library, 11 (London: Penguin, 1991), pp. 409–25

——, 'Inhibitions, Symptoms and Anxiety', in *The Standard Edition of the Complete Psychological Works of Sigmund Freud (Volume XX)*, ed. and trans. by James Strachey et al. (London: Hogarth, 1959), pp. 75–175

Fumagalli, Vito, *Landscapes of Fear: Perceptions of Nature and the City in the Middle Ages*, trans. by Shayne Mitchell (Cambridge: Polity, 1994)

Gager, John C., *Curse Tablets and Binding Spells from the Ancient World* (Oxford: Oxford University Press, 1992)

Gallais, Pierre, 'L'Hexagone logique et le roman médiéval', *Cahiers de Civilisation Médiévale*, 18 (1975), 1–14 and 113–48

——, 'Hexagonal and Spiral Structure in Medieval Narrative', *Yale French Studies*, 51 (1974) 115–32

——, *Dialectique du récit médiéval: Chrétien de Troyes et l'hexagone logique*, Faux Titre, 9 (Amsterdam: Rodopi 1982)

Gasparri, Françoise, Genevieve Hasenohr and Christine Ruby, 'De l'écriture à la lecture: réflexion sur les manuscrits d'*Erec et Enide*', in *Les Manuscrits de Chrétien de Troyes*, I, pp. 97–148

Gaudet, Minette, 'The Denial of Feminine Subjectivity in Chrétien's Enide', *Romance Languages Annual*, 5 (1993), 40–6

Gaunt, Simon, *Troubadours and Irony*, Cambridge Studies in Medieval Literature, 3 (Cambridge: Cambridge University Press, 1989)

——, *Gender and Genre in Medieval French Literature*, Cambridge Studies in French, 53 (Cambridge: Cambridge University Press, 1995)

——, 'Straight Minds/ Queer Wishes in Old French Hagiography: *La Vie de Sainte Euphrosine*', in *Premodern Sexualities*, ed. by Louise Fradenburg and Carla Freccero (New York and London: Routledge, 1996), pp. 155–73

——, ' "The Look of Love": The Gender of the Gaze in Troubadour Lyric', in *Troubled Vision: Gender Sexuality and Sight in Medieval Text and Image*, ed. by Emma Campbell and Robert Mills (New York and Basingstoke: Palgrave MacMillan, 2004), pp. 79–95

——, *Love and Death in Medieval French and Occitan Courtly Literature: Martyrs to Love* (Oxford: Oxford University Press, 2006)

Gayraud, Jean-François and David Sénat, *Le Terrorisme*, Que Sais-Je? (Paris: Presses Universitaires de France, 2002)

Geertz, Clifford, 'Deep Play: Notes on the Balinese Cock-Fight', in *The Interpretation of Culture: Selected Essays* (New York: Basic, 1973), pp. 412–53

——, *Negara: The Theatre State in Nineteenth Century Bali* (Princeton and Guilford: Princeton University Press, 1980)

Genaust, Helmut, *Die Struktur der altfranzösischen antikisierenden Lais* (Hamburg, 1965)

Genette, Gérard, *Palimpsestes: la littérature au second degré*, Poétique (Paris: Seuil, 1982)

Gertz, SunHee Kim, 'Rhetoric and the Prologue to Chrétien de Troyes' *Erec et Enide*', *Essays in French Literature*, 25 (1988), 1–8

Gier, Albert, 'Zu einer neuen Interpretation von Chretiens *Erec et Enide*', *Zeitschrift fur Romanische Philologie*, 95 (1979), 92–103

——, ' "Cil dormi et cele veilla": Ein Reflex des literarischen Gesprächs in den Fabliaux', *Zeitschrift fur Romanische Philologie*, 102:1–2 (1986), 88–93

Gilbert, Jane, ' "Boys Will Be... What?" Gender, Sexuality and Childhood in *Floire et Blancheflor* and *Floris et Lyriope*', *Exemplaria*, 9:1 (1997), 40–61

——, 'The Practice of Gender in *Aucassin et Nicolette*', *Forum for Modern Language Studies*, 33:3 (1997), 215–28

——, 'Men Behaving Badly: Linguistic Purity and Sexual Perversity in Derrida's *Monolinguisme de l'autre* and Gower's *Traitié pour essampler les amantz marietz*', *Romance Studies*, 24 (2006), 77–89

Girard, René, *Violence and the Sacred*, trans. by Patrick Gregory (Baltimore and London: Johns Hopkins, 1979)

Godelier, Maurice, *The Enigma of the Gift*, trans. by Nora Scott (Cambridge: Polity, 1999)

Gontero, Valérie, 'Les Gemmes dans l'oeuvre de Chrétien de Troyes (*Erec et Enide*, *Cligès*, le *Chevalier de la Charrette*, le *Chevalier au Lion*, *Perceval*)', *Cahiers de Civilisation Médiévale*, 45:179 (2002), 237–54

Gonthier, Nicole, *Le Châtiment du crime au Moyen Age: XIIe–XVIe siècles* (Rennes: Presses Universitaires de Rennes, 1998)

Goodich, Michael, 'Biography 1000–1350', in *Historiography in the Middle Ages*, ed. by Deborah Mauskopf Deliyannis (Leiden and Boston: Brill, 2003), pp. 353–85

Gössman, Elisabeth, *Antiqui und Moderni im Mittelalter: eine geschichtliche Standordbestimmung*, Veröffentlichungen des Grabmann-Institutes, New Series, 23 (Munich: Schöningh, 1974)

Goulden, Oliver, '*Erec et Enide*: The Structure of the Central Section', *Arthurian Literature*, 9 (1989), 1–24

——, '*Erec et Enide*: le masque de la courtoisie', in *Le Monde des héros dans la culture médiévale*, ed. by Danielle Buschinger and Wolfgang Spiewok, WODAN, 35 (Greifswald: Reineke, 1994), pp. 115–29

Gouttebroze, Jean-Guy, 'La Chasse au blanc cerf et la conquête de l'épervier dans *Erec et Enide*', in *Mélanges de langue et de littérature médiévales offerts à Alice Planche*, ed. by Maurice Accarie and Ambroise Queffélec (Paris: Belles Lettres, 1984), pp. 213–24

——, 'Le Statut sociologique du mariage d'Erec et d'Enide', in *Actes du 14e Congrès International Arthurien*, ed. by Charles Foulon and others, 2 vols (Rennes: Presse Universitaire de Rennes 2, 1985), I, pp. 218–40

Gouttebroze, Jean-Guy, 'Entre le nu et le vêtu: le transparent', in *Le Nu et le vêtu au Moyen Age (XIIe-XIIIe siècles): Actes du 25e colloque du CUERMA, 2-4 mars 2000*, Senefiance, 47 (Aix-en-Provence: CUERMA, 2001), 153–64

Graevenitz, Gerhart, '*Contextio* und *conjointure*, Gewebe und Arabeske: Über Zusammenhänge mittelalterlicher und romantischer Literaturtheorie', in *Literatur, Artes und Philosophie*, ed. by Walter von Haug and Burghart Wachinger (Tübingen: Niemeyer, 1992), pp. 229–57

Gravdal, Kathryn, *Vilain and Courtois: Transgressive Parody in French Literature of the Twelfth and Thirteenth Centuries* (Lincoln N and London: University of Nebraska Press, 1985)

— —, *Ravishing Maidens: Writing Rape in Medieval French Literature and Law* (Philadelphia: University of Pennsylvania Press, 1991)

Green, O. H., *The Emotions: A Philosophical Theory*, Philosophical Studies Series, 53 (Dordrecht and Boston: Kluwer, 1992)

Greenblatt, Stephen, *Renaissance Self-Fashioning: From More to Shakespeare* (Chicago: University of Chicago Press, 1980)

Greene, Virginie, 'Le Deuil, mode d'emploi, dans deux romans de Chrétien de Troyes', *French Studies*, 52:3 (1998), 257–78

Greer, Germaine, *The Boy* (London: Thames and Hudson, 2003)

Greiner, Thorsten, 'Das Erzählen, das Abenteuer und ihre "sehr schöne Verbindung": Zur Begründung fiktionalen Schreibens in Chrétiens de Troyes *Erec*-Prolog', *Poetica: Zeitschrift fur Sprach- und Literaturwissenschaft*, 24:3–4 (1992), 300–16

Grimbert, Joan Tasker, 'Misrepresentation and Misconception in Chrétien de Troyes: Nonverbal and Verbal Semiotics in *Erec et Enide* and *Perceval*', in *Sign, Sentence, Discourse: Language in Medieval Thought and Literature*, ed. by Julian N. Wasserman and Lois Roney (Syracuse: Syracuse University Press, 1989), pp. 50–79

Guenée, Bernard, *Histoire et culture historique dans l'Occident médiéval* (Paris: Aubier Montaigne, 1980)

Guerin, M. Victoria, *The Fall of Kings and Princes: Structure and Destruction in Arthurian Tragedy*, Figurae: Reading Medieval Culture (Stanford: Stanford University Press, 1995)

Guerreau-Jalabert, Anita, 'Le Cerf et l'épervier dans la structure du prologue d'Erec', in *La Chasse au Moyen Age: société, traités, symboles*, ed. by Agostino Paravicini Bagliani and Baudouin Van Den Abeele, Micrologus Library, 5 (2000), 203–19

Guyer, F. E., 'The Influence of Ovid on Crestien de Troyes', *Romanic Review*, 12 (1921), 97–134 and 216–47

Haas, Kurtis B., 'Erec's Ascent: The Politics of Wisdom in Chrétien's *Erec et Enide*', *Romance Quarterly*, 46:3 (1999), 131–40

Haidu, Peter, *The Subject of Violence: The 'Song of Roland' and the Birth of the State* (Bloomington and Indianapolis: Indiana University Press, 1993)

Han, F., 'Enide et Yseut', *Europe*, 427–8 (1964), 14–24

Hanning, Robert W., *The Vision of History in Early Britain: From Gildas to Geoffrey of Monmouth* (New York and London: Columbia University Press, 1966)

——, *The Individual in Twelfth-Century Romance* (New Haven CT and London: Yale University Press, 1977)

Harari, Roberto, *Lacan's Seminar on 'Anxiety': An Introduction* (New York: Other, 2001)

Harper, James G., 'Turks as Trojans; Trojans as Turks: Visual Imagery of the Trojan War and the Politics of Cultural Identity in Fifteenth-Century Europe', in *Postcolonial Approaches to the European Middle Ages: Translating Cultures*, ed. by Ananya Jahanara Kabir and Deanne Williams, Cambridge Studies in Medieval Literature (Cambridge: Cambridge University Press, 2005), pp. 151–79

Harris, R., 'Et Liconaus ot non ses pere', *Medium Aevum*, 26 (1957), 32–5

——, 'The White Stag in Chrétien's *Erec et Enide*', *French Studies*, 10 (1956), 55–61

Harris Stabelein, Patricia, '*Erec et Enide*: l'ouverture du sacrifice arthurien', in *Erec ou l'ouverture du monde Arthurien: Actes du colloque du Centre d'Etudes Médiévales de l'Université de Picardie-Jules Verne, Amiens 16–17 janvier 1993*, ed. by Danielle Buschinger and Wolfgang Spiewok, WODAN, 18 (Greifswald: Reineke, 1993), 51–61

Hart, Thomas Elwood, 'The Quadrivium and Chrétien's Theory of Composition: Some Conjunctures and Conjectures', *Symposium*, 35:1 (1981), 57–86

——, 'Chrestien, Macrobius and Chartrean Science: The Allegorical Robe as Symbol of Textual Design in the Old French *Erec*', *Mediaeval Studies*, 43 (1981), 250–97

Harvey, Ruth, 'Eleanor of Aquitaine and the Troubadours', in *The World of Eleanor of Aquitaine*, pp. 101–14

Harward, V. J., *The Dwarfs of Arthurian Romance and Celtic Tradition* (Leiden: Brill, 1958)

Haug, Walter, 'O Fortuna: eine historisch-semantische Skizze zür Einführung' in *Fortuna*, ed. by Walter Haug and Burghart Wachinger (Tübingen: Niemeyer, 1995), pp. 1–22

——, Walter, 'Eros und Fortuna: der höfische Roman als Spiel von Liebe und Zufall', in *Fortuna*, ed. by Walter Haug and Burghart Wachinger (Tübingen: Niemeyer, 1995), pp. 52–75

——, 'Die Rollen des Begehrens: Weiblichkeit, Männlichkeit und Mythos im arthurischen Roman', in *Literarische Leben: Rollenentwürfe in der Literatur des Hoch- und Spätmittelalters. Festschrift für Volker Mertens zum 65. Geburtstag*, ed. by Matthias Meyer and Hans-Jochen Schiewer (Tübingen: Niemeyer, 2002), pp. 247–67

Hedges, Warren, 'Queer Theory Explained', www.sou.edu/English/Hedges/Sodashop/RCenter/Theory/Explaind/queer.htm, accessed 04/09/07

Heers, Jacques, *Family Clans in the Middle Ages: A Study of Political and Social Structures in Urban Areas*, Europe in the Middle Ages Selected Studies, 4 (Amsterdam and New York: North-Holland, 1977)
Heine, Thomas, 'Shifting Perspectives: The Narrative Strategy in Hartmann's *Erec*', *Orbis Litterarum*, 36:2 (1981), 95–115
Heller-Roazen, Daniel, *Fortune's Faces: The 'Roman de la rose' and the Poetics of Contingency*, Parallax: Revisions of Culture and Society (Baltimore and London: Johns Hopkins University Press, 2003)
Helm, Joan, The Celestial Circle: *Fées*, Philosophy and Numerical Circularity in Medieval Arthurian Romances', *Arthurian Interpretations*, 3:1 (1988), 25–36
——, 'Nature's Marvel: Enide as Earth's Measure in an Early Arthurian Manuscript', *Quondam et Futurus*, 1:3 (1991), 1–24
——, '*Erec*, the Hebrew Heritage: Urban Tiger Holmes Vindicated', *Quondam et Futurus*, 2:1 (1992), 1–15
——, 'Deus si beles ymages, une molt bele conjointure', *AUMLA: Journal of the Australasian Universities Language and Literature Association*, 84 (1995), 85–110
Heng, Geraldine, *Empire of Magic: Medieval Romance and the Politics of Cultural Fantasy* (New York: Columbia University Press, 2003)
——, 'The Romance of England: *Richard Coer de Lyon*, Saracens, Jews and the Politics of Race and Nation', in *The Postcolonial Middle Ages*, ed. by Cohen, The New Middle Ages (Basingstoke and New York: MacMillan, 2000), pp. 135–71
Henwood, Dawn E., 'Le Narrateur dans *Erec et Enide* de Chrétien de Troyes', *Initiales/Initials*, 10–11 (1990–1991), 3–9
Hill, Thomas D., 'Enide's Colored Horse and Salernitan Color Theory: *Erec et Enide*, ll. 5268–81', *Romania*, 108:4 (1987), 523–27
Hindman, Sandra, *Sealed in Parchment: Rereadings of Knighthood in the Illuminated Manuscripts of Chrétien de Troyes* (Chicago and London: University of Chicago Press, 1994)
Hoepffner, E., 'La *Philomena* de Chrétien de Troyes', *Romania*, 57 (1931), 13–74
Holzbacher, Ana-María, 'Chrétien de Troyes et le theme de la *recréantise*', in *Boletín de la Real Academia de Buenas Letras de Barcelona*, 43 (1991), 125–52
Houdeville, Michelle, 'Le Beau et le Laid: Fonction et signification dans *Erec et Enide* de Chrétien de Troyes', in *Le Beau et le laid au Moyen Age* (Aix-en-Provence: Université de Provence, 2000), pp. 229–37
Hruby, A., 'Das Sinngefüge der Galoainepisode in Chrétiens *Erec*', *Neophilologus*, 50 (1966), 219–34
Huchet, Jean-Charles, *Le Roman médiéval*, Littératures Modernes (Paris: Presses Universitaires de France, 1984)
——, *L'Amour discourtois: la 'fin'amors' chez les premiers troubadours* (Toulouse: Privat, 1987)

——, *Littérature médiévale et psychanalyse: pour une clinique littéraire*, Ecriture (Paris: Presses Universitaires de France, 1990)
——, *Essais de clinique littéraire du texte médiéval*, Medievalia (Orléans: Paradigme, 1998)
——, 'Troubadour Lyric and Old French Narrative', in *The Troubadours: An Introduction*, ed. by Gaunt and Kay (Cambridge: Cambridge University Press, 1999), pp. 263–78
Hult, David F., 'Author /Narrator /Speaker: The Voice of Authority in Chrétien's *Charrete*'; in *Discourses of Authority in Medieval and Renaissance Literature*, ed. by Walter Stephens and Kevin Brownlee (Hanover and London: University Press of New England, 1989), p. 76–96
Huizinga, Johan, *Herfsttij der Middeleeuwen: Studie over Levens- en Gedachtenvormen der Veertiende en Vijftiende eeuw in Frankrijk en de Nederlanden* (Haarlem: Tjeenk Willink, 1919)
——, *The Waning of the Middle Ages: A Study of the Forms of Life, Thought and Art in France and the Netherlands in the Fourteenth and Fifteenth Centuries*, trans. by F. Hopman (London: Penguin, 1955)
——, *The Autumn of the Middle Ages*, trans. by Rodney J. Payton and Ulrich Mammitzsch (Chicago: Chicago University Press, 1996)
Hunt, Alan, *Governance of the Consuming Passions: A History of Sumptuary Laws* (London: MacMillan, 1996)
Hunt, Tony, 'The Rhetorical Background to the Arthurian Prologue: Tradition and the Old French Vernacular Prologues', *Forum for Modern Language Studies*, 6 (1970), 1–20
——, 'Tradition and Originality in the Prologues of Chrétien de Troyes', *Forum for Modern Language Studies*, 8 (1972), 320–44
——, 'Abelarian Ethics and Béroul's *Tristan*', *Romania*, 98 (1977), 501–40
——, 'Chrestien de Troyes: The Textual Problem', *French Studies*, 33:3 (1979), 257–71
——, 'Chrestien and Macrobius', *Classica et Mediaevalia*, 33 (1982), 211–27
——, *Chrétien de Troyes: 'Yvain'*, Critical Guides to French Texts (London: Grant and Cutler, 1986)
——, 'Redating Chrestien de Troyes', *Bulletin bibliographique de la Société Internationale Arthurienne*, 30 (1987), 209–37
Huot, Sylvia, 'Troubadour Lyric and Old French Narrative', in *The Troubadours: An Introduction*, ed. by Simon Gaunt and Sarah Kay (Cambridge: Cambridge University Press, 1999), pp. 263–78
——, *Madness in Old French Literature: Identities Found and Lost*, (Oxford: Oxford University Press, 2003)
——, 'Cultural Conflict as Anamorphosis: Conceptual Spaces and Visual Fields in the *Roman de Perceforest*', *Romance Studies*, 22:3 (2004), 185–95
Hurst, Peter W., 'The Encyclopaedic Tradition, the Cosmological Epic and the Validation of the Medieval Romance', *Comparative Criticism*, 1 (1979), 53–71

Husemuller, Jeanne Nightingale, 'Court, Cosmos, and Conjointure: A Study of Chartrian Patterns of Thought in the Imagination of Chrétien de Troyes', *Dissertation Abstracts International* 47:11 (1987 May), p. 4081A
Illingworth, R. N., 'Structural Interlace in "Li Premiers Vers" of Chrétien's *Erec et Enide*', *Neuphilologische Mitteilungen*, 89:3 (1988), 391–405
Innes, Matthew, '"A Place of Discipline": Carolingian Courts and Aristocratic Youth', in *Court Culture in the Middle Ages: The Proceedings of the First Alcuin Conference*, ed. by Catherine Cubitt, Studies in the Early Middle Ages (Turnhout: Brepols, 2003), pp. 59–76
Irigaray, Luce, *Speculum of the Other Woman*, trans. by Gillian C. Gill (Ithaca NY: Cornell University Press, 1985)
Iyasere, Marla W. M., 'The Tripartite Structure of Chrétien's *Erec et Enide*', *Mediaevalia*, 6 (1980), 105–21
Jaeger, Stephen C., *The Origins of Courtliness: Civilizing Trends and the Formation of Courtly Ideals 939-1210* (Philadelphia: University of Pennsylvania Press, 1985)
——, *The Envy of Angels: Cathedral Schools and Social Ideals in Medieval Europe, 950–1200*, The Middle Ages (Philadelphia: University of Pennsylvania Press, 1994)
——, *Ennobling Love: In Search of a Lost Sensibility* (Philadelphia: University of Pennsylvania Press, 1999)
James, Susan, *Passion and Action: The Emotions in Seventeenth-Century Philosophy* (Oxford: Clarendon, 1997)
Jauss, Hans Robert, 'Chanson de geste et roman courtois: analyse comparative du *Fierabras* et *Le Bel Inconnu*', in *Chanson de geste und höfischer Roman*, ed. by Pierre le Gentil and others, Studia Romanica, 4 (Heidelberg: Winter, 1963), pp. 61–77
Jeffrey, David L., 'Literature in an Apocalyptic Age: Or, How to End a Romance', *Dalhousie Review*, 61:3 (1981), 426–46
Jordan, Mark D., *The Invention of Sodomy in Christian Theology* (Chicago and London: University of Chicago Press, 1997)
Kaeuper, Richard, *Chivalry and Violence in Medieval Europe* (Oxford: Oxford University Press, 1999)
——, 'Introduction', in *Violence in Medieval Society*, ed. by Kaeuper (Woodbridge: Boydell, 2000), pp. ix–xiii
——, 'Chivalry and the "Civilising Process"', in *Violence in Medieval Society*, pp. 21–35
Kalinke, Jane A., *The 'Erex saga' and Its Relation to Chretien de Troyes' 'Erec et Enide'*, Dissertation Abstracts International, 31 (1970), p. 1280A
Kalinke, Marianne, 'A Structural Comparison of Chrétien de Troyes' *Erec et Enide* and the Norse *Erex saga*', *Mediaeval Scandinavia*, 4 (1971), 54–65
Kantorowicz, Ernst Hartwig, *The King's Two Bodies: A Study in Medieval Political Theology* (Princeton: Princeton University Press, 1957)

Katzenmeier, Ursula, *Das Schachspiel des Mittelalters als Strukturierungsprinzip der 'Erec'-Romane*, Beiträge zur Älteren Literaturgeschichte (Heidelberg: Winter, 1989)
Kay, Sarah, 'The Character of Character in the Chanson de geste', in *The Craft of Fiction: Essays in Medieval Poetics*, ed. by Leigh A. Arrathoon (Rochester Mich.: Solaris, 1986), pp. 475–98
——, *Subjectivity in Troubadour Poetry*, Cambridge Studies in French, 31 (Cambridge: Cambridge University Press, 1990)
——, 'Who Was Chrétien de Troyes?', *Arthurian Literature*, 15 (1997), 1–35
——, 'The Sublime Body of the Martyr: Violence in Early Romance Saints' Lives', in *Violence in Medieval Society*, ed. by Kaeuper (Woodbridge: Boydell, 2000), pp. 3–20
——, 'Courts, Clerks and Courtly Love', in *The Cambridge Companion to Medieval Romance*, ed. by Roberta L. Krueger (Cambridge: Cambridge University Press, 2000), pp. 81–96
——, *Courtly Contradictions: The Emergence of the Literary Object in the Twelfth Century*, Figurae: Reading Medieval Culture (Stanford: Stanford University Press, 2001)
——, *Žižek: An Introduction*, Key Contemporary Thinkers (Cambridge: Polity, 2003)
Keen, Maurice H., *The Laws of War in the Late Middle Ages* (London: ?WEB, 1965 [repr. London: Gregg Revivals, 1993])
——, *Chivalry* (New Haven and London: Yale University Press, 1984)
Kellogg, Judith L., 'Economic and Social Tensions Reflected in the Romances of Chrétien de Troyes', *Romance Philology*, 39:1 (1985), 1–21
——, *Medieval Artistry and Exchange: Economic Institutions, Society and Literary Form in Old French Narrative*, American University Studies Series, 2; Romance Languages and Literature, 123 (New York: Peter Lang, 1989)
Kelly, Douglas, '*Fin'amors* and *recreantise* in Chrétien's *Erec*', *Bulletin Bibliographique de la Société Internationale Arthurienne*, 21 (1969), 141
——, 'The Composition of Aimon de Varennes's *Florimont*', *Romance Philology*, 23 (1969), 277–92
——, 'The Source and Meaning of *Conjointure* in Chrétien's *Erec*, l. 14', *Viator*, 1 (1970), 179–200
——, 'La Forme et le sens de la quête dans l'*Erec et Enide* de Chrétien de Troyes', *Romania*, 92 (1971), 326–58
——, '*Matiere* and *genera dicendi* in Medieval Romance', *Yale French Studies*, 51 (1974), 147–59
——, 'Narrative Poetics: Rhetoric, Orality and Performance', in *A Companion to Chrétien de Troyes*, ed. by Norris J. Lacy and Joan Tasker Grimbert, Arthurian Studies, 63 (Woodbridge: Brewer, 2005), pp. 52–63
Kershaw, Ian, *Hitler 1936–1945: Nemesis* (London: Penguin, 2001)

Kibler, William W. (ed.), *Eleanor of Aquitaine: Patron and Politician*, ed., University of Texas Symposia in the Arts and Humanities, 3 (Austin TX: University of Texas Press, 1976)

Kipling, Gordon, *Enter the King: Theatre, Liturgy and Ritual in the Medieval Civic Triumph* (Oxford: Clarendon, 1998)

Köhler, Erich, *Ideal und Wirklichkeit in der höfischen Epik: Studien zur Form der frühen Artus- und Graldichtung*, Beihefte zur Zeitschrift für Romanische Philologie, 97 (Tübingen: Niemeyer, 1956)

——, 'Le Rôle de la coutume dans les romans de Chrétien de Troyes', *Romania*, 81 (1960), 386–97

——, *L'Aventure chevaleresque: idéal et réalité dans le roman courtois*, trans. by Eliane Kaufholz, Bibliothèque des Idées (Paris: Gallimard, 1974)

Kors, Alan C. and Edward Peters (eds), *Witchcraft in Europe, 1100–1700: A Documentary History* (London: Dent, 1973)

Koziol, Geoffrey, *Begging Power and Favour: Ritual and Political Order in Early Medieval France* (Ithaca and London: Cornell University Press, 1992)

Krueger, Roberta L., *Women Readers and the Ideology of Gender in Old French Verse Romance*, Cambridge Studies in French, 43 (Cambridge: Cambridge University Press, 1993)

— (ed.), *The Cambridge Companion to Medieval Romance* (Cambridge: Cambridge University Press, 2000)

Kullmann, Dorothea, 'Hommes amoureux et femmes raisonnables: *Erec et Enide* et la doctrine ecclésiastique du mariage', in *Arthurian Romance and Gender/ Masculin/ Féminin dans le roman arthurien médiéval/Geschlechterrollen im mittelalterlichen Artusroman*, ed. by Friedrich Wolfzettel (Amsterdam: Rodopi, 1995), pp. 119–29

Labarge, Margaret Wade, *Henry V: The Cautious Conqueror* (London: Secker and Warburg, 1975)

Lacan, Jacques, *Ecrits*, Le Champ Freudien (Paris: Seuil, 1966)

——, *Ecrits: A Selection*, trans. by Bruce Fink (New York and London: Norton, 2004)

——, *The Seminar of Jacques Lacan (Book I): Freud's Papers on Technique (1953–1954)*, ed. by Jacques-Alain Miller, trans. by John Forrester (London and New York: Norton, 1991)

——, *Le Séminaire de Jacques Lacan (livre III): les psychoses (1955–1956)*, ed. by Jacques-Alain Miller, Le Champ Freudien (Paris: Seuil, 1981)

——, *Le Séminaire de Jacques Lacan (livre IV): la relation d'objet (1956–1957)*, ed. by Jacques-Alain Miller, Le Champ Freudien (Paris: Seuil, 1994)

——, *Le Séminaire de Jacques Lacan (livre VII): l'ethique de la psychanalyse (1959-1960)*, ed. by Jacques-Alain Miller, Le Champ Freudien (Paris: Seuil, 1986)

——, *Le Séminaire de Jacques Lacan (livre X): l'angoisse (1962–1963)*, ed. by Jacques-Alain Miller, Le Champ Freudien (Paris: Seuil, 2004)

——, *Le Séminaire de Jacques Lacan (livre XI): les quatre concepts fondamentaux de la psychanalyse (1963–4)*, ed. by Jacques-Alain Miller, Le Champ Freudien (Paris: Seuil, 1973)

——, *Le Séminaire de Jacques Lacan (livre XX): encore (1972–1973)*, ed. by Jacques-Alain Miller, Le Champ Freudien (Paris: Seuil, 1975)

Lacy, Norris J., 'Thematic Analogues in *Erec*', *Esprit Créateur*, 9 (1969), 267–74

——, 'The Conjointure of Chrétien's *Erec*', *Bulletin Bibliographique de la Société Internationale Arthurienne*, 21 (1969), 141–42

——, 'Narrative Point of View and the Problem of Erec's Motivation', *Kentucky Romance Quarterly*, 19 (1972), 355–62

——, *The Craft of Chrétien de Troyes: An Essay on Narrative Art*, Davis Medieval Texts and Studies, 3 (Leiden: Brill, 1980)

——, 'Gauvain and the Crisis of Chivalry in the *Conte del graal*', in *The Sower and his Seed: Essays on Chrétien de Troyes*, ed. by R. T. Pickens (Lexington KY: French Forum, 1983), pp. 155–64

——, 'Motivation and Method in the Burgundian *Erec*', in *Conjunctures*, ed. by Keith Busby and Norris J. Lacy (Amsterdam: Rodopi, 1994), pp. 271–92

——, 'Arthurian Research in a New Century: Prospects and Projects', in *New Directions in Arthurian Studies*. ed. by Alan Lupack, Arthurian Studies, 51 (Cambridge: Brewer, 2002), 1–20

——, 'Medieval McGuffins: The Arthurian model', *Arthuriana*, 15:4 (2005), 53–64

——, 'On Armour and Identity: Chrétien and Beyond', in *'De sens rassis': Essays in Honor of Rupert T. Pickens*, ed. by Keith Busby, Bernard Guidot and Logan E. Whalen, Faux Titre, 259 (Amsterdam: Rodopi, 2005), pp. 365–74

Laidlaw, J. C., 'Rhyme, Reason and Repetition in *Erec et Enide*', in *The Legend of Arthur in the Middle Ages: Studies Presented to A. H. Diverres by Colleagues, Pupils, and Friends*, ed. by P. B. Grout, R.A. Lodge, C. E. Pickford, K. Varty (Cambridge: Brewer, 1983), pp. 129–37

Laurie, Helen C.R. 'The Arthurian World of *Erec et Enide*', *Bulletin Bibliographique de la Société Internationale Arthurienne*, 21 (1969), 111–19

—,'The Testing of Enide', *Romanische Forschungen*, 82 (1970), 353–64

Le Rider, Paule, 'L'Episode de l'épervier dans *Erec et Enide*', *Romania*, 116:3–4 (1998), 368–93

Leeker, Joachim, *Die Darstellung Cäsars in den romanischen Literaturen des Mittelalters*, Analecta Romanica, 50 (Frankfurt-am-Main: Vittorio Klostermann, 1986)

Lefay-Toury, Marie-Noëlle, *La Tentation du suicide dans le roman français du XIIe siècle* (Paris: Champion, 1979)

Léglu, Catherine and Marcus Bull, 'Introduction', in *The World of Eleanor of Aquitaine: Literature and Society in Southern France between the Eleventh and Thirteenth Centuries*, ed. by Marcus Bull and Catherine Léglu (Woodbridge: Boydell, 2005), pp. 1–12

Lejeune, Rita, 'Le Rôle littéraire d'Aliénor d'Aquitaine et de sa famille', *Cultura Neolatina*, 14 (1954), 1–57

——, 'Le Rôle littéraire de la famille d'Aliénor d'Aquitaine', *Cahiers de Civilisation Médiévale*, 1 (1958), 551–91

Levinas, Emmanuel, *Le Temps et l'autre* (Paris: Quadrige and Presses Universitaires de France, 1996)

Levi, Anthony, *French Moralists and the Theory of the Passions 1585–1649* (Oxford: Clarendon, 1964)

Levy, Brian and Lesley Coote, 'The Subversion of Medievalism in *Lancelot du Lac* and *Monty Python and the Holy Grail*', in *Postmodern Medievalisms*, ed. by Richard Uz and Jesse G. Swan, Studies in Medievalism, 13 (Cambridge: Brewer, 2005), pp. 99–126

Lévy-Gires, Noëlle, 'Se coiffer au Moyen Age ou l'impossible pudeur', in *La Chevelure dans la littérature et l'art du Moyen Age*, ed. by Chantal Connochie-Bourgne, Senefiance, 50 (Aix-en-Provence: Publications de Université de Provence, 2004), pp. 279–90

Liebertz-Grün, Ursula, 'Kampf, Herrschaft, Liebe: Chrétiens und Hartmanns *Erec*- und *Iweinromane* als Modelle gelungener Sozialisation im 12. Jahrhundert', in *The Graph of Sex and the German Text: Gendered Culture in Early Modern Germany 1500–1700*, ed. by Lynne Tatlock (Amsterdam: Rodopi, 1994)

Lloyd, Terry, *Worlds of Arthur: King Arthur in History, Legend and Culture* (Stroud: Tempus, 1998)

Loomis, Roger Sherman, 'Arthurian Influence on Sport and Spectacle', in *Arthurian Literature in the Middle Ages: A Collaborative History*, ed. by Loomis (Oxford: Clarendon, 1959), pp. 553–9

LoPrete, Kimberly A., 'Le Conflit plantagenêt-capétien vu des frontières', in *Capétiens et Plantagenêts: confrontations et héritages*, ed. by Martin Aurell and Noël-Yves Tonnerre, Histoires de Famille: La Parenté au Moyen Age, 4 (Turnhout: Brepols, 2006), pp. 359–75

Lot, F., 'Les Noces d'Erec et d'Enide', *Romania*, 46 (1920), 42–5

Luttrell, Claude, *The Creation of the First Arthurian Romance: A Quest* (London: Edward Arnold, 1974)

——, 'Chrestien and Alan of Lille', *Bulletin Bibliographique de la Société Internationale Arthurienne*, 32 (1980), 250–75

——, 'La Nouveauté significative dans *Erec et Enide*', *Romania*, 101 (1980), 277–80

Lutz, Eckart Conrad, 'Herrscherapotheosen: Chrestiens *Erec*-Roman und Konrads *Karls*-Legende im Kontext von Herrschaftslegitimation und Heilssicherung', in *Geistliches in weltlicher und Weltliches in geistlicher Literatur des Mittelalters*, ed. by Christoph Huber, Burghart Wachinger and Hans-Joachim Ziegeler (Tübingen: Niemeyer, 2000), pp. 89–104

Maddox, Donald, 'Nature and Narrative in Chretien's *Erec et Enide*', *Mediaevalia*, 3 (1977), 59–82

——, 'The Structure of Content in Chrétien's *Erec et Enide*', in *Mélanges de philologie et de littératures romanes offerts à Jeanne Wathelet-Willem*, ed. by Jacques de Caluwé, (Liège: Cahiers de l'A. R. U., 1978), pp. 381–94

——, *Structure and Sacring: The Systematic Kingdom in Chretien's 'Erec et Enide'* (Lexington KY: French Forum 1978)

——, 'Pseudo-Historical Discourse in Fiction: *Cligés*', in *Essays in Early French Literature Presented to Barbara M. Craig*, ed. by Norris J. Lacy and Jerry Nash (Columbia SC: French Literature, 1982), pp. 9–24

——, *The Arthurian Romances of Chrétien de Troyes: Once and Future Fictions* (Cambridge: Cambridge University Press, 1991)

——, 'Lévi-Strauss in Camelot: Interrupted Communication in Arthurian Fictions', in *Culture and the King: The Social Implications of the Arthurian Legend (Essays in Honour of Valerie M. Lagorio)*, ed. by Shichtman and Carley (Albany NY: State University of New York Press, 1994), pp. 35–53

Maddox, Donald and Sara Sturm-Maddox, 'Erec et Enide: the First Arthurian Romance', in *A Companion to Chrétien de Troyes*, ed. by Norris J. Lacy and Joan Tasker Grimbert, Arthurian Studies, 63 (Woodbridge: Brewer, 2005), pp. 103–19

Mandach, André de, '*Erec et Enide*: Le Clair-obscur de leur préhistoire', in *Lancelot-Lanzelet: Hier et aujourd'hui*, ed. by Danielle Buschinger and Michel Zink (Greifswald: Reineke, 1995), pp. 133–36

——, 'Les Modèles anglo-normands de Chrétien: Chrétien en Angleterre, *Romanistische Zeitschrift für Literaturgeschichte*, 25:3–4 (2001), 283–93

Mandel, Jerome, 'The Ethical Context of Erec's Character', *French Review*, 50 (1976), 421–28

——, 'The Idea of Family in Chrétien de Troyes and Sir Thomas Malory', *Arthuriana*, 12:4, (2002), 90-99

Margherita, Gayle, *The Romance of Origins: Language and Sexual Difference in Middle English Literature* (Philadelphia: University of Pennsylvania Press, 1994)

Masi, Michael, 'Introduction', in *Boethius and the Liberal Arts: A Collection of Essays*, ed. by Masi, Utah Studies in Literature and Linguistics, 18 (Bern: Peter Lang, 1981), pp. 9–16

Mauss, Marcel, *The Gift: The Form and Reason for Exchange in Archaic Societies*, trans. by W. D. Halls (London: Routledge, 1990)

May, Rollo, *The Meaning of Anxiety* (London and New York: Norton, 2004)

McCracken, Peggy, 'The Body Politic and the Queen's Adulterous Body in French Romance', in *Feminist Approaches to the Body in Medieval Literature*, ed. by Linda Lomperis and Sarah Stanley, New Cultural Studies (Philadelphia: University of Pennsylvania Press, 1993), pp. 38–64

——, 'Silence and the Courtly Wife: Chrétien de Troyes's *Erec et Enide*', *Arthurian Yearbook*, 3 (1993), 107–26

——, *The Romance of Adultery: Queenship and Sexual Transgression in Old French Literature*, The Middle Ages (Philadelphia: University of Pennsylvania Press, 1998)

——, 'Scandalising Desire: Eleanor of Aquitaine and the Chroniclers', in *Eleanor of Aquitaine: Lord and Lady*, ed. by Bonnie Wheeler and John Carmi Parsons, The New Middle Ages (New York and Basingstoke: Palgrave MacMillan, 2003), pp. 247–63

McDonald, Jill Pamela, *Hartmann von Aue's 'Erec' and Chretien de Troyes's 'Erec et Enide': The Extent and Logic of Hartmann's Transformations of Chretien's Romance*, Dissertation Abstracts International, 39 (1978), p. 3610A–11A

McDonald, William, 'The Crown Endures: Concerning Heraldry as Narrative Discourse in the *Erec* of Hartmann von Aue', *Colloquia Germanica: Internationale Zeitschrift für Germanistik*, 33:4 (2000), p. 317–32

McMahon, J. V., 'Enite's Relatives: The Girl in the Garden', *Modern Language Notes*, 85 (1970), 367–72

Mehl, Jean-Michel, 'Games in their Seasons', in *Custom, Culture and Community: A Symposium*, ed. by Thomas Pettit and Leif Sondergaard (Odense: Odense University Press, 1994), pp. 71–83

Méla, Charles, *La Reine et le Graal: la conjointure dans les romans du Graal de Chrétien de Troyes au Livre de Lancelot* (Paris: Seuil, 1984)

Mellinkoff, Ruth, *Outcasts: Signs of Otherness in Northern European Art of the Late Middle Ages*, 2 vols (Berkeley and Oxford: University of California Press, 1993)

Ménage, René, '*Erec et Enide*: Quelques pièces du dossier', *Marche Romane*, 30:3–4 (1980), 203–21

——, 'Erec et les intermittences du coeur', in *Marche Romane*, 32:2–4 (1982), 5–14

Ménard, Philippe, 'Le Temps et la durée dans les romans de Chrétien de Troyes', *Le Moyen Age*, 73 (1967), 375–401

——, 'Réflexions sur les coutumes dans les romans arthuriens', in *Por le soie amisté. Essays in Honour of Norris J. Lacy*, ed. by Keith Busby and Catherine M. Jones (Amsterdam: Rodopi, 2000), pp. 357–70

Meneghetti, Maria Luisa, ' "Joie de la Cort": Intégration individuelle et métaphore sociale dans *Erec et Enide*', *Cahiers de Civilisation Médiévale*, 19 (1976), 371–79

Mezghani-Manal, Mounira, 'La Description de l'œuvre d'art entre esthétique et technique', in *La Description au Moyen Age: Actes de Colloque de janvier 2002 à Amiens*. ed. by Danielle Buschinger, Médiévales, 24 (Amiens: Centre d'Etudes Médiévales, Université de Picardie–Jules Verne, 2002), pp. 76–87

Micha, Alexandre, *La Tradition manuscrite des romans de Chrétien de Troyes* (Geneva: Droz, 1966)

Mickel, Emmanuel J., 'A Reconsideration of Chrétien's *Erec*', *Romanische Forschungen*, 84 (1972), 18–44

— —, 'Mercury's Philologia and Erec's Enide', *Romance Philology*, 56:1 (2002), 1–22
Middleton, Roger, 'Erec's Coronation Robe', *Bulletin Bibliographique de la Société Internationale Arthurienne*, 27 (1975), 224
— —, 'Le Grand d'Aussy's *Erec et Enide*', *Nottingham French Studies*, 25:2 (1986), 14–41
— —, 'Structure and Chronology in *Erec et Enide*', *Nottingham French Studies*, 30:2 (1991), 43–80
— —, 'Coloured Capitals in the Manuscripts of *Erec et Enide*', in *Les Manuscrits de Chrétien de Troyes*, I, pp. 149–93
— —, 'Enide's See-Through Dress', *Arthurian Studies in Honour of P.J.C. Field*, ed. by Bonnie Wheeler, Arthurian Studies, 57 (Cambridge: Brewer, 2004), 143–63
Miller, J. Hillis, *Topographies*, Meridian: Crossing Aesthetics (Stanford: Stanford University Press, 1995)
Misrahi, Jean, 'More Light on the Chronology of Chrétien de Troyes?', *Bulletin Bibliographique de la Société Internationale Arthurienne*, 11 (1959), 89–120
— —, 'Symbolism and Allegory in Arthurian Romance', *Romance Philology*, 17 (1964), 555–69
Moore, R. I., *The Formation of a Persecuting Society: Power and Deviance in Western Europe, 950–1250* (Oxford: Blackwell, 1990 [1996 printing])
Morris, Rosemary, *The Character of King Arthur in Medieval Literature*, Arthurian Studies, 4 (Woodbridge: Brewer, 1985)
Mosse, George, review of Elias, *The Civilising Process*, *New German Critique*, 15 (1978), 178–83)
Mühlethaler, Jean-Claude, 'Mourir à table: contextualisation et enjeux d'une séquence narrative au XIIe siècle (de la *Chanson de Guillaume* à *Erec et Enide*)', in *Banquets et manières de table au Moyen Age,* Senefiance, 38 (Aix-en-Provence: Centre Universitaire d'Etudes et de Recherches Médiévales d'Aix, Publication: 1996), pp. 215–34
Mullally, Evelyn, *The Artist at Work: Narrative Technique in Chrétien de Troyes*, Transactions of the American Philosophical Society, 78:4 (Philadelphia: The American Philosophical Society, 1988)
Mulvey, Laura, 'Visual Pleasure and Narrative Cinema', *Screen*, 16:3 (1975), 6–18
Murphy, Margueritte S., 'The Allegory of "Joie" in Chrétien's *Erec et Enide*', in *Allegory, Myth, and Symbol*, ed. by, Morton W. Bloomfield (Cambridge MA: Harvard University Press, 1981)
Murray, Alexander, *Suicide in the Middle Ages: 1) The Violent Against Themselves* (Oxford: Oxford University Press, 1998)
— —, *Suicide in the Middle Ages: 2) The Curse of Self-Murder* (Oxford: Oxford University Press, 2000)
Murray, Erin, 'The Masculinization of Enide's Voice: An Ambiguous Portrayal of the Heroine', *Romance Languages Annual*, 8 (1996), 79–83

Mussetter, Sally, 'The Education of Chrétien's Enide', *Romanic Review*, 73:2 (1982), 147–66
— —, 'The Fairy Arts of *Mesure* in Chrétien's *Erec*', *Romance Quarterly*, 31:1 (1984), 9–22
Myers, Tony, *Slavoj Žižek* (London and New York: Routledge, 2003)
Nelson, Deborah, 'Enide: *amie* or *femme*?', *Romance Notes*, 21:3 (1981), 358–63
— —, 'The Role of Animals in *Erec et Enide*', *Romance Quarterly*, 35:1 (1988), 31–38
Nelson, Jan A., 'A Jungian Interpretation of Sexually Ambiguous Imagery in Chrétien's *Erec et Enide*', in *The Arthurian Tradition: Essays in Convergence*, ed. by Mary Flowers Braswell, and John Bugge (Tuscaloosa: University of Alabama Press, 1988), pp. 75–89
Nelson, Janet L., *Charles the Bald*, The Medieval World (London and New York: Longman, 1992)
— —, Nelson, 'Did Charlemagne have a Private Life?', in *Writing Medieval Biography, 750–1250: Essays in Honour of Professor Frank Barlow* (Woodbridge: Boydell, 2006), pp. 15–28
Newstead, H., 'The *Joie de la Cort* Episode in *Erec* and the Horn of Bran', *Publications of the Modern Language Association*, 51 (1936), 13–25
Nickel, Helmut, 'About a Crown Found and a Grail Tournament Held at the "Castle of the Maiden"', *Arthuriana*, 7:3 (1997), 36–44
Niemeyer, K. H., 'The Writer's Craft: The *Joie de la Cort*', *L'Esprit Créateur*, 9 (1969), 286–92
Nightingale, Jeanne A., 'The Romances of Chrétien de Troyes as Adventures in Interpretation', *Cincinnati Romance Review*, 7 (1988), 11–28
— —, 'Chrétien de Troyes and the Mythographical Tradition: The Couple's Journey in *Erec et Enide* and Martianus' *De Nuptiis*', in *King Arthur through the Ages, I*, Valerie M. Lagorio and Mildred Leake Day (New York: Garland, 1990)
— —, 'From Mirror to Metamorphosis: Echoes of Ovid's *Narcissus* in Chrétien's *Erec et Enide*', in *The Mythographic Art: Classical Fable and the Rise of the Vernacular in Early France and England*, ed. by Jane Chance (Gainsville: University of Florida Press, 1990), pp. 47–82
— —, 'Erec in the Mirror: The Feminization of the Self and the Re-Invention of the Chivalric Hero in Chrétien's First Romance', in *Arthurian Romance and Gender/ Masculin/ Féminin dans le roman arthurien médiéval/ Geschlechterrollen im mittelalterlichen Artusroman*, ed. by Friedrich Wolfzettel (Amsterdam: Rodopi, 1995), pp. 130–46
Nirenberg, David, *Communities of Violence: Persecution of Minorities in the Middle Ages* (Princeton: Princeton University Press, 1996)
Nitze, W. A., 'The Exhumation of King Arthur at Glastonbury', *Speculum*, 9:4 (1934), pp. 355–61
— —, 'Conjointure in *Erec*, l 14', *Modern Language Notes*, 69:3 (1954), 180–81
— —, 'Erec and the Joy of the Court', *Speculum*, 29:4 (1954), 691–701

Nixon, Terry, '*Amadas et Ydoine* and *Erec et Enide*: Reuniting Membra Disjecta from Early Old French Manuscripts', *Viator*, 18 (1987), 227–51

Noacco, Cristina, 'La Dialectique du don dans la quête de la Joie d'*Erec et Enide*', in *Guerres, voyages et quêtes au Moyen Age. Mélanges offerts à Jean-Claude Faucon*, ed. by Alain Labbe, Daniel W. Lacroix and Danielle Queruel, Colloques, Congrès et Conférences sur le Moyen Age, 2 (Paris: Champion, 2000), 299–311

Noble, Peter S., *Love and Marriage in Chrétien de Troyes* (Cardiff: University of Wales Press, 1982)

Nykrog, Per, *Chrétien de Troyes: romancier discutable*, Publications Romanes et Françaises, 213 (Geneva: Droz, 1996)

O'Callaghan, Tamara F., 'Tempering Scandal: Eleanor of Aquitaine and Benoît de Sainte-Maure's *Roman de Troie*', in *Eleanor of Aquitaine: Lord and Lady*, ed. by Bonnie Wheeler and Parsons, The New Middle Ages (New York and Basingstoke: Palgrave MacMillan, 2003), pp. 301–17

Ogle, M. B., 'The Sloth of Erec', *Romanic Review*, 9 (1918), 1–20

Okken, Lambertus, 'Chrétien/Hartmann und Seneca, *De beneficiis*', *Amsterdamer Beitrage zur Alteren Germanistik*, 35 (1992), 21–36

Ollier, M.-L., 'Modernité de Chrétien de Troyes', *Romanic Review*, 71 (1980), 413–44

— —, 'The Author in the Text: The Prologues of Chrétien de Troyes', *Yale French Studies*, 51 (1974), 26–41

Orr, Mary, *Claude Simon: The Intertextual Dimension* (Glasgow: University of Glasgow French and German Publications, 1993)

Owen, D. D. R., 'Reward and Punishment in Chrétien's *Erec* and Related Texts', in *Rewards and Punishments in the Arthurian Romances and Lyric Poetry of Mediaeval France*, ed. by Peter V. Davies and Angus Kennedy (Cambridge: Brewer, 1987), pp. 119–32

— —, *Eleanor of Aquitaine: Queen and Legend* (Oxford: Blackwell, 1993)

Paden, William D., 'Scholars at a Perilous Ford', in *The Future of the Middle Ages: Medieval Literature in the 1990's*, ed. by Paden (Gainsville: University of Florida Press, 1994), pp. 3–31

Paris, Gaston, Review of Wendelin Foerster (ed.), *Erec und Enide*, *Romania*, 20 (1891), 148–66

Parker, Ian, *Slavoj Žižek: A Critical Introduction* (London: Pluto, 2004)

Parsons, John Carmi, 'Damned If She Didn't and Damned When She Did: Bodies, Babies and Bastards in the Lives of Two Queens of France', in *Eleanor of Aquitaine: Lord and Lady*, ed. by Bonnie Wheeler and Parsons, The New Middle Ages (New York and Basingstoke: Palgrave MacMillan, 2003), pp. 267–99

Pastoureau, Michel, *Une histoire symbolique du Moyen Age occidentale*, La Librairie du XXIe Siècle (Paris: Seuil, 2004)

Patterson, Lee, *Negotiating the Past: The Historical Understanding of Medieval Literature* (Madison: University of Wisconsin Press, 1987)
Peek, Wendy Chapman, *Vision, Language, Spectacle: Ekphrasis in the 'Aeneid' and Medieval Romance*, Dissertation Abstracts International 53:10 (1993), p. 3522A
Pérennec, René, 'La "Faute" d'Enide: transgression ou inadéquation entre un projet poétique et des stéréotypes de comportement?', in *Amour, mariage et transgressions au Moyen Age: Actes du colloque des 24–27 mars 1983, Université de Picardie, Centre d'Etudes Médiévales*, ed. by Danielle Buschinger and André Crépin, Göppinger Arbeiten zur Germanistik 420 (Göppingen: Kümmerle, 1984), pp. 153–9
— —, 'Adaptation et société: l'adaptation par Hartmann d'Aue du roman de Chrétien de Troyes: *Erec et Enide*', *Etudes Germaniques*, 28 (1973), 289–303
Peters, Edward, 'What Was God Doing Before He Created the Heavens and the Earth?', *Augustiniana*, 34:1–2 (1984), 53–74 reprinted in *Limits of Thought and Power in Medieval Europe*, Variorum Collected Studies (Aldershot and Burlington: Ashgate, 2001)
Philips, Adam, *On Kissing, Tickling and Being Bored* (London: Faber and Faber, 1993)
Pickens, Rupert T., 'Estoire, Lai and Romance: Chrétien's *Erec et Enide* and *Cligès*', *Romanic Review*, 66 (1975), 247–62
Pickering, Frederick, P., *Augustinus oder Boethius? Geschichtsschreibung und epische Dichtung im Mittelalter und in der Neuzeit*, Philologische Studien und Quellen, 39 and 80, 2 vols (Berlin: Schmidt, 1967–1976)
Pickford, Cedric E., 'La Transformation littéraire d'Erec: le fils "Lac"', in *Mélanges de philologie et de littératures romanes offerts à Jeanne Wathelet-Willem*, ed by Jacques de Caluwé (Liège: Cahiers de l'A. R. U., 1978), pp. 477–94
Pintarič, Miha, 'Le Rôle de la violence dans le roman médiéval: l'exemple d'*Erec et Enide*', in *La Violence dans le monde médiéval*, Senefiance, 36 (Aix-en-Provence: CUERMA, 1994), pp. 413–23
Pirenne, Henri, *Histoire de Belgique*, 8 vols, rev. edn (Brussels: Lamertin, 1922–32)
Pirot, F., *Recherches sur les connaissances littéraires des troubadours occitans et Catalans des XIIe et XIIIe siècles*, Memorias de la Real Academia de Buenas Lettras de Barcelona (Barcelona: Real Academia de Buenas Lettras, 1972)
Pitkin, Hanna Fenichel, *Fortune is a Woman: Gender and Politics in the Thought of Niccolò Machiavelli* (Berkeley and London: University of California Press, 1984)
Plummer, John F., '*Bien dire* and *bien aprandre* in Chretien de Troyes's *Erec et Enide*', *Romania*, 95 (1974), 380–94
Power, Dan, 'The Stripping of a Queen: Eleanor of Aquitaine in Thirteenth-Century Norman Tradition', in *The World of Eleanor of Aquitaine: Literature and Society in Southern France between the Eleventh and Thirteenth Centuries*, ed. by Marcus Bull and Catherine Léglu (Woodbridge: Boydell, 2005), pp. 115–35

Prakash, Gyan, 'Subaltern Studies as Postcolonial Criticism', *American Historical Review*, 99:5 (1994), 1475–90

Press, A. R., 'Le Comportement d'Erec envers Enide dans le roman de Chrétien de Troyes', *Romania*, 90 (1956), 529–38

— —, 'Death and Lament in Chrétien de Troyes's Romances: The Dialectic of Rhetoric and Reason', *Forum for Modern Language Studies*, 23:1 (1987), 11–20

Purdie, Rhiannon and Nicola Royen (eds), 'Introduction: Tartan Arthur?', in *The Scots and Medieval Arthurian Legend*, Arthurian Studies (Woodbridge: Brewer, 2005), pp. 1–7

Putter, Ad, 'Finding Time for Romance: Medieval Arthurian Literary History', *Medium Aevum*, 53 (1994), 1–16

— —, 'Knights and Clerics in the Court of Champagne: Chrétien de Troyes's Romances in Context', in *Medieval Knighthood V: Papers from the Sixth Strawberry Hill Conference 1994*, ed. by Steven Church and Ruth Harvey (Woodbridge: Boydell and Brewer, 1995), pp. 243–66

Ramey, Lynn Tarte, 'Representations of Women in Chrétien's *Erec et Enide*: Courtly Literature or Misogyny?', *Romanic Review*, 83:4 (1993), 377–86

Reuter, Tim, 'Assembly Politics in Western Europe from the Eighth Century to the Twelfth', in *The Medieval World*, ed. by Peter Linehan and Janet L. Nelson (London and New York: Routledge, 2001), pp. 432–50 rev. edn in *Medieval Polities and Modern Mentalities*, ed. by Nelson (Cambridge: Cambridge University Press, 2006), pp. 193–216

Ricoeur, Paul, *Temps et récit*, L'Ordre Philosophique, 3 vols (Paris: Seuil, 1983–1985)

Ribémont, Bernard, *La 'Renaissance' du XIIe siècle et l'encyclopédisme*, Essais sur le Moyen Age (Paris: Honoré Champion, 2002).

Roach, Eleanor A., *Considerations of Chrétien de Troyes' 'Erec et Enide'*, Dissertation Abstracts International, 32 (1971), p. 398A

Robertson, D. W., Jr. 'A Further Note on Conjointure', *Modern Language Notes*, 70:6 (1955), 415–16

— —, *A Preface to Chaucer: Studies in Medieval Perspectives* (Princeton: Princeton University Press, 1962)

Rollo, David, 'From Apuleius's *Psyche* to Chrétien's *Erec and Enide*', in *The Search for the Ancient Novel*, ed by James Tatum (Baltimore: Johns Hopkins University Press, 1994), pp. 347–69

Roloff, Volker, ' "Parole" und "teisir" in Chrétien de Troyes *Erec et Enide*', in *Reden und Schweigen: zur Tradition und Gestaltung eines mittelalterlichen Themas in der französischen Literatur*, ed. by Volker Roloff, Münchener Romanistische Arbeiten, 34 (Munich: Fink, 1973), pp. 117–38

Roncaglia, Alfredo, 'Carestia', *Cultura Neolatina*, 18 (1958), 121–37

Rorty, Amélie Oksenberg, 'Explaining Emotions', in *Explaining Emotions*, ed. by Rorty (Berkeley: University of California Press, 1980), pp. 104–26

Rosen, Stanley, *The Quarrel Between Poetry and Philosophy: Studies in Ancient Thought* (London and New York: Routledge, 1988)
Roussel, Claude, 'Courtoisie', in *Dictionnaire raisonné de la politesse et du savoir-vivre du Moyen Age à nos jours*, ed. by Alain Montaudon (Paris: Seuil, 1994), pp. 175–96
Royle, Nicholas, *Telepathy and Literature: Essays on the Reading Mind* (Oxford: Blackwell, 1990)
— —, *After Derrida* (Manchester and New York: Manchester University Press, 1995)
Ruberg, Uwe, 'Die Königskrönung Erecs bei Chrétien und Hartmann im Kontext arthurischer Erzählschlüsse', *LiLi: Zeitschrift für Literaturwissenschaft und Linguistik*, 25:99 (1995), 69–82
Ruden, Randi Diane, *War and Peace/Man and Woman: Virgil's 'Aeneid' to Chrétien de Troyes' 'Erec et Enide'*, Dissertation Abstracts International 53:6 (1992 Dec), p. 1903A
Salecl, Renata, *On Anxiety*, Thinking in Action (London and New York: Routledge, 2004)
Salinero, Ma Jesús, 'Introducción a "l'imaginaire" de Chrétien de Troyes: la feminidad causa de "conflicto heroico" en *Erec*, *Cligès*, *Perceval*', *Cuadernos de Investigacion Filologica*, 11:1–2 (1985 May-Dec.), 167–85
Salisbury, Joyce E. *The Beast Within: Animals in the Middle Ages* (London and New York: Routledge, 1994)
Sargent-Baur, Barbara Nelson, 'Petite Histoire de Maboagrain (à propos d'un article recent)', *Romania*, 93 (1972), 97–96
— —, 'Erec's Enide: "sa fame ou s'amie"?', *Romance Philology*, 33 (1979), 373–87
— —, 'Erec, "novel seignor" à nouveau', *Romania*, 105:4 (1984), 552–58
— —, 'Promotion to Knighthood in the Romances of Chrétien de Troyes', *Romance Philology*, 37:4 (1984), 393–408
Scaglione, Aldo, *Knights at Court: Courtliness, Chivalry and Courtesy from Ottonian Germany to the Italian Renaissance* (Berkeley and Oxford: University of California Press, 1991)
Schibanoff, Susan, 'Sodomy's Mark: Alan of Lille, Jean de Meun and the Medivel Theory of Authorship', in *Queering the Middle Ages*, ed. by Burger and Kruger, Medieval Cultures, 27 (Minneapolis and London: University of Minnesota Press, 2001), pp. 28–56
Schleiner, W., 'Rank and Marriage: A Study of the Motif of "Woman Wilfully Tested"', *Comparative Literature Studies*, 9 (1972), 365–75
Schmitt, Jean-Claude, ' "Façons de sentir et de penser": Un tableau de la civilisation ou un histoire-problème', in *Marc Bloch aujourd'hui: Histoire comparée et sciences sociales*, ed. by Hartmut Atsma and André Burguière (Paris: Editions de l'Ecole des Hautes Etudes en Sciences Sociales, 1990)
Schmolke-Hasselmann, Beate, 'Henry II Plantagenet, roi d'Angleterre, et la genèse d'*Erec et Enide*', *Cahiers de Civilisation Médiévale*, 24:3–4 (1981), 241–46

——, *The Evolution of Arthurian Romance: The Verse Tradition from Chrétien to Froissart* (Cambridge: Cambridge University Press, 1998)

Scully, Terence, 'The *Sen* of Chrétien de Troyes's *Joie de la cort*', in *The Expansion and Transformations of Courtly Literature*, ed. by Nathaniel B. Smith and Joseph T. Snow (Athens GA: University of Georgia Press, 1980), pp. 71–94

Sedgwick, Eve Kosofsky, *Between Men: English Literature and Male Homosocial Desire*, rev. edn (New York: Columbia University Press, 1985)

Seebass-Linggi, Claudia, *Lecture d''Erec': traces épiques et troubadouresques dans le conte de Chrétien de Troyes*, French Language and Literature, 211 (Bern: Peter Lang, 1996)

Senellart, Michel, *Les Arts de gouverner: du 'regimen' médiéval au concept du gouvernement*, Des Travaux (Paris: Seuil, 1995)

Sheldon, E. S., 'Why Does Erec Treat Enide So Harshly?', *Romanic Review*, 5 (1914), 115–26

Shichtman, Martin B. and James P. Carley, 'Introduction: The Social Implications of the Arthurian Legend', in *Culture and the King: The Social Implications of the Arthurian Legend (Essays in Honour of Valerie M. Lagorio)*, ed. by Shichtman and Carley (Albany NY: State University of new York Press, 1994), pp. 4–12

Shippey, T. A., The Uses of Chivalry: *Erec* and *Gawain*', *Modern Language Review*, 61 (1971), 241–50

Short, Ian, 'Patrons and Polyglots: French Literature in Twelfth-Century England', *Anglo-Norman Studies*, 14 (1991), 229–49

Simmel, Georg, 'Culture of Interaction', in *Simmel on Culture: Selected Writings*, ed. by David Frisby and Mike Featherstone, Theory, Culture and Society (London: Sage, 1997), pp. 109–35

Simpson, James, *Sciences of the Self in Medieval Poetry: Alan of Lille's 'Anticlaudianus' and John Gower's 'Confessio Amantis'*, Cambridge Studies in Medieval Literature, 25 (Cambridge: Cambridge University Press, 1995)

Simpson, James R., *Animal Body, Literary Corpus: The Old French 'Roman de Renart'* (Amsterdam: Rodopi, 1996)

——, *Fantasy, Identity and Misrecognition in Medieval French Narrative* (Bern: Peter Lang, 2000)

Small, Graeme, *Georges Chastelain and the Shaping of Valois Burgundy: Political and Historical Culture at Court in the Fifteenth Century* (Woodbridge: Boydell, 1997)

Smoller, Laura Ackerman, *History, Prophecy and the Stars: The Christian Astrology of Pierre d'Ailly, 1350–1420* (Princeton: Princeton University Press, 1994)

Solterer, Helen, *The Master and Minerva: Disputing Women in Medieval French Culture* (Berkeley: University of California Press, 1995)

Sorabji, Richard, *Emotion and Peace of Mind: From Stoic Agitation to Christian Temptation*, The Gifford Lectures (Oxford: Oxford University Press, 2000)

Southern, R. W., *The Making of the Middle Ages* (London: Cresset, 1967; repr. 1987)

Spearing, Tony, *The Medieval Poet as Voyeur: Looking and Listening in Medieval Love Narratives* (Cambridge: Cambridge University Press, 1992)
Spence, Sarah, *Rhetorics of Reason and Desire: Virgil, Augustine, and the Troubadours* (Ithaca and London: Cornell University Press, 1988)
Spensley, R.M., 'Allusion as a Structural Device in Three Old French Romances', *Romance Notes*, 15 (1973), 349–54
Spiegel, Gabrielle M., *Romancing the Past: The Rise of Vernacular Prose Historiography in Thirteenth Century France* (Berkeley and Oxford: University of California Press, 1993)
Spivak, Gayatri Chakravorty, 'Can the Subaltern Speak?', in *Marxism and the Interpretation of Culture*, ed. by Cary Nelson and Lawrence Grossberg (Urbana: University of Illinois Press, 1988), pp. 271–313
Stahuljak, Zrinka, *Bloodless Genealogies of the French Middle Ages: Translatio, Kinship, and Metaphor* (Gainsville: University Press of Florida 2005)
Stanbury, Sarah, 'Feminist Film Theory Seeing Chrétien's Enide', *Literature and Psychology*, 36:4 (1990), 47–66
Steinhart, Margot Michele, *Joy in Chretien de Troyes' 'Erec et Enide'*, Dissertation Abstracts International, 41 (1980), p. 2597A
Strathern, Marilyn, *The Gender of the Gift: Problems with Women and Problems with Society in Melanesia* (Berkeley and London: University of California Press, 1988)
Strickland, Debra Higgs, *Saracens, Demons and Jews: Making Monsters in Medieval Art* (Princeton: Princeton University Press, 2003)
Strickland, Matthew, *War and Chivalry: The Conduct and Perception of War in England and Normandy, 1066-1217*, Cambridge Studies in Medieval Life and Thought (Cambridge: Cambridge University Press, 1996)
Strohm, Paul, *Theory and the Premodern Text*, Medieval Cultures, 26 (Minneapolis and London: University of Minnesota Press, 2000)
Sturm-Maddox, Sara, '*Hortus non Conclusus*: Critics and the Joie de la Cort', *Oeuvres et Critiques*, 5:2 (1980–1981), 61–71
— —, 'Description in Medieval Narrative: Vestimentary Coherence in Chrétien's *Erec et Enide*', *Medioevo Romanzo*, 9:1 (1984), 51–64
— —, 'The "Joie de la cort": Thematic Unity in Chrétien's *Erec et Enide*', *Romania*, 103 (1982), 513–28
— —, 'The Presentation of Enide in the "Premier vers" of Chrétien's *Erec et Enide*', *Medium Aevum*, 52:1 (1983), 77–89
— —, ' "Tenir sa terre en pais": Social Order in the *Brut* and in the *Conte du Graal*', *Studies in Philology*, 81:1 (1984), 28–41
Suard, François, 'La Réconciliation d'Erec et d'Enide: de la parole destructrice à la parole libératrice (*Erec*, 4879–4893)', in *'Bien dire et bien aprandre': Bulletin du Centre d'Etudes Médiévales et Dialectales de l'Université de Lille III*, Bien Dire et Bien Aprandre, 1 (Lille: Centre de Gestion de L'Edition Scientifique, 1978), pp. 86–105

Sullivan, Penny, 'The Education of the Heroine in Chrétien's *Erec et Enide*', *Neophilologus*, 69:3 (1985), 321–31

Taylor, Jane H. M., The Significance of the Insignificant: Reading Reception in the Burgundian *Erec* and *Cligès*', *Fifteenth-Century Studies*, 24 (1998), 183–97

Tester, S. J., *A History of Western Astrology* (Woodbridge: Boydell, 1987)

Thomas, Keith, review of Elias, *The Civilising Process*, *The New York Review of Books*, 25:3 (1978), 28–31

Thomas, Roscoe A., *Symmetrical Composition in Chretien de Troyes' 'Erec et Enide'*, Dissertation, Abstracts, 28 (1967), p. 2266A

Timelli, Maria Columbo, 'De l'*Erec* de Chrétien de Troyes à la prose du XVe siècle: le Traitement des proverbes', *Moyen Français*, 42 (1998), 87–113

Töbler, Adolf and Erhard Lommatzsch, *Alfranzösisches Wörterbuch*, 10 vols (Wiesbaden: Steiner, 1925–2002)

Topsfield, Leslie T., *Chrétien de Troyes: A Study of the Arthurian Romances* (Cambridge: Cambridge University Press, 1981)

Türk, Egbert, *Nugae curialium: le règne d'Henri II Plantegenêt (1145–1189) et l'éthique politique*, Hautes Etudes Médiévales et Modernes, 28 (Geneva: Droz, 1977)

Turner, Victor, *The Forest of Symbols: Aspects of Ndembu Ritual* (Ithaca and London: Cornell University Press, 1967)

Uebel, Michael, *Ecstatic Transformation: On the Uses of Alterity in the Middle Ages*, The New Middle Ages (London: Palgrave MacMillan, 2005)

Uhlfelder, Myra L., 'The Role of Liberal Arts in Boethius' *Consolatio*', in *Boethius and the Liberal Arts*, pp. 17–34

Uitti, Karl D. 'Vernacularisation and Old French Romance Mythopoesis with Emphasis on Chrétien's *Erec et Enide*', in *The Sower and His Seed: Essays on Chrétien de Troyes*, ed. by Rupert T. Pickens (Lexington, KY: French Forum, 1983), pp. 81–115

Uitti, Karl D. and Eric Hicks 'A propos de philologie', *Littérature*, 41 (1981), 30–46

Vance, Eugene, 'Le Combat érotique chez Chrétien de Troyes: de la figure à la forme', *Poétique*, 12 (1972), 544–71

— —, *From Topic to Tale: Logic and Narrativity in the Middle Ages* (Minneapolis: University of Minnesota Press, 1987)

Varty, Kenneth, 'On Birds and Beasts, "Death" and "Resurrection", Renewal and Reunion in Chrétien's Romances', in *The Legend of Arthur in the Middle Ages: Studies Presented to A. H. Diverres by Colleagues, Pupils and Friends*, ed. by, P. B. Grout, R. A. Lodge, C. E. Pickford and K. Varty (Cambridge: Brewer, 1983), pp. 194–212

— —, 'The Giving and Withholding of Consent in Late Twelfth-Century Literature', *Reading Medieval Studies*, 12 (1986), 27–49

Vigarello, Georges, 'The Upward Training of the Body from the Age of Chivalry to Courtly Civility', in *Fragments for a History of the Human Body*, ed. by

Michael Feher, Ramona Nadaff and Nadia Tazi, 3 vols (New York: Zone, 1989), II, pp. 148–99

Villena, Juanita, 'Harmonizing Spatial and Sentimental Aspects of Four Romances of Chrétien de Troyes: *Erec et Enide, Yvain, Cligès* and *Lancelot*', *Tropos*, 17:1 (1991), 71–80

Virillio, Paul, *Ground Zero*, trans. by Chris Turner (London and New York: Verso, 2003)

Vitz, Evelyn Birge, 'Chrétien de Troyes: clerc ou ménestrel—problèmes des traditions orale et littéraire dans les cours de France au XIIe siècle', *Poétique*, 21:81 (1990), 21–42

Wallen, Martha L., *The Art of Adaptation in the Fifteenth-Century 'Erec et Enide' and 'Cligès'*, Dissertation Abstracts International, 33 (1973), pp. 3678A-79A

——, 'Significant Variations in the Burgundian Prose Version of Erec et Enide', *Medium Aevum*, 51:2 (1982), p. 187–96

Walter, Philippe, *La Mémoire du temps: fêtes et calendriers de Chrétien de Troyes à 'La Mort Artu'*, Nouvelle Bibliothèque du Moyen Age, 13 (Paris: Champion; Geneva: Slatkine, 1989)

——, 'Erec et le cocadrille: Note de philologie et de folklore médiéval', *Zeitschrift für Romanische Philologie*, 115:1 (1999), 56–64

Warren, Michelle R., *History on the Edge: Excalibur and the Borders of Britain, 1100–1300*, Medieval Cultures, 22 (Minneapolis and London: University of Minnesota Press, 2000)

Warren, W. L., *Henry II*, Yale English Monarchs (New Haven and London: 2000)

Watt, Diane, *Amoral Gower: Language Sex and Politics*, Medieval Cultures, 38 (Minneapolis and London: University of Minnesota Press, 2003)

Weber, Max, *Economy and Society: An Outline of Interpretative Sociology*, ed. by Gunther Roth and Claus Wittich, trans. by Roth, Wittich et al., 3 vols (New York: Bedminster, 1968)

de Weever, Jacqueline, *Sheba's Daughters: Whitening and Demonizing the Saracen Woman in Medieval French Epic*, Garland Reference Library of the Humanities, 2077 (New York and London: Garland, 1998)

Weston, Jessie, 'Who Was Brian des Illes?', *Modern Philology*, 22 (1924), 4–11

Wetherbee, Winthrop, *Platonism and Poetry in the Twelfth Century: The Literary Influence of the School of Chartres* (Princeton: Princeton University Press, 1972)

Wheeler, Bonnie and James Carmi Parsons (eds), *Eleanor of Aquitaine: Lord and Lady*, The New Middle Ages (New York and Basingstoke: Palgrave Macmillan, 2002)

White, Catherine L., 'Not So Dutiful Daughters: Women and Their Fathers in Three French Medieval Works: *Le Roman de Silence, Erec et Enide* and *Le Livre de la cité des dames*', *Cincinnati Romance Review*, 18 (1999), 189–99

White, Stephen D., 'The Politics of Anger', in *Anger's Pasts*, ed. by Rosenwein, pp. 127–52

Williams, M., ' "Kerrins li viauz rois de Riel" (*Erec*, l. 1985)', in *Studies Presented to Mildred K. Pope*, (Manchester: Manchester University Press, 1939), pp. 405–12
— —, 'Eleanor of Aquitaine and the Arthurian Romances', *The Durham University Journal*, 42 (1949), 1–7
Williams, Simon J., *Emotions and Social Theory* (London: Sage, 2001)
Wittig, Joseph S., 'The Aeneas-Dido Allusion in Chrétien's *Erec et Enide*', *Comparative Literature*, 22 (1970), 237–53
Woledge, Brian, 'Bons vavasseurs et mauvais seneschaux', in *Mélanges offerts à Rita Lejeune, professeur à l'Université de Liège*, 2 vols (Gembloux: Duculot, 1969), II, pp. 1263–77
Wolf, Alois, 'Die "Grosse Freude": Vergleichende Betrachtungen zur Eros-exsultatio in Minnekanzonen, im *Erec* und im *Tristan*', *Literaturwissenschaftliches Jahrbuch im Auftrage der Görres-Gesellschaft*, 34 (1993), 49–79
Wolfzettel, Friedrich, '*Le Roman d'Erec en prose* du XIIIe siècle: Un Anti-*Erec et Enide*?', in *The Legacy of Chrétien de Troyes*, ed. by Norris J. Lacy, Douglas Kelly and Keith Busby, 2 vols (Amsterdam: Rodopi, 1988), II, pp. 215–28
Wolfzettel, Friedrich, 'Doppelweg und Biographie', in *Erzählstrukturen der Artusliteratur: Forschungsgeschichte und neue Ansätze*, ed. by Friedrich Wolfzettel and Peter Ihring (Tübingen: Niemeyer, 1999), pp. 119–41
— —, 'Temps et histoire dans la littérature arthurienne', in *Temps et histoire dans le roman arthurien*, ed by Jean-Claude Faucon (Toulouse: Editions Universitaires du Sud, 1999), pp. 9–32
Zaddy, Zara P., *Chrétien Studies: Problems of Form and Meaning in 'Erec', 'Yvain', 'Cligès' and the 'Charrete'* (Glasgow: Glasgow University Press, 1973)
Zai, Marie-Claire, *Les Chansons courtoises de Chrétien de Troyes*, Europäische Hochschulschriften, 13:27 (Bern: Peter Lang, 1974)
Zak, Nancy Carpenter, *The Portrayal of the Heroine in Chrétien de Troyes' 'Erec et Enide', Gottfried von Strassburg's 'Tristan', and 'Flamenca'*, Göppinger Arbeiten zur Germanistik, 347 (Göppingen: Kümmerle, 1983)
Zapperi, Roberto, *The Pregnant Man*, ed. and trans. by Brian Williams, rev. edn (Chur and London: Harwood Academic, 1991)
Zeikowitz, Richard E., *Homoeroticism and Chivalry: Discourses of Male Same-Sex Desire in the Fourteenth Century*, The New Middle Ages (New York and Basingstoke: Palgrave MacMillan, 2003)
Ziltener, W., *Chrétien und die 'Aeneis': eine Untersuchung des Einflusses von Virgil auf Chrétien von Troyes* (Graz: , 1969)
Zink, Michel, *The Invention of Literary Subjectivity*, trans. by David Sices, Parallax: Re-Visions of Culture and Society (Baltimore and London: Johns Hopkins University Press, 1999)
Ziolkowski, Jan, *Alan of Lille's Grammar of Sex: The Meaning of Sex to a Twelfth-Century Intellectual*, Speculum Anniversary Monographs, 10 (Cambridge MA: Medieval Academy of America, 1985)

Žižek, Slavoj, *Enjoy Your Symptom!: Jacques Lacan In and Out of Hollywood* (London and New York: Routledge, 1992)
——, *The Sublime Object of Ideology*, Phronesis (London and New York: Verso, 1989)
——, *Looking Awry: An Introduction to Jacques Lacan through Popular Culture*, October (Cambridge, MA and London: MIT Press, 1992)
——, *Tarrying with the Negative: Kant, Hegel and the Critique of Ideology* (Durham NC: Duke University Press, 1993)
——, *The Metastases of Enjoyment: Six Essays on Woman and Causality*, Wo Es War (London and New York: Verso, 1994)
——, *The Plague of Fantasies*, Wo Es War (London and New York: Verso, 1997)
——, *The Art of the Ridiculous Sublime: On David Lynch's 'Lost Highway'*, Walter Chapin Simpson Center Occasional Papers, 1 (Seattle: Walter Chapin Simpson Center for the Humanities, University of Washington, 2000)
——, *The Fragile Absolute – Or, Why Is the Christian Legacy Worth Fighting For?*, Wo Es War (London and New York: Verso, 2000)
——, *The Ticklish Subject* (London and New York: Verso, 2000)
——, *Did Somebody Say Totalitarianism? Four Interventions in the Misuse of a Notion* (London and New York: Verso, 2001)
——, *On Belief*, Thinking in Action (London and New York: Routledge, 2001)
——, *Welcome to the Desert of the Real: Five Essays on 11 September and Related Dates* (London and New York: Verso, 2002)
——, *The Puppet and the Dwarf: The Perverse Core of Christianity*, Short Circuits (Cambridge MA and London: MIT, 2003)
——, *Iraq: The Borrowed Kettle* (London and New York: Verso, 2004)
——, *Organs Without Bodies: Deleuze and Consequences* (London and New York: Routledge, 2004)
——, 'What Lies Beneath', *Guardian Review*, May 1st, 2004, p. 7
——, *How to Read Lacan* (London: Granta, 2006)
——, 'Robespierre or the "Divine Violence" of Terror', in *Virtue and Terror*, ed. by Jean Ducange, trans. by John Howe, Revolutions (London and New York: Verso: 2007), pp. vii–xxxix
Žižek, Slavoj and Glyn Daly, *Conversations with Žižek* (Cambridge: Polity, 2003)
Zumthor, Paul, 'Roman et histoire: aux sources d'un univers narratif', in *Langue, texte, enigme* (Paris: Seuil, 1975)
Zupančič, Alenka, *Ethics of the Real: Kant, Lacan*, Wo Es War (London and New York: Verso, 2000)

Filmography

Adamson, Andrew and Vicky Jenson (dir.), *Shrek* (2001)
Adamson, Andrew and Kelly Ashbury (dir.), *Shrek 2* (2004)
Boorman, John (dir.), *Deliverance* (1972)
Bresson, Robert (dir.), *Lancelot du lac* (1974)
Campbell, Martin (dir.), *The Mask of Zorro* (1998)
Curtiz, Michael (dir.), *Casablanca* (1942)
Fiennes, Sophie (dir.), *The Pervert's Guide to Cinema* (2006)
Fincher, David (dir.), *Fight Club* (1999)
Fuqua, Antoine (dir.), *King Arthur* (2004)
Gilliam, Terry and Terry Jones (dirs), *Monty Python and the Holy Grail* (1975)
Hitchcock, Alfred (dir.), *Rope* (1948)
—— (dir.), *Vertigo* (1958)
Hynter, Nicholas (dir.), *The Madness of King George* (1994)
Jarmusch, Jim (dir.), *Ghost Dog: The Way of the Samurai* (1999)
Kitano, Takeshi (dir.) *Zatoichi* (2003)
Kubrick, Stanley (dir.) *Eyes Wide Shut* (1999)
Lynch, David (dir.) *Blue Velvet* (1986)
Roach, Jay (dir.), *Austin Powers: International Man of Mystery* (1997)
—— (dir.), *Austin Powers: The Spy Who Shagged Me* (1999)
Rodriguez, Robert (dir.), *El Mariachi* (1992)
—— (dir.), *Desperado* (1995)
—— (dir.), *Once Upon a Time in Mexico* (2003)
Scott, Ridley (dir.), *Blade Runner* (1982)
Spielberg, Steven (dir.), *Saving Private Ryan* (1998)
Syberberg, Hans-Jürgen (dir.), *Parsifal* (1982)
Tarantino, Quentin (dir.), *Pulp Fiction* (1994)

Index

Absalom
    Chrétien de Troyes, 244
    Walter Map, 129
Adams, Alison, 87
Adler, Alfred, 372
Alan of Lille, 10, 20, 138
    Hymenaeus, 260
    Joci ('Sports'), 160
Albertus Magnus, 137, 160
Alcuin of York, 83
Ale-Hood (Old Norse), 135
Allard, Jean-Paul, 384, 413
Anamorphosis
    Holbein, Hans, 42
Anger, 110–14
    Alcuin of York, 112
    Althoff, Gerd, 113
    Bernard of Clairvaux, 202
    Henry II, 110, 114
    John of Salisbury, 112
    Kaeuper, Richard, 111
    Orderic Vitalis, 111
    Peter of Blois, 114
    White, Stephen, 112
    Wolfram von Eschenbach, 113
Anseïs de Carthage (epic), 128
Anxiety
    Anxiety and king figures, 35–38
    Neighbour and anxiety, 33–35
Arthur (King)
    as Caesar-figure, 105–10
    as model, 1–2
    Geoffrey of Monmouth, 107–8
    Glastonbury
        Ovid, 105
Aucassin et Nicolette, 92, 152, 227, 420

Auerbach, Eric, 84
Augustine of Hippo, 25, 105, 110, 261, 353, 399, 468
    Against Julian, 159
    Astrology, 381, 436, 452
    City of God, 25
    Confessions, 425
    Demonic power, 181
    Fortune, 441
    Sexual arousal, 135
    Suicide, 365, 442
        Lucretia, 55, 337, 367–69, 390
        Marcus Regulus, 370, 383, 435
    Suicide, 365
    Time, 44, 94, 126
    Will, 441
Barber, Richard, 21, 22
Barthes, Roland, 193, 242
Barton, Richard E., 114
Beauvoir, Simone de, 4, 60, 166, 373, 395, 433
Bel Inconnu, 33–35, 138
Benjamin, Walter, 41
Benton, John F., 13
Berangier au long cul (fabliau), 327
Bernardus Silvestris, 392, 397
Bernart de Ventadorn, 22
Bezzola, Reto, 47, 131, 141, 143, 149, 177
Biddick, Kathleen, 241, 303, 342, 343
Blaess, Madeleine, 105
Bloch, R. Howard, 153, 219, 291, 298
Boethius, 21, 25, 54, 98, 170, 352, 353, 373, 393, 453
    Consolation of Philosophy, 25
Bourdieu, Pierre, 7, 96
Broadhurst, Karen, 20

515

Brooke, Christopher, 129
Bull, Marcus, xii, 14, 141
Burger, Glenn, 48
Burgess, Glyn S., 47, 90, 140, 143, 159, 256, 277, 284, 314, 325, 393, 400
Burgwinkle, Bill, 378
Burgwinkle, William, 430, 431
Burke, Edmund, 4
Burns, E. Jane, 131, 144, 254, 436
Busby, Keith, 116
Butler, Judith, 1, 10
Camus, Albert, 98
   Caligula (play), 435
Casablanca (film), 296
Chakrabarty, Dipesh, 32, 38, 39, 40, 41, 73, 95, 122, 172, 242
   Provincialisation, 27
Chandès, Gérard, 93
Chanson de Roland (Châteauroux), 105
Chanson de Roland (Oxford), 146, 149, 158, 268
Chanson de Roland (Paris), 365
Charisma, 36, 37
Charms, 296, 299
Chaucer, Geoffrey, 179
   Wife of Bath, 134
Chesterton, G. K., 32
Chevalier à l'épée (romance), 226, 227, 252
Chevalier qui fist parler les cons (fabliau), 220
Chrétien de Troyes
   Chevalier au lion, 220, 306, 307, 308, 309, 371
   Chevalier de la charrette, 35, 153, 233, 373
   Cligés, 35, 130, 182–83, 251, 267
   Conte du graal, 138, 204, 232
   Erec et Enide

Cadoc of Tabriol, 24, 48, 53, 54, 144, 304, 332–44, 353, 354, 358, 362, 364, 414
Consent, 153
Court as context, 13–27
Departure from Carnant, 270–80
Enide and the Joy, 436–40
Erec's beauty, 125–28
Evrain, 443
Galoain, 52, 304–17, 318, 325, 326, 330, 334, 353, 372
Gauvain, 50, 53, 90, 93, 95, 130, 139, 149, 150, 155, 217, 221, 244, 270, 280, 304, 326, 327, 328, 330, 331, 329–31, 333, 340, 394, 458
Gringalet, Le, 53, 304, 328, 333, 348
Guinevere, 25, 49, 130, 133, 139, 149, 168, 189, 201, 207, 208, 219, 222, 229, 233, 234, 257, 272, 316, 357, 378, 421, 428, 458, 459
Guinevere's handmaiden, 130–45
Guivret, 24, 53, 55, 196, 242, 265, 304, 315, 317–26, 327, 364, 381, 385, 386, 379–87, 388, 389, 390, 400, 401, 404, 407, 414, 415, 434, 458
Hunt, 87–97
Joy of the Court, 56, 399–443
Kay, 326–29
King as masochist, 151–57
Maboagrain, 56, 413–21, 425–35
Oringle of Limors, 54, 242, 260, 275, 279, 335, 364–75, 381
Parsome, 42–44, 97, 207, 235, 254, 261, 264, 277, 286, 393

516

Prologue, 79–87
Recreantise, 255–70
Suicide, 354–73
Lyric poems
   Amors tençon et bataille, 183–84
   D'amors qui m'a tolu a moi, 184–86
Manuscripts
   B. N. fonds fr. 1376, 17, 52, 80, 81, 86, 221, 262, 263, 392, 393, 458, 462
   B. N. fonds fr. 24403, 80, 87, 338, 420
   B. N. fonds fr. 794, 262, 458
   Chantilly, Condé 472, 458, 461
Philomena, 45, 173, 171–82, 218, 228, 233, 263, 275, 338, 390
   Pandion, 313
   Philomena, 50, 226, 246, 292, 313, 314, 335, 366, 380, 381, 393
   Tereüs, 234, 237, 313, 314, 330
Cicero, Marcus Tullius
   On Duties, 107
   On the Orator, 255, 266
Cixous, Hélène, 433
Cleland, John
   Memoirs of a Woman of Pleasure, 48
Cohen, Jeffrey, 49, 134, 152, 153, 305, 306, 308, 315, 327, 345, 366
Couronnement de Louis, 146
Court behaviour
   Hincmar of Rheims, 5–7
Crane, Susan, 1, 8
Danton, Georges, 468
Davis, R. H. C., 159
Deleuze, Gilles, 97, 153
Denis Piramus
   Vie de saint Edmund le rei, 82
Derrida, Jacques, 110, 118, 138
   Gift, 344

Diana, Princess of Wales, 467
Diderot, Denis
   La Religieuse, 171
Dinshaw, Carolyn, 118, 333, 433
Douglas, Mary, 11
Duby, Georges, 446
Duggan, Joseph, 22, 47, 173
Edge, David, 202
Eleanor of Aquitaine, 20, 21, 23, 25, 48, 51, 219, 227, 230
Elias, Norbert, 36, 37, 78
Evergates, Theodore, 46
Eyes Wide Shut (film), 252, 253, 254
Firestone, Ruth, 21, 393, 394
Florimont (romance), 81, 86
Foucault, Michel, 153
Foulon, Charles, 96
Frappier, Jean, 47, 74, 159, 198, 224
Freedman, Paul, 38
Freud
   Schreber, 294
Freud, Sigmund
   Anxiety, 31, 139, 430
   Dora, 192, 312, 344
   Fort-da game, 36
   Neighbour, 33, 169
   Schreber, 253
   Vorlust, 30
Fritz, Jean-Marie, 261, 262
Fulgentius, 392
Garin de Monglane (epic), 80
Gaston Fébus
   Livre de la chasse, 141, 161
Gaunt, Simon, 18, 23, 68, 117, 135, 227, 316, 345, 444
Geertz, Clifford, 192, 303, 342
   Ritual deactivation, 37
Geoffrey (son of Henry II), 20
Geoffrey le Bel, 166, 205
Geoffrey of Monmouth, xii, 26, 35, 40, 48, 54, 78, 98, 101, 109, 122, 209, 306, 337, 339, 361–63
Georges Chastellain, 1

517

Gerald of Wales, 303
Ghost Dog (film), 377
Gilbert, Jane, 162, 226
Girard, René, 10, 35, 37, 72, 286
Gladiator (film), 425
Gravdal, Kathryn, 144, 231, 233, 254, 293, 369
Guenée, Bernard, 120
Guerin, Victoria, 35
Hanning, Robert W., 251
Harvey, Ruth, 22
Henry II, 20, 21, 23, 49, 136, 203, 224
   Astrology, 453
Henry, the 'Young King' (son of Henry II), 21, 22, 244, 277
Hincmar of Rheims, 5, 127
Hindman, Sandra, 80, 87, 116, 419, 420
Hitchcock, Alfred
   Rope, 444
   Vertigo, 314
Hoepffner, E., 74
Holbein, Hans, 84, 99, 148, 260, 332, 378, 394, 409
Horses
   Sexuality
      Bayeux tapestry, 134
      Isidore of Seville, 134
      Teaser, 138
Huchet, Jean-Charles, 396
Hugh of St Victor, 277
Huizinga, Johan, 2, 10, 95
Hult, David, 83
Hunt, Tony, 20, 200, 262
Jaeger, C. Stephen, 6, 7, 10, 311
James, M. R., 375
John Dymmock (champion of Richard II), 96, 326
John of Salisbury, 29, 110, 160, 239, 306, 378
   Astrology, 453
   Witchcraft, 181

Julius Caesar, 99–105
   Augustine of Hippo, 102
   Fait des Romains, 103–4
   Gerald of Wales, 103
   John of Salisbury, 100, 102
   Ovid, 83, 101
   Plutarch, 100, 104, 120, 280
   Roman d'Eneas, 102
   Roman de Jules Cesar, 104–5
   Suetonius, 13, 99, 101, 102, 103, 109, 120
   Walter Map, 79
Juvenal, 431, 432
Kaeuper, Richard, 122
Katherine of Aragon, 176
Kay, Sarah, 13, 251, 276, 336, 358
Kershaw, Ian, 164
King Arthur (film), 77
Knight's Tale, A (film), 382
Köhler, Erich, 32, 167, 170, 209
Koziol, Geoffrey, 87, 166, 167, 206
Krueger, Roberta, 469
Kruger, Steven, 48
La Bruyère, Jean de, 3, 304
Lacan, Jacques, 28, 40, 264, 294, 363, 402, 420
   Anamorphosis, 73, 148
   Antigone, 347
   Anxiety, 27, 31, 34, 35, 254, 430
   Barred Subject, 261
   Courtly love, 29, 70
   Desire, 92
   émoi, 34, 35
   Full Speech, 28, 42
   Imaginary, 315
   Imaginary Father, 274
   Law, 175
   Little Hans, 71
   Love, 155, 279
   Masochism, 31
   Need, demand and desire, 257
   Not all, 314, 407
   Perversion, 70

Psychosis, 252, 294
Sadism, 253, 344
Superego, 427
Want-to-be (*manque-à-être*), 308
Lefay-Toury, Marie-Nöelle, 373
Levinas, Emmanuel, 100
Lévy-Gires, Noëlle, 174
Louis VII, 46
Lucan, 25, 40, 76, 81, 84, 100, 103, 104, 108, 145, 245, 261, 313, 344
Luttrell, Claude, 20, 224
Machiavelli, Niccolò, xii, 87, 209
Maddox, Donald, 2, 47, 117, 130, 137
Madness of King George (film), 326, 331
Marie de France
  Chaitivel, 244
  Chevrefeuille, 279
  Lanval, 172, 312
McCracken, Peggy, 22, 177, 191, 373
Middleton, Roger, 116
Miller, J. Hillis, 13
Monty Python and the Holy Grail (film), 79, 345, 385
Mort le roi Artu, 36, 96, 146, 172, 281, 283
  Fortune's wheel, 98–99
Naissance du chevalier au cygne (epic), 105
Napoleon, 468
Nelson, Deborah, 198
Nelson, Janet L., 5
Nitze, W. A., 74
Noble, Peter, 47
Noble, Peter S., 159
Ogier le Danois (epic), 80
Ovid, 25, 50, 76, 81, 83, 172, 175, 177, 178, 179, 181, 182, 208, 276, 367, 399
Ovide moralisé, 172
Owen, D.D.R., 20
Paris, Gaston, 74
Patterson, Lee, 180

Pèlerinage de Charlemagne à Constantinople (epic), 15
Perversion, 29–31
Peter of Blois, 110
Peter the Lombard, 137, 153
Philip the Good, 1
Philippe Auguste, 431
Philippe Pot, 1, 468
Philips, Adam, 231
Pintarič, Miha, 93
Plummer, John, 372, 469
Pompey
  Lucan, 106
  Plutarch, 106
Power, Dan, 22
Pseudo-Turpin Chronicle, 15
Pulp Fiction (film), 333, 339, 420, 433
Putter, Ad, 13
Queen, The (film), 467
Queer theory and queering, 48–49
Quintilian, 145
Raimon de Miraval (troubadour), 225
Raoul de Cambrai (epic), 298
Renaut de Montauban, 306
Reuter, Tim, 76
Richard Coer de Lyon, 307
Richard of Devizes, 432
Richard of Devizes, 430
Richard the Lionheart, 12, 431
Ridicule (film), 29
Roger of Hoveden, 203
Roman d'Eneas, 23, 26, 46, 49, 51, 53, 54, 56, 84, 87, 103, 135–36, 138, 168, 177, 227, 251, 252, 261, 265, 290, 293, 306, 320, 327, 336, 342, 361, 363, 367, 390, 391, 392, 394, 400, 429, 430, 431, 461
Roman de Perceforest, 283
Roman de Renart, 11
Roman de Silence, 172
Roman de Thèbes, 23, 79, 81, 82, 306
Roman d'Eneas, 24

519

Roman d'Erec, 280–83
Sade, Marquis de
   Justine ou les malheurs de la vertu, 171
   Philosophie dans le boudoir, 253, 293
Salisbury, Joyce, 135
Saving Private Ryan (film), 290
Schmolke-Hasselmann, Beate, 20
Schnitzler, Arthur
   Traumnovelle, 252
Seebass-Linggi, Claudia, 47, 79, 186, 201, 286, 314, 361, 374, 451
Shakespeare, William, xii, 94, 213, 230, 304, 369
Short, Ian, 21
Shrek (film), 160, 347
Simmel, Georg, 127
Simpson, James, 27
Spence, Sarah, 26, 69, 399
Spivak, Gayatri Chakravorty, 38
Stabelein, Patricia Harris, 82
Stahuljak, Zrinka, 136
Strickland, Matthew, 67
Strohm, Paul, 96
Subaltern studies, 28, 38–40
Suetonius, 18, 99, 101, 102, 103, 109
Thorpe, Lewis, 12
Topsfield, Leslie, 47, 166, 167, 195, 349
Trubert, 152, 154, 227
Virgil, 25, 26, 90, 110, 135, 180, 205, 392, 393, 399
Voltaire
   Candide, 171
Wace, Robert, 23
   Roman de Brut, 40, 78, 106, 144, 337, 339, 361, 363
Walter Map, 3, 94, 110, 114, 255
   Cistercians, 9
   Henry II, 9

Henry, the 'Young King' (son of Henry II), 29, 129–30, 244, 277
Walter, Philippe, 93, 381
Weber, Max, 36
Whitman, Walt, 116
Will
   Augustine of Hippo, 365–72
   Chrétien de Troyes, 79–97
   John of Salisbury, 29
   Ovid, 83
William IX (troubadour), 22, 51, 79, 216, 219, 224, 230, 361
Witchcraft, 297
Wittig, Joseph, 392
Yamamoto, Tsunemoto
   Book of the Samurai, 374
Zaddy, Zara, 47, 74
Zatoichi (film), 287, 514
Zink, Michel, 82, 161
Žižek, Slavoj, 41, 364, 467
   Anamorphosis, 73
   Anti-Semitism, 71
   Christianity as perverse, 32
   Coke as sublime object, 470
   Cuba and revolution, 41
   Dirty secrets, 156, 163
   Eyes Wide Shut (film), 294
   Fantasy, 154, 312, 344, 363
   Fetishism, 424
   Fight Club (film), 163
   Law, 267, 297, 337
   Masochism, 162
   Masochism and anxiety, 154
   Neighbour, 33, 166, 192
   Parsifal, 147, 161
   Perversion, 30, 70
   Rape in war, 349
   Subjective interpellation, 265, 295
   Theft of enjoyment, 30
   Universalism, 40

Medieval and Early Modern French Studies

Series Editor
Noël Peacock

Striking and stimulating contributions continue to be made to French studies and cultural studies of the medieval and early modern periods. This series aims to publish work of the highest quality in these areas. The series will include monographs and collaborative or collected works from both established and younger scholars, and will encompass a wide range of disciplines and theoretical approaches. Contributions will be welcomed in French or English.

Volume 1
Forthcoming.

Volume 2
William Brooks and Rainer Zaiser (eds):
> Theatre, Fiction, and Poetry in the French Long Seventeenth Century / Le Théâtre, le roman, et la poésie à l'âge classique. 2007. 322 pages. ISBN 978-3-03911-103-9

Volume 3
William Brooks and Rainer Zaiser (eds):
> Religion, Ethics, and History in the French Long Seventeenth Century / La Religion, la morale, et l'histoire à l'âge classique. 2007. 348 pages. ISBN 978-3-03911-104-6

VOLUME 4

Forthcoming.

VOLUME 5

James R. Simpson
  Troubling Arthurian Histories. Court Culture, Performance and Scandal in Chrétien de Troyes's *Erec et Enide*. 2007. 520 pages. ISBN 978-3-03911-385-9